SENTENCING
A MODERN INTRODUCTION

SENTENCING
A MODERN INTRODUCTION

THOMAS O'MALLEY
Senior Counsel

CLARUS
PRESS

Published by
Clarus Press Ltd,
Griffith Campus,
South Circular Road,
Dublin 8.
www.claruspress.ie

Typeset by
Gough Typesetting Services,
Dublin

Printed by
Sprint Books,
Dublin

ISBN
978-1-911611-75-2

A catalogue record for this book is available from the British Library

PREFACE

Sentencing has only recently come to be accepted as a branch of law worthy of study in its own right. University law schools traditionally ignored it entirely or else treated it as a small component of their core criminal law courses that were otherwise devoted to the principles of criminal liability and offence definitions. It fared little better in professional practice courses for future solicitors and barristers. Granted, until well into the twentieth century, there was little by way of sentencing legislation or case law, certainly not enough to justify a full academic course or provide a basis for much academic research.[1] All this has changed radically. There is now an abundance of sentencing legislation and case law in all common-law jurisdictions, including Ireland. More fundamentally, sentencing is no longer treated as a topic about which there is little to be said. It used to be viewed, within legal circles at least, as a task best left to the wisdom and discretion of trial judges, with the added safeguard of an appeals system to reduce excessively severe sentences. Academic research on sentencing was treated with suspicion at best, mainly because of fears that its agenda might be to constrain, if not eliminate, judicial discretion. In Ireland, the problem was further compounded by a dearth of detailed and reliable criminal justice statistics, a problem that remains to some degree. However, the volume of Irish sentencing case law has greatly increased, especially since the establishment of the Court of Appeal in 2014, which means that there is a great deal more judicial analysis of fundamental sentencing principles. There is also a growing corpus of offence-specific guideline judgments (discussed in Chapter 13), and steps are being taken to collect and analyse data on current sentencing practice. Opportunities for academic research on sentencing have never been better, and it is to the credit of the courts, especially the Supreme Court and Court of Appeal, that they are willing to consider published academic work, from both at home and abroad, whenever it appears relevant to the cases they have to decide.

Most of all, we have come to realise that sentencing matters. It represents

1 It took some time for criminal law more generally to gain a foothold in the academic curriculum. Giving evidence before a Select Committee on Legal Education in 1846, Mountiford Longfield, Regius Professor of Feudal and English Law at Trinity College Dublin, said that he never lectured on criminal law because there were "no fixed principles in it, except that men must not commit certain crimes, and if they do, there are certain punishments" (quoted in VTH Delany, "The history of legal education in Ireland" (1960) 12 *Journal of Legal Education* 396, 403).

the ultimate coercive power of the state over persons within its jurisdiction, a power that can extend to the deprivation of liberty and, in some countries, life. Significant numbers of our fellow citizens are sentenced annually to various kinds of penalties including imprisonment. There were 7,000 committals to Irish prisons in 2022, almost 1,000 more than in the previous year. In mid-June 2024, there were almost 5,000 prisoners in custody (including 924 on remand), compared with 3,780 at the end of 2021. This has left the prison system operating at 111 per cent capacity, compared with 86 per cent capacity in December 2021. The total budget for the Prison Service in 2022 was €414 million. Meanwhile in 2021 the Probation Service worked with 15,400 offenders in the community and with 2,730 prisoners. In June 2024, the United Kingdom had a total prison population of 97,500, including 87,317 in England and Wales where the prison population is projected to rise to 106,000 by 2027.[2] The cost of sentencing should never, of course, be assessed solely in financial terms. The human and social costs of imprisonment in particular, not only for offenders but also for their families and dependants, can be very significant indeed.[3]

Sentencing matters also because it tells us much about the society in which we live. Fundamentally, the criminal law consists of a set of proscriptions and penalties that are intended to dissuade us from harming other individuals or the broader community. But the study of criminal law is no less important for the light it sheds on prevailing social and moral values. Those values vary across time and space, as even a cursory study of legal history and comparative law will reveal. Granted, the criminal law, like law in general, can be slow to change, but eventually it catches up with contemporary views (or majoritarian views at least) about acceptable standards of behaviour. Gradually or otherwise, it develops to reflect the shifting balance between personal autonomy and liberty on the one hand, and social protection on the other. In the area of sexual offences, for example, legal moralism has yielded to a more liberal, harm-to-others approach as reflected in the decriminalisation of consensual adult homosexual activity and the more intensive criminalisation of child sexual abuse and exploitation. The growth in so-called regulatory offences, including much of what we call white-collar crime, reflects a heightened awareness of the real harm caused by fraudulent transactions and corporate misconduct. It is reasonable to predict that harming the natural environment will be treated more seriously and punished more severely in the future. Meanwhile, the prosecution and punishment of

---

2 Georgina Sturge, *UK Prison Population Statistics* (House of Commons Library, 2023).

3 The impact of parental imprisonment on children is briefly discussed in Chapter 5 below. See also David Ormerod, "The need for a criminal division of the High Court" (2023) 76 *Current Legal Problems* 403, 405 ("Lives are changed fundamentally whenever liberty is at stake. The stigma of a criminal conviction is unique").

climate activists whose protests involve violations of the criminal law will probably become more controversial.[4]

Likewise, the penalties attaching to criminal offences and judicial sentencing practices are instructive about prevailing social priorities and values. From a global perspective, imprisonment rates and the length of prison terms (not to mention the availability or otherwise of capital punishment) reveal how concepts of penal deservedness and severity vary across national frontiers, and how some political regimes are more willing than others to prioritise social reintegration over retribution in the treatment of offenders. At a more local level, statutory rules, judicially developed principles and current sentencing practice reflect contemporary evaluations of the harmfulness of various kinds of criminal conduct and the risks posed by certain categories of offender. To this extent, it mirrors developments in the substantive criminal law. However, judicial sentencing has a special role in this regard, largely because it is an iterative as well as a highly visible process. Courts are constantly and publicly sentencing for the same offences (though committed by different offenders). Every sentence amounts to a public reaffirmation of the wrongfulness of the offence and the degree of censure it merits. Consequently, sentencing practice can, and normally does, reflect prevailing public opinion about the comparative gravity of different kinds of offending and the extent to which they call for disapprobation and condemnation.

Public and political interest in sentencing has grown exponentially in recent decades, as might be expected with the steady increase in both the volume of recorded crime and the prison population. Unfortunately, interest is not always matched with knowledge. Those who complain most vociferously about the operation of the sentencing system are often poorly informed about current sentencing law and practice. Judicial sentencing decisions are frequently criticised as being inconsistent and unduly lenient. More often than not, those claims are unsupported by any empirical evidence (which admittedly can be hard to find) and they typically ignore factors such as the existence of sentencing guidelines and the DPP's power to request the Court of Appeal to review unduly lenient sentences for serious offences. In recent years the vast majority of undue leniency applications have been successful (31 out of 38 in 2022), and in most of those cases sentences have been increased.[5]

The findings of two recent English reports should resonate in Ireland as well. A report published by the Sentencing Academy in January 2022 examined public knowledge of custody rates and average prison sentence lengths over the period 1996-2021.[6] A majority of respondents were unaware of increases in sentence lengths during the period, and the

---

4 See, for example, *R v Trowland and Decker* [2023] EWCA Crim 919; [2024] 1 WLR 1164; [2024] 1 Cr App R(S) 13, discussed further in Chapter 5.

5 Chapter 2 below.

6 Sentencing Academy, *Public Knowledge of Sentencing Practice and Trends* (Sentencing Academy, 2022), at https://www.sentencingacademy.org.uk.

report concluded that there was a clear relationship between knowledge of sentencing and attitudes towards sentence severity. Those who believed that sentences were too lenient were generally ill-informed about current sentencing practices. In fact, other empirical studies have shown that when people who complained about sentences being too lenient were asked, as part of a research exercise, to suggest appropriate sentences in cases for which they were given all the relevant facts, the sentences they recommended were often less severe than those that had actually been imposed by the courts in those cases. Another report on the same topic was published by the House of Commons Justice Committee in September 2023.[7] It too concluded that the public does not have a good knowledge of the sentencing system or of the role played by different state institutions (e.g. prosecutors, courts, parole authorities) in that system. Both reports recommended that greater efforts be made to educate the public about sentencing and, in particular, about current judicial sentencing practice.

Public education is important for several reasons. Courts, when sentencing offenders, are acting on behalf of the community and, in many instances, spending significant amounts of public money by imposing prison sentences. Members of the public are therefore entitled to reliable information about how the courts discharge this function. Secondly, there is nothing more certain to undermine public confidence in the criminal justice system than a widespread belief or perception that sentencing decisions are unfair, arbitrary, discriminatory or inconsistent. It can never, of course, be presumed that any sentencing system is flawless in this regard. But to test the accuracy of any such perception, one must have access to reliable data on sentencing practice. Otherwise, claims of arbitrariness, inconsistency and so forth cannot properly be evaluated and, if found to be inaccurate, refuted. Thirdly, and closely related to what has just been said, mounting public protests about excessively lenient or inconsistent sentencing, again however ill-founded, can pressurise politicians to legislate for more severe or repressive sentencing laws for which, in truth, there may be no need and which, in the long run, may cause more problems than they solve. Robert Dahl once wrote that "there is a great variety of empirical facts that one needs to know... before one can rationally decide on the kinds of political rules one wants to follow in the real world."[8] This certainly holds true of criminal justice policy making.

There has been one positive development in this regard in Ireland. The powers and functions of the Sentencing Guidelines and Information Committee established by the Judicial Council Act 2019 include the preparation and dissemination of information about sentences imposed

---

7 House of Commons Justice Committee, *Public Opinion and Understanding of Sentencing*, 10th Report of Session 2022-23, at https://committees.parliament.uk/publications/41844/documents/207521/default/ .

8 Robert A Dahl, *A Preface to Democratic Theory* (University of Chicago Press, 1956), 52. See also John Rappaport, "Some doubts about 'democratizing' criminal justice" (2020) 87 Univ. Chicago LR 71

by the courts.[9] The Committee's primary function is to prepare draft sentencing guidelines for review by the Board of the Council, but it will hopefully be sufficiently resourced to fulfil its additional role in educating the public about sentencing practice. Ideally, there should be some body, whether under the aegis of the Judicial Council or otherwise, charged with publicising and analysing sentencing developments more generally. Judicial sentencing practice is, of course, vitally important but it is only one element of the overall sentencing process. Statutory developments, including those creating new offences, revising maximum sentences, establishing general sentencing rules and specifying parole eligibility can be even more influential in determining the sentences that are imposed and served. These too are matters about which the public should be kept informed. The London-based Sentencing Academy, which operates as charity, provides an excellent model for such a body as it is dedicated to providing reliable and well-researched, but also accessible and freely-available, information on sentencing.

No less important than the provision of information is the need for realism about what sentencing can achieve. Perhaps because it is the most visible component of the overall criminal process, sentencing is often assumed to be capable of achieving all kinds of worthy goals, mostly connected with crime reduction. This is reflected in regular calls for more severe penalties, often in the form of mandatory minimums, for certain offences, typically in the aftermath of an offence or spate of offences that has attracted intense media interest. Yet, all a sentencing system can be guaranteed to deliver is just punishment for persons duly convicted of criminal offences, and to achieve even this the system must be principled, proportionate and moderate. Of course, sentencing *can* sometimes advance utilitarian goals such as deterrence and reform as well, but it would be a serious mistake to assume that sentencing policy can be tweaked or revised to eliminate or significantly diminish the incidence of crime. The causes of serious crime are manifold and complex. They include individual and socio-economic factors, some of which can undoubtedly be addressed, but only through effective political, social and economic policies. Sentencing, by itself, can achieve very little in this regard.[10] At a minimum, commentators and critics should always clarify their own observational standpoint, to adopt the language of the New Haven school of jurisprudence. As three leading exponents of that school have written:

> "Perception of the same phenomenon may vary depending on the culture, class, gender, age, or, in particular, by the profound influence of crisis-experience or trauma on the observer. Even within the formal institutions of the legal establishment, reference and content will vary depending on

---

9 Judicial Council Act 2019, s 23. See Chapter 13 below.

10 Norval Morris once remarked, in an American context, that "[t]he public has been led to expect too much of the criminal justice system generally and grossly too much from sentencing reform." (Morris, "Towards principled sentencing" (1977) 37 Maryland LR 267, 268). The same holds true in most jurisdictions today.

> whether the observer is a legislator, a judge, a prosecutor, a juryman, a defence attorney, an accused, or a victim."[11]

When evaluating the justice or legitimacy of a sentencing decision or the sentencing system more generally, one must always be conscious of the standpoint from which one is viewing it. A given sentence may seem appropriate or inappropriate depending on whether it is viewed from the perspective of the offender, the victim, a criminal law practitioner or, indeed, a member of the public who may or may not be well informed about the facts of the case and the operation of the system.

One of the more contentious issues in sentencing today might be encapsulated in the question: *cui bono*? For whose benefit or in whose interests are sentences imposed? Private law scholars have devoted much attention to the "other-regarding" nature of certain legal relationships and powers. Trustees, company directors and others with fiduciary obligations must exercise their powers, not to advance their own personal interests or preferences, but solely for the benefit of others.[12] The same applies in the realm of public law. In fact, public administration is, or should be, entirely other-regarding. Public officials may never use the power and resources entrusted to them to increase their own wealth or further their own interests. This obviously applies to everyone engaged in the administration of criminal justice, including sentencing judges. Selection of penalty is quintessentially an other-regarding function. But who exactly is "the other" in these circumstances? The offender is undoubtedly one such person. After all, it is he or she who must undergo the hard treatment which the penalty entails, and who has both a moral and constitutional right to proportionate punishment. Society is also an important "other." As the entity on whose behalf sentences are passed, society has an interest in having offenders punished fairly and effectively, bearing in mind that effectiveness is not always to be equated with severity. This leaves the victim, where there is an identifiable one. Some nowadays claim that the victim's interests, or even wishes, should take priority in sentencing. The injury or harm caused to the victim is, of course, a key consideration when determining an appropriate penalty. Victims will naturally have a strong interest in the sentences imposed on those who have harmed them. But this does not entitle them to decide or influence what those sentences should be. Victims are entitled to see justice done at sentencing, but they have that entitlement as members of the public and not as individuals. It is primarily to the public as well as to offenders that courts owe their obligation to impose just sentences.

This book in intended primarily as an educational text, though it will hopefully be of broader use as well. Sentencing has become a significant and increasingly intricate area of legal practice. General principles of

---

11 W Michael Reisman, Siegfried Wiessner and Andrew R Willard, "The New Haven School: A brief introduction" (2007) 32 *Yale Journal of International Law* 575, 579.

12 Lionel Smith, *The Law of Loyalty* (Oxford University Press, 2023).

sentencing are constantly being developed and refined. Lawyers and judges must also keep abreast of the growing number of judicially developed guidelines which will soon be supplemented with, if not replaced by, formal guidelines drawn up by the Judicial Council. The main purpose of this book is to provide students, whether at the academic or professional stage of their legal education, with a reasonably thorough account of the fundamentals of sentencing. It concentrates on general sentencing principles, the moral justifications for state punishment and strategies such as guidelines for structuring judicial sentencing discretion. The procedural aspects of sentencing are dealt with only briefly, in Chapter 2. As against this, every effort has been made to present a holistic account of the topic by showing how sentencing, as we normally understand the term, is merely one official strategy for punishing various kinds of transgressive conduct.[13] Moreover, the judicially imposed penalty is often only part of the overall punishment an offender suffers for the offence. Collateral consequences can be equally punitive and often more enduring in their impact.[14] Further, and as discussed in Chapter 14, executive decisions on prisoner release determine the amount of punishment imprisoned offenders undergo, and that may be significantly less than what was judicially imposed. We tend to think of sentencing as an event – the judicial imposition of a penalty – whereas in reality it is a process extending from the legislative decision to create an offence to the point at which the sentence imposed for a specific offence is finally served.

This book has been a long time in the making, and it was eventually delivered to the publisher years later than originally promised. My first debt of gratitude, therefore, is to David McCartney of Clarus Press who has been unfailingly patient, helpful and encouraging throughout the entire process. The Irish legal community is extremely fortunate to have such a committed and professional publisher. I am also most grateful to Professor Julian Roberts of Oxford University who read an early draft of the chapter on sentencing guidelines (now Chapter 13) and offered many valuable comments on it. Finally, I should thank the University of Galway, from which I have recently retired, for giving me the time, space and resources to pursue research for this book and, indeed, for several earlier ones.

Tom O'Malley
7 February 2025

---

[13] Chapter 1 below.
[14] Chapter 7 below.

TABLE OF CONTENTS

TABLE OF CASES

TABLE OF LEGISLATION

Constitutional Provisions

Pre-1922 Statutes

Acts of the Oireachtas

Statutory Instruments Ireland

European Union

Directives European Union

Other Jurisdictions

Statutes Australia

Statutes Canada

Statutes New Zealand

Statutes United Kingdom

Statutes and Codes USA

Constitution of Belize

Constitution of Canada

International

CHAPTER 1

SENTENCING IN CONTEXT

Viewed as a body of scholarship, sentencing consists of contributions from many disciplines including law, philosophy, sociology, psychology and history. It might, therefore, be viewed as a 'rendezvous discipline', as criminology was once aptly described, because it represents the confluence of several branches of knowledge.[1] Ideally, sentencing scholars should try to draw on the insights and research findings of all the contributing disciplines – and some make brave efforts to do so – but the sheer volume of research now being produced within each of them means that many of us must, reluctantly or otherwise, remain largely within the confines of our own area. It calls to mind Ashburner's fluvial metaphor, familiar to generations of law students, describing the co-existence of law and equity in the wake of the Judicature Acts. He wrote that "though [common law and equity] run in the same channel, [they] run side by side and do not mingle their waters".[2] Much the same can be said of the various disciplines constituting sentencing scholarship, although they do mingle to some degree. Even when sentencing is being studied or analysed primarily from a legal perspective, as in this book, insights from other disciplines must also be considered. The fundamental question of why the state is morally justified in punishing convicted offenders is clearly one of moral and political philosophy. Any discussion of this question must, therefore, engage with the various penal theories advanced by philosophers from classical times onwards. Likewise, empirical analyses of the use of various sentencing options and their effectiveness in producing desired outcomes, such as desistance from crime, must be considered in any evaluation of a sentencing system. Social science research can also shed light on many other sentencing issues including the differential treatment of various population groups.[3] **1–01**

This first chapter aims to locate sentencing within the broader legal system by concentrating on some key contextual issues. Sentencing must be viewed as a process beginning with a political decision to criminalise certain conduct and ending when the penalty ultimately imposed – **1–02**

---

1 The expression 'rendezvous discipline' is usually attributed to Professor David Downes, a leading British criminologist.

2 Walter Ashburner, *Principles of Equity* (Butterworth, 1902), 23.

3 On the evolution of 'punishment and society' as a distinct area of research, see Jonathan Simon and Richard Sparks, "Punishment and society: The emergence of an academic field" in Jonathan Simon and Richard Sparks (eds), *The SAGE Handbook of Punishment and Society* (Sage, 2013).

whether by the trial court or an appeal court – on an individual offender has been fully served or is deemed to have been served. Of course, many offenders will never be sentenced because they escape detection or their offences are never reported, or it is decided, for one reason or another, not to prosecute them. However, our primary concern here is with those cases that reach the point at which a penalty is imposed. The process does not always end there. Courts may be exclusively responsible for imposing sentence, but they cannot as a rule determine how much of a sentence will actually be served, a topic addressed in Chap 14. Part 1 of this chapter deals with criminalisation and the setting of maximum penalties – both fo which are the product of political policy making. Part 2 deals with sentencing as a process. Part 3 deals with the relationship between sentencing and other sanctioning mechanisms such as punitive damages in tort actions, penalties imposed by official regulators and deferred prosecution agreements. It also asks if there is still anything special about the criminal law as a means of securing compliance with social norms. Part 4 deals with restorative justice and its relationship with sentencing.

1. Criminalisation and Maximum Penalties

Criminalisation

1–03 The risk of being subjected to criminal punishment depends, first and foremost, on the range of conduct criminalised within the jurisdiction.[4] Nowadays, the creation of new criminal offences and the amendment of existing offence definitions are exclusively political functions. While the Constitution of Ireland closely regulates the investigation and trial of criminal offences, it imposes few restraints on offence creation.[5] The legislature has largely a free hand in the matter. The principle of legality, a key element of the rule of law, prohibits both the retroactive application of new criminal offences and the imposition of a more severe punishment than applied when the offence was committed. It also requires that criminal offences be clearly and specifically defined so that people may know, or be reasonably able to ascertain, what the law forbids.[6] However, what the legality principle does *not* do is limit the range of conduct

[4] Thomas Sobirk Petersen, *Why Criminalize? New Perspectives on Normative Principles of Criminalization* (Springer, 2020), 4 ("[T]he more acts that are criminalized, the higher the risk of transgressing the criminal law will usually become; and a higher risk of being punished will normally follow that. Furthermore, the risk of being a victim of a crime also depends on which kinds of conduct a state decides to write into the criminal law.").

[5] William J Stuntz, "The political constitution of criminal justice" (2006) 119 Harvard LR 780, 790 makes a similar point about American law. He notes that apart from crimes involving speech, consensual sex, human reproduction and offences such as vagrancy, that may be void for vagueness, the federal constitution places few limits on crime definition.

[6] John Rawls, *A Theory of Justice* (Oxford University Press, 1973), 238 ("For if, say, statutes are not clear in what they enjoin and forbid, the citizen does not know how he is to behave"). It is generally accepted that there will always be some degree of imprecision in legal definitions, a reality that has troubled legal

that may be criminalised. All it demands is that the law be made by the appropriate sovereign, that it be prospective in its application and clear in its meaning.[7] This is not to deny that other dimensions of the rule of law, depending on how that concept is understood, might restrict the range of conduct that may be outlawed. If, as some persuasively argue, the rule of law imposes an obligation to respect fundamental human rights, it would preclude the creation of offences that prohibited or unreasonably restricted the exercise of any of those rights.[8] As we shall see, however, international human rights instruments have also been interpreted to require the creation of criminal offences or to provide for heavier penalties for certain kinds of criminal conduct.

Criminalisation has attracted much academic interest in recent decades, and this is scarcely surprising given the exponential growth in the number of criminal offences. As Lindsay Farmer remarks at the conclusion of his study of the topic: **1–04**

> "The paradox of the modern criminal law is that despite being shaped by a liberal sensibility about the scope of state power and the desire to respect individual rights and liberties, it has expanded in scope, more or less continually, since the late eighteenth century."[9]

The publication of Douglas Husak's *Overcriminalization* in 2007, with its insistence on the need for a general normative theory to determine when criminal offences and the punishments attached to them are justified, sparked a debate that has continued ever since.[10] A decade earlier, Andrew Ashworth had drawn attention to the same phenomenon in England and Wales.[11] The matter received renewed attention when political and media sources claimed that the New Labour Government had created more than 3,500 new offences while in office from 1997 to 2010.[12] Tracking **1–05**

---

theorists. See, for example, Timothy Endicott, "Vagueness and legal theory" (1997) 3 *Legal Theory* 37.

7 The classic account of the law's 'inner morality' in this sense is Lon Fuller, *The Morality of Law*, rev. ed. (Yale University Press, 1969). See also Jeremy Waldron, *Thoughtfulness and the Rule of Law* (Harvard University Press, 2023).

8 On the various versions of the rule of law, see Jonathan Rose, "The rule of law in the western world: An overview" (2004) 35 *Journal of Social Philosophy* 457; Brian Tamanaha, "The rule of law for everyone?" (2002) 55 *Current Legal Problems* 97; TH Bingham, *The Rule of Law* (Allen Lane, 2010) presents an account of the more inclusive version.

9 Lindsay Farmer, *Making the Modern Criminal Law: Criminalization and Civil Order* (Oxford University Press, 2016), 298. See also AP Simester *et al*, *Simester and Sullivan's Criminal Law*, 6th ed. (Bloomsbury, 2016), Chap 16.

10 Douglas Husak, *Overcriminalization: The Limits of the Criminal Law* (Oxford University Press, 2007).

11 Andrew Ashworth, "Is the criminal law a lost cause?" (2000) 116 LQR 116 and reprinted in Ashworth, *Positive Obligations in Criminal Law* (Hart Publishing, 2013). See also Ashworth "Conceptions of Overcriminalization" (2008) 5 *Ohio State Journal of Criminal Law* 407.

12 David Hare, "Labour's criminal record – 3,600 new offences and 86,637 inmates", *The Guardian*, 8 April 2010.

the creation of new criminal offences can be quite complex, as scholars have shown,[13] but it is undoubtedly true that many offences are created because the criminal process happens to be the most effective and efficient way of controlling the conduct they prohibit. Further, a distinction must be drawn between formal and substantive criminalisation.[14] Formal criminalisation occurs when the legislature creates new criminal offences, often in response to pressure of one kind or another. Whether this law is ever enforced – substantive criminalisation – depends on policies adopted and decisions made by law enforcement authorities, notably police and prosecutors, and on the resources available to them.

1–06 Theorising about the proper scope and function of the criminal law is by no means new. In the mid-twentieth century, for example, it focused on the relationship between law and morality, as reflected in the Hart-Devlin debate.[15] Hart espoused the liberal approach associated with John Stuart Mill who had claimed that the law may intervene in peoples' lives only to prevent harm to others.[16] Devlin was more inclined to legal moralism, arguing that a society is entitled to protect its moral integrity just as much as its physical or territorial integrity, and that a rigid separation of law and morality is therefore inappropriate. In most Western countries, the Mill-Hart approach has triumphed, as reflected, for example, in measures decriminalising consensual homosexual acts and, more recently, permitting same-sex marriage. Granted, the concept of "harm to others" is more problematic than Mill and some of his later disciples acknowledged. Ideas about what constitutes 'harm', whether to oneself or others, change and develop across time and place.[17] However, there are now few vestiges of legal moralism.

1–07 Concern about criminalisation now centres mainly on the number of new offences being created, and the extent to which some of them outlaw conduct that would not traditionally have come within the definition of inchoate, let alone completed, offences.[18] Many of them are designed to counteract perceived risks rather than respond to harm already done

---

13 James Chalmers and Fiona Leverick, "Tracking the creation of criminal offences" [2013] Crim LR 543; James Chalmers, Fiona Leverick and Alasdair Shaw, "Is formal criminalisation really on the rise; Evidence from the 1950s" [2015} Crim LR 177; James Chalmers and Fiona Leverick, "Criminal law in the shadows: Creating offences in delegated legislation" (2018) 38 *Legal Studies* 321.

14 Nicola Lacey and Lucia Zedner, "Criminalization: Historical, legal, and criminological perspectives" in Alison Liebling, Shadd Maruna and Lesley McAra (eds), *The Oxford Handbook of Criminology*, 6th ed. (Oxford University Press, 2017), 57, 59.

15 HLA Hart, *Law, Liberty, and Morality* (Oxford University Press, 1963); Patrick Devlin, *The Enforcement of Morals* (Oxford University Press, 1965).

16 John Stuart Mill, *On Liberty* (Penguin Books, 1982), 68 (first published 1859).

17 Bernard Harcourt, "The collapse of the harm principle" (1999) 90 *Journal of Criminal Law and Criminology* 109.

18 Husak, note 10 above; RA Duff et al. (eds), *Criminalization: The Political Morality of the Criminal Law* (Oxford University Press, 2014); RA Duff, *The Realm of Criminal Law* (Oxford University Press, 2018).

which, historically, was the criminal law's primary concern. As Lucia Zedner has observed:

> "In important respects we are on the cusp of a shift from a post- to a pre-crime society, a society in which the possibility of forestalling risks competes with and even takes precedence over responding to wrongs done. In consequence, the post-crime orientation of criminal justice is increasingly overshadowed by the pre-crime logic of security."[19]

The liberal model of criminal law is based on the principle that the purpose of that law is to punish and censure those duly proved guilty of criminal offences, while respecting the dignity and autonomy of the persons concerned.[20] Moreover, the primary purpose of the criminal law, according to this model, is to punish past wrongdoing, meaning harm already caused with the requisite degree of culpability. Of course, even liberal theorists accept that the law must also do what it reasonably can to prevent people from harming others. This is the underlying rationale of inchoate offences such as attempt. During the past few decades, however, the criminal law has taken a distinct 'preventive turn' with a much greater emphasis on proscribing and punishing conduct that is deemed to pose a risk to personal safety and security, even where that conduct is quite remote from the apprehended harm.[21] **1–08**

Security has become a major preoccupation of governments, especially since the 9/11 attacks in the United States in 2001. In many countries, legislation has been enacted that is designed to promote personal or subjective feelings of security. To this end, offences were created that prohibited "not only conduct that undermines our feelings of security but also conduct that *might* undermine them, conduct that manifests an indifference to others' feelings of security."[22] Terrorism-related offences are often cited as exemplifying this phenomenon. For instance, the (British) Terrorism Act 2006 (s 5(1)) provides: **1–09**

> "A person commits an offence if, with the intention of (a) committing acts of terrorism, or (b) assisting another to commit such acts, he engages in any conduct in preparation for giving effect to his intention."

Conduct "in preparation for giving effect" to the relevant intention could be very far removed from the completed offence which might never, of course, occur. Another pertinent example is s 58 of the (British) **1–10**

---

19 Lucia Zedner, "Pre-crime and post-criminology?" (2007) 11 *Theoretical Criminology* 261, 262.

20 Andrew Ashworth and Lucia Zedner, "Defending the criminal law: Reflections on the changing character of crime, procedure, and sanctions" (2008) 2 *Criminal Law and Philosophy* 21.

21 Henrique Carvahlo, *The Preventive Turn in Criminal Law* (Oxford University Press, 2017), Chap 1 has a excellent account of the tension between liberal and preventive models of criminal law.

22 Peter Ramsay, *The Insecurity State: Vulnerable Autonomy and the Right to Security in the Criminal Law* (Oxford University Press, 2012), 2.

Terrorism Act 2000 which makes it an offence punishable with up to 15 years' imprisonment to (a) collect or record information of a kind likely to be useful to a person committing or planning an act of terrorism; (b) to possess material of this kind, or (c) view or accesses such material on the internet.[23] As we shall see in Chap 5, when discussing harm, many "ordinary" criminal offences such as corruption[24] and the growing number of possession-based offences may also be committed without proof of any actual harm having occurred.[25] This is not to say that the criminalisation of all such conduct is unjustified or unnecessary, but it undoubtedly extends the reach of state power and can pose difficulties in identifying appropriate sentences.

1–11 Preventive justice includes much more than terrorism-related measures. It manifests itself most noticeably in the growing number of statutory provisions authorising courts to make civil orders, the breach of which is a criminal offence. These orders typically relate to anti-social or threatening conduct of one kind or another. The best-known example in these islands is the Anti-Social Behaviour Order (ASBO) introduced in England and Wales in 1998.[26] Such an order could be granted by a magistrates' court on the application of a local authority or senior police officer if it appeared to the applicant that a person had caused or was likely to cause harassment, alarm or distress to others and that the order was necessary to protect others from further anti-social conduct by that person. Magistrates could make an order, which had to last for at least two years, prohibiting the person from doing anything described in the order. A breach of the order was an offence punishable with up to six months' imprisonment following summary conviction or five years following conviction on indictment. ASBOs were abolished in 2014 but replaced with a range of other orders that are rather similar in nature.[27] Ireland has a growing number of such

---

23 In *R v John (Ben)* [2022] EWCA Crim 54; [2022] 2 Cr App R (S) 20, the defendant, shortly before his 20th birthday, was found in possession of a large quantity of far-right extremist material as well as a copy of *The Anarchist Cookbook* which contained instructions on how to make explosive devices. Having been convicted solely on the charge of possessing *The Anarchist Cookbook* (which he had downloaded at the age of 13), he was given a two-year sentence suspended on rather unusual conditions, including a requirement that he read the works of Jane Austen. However, following an undue leniency application by the Attorney General, the Court of Appeal substituted a sentence of two years' immediate imprisonment.

24 Criminal Justice (Corruption Offences) Act 2018, s 5.

25 Jeremy Horder, "Harmless wrongdoing and the anticipatory perspective on criminalisation" in GR Sullivan and Ian Dennis (eds), *Seeking Security: Pre-Empting the Commission of Criminal Harms* (Hart Publishing, 2012), Chap 4.

26 Crime and Disorder Act 1998, s 1 (since repealed).

27 Anti-social behaviour, Crime and Policing Act 2014. See Rory Kelly and Andrew Ashworth, "State responses to criminal offences in England and Wales and the problem of equality" in Matthew Dyson and Benjamin Vogel (eds), *The Limits of Criminal Law: Anglo-German Concepts and Principles* (Insentia, 2018), Chap 17. For more detailed discussion and criticism of the ABSO while it existed, see Andrew Ashworth and Lucia Zedner, *Preventive Justice* (Oxford University Press, 2015), Chap 4; Ramsay, note 22 above, Chap 2; Ian Dennis, "Security,

provisions, as exemplified by s 115 of the Criminal Justice Act 2006 which permits the District Court to grant a 'civil order' which is effectively an ASBO in everything but name.[28] A breach of such an order is an offence punishable with up to six months' imprisonment. The Criminal Justice (Miscellaneous Provisions) Act 2023 authorises the District Court to grant "civil orders against relevant conduct" to prevent harassment, stalking and other conduct of that nature. The breach of such an order is an offence punishable with up to 12 months' imprisonment.[29]

International human rights law has been another driver of criminalisation, though its influence in this regard tends to be overstated. The relationship between human rights and criminal law has been described as paradoxical.[30] Originally, international human rights law was primarily concerned with protecting individuals from unfair application of the criminal law (in both its substantive and procedural dimensions) and from excessive punishment. That remains one of its more important functions. However, human rights bodies have increasingly looked to criminalisation and, at times, insisted on it as a human rights protection mechanism. Christine Van den Wyngaert, a former judge of the International Criminal Court and a leading international criminal law scholar, is accredited with developing the 'shield and sword' metaphor.[31] At one time, human rights were seen as providing a defence or a shield against the application of the criminal law, but over time it has weaponised the criminal law as a protective mechanism.[32] Increasingly, international human rights instruments and EU directives demand the criminalisation of certain kinds of conduct. Further, the European Court of Human Rights has occasionally found states to be in violation of the European Convention on Human Rights because of gaps in substantive criminal law or because of failure to impose sufficiently severe punishment.[33] **1–12**

There is a common tendency to treat criminalisation as morally **1–13**

risk and preventive orders" in Sullivan and Dennis, note 25 above, Chap 8. On the anti-social behaviour injunction introduced by s 1 of the 2014 Act, see Rory Kelly, "Reconsidering the punishment-prevention divide" (2019) 135 LQR 12, dealing with *Jones v Birmingham City Council* [2018] EWCA Civ 1189; [2019] QB 521; [2018] 2 Cr App R 23.

[28] For an analysis of this provision, see *Tallon v DPP* [2022] IEHC 322.

[29] Likewise, a breach of various civil orders introduced in the Domestic Violence Act 2018 constitutes a criminal offence.

[30] Mireille Delmas-Marty, "Le paradox pénal" in M Delmas-Marty and C Lucas de Leyssac (eds), *Libertés et Droits Fondamentaux* (Seuil, 1996), 368.

[31] Françoise Tulkens, "The paradoxical relationship between criminal law and human rights" (2011) 9 *Journal of International Criminal Justice* 577.

[32] Mattia Pinto, "Historical trends of human rights gone criminal" (2020) 42 *Human Rights Quarterly* 729; Mattia Pinto, "Awakening the Leviathan through human rights law – How human rights bodies trigger the application of criminal law" (2018) 34 *Utrecht Journal of International and European Law* 161; Karen Engle, "Anti-impunity and the turn to criminal law" (2015) 100 Cornell LR 1069.

[33] See, for example, *Stoyanova v Bulgaria* (2022) 75 EHRR 27; *Gäfgen v Germany* (2011) 52 EHRR 1; *Okkali v Turkey* (2010) 50 EHRR 43.

problematic, but it is often necessary and, indeed, beneficial. When evidence emerges of new or newly-discovered behaviour that is seriously harmful or injurious to others, the state is obliged to take all appropriate steps to prevent it. The criminal law is usually the most appropriate means of doing so. Modern examples of such behaviour include human trafficking, forced labour and slavery. Heightened social awareness of the harmfulness of conduct that was not traditionally treated very seriously may also justify the creation of new criminal offences or the prescription of more severe punishment than hitherto applied. Harassment and domestic violence (including the offence of coercive control) would fall into this category.[34] Technology, for all its benefits, has also engendered new kinds of criminal activity and facilitated the commission of existing criminal conduct in novel ways. Child pornography, for example, existed long before the internet, but it began to proliferate to an alarming extent once its producers and users began to take advantage of the internet. This led many countries to introduce new laws prohibiting the production, distribution and possession of child pornography.[35] The same holds true of various kinds of fraudulent transactions.

1–14 As will be evident from this brief and necessarily incomplete survey of recent trends in criminalisation, the offences now known to our law vary enormously in terms of the motivation for their creation, the harm they are designed to prevent and punish, and the distance between the prohibited conduct and the apprehended harm. A consequent challenge for the sentencing system, if it aims to respect ordinal proportionality, is to identify and develop a method for assessing the comparative gravity of the myriad offences now known to our law and, especially, those designed to prevent remote harms. Should risk-based offences always attract less punishment than those offences, such as assaults and robberies, that inflict immediate harm? To what extent should the nature of the apprehended harm, irrespective of its remoteness from the prohibited conduct, determine where an offence should be located on the overall scale of gravity? Questions such as these underscore the need for a holistic and comprehensive approach to the formulation of sentencing principles and guidelines. Practice-derived sentence ranges may be acceptable on an offence-specific basis, but they may fail to reflect the relative gravity of the offending conduct when viewed within the context of the criminal law as a whole.

Maximum Penalties

1–15 Virtually all offences known to Irish law carry maximum, as opposed to mandatory, sentences. Murder is the only commonly prosecuted offence that is punishable with a truly mandatory sentence (life imprisonment).[36]

---

34 Non-Fatal Offences Against the Person Act 1997, s 10 (harassment); Domestic Violence Act 2018, Pt 3.

35 In Ireland, this was accomplished with the Child Trafficking and Pornography Act 1998.

36 Criminal Justice Act 1990, s 2.

A small number of drug and firearms offences are subject to presumptive minimum sentences, but courts may impose sentences below the specified minimums in certain circumstances.[37] A maximum sentence both confers and limits judicial discretion; a court may impose any penalty up to, but not beyond, the specified maximum. In practice, however, maximum sentences seldom curb judicial discretion to any appreciable extent, as they tend to be pitched at a high level. Many serious offences, including manslaughter, rape, robbery and drug dealing carry maximum sentences of life imprisonment which means that, in theory at least, they may be punished with determinate prison sentences of any length or with a life sentence which is effectively indeterminate. Thirty years may be a long sentence but it is, again in theory, less than life (though in reality, of course, this depends on the offender's age at the time of sentence). It can also happen, usually for historical reasons, that a maximum sentence may be remarkably low by today's standards and values, although recent law reform has largely solved this problem. Under the Children Act 1908 (s 12), for example, the maximum sentence for cruelty to a child was a fine of £100, two years' imprisonment or both. It is now the Euro equivalent of £10,000, seven years' imprisonment or both.[38] A further reason why maximum sentences often have little practical effect is that a significant percentage of offenders are sentenced at the same time for more than one offence, or they are already serving a prison sentence following an earlier conviction. Courts have considerable discretion in ordering prison sentences to run concurrently or consecutively, and fines may also be cumulative.[39] The cumulative sentence imposed for several offences may well exceed the maximum available for any one of them.

Statutory maximum penalties have assumed greater significance with the **1–16** advent of sentencing guidelines. It is already a well-established sentencing principle that a court must always have regard to the maximum when deciding on the penalty in a specific case. This stands to reason. A court must begin, as a rule, by locating the offence on the overall scale of gravity which will have a penalty range typically extending from zero to the specified maximum. The chosen location on the scale will determine the headline sentence to which further adjustments must be made to reflect offender-related factors. Judicially-developed guidelines in this jurisdiction consist mainly of recommended sentence ranges.[40] Typically, though not invariably, the overall statutory penalty range is divided into three equal, or roughly equal, parts. Thus, for an offence with a maximum sentence of nine years' imprisonment, the guideline ranges will be zero to three years, three to six years and six to nine years. Where an offence carries a maximum sentence of life imprisonment, the Court of Appeal usually proceeds on the basis that the effective maximum is in the region of 15 years.[41] The recommended guideline ranges will, therefore, probably

---

[37] Chap 10 below.
[38] Children Act 2001, s 246.
[39] See Chap 5 on consecutive and concurrent sentences.
[40] Chap 13 below.
[41] See, for example, *People (DPP) v Byrne* [2018] IECA 120, para 60.

be zero to five years, five to 10 years and 10 to 15 years, subject to the caveat that sentences in excess of 15 years will be appropriate in some cases.

1–17 In a guideline system of this nature, the significance of statutory maximum penalties is self-evident. The higher the maximum, the more severe each of the recommended ranges will be. By way of illustration, in *People (DPP) v Lennon*[42] the Court of Appeal offered guidance on sentencing for witness intimidation. When first introduced under the Criminal Justice Act 1999 (s 41), this offence carried a maximum sentence of 10 years' imprisonment, but this was increased, for no particularly compelling reason, to 15 years under the Criminal Justice (Amendment) Act 2009 (s 16). In *Lennon* the court adopted the standard tripartite approach and recommended sentence ranges of zero to five years, five to 10 years and 10 to 15 years. It held that the more serious of the two intimidation offences in that case fell into the middle range and merited a headline sentence of eight years' imprisonment, reduced to six years in recognition of a guilty plea. Other sentences were ordered to run concurrently or taken into consideration. Had the maximum sentence for witness intimidation remained at 10 years, the recommended guideline ranges would have been commensurately lower and, in all probability, the sentences ultimately imposed in this case would have been somewhat lower as well. The same holds true of the offence of participating in the activities of a criminal organisation which, when first introduced by the Criminal Justice Act 2006 (s 72), carried a maximum sentence of five years but this too was increased to 15 years by the Criminal Justice (Amendment) Act 2009 (s 6) which also substituted a new definition of the offence.[43]

1–18 The major problem with maximum sentences is that they are often the product of historical accident and cannot therefore be relied upon to produce true proportionality in sentencing practice.[44] It would be all very well if maximum sentences were chosen according to a rational scheme in which each was carefully ranked, having regard to the inherent gravity of the offence to which it attached compared with the gravity of other offences. Historically, at least, this seldom happened, with the result that there were some extraordinary anomalies. In 1965, Rupert Cross devoted part of his inaugural lecture at Oxford to listing some of these anomalies including, for example, the two-year maximum for indecent assault upon a female compared with a maximum of 10 years for indecent assault on a male (a differential that later led to a successful constitutional challenge in Ireland).[45] About the same time, HLA Hart noted that under the Malicious Damage Act 1861 (ss 14 and 39), maliciously damaging a work of art was punishable with a maximum of six months' imprisonment whereas

---

42 [2021] IECA 30.

43 See *People (DPP) v Aylmer* [2020] IECA 106.

44 Rory Kelly, "Reforming maximum sentences and respecting ordinal proportionality" [2018] Crim LR 450.

45 ARN Cross, *Paradoxes in Prison Sentences* (Clarendon Press, 1965). See *M(S) v Ireland (No.2)* [2007] IEHC 280; [2007] 4 IR 369, and *People (DPP) v Maher* [2016] IESC 31; [2016] 2 IR 634.

maliciously damaging textiles was punishable with a maximum of life imprisonment.[46] Many of these anomalies have been ironed out in the meantime. All sexual assaults are now punishable with a maximum 10 years' imprisonment, or 14 years where the victim was under 17 years at the time of the assault.[47] Virtually all of the Malicious Damage Act 1861 was repealed by the Criminal Damage Act 1991 which created three general offences related to damaging property. Following conviction on indictment, these are punishable with a maximum of 10 years' imprisonment or life imprisonment where the damage was caused by arson. As discussed in Chap 5, in the context of proportionality, a court must always have regard to statutory changes in maximum sentences when selecting penalties in specific cases and also when indicating guideline ranges. However, the fact remains that true sentencing consistency is impossible to attain unless maximum sentences are ordinally proportionate.

2. Sentencing as Process

Sentencing is often viewed as an event that begins and ends with the judicial imposition of a penalty on a convicted person. This is indeed a crucial moment, but it is only one step in a process that will have begun much earlier and, in many instances, will end much later. The process may be said to begin with the political decision to criminalise the relevant conduct and prescribe a maximum sentence for it. Where it ends depends on how an individual case unfolds. A recorded offence may never result in a prosecution (perhaps because the perpetrator cannot be identified or apprehended) and, even it does, the defendant may be acquitted. Where there is a conviction, especially for a serious offence, the imposition of sentence by the trial court is seldom the end of the matter. There may be an appeal against conviction, sentence or both. If a prison sentence is ultimately imposed, a decision must later be taken as to when the offender should be released, conditionally or otherwise. James Q Whitman identifies ten "decision points" in the criminal process, beginning with legislative criminalisation and ending with the termination of punishment, with some measure of discretion being exercised by some official or group at each point.[48] He was writing in an American context but his analysis is broadly applicable in these islands as well. William J Stuntz invites us to imagine the criminal process as a giant funnel which a large number of people (millions in the American context in which he was writing) enter annually through being investigated or arrested. But relatively few emerge from the narrow end, in the sense of being convicted and sentenced.[49] **1–19**

[46] HLA Hart, *Punishment and Responsibility: Essays in the Philosophy of Law*, 2nd ed. (Oxford University Press, 2008), 116. First published 1968.

[47] Criminal Law (Rape) (Amendment) Act 1990, s 2 as amended by Sex Offenders Act 2001, s 37.

[48] James Q Whitman, "Equality in criminal law: The two divergent Western roads" (2009) 1 *Journal of Legal Analysis* 119, 121-122.

[49] Stuntz, note 5 above, at 782.

1–20 In institutional terms, the criminal justice system operates through a subtle mix of independence and collaboration. Each of the principal institutions – police, prosecutors, courts, prisons, probation service, parole authority – is to a great extent operationally independent of the others. In Ireland, for example, the prosecution of serious offences is constitutionally assigned to the Director of Public Prosecutions, just as the trial of offences is assigned to the courts.[50] Yet, decisions taken by one agency can determine or significantly influence the choices available to another. The charge preferred by a prosecutor against an accused will determine the maximum sentence that may be imposed in the event of a conviction. At the other end of the spectrum, courts impose but do not implement sentences. Implementation is the responsibility of the executive branch of government. Therefore, a judicially-imposed prison sentence represents the maximum the offender will be required to serve. In all probability, through the operation of remission, parole and other early release mechanisms, the term served will be shorter, and perhaps considerably shorter, that than imposed by the court.

1–21 Prosecutors exercise considerable influence over sentence. In fact, by exercising their well-established discretion not to prosecute even where there is sufficient evidence to justify so doing, they can exempt offenders from any censure or punishment. (This is not a decision to be made arbitrarily; there must be a good reason, having regard to the public interest, for refraining from prosecuting in these circumstances).[51] As James Edwards notes, "many criminal offences now exist alongside guidance that instructs prosecutors to refrain from prosecuting offenders whose acts are morally innocuous".[52] Of equal importance, prosecutors usually enjoy considerable discretion in deciding on the charges to be brought and, increasingly, on the mode of trial. They are not obliged to charge the most serious offence the available evidence might support.[53] In any event, the alleged conduct may come within the definition of more than one offence. Further, the proliferation of hybrid offences that may be prosecuted either summarily or on indictment at the election of the prosecutor means that, in many instances, the prosecutor can effectively

---

50 Constitution of Ireland, Arts 30.3 and 34 respectively; Prosecution of Offences Act 1974.

51 Most common law countries, including Ireland, apply some version of the Shawcross doctrine which holds that not all offences need be prosecuted, even where it is legally possible to do so. See Thomas O'Malley, *The Criminal Process* (Round Hall, 2009), 382-388. This is reflected in the DPP's *Guidelines for Prosecutors,* 5th ed (Office of the DPP, 2019).

52 James Edwards, "Master principles of criminalisation" (2016) 7 *Jurisprudence* 138, 147-148, referring to Jonathan Rogers, "The role of the public prosecutor in applying and developing the substantive criminal law" in RA Duff et al (eds), *The Constitution of the Criminal Law* (Oxford University Press, 2013). See also Kenneth J Melilli, "Prosecutorial discretion in an adversary system" [1992] BYU LR 669; Shima Baradaran Baughman, "Can prosecutorial declination end overincarceration?" at https://papers.ssrn.com/so13/papers,cfm?abstract_id=4842851> accessed 27 November 2024.

53 *People (DPP) v J (D)* [2017] IECA 181; [2017] 3 IR 677.

determine the upper limit of the punishment to which an accused, if convicted, will be subject. The maximum custodial sentence following summary conviction will never exceed 12 months, whereas it could be 10 years or more following conviction on indictment.[54]

The second additional actor is the executive branch of government which is responsible for the implementation of judicially-imposed sentences, as described in Chap 14. Suffice it to note here that the executive has a constitutional prerogative to commute or remit any punishment,[55] as well as statutory powers to grant various kinds of early release to prisoners. As already mentioned, most prisoners are released before they have served their sentences in full. Yet, executive release decisions are of very low visibility compared with judicial sentencing decisions. They are made away from the public gaze and, even when they become known, are unlikely to attract media attention except in the very rare case of a high-profile offender. However, the visibility levels of key decisions affecting sentence bear little relationship to their impact on the punishment, if any, which an offender will undergo. **1–22**

3. Sentencing, Punishment and Regulation

The criminal law is just one legal strategy for regulating human and corporate conduct. In fact, the law in its totality is only one means of promoting conformity with social norms. Custom, convention, etiquette, religious beliefs, philosophical commitments and fear of social disapproval all provide reasons and incentives, at least at certain times and for certain people, to adhere to acceptable standards of behaviour. But even within the broad realm of the law itself, the criminal law (with its penalty system) is but one of the strategies for responding to illegal conduct, including conduct coming within the definition of established criminal offences. Tort law, regulatory regimes, confiscation of assets and diversionary schemes are among the others.[56] With the growing use of regulatory sanctions in particular, sentencing is no longer co-extensive with officially imposed punishment. Regulatory agencies, especially those regulating financial services, nowadays have significant enforcement powers, including the authority to impose very heavy monetary penalties. Further, in some jurisdictions at least, courts are willing to award substantial punitive damages to successful plaintiffs in tort actions. Criminal sentencing is therefore part of a network of official responses to wrongdoing. It will not always be the most punitive or, in some instances, the most effective of those responses. This observation has little relevance to 'core' crimes **1–23**

---

54 This is true of theft (Criminal Justice (Theft and Fraud Offences) Act 2001, ss 4 and 53), although this is a rare instance where the accused as well as the prosecutor must consent to summary trial.

55 Constitution of Ireland, Art 13.6.

56 For an excellent collection of essays on this topic, see Elise Bant, Wayne Courtney, James Goudkamp and Jeannie Marie Patterson (eds), *Punishment and Private Law* (Hart Publishing, 2021).

such as offences against the person and the traditional offences against property, but it has considerable relevance to white-collar and corporate crime which is widely assumed to be under-reported, under-investigated and under-prosecuted. Empirical verification of this claim may be difficult but, whether objectively true or not, it must be considered against the backdrop of the broader sanctioning network just mentioned. Financial malpractice, for example, may be punished with heavy regulatory fines, just as misconduct by public officials may result in punitive damages being awarded to the injured party. Assets suspected of being the proceeds of crime may be seized by the Criminal Assets Bureau and ultimately confiscated by the State through a process that is entirely civil rather than criminal. Deferred prosecution agreements, now available in some jurisdictions, permit corporations (and in some instances individuals) to avoid prosecution and the conviction that might follow, but usually in return for paying a heavy financial penalty and fulfilling other, sometimes onerous, conditions.

1–24 This multiplicity of sanctioning strategies is by no means a recent phenomenon. 30 years ago, Abraham Goldstein wrote that America had "a helter-skelter cumulation of processes and sanctions. Civil processes and sanctions have emerged that are often more punitive than criminal processes but equally stigmatising".[57] Indeed, Sanford Kadish made similar observations in the early 1960s.[58] The same may now be said of Ireland and many other countries. Some scholars attribute this to the economic theory of law with its emphasis on efficiency and utilitarian objectives, including deterrence. Carol Steiker, for example, claims that the growth of this theory correlates "with the expansion of 'hybrid' sanctioning authority in the administrative state."[59] The law and economics movement cannot be held entirely responsible because hybrid sanctioning existed long before that movement began to make its presence felt. However, it has probably had an accelerating effect. Some of its leading exponents hold that where tort remedies, including punitive damages, provide an adequate deterrent, there is no need to resort to criminal law. Recognising that many wrongdoers cannot afford to pay damages, punitive or otherwise, they are content to let the criminal law apply primarily to the 'nonaffluent'.[60]

---

57 Abraham Goldstein, "White-collar crime and civil sanctions" (1992) 101 Yale LJ 1895, 1899.

58 Sanford H Kadish, "Some observations on the use of criminal sanctions in enforcing economic regulations" (1963) 30 Univ Chicago LR 423.

59 Carol S Steiker, "Punishment theory and the criminal-civil divide" (1997) 85 Georgetown LJ 775, 780. She also writes (p 784): "Economic analysis of law has fundamentally recast the nature of civil and criminal sanctions in a way that portrays them as related parts of a unitary scheme of state control of private behaviour."

60 Richard A Posner, "An economic theory of the criminal law" (1985) 85 Columbia LR 1993, 1204.

Punitive Damages

Tort law differs from criminal law in some important respects. Under tort law, it is up to the injured party to institute proceedings against the alleged wrongdoer. A successful tort action ordinarily results in the wrongdoer being ordered to provide redress, usually in the form of monetary damages, to the injured party. It is, after all, a system of personal redress, and a means of repairing wrongful losses.[61] A further difference is that compensation may be paid by a third party rather than by the wrongdoer personally. What matters is that it should be paid.[62] (The same admittedly is true of a criminal fine.) There are several theories of tort law, but the corrective justice theory has gained considerable academic support in recent years. Corrective justice "demands that wrongful (or unjust) gains and losses be rectified, eliminated, or annulled".[63] The idea can be traced back to Aristotle who drew a distinction between distributive justice and corrective justice, the former being transactional in nature. A person who wrongfully possesses something that rightfully belongs to another must, as a matter of justice, be obliged to restore it to its rightful owner.[64] This captures the essence of corrective justice, even as it is understood today, although the range of conduct recognised as tortious has expanded greatly since Aristotle's time. The very notion of corrective justice suggests that the purpose of any remedy granted in its name is compensatory. It is to put the plaintiff in the position he or she would have been in if the tortious act had not occurred, in so far as that is practically possible.[65] Granted, compensation is often an imperfect remedy for plaintiffs who have sustained serious personal injuries; no amount of money may be capable of restoring them to the state of health or ability they enjoyed before the injury was inflicted.[66] **1–25**

In practice, however, damages may be used to punish the wrongdoer in addition to compensating the victim.[67] Lord Mansfield's declaration **1–26**

---

61 John CP Goldberg, "Twentieth-century tort theory" (2003) 91 Georgetown LJ 513.

62 Jules Coleman, "Theories of tort law", *Stanford Encyclopedia of Philosophy* at https://stanford.library.usyd.edu/ > accessed 27 November 2024.

63 Jules Coleman, "Tort law and the demands of corrective justice" (1992) 67 Indiana LR 349, 357. See also Jules Coleman, *Risks and Wrongs* (Cambridge University Press, 1992), 324.

64 Aristotle, *Nicomachean Ethics,* translated by JAK Thomson, (Penguin Books, 1976), Chap 5, iv (where the translator prefers the term 'rectificatory justice'). See also Ernest Weinrib, "Corrective Justice" (1992) 77 Iowa LR 403; Stephen R Perry, "The moral foundations of tort law" (1992) 77 Iowa LR 449; John Rawls, *A Theory of Justice* (Oxford University Press, 1972), 10.

65 *Island Ferries Teoranta v Minister for Communications* [2012] IEHC 256, para 29. Cass Sunstein, "The limits of compensatory justice" in John W Chapman (ed), *Compensatory Justice,* Nomos XXXIII (New York University Press, 1991), 281, 282 (where he goes on to say that it is not the purpose of the remedy "to engage in any kind of social reordering or social management except in so far as these functions are logically entailed by the principle of compensation").

66 *Reddy v Bates* [1983] IR 141, 150 (McCarthy J).

67 *United States v Halper* 490 US 435, 447 (1989) ("It is commonly understood that

in 1775 that "there is no distinction better known, than the distinction between civil and criminal law, or between criminal prosecutions and civil actions"[68] may have been largely true at the time, but a decade earlier the distinction had already become blurred with the award of punitive damages in two well-known cases, *Wilkes v Wood*[69] and *Huckle v Money*.[70] In *Wilkes*, Pratt CJ instructed the jury that damages could be awarded, not only to compensate, "but likewise as a punishment to the guilty, to deter from such proceeding for the future, and as a proof of the detestation of the jury to the action itself". This encapsulates the essential purposes of punitive damages today – retribution, deterrence and condemnation. Modern case law from both sides of the Atlantic is suffused with statements to this effect. In Ireland, at least as far back as 1920, it was held that such damages were intended "to punish the defendant in an exemplary manner".[71] In *Rookes v Barnard*, a leading English authority, Lord Devlin stated that the object of exemplary damages "is to punish and deter".[72] (The terms 'exemplary damages' and 'punitive damages' are used interchangeably in English and Irish law,[73] though in the United States the term 'punitive damages' is preferred.) Likewise, the Canadian Supreme Court, in holding that punitive damages could be awarded for breach of contract, stated quite categorically that the purpose of such damages was to punish the defendant[74] and the United States Supreme Court has held that punitive damages serve the same purposes as criminal penalties.[75] Ireland is no different. In *Conway v Irish National Teachers Organisation*,[76] the Supreme Court held that Irish law recognises three different heads of damages for torts and breaches of constitutional rights: (1) compensatory damages; (2) aggravated damages; and (3) punitive damages. All three members of the court stressed that punitive damages were intended to mark disapproval of the defendant's conduct, to punish that conduct and to deter others.[77] McCarthy J likened the power to award punitive damages

civil proceedings may advance punitive as well as remedial goals…").

68 *Atcheson v Everitt* (1775) 1 Cowp 382; 98 Eng Rep 1142, 1147.

69 (1763) Lofft 1; 98 Eng Rep 489.

70 (1763) 2 Wils KB 205; 95 Eng Rep 768.

71 *Worthington v Tipperary County Council* [1920] 2 IR 233, 245.

72 [1964] AC 1129, 1221.

73 *McIntyre v Lewis* [1991] 1 IR 121, 139. Both terms are used in the Civil Liability Act 1961. In fact, both terms are now used in the same section (s 7) as a result of the insertion of new subsection.

74 *Whiten v Pilot Insurance Co.* [2002] 1 SCR 595. For a critique of this decision, see Ernest Weinrib, *Corrective Justice* (Oxford University Press, 2012), Chap 5. Several American states also permit recovery of punitive damages for breach of contract; see *Pacific Mutual Life Insurance v Haslip* 499 US 1 (1991), O'Connor J dissenting.

75 *State Farm Mut Auto Ins Co v Campbell* 538 US 408, 417 (2003) where the court added that defendants subjected to punitive damages are not accorded the protections applicable in criminal proceedings. See also *BMW of North America Inc v Gore* 517 US 559 (1996) which has a good discussion of the history and purposes of punitive damages.

76 [1991] 2 IR 305.

77 [1991] 2 IR 305, 317 (Finlay CJ), 323 (Griffin J) and 326 (McCarthy J). See also *McIntyre v Lewis* [1991] 1 IR 121.

to a court's duty to vindicate constitutional rights, drawing a comparison for this purpose with the power to exclude unconstitutionally obtained evidence. More recently, courts have tended to award punitive damages in respect of torts that also constituted breaches of constitutional rights.[78] A breach of rights, even a grave breach, will not automatically entitle a plaintiff to punitive damages, but they are likely to be awarded where the defendant's conduct was particularly objectionable, or degrading towards the plaintiff.[79] Whatever the reason for awarding such damages in any particular case, the policy objective is unambiguously punitive. Indeed, it has been said that while punitive damages take the form of a financial penalty, they are in substance a moral sanction.[80]

Anomalous therefore though it may seem when viewed through the lens of corrective justice, tort law (and, in jurisdictions such as Canada, contract law) can accomplish goals that are primarily associated with the criminal law, namely, to censure, punish and deter. Moreover, the conduct being punished might well come within the definition of a criminal offence such as assault, harassment or interception of communications, as exemplified by some recent Irish cases where punitive damages were awarded.[81] A tort action in these circumstances bears some similarity to a private prosecution, save that the plaintiff's sole purpose is to secure compensation, even if this entails some degree of punishment for the offender. Punitive damages, when awarded in these circumstances, might be viewed as a fine or monetary penalty payable to the injured party rather than to the State. All this, of course, rests on the assumption that it is the actual wrongdoer who is being punished but that is not always, or even commonly, the case. Where the actual wrongdoer is an agent of the state or a member or employee of a corporate entity, he or she is unlikely to be personally liable for the payment of damages, punitive or otherwise. (The wrongdoer might, of course, be subject to some kind of disciplinary sanction within the organisation.) **1–27**

A recent empirical study in England and Wales showed that punitive damages were awarded more frequently against natural persons than against corporations or public bodies. Further, the mean awards were relatively modest. Adjusted for inflation, they worked out at approximately £16,000 for natural persons, £35,000 for corporations and almost £15,000 for public bodies.[82] There does not seem to be any similar research in **1–28**

---

78 *McDonnell v Ireland* [1998] 1 IR 134 at 148, *O'Connell v Building and Allied Trades Union* [2021] IECA 265, para 47.

79 *Conway v Irish National Teachers Organisation* [1991] 2 IR 305, 321; *Shortt v Commissioner of An Garda Síochána* [2007] IESC 9; [2007] 4 IR 587, para 120 (Murray CJ). See also *Sullivan v Boylan* [2013] IEHC 104; [2013] 1 IR 510; *Savickis v Governor of Castlerea Prison* [2016] IECA 310; *Herrity v Associated Newspapers (Ireland) Ltd* [2008] IEHC 249; [2009] 1 IR 316.

80 *Shortt v Commissioner of An Garda Síochána* [2007] IESC 9; [2007] 4 IR 587, para 110.

81 See, for example, *Savickis v Governor of Castlerea Prison* [2016] IECA 310; *Sullivan v Boylan* [2013] IEHC 104.

82 James Goudkamp and Eleni Katsampouka, "An empirical study of punitive

Ireland, but some very significant sums have been awarded here, notably the €1 million in punitive damages, in addition to more than €3.5 million in general and special damages, awarded in *Shortt v Commissioner of An Garda Síochána.*[83] It has been suggested that there has emerged a pattern of fixing punitive damages at about half the amount awarded by way of compensatory damages. However, this assertion was based on awards made in only two previous cases and it is unlikely that it can be treated as a rule of practice.[84] In *Shortt,* Murray CJ disagreed with the notion that punitive damages should always be a fraction of compensatory damages. He said that the amount was at the court's discretion to be exercised according to the circumstances of each case.[85] This is surely the correct approach. The means of the parties are irrelevant in the assessment of compensatory damages, but the defendant's means are material when assessing punitive damages, as would be the case when determining a fine following a criminal conviction.[86]

Regulation

1–29 Regulatory agencies are now part of state machinery in many countries, and there is a significant body of scholarship on the growth of the 'regulatory state".[87] The evolution of the regulatory state is often attributed, in large part at least, to privatisation and a retreat from *dirigisme.* As the ideal and practice of public ownership declined and as the state withdrew from the direct provision of services, such as postal and telephone services, public transport and aviation, it felt compelled to introduce some mechanism to deal with market failure.[88] These vital services were now left to the market which, while having some advantages, is far from perfect. Regulation was the favoured control mechanism in most Western countries and the upshot, in institutional terms, was the creation of an army of regulators with oversight of various utilities and services including telecommunications, transport and financial services. Rather than directly providing or distributing goods and services, the government is steering a system that is essentially market-based. Or, as it has been put, the state was no longer there to row but to steer.[89]

---

damages" (2018) 38 *Oxford Journal of Legal Studies* 90.

[83] [2007] IESC 9; [2007] 4 IR 587.

[84] The statement was made in *Savickis v Governor of Castlerea Prison* [2016] IECA 310, and the two previous cases were *Herrity v Associated Newspapers Ltd* [2008] IEHC 249 and *Sullivan v Boylan (No 2)* [2013] IEHC 104; [2013] 1 IR 510.

[85] [2007] IESC 9; [2007] 4 IR 587, para 117.

[86] *McIntyre v Lewis* [1991] 1 IR 121.

[87] Giandomenico Majone, "The rise of the regulatory state in Europe" (1994) 12 *Western European Politics* 77; Michael Moran, "Review article: Understanding the regulatory state" (2002) 32 *British Journal of Political Science* 391; John Braithwaite, "The regulatory state?" in Robert E. Goodin (ed.), *The Oxford Handbook of Political Science* (Oxford University Press, 2011).

[88] Giandomenico Majone, *Regulating Europe* (Routledge, 1996).

[89] David Osborne and Ted Gaebler, *Reinventing Government: How the Entrepreneurial Spirit is Transforming the Public Sector* (Plume, 1993).

Regulators usually have multiple functions – setting standards, monitoring compliance, conducting investigations and enforcement. Our concern here is with enforcement which, in turn, can take many forms. Leading empirical studies of regulatory practices, though dating mainly from the 1980s, have shown that regulators are primarily concerned with securing compliance rather than initiating prosecutions once any breach of the criminal law has been identified.[90] Albert Reiss is usually credited with drawing a distinction between compliance and deterrence.[91] Compliance strategies, by his account, are intended to induce conformity and reduce harm to the greatest extent possible, while deterrence is premised on the belief that the imposition of penalties (most likely criminal penalties) will prevent future violations. Yet it would be a mistake to assume that regulatory enforcement is all about compliance while the police (in the sense of a police force such as An Garda Síochána in Ireland) invariably treat prosecution as the strategy of first resort. Police often deal with tense situations by issuing a warning or advice, even where a prosecution might be legally possible. They may also issue cautions under juvenile diversion or adult cautioning schemes. Conversely, regulators, even those who generally favour compliance, often prosecute for particularly serious violations, as well as in situations where all reasonable efforts to secure compliance have failed. Braithwaite and his colleagues refer to an enforcement pyramid with persuasion, the most common tactic, at the base with severe penalties, criminal or otherwise, at the top.[92] These penalties may seldom be imposed but they sometimes are. **1–30**

Civil and administrative penalties, mostly imposed by regulatory bodies, form part of the broader sanctioning network mentioned earlier. It is beyond the scope of this discussion to offer any assessment of the justice of these penalties, individually or collectively. They may well be fully deserved though they are often very severe indeed. In Ireland, for example, the Central Bank Act 1942 (s 33AQ) provides that where the Bank finds a regulated service provider has committed a contravention, it may impose one or more sanctions ranging from a reprimand to a monetary penalty not exceeding the greater of €10 million or "an amount equal to 10 per cent of the turnover of the body for its last complete financial year before the finding is made". For a human person, the maximum penalty is currently €1 million. The Bank may also revoke a service provider's authorisation in respect of one or more of its activities for a maximum term of 12 months. **1–31**

---

90 Keith Hawkins, *Environment and Enforcement: Regulation and the Social Definition of Crime* (Clarendon Press, 1984); Bridget Hutter, *The Reasonable Arm of the Law? The Law Enforcement Procedures of Environmental Health Officers* (Clarendon Press, 1988); Peter Grabosky and John Braithwaite, *Of Manners Gentle: Enforcement Strategies of Australian Business Regulatory Agencies* (Oxford University Press, 1986), in particular, Chap 15.

91 Albert J Reiss Jr, "Consequences of compliance and deterrence models of law enforcement for the exercise of police discretion" (1984) 47 *Law and Contemporary problems* 83.

92 Ian Ayres and John Braithwaite, *Responsive Regulation: Transcending the Deregulation Debate* (Oxford University Press, 1992).

1–32 By autumn 2022, the Central Bank had concluded 152 enforcement actions, with the total fines imposed amounting to €400 million. Some of the individual penalties have been very high, at least when compared with fines imposed by courts following criminal conviction. In September 2022, the Central Bank fined Bank of Ireland over €100 million for failings in respect of about 16,000 tracker mortgages between 2004 and 2022. In fact, the appropriate fine was assessed at €143.6 million but that was reduced to reflect a settlement discount. About the same time, the Central Bank fined Danske Bank A/S €1.82 million for breaches of money laundering legislation. Other regulators, including the Data Protection Commission, the Commission for Communications Regulation and the Competition and Consumer Protection Commission are also empowered to impose administrative fines. In September 2022, the Data Protection Commission fined Instagram €405 million for breaches of the GDPR and failing to protect children's information (at the time of writing, that fine is under appeal to the High Court.) A year later, it fined TikTok €345 million for similar breaches. In 2021, another Meta-owned platform, WhatsApp, was fined €225 million for infringements of privacy laws.[93] The Data Protection Commission is reported to have imposed more than €1.64 billion in fines between January 2022 and January 2023.

1–33 The Competition (Amendment) Act 2022 empowers independent regulators to impose administrative sanctions (which may include very heavy fines) for breaches of competition law. It gives effect to a European Union directive, the express purpose of which is "to empower the competition authorities of the member states to be more effective enforcers and to ensure the proper functioning of the internal market".[94] Many of the key provisions of the 2022 Act directly reflect (as they must) the terms of the Directive. For example, sanctions must be "effective, proportionate and dissuasive" (an expression found in most EU criminal law). The Directive (art 15) requires member states to ensure that a national authority may impose a fine of not less than 10 per cent of an undertaking's total worldwide turnover for the preceding year. This is included in the Act as are other Directive provisions relating to periodic penalty payments, leniency programmes and fine reduction. Importantly, however, the Act also allows for an appeal against the sanctioning authority's decision to the High Court and, even in the absence of an appeal, the authority must apply to that court for confirmation of its decision. The court, on hearing the application, must confirm unless satisfied that there is a serious error of law manifest in the decision or that the sanction or remedy imposed was disproportionate or in excess of what was required for the sanction to be dissuasive or effective.[95] The Government claimed that this element of judicial oversight was included in the legislation to conform with the

[93] Cristina Criddle, "Irish regulator fines Instagram €405m for failing to protect children's data", *Financial Times,* 5 September 2022.

[94] Directive (EU) 2019/1 of the European Parliament and Council of 11 December 2018.

[95] Competition Act 2002, s 15AZ, inserted by Competition (Amendment) Act 2022, s 13.

Supreme Court judgment in *Zalewski v Workplace Relations Commission*[96] although there was already a rather similar provision in the Data Protection Act 2018 (s 143) and more recently such an arrangement is provided for in the Central Bank (Individual Accountability Framework) Act 2023.

Regulatory penalties are now criminal sentencing's strongest competitor in the areas of white-collar and corporate crime, but they remain underresearched as a form of punishment. A good deal of attention has been paid to responsive regulation which generally denotes a set of practices whereby regulators endeavour to secure compliance through various persuasive strategies with the possibility of criminal prosecution if all else fails.[97] Yet, the rationale for some of the enormous penalties now being imposed by regulators, even where they are formally classified as 'settlements', is often far from clear. They demand far more scrutiny that they have so far received. This is not to suggest that the amounts in question are invariably too high; in some instances, they may be too low. However, given how punitive they can be, often exceeding in severity any monetary penalty ever imposed by a criminal court, their selection should be governed by the same values and principles – rationality, proportionality, transparency, procedural fairness and consistency of approach – as apply in the criminal sentencing system. In this context, it is noteworthy that in June 2024, a majority of the United States Supreme Court held a person against whom the Securities and Exchange Commission (SEC) seeks a civil penalty for securities fraud is entitled to jury trial under the Seventh Amendment to the Constitution. Prior to that, the SEC could simply impose the penalty itself.[98] Criminal courts on this side of the Atlantic do occasionally impose very heavy fines for financial crime. In England in 2021, for instance, National Westminster Bank, on pleading guilty to three money laundering offences, was fined almost £265 million as well as being ordered to pay £4.3 million in costs. There was also a confiscation order in the amount of £460,000.[99] However, judicially imposed financial penalties of this order have, so far at least, been exceedingly rare. **1–34**

[96] [2021] IESC 24; [2022] IR 421. See remarks of Minister for State at Department of Enterprise, Trade and Employment at Second Reading of the Competition (Amendment) Bill (Seanad Debates, Vol 285, 26 May 2022).

[97] Ian Ayres and John Braithwaite, *Responsive Regulation: Transcending the Deregulation Debate* (Oxford University Press, 1992); John Braithwaite, "The essence of responsive regulation" (2011) 44 Univ British Columbia LR 475; Neil Cunningham, "Enforcement and compliance strategies" in Robert Baldwin, Martin Cave and Martin Lodge (eds), *The Oxford Handbook of Regulation* (Oxford University Press, 2010).

[98] *Securities and Exchange Commission v Jarkesy* 603 US – (2024) (27 June 2024).

[99] *R (The Financial Conduct Authority) v National Westminster Bank*, Southwark Crown Court, 13 December 2021. See Jay Gormley, *Fines: A Review of the Sanction, its Use and Operation, and Research Evidence* (Sentencing Academy, 2022), 6.

Confiscation of Assets

1–35 Confiscating the proceeds of criminal activity is seen as an effective means of combatting crime, and organised crime in particular. Drug trafficking, for example, can generate enormous profits which are typically held in various bank accounts or converted into other assets consisting of real or personal property. Those planning to engage in organised crime may be dissuaded (though, realistically, only to a limited extent) by the knowledge that they will sooner or later be deprived of the proceeds of their criminal activities. Confiscation may operate, in effect, as part of a sentence imposed on a convicted person. The Criminal Justice Act 1984 provides that at or after the sentencing of a person convicted on indictment, the court may, on the application of the Director of Public Prosecutions, make a confiscation order requiring the offender to pay to the court such sum as the court thinks fit.[100] Where a person has been convicted of a drug trafficking offence, the court *must* determine if he or she has benefited from the trafficking. If so satisfied, the court shall make a confiscation order.[101] Post-conviction orders of this nature operate *in personam.* They are part of the punishment imposed on offenders, although any question as to whether an offender has benefited financially from the offending conduct or as to the amount to be recovered is determined by applying the civil standard of proof. A European Union directive dating from 2014 requires member states to provide for the confiscation of criminal proceeds following a final conviction for an offence.[102]

1–36 However, Ireland, like many other countries, operates a parallel system of non-conviction-based asset forfeiture. The rationale for this system was recently explained by the European Commission:

> "Traditional – conviction-based – confiscation did not equip law enforcement authorities and judicial authorities with the necessary and effective tools that enable the confiscation of a satisfactory percentage of the proceeds of organised criminal activities. The reasons for this might be that a conviction for an alleged criminal offence may not be possible, in spite of the presence of potential proceeds of illicit activity which could justify confiscation. It might also be difficult to link the obtained assets to a criminal conviction. Another reason is that at times the conviction of an accused is barred because of his/her immunity, death, absconding or illness. Non-conviction-based confiscation measures enable to bridge that gap and seize criminal assets through separate judicial proceedings that might be of criminal, civil or administrative nature."[103]

---

[100] Criminal Justice Act 1994, s 9.

[101] Criminal Justice Act 1994, s 4 as substituted by Criminal Justice Act 1999, s 25.

[102] Directive 2014/42/EU of the European Parliament and Council of 3 April 2014 on the freezing and confiscation of instrumentalities and proceeds of crime in the European Union.

[103] European Commission, *Analysis of non-conviction-based confiscation measures in the European Union,* SWD(2019) 1050 final, p 2. See also Council of Europe, *The Use of Non-Conviction Based Seizure and Confiscation* (2020) at www.coe.int/econcrime> accessed 27 November 2024.

Asset confiscation of this nature operates *in rem*. It targets property believed to be the proceeds of crime, even though the perpetrator of the crime may never be prosecuted, convicted or even identified. Unexplained wealth, in the sense of a disproportion between a person's assets and his or her declared income, may also provide a basis for confiscation proceedings. Granted, the Irish statutory regime governing the seizure and confiscation of assets in these circumstances provides many procedural safeguards for persons affected. The Proceeds of Crime Acts 1996-2016 set out all the steps to be taken from the initial seizure and detention of property until the point at which it can be transferred to the State. Apart from the initial seizure, all further steps must be authorised by the High Court with due notice being given, where possible, to the person in possession or control of the property. A final order transferring the property to the State may not be made until an interlocutory order has been in force for at least seven years (although it is now proposed to reduce this period to two years). These safeguards are necessitated by the strong protection afforded to property rights by the Constitution of Ireland.[104] **1–37**

Asset confiscation of this nature amounts to civil forfeiture which, as noted, is subject to important procedural safeguards, but it still allows for the range of due process requirements that must be observed in criminal proceedings to be avoided.[105] By focusing on the property and its alleged provenance rather than on the guilt of any individual, civil forfeiture depersonalises the process. One can, of course, argue that it should not be viewed as a punishment because it merely involves depriving people of property to which they never had any moral entitlement. However, it is so viewed by those who illegally acquired the property in question. In fact, its acquisition may have provided the sole motivation for their crimes in the first instance. To this extent, it is a punishment and one that can be quite effective, especially in circumstances where, for whatever reason, the perpetrators of the crimes that produced the property cannot be brought to justice. It may also have a deterrent effect, and that is one of its underlying rationales, though how well it succeeds in this respect is open to question. **1–38**

Deferred Prosecution Agreements

Deferred prosecution agreements (DPAs) and non-prosecution agreements (NPAs) generally operate within the criminal justice system, to the extent they require active engagement by prosecutors. But they still operate as alternatives to prosecution thereby allowing those to whom they apply to avoid conviction and sentence. DPAs, to which we shall confine our attention here, may potentially apply to individual and corporate offenders, though in the United Kingdom they apply to corporate offenders only. Their introduction has generally been motivated **1–39**

---

104 Arts 40.3 and 43.

105 Liz Campbell, "Theorizing asset forfeiture in Ireland" (2007) 71 *Journal of Criminal Law* 441.

by two primary considerations. One is that compliance strategies are often preferable to prosecution and punishment as a response to certain kinds of wrongdoing, and in particular to what may loosely be described as regulatory offences (though some of these can be very serious because of the injuries and loss they inflict). Secondly, DPAs can spare offenders the significant collateral consequences that may result from a criminal conviction. Being indicted, let alone convicted, may have profound implications for large corporations, as illustrated by the experience of Arthur Andersen in 2002 when it was indicted and later convicted on a charge of obstructing justice in connection with the collapse of Enron, one of its major clients.[106] Approximately 85,000 Arthur Andersen employees lost their jobs, although most had no involvement in the Enron business. Nor did it help that three years later, the United States Supreme Court unanimously reversed the conviction because the jury had been wrongly instructed on the elements of the offence charged.[107] The cataclysmic collapse of Arthur Andersen, probably more than any other event, caused American law enforcement authorities to turn increasingly to DPAs to avoid the collateral consequences of formal indictment and conviction.[108] A criminal conviction may also disbar a company from tendering for government contracts or conducting business with certain foreign governments. Yet, a further consideration prompting the introduction and use of DPAs in England and Wales was that the identification doctrine as a means of attributing criminal responsibility can make it difficult to mount a successful prosecution of a corporation.[109] From a prosecution perspective, DPAs therefore "provide a more effective and efficient way of holding offending corporations to account without the cost and uncertainty of a criminal trial".[110] DPAs have not yet been introduced in Ireland.[111]

---

[106] For more background detail, see James Kelly, "The power of an indictment and the demise of Arthur Andersen" (2006-2007) 48 S Texas LR 509; Gabriel Markoff, "Arthur Andersen and the myth of the corporate death penalty: Corporate criminal convictions in the twenty-first century" (2013) 15 *University of Pennsylvania Journal of Business Law* 797; Wulf A. Kaal and Timothy A. Lacine, "The effect of deferred and non-prosecution agreements on corporate governance: Evidence from 1993-2013" (Winter 2014/2015) 70 *The Business Lawyer* 61.

[107] *Arthur Andersen LLP v United States* 544 US 696 (2005).

[108] Note, "*United States v Fokker Services BV* 818 F3d 733 (DC Cir 2016)" (2017) 130 Harvard LR 1048; Joseph A. Grundfest, "Over before it started", *New York Times*, 14 June 2005; Scott Resnik and Keir N Dougall, "The rise of deferred prosecution agreements", *New York Law Journal*, 18 December 2006.

[109] Karl Laird, "Deferred prosecution agreements: The latest developments" [2021] Crim LR 283.

[110] Liz Campbell, "Revisiting and re-situating deferred prosecution agreements in Australia: Lessons from England and Wales" (2021) 43 Sydney LR 187.

[111] Under the Communications Regulation Act 2002, s 44 (as substituted and amended), if the Commission for Communications Regulation believes that a person has committed one of the summary offences specified in the section, it may give the person notice to that effect and allow that person 21 days to remedy the matter in question and pay a fee. No prosecution will follow if

While the rules governing the operation of DPAs vary across jurisdictions, the common thread running through them is that a prosecuting authority will refrain from bringing or proceeding with charges provided the corporation agrees to specified conditions, which may include accepting the facts alleged by the prosecution.[112] The conditions almost invariably include payment of a substantial penalty and possibly restitution, compensation or disgorgement of profits was well.[113] Moreover, DPAs usually include specific mandates designed to reduce the risk of reoffending.[114] This may involve significant corporate restructuring or the introduction of new compliance mechanisms. No prosecution will follow provided the corporation has complied with all the conditions within the specified period. A defendant is never obliged to enter a DPA, nor is the prosecution ever obliged to offer one.[115] **1–40**

DPAs were introduced in the United Kingdom by the Crime and Courts Act 2013 (s 45 and Sch 17).[116] A designated prosecutor, either the DPP or the Serious Fraud Office (SFO), may enter into an agreement with a corporation, partnership or unincorporated association after proceedings have been issued charging the entity in question with an alleged offence. After negotiations between the parties have begun but before the terms are agreed, an application must be made to the Crown Court for a declaration that entering into the DPA is likely to be in the interests of justice and that the proposed terms are fair, reasonable and proportionate. After agreement has been reached, a application must be made to the same court for a further declaration that in the same terms. The DPA must include an expiry date and the requirements, as set out in Sch 17, may include: payment of a financial penalty, compensation to victims, donation of money to charity, disgorgement of profits, implementation of a compliance programme and payment of prosecutor's reasonable costs. **1–41**

---

the matter is remedied to the Commission's satisfaction. While not a DPA, the underlying idea is broadly the same.

112 David M. Uhlmann, "Deferred prosecution and non-prosecution agreements and the erosion of corporate criminal liability" (2013) 72 Maryland LR 1295; Andrew Murphy, "Deferred prosecution agreements: Lessons from a comparative analysis for Irish corporate enforcement" (2021) 21 University College Dublin LR 1.

113 See, for example, *Serious Fraud Office v Standard Bank plc* [2016] Lloyd's Rep FC 102, the first DPA approved in England and Wales, and comment by Nicola Padfield [2016] Crim LR 449.

114 Brandon L. Garrett, "The public interest in corporate settlements" (2017) 58 Boston College LR 1483.

115 Michael Bisgrove and Mark Weekes, "Deferred prosecution agreements: A practical consideration" [2014] Crim LR 416.

116 For an excellent description of the system as it operates in England and Wales and an analysis of relevant the jurisprudence, see Karl Laird, "Deferred prosecution agreements and the interests of justice: a consistency of approach" [2019] Crim LR 486. See also Laird, note 109 above, and Colin King and Nicholas Lord, "Deferred prosecution agreements in England and Wales: Castles made of sand?" [2020] *Public Law* 307. The system is concisely described by Sir Brian Leveson (then President of the Queen's Bench) in *SFO v Standard Bank plc* [2016] Lloyd's Rep FC 102.

The amount of any financial penalty "must be broadly comparable to the fine that a court would have imposed on [the entity] on conviction for the alleged offence following a guilty plea".[117]

1–42 By early 2024, the SFO had entered into about a dozen DPAs. In all cases, the offence was of a very serious nature, often involving bribery and corruption to secure contracts in foreign countries. The financial penalties, including disgorgement of profits in many instances, have often been extremely high, especially when compared with court fines. For instance, the DPA entered into with Airbus in 2021 imposed a total financial sanction of almost €1 billion, consisting of a penalty of almost €400 million and disgorgement of profits of about €586 million. As the President of the Queen's Bench noted when approving the agreement, the overall amount exceeded the total of all the sums paid under previous DPAs and was more than double the total of all the fines paid in respect of criminal conduct in England and Wales in 2018.[118] In fact, this was merely part of a total sanction of €3.5 billion which Airbus had to pay because of equivalent proceedings in France and the United States. The SFO investigation related to bribery offences in Malaysia, Ski Lanka, Taiwan, Indonesia and Ghana.

1–43 DPAs have been criticised on a number of grounds. Historically, they were introduced in the United States and, apparently in England, in the early 20th century to deal with offenders such as juveniles, persons addicted to drugs and those involved in prostitution, whose offending could in one way or another be attributed to social disadvantage or deprivation. It was considered that, in many such cases, it would be better to provide the defendants with an opportunity to engage with social services and avail themselves of rehabilitation programmes rather than simply prosecute them.[119] Prosecution would, therefore, be deferred and ultimately dropped if the defendants took advantage of the opportunity offered to them. However, in the late 20th century, DPAs came to be used predominantly to deal with serious white-collar and corporate crime. Therefore, a strategy that was introduced to deal with the least privileged came to be used to assist the most privileged. In the United States, DPAs have come in for particularly strong criticism where they have been used in response to serious corporate misconduct that has resulted in multiple fatalities, such as the DPA offered to (and unsurprisingly accepted by) Boeing after two of its 737 Max aircraft crashed in 2018 and 2019 with the loss of 346 lives. This decision has come in for some damning criticism.[120] As one critic of the use of DPAs in these circumstances has written:

---

[117] Crime and Courts Act 2013, Sch 17, para 5(4).

[118] *SFO v Airbus SE* [2021] Lloyd's Rep FC 159, para 1.

[119] Benjamin M Greenblum, "What happens to a prosecution deferred? Judicial oversight of corporate deferred prosecution agreements" (2005) 105 Columbia LR 1863. This original purpose of deferred prosecution was also reflected in the (United States) Speedy Trial Act 1974 which permitted certain offenders, such as those mentioned above, to be given a second chance.

[120] See, in particular, John C Coffee, "Nosedive: Boeing and the corruption of

> "Leadership in American business has internalised the idea that it is sometimes possible to engage in serious wrongdoing with relative impunity – no job loss, no trial, no guilty verdict, and no jail time or other serious punishment for wrongdoers. Instead the company agrees to admit misconduct, cooperate with the government, and pay a fine – a process and penalty that can become just another cost of doing business."[121]

1–44 Another criticism of DPAs, though this is mainly applicable in the United States, is that they can confer virtually unfettered discretion on prosecutors to give effect to their own preferences, which may or may not be well informed, as to how companies should be managed. It has also been argued that DPAs infringe the presumption of innocence and are contrary to the rule of law.[122] The legitimacy of these objections depends on how DPAs operate, which varies from one jurisdiction to another. American versions of the DPA have been strongly and justifiably criticised for the largely uncontrolled power they vest in prosecutors and state agencies, with no meaningful judicial supervision.[123] However, the English experience to date shows that DPAs can work reasonably well, largely because of the degree of judicial supervision to which they are subject in that jurisdiction and the requirement that the financial penalty, although typically only one element of an agreement, should not exceed the fine that would be imposed by a court for the offending conduct.

4. Is There Still Anything Special About the Criminal Law?

1–45 The existence of the various civil sanctioning mechanisms that have just been outlined raises a question as to what role the criminal law, with its penalty system, can or should play in enforcing standards of human and corporate conduct. As already mentioned, those alternative sanctioning strategies have little or no application to core criminal offences such as offences against the person and the more traditional offences against

---

the deferred prosecution agreement" (2022) at https://papers.ssrn.com/so13/papers.cfm?abstract_id=4105514> accessed 12 March 2023.

[121] Peter R Reilly, "Outlawing corporate prosecution deals when people have died" (2023) 55 Arizona LR 1351, 1356. The DPA entered into by Boeing in 2021 included the payment of $2.5 billion by way of monetary sanction and compensation.

[122] Douglas Husak, "Social engineering as an infringement of the presumption of innocence: The case of corporate criminality" (2014) 8 *Criminal Law and Philosophy* 353, 359 (American prosecutors "increasingly use their powers not to seek conventional punishments, but to change the ways corporate entities do business"). See also Jennifer Arlen, "Prosecuting beyond the rule of law: Corporate mandates imposed through deferred prosecution agreements" (2016) 8 *Journal of Legal Analysis* 11. Roger A Shinor and Hiney Ho, "Deferred prosecution agreements and the presumption of innocence" (2018) 12 *Criminal law and Philosophy* 707 (arguing that DPAs do not infringe the presumption of innocence).

[123] Brandon Garrett, *Too Big to Jail: How Prosecutors Compromise with Corporations* (Harvard University Press, 2014); Peter Reilly, "Sweetheart deals, deferred prosecution, and making a mockery of the criminal justice system: U.S. corporate DPAs rejected on many fronts" (2018) 50 Arizona LJ 1113.

property. They are mainly relevant to white-collar and corporate misconduct, criminal or otherwise. The real question then is whether the criminal law has anything special to offer as a response to offending of that nature. The criminal law is itself a form of regulation; it aims to shape and influence behaviour, mainly through the threat of punishment. But the same may be said of civil sanctioning systems. The distinctive characteristic of the criminal law, it is often said, is its unique capacity to censure and condemn.[124] It has a 'moral voice' that the civil law lacks.[125] Yet, there are times when a civil sanction may carry a significant social stigma. For example, Davy Stockbrokers came in for very considerable public criticism after being fined more than €4 million by the Central Bank of Ireland for breaches of financial regulations involving conflict of interest and personal account dealing. Effectively, the firm had acted as broker and buyer in the offending transaction.[126]

1–46 However, this is probably an exception. Civil penalties, whether in the form of punitive damages or regulatory fines, seldom attract sustained public attention, if any, even when they run to millions or hundreds of millions of Euro. A criminal conviction, on the other hand, impresses a stamp of disapproval and condemnation that civil penalties cannot ordinarily convey. A judicially imposed sentence intensifies and reinforces the condemnatory message inherent in the conviction. Imprisonment is obviously the most potent signal of disapproval, and it is a sanction that no authority other than a court may impose. Likewise, a suspended prison sentence expresses strong denunciation of the offending conduct, even if there is some countervailing factor to justify leaving the offender at conditional liberty.[127]

1–47 Equally important is the procedural dimension of the criminal law. Nobody, whether a natural person or a corporate body, may be convicted of any offence save in due course of law.[128] This requires, at a minimum, that the prosecution prove each element of the offence charged and satisfy the tribunal of fact beyond a reasonable doubt of the defendant's guilt. Even where the law provides for presumptions or reverse burdens of proof in respect of certain matters, the prosecution must still establish the essential facts on which it is relying to establish the defendant's criminal liability. To discharge this obligation, the prosecution (and the investigating authorities) must painstakingly gather and analyse all the

---

[124] Matthew Gibson, "Three justifications of fair labelling" (2024) 140 LQR 431, 448 (the criminal law "acts as a uniquely coercive punishment-imposing institution, whose offences should paradigmatically target fault-based conduct.").

[125] AP Simester and Andreas von Hirsch, *Crimes, Harms, and Wrongs: On the Principles of Criminalisation* (Hart Publishing, 2011), 4.

[126] Simon Carswell, "Fine against Davy over 2014 bond deal could be 'problematic' for criminal probe", *Irish Times,* 14 March 2022. The fine and ensuing controversy led to the resignation of several senior managers and employees and the sale of the firm to the Bank of Ireland (though for several hundred million Euro).

[127] Chapter 12 below.

[128] Constitution of Ireland, Art 38.1.

available evidence in order to construct a convincing case. When the case comes on for trial, that evidence will be rigorously tested by the defence, and some of it may be declared inadmissible. All this imposes a heavy burden on the prosecution, especially in complex cases involving various kinds of economic crime. But it is also the great strength of the criminal law. Nobody may be convicted without a trial in which the alleged misconduct is described and analysed in detail, and ultimately proved beyond a reasonable doubt. Moreover, all this must be done in a public trial. Regulatory proceedings must, of course, be conducted in accordance with the requirements of procedural fairness and constitutional justice, but they still lack the all-important public element of criminal proceedings and the rigour with which allegations are tested in the course of those proceedings.

5. Restorative Justice

The term 'restorative justice' now covers a wide range of practices **1–48** occurring at different stages of the criminal process. It may involve diversion from the courts entirely, or it may operate in tandem with criminal proceedings. Indeed, it can also be employed at the post-conviction stage in the form of a structured meeting between an offender and victim while the offender is still serving a sentence. Our main concern here is with restorative processes as an alternative to conventional criminal proceedings.[129] This might entail conferencing, especially for children and young offenders, as pioneered in Australia and New Zealand, but it could potentially involve any arrangement in which the conflict created by an offence is resolved through a meeting between offender, victim and other interested parties, irrespective of the offender's age or the nature of the offence.[130] Processes of this kind tend to be used mainly for less serious offences, though some restorative justice advocates argue that they could usefully be employed for more serious offences as well.[131] This is effectively a system of victim-offender mediation. A similar process might operate within the criminal process in the sense that a judge, before imposing sentence, would request the relevant parties to engage in discussions with

[129] For an account of the various restorative justice practices so far undertaken in Ireland and how they might further develop, see Ian Marder, "Mapping restorative justice and restorative practices in criminal justice in the Republic of Ireland" (2022) 70 *International Journal of Law, Crime and Justice* 100544 and Ian Marder, "Restorative justice as the new default in Irish criminal justice" (2019) 16 *Irish Probation Journal* 60.

[130] On juvenile justice conferencing in Australia, New Zealand and elsewhere, see Allison Morris and Gabrielle Maxwell (eds), *Restorative Justice for Juveniles: Conferencing, Mediation and Circles* (Hart Publishing, 1998). See also Hennessey Hayes and Kathleen Daly, "Youth justice conferencing and reoffending" (2009) 20 *Justice Quarterly* 725.

[131] Nikki D'Souza and Joanna Shapland, "The exclusion of serious and organised offenders and their victims from the offer of restorative justice: Should this be so and what happens when the offer is put on the table?" (2023) 23 *Criminology and Criminal Justice* 60.

a view to recommending a sentence that, ideally at least, is satisfactory to all. There may be a presumption that this sentence will be imposed, though the judge will not be bound by it. This is essentially how sentencing circles operate in Canada, mainly for aboriginal offenders, and how various kinds of victim-offender conferences operate as part of the sentencing process in South Africa and New Zealand.[132]

1–49 Two definitions of restorative justice are widely quoted, though they may not cover all varieties of restorative processes. According to Tony Marshall:

> "Restorative justice is a process whereby all parties with a stake in a specific offence come together to resolve collectively how to deal with the aftermath of the offence and its implications for the future."[133]

1–50 Howard Zehr, regarded as a pioneer in the field, has offered a somewhat different definition:

> "Restorative justice is a process to involve to the greatest extent possible those who have a stake in a specific offence to collectively identify and address harms, needs and obligations in order to heal and put things as right as possible."[134]

1–51 The question that both of these definitions, taken in isolation, leave unanswered is who exactly has a stake in the offence. Participants should clearly include the offender and victim as well as any of the victim's family members or close associates who have also been harmed or affected by the offence. Some family members or supporters of the offender might also be present. However, it is often envisaged that, additionally, there should be some "community representatives" though this immediately raises the question of how the relevant community is to be identified. We all belong to several overlapping or cross-cutting communities of which geographical community is but one. The community with 'a stake' in the process, as envisaged by Marshall and Zehr, might therefore depend on the nature and circumstances of the offence. For instance, if the offence were committed against a member of a racial minority, and especially if the victim's race seemed to be a motivating factor, the relevant community might be members of that minority. Having said this, the Marshall and

---

132 Annette van der Merwe and Ann Skelton, "Victims' mitigating views in sentencing decisions: A comparative analysis" (2014) 35 *Oxford Journal of Legal Studies* 355, describing South African and New Zealand cases involving such a process. On sentencing circles in Canada, see Jon Nadler, "Sentencing circles: A way to envision justice as a community responsibility", paper presented to 30th Annual Criminal Law Conference of County of Carleton Law Association, October 2018, available at https://canlii.ca/t/sqvw> accessed 2 January 2023.

133 Tony Marshall, "The evolution of restorative justice in Britain" (1996) 4 *European Journal on Criminal Policy and Research* 21. For a critical, though by no means negative, analysis of restorative justice, see Adriaan Lanni, "Taking restorative justice seriously" (2021) 69 Buffalo LR 635. See also Victoria McGeer and Philip Pettit, "The desirability and feasibility of restorative justice" (2015) 57 *Raisons Politiques* 17.

134 Howard Zehr, *The Little Book of Restorative Justice* (Good Books, 2002), 37.

Zehr definitions, with their emphasis on collective resolution, capture the essence of restorative processes. Susan Sharpe has offered a more elaborate account of restorative justice by identifying five key principles by which it should be informed. It should (1) invite full participation and consensus by the relevant parties; (2) seek to heal what is broken; (3) seek full and direct accountability; (4) seek to reunite what has been divided and (5) seek to strengthen the community in a way that will prevent further offending.[135] In connection with the third principle, she makes the important point that while at the outset the offender and victim see themselves, and are seen, as such, those descriptions should not become permanent. The restorative process should enable each of them to transcend their status as offender or victim, as the case may be, and look to a future in which they will no longer be defined as the perpetrator or victim of the offence, but as members of the same community.

Where restorative justice functions as an alternative to criminal justice, it **1–52** spares the offender the more onerous sanctions, such as imprisonment, that may be judicially-imposed following conviction. The offender may nonetheless be obliged to take some reparative steps by, for example, apologising to the victim, making restitution or embarking on some course of action that will benefit the wider community.[136] From a victim's perspective, restorative processes provide an opportunity to confront the offender and impress on him or her the impact of the offence, both at the time of its commission and later. Victim impact evidence at sentencing serves a rather similar purpose, but with one significant difference. At a sentencing hearing, the victim is essentially addressing the court, though usually aware that the offender is listening as well. Indeed, victim impact statements often include a direct message to the offender. What is missing, however, is dialogue. The offender will not respond to the victim's statement except, perhaps, by making a formal apology and even that is usually conveyed to the court by defence counsel. Restorative justice processes have the advantage of facilitating a direct and meaningful dialogue that can generate mutual understanding. Just as the victim can impress upon the offender how he or she was affected by the offence, the offender can inform the victim of any background factors or personal difficulties that contributed to the commission of the offence (not that these circumstances will always be excusing). The process puts a human face on the offender as well as the victim. Equally importantly, a restorative justice process has "the potential to change an offender's perspective – to make them fully appreciate the human side of the harm they have done – which can change their behaviour when an opportunity for crime arises in the future".[137]

---

[135] Susan Sharpe, *Restorative Justice: A Vision for Healing and Change* (Edmonton Victim Offender Mediation Society, 1998).

[136] Sara Sun Beale, "Still tough on crime? Prospects for restorative justice in the United States" [2003] Utah LR 413, 418.

[137] Paul H Robinson, "The virtues of restorative processes, the vices of 'restorative justice'" [2003] Utah LR 375, 375.

1–53 As against all this, restorative justice runs the risk of unduly privatising the conflict that arises from the commission of an offence. The essence of a crime, as reiterated throughout this book, is that it constitutes a wrong against society as well as against the victim (where there is one). A crime, as opposed to a civil wrong, involves conduct about which society has a right and duty to be concerned. Of equal importance, society has a duty to ensure, through the medium of its criminal justice system, that persons suspected or accused of criminal offences are treated fairly and accorded all the procedural protections inherent in the concept of due course of law. Penalties imposed on those duly convicted must be proportionate to the gravity of their offences and their relevant personal circumstances. Restorative processes could be arranged, as some are, to involve community representatives, but this provides no guarantee that the offender will be afforded the procedural protections to which he or she would be entitled if prosecuted and put on trial. More pertinently in the present context, there is no guarantee that the penalty (even if not so described) imposed on the offender will be proportionate to the offending conduct or that it will serve any of the traditional purposes of criminal punishment, including offender rehabilitation.[138]

1–54 These reservations about restorative justice apply mainly where it operates as an alternative or competitor to criminal justice. There may be less cause for concern about restorative processes that operate within the criminal justice system as when, for example, a meeting between the offender, the victim and others takes place prior to sentencing (which, as already noted, is possible in some jurisdictions). Irrespective of any recommendation emerging from such a meeting, the final sentencing decision rests with the judge who will ordinarily have regard to the recommendation but who must still ensure that the sentence is fair and proportionate. This is not to belittle restorative processes that operate as an alternative to criminal justice, because they can undoubtedly have the advantages mentioned earlier. But any such process must be designed to ensure that no penalty (however described) imposed on the offender is disproportionality severe, having regard to all the factors that would be relevant if the penalty were being judicially determined following conviction.

---

[138] For further and much more detailed analysis of the issues raised in this paragraph, see three articles by Andrew Ashworth: "Some doubts about restorative justice" (1993) 4 *Criminal Law Forum* 277; "Is restorative justice the way forward for criminal justice?" (2001) 54 *Current Legal Problems* 347; "Responsibilities, rights and restorative justice" (2002) 42 Brit J Criminology 578. See also Andrew von Hirsch *et al* (eds), *Restorative Justice and Criminal Justice: Competing or Reconcilable Paradigms?* (Hart Publishing, 2003).

CHAPTER 2

THE SENTENCING PROCESS

The purpose of this chapter is to describe, in a simplified outline, some important elements of sentencing procedure with particular emphasis on the jurisdiction of the criminal courts and the appeals system. It is intended to help readers without experience of legal practice or any detailed knowledge of criminal procedure to understand the framework in which sentences are imposed and, in many cases, reviewed by appeal courts. Procedure and substance are closely intertwined. This holds true of law generally, and sentencing is no exception. For example, the capacity of the senior appeal courts to develop sentencing principles and guidelines depends on the jurisdiction that has been constitutionally and legislatively conferred upon them. It has been said that the contract law of a country depends largely on the kinds of cases that historically reached its highest courts. Where those cases mostly involved large commercial enterprises, as was true in Britain in the 18th and 19th centuries, the courts developed quite strict rules in relation to matters such as time clauses because parties with significant resources at their disposal could reasonably be expected to observe those rules. In countries where cases reaching the highest courts involved more consumer-type contracts and the parties were often 'ordinary' individuals, judicially-developed rules were distinctly more flexible.[1] A similar observation may be made about sentencing. Higher appeal courts, such as the Supreme Court and Court of Appeal in Ireland, are generally confined to entertaining appeals in respect of persons convicted on indictment although these account for only a small proportion of all those convicted of criminal offences in any year. The remainder will have been convicted in summary jurisdiction courts such as the District Court in Ireland. Sentencing jurisprudence emanating from the higher courts therefore consists predominantly of principles and guidelines applicable to serious offences only. It has little to say about the vast range of offences that are disposed of summarily. **2–01**

1. Allocation of Sentencing Powers

Each branch of government has a distinct role in the overall sentencing process. The legislature which, by virtue of Art 15.2 of the Constitution, has the sole and exclusive power to make laws for the State, is responsible **2–02**

1 MP Ellinghaus, "An Australian contract law?" (1989) 2 *Journal of Contract Law* 13, 19-20; Hein Kötz, "The common core of European private law" (1997) 5 *European Review of Private Law* 549, 551.

for the creation of criminal offences and for specifying the maximum, mandatory or minimum sentences applicable to them. Almost all offences carry maximum sentences, an arrangement that effectively confers discretion on trial judges to decide on the appropriate sentence in each case. Other more general matters governed by legislation include the range of available sentencing options such as imprisonment, probation, community service, fines and suspended sentences, the allocation of jurisdiction among the various criminal courts, special sentencing arrangements for young offenders, and (increasingly) provision for ancillary measures such as disqualification, confiscation of assets and notification requirements that may or must be imposed on persons convicted of certain offences. The judiciary is exclusively responsible for the selection and imposition of sentence whenever there is a selection to be made.[2] The executive branch of government, apart from being obliged to ensure that the criminal justice system is adequately resourced with police, courts, prisons, probation services and a parole system, is also responsible for sentence implementation. Judges have the difficult task of selecting sentences, but ultimately all they can do is speak the words of imposition.[3] The executive must then assume responsibility for implementing those sentences although, as we shall see in Chap 14, it enjoys extensive discretion in deciding the extent to which offenders are required to serve their sentences. As mentioned in Chap 1, the judicial role remains by far the most visible. Judges must always pronounce sentence in public and, at least in the case of serious offences, give reasons for the sentences they impose. Public discourse tends to concentrate almost entirely on the judicial role. Executive decisions, on the other hand, seldom attract much public attention, but they are no less important. Serving prisoners are constantly being granted various kinds of early release, as is legally permissible, but, except in rare cases involving high-profile offenders, those release decisions are never reported or publicly commented upon.

2. The Trial Courts

2–03 Ireland has four criminal trial courts: District Court, Circuit court, Central Criminal Court and Special Criminal Court. The District Court is a court of summary jurisdiction which means that it is a non-jury court where all matters of law and fact are determined by the presiding judge. Summary proceedings are meant to be reasonably informal and expeditious, though not to the extent of depriving any party, including a criminal defendant, of their constitutional rights to fair procedures, due process and observance of the rule of law. All Irish courts, including the District Court, are staffed by professional judges who will have practised for several years as solicitors or barristers before being appointed to the bench. In England and Wales, on the other hand, summary justice is administered largely by lay magistrates.[4] Under the Constitution of Ireland (Art 38.2), the District

2 *Deaton v Attorney General and Revenue Commissioners* [1963] IR 170.

3 Robert M Cover, "Violence and the Word" (1986) 95 Yale LJ 1601.

4 Penny Darbyshire, *Darbyshire on the English Legal System*, 12th ed (Sweet and

Court is confined to dealing with minor offences. These in turn consist of summary offences which may be tried in the District Court only, as well as more serious, indictable offences that are deemed, on the particular facts, to be minor in nature (meaning, in effect, that in the event of a conviction, the defendant will not merit a heavier penalty than the District Court may lawfully impose). Thus, assault contrary to s 2 of the Non-Fatal Offences against the Person Act 1997 is a summary offence only, with a maximum prison sentence of six months. Theft, on the other hand, is an indictable offence punishable with a maximum of 10 years' imprisonment.[5] Yet, as might be expected, the vast bulk of theft prosecutions are dealt with in the District Court because they involve offending of a minor nature.[6] By virtue of the Criminal Procedure Act 1967 (s 13), the District Court may deal with a wide variety of indictable offences, apart from very serious ones such as murder and rape, if the accused pleads guilty and the prosecutor agrees to the matter being dealt with summarily. In 2021, the District Court dealt summarily with 53,000 indictable offences, including 22,500 drug offences, and 20,500 theft and related offences. In the same year, it dealt with 211,000 summary offences. More than 68 per cent of these were road traffic offences.[7]

The Constitution, while confining the District Court's jurisdiction to the trial of minor offences, provides no definition of a minor offence. **2–04**
However, it has been judicially decided that the primary consideration in determining if an offence is minor is the punishment that it may attract.[8] An offence may be treated as minor where the maximum prison sentence is 12 months or less. The highest level of fine that may be attached to a minor offence will naturally vary over time, with fluctuations in the value of money. At present a maximum fine of €5,000 or perhaps somewhat higher is considered acceptable. The maximum penalties attaching to purely summary offences are always kept within those limits. When the District Court deals with an indictable offence which it holds to be minor in nature, it may not impose a prison sentence in excess of 12 months for any one such offence[9] or an aggregate term exceeding two years for a combination of offences.[10] A class A fine (which has a current maximum of €5,000) may also be imposed. When deciding if an offence is minor, the court has regard only to the primary punishment, such as the amount of fine or term of imprisonment, that may be imposed. Other ancillary penalties, severe though they may be, such as disqualification from driving, are generally

Maxwell, 2017), Chap 7 (describing the courts system in England and Wales).

5 Criminal Justice (Theft and Fraud Offences) Act 2001, s 4.

6 The Criminal Justice (Theft and Fraud Offences) Act 2001, s 53, specifically permits the summary disposal of any offence under the Act provided both defence and prosecution consent and the District Court is satisfied that the facts disclose a minor offence fit to be tried summarily. See *Gifford v DPP* [2017] IEHC 423; [2017] 2 IR 761.

7 Courts Service Annual Report 2021, pp 90-91.

8 *Conroy v Attorney General* [1965] IR 411.

9 Criminal Justice Act 1951, s 4 as amended by Fines Act 2010, s 10; Criminal Procedure Act 1967, s 13(3) as amended by Fines Act 2010, s 10.

10 Criminal Justice Act 1951, s 5 as amended by Criminal Justice Act 1984, s 12.

disregarded for this purpose.[11] The maximum penalty is not the sole consideration in determining if an offence is minor. The moral quality of the alleged conduct is another.[12] Therefore, an offence such as rape may never be treated as minor. In any event, by virtue of statute, rape and aggravated sexual assault are excluded from the jurisdiction of the District Court, even if the accused is willing to plead guilty. A person who pleads guilty to such an offence in the District Court, as occasionally happens, must be sent forward for sentence to the Central Criminal Court.[13] In effect, therefore, the sentencing powers of the District Court are subject to two statutory limits. First, it may not impose a sentence in excess of the statutory maximum for the relevant offence (such as the six months' imprisonment for a basic assault offence). Secondly, even when dealing with an indictable offence (which may have a high maximum sentence), it may not impose more than 12 months' imprisonment for one offence or a total of two years for a combination of offences.

2–05 An indictable offence is essentially one that carries the right to trial by jury. As might be expected, all serious offences such as murder, rape, robbery and drug trafficking are indictable. Only a minority of those charged with indictable offences end up being tried by a jury. As already noted, many such offences are disposed of in the District Court because they happen to be minor in nature. Furthermore, many defendants charged with indictable offences plead guilty, thereby removing the need for trial. Those who plead not guilty to an offence prosecuted on indictment will go on trial in the Circuit Court, the Central Criminal Court or the Special Criminal Court. The Circuit Court deals with almost all indictable offences, apart from the few such as murder and rape that are within the exclusive jurisdiction of the Central Criminal Court. In 2021, 6,313 defendants were sent forward to the Circuit Court charged with 18,676 offences, mainly serious property offences, assaults, drug dealing and firearms offences. Again, there is a high rate of guilty pleas. In 2021, 14,673 offences (as opposed to individual defendants, many of whom were charged with more than one offence) were resolved one way or another in the Circuit Court. More than 10,000 (70 per cent) were resolved by way of a guilty plea, with 409 convictions resulting from a trial, though there were also 514 acquittals, again for offences rather than defendants, following trial.[14] The Circuit Court has far more ample sentencing powers than the District Court. It may impose any sentence up to the maximum specified by statute. Thus, it may impose up to 10 years' imprisonment for theft, 14 years for burglary and 10 years for assault causing harm.[15] Indeed, it may

---

[11] *Conroy v Attorney General* [1965] IR 411.

[12] *State (Rollinson) v Kelly* [1984] IR 248 at 260.

[13] Criminal Law (Rape) (Amendment) Act 1990, s 20. The same applies, for example, to a drug dealing offence contrary to s 15A of the Misuse of Drugs Act 1977 (as amended) save that, in relation to that offence, a defendant who pleads guilty is forward for sentence to the Circuit Court.

[14] Courts Service Annual Report 2021, p 93.

[15] The maximum sentence for assault causing harm was raised from five to 10 years by the Criminal Justice (Miscellaneous Provisions) Act 2023, s 20.

impose anything up to life imprisonment for several offences including robbery, aggravated burglary, manslaughter, defilement of a child under the age of 15 years and possession of controlled drugs for sale or supply.

The Central Criminal Court is the High Court exercising criminal jurisdiction. Its procedures and sentencing powers are, for all practical purposes, the same as those of the Circuit Court, save that it is presided over by a High Court judge. Its range of jurisdiction is quite limited, being confined to murder, rape, aggravated sexual assault and a few other offences that are seldom prosecuted such as breaches of competition law. As with the Circuit Court, the only formal constraint on its sentencing powers is the maximum sentence specified by statute. Murder carries a mandatory sentence of life imprisonment which means that the court has no option but to impose that sentence on every adult convicted of murder, even when the conviction results from a guilty plea. Manslaughter is available as an alternative verdict to murder, and murder defendants are occasionally convicted of the lesser offence of manslaughter which carries a maximum sentence of life imprisonment. The judge therefore has a discretion as to the sentence to be imposed, though in a case of assault manslaughter, regard must now be had to the guidelines established by the Supreme Court in *People (DPP) v Mahon*.[16] **2–06**

The Special Criminal Court is a non-jury court which potentially has jurisdiction over any offence but, by virtue of the Constitution and the governing legislation, it is confined to dealing with cases in respect of which it has been determined that "the ordinary courts are inadequate to secure the effective administration of justice, and the preservation of public peace and order".[17] In effect, a case is most likely to be referred to the Special Criminal Court where there is a fear of jury intimidation as might occur in trials for offences of a political nature (such as involvement in an illegal organisation), organised crime or gangland crime. Nowadays, the court consists of a bench of three judges, one each from the High Court, Circuit Court and District Court. Its caseload is relatively light compared with other trial courts. In 2021, there were 15 trials involving 26 defendants. It has the same sentencing powers as the Central Criminal Court and Circuit Court, save that it may not make a community service order.[18] **2–07**

3. Appeals Against Sentence

The Role of Appeal Courts

Historically, the right to appeal against conviction and sentence was hard **2–08**

---

16 [2019] IESC 24; [2019] 3 IR 151; [2019] 2 ILRM 81.

17 Constitution of Ireland, Art 38.3.1°; Offences Against the State Act 1939, s 36. See GW Hogan, GF Whyte, D Kenny and R Walsh, *Kelly: The Irish Constitution*, 5th ed (Bloomsbury Professional, 2018), 1404-1429.

18 Criminal Justice (Community Service) Act 1983, s 1.

won, and it is salutary to recall that it is barely a century old in Ireland.[19] However, criminal appeals are now well established and they serve several purposes within the legal system.[20] From a psychological perspective, they provide disappointed litigants and defendants with the hope of a more favourable result than they obtained in the trial court. Even if they are eventually disappointed, the interval between the first-instance decision and the appeal gives them time to adjust psychologically to the possibility of having to live with the first-instance decision, while fortified with the hope that they may do better on appeal. The availability of a right to appeal is also essential for preserving the rule of law and, in a criminal law context, for safeguarding a defendant's right to trial in due course of law which, in turn, has many constituent elements including the right to a fair and proportionate sentence. The trial court may have erred in drawing inferences from established facts, in interpretating the applicable law or, more pertinently in the present context, in identifying and applying the relevant sentencing principles. The primary function of an appeal court is to correct any such errors. A senior appeal court has yet another important function and that is to ensure uniformity among the lower courts over which it has appellate jurisdiction.[21] In a sentencing context, uniformity signifies consistency of approach. Permitting trial court judges to sentence according to criteria and principles of their own personal choosing would be anathema to both the rule of law and the individual's constitutional right to procedural fairness. Outcomes will inevitably vary to some degree even when settled principles are consistently applied, but it is critical that those principles should be consistently applied by all trial courts. An appeal court must take the necessary corrective action when they are not.

---

[19] Courts of Justice Act 1924, ss 8 and 28-34. On the history of criminal appeals in common law and continental European jurisdictions, see Peter D Marshall, "A comparative analysis of the right to appeal" (2011) 22 *Duke Journal of Comparative and international Law* 1. See also Rosemary Pattenden, *English Criminal Appeals 1844-1994: Appeals against Conviction and Sentence in England and Wales* (Clarendon Press, 1996); John H Langbein, Renée Lettow Lerner and Bruce P Smith, *History of the Common Law: The Development of Anglo-American Legal Institutions* (Aspen Publishers 2009); Leon Radzinowicz and Roger Hood, *The Emergence of Penal Policy in Victorian and Edwardian England* (Clarendon Press, 1990), Chap 23. The right to appeal is recognised in the main international human rights instruments including the European Convention on Human Rights, Protocol 7, art 2 and the International Covenant on Civil and Political Rights, art 14 (which is discussed in detail by Marshall, above). On the early history of the Irish Court of Criminal Appeal, see VTHD, "The Irish Court of Criminal Appeal: The first thirty years" (1952) 18 *Irish Jurist* 33.

[20] The English Law Commission in its *Issues Paper on Criminal Appeals* (2023), 6, lists the main purposes of criminal appeals as safeguarding against wrongful convictions, remedying violations of the right to a fair trial, providing consistency in the interpretation and application of the law, encouraging better decision making at trial court level, and enabling the development of substantive and procedural doctrine.

[21] Martin Shapiro, "Appeal" (1980) 14 *Law & Society Review* 629. He also writes (at 631): "[A]ppeal is the handmaiden of certain fundamental legal values: it seeks to ensure that the law shall be uniform, impersonal, impartial, principled, and clearly elaborated."

When performing the last of these functions in a sentencing context, a senior appeal court (such as the Supreme Court or Court of Appeal in Ireland) has the opportunity and, indeed, an obligation to develop sentencing jurisprudence, a role that the legislature has implicitly assigned to the judiciary. Statutory sentencing provisions tend to be phrased in broad terms. In most cases, the only statutory guidance on the sentencing of a particular offence is the specified maximum penalty. Even where statute law elaborates somewhat on the approach to be adopted in sentencing certain offences, it will probably employ terms such as "exceptional and specific circumstances" which, in turn, will fall to be interpreted and applied by the courts.[22] An appeal court must therefore be a forum of principle as well as a decision-making tribunal. Individual appeals provide a context or framework in which general sentencing principles and guideline ranges can be articulated, re-affirmed, developed or refined as the need arises. Most sentence appeals are routine in nature and require no more than a decision as to whether the sentence should be upheld or varied. Some, however, furnish an opportunity to elaborate more generally on the rules or principles that should govern the outcome. Henry Hart once claimed that the United States Supreme Court is predestined "to be a voice of reason, charged with the creative function of discerning afresh and of articulating and developing impersonal and durable principles of constitutional law."[23] In a similar vein, senior appeal courts exercising criminal jurisdiction have a duty to develop fair, rational, effective and durable principles of sentencing, and to ensure, as far as they can, that those principles are consistently applied. **2–09**

Appeal courts therefore exercise a supervisory role in respect of trial courts but in a manner that differs greatly from our ordinary understanding of supervision. In an employment context, for example, supervision is based on direct communication. The subordinate or supervisee can seek advice or direction from the supervisor on how to approach a task or on the decision to be made in a specific case. The supervisor, in turn, can advise, correct or reprimand a subordinate who has somehow erred or fallen short in the performance of their duties. Judicial supervisory systems operate very differently. Apart from case stated proceedings, described below, trial judges cannot seek advice or guidance from an appeal court on any decision they are about to make. A trial judge may not, for example, ask the Court of Appeal if a particular sentence that he or she is minded to impose would be acceptable to it. The judge must simply decide on a sentence and let the defence or prosecution, if they are dissatisfied with it, seek to have it varied on appeal. By the same token, the Court of Appeal cannot interfere with a sentence which it regards as manifestly wrong in principle unless that sentence is the subject of a defence appeal or an undue leniency application by the prosecution. Moreover, an appeal court decision never takes the form of direct communication with the trial judge. **2–10**

[22] See, for example, Misuse of Drugs Act 1977, s 27(3D), as substituted by Criminal Justice Act 2007, s 33 on the sentencing of s 15A drug offences.

[23] Henry M Hart, Jr, "The Supreme Court 1958 term: Foreword: The time chart of the Justices" (1959) 73 Harvard LR 84, 99.

Rather it is conveyed in a judgment addressed primarily to the parties and, when in published form, to the world at large.[24]

Defence Appeals

2–11 A person convicted and sentenced in the District Court has an automatic right of appeal to the Circuit Court.[25] An appeal against conviction involves a complete rehearing of the case (a *de novo* hearing) whereas in an appeal against sentence only, the Circuit Court will hear so much of the case as is necessary to determine the matter.[26] The Circuit Court's decision is final and unappealable, though it may be challenged on limited grounds by way of judicial review as described below. Once an appeal against a District Court conviction or sentence is properly lodged, it operates as a stay of execution. The penalty, even if it is one of imprisonment, will not come into effect until the matter has finally been determined by the Circuit Court. Any penalty substituted by that court following the hearing of an appeal must be one that would have been within the jurisdiction of the District Court.

2–12 The system of appeals in respect of offences dealt with on indictment in the Central Criminal Court, Special Criminal Court and Circuit Court underwent a significant change following the adoption of the 33rd Amendment of the Constitution in 2013 which provided for the establishment of a permanent Court of Appeal. Prior to that, all such appeals went to the Court of Criminal Appeal which was originally established under the Courts of Justice Act 1924, though it never had an express constitutional foundation. The Court of Criminal Appeal sat at least once a week and consisted of one Supreme Court judge and two High Court judges. The membership tended to vary from one sitting to the next. Its decision in any appeal against conviction or sentence was final unless it issued a certificate to the effect that the case involved a point of law of exceptional public importance which justified a further appeal to the Supreme Court. The Attorney General and the Director of Public Prosecutions were also empowered to issue such a certificate.[27] Following the 2013 constitutional amendment, the Court of Criminal Appeal was abolished, and its jurisdiction transferred to the new Court of Appeal.[28] The new court, unlike its predecessor, has a permanent judiciary, currently consisting of 18 judges, including the President.[29] It deals with civil appeals

---

[24] Note, "Courting reversal: The supervisory role of state supreme courts" (1978) 87 Yale LJ 1191, 1194.

[25] Courts of Justice Act 1928, s 18.

[26] Courts (Supplemental Provisions) Act 1961, s 50. See *State (Aherne) v Cotter* [1982] IR 188; [1983] ILRM 17.

[27] Courts of Justice Act 1924, s 29. See, for example, *People (DPP) v Wharrie* [2017] 2 IR 743 which seems to be the last such appeal dealt with by the Supreme Court under the old system. The leading case of *People (DPP) v Tiernan* [1988] IR 250; [1989] ILRM 149 on sentencing for rape came before the Supreme Court following the issue of a certificate by the Attorney General.

[28] Court of Appeal Act 2014.

[29] Courts Act 2023, s 2.

from the High Court as well as those criminal appeals that formerly went to the Court of Criminal Appeal. Unlike its English counterpart, the Irish Court of Appeal does not have formal civil and criminal divisions but, in effect, it has a criminal law division in the sense that a bench of three judges sits almost daily in the Criminal Courts of Justice to deal with appeals against conviction, sentence or both. A decision of the Court of Appeal is final and conclusive, but it is possible to apply to the Supreme Court for a determination that the decision involves a matter of general public importance or that the interests of justice render it necessary that there should be a further appeal to the Supreme Court.[30] The decision on the grant of leave for such further appeal rests with the Supreme Court itself. Since the new system became operative in 2014, the Supreme Court has heard and decided some significant sentencing cases under this rubric, including *People (DPP) v Mahon*[31] (sentencing for assault manslaughter), *People (DPP) v E(F)*[32] (sentencing for rape) and *Ellis v Minister for Justice and Equality*[33] (striking down mandatory minimum sentence for repeat firearms offence).

2–13 A convicted person appealing against severity of sentence must satisfy the Court of Appeal that the trial court committed an error of principle. This longstanding rule originated in *R v Sidlow*,[34] one of the earliest cases decided by the English Court of Criminal Appeal. There the Court is recorded as having said that it would not interfere with a sentence "unless it was apparent that the judge at trial had proceeded upon wrong principles, or given undue weight to some of the facts proved in evidence". The 'error of principle' criterion was adopted by the Irish Court of Criminal Appeal very soon after its establishment in 1924 and, indeed, by equivalent courts in other common law jurisdictions. For instance, in *R v House*[35] the High Court of Australia held that, before an appeal court could interfere with a sentence, the trial judge must have made some error in the exercise of his or her discretion. In Ireland, a sentence may also be challenged if the trial court made a material error of law or fact or if it acted outside of its jurisdiction.[36] However, almost all defence appeals are based on an alleged error of principle. Such an error may be found where the sentence is manifestly excessive or where the trial court failed to take account of a relevant factor, such as a guilty plea, or attributed inadequate weight to a relevant factor of which it took

30 Constitution of Ireland, Art 34.5.3^{0}.

31 [2019] IESC 24; [2019] 3 IR 151; [2019] 2 ILRM 81.

32 [2019] IESC 85 and [2020] IESC 5; [2021] 1 IR 217; [2020] 1 ILRM 517 and [2020] 2 ILRM 153. See also *People (DPP) v Molloy* [2021] IESC 44; [2021] 2 ILRM 278 (conditions attached to suspended sentence and guidelines on sentencing for harassment); *People (DPP) v Duffy* [2023] IESC 1 (victim's views on sentence and use of compensation orders); *People (DPP) v Faulkner* [2024] IESC 16 (sentencing for burglary and sentencing principles more generally).

33 [2019] IESC 30; [2019] 3 IR 511; [2019] 2 ILRM 420.

34 (1909) 1 Cr App R 28.

35 (1936) 55 CLR 499.

36 In *People (DPP) v McGrane* [2020] IECA 369, for example, the trial court erred in relation to the applicable maximum sentence.

some account. Failure on the part of the trial judge to permit a convicted person, through counsel or otherwise, to make a plea in mitigation and address any other issues that might have a material bearing on sentence would also amount to an error which would almost certainly lead to the sentence being quashed, even if the sentence did not seem inappropriate in the circumstances.[37]

2–14 Having heard an appeal against sentence, the Court of Appeal may uphold the sentence or quash it and replace it with such sentence or other order as it considers appropriate, being a sentence or order that could have been imposed on the appellant by the trial court.[38] A sentence may therefore be increased as well as reduced following a defence appeal, although this rarely happens[39] Where a defence appeal seems patently unmeritorious and the original sentence seems, if anything, to be too lenient, the court generally advises the appellant of its power to increase sentence. More often than not, this leads to an application to withdraw the appeal, an application that is usually granted. The English Court of Appeal had a similar power until 1966 when it was removed, apparently because it was felt that it might deter genuine appeals and that it was unfair that convicted persons who believed their sentences were too severe should end up with sentences that were even more severe.[40] However, English law has a different kind of deterrent against unmeritorious appeals, and this is the "loss of time" order. If satisfied that an appeal against conviction or sentence is clearly unmeritorious, the Court of Appeal may direct that the time spent in custody by the applicant pending the determination of the appeal is not to be reckoned as part of the sentence to which he or she is subject.[41] When the court exercises this power, it seldom adds more than a few weeks to the sentence. For instance, in *R v Jan*[42]it added 28 days. In *Ali v Trinidad and Tobago*[43]the Privy Council considered a similar statutory provision and indicated certain principles that should govern its application. A loss of time order should not be made to reflect the seriousness of the offence or lack of remorse as these are matters solely relevant to the original sentence. An order, when made to discourage

---

37 *Moss v The Queen* [2013] UKPC 32; [2013] 1 WLR 3884; *R v Watson* [2023] UKPC 32.

38 Criminal Procedure Act 1993, s 3(2).

39 However, in *People (DPP) v O'Haire* [2022] IECA 36, the Court of Appeal increased the sentence by reducing the suspended portion of a five-year sentence from 24 months to 15 months. More recently, the Court significantly increased the sentence in *People (DPP) v McM(J)* [2024] IECA 220.

40 AJ Ashworth, "Prosecution and procedure in criminal justice" [1979] Crim LR 480, 489; David Thomas "Increasing sentences on appeal: A re-examination" [1972] Crim LR 288.

41 Criminal Appeal Act 1968, s 29(1). Cases dealing with this provision include *R v Wilson* [2014] EWCA Crim 2336; *R v Fortean* [2009] EWCA Crim 437; *R v Hart* [2007] 1 Cr App R 31; *R v Gray* [2014] EWCA Crim 2372; [2015] 1 Cr App R (S) 27 (and see detailed comment on *Gray* by Paul Taylor at [2015] Crim LR 352).

42 [2023] EWCA Crim 164.

43 [2005] UKPC 41; [2006] 1 WLR 269.

unmeritorious appeals, should not inflict an unfairly long extension of imprisonment. The English loss of time provision was unsuccessfully challenged before the European Court of Human Rights in *Monnell and Morris v United Kingdom.*[44] The court found that it conflicted with neither art 5 nor art 6 of the European Convention on Human Rights (ECHR), though two judges dissented on the art 5 point.

The English power to make a loss of time order and the Irish power to increase sentence following a defence appeal are similar to the extent that both can lead to a longer term of imprisonment than that imposed by the trial court. They differ however in their purpose and rationale. In Ireland, a sentence will be increased because the Court has determined that it was disproportionately lenient. In England and Wales, a loss of time order operates, in effect, as a punishment for having brought an unmeritorious appeal as opposed to a punishment for the offence. One might of course argue that the Irish provision also acts as a disincentive to bringing appeals that seem bound to fail. However, it is more properly seen as a power vested in the Court of Appeal to ensure that offences are punished appropriately and to correct a sentence that seems too lenient. Whether such a power is any longer necessary in view of the entitlement of the Director of Public Prosecutions to bring an undue leniency application (described immediately below) remains debatable. **2–15**

Persons convicted on indictment have a right to appeal directly to the Court of Appeal against conviction, sentence or both. There is no screening mechanism to eliminate appeals that seem bound to fail. In England and Wales, an application for leave to appeal to the Court of Appeal (Criminal Division) is first considered by a single judge of the Court. A person refused leave may renew the application before the full court. In 2015, for example, there were more than 4,444 leave applications of which 1,385 were granted.[45] In Ireland, the number of criminal appeals is much lower. In 2021, 248 criminal appeals were lodged with the Court of Appeal and it disposed of 282, including 79 appeals against conviction, 162 against severity of sentence and 36 undue leniency applications.[46] While the number of appeals is substantial in light of the resources available to the court, which also has an extensive civil jurisdiction, it probably does not justify the introduction of a screening system similar to that operating in England and Wales. **2–16**

As already noted, a decision of the Court of Appeal is ordinarily final and conclusive, but leave may sought to take a further appeal to the Supreme Court on the basis that the decision involves a matter of general public importance or that it is necessary in the interests of justice to have a further appeal. It is for the Supreme Court itself to decide if leave should be granted in any case. A sentencing decision, like any other decision of **2–17**

---

44 (1988) 10 EHRR 205.

45 Andrew Ashworth, "The evolution of English sentencing guidance in 2016" [2017] Crim LR 507 at 508

46 Courts Service Annual Report 2021, 103.

the Court of Appeal, may be subject to a further appeal to the Supreme Court. Such an appeal may be initiated by either the defence or the prosecution if it is believed that the Court of Appeal erred in principle. If the Supreme Court finds that the Court of Appeal did so err, it is not confined to making a declaration to that effect. Rather, as the Supreme Court held in *People (DPP) v E (F)*,[47] which happened to arise from an appeal by the prosecution, when it entertains an appeal from the Court of Appeal or directly from the Central Criminal Court (which is also possible), it is exercising the same powers of appeal and correction as the Court of Appeal would possess in a similar case. It may therefore vary the sentence if it deems it necessary to do so. In *E (F)* itself, the Supreme Court, having determined that the Court of Appeal erred in reducing the sentence (for rape in that instance), restored the sentence imposed by the Central Criminal Court.

2–18 A 'one judgment' rule applies when the Court of Appeal is deciding a 'criminal matter'. The current statutory provision, dating from 2014, provides:

> "Where the Court of Appeal is exercising its jurisdiction in respect of a criminal matter before it, then unless the matter is one which involves a question as to the validity of any law having regard to the provisions of the Constitution, the decision of the majority of the judges of the Court hearing the case shall be the decision of the Court of Appeal and it shall be pronounced by such one of the judges of the Court as that Court shall direct and no other opinion whether assenting or dissenting shall be pronounced, nor shall the existence of any such other opinion be disclosed."[48]

2–19 The former Court of Criminal Appeal was subject to a similar rule by virtue of the Courts of Justice Act 1924 (s 28). There are conflicting views about the wisdom of this rule which has no application in civil appeals, including judicial review applications arising from criminal proceedings in the lower courts.[49] Defenders of the rule claim that it obviates appearances of uncertainty which might be undesirable in criminal appeals. They also say that it could be unfair to a successful appellant if two members of the court decided to quash a conviction while the third member, dissenting, argued that the conviction should be upheld.[50] On the other hand, the Supreme Court is subject to no such restriction. Members of that court are free to deliver individual judgments, whether concurring or dissenting,

---

47 [2020] IESC 5; [2021] 1 IR 217.

48 Courts (Supplemental Provisions) Act 1961, s 7A(7), inserted by Court of Appeal Act 2014, s 8.

49 For a more detailed analysis, see Rory Kelly, "Criminalising dissent" (2022) 138 LQR 432. See also JD Heydon, "Threats to judicial independence: The enemy within" (2013) 129 LQR 205, and Peter W Hogg and Ravi Amarnath, "Why judges should dissent" (2017) 67 University of Toronto LJ 126.

50 RM Chitty, "Dissenting judgments in criminal appeals are undesirable" (1967) 15 Chitty's LJ 335.

even in appeals against conviction or sentence.[51] As a matter of practice, a one-judgment rule applies in the English Court of Appeal (Criminal Division), although the governing legislation provides that the presiding judgment may determine that the question is "one of law on which it is convenient that separate judgments should be pronounced by members of the court".[52] In Canada, by contrast, multiple judgments are permitted in criminal cases in intermediate appeal courts as well as in the Supreme Court.[53]

4. Undue Leniency Applications

Since 1993, the Director of Public Prosecutions has been empowered to bring what is in effect a prosecution appeal against leniency of sentence. What the relevant statute, the Criminal Justice Act 1993 (the '1993 Act') (s 2), actually provides is that the Director, if she considers the sentence imposed on a person convicted on indictment to be unduly lenient, may apply to the Court of Appeal to review that sentence. Having considered the application, the Court of Appeal may (1) quash the sentence and substitute another which it considers appropriate or (2) refuse the application. Between 2012 to 2021, the DPP made a total of 493 undue leniency applications, and a total of 434 were heard during that period. Of these 272 (63%) were successful, 131 (30%) were refused and 31 (7%) were withdrawn or struck out. The success rate has increased in recent years. In 2021, for example, 27 applications were successful while 5 were refused.[54] Courts in other jurisdictions with a similar provision have sometimes held that the prosecution power to appeal against leniency of sentence should be sparingly used, and that such appeals are expected to be rare.[55] In Ireland, however, the 1993 Act (s 2) merely provides: "If it appears to the Director of Public Prosecutions that a sentence imposed by a court... on conviction of a person on indictment was unduly lenient, he may apply to the [Court of Appeal] to review the sentence". There is nothing in this provision to suggest that such application should be either rare or exceptional, save to the extent that the sentence must be viewed by the DPP as *unduly* lenient. As a matter of probability, only a small minority of cases are likely to be so regarded. The Court of Appeal has occasionally found a sentence to be very lenient but not so unduly lenient as to warrant intervention.[56] One reason why appeal courts have been inclined to treat **2–20**

---

[51] See, for example, *People (DPP) v N (F)* [2022] IESC 22; [2022] 2 ILRM 279; *People (DPP) v Duffy* [2023] IESC 1.

[52] Supreme Court Act 1981, s 59. See Roderick Munday, "'All for one and one for all': The rise to prominence of the composite judgment within the civil division of the Court of Appeal" (2002) 61 Cambridge LJ 321, 340-345.

[53] See, for example, *R v S (R)* 2023 ONCA 608.

[54] Office of the Director of Public Prosecutions, *Annual Report 2021* (2022), 35.

[55] This has been the policy of Australian courts in particular. See *Griffiths v The Queen* [1977] HCA 44; (1977) 137 CLR 293 and *Everett v The Queen* [1994] HCA 49; (1994) 181 CLR 295.

[56] See, for example, *People (DPP) v Hanney* [2017] IECA 209; *People (DPP) v Bannerton* [2022] IECA 191.

as exceptional the jurisdiction to review sentences for undue leniency is that, traditionally, an offender was entitled to assume that the sentence imposed by the trial court was final unless varied following a defence appeal, but it was up to the offender to decide if any such appeal should be taken. Now that undue leniency applications have become deeply embedded in the system, the expectation of finality may no longer be as legitimate as it once was. The Director of Public Prosecutions must nonetheless act expeditiously in seeking review. The application must be made, on notice to the offender, within 28 days of the date of sentence or, with the permission of the Court of Appeal, within a longer period not exceeding 56 days.[57]

2–21 Both the former Court of Criminal Appeal and the present Court of Appeal have consistently stressed that the Director of Public Prosecutions must demonstrate that the sentence is *unduly* lenient, in the sense that it is clearly beyond the parameters of what could be considered an appropriate sentence in light of all the circumstances of the case.[58] As recently phrased by the Supreme Court, the question is "whether there is a substantial divergence from what would be considered the appropriate sentence, taking into account the particular features of the crime and the accused".[59] It is not sufficient that the appeal court or any individual members of it might have imposed a heavier sentence if they had been dealing with it at first instance. The sentence must, objectively viewed, represent a significant departure from the norm.[60] In evaluating the sentence, the Court of Appeal, like the trial court, must take all relevant factors into consideration, including the offender's culpability.[61] If the court decides to quash a sentence and substitute another it considers appropriate, in accordance with the terms of s 2 of the 1993 Act, appropriateness must be evaluated by reference to the circumstances existing at the time of resentencing. It must therefore consider any changes in the circumstances of the defendant or other persons involved as well as the period of

---

57 Criminal Justice Act 1993, s 2(2) as amended by Criminal Justice Act 2006, s 23.

58 The principles governing undue leniency appeals have been set out in many cases including *People (DPP) v Byrne* [1995] 1 ILRM 279; *People (DPP) v McCormack* [2000] 4 IR 356; *People (DPP) v Stronge* [2011] IECCA 79; *People (DPP) v Byrne* [2018] IECA 120.

59 *People (DPP) v Duffy* [2023] IESC 1, para 37 where the court further said that the answer to this question will normally involve consideration of any applicable guideline.

60 In *People (DPP) v Bannerton* [2022] IECA 191, for example, the sentence did not represent a sufficient departure from the norm to justify a finding of undue leniency. See also *People (DPP) v M (N)* [2020] IECA 25. The same criterion applies in England and Wales. In *Attorney General's Reference No 4 of 1989* [1990] 1 WLR 41, 46; (1989) 11 Cr App R (S.) 517 the Court of Appeal held that a sentence is unduly lenient "where it falls outside the range of sentences which the judge, applying his mind to all the relevant factors, could reasonably consider appropriate".

61 *People (DPP) v R (M)* [2022] IECA 192 (application refused because of defendant's mental health issues); *People (DPP) v Wallace* [2016] IECA 57 where the defendant's physical disability was a factor in the refusal of the application.

uncertainty and, where relevant, that the defendant has been released from prison.[62]

Even where the Court decides to grant an application and increase a sentence, it usually makes some reduction for the so-called disappointment factor. This is done in recognition of the fact that a convicted person is generally entitled to assume that the sentence imposed by the trial judge is the final sentence, subject to any adjustment made following a defence appeal.[63] Further, it is accepted that the sense of disappointment will be all the greater where a successful prosecution appeal results in a person who was given a non-custodial penalty by the trial court being sent to prison or where the person has already served the prison sentence originally imposed and must now return to serve a further term. **2–22**

The power vested in the Court of Appeal to determine if a sentence is unduly lenient may be justified on various policy grounds. First, it permits the correction of a serious error in sentencing. Respect for the proportionality principle (described in Chap 5 below) demands that sentences should not be disproportionately and unjustifiably lenient any more than they should be disproportionately severe. Secondly, it allays public concern in any case where a sentence widely perceived to be unduly lenient is passed, an issue that is most likely to arise in respect of sexual or other violent offences. Thirdly and more generally, having a formal process to review apparently unduly lenient sentences helps to maintain public confidence in the criminal justice system.[64] For this reason, in a case where the defendant has been sentenced to several terms of imprisonment, some of them consecutive, the Court of Appeal may be satisfied with the cumulative sentence, but it may increase some of the individual sentences to reflect more accurately the gravity of the offences to which they relate. The revised sentences may then be ordered to run in a way that will leave the original cumulative sentence intact.[65] **2–23**

Even where the Court of Appeal is satisfied that a sentence is unduly **2–24**

---

62 *People (DPP) v Egan* [2001] 2 ILRM 299, 307. See also *People (DPP) v O'Connor* [2023] IECA 306 where the sentence, despite being declared unduly lenient, was not increased largely because of the lapse of time between the commission of the offence and sentence, and between the imposition of sentence and the hearing of the undue leniency application. In *People (DPP) v O'Flaherty* [2021] IECA 43, where a fine had been imposed, the Court of Appeal added a term of imprisonment but suspended it in recognition of mitigating factors.

63 Among many examples, see *People (DPP) v Connor* [2020] IECA 255; *People (DPP) v Murphy* [2020] IECA 244; *People (DPP) v Maxwell* [2020] IECA 62; *People (DPP) v Cummins* [2020] IECA 42.

64 *Attorney General's Reference No 132 of 2001 (R v Johnson)* [2002] EWCA Crim 1418; [2003] 1 Cr App R (S) 41, para 24; *R v Bremakumar* [2023] EWCA Crim 545, para 24.

65 See, for example, *R v Wacker* [2002] EWCA Crim 1944; [2003] QB 1207; [2003] 1 Cr App R (S) 92 where the English Court of Appeal adopted this approach when resentencing for multiple manslaughters and conspiracy.

lenient, it is not obliged to substitute a more severe penalty. The Criminal Justice Act 1993 (s 2(3)) provides:

> "On such an application, the Court may either (a) quash the sentence and in place of it impose on the convicted person such sentence as it considers appropriate, being a sentence which could have been imposed on him by the sentencing court concerned, or (b) refuse the application."

2–25 It seems clear from this wording that an application may be refused even where undue leniency has been established. Alternatively, having made a finding of undue leniency, the Court of Appeal may adjust the sentence in such a way that the defendant will not have to spend any time in immediate custody or any longer than required under the original sentence. (After all, s 2(3) authorises the court to substitute such sentence as it considers appropriate and this does not necessarily have to be a longer custodial sentence). Such a response might serve the interests of justice if, for example, a considerable period of time had elapsed since the sentence was imposed or since the offender was released from prison on having served the original sentence, or there was unwarranted delay at some point during the overall proceedings.[66] It might also be appropriate if the offender was engaging effectively with rehabilitation services or otherwise seemed to making genuine efforts at desistance.[67] In *People (DPP) v Zinck*,[68] for example, the Court of Appeal substituted a ten-year sentence but suspended it entirely because of the "wholly exceptional" progress and transformation on the defendant's part since his arrest. The court may also increase the sentence but suspend such a portion of it as will ensure that the offender spends no longer in prison.[69] In other circumstances, a factor of this nature may justify increasing the sentence to a lesser extent than would otherwise be appropriate.[70] In England and Wales, where prosecution appeals against unduly lenient sentences were introduced in 1988, and where the relevant statutory provision is broadly similar to the current Irish law, a similar discretion applies.[71] As the Court of Appeal said in one of the earliest references:

> "The second thing to be observed about the section is that, even where it considers that the sentence was unduly lenient, this court has a discretion as to whether to exercise its powers. Without attempting an exhaustive

---

66 *People (DPP) v Naylor and Goddard* [2020] IECA 166; *People (DPP) v O'Connor* [2023] IECA 306 where lapse of time was one of the reasons why the Court of Appeal dismissed the DPP's application.

67 *People (DPP) v Matthews* [2019] IECA 365; *People (DPP) v W(A)* [2023] IECA 204. English courts occasionally do the same. See, for example, *R v Feve* [2024] EWCA Crim 286.

68 [2016] IECA 368 and [2017] IECA 33 (a s 15A drug case where the original sentence was nine years fully suspended).

69 *People (DPP) v Berney* [2021] IECA 226.

70 *People (DPP) v Joyce* [2021] IECA 124.

71 Criminal Justice Act 1988, s 36, provides that where the Attorney General seeks review of an unduly lenient sentence, the Court of Appeal *may* quash the sentence and substitute such sentence as it considers appropriate, being a sentence that could have been imposed by the trial court.

> definition of the circumstances in which this court might refuse to increase an unduly lenient sentence, we mention one obvious instance: where in the light of events since the trial it appears either that the sentence can be justified or that to increase it would be unfair to the offender or detrimental to others for whose well-being the court ought to be concerned."[72]

Significantly also, the court went on to say that the trial judge is particularly well placed to assess the weight to be given to the various competing considerations, and that "leniency is not in itself a vice. That mercy should season justice is a proposition as soundly based in law as it is in literature".[73] **2–26**

5. Judicial Review and Case Stated Procedures

As already noted, a decision of the Circuit Court in an appeal against conviction or sentence from the District Court is final and unappealable. Circuit Court decisions are seldom, if ever, reported. It is therefore useful to have some mechanism for bringing important points of law and procedure before the Superior Courts (the High Court, Court of Appeal and Supreme Court) for an authoritative determination. This is most commonly done by way of judicial review, but occasionally by way of case stated instead. Judicial review proceedings may not be initiated in any court other than the High Court which has an inherent power to exercise a supervisory jurisdiction over decision-making by public bodies which, for this purpose, include the lower courts (the District Court, Circuit Court and Special Criminal Court). It is beyond the scope of this work to describe the judicial review process in any detail but there are a few salient points to note.[74] First, judicial review is not concerned with the merits of a challenged decision (that is the purpose of an appeal), but rather with the manner in which the decision was reached. Typically, the applicant will be arguing that the respondent body (such as the District Court) exceeded its jurisdiction, committed a significant legal error, abused its discretion or failed to exercise it, or failed to observe the principles of natural and constitutional justice. As the High Court said in *Connors v DPP*,[75] judicial review "is concerned principally with the legality of the decision-making process and not with the underlying merits of the decision under challenge (save in cases of irrationality)". In that case, it was held that the trial judge's refusal to grant a short adjournment to allow **2–27**

---

72 *Attorney General's Reference No 4 of 1989* [1990] 1 WLR 41, 46; (1989) 11 Cr App R (S) 517.

73 [1990] 1 WLR 41, 46; (1989) 11 Cr App R (S.) 517.

74 For detailed accounts of judicial review procedure, see Mark de Blacam, *Judicial Review*, 3rd ed (Bloomsbury Professional, 2017); David Gwynn Morgan, Paul Daly and Gerard W Hogan, *Hogan and Morgan's Administrative Law*, 4th ed (Thomson Reuters, 2012); Anthony M Collins and James O'Reilly, *Civil Proceedings and the State*, 3rd ed (Round Hall, 2019).

75 [2023] IEHC 8, para 14. See also *R (E) v DPP* [2019] IESC 86, para 17 of judgment of Charleton J ("Judicial review is about process, jurisdiction and adherence to a basic level of sound procedures".) and *Sweeney v Fahy* [2014] IESC 50.

the defendant, who had pleaded guilty, to have a consultation with his defence counsel prior to the sentencing hearing amounted to a breach of the defendant's constitutional right to fair hearing. It was therefore one of those cases where a challenge by way of judicial review as opposed to an appeal was appropriate.

2–28 Secondly, there are certain public law remedies, notably certiorari, mandamus and prohibition, that are available by way of judicial review only. In a criminal law context, the remedy most frequently sought is certiorari which is effectively a quashing order (as it is now known in England and Wales). When the High Court grants certiorari, it quashes the challenged decision, although it usually has a discretion to remit the matter back to the respondent body or court, so that the decision can be made again, but properly this time around. An order of mandamus has the effect of compelling a public body to do something it is legally obliged to do, while an order of prohibition, as the name suggests, restrains the respondent from taking some step or from continuing with some procedure, such as a prosecution, on which it has embarked. Thirdly, an application for relief by way of judicial review involves a two-stage process. The applicant must first seek leave from the High Court to proceed with judicial review. Such an application is usually made *ex parte*, meaning that the applicant alone is heard; the intended respondent need not be on notice of the application at that point. Only if leave is granted by the High Court (or, if it refuses leave, by the Court of Appeal) does the matter then proceed to a full hearing. Obviously, all parties to the case are heard at that point. Fourthly, judicial review proceedings are always civil in nature, even when they are challenging the outcome of criminal proceedings. This means that the applicant who, in the present context, will typically be a person convicted in one of the lower courts, bears the burden of proof but to the civil standard (on the balance of probabilities).

2–29 By way of example, a person who was sentenced to six months' imprisonment following conviction in the District Court and who felt that this sentence was too severe should appeal to the Circuit Court. The complaint in this instance is about the substance of the challenged decision. The convicted person is not saying that the sentencing decision was illegally or improperly made but rather than it was wrong in principle. The Circuit Court's role will be to examine the circumstances of the offence and the offender and then decide if the sentence was appropriate. In other words, it must decide on the merits of the case. However, there are other situations where judicial review is the more appropriate remedy. Suppose, for example, the person was convicted of several offences at the same District Court hearing and sentenced to a total of three years' imprisonment. Here, the District Court would have acted unlawfully and outside its jurisdiction because the maximum custodial sentence it may legally impose in these circumstances is two years' imprisonment. The convicted person, who would become the applicant in judicial review proceedings, would seek, and almost certainly obtain, from the High Court an order of certiorari quashing the three-year sentence. The High Court, in this instance, would not be concerned with the question of whether the sentence was deserved having regard to the offences of conviction; that would be going to the merits of the case. Rather it would have to decide if the District Court order (the three-year sentence in this example) was in accordance with law and made within jurisdiction. In Ireland, unlike England and Wales, when the High Court quashes a sentence, it has no power to substitute a new sentence in its place. That will be a matter for the original trial court if the High Court remits the case back to it.

Judicial review would also be appropriate if the District Court judge, while imposing a sentence that was entirely lawful and within jurisdiction, had conducted the proceedings in an unfair manner. For example, the judge might have prevented the defendant's legal representative from cross-examining a witness, or refused to entertain a plea in mitigation. In either event, there would be a breach of natural and constitutional justice.[76] A sentence may also be quashed by way of certiorari if is found to be unreasonable. This very rarely happens, because the applicable test is a very demanding one. The applicant must ordinarily satisfy the High Court that the challenged decision was so unreasonable that it "[flew]in the face of fundamental reason and common sense".[77] In *Mooney v DPP*[78] the High Court quashed a sentence imposed by the District Court for a harassment offence. The sentence included a restraining order under s 10(3) of the Non-Fatal Offences Against the Person Act 1997 which prohibited the offender from residing within eight kilometres of the victim. This restriction was apparently intended to last for the offender's lifetime, as it was not expressed to apply for any specific period. A similar condition applied to the portion of the prison sentence that was suspended. The High Court quashed these orders (and the sentence in its entirety) because they were "disproportionate", though it might be inferred from an earlier portion of the judgment that this term was being used in the sense of "unreasonable". The court had said that a sentence, even if formally within a court's jurisdiction, "may nevertheless be so far outside the *reasonable* discretionary limits that it amounts to an error of law".[79] Any claim that a sentence is disproportionately severe, though not to an unreasonable extent, should be addressed by way of appeal. **2–30**

The High Court has, however, occasionally quashed sentences because the respondent judge failed to exercise discretion. When the law confers discretion on a judge or other public official, it requires that an individualised decision be made in each case. The legislature, when it makes an offence punishable with a maximum rather than a mandatory **2–31**

[76] See, for example, *Nevin v Crowley* [1999] 1 ILRM 376 (High Court); [2001] 1 IR 113 (Supreme Court).

[77] *O'Keeffe v An Bord Pleanála* [1993] 1 IR 39; [1992] ILRM 237. In *O'Brien v Coughlan* [2015] IECA 245, the Court of Appeal found a 40-year driving ban to be unreasonable in the circumstances, although it upheld the remainder of the sentence.

[78] [2019] IEHC 625.

[79] [2019] IEHC 625, para 22 (mphasis in original).

sentence, is effectively conferring upon trial judges a discretion which they are bound to exercise. A judge who adopted a fixed or rigid policy as to the sentence that should be imposed for a given offence (eg 'everyone convicted of this offence in my court gets three months' imprisonment and that is the end of the matter') would thereby be failing to exercise the necessary discretion.[80] This does not preclude the establishment of guidelines which judges are required to follow, provided the guidelines are sufficiently flexible, as they almost invariably are, to allow for all the relevant circumstances of a case to be duly considered.

2–32 Case stated procedure may be briefly described. It often serves the same purpose as judicial review to the extent that it permits the High Court or Court of Appeal to answer a legal question posed by a judge of the District Court or Circuit Court.[81] Decisions of the District Court may be subject to an appeal by way of case stated, meaning that the District Court judge agrees to state a case for the High Court asking if he or she was correct in law in reaching a particular decision based on the facts of the case in question. This will normally be done at the request of either the defence or the prosecution. Many cases stated under this procedure deal with aspects of road traffic law though they may, of course, relate to any matter within the District Court's jurisdiction. An appeal against the High Court's decision lies to the Court of Appeal. A District Court judge may also state a consultative case to the High Court. This involves seeking a ruling from the High Court on a point of law that has arisen during the District Court hearing. For instance, in *DPP (Purtill) v Murray*[82] a District Court judge stated a consultative case asking if the common law power to suspend a prison sentence had survived the enactment of s 99 of the Criminal Justice Act 2006 which had provided a statutory basis for suspension of sentence, though without expressly abolishing the common law power. The High Court answered this question in the negative. A Circuit Court judge may state a consultative case for the Court of Appeal (formerly for the Supreme Court), again seeking a ruling on some point of law.[83] In *DPP v S (A)*,[84] for example, a Circuit Court judge stated a consultative case asking if a sentence of detention imposed on a young offender under the Children Act 2001 could lawfully be suspended in whole or in part. This question too was answered in the negative. More recently, *People (DPP) v O'Leary*[85] came before the Court of Appeal by way of a consultative case stated on the operation of s 144 of the Children Act 2001 which permits the imposition of deferred detention order. The court

80 *Lacatus v DPP* [2023] IEHC 328 (where earlier authorities are reviewed); *People (DPP) v O'D (R)* [2000] 4 IR 361; *Pudliszewski v Coughlan* [2006] IEHC 304. See also Thomas O'Malley, *Sentencing Law and Practice*, 3rd ed (Round Hall, 2016), 87-88.

81 For a detailed description of case stated procedures see Collins and O'Reilly, note 74 above, Chaps 1 and 2.

82 [2015] IEHC 782; [2015] 4 IR 405.

83 Courts of Justice Act 1947, s 16

84 [2017] IECA 310

85 [2023] IECA 48

provided useful clarification on the options open to a judge where the offender has reached the age of 18 years on the resumed hearing date.[86]

[86] This is discussed further in Chap 9 below.

CHAPTER 3

WHY PUNISH?

Because punishment involves the infliction of hard treatment, it needs to be morally justified. Judicially imposed penalties usually entrench upon liberty or property rights that are otherwise constitutionally protected. Those rights are not absolute; they may be limited or restricted to promote certain social goals that must occasionally trump individual rights and interests. The detection, investigation, prosecution and punishment of crime are undoubtedly legitimate social goals. People who are suspected, accused or convicted of criminal offences may therefore be deprived of their liberty through being detained for questioning, held in custody pending trial and sentenced to imprisonment if found guilty. A fine, which happens to be the most commonly imposed penalty, is clearly a restriction on property rights. Restrictions on fundamental rights must always be authorised by law – that is a minimum requirement – but they must also be justifiable in a rational and principled manner, especially when they entail suffering or deprivation.[1] So why exactly is the State justified in punishing convicted offenders? This is essentially a question of moral philosophy, but it is also, as we shall see, one of great practical importance. **3–01**

To understand the various theories that have been advanced to justify state punishment (which is effectively what judicial sentencing amounts to), we must first reflect on how the morality of human action is evaluated more generally. Most of our routine activities do not call for any deep philosophical reflection, but some actions can be morally contentious. Advances in medical research, for instance, occasionally produce ethical dilemmas that force us to reflect on the criteria according to which we should judge the morality of human action. Stem cell research is a case in point. Where this research involves the destruction of human embryos, it is regarded by some as intrinsically wrong and ethically unacceptable. Yet it seems that the fruits of this research may permit the alleviation or even the cure of certain serious degenerative diseases.[2] Opponents of **3–02**

---

1 John Gardner, *From Personal Life to Private Law* (Oxford University Press, 2018), 3 ("[I]t is very hard to justify revenge. Actually, it is hard to justify even extremely mild punishment. For both revenge and punishment involve the intentional infliction of suffering or deprivation. If the person at the sharp end does not suffer and is not deprived, the act of revenge or punishment has failed. It is extremely hard to explain why anyone should aim to bring extra suffering or deprivation into the world, especially in the name of setting right suffering or deprivation already brought about".)

2 Anne McLaren, "Ethical and social considerations of stem cell research" (2001)

destructive human embryo research invoke the moral imperative that it is wrong to kill, and they see embryonic destruction as tantamount to murder. Its supporters, on the other hand, justify it by pointing to the benefits it will produce. This example illustrates the distinction between deontological and teleological approaches to ethical problems.[3] The word "deontological" is derived from the ancient Greek *dei*, meaning that which is right or proper, while "teleological" derives from *telos*, meaning "end". Deontology is therefore grounded on the notion of moral imperatives. It holds that some choices are morally forbidden, simply because they are intrinsically wrong. A teleological or consequentialist approach, on the other hand, assesses moral choices according to the results they will bring about. The rightness or wrongness of an act is to be judged solely by how much good it will produce.[4] Utilitarianism is, strictly speaking, a variety of consequentialism though the two are often treated as synonymous. In its classical form, as developed by Jeremy Bentham (1748-1832) and John Stuart Mill (1806-1873), utilitarianism equated the good with pleasure. But, for our purposes, teleology, consequentialism and utilitarianism may be treated as synonymous. Absolute moral imperatives can be difficult to defend if carried to extremes. That is why some, such as Michael Moore, describe themselves as "threshold deontologists" because they accept that deontological principles may occasionally have to yield to consequentialist ones.[5] Moore argues, for example, that a deontologist would not countenance torturing or killing an innocent person just to save a few other innocent people being tortured or killed. But it might be different if torturing or killing an innocent person saved the lives of hundreds of others. In his view, consequentialism might then have to win out.

3–03 The distinction between deontology and consequentialism becomes highly relevant in the context of justifying state punishment.[6] According to one line of argument, offenders should be punished simply because it is the right thing to do. They have broken the law and, in so doing, they may have caused or risked considerable harm to individuals or society at large. For that reason alone, they deserve to be punished and no further justification is needed. This point of view may be described as deontological because it reflects a commitment to a moral principle that those who voluntarily engage in criminal conduct should be punished,

---

414 *Nature* 129.

3 For a more detailed but lucid discussion of these concepts, see Michael J Sandel, *Justice: What's the Right Thing to do?* (Penguin Books, 2010).

4 JJC Smart, "Hedonistic and Ideal Utilitarianism" (1978) 3:1 *Midwest Studies in Philosophy* 240.

5 Michael S Moore, "Torture and the balance of evils" (1989) 23 Israel LR 280, reprinted in Michael S Moore, *Placing Blame: A General Theory of the Criminal Law* (Clarendon Press, 1997), Chap 17. Robert Nozick suggests something similar in *Anarchy, State, and Utopia* (Harvard University Press, 1974), 30. See also Larry Alexander, "Deontology at the threshold" (2000) 37 San Diego LR 893.

6 For a good account of the justifications for punishment, see Richard S Frase, "Punishment purposes" (2005) 58 Stanford LR 67.

unless they can rely on a recognised excuse, justification or exemption. It is an approach most often associated with Immanuel Kant (1724-1804) who viewed the punishment of offenders as a moral imperative and rejected any utilitarian considerations that might reduce the punishment an offender deserved. He wrote:

> "Punishment by a court... can never be inflicted merely as a means to promote some other good for the criminal himself or for civil society. It must always be inflicted upon him only because he has committed a crime. For a human being can never be treated merely as a means to the purposes of another or be put among the objects of rights to things: his innate personality protects him from this, even though he can be condemned to lose his civil personality."[7]

Later in the same passage, he says:

> "The law of punishment is a categorical imperative, and woe to him who crawls through the windings of eudaimonism in order to discover something that releases the criminal from punishment or even reduces its amount by the advantages it promises..."

As against this, it might be argued that punishment, because it inflicts suffering or imposes a detriment of some kind, is morally objectionable unless it can be shown to produce some future good, whether by way of deterrence, rehabilitation, risk reduction or incapacitation. This reflects a teleological or consequentialist approach because it judges the legitimacy or the worth of an action, such as the infliction of punishment, according to the results it will produce. Those results are morally tolerable only if their value outweighs the evil or harmfulness of the action itself. All these rival conceptions of punishment have had their own champions throughout history. Notable supporters of a utilitarian approach include Plato in the fifth century BC, Thomas Hobbes in the 17th century, Cesare Beccaria and Jeremy Bentham in the 18th century. Kant, as we have seen, favoured a more deontological approach, as did some 20th century philosophers such as JD Mabbott.[8] **3–04**

Punishment theorists tend to concentrate on the justifications for punishing individual offenders and they usually strive to defend a theory that is sufficiently comprehensive to cover all cases, irrespective of the nature of the offence. (However, they are mostly willing to make exceptions for certain categories of offenders such as children and persons with mental disabilities.) Much of this chapter will be devoted to a discussion of the traditional theories of punishment such as retribution and deterrence, but first we should note an important distinction between the overall purpose **3–05**

---

[7] Immanuel Kant, *The Metaphysics of Morals* in Immanuel Kant, *Practical Philosophy*, translated and edited by Mary J Gregor (Cambridge University Press, 1996) 353, 473. *The Metaphysics* originally appeared in 1797. Elsewhere in his work, Kant seems more inclined to a utilitarian view. See Jeffrie G Murphy, "Does Kant have a theory of punishment?" (1987) 87 Columbia LR 509.

[8] JD Mabbott, "Punishment" (1939) 48 *Mind* 152.

of the criminal law (including the institution of punishment) and the purposes that should inform the sentencing of individual offenders. The genesis of this distinction may be traced back to the works of David Hume and John Austin in the 18th and early 19th centuries, but it is now most closely associated with an early essay by John Rawls and another by HLA Hart entitled "Prolegomenon to the Principles of Punishment".[9] Rawls reminded us of the conceptual difference between justifying a general practice (such as the punishment of offenders) and justifying a particular action falling under that practice (such as the sentencing of an individual offender for a specific crime). Hart built on this by distinguishing between what he called the general justifying aim of punishment and the aim(s) that may be pursued when sentencing specific breaches of the criminal law. The general justifying aim may well be deterrence although it might also be argued that the dominant purpose of the criminal law with its system of sanctions is to express and routinely reaffirm fundamental social values and shared conduct norms. But let us assume, for the sake of argument, that deterrence is the general justifying aim. After all, the prime political motivation for creating criminal offences and attaching penalties to them is to dissuade people from engaging in the proscribed conduct. Hart's point is that the adoption of deterrence as the general justifying aim does not preclude the adoption of some other rationale when selecting sentence in a specific case. Desert might well be the governing distributive principle, and Hart seems to suggest that it should be. This remains a valuable insight and it helps to dispel some of the confusion that can surround the debate about the proper purpose of criminal punishment.

3–06 The question of why punishment is morally justified has occupied minds for thousands of years. In one of Plato's dialogues, written in the early 4th century BCE, Protagoras, a leading 5th century sophist, is recorded as saying:

> "If you will think, Socrates, of the nature of punishment, you will see at once that in the opinion of mankind virtue may be acquired; no one punishes the evil doer under the notion, or for the reason, that he has done wrong; only the unreasonable fury of a beast acts in that manner. But he who desires to inflict rational punishment does not retaliate for a past wrong which cannot be undone; he has regard to the future, and is desirous that the man who is punished, and he who sees him punished, may be deterred from doing wrong again. He punishes for the sake of prevention, thereby clearly implying that virtue is capable of being taught."[10]

3–07 This does not necessarily represent Plato's view. It is simply a statement put in the mouth of Protagoras who is arguing that virtue can be taught. But the modern reader finds it strikingly familiar in both content and

---

9 John Rawls, "Two concepts of rules" (1955) 64 *The Philosophical Review* 3. Hart's paper was delivered in 1959 and forms the opening chapter of his *Punishment and Responsibility: Essays in the Philosophy of Law,* 2nd ed (Oxford University Press, 2008), first published 1968.

10 Plato, *Protagoras,* 324a-b, translated by Benjamin Jowett, *The Dialogues of Plato,* 4th ed (Clarendon Press, 1953), Vol 1.

language. Today, we might not condemn retributivists as acting 'with the unreasonable fury of a beast', but we understand utilitarian justifications for punishment, especially deterrence, largely in the terms here attributed to Protagoras. The rationale for punishment, whether inflicted by public authorities or private individuals, has therefore been a topic of perennial interest. It was being debated long before Kant and Bentham whose works often provide the starting point for modern discussions of the topic.

1. Retribution, Desert and Penal Censure

At one time, retribution was understood to mean that punishment should equal the crime, but that would be practically impossible in most cases and decidedly inhumane in some. Today, we think more in terms of desert – what the offender deserves by way of punishment for the offence.[11] Since the mid-1970s, there has been a growing attachment to the notion of 'just deserts' which holds that punishment should be proportionate to the gravity of the offence.[12] Gravity, in turn, is to be assessed by reference to both the harm caused, foreseen or risked by the offending conduct and the offender's degree of culpability. According to this theory of punishment, more serious offences should generally attract heavier penalties than less serious ones, and the penalty imposed for a specific offence should reflect the gravity of the offender's actual conduct. Murder should therefore carry a heavier penalty than assault and, in the case of assault, the infliction of a minor injury calls for a more lenient penalty than the infliction of a life-threatening injury. A policy of just deserts emphasises proportionality as opposed to equality of punishment. We no longer hold that murder must be punished with death; most countries have abolished the death penalty in any event. However, a just deserts philosophy would insist that murder should ordinarily attract the most severe penalty available within the jurisdiction. This may be a life sentence or a substantial determinate period of imprisonment. **3–08**

To be truly convincing, a retributivist or desert-based theory must do more than simply assert that offenders deserve to be punished; it must try to explain why this is so. Various explanations have been advanced by theorists over the years. One is the unfair advantage theory, most closely associated with an essay by Herbert Morris in which he argued that one of the benefits members of a civilised society enjoy is non-interference with their basic rights (to life, bodily integrity, private property and so forth). Such rights can be secure only if members of society are willing to exercise self-restraint and refrain from infringing the rights of others. To this end, we must all assume what Morris called a burden of self-restraint. **3–09**

---

[11] J Angelo Corlett, "Punishment and the Socratic Roots of Retributivism" in Jesper Ryberg and J Angelo Corlett (eds), *Punishment and Ethics: New Perspectives* (Palgrave Macmillan, 2010), 1 ("all retributivists hold that the notion of desert is central to why, if ever, punishment and punishments are morally justified").

[12] Andrew von Hirsch and Andrew Ashworth, *Proportionate Sentencing: Exploring the Principles* (Oxford University Press, 2005).

The offender is somebody who chooses to renounce the burden that others have voluntarily assumed. Morris therefore argued that just punishment "restores the equilibrium of benefits and burdens by taking from the individual what he owes, that is, exacting the debt".[13] John Finnis similarly argued that a criminal act represents gaining an advantage "which the law-abiding members of society have as such denied themselves, namely the advantage of indulging one's will, of exercising one's freedom beyond the restrictions imposed by law".[14] Critics of this explanation argue (among other things) that many crimes, such as homicides and assaults, can scarcely be viewed as instances of unfair advantage because an offender seldom gains anything tangible from them.[15] A counter argument might be that the perpetrators of such crimes clearly subordinated the lives or wellbeing of others to their own immediate desires and, to that extent, gained an unfair advantage.

3–10 That counter argument connects with another suggested justification for retribution, this one associated with Jean Hampton. She argued that those who commit crimes are asserting their own moral superiority over their victims. Offenders are effectively proclaiming that their interests are of greater moral value than those of their victims. (Hegel had made a rather similar argument: the offender uses his freedom to negate or deny the rights and freedoms of others, and is thereby asserting his superiority over his victims.)[16] Punishment is therefore intended to vindicate the value and inherent human dignity of the victim and to repudiate the offender's implicit claim that the victim is somehow less equal as a human being and less worthy of respect.[17] This is quite an attractive and convincing argument though it has its limitations, the most obvious one being that it applies, directly in any case, only where there is an identifiable victim. Many serious crimes, such as possession of drugs for sale or supply or possession of firearms, have no immediate, identifiable victims. Even then, one might argue that the offender is claiming moral superiority over those who are at risk of being harmed by the conduct constituting the offence. The same might be said of offences such as tax evasion where offenders are effectively prioritising their own interests over those of their fellow citizens who may suffer in one way or another through a shortfall in exchequer revenue. In its pure form, this retributive theory fails to account

---

13 Herbert Morris, "Persons and Punishment" (1968) 52 *The Monist* 475, 478.

14 JM Finnis, "Meaning and ambiguity in punishment (and penology)" (1972) 10 Osgoode Hall LJ 264 ,265.

15 For a more detailed critique, see DJ Galligan, "The return to retribution in penal theory" in Colin Tapper (ed.), *Crime, Proof and Punishment: Essays in Memory of Sir Rupert Cross* (Butterworths, 1981), Chap 8.

16 GWF Hegel, *The Philosophy of Right,* translated by TM Knox (Clarendon Press, 1942), 246.

17 Jean Hampton, "Correcting harms versus righting wrongs: The goal of retribution" (1992) 39 UCLA L E 1659. Her earlier writings on the topic include "A new theory of retribution" in RG Frey and Christopher W Morris (eds), *Liability and Responsibility: Essays in Law and Morals* (Cambridge University Press, 1991) and "An expressive theory of retribution" in Wesley Cragg (ed), *Retributivism and its Critics* (Franz Steiner Verlag, 1992).

for factors such as extreme deprivation or mental illness which may partly excuse the offending conduct or justify mitigated punishment.[18] However, the theory could possibly be adjusted to cater for these circumstances.

A third rationale for retributive sentencing, and currently the most popular one, rests on the notion of censure. State punishment undoubtedly has an expressive quality and function. As Joel Feinberg wrote in his classic article on the topic: **3–11**

> "Punishment is a conventional device for the expression of attitudes of resentment and indignation, and of judgments of disapproval and reprobation, either on the part of the punishing authority himself or of those 'in whose name' the punishment is inflicted."[19]

Feinberg was concerned to show that punishment served an expressive *function*. He was not so much concerned with the fundamental moral justifications for the practice of state punishment. He was undoubtedly correct in identifying moral condemnation as an essential characteristic of punishment. A fine and a tax may impose the same financial burden on an individual. Yet, a fine expresses condemnation in a way that a tax does not. The same might be said of the difference between committal to prison and committal to a psychiatric hospital.[20] The idea that the essential purpose of punishment is to censure criminal conduct has been central to the work of modern desert theorists such as Andrew von Hirsch.[21] The sentence imposed by a court is meant to express disapproval and condemnation of what the offender has done. Of course, the pronouncement of the sentence (or even the verdict of guilty) could of itself be deemed sufficient censure.[22] This, in turn, raises the question of why a sentence should also include a 'hard treatment' element such as a fine or term of imprisonment. von Hirsch's answer is that the hard treatment is best explained as a prudential supplement, meaning that it provides an additional incentive to obey the law for those who would not be sufficiently motivated to do so if they were just verbally censured. To this extent, his theory includes a crime prevention as well as a retributive element.[23] Antony Duff proffers a rather different explanation, though one that is less convincing given the real- **3–12**

---

18 Richard L Lippke, "Diminished opportunities, diminished capacities: Social deprivation and punishment" (2003) 29 *Social Theory and Practice* 459, 476-477,

19 Joel Feinberg, "The expressive function of punishment" (1965) 49 *The Monist* 397, 400.

20 Henry M Hart, "The aims of the criminal law" (1958) 23 *Law and Contemporary Problems* 401, 404-406. See also Robert Cooter, "Prices and sanctions" (1984) 84 Columbia LR 1523, 1524-1525.

21 von Hirsch's extensive writings on the topic include *Censure and Sanctions* (Clarendon Press, 1993) and *Deserved Criminal Sentences: An Overview* (Hart Publishing, 2017).

22 CL Stevenson, *Ethics and Language* (Yale University Press, 1944), 307 (blaming as "verbally mediated punishment").

23 Andrew von Hirsch, "Punishment, penance, and the State" in Matt Matravers (ed), *Punishment and Political Theory* (Hart Publishing, 1999), Chap 4; AP Simester and Andreas von Hirsch, *Crimes, Harms, and Wrongs: On the Principles of Criminalization* (Hart Publishing, 2011), 14.

world conditions in which crimes are committed and punished. He sees punishment as a communicative exercise, but one that involves two-way communication. The court communicates its censure to the offender, and the offender then expresses repentance by undergoing the specified punishment, thereby restoring himself to the law-abiding community. This mode of expressing repentance is an implied acknowledgment by the offender of his or her wrongdoing.[24] John Kleinig provides what is perhaps the most convincing justification for hard treatment by arguing that "(h)ard treatment may register where words fail".[25] He says that unless offenders see or experience some form of hard treatment, they are likely to remain "anesthetized" to the significance of their harmful actions.[26] Purely verbal censure cannot adequately impress upon offenders (and those affected by their crimes) the moral unacceptability of the offending conduct. It also follows that the hard treatment should be proportionate to the gravity of that conduct. In fact, von Hirsch has more recently refined his defence of hard treatment, bringing it more into line with Kleinig's approach. He now appears to accept, like Kleinig, that hard treatment has an amplifying function, meaning that it can convey disapprobation much more effectively than mere words. He adds that it also serves a 'grading' function, "by scaling the degrees of disapprobation expressed by the penal responses – so as to reflect crimes' varying degrees of seriousness, as a desert rationale requires".[27]

3–13 Desert theorists also disagree on the question of whether retributivism demands that all offenders *must* be punished or merely permits them to be punished. Adherents of 'strong' retributivism regard the punishment of offenders as a categorical imperative. Offenders should be punished simply because they deserve it, and no guilty person should be exempt from punishment, even on strong utilitarian grounds.[28] Others are prepared to adopt a more flexible or permissive approach, accepting that there may be good reasons for declining to punish in some circumstances.[29]

---

24 RA Duff, *Trials and Punishments* (Cambridge University Press, 1986); RA Duff, "Punishment, communication, and community" in Matravers, note 23 above, Chap 3.

25 John Kleinig, "Punishment and moral seriousness" (1991) 25 Israel LR 401, 417,

26 A similar argument had been made by AC Ewing, *The Morality of Punishment* (Kegan, 1929), 84 ("The infliction of pain is society's way of impressing on [the offender] that he has done wrong.") See also Igor Primoratz, "Punishment as language" (1989) 64 *Philosophy* 187 who adds that punishment is not just about communicating a message to the offender but also to the victim and the public at large. The message would be largely empty without some element of hard treatment.

27 Andreas von Hirsch, "Censure and hard treatment in the general justification for punishment: A reconceptualisation of desert-oriented penal theory" in Antje du Bois-Pedain and Anthony E Bottoms, *Penal Censure: Engagements Within and Beyond Desert Theory* (Hart, 2019), Chap 5.

28 Michael S Moore, "Justifying retributivism" (1993) 27 Israel LR 15, arguing along these lines.

29 Larry Alexander, "Retributivism and the inadvertent punishment of the innocent" (1983) 2 *Law and Philosophy* 233, 241, describing this approach as

For example, an offender may be granted immunity from prosecution if he or she is willing to provide evidence that may help to convict more serious offenders. Certain kinds of criminal conduct, such as cartel agreements in violation of competition law, are virtually impossible to detect unless some participants are willing to act as informers in return for immunity from prosecution or lenient sentences in the event of conviction. Some people, notably diplomats, may be legally entitled to immunity from criminal prosecution. Whatever the strength of the various theoretical arguments, therefore, a desert-based sentencing system must inevitably accept the reality that, for entirely prudential reasons, some known offenders must either escape punishment entirely or receive less than they objectively deserve.

Retribution must be carefully distinguished from revenge and retaliation. **3–14**
Indeed, the distinction has been recognised since classical times. Gregory Vlastos, a leading scholar of classical philosophy, has said that this distinction, especially as drawn by Plato in *Protagoras*, "must be regarded as one of the most momentous of the conceptual discoveries ever made by humanity in the course of its slow, tortuous, precarious emergence from barbaric tribalism".[30] As he says, the *lex talionis* "put a lid on the extravagance of passion by stipulating that for any given harm no greater may be inflicted in return". Many modern philosophers and theorists have also emphasised the distinction. Robert Nozick, for example, identifies five differences between retribution and revenge which may briefly be summarised as (1) retribution is for a wrong (presumably meaning a legal wrong), whereas revenge can be for an injury or a slight; (2) retribution sets an internal limit on the amount of punishment that may be inflicted, but revenge does not; (3) revenge requires some personal tie to the victim, while retribution, being impersonal, does not; (4) revenge is usually emotional, eg gaining pleasure from the suffering of another, a quality that is absent from retribution; (5) retribution has a 'generality', meaning that similar punishments are (or should be) inflicted in similar circumstances; revenge has no such concern.[31] In short, a retributive response, in contrast to a vengeful one, should be characterised by rationality, objectivity, fairness and consistency of approach.

One advantage of desert theory, whatever its moral foundation, is that it **3–15**
treats individual offenders as moral agents who are entitled to be punished

---

"weak retributivism" and arguing that "treating people better than they deserve is not wrong".

[30] Gregory Vlastos, *Socrates: Ironist and Moral Philosopher* (Cambridge University Press, 1991), 187. The relevant passage from *Protagoras* is cited above, note 10 and accompanying text. Later, we find Aristotle claiming that "punishment is for the sake of the person punished, revenge for that of the avenger so that he may be satisfied". (Aristotle, *The Art of Rhetoric*, translated by HC Lawson-Tancred (Penguin Books, 2004), 114). See also Leo Zaibert, "Punishment and revenge" (2006) 25 *Law and Philosophy* 81.

[31] Robert Nozick, *Philosophical Explanations* (Harvard University Press, 1981), 366, For a critique, see Nigel Walker, "Nozick's revenge" (1995) 70(274) *Philosophy* 581.

for the crimes that they have committed, and for those crimes only. In this regard, it conforms with the Kantian imperative that human beings should always be treated as ends in themselves and never as means to achieving some further goal. Some consequentialist theories, as we shall see, can be criticised for failing to adhere to this principle. Secondly, a desert-based sentencing system provides judges with some guidance as to the degree of punishment appropriate in a given case. Granted, this guidance is of a very general nature and will seldom, if ever, point to a specific penalty. But at least it requires a judge to anchor the penalty at a point on the scale that fairly reflects the gravity of the offence. This is not something that can be said of a system solely or primarily informed by a policy of general deterrence, incapacitation or even rehabilitation.

3–16 A desert-based sentencing system may also have some utilitarian value.[32] Offenders may be deterred from committing serious offences in a jurisdiction that has a clear policy of imposing appropriately severe punishment for serious offences. As discussed further below in the context of deterrence, many offenders probably never consider the likely consequences of their conduct or else they underestimate the severity of the penalties they are likely to incur. But it is also probable that some more calculating individuals will weigh up the consequences of engaging in one kind of crime rather than another, or of committing a crime of any description. The decisions they reach may well be strongly influenced by an awareness of the 'going rate' for particular offences, and they may be less inclined to commit offences for which the proportionate punishment is generally severe. A retributive sentence, if one of imprisonment, will also be incapacitative while it lasts. The incarcerated offender will be unable to commit any further offences within the community, whatever about within the prison itself.

Limiting Retributivism

3–17 The notion of limiting retributivism is most closely associated with Norval Morris who developed it in a number of highly influential works on sentencing and imprisonment in the 1970s and 1980s, although it had earlier been mooted by Lord Longford and Nigel Walker.[33] In *The Future of Imprisonment*[34] Morris noted that since desert is not precisely quantifiable,

---

[32] Paul H Robinson and John M Darley, "The utility of desert" (1997) 91 Northwestern Univ LR 453; John Wilson, "The purposes of retribution" (1983) 58(226) *Philosophy* 521, 525 ("Obviously enough, the same treatment or behaviour may meet the demands of retribution and also be deterrent and (in a more general way) reformative – just as it may be more expensive or fashionable or many other things.")

[33] Frank Pakenham (Lord Longford), *The Idea of Punishment* (Geoffrey Chapman, 1961), 61 ("Retribution, in short, provides a justification for *some* punishment and sets a limit to the amount of punishment justifiable."); Nigel Walker, *Sentencing in a Rational Society* (Penguin Books Ltd., 1972), 30-31.

[34] Norval Morris, *The Future of Imprisonment* (University of Chicago Press, 1974).

the deserved punishment, however assessed, should limit rather than determine the sentence to be imposed. He wrote:

> "To say that a punishment is deserved, in this sense, is not to say that it ought to be imposed. The concept of desert here advanced is one of retributive maximum; a license to punish the criminal up to that point but by no means an obligation to do so. For example, the principle of parsimony should also infuse all decisions as to the proper punishment to impose. Mercy, clemency, the avoidance of severing the convicted criminal's social ties by imposing a term of imprisonment, are all values of importance to be served up to the proper limits of the larger social utility. The criminal law has general preventive purposes in relation to crime, cohesive functions in relation to society, educative and deterrent functions in relation to potential criminals, all of which bear upon the determination of the proper punishment. The punishment equation relates these social purposes to the sentence on the convicted criminal up to the deserved punishment."[35]

He resumed the argument in *Madness and the Criminal Law* where he asserted that it is rarely possible to say with confidence, "that is the deserved punishment". The best one can usually say is that it is not an undeserved punishment.[36] Desert therefore justifies and limits eligibility for punishment, but it cannot claim to identify precisely the appropriate penalty in any case, because other factors must also enter the equation.[37] In later work, Morris was prepared to accept that longer sentences might be imposed on dangerous offenders, but again within the bounds of proportionality.[38] **3–18**

This concept of limiting retributivism has proved to be very influential. It is reflected in modern sentencing guideline systems that establish a range of permissible punishment, rather than specific penalties, for the offences to which they apply. Morris, admittedly, treated desert solely as a means of identifying an upper limit on sentence, whereas guideline ranges also specify a lower limit. Most guideline systems allow for departure in exceptional cases. In any event, limiting retributivism allows for a measure of judicial discretion, albeit bounded discretion. As Richard Frase writes: **3–19**

> "Limiting retributivism is popular with practitioners and makes good sense as a matter of policy, because it strikes an appropriate balance between the conflicting punishment goals and values that are recognised in almost all western countries. The theory accommodates retributive values (especially

---

35 Morris, note 34 above, at 75.

36 Norval Morris, *Madness and the Criminal Law* (University of Chicago Press, 1982), 148. See also Norval Morris and Michael Tonry, *Between Prison and Probation: Intermediate Punishments in a Rational Sentencing System* (Oxford University Press, 1990).

37 For further discussion of limiting retributivism, see Richard Frase, *Just Sentencing: Principles and Procedures for a Workable System* (Oxford University Press, 2013), in particular the Introduction and Chap 2; Andrew von Hirsch and Andrew Ashworth, *Proportionate Sentencing: Exploring the Principles* (Oxford University Press, 2005), App 2.

38 Norval Morris and Marc Miller, "Predictions of Dangerousness" (1985) 6 *Crime and Justice: An Annual Review of Research* 1.

the important, human rights-based need to avoid excessively severe penalties) along with crime control goals such as deterrence, incapacitation, rehabilitation and moral education."[39]

3–20 The revised sentencing provisions of the American Model Penal Code also adopt limiting retributivism as the dominant sentencing policy. It provides that courts should "render sentences in all cases within a range of severity proportionate to the gravity of offences, the harms done to crime victims, and the blameworthiness of offenders".[40] The Code further provides that courts may pursue what the commentary describes as the "legitimate and desirable purposes" of rehabilitation, deterrence, incapacitation, restitution to victims, preservation of families and offender reintegration, provided these goals are pursued within the boundaries of proportionality. No crime-prevention or other utilitarian purpose may be invoked to justify a sentence outside that range. While clearly influenced by Norval Morris's ideas, to which they refer, the drafters of the revised Code treat limiting retributivism as providing a floor as well as a ceiling to deserved punishment. Sentences should not be disproportionately severe, but neither should they be disproportionately lenient.

3–21 Proportionality, although a distributive principle rather than a justification for punishment, may be viewed in the same way. Just as the application of a desert-based philosophy cannot realistically point to a 'right' sentence, a proportionality standard must also allow for some degree of elasticity. This, in fact, is how courts usually interpret it. Appeal courts will uphold a sentence if it falls within an acceptable range, which may or may not be set out in a guideline. They never proceed on the basis that there is an exactly right sentence, however discoverable, for the offence in question. Proportionality, as thus interpreted, sets upper and lower limits on permissible punishment and, within those limits, effect may be given to a variety of goals, including deterrence and rehabilitation. Some desert theorists object to the notion of limiting retributivism on the basis that it can lead to inequality and disparity.[41] If courts are permitted to sentence within a range, they may often end up imposing markedly different punishments on offenders convicted of similar offences. This point is well taken, especially if the range is reasonably extensive. In a system where, for example, a certain kind of residential burglary was punishable with a range of two to five years' imprisonment, one burglar might receive a sentence twice as long as the other, despite their offences and personal circumstances being broadly similar. Given the undoubted impossibility of identifying an exactly right sentence for any offence, the best solution to this problem is to devise further guidance for appropriately locating offences within the relevant range. This might be done through formal guidelines or, failing that, through judicially developed principles

39 Frase, note 37 above at p 4.

40 Model Penal Code: Sentencing, §1.02(2)(a)(i) (American Law Institute, Proposed Final Draft, 2017).

41 von Hirsch, *Deserved Criminal Sentences*, note 21 above, Chap 5.

indicating the factors to be considered when deciding where an offence should be placed within a range.

Desert as a Static or Dynamic Concept

The concept of desert as it developed in modern times through the work of Andrew von Hirsch and others was essentially static in nature.[42] A sentence was to be determined by reference to the gravity of the offence which, in turn, consisted of the harm caused or risked and the offender's culpability at the time of committing the offence. The offender's desert therefore became fixed at the time of the offence, and neither the passage of time nor any evidence of reformation on the part of the offender should affect the sentence. If a court imposed a five-year prison sentence, that sentence should be served in full (less remission where it applies), irrespective of whether the offender, while serving the sentence, underwent a significant change in outlook, came to appreciate the wrongfulness of his or her conduct, experienced and expressed genuine remorse, or even made reparation in some way or other to the victim. **3–22**

Some more recent scholarship has urged that desert or, more precisely, penal censure should be viewed as a dynamic concept. This would mean that the degree of censure (and consequently the degree of the accompanying hard treatment) merited by an offender might, in certain circumstances, diminish over time.[43] This would occur only where the offender took some action or engaged in an exercise that directly related to the offence of conviction. Such an initiative would show that the offender was now a demonstrably different and better person than when he or she committed the offence. The notion of dynamic desert has therefore been described as 'responsive censure' because the degree of deserved censure could vary during the term of the sentence or, indeed, during the interval between offence and sentence, if the offender responded in an appropriate manner. The response might consist of a clear acknowledgement of the harm inflicted on the victim or the broader community, a sincere apology or some effort at making reparation. **3–23**

Parole and other early release arrangements already allow for the executive reduction of custodial sentences, sometimes quite substantially, but parole decisions are almost invariably based on risk assessment. The question for parole authorities is not if individual prisoners have **3–24**

---

[42] See, for example, Andrew von Hirsch, *Doing Justice: The Choice of Punishments* (Hill and Wang, 1976).

[43] Julian V Roberts and Netanel Dagan, "The evolution of retributive punishment: From static desert to responsive penal censure" in Du Bois-Pedain and Bottoms, note 27 above, Chap 8 makes a strong argument for the adoption of this approach. See also Hadar Dancig-Rosenberg and Netanel Dagan "Retributarianism: A new individualization of punishment" (2019) 13 *Criminal Law and Philosophy* 129; Paul H Robinson and Muhammad Sarahne "After the crime: Rewarding offenders' positive post-offence conduct" (2021) 24 *New Criminal Law Review* 367.

suffered as much as they deserve on retributive grounds, but rather if it is safe to release them. At least, that is how it should be. The tension between desert-based sentencing and parole is well acknowledged and discussed further in Chap 14. However, the concept of dynamic censure, as elaborated by Julian Roberts and Netanel Dagan, is quite different.[44] Desert, or penal censure, remains the animating purpose throughout the entire term of the sentence. But the degree of censure merited by the offender may diminish – Roberts and Dagan are careful to say that it should never increase – because of some transformation undergone by the offender during the currency of the sentence.

3–25 The idea of dynamic desert or responsive censure has considerable appeal as a means of addressing problems posed by very long prison sentences, often exceeding an offender's natural life span, which are particularly common in the United States. Measures have however been introduced in some American jurisdictions to permit courts to review long sentences. In the federal system, parole was abolished by the Sentencing Reform Act 1984 which introduced sentencing guidelines but, to compensate (though only to a very minor extent), the Act permitted courts to entertain applications from prisoners seeking what became known as compassionate release. This was largely ineffective because such an application could be made only by the Bureau of Prisons. In 2018, Congress passed the First Step Act which allows prisoners themselves to petition federal district courts for release. This, in turn, means that federal judges now frequently find themselves reviewing sentences, a practice that hitherto was largely unknown. Hundreds of thousands of applications have already been made under the First Step Act, especially during the Covid-19 pandemic, though only a small minority have resulted in release.[45] Procedures of this kind, though not necessarily those prescribed by the First Step Act itself, would be compatible with the notion of dynamic desert.

2. Deterrence

3–26 Deterrence may be either general or specific. General deterrence is concerned with dissuading others from engaging in the conduct of which the offender has been convicted.[46] Specific or individual deterrence is concerned with dissuading the individual being sentenced from engaging in further crime.[47] Occasionally, the same penalty might serve

---

44 Note 43 above.

45 On the operation of the First Step Act, see Michael J Hamilton, "Opening the safety valve: A second look at compassionate release under the First Step Act" (2022) 90 Fordham LR 1743; Colleen McMahon, "(Re)views from the bench: A judicial perspective on second-look sentencing in the federal system" (2021) 58 American Crim LR 1617; *United States v Brooker* 976 F3d 228 (2nd Cir, 2020).

46 Dan Kahan, "The secret ambition of deterrence" (1999) 113 Harvard LR 413 , 415 (deterrence depicts punishment "as a policy aimed at creating efficient behavioural incentives").

47 The distinction has long been recognised. Jeremy Bentham in *The Rationale of Punishment*, Bk 1, chap III (1830) wrote of "[p]articular prevention, which

both purposes. Both forms of deterrence are clearly utilitarian. They are intended to achieve a future goal, crime reduction in this instance. Nobody would seriously deny that punishment deters. Certain kinds of criminal conduct would probably be more prevalent were it not for fear of the penalties they will attract if detected. A conviction for drink driving leads to the loss of a driver's licence, sometimes for a lengthy period, while other road traffic offences are punishable with penalty points which, when they reach a certain aggregate, also lead to loss of licence. These are consequences that drivers wish to avoid at all costs, so it is reasonable to assume that the fear of incurring them influences driver behaviour for the better. The extent to which people are deterred by the fear of punishment is unknowable, but what we do know is that the threat or prospect of punishment is not an entirely effective deterrent. Murder carries a mandatory sentence of life imprisonment, but that does not prevent many murders being committed each year. The same held true when it was a capital offence, as it remains in some countries today. Many other offences that are virtually guaranteed to attract heavy sentences following conviction also remain prevalent. For the past 25 years in Ireland, the possession for sale or supply of drugs with a street value of €13,000 or more has carried a presumptive minimum sentence of 10 years' imprisonment.[48] Even those offenders who escape the minimum are very likely to receive sentences ranging from five to 10 years. In November 2022, there were 386 prisoners serving sentences for drug offences, with about 60 per cent of these serving sentences of three years or longer.[49] Yet drug crime continues unabated with 4,000 to 5,000 offences of possessing drugs for sale or supply and importing drugs recorded in recent years.[50] Again, it may be that drug dealing and other serious offences would be even more prevalent were it not for the penalties they attract.

Deterrence, whether general or specific, is premised on the notion that offenders and would-be offenders are rational actors with both the capacity and inclination to weigh up the consequences of their contemplated actions. As such, they will calculate both the benefit and the detriment that are likely to accrue from the crime, the detriment being the penalty that would follow a conviction. In terms of abstract logic at least, a rational actor will refrain from a course of conduct if there is a reasonably strong probability that the detriment will exceed the benefit. This is the assumption underpinning most economic analyses of criminal law.[51] **3–27**

applies to the delinquent himself, and general prevention, which is applicable to all the members of the community, without exception".

48 The presumptive minimum was first introduced under the Criminal Justice Act 1999 (s 5), amending the Misuse of Drugs Act 1977, s 27.

49 Irish Prison Service Annual Report 2021, p 65.

50 These figures are based on information published by the Central Statistics Office.

51 Gary S Becker, "Crime and punishment: An economic approach" (1968) 76 *Journal of Political Economy* 169; Richard A Posner, "An economic theory of the criminal law" (1985) 85 Columbia LR 1193. For a critical analysis, see David A Anderson, "The deterrence hypothesis" (2009) 4 *American Law and Economics Review* 295.

Some potential offenders may engage in this kind of rational calculation but many, probably most, do not. White-collar crime is often cited as an example of rational planning, and sometimes it may be. A person planning a fraud, a tax evasion scheme or the creation of a cartel in contravention of competition law may well try to evaluate the likely gains, the penalties if caught and, importantly, the probability of being caught, a matter to which we shall return. Yet, experience shows that this is not always so. Some who engage in fraudulent conduct, such as stealing from their employers or clients, have a gambling or other addiction which may detract from their ability to think rationally or plan strategically. Others will simply have acted impulsively or opportunistically. Violent crimes are even less likely to be the product of rational choice. According to Michael Tonry:

> "Many of these [violent and other serious] crimes are impulsive or are committed under the influence of drugs, alcohol, peer influences, powerful emotions or situational pressures. Many are committed by people who are already deeply socialised into deviant values and lifestyles. These characteristics of many would-be offenders do not mean that it is a priori impossible to affect would-be offenders' criminal choices by means of legal threats. They do mean that doing so is far from being a matter of enacting harsher laws, imposing harsher penalties, or adopting more aggressive policing strategies."[52]

3–28 He may have been writing from an American perspective, but his observations are probably universally true. Certainly, it would be difficult for an Irish or British lawyer to disagree with them. Further even a rational choice explanation of criminal behaviour, as advanced most notably by Clarke and Cornish, must account for bounded rationality, meaning that a person's choices and decisions are typically constrained by available information, the actor's cognitive abilities and personal circumstances.[53] Therefore, any claim that a given offence was the product of rational choice must be tempered with an acceptance that the offender's reasoning process may have been influenced by factors over which he or she had limited, if any, control.

3–29 General deterrence is subject to the moral objection that it treats offenders instrumentally rather than as persons who deserve to be treated individually according to their degree of guilt and relevant personal circumstances. As such, it falls foul of the Kantian imperative that human beings should always be treated as ends in themselves and never as means. Punishment, according to Kant, should not be inflicted to produce some future good, but solely because the offender deserves it.[54] Bentham, by

---

[52] Michael Tonry, "Learning from the limitations of deterrence research" (2008) 37 *Crime and Justice* 279 at 282.

[53] Ronald V Clarke and Derek B Cornish, "Modeling offenders' decisions: A framework for research and policy" (1985) 6 *Crime and Justice* 147; Derek B Cornish and Ronald V Clarke, "Understanding crime displacement: An application of rational choice theory" (1987) 25 *Criminology* 933.

[54] Immanuel Kant, *Groundwork of the Metaphysics of Morals* (1797) in Immanuel

contrast, as a committed utilitarian, regarded punishment as an evil that is justified only where it achieves or promotes crime prevention. He wrote:

> "The general object which all laws have, or ought to have, in common, is to augment the total happiness of the community; and therefore, in the first place, to exclude, as far as may be, every thing that tends to subtract from that happiness; in other words, to exclude mischief.
>
> But all punishment is mischief: all punishment in itself is evil. Upon the principle of utility, if it ought to be at all to be admitted, it ought only to be admitted in as far as it promises to exclude some greater evil."[55]

Specific deterrence may be compatible with the Kantian imperative in the sense that it calls for a sentence that will deter the individual offender from committing further crimes. As such, it is not treating the offender instrumentally to the same extent as general deterrence. Both kinds of deterrence nonetheless raise the fundamental question of whether it is ever just to impose a disproportionately severe penalty to advance some social goal, however worthy that goal might seem. The emphasis here is on *disproportionately* severe penalties. A proportionate penalty, especially if severe, can have a deterrent effect. **3–30**

The second major objection to deterrence, and especially to general deterrence, is more empirical in nature. It is popularly assumed that increased penalties will reduce crime. According to this line of thinking, an offence now attracting an average sentence of three years' imprisonment should become considerably less prevalent if the average sentence were raised to five years' imprisonment. In fact, it probably will not, and there are several reasons for this. What we are discussing here is often known as marginal deterrence, the assumption being, as Andrew Ashworth says in a perceptive analysis of the topic, that there is a hydraulic relationship between punishment and crime.[56] More punishment should mean less crime. An increase in punishment by a certain margin should reduce crime by roughly the same margin. Several major empirical studies and research reviews have shown that this is simply not the case.[57] Increased punishment may lead to some reduction in the incidence of the offence to **3–31**

Kant, *Practical Philosophy*, translated by Mary J Gregor (Cambridge University Press, 1996).

55 Jeremy Bentham, *Introduction to the Principles of Morals and Legislation* (Blackwell Publishers, 1948), Chap XIII, s 1 (first published 1789).

56 Andrew Ashworth, "The common sense and complications of general deterrent sentencing" [2019] Crim LR 564.

57 See, in particular, Andrew von Hirsch, Anthony E Bottoms, Elizabeth Burney and Per-Olof Wikström, *Criminal Deterrence and Sentence Severity: An Analysis of Recent Research* (Hart Publishing, 1999); Cheryl Marie Webster and Anthony N Doob, "Searching for Sasquatch: Deterrence of crime through sentence severity" in Joan Petersilia and Kevin R. Reitz (eds), *The Oxford Handbook of Sentencing and Corrections* (Oxford University Press, 2012), chap 7; Tonry, note 52 above; Daniel S Nagin, "Criminal deterrence research at the outset of the twenty-first century" (1998) 23 *Crime and Justice* 1; Daniel S Nagin, "Deterrence in the twenty-first century" (2013) 42 *Crime and Justice* 199.

which it applies, but only to a slight degree. As Daniel Nagin, a leading scholar in this field, has written:

> "[T]here is little evidence that increases in the length of already long prison sentences yield general deterrent effects that are sufficiently large to justify their social and economic costs.... [T]here is substantial evidence that increasing the visibility of the police by hiring more officers and allocating existing officers in ways that materially heightens the perceived risk of apprehension can deter crimes."[58]

3–32 One important, though often overlooked, point is that increases in sentence, however significant, are unlikely to have any impact unless potential offenders become aware of them.[59] One American study based on interviews with 278 incarcerated males, found that 63 per cent either did not think they would be apprehended or did not think about the possibility, while 53 per cent did not know, or did not think about, what the punishment would be if they were convicted.[60] There are two other reasons why the threat of punishment, however severe, may not deter. For many offenders, the criminal law is what Hans von Hentig described as a "long-distance danger".[61] He claimed that criminals belong to a species whose appetites and desires are attracted by a "near subject" meaning, in effect, that they are so preoccupied with immediate or short-term gratification that, at the time of criminal act, they fail to consider or care very much about the legal consequences. One need not subscribe to his view that offenders constitute a distinct species or that they are "feebleminded" as he suggested in the same passage. Experience strongly suggests that his observation about the possibility of prosecution, conviction and punishment being a "long-distance danger" holds true of many who commit criminal acts, and violent acts in particular. The second, and related, reason why the threat or prospect of penalties may provide a weak deterrent derives from what economists describe as subjective discount rates. We tend to underestimate the impact of costs we will not have to incur until sometime in the future (for example, when we pay with a credit card rather than cash).[62] For some offenders, likewise, punishment (in so far as they contemplate it at all) is something they will possibly have to endure in the future, but it is merely a prospect and not of such immediacy as to dissuade them from their criminal conduct.

3–33 A strong probability of being detected and convicted seems to be a more effective deterrent than increased punishment. This was intuitively recognised long before there was any empirical research on the matter. Beccaria, in his essay, *On Crimes and Punishments,* published in 1764,

58 Nagin, "Deterrence in the twenty-first century", note 57 above, at 201.

59 Webster and Doob (note 57 above), p 181 make a similar point: "Consequences that are unknown to potential offenders cannot affect their behaviour".

60 Anderson, note 51 above.

61 Hans von Hentig, "The limits of deterrence" (1938) 29 *Journal of Criminal Law and Criminology* 555 at 559.

62 Raymond Paternoster, "How much do we really know about criminal deterrence?" (2010) 100 *Journal of Criminal Law and Criminology* 765, 805.

argued that punishment will deter rational agents provided it is severe, certain and swift.[63] He wrote that "(t)he certainty of a punishment, even if it be moderate, will always make a stronger impression than the fear of another which is more terrible but combined with the hope of impunity." Research suggests that a strong probability of being detected or apprehended is more likely to deter than the prospect of punishment.[64]

3. Rehabilitation

A distinction must be drawn between rehabilitation as a purpose of sentencing and the provision of rehabilitative opportunities for offenders while they are serving their sentences. A sentence may well be selected by reference to some other rationale such as desert or deterrence, but that does not preclude the executive branch of government from adopting measures to ensure, for example, that persons serving custodial sentences can participate in education and training programmes and avail themselves of appropriate counselling and treatment facilities within a humane environment. Indeed, there is a growing view that offenders, especially those undergoing imprisonment, should have access to rehabilitation as of right. This is reflected in recent jurisprudence of the European Court of Human Rights.[65] In *Vinter v United Kingdom*, for example, the Court said: **3–34**

> "Indeed, there is now clear support in European and international law for the principle that all prisoners, including those serving life sentences, be offered the possibility of rehabilitation and the prospect of release if that rehabilitation is achieved."[66]

3–35 It went on to say that while punishment remains an important aim of imprisonment, the emphasis in European penal policy has now shifted to rehabilitation, especially towards the end of long sentences. In this regard, the Court favours a 'progression principle' whereby, irrespective of the original penological purpose of the sentence, during the later stages of a prison term the emphasis should be on preparation for release and progressive social reintegration.[67] Prisoners subject to indefinite detention should be provided with reasonable opportunities to undertake courses designed to help them address their offending behaviour.[68]

---

63 Cesare Beccaria, *On Crimes and Punishments*, ed by Richard Bellamy (Cambridge University Press, 1995).

64 Daniel S Nagin, "Deterrence" in Erik Luna (ed), *Reforming Criminal Justice*, Vol 4, *Punishment, Incarceration, and Release* (Arizona State University, 2017).

65 For a comprehensive analysis, see Adriano Martufi, "The paths of offender rehabilitation and the European dimension of punishment: New challenges for an old ideal?" (2018) 25 *Maastricht Journal of European and Comparative Law* 672.

66 (2016) 63 EHRR 1, para 114.

67 *Dickson v United Kingdom* (2008) 46 EHRR 41, para 28; *Boulois v Luxembourg* (2012) 55 EHRR 32, para 83.

68 *James v United Kingdom* (2013) 56 EHRR 12, para 218. On the later treatment of this judgment by the United Kingdom Supreme Court, see Sebastian Walker and Karl Laird, "A prisoner's right to rehabilitation" (2018) 134 LQR 527.

3–36 A well-resourced range of community-based penalties is also essential for promoting offender rehabilitation. Terms such as 'rehabilitation', 'reform' and 'risk reduction' are sometimes used interchangeably, although they have different shades of meaning. Reform has, in the past at least, been associated with moral reform and the notion of changing an offender's outlook, attitudes and behaviour to bring them into line with those of the wider community. This approach is always in danger of ignoring the extent to which some offenders, because of background or poverty, may have good reason to resent mainstream values that have deprived them of many advantages enjoyed by those who are now urging them to conform. Risk reduction and rehabilitation are certainly not synonymous, because risk reduction might be achieved by incapacitation or severe deterrent penalties. Of course, rehabilitation, whatever form it may take, is meant to promote desistance and thus sometimes described as 'assisted desistance'. Scholars and policy makers have long debated what rehabilitation really means and how it can be most effectively delivered.[69] Edgardo Rotman has suggested that rehabilitation may be defined as "a right to an opportunity to return to (or remain in) society with an improved chance of being a useful citizen and staying out of prison".[70] The reference to 'opportunity' is significant as it underscores the importance of voluntary participation in rehabilitative programmes as opposed to any kind of repressive welfarism, or coerced cure as Norval Morris described it.[71]

3–37 Rehabilitation as the guiding rationale of sentencing is a decidedly more difficult issue. To treat it as the sole or dominant purpose could imply that crime should be viewed as a disease, that the offender is sick and in need of treatment, a perspective that was roundly and convincing condemned by CS Lewis and Herbert Morris more than half a century ago.[72] In fact, an essay published in 1900 by an English barrister, Montague Crackanthorpe, made the same point quite eloquently:

> "The reformatory principle cannot be always and everywhere the dominant principle, since it is clear that we should punish the hardened offender even though to reform him would be hopeless. But there are other reasons for not dwelling on it here. If we invest it with exaggerated importance, if we assign to it the first place, we are driven to adopt the 'indeterminate sentence' – that is to say, we must treat the criminal as a sick man, and keep him in gaol until we have completed his cure. In that case, we do not want any standard of punishment at all, we only require a high penal maximum so as to allow time for a protracted course of treatment in the event of the disease

69 Fergus McNeill, "Four forms of 'offender' rehabilitation: Towards an interdisciplinary perspective" (2012) 17 *Legal and Criminological Psychology* 18; Rob Canton, "Censure, dialogue and reconciliation" in Du Bois-Pedain and Bottoms, note 27 above, Chap 13.

70 Edgardo Rotman, *Beyond Punishment: A New View on the Rehabilitation of Offenders* (Greenwood Press, 1990).

71 Morris, note 34 above.

72 CS Lewis, "The humanitarian theory of punishment" (March 1949) 3:3 *The Twentieth Century: An Australian Quarterly Review* 5; Herbert Morris, note 13 above.

> becoming deep-seated. Further the entire subject of reformation belongs rather to the ethics of prison discipline than to the ethics of sentencing."[73]

Proportionality and consistency would be difficult to achieve if sentencing courts were obliged to select measures that, in their view, would be most effective in rehabilitating individual offenders. Those measures would naturally vary enormously. Further, some offenders (such as those convicted of white-collar crimes) might not need any rehabilitation, at least as that term is conventionally understood. **3–38**

This is not to deny that rehabilitation can be a legitimate consideration at sentencing. It is routinely listed as a statutory sentencing purpose in those jurisdictions, including England and Wales, Canada and New Zealand, that have legislated on the matter, and is recognised in Ireland as a matter of common law.[74] Further, certain sentencing measures, notably probation, have a clear rehabilitative purpose. The idea that imprisonment may rehabilitate is reflected in parole legislation which is generally premised on the assumption that an offender, on having served some portion of a custodial sentence, may be sufficiently rehabilitated to justify his or her release back into the community. In Ireland, for example, the Parole Act 2019 (s 27) provides that the Parole Board may release a prisoner if satisfied that he or she would not pose an undue risk to the safety and security of others and "has been rehabilitated and would, upon being released, be capable of reintegrating back into society". **3–39**

Where proportionality is the dominant distributive principle of sentencing, rehabilitative objectives can be accommodated in various ways. It may be accorded priority over other objectives where, for example, it appears that the offender will benefit from probation supervision or some therapeutic measure that will assist his or her social integration and desistance for further crime, which will ultimately benefit society as well as the offender. The nature of the offence and/or the offender's circumstances may indicate that these objectives can be most effectively advanced by sparing the offender the experience of imprisonment or other overtly punitive measure. Alternatively, where the offence is sufficiently serious to warrant a custodial sentence on desert-based grounds, a court may suspend some portion of the sentence to incentivise rehabilitation. As discussed further in Chap 12 in connection with the suspended sentence, part-suspension for this purpose is generally granted only where there are good grounds to believe that it will promote the offender's rehabilitation. Finally, it must be stressed that an offender sentenced to a term of imprisonment, whether part-suspended or otherwise, should always have access to suitable rehabilitative opportunities while in custody. Incentives such as the possibility of enhanced remission or release on parole, both discussed in Chap 14, are important in providing encouragement for sentenced prisoners to avail themselves of any rehabilitative opportunities on offer. **3–40**

---

[73] Montague Crackanthorpe, "Can sentences be standardised?" (January 1900) 47 *The Nineteenth Century* 103 at 106.

[74] Discussed further below under "Translating Theory into Practice".

3–41 One perennial problem with rehabilitation, as reflected in the academic literature on the topic, is the absence of consensus on what exactly it means and how it should be delivered.[75] The Risk-Need-Responsivity (RNR) model developed in Canada in the 1980s has proved influential. This model attempts to identify 'criminogenic needs', meaning risk factors that point to recidivism, and to address those needs. The risk element entails matching the degree of intervention with the offender's apparent risk of re-offending. The greater the risk, the more intensive the required intervention. Need refers to criminogenic needs, namely dynamic factors, such as antisocial associates and substance abuse. Responsivity means tailoring the rehabilitative interventions to the learning style, motivation, abilities and strengths of the offender.[76] Research has shown that interventions adhering to these principles are effective in reducing recidivism, certainly more effective than those that do not.[77] If the RNR model is associated with Canada, its main competitor, the Good Lives Model (GLM) originated in New Zealand through the work of Tony Ward and his colleagues. This model has gone through various refinements but in its original form, it was critical of the RNR model because of its strong focus on criminogenic needs and risk reduction, and its preoccupation with reducing the likelihood of re-offending.

3–42 The Good Lives Model bears a close relationship to, and seems to have been influenced by, positive psychology which, rather than being preoccupied with addressing problems, is more concerned with enabling people to flourish and achieve their full human potential.[78] It emphasises the need to respect offenders as individuals who are entitled to be treated with dignity and with respect for their human rights. More specifically, it recognises the offenders, like everyone else, can and should have plans as to how they want to live their lives, though with the important caveat that this should be in a law-abiding way. The offender is therefore seen as someone who engages in crime as a result of lacking "the capabilities to realise valued outcomes in personally fulfilling and socially acceptable ways".[79] He or she should therefore be equipped with the skills, values

---

[75] Tony Ward and Shadd Maruna, *Rehabilitation: Beyond the Risk Paradigm* (Routledge, 2007).

[76] JA Andrews, James Bonta and J Stephen Wormith, "The Risk-Need-Responsivity (RNR) Model. Does adding the Good Lives Model contribute to effective crime prevention?" (2011) 38 *Criminal Justice and Behaviour* 735, 738.

[77] Andrews et al, note 76 above.

[78] Shelly L Gable and Jonathan Haidt, "What (and why) is positive psychology?" (2005) 9 *Review of General Psychology* 103; Jennifer S Cheavens and David B Feldman, *The Science and Application of Positive Psychology* (Cambridge University Press, 2022).

[79] Tony Ward, Ruth E Mann and Theresa A Gannon, "The good lives model of offender rehabilitation: Clinical implications" (2007) 12 *Aggression and Violent Behaviour* 87, 90. See also Tony Ward and Claire A Stewart, "The treatment of sex offenders: Risk management and good lives" (2003) 34 *Professional Psychology: Research and Practice* 353; Tony Ward and Mark Brown, "The good lives model and conceptual issues in offender rehabilitation" (2004) 10 *Psychology, Crime & Law* 243; Clare-Ann Fortune, Tony Ward and Ruth Mann, "Good lives and the

and attitudes to embark on a lifestyle and set about achieving realistic goals in a manner that will be personally satisfying without, of course, inflicting harm on others. Offenders should therefore be encouraged to think about what would be a good life for them individually and then be equipped with the internal and external resources to enable them to realise their plans (or, at least, every effort should be made by practitioners to do this).[80] Such an approach, it is believed, can improve treatment compliance and reduce recidivism.

4. Incapacitation

The belief that certain offenders, whether because of the nature of their offence, their criminal history or both, should be removed from society is reflected in penal practice from ancient times right down to the present day. The death penalty, which still exists in many countries, including parts of the United States, is clearly the ultimate incapacitating measure.[81] But there are other less drastic means including banishment and exile that were commonly practised in the ancient world, sometimes as alternatives to capital punishment. Transportation, first to America and later to Australia, was widely used as a sentencing measure in these islands between the beginning of the 18th and the middle of the 19th century. As many as 200,000 in all may have been transported during this era, including about 40,000 from Ireland.[82] Penal strategies of this kind are generally based on the conviction that society is safer and better off if it can be rid of the depredations and malign influence of serious or habitual criminals. Social Darwinism began to make its presence felt in the late 19th century, as reflected in an essay by the Oxford philosopher, FH Bradley where he referred to "social surgery" and observed how the "right and duty of the organism to suppress its undesirable growths is the idea of punishment directly suggested by Darwinism".[83]This was also an era in which there was a growing preoccupation with habitual criminals and the need to control them.[84] Even in the late 1930s, a Harvard anthropologist, **3–43**

rehabilitation of sex offenders: A positive approach to treatment" in Stephen Joseph (ed), *Positive Psychology in Practice,* 2nd ed (John Wiley and Sons, 2015), Chap 37,

80 Tony Ward and Clare-Ann Fortune, "The good lives model: Aligning risk reduction with promoting offenders' personal goals" (2013) 5(2) *European Journal of Probation* 29.

81 On the present use of the death penalty internationally, see Chap 12, note 1 below.

82 The overall figure of 200,000 is suggested by Leon Radzinowicz and Roger Hood, *The Emergence of Penal Policy in Victorian and Edwardian England* (Clarendon Press, 1990), p 468, though the authors acknowledge the difficulty in reaching a reliable estimate. On transportation to Australia, see AGL Shaw, *Convicts and the Colonies: A Study of Penal Transportation from Great Britain and Ireland to Australia and other parts of the British Empire* (Irish Historical Press, 1998), first published by Faber and Faber, London in 1966.

83 FH Bradley, "Some remarks on punishment" (1894) 4:3 *International Journal of Ethics* 269.

84 *The Times* (6 January 1857) described the habitual criminal as "educated and

Earnest A Hooton, controversially concluded, following a major study of American criminals, that they were "organically inferior beings" and that crime could be eliminated "only by the extirpation of the physically, mentally or morally unfit, or by their complete segregation in a socially aseptic environment."[85] Today, we would find such sentiments repulsive, as did many of Hooton's contemporary critics.[86] But modern societies have their own, less drastic, exclusionary strategies including various ancillary measures, such as disqualification from driving or acting as a company director, which are designed to incapacitate an offender from engaging in specified activities. Those measures cannot always be guaranteed to succeed as shown, for example, by the number of people convicted each year of driving while disqualified. Tribal courts in Canada and the United States still use banishment as a form of punishment.[87] Elsewhere, various forms of spatial exclusion are widely used as means of social control.[88]

3–44 As a rationale for punishment, incapacitation has very limited ambition. It aims to take offenders out of circulation and prevent them from committing further offences within the community. It does not aspire to deter or rehabilitate, though it may incidentally achieve those goals to some degree.[89] Incapacitating offenders through long-term or extended imprisonment is often the product of an actuarial approach to punishment, to use the phrase made famous by Malcolm Feeley and Jonathan Simon.[90] Actuarial justice is focused on risk and on classifying offenders, not by reference to their individual histories and circumstances, but according to their estimated risk of re-offending. It is usually about managing rather than seeking to transform or rehabilitate. More often than not, in the case of high-risk offenders, management consists of long-term incarceration.[91] This in turn leads to the 'warehousing' of offenders, mainly in prison or sometimes nowadays through intensive community-based supervision.[92]

---

hardened in crime… talks the slang, frequents the haunts, loves the fraternity, of crime… despises every form of honesty, industry, and goodness and a milksop and unmanly weakness." (Quoted in Leon Radzinowicz and Roger Hood, "Incapacitating the habitual criminal" (1980) 78 Michigan LR 1305 at 1311).

85 Earnest A Hooton, *The American Criminal: An Anthropological Study* (Harvard University Press, 1939), 309.

86 Robert K Merton and MF Ashley-Montague, "Crime and the anthropologist" (1940) 43 *American Anthropologist* 384.

87 Colin Miller, "Banishment from within and without: Analysing indigenous sentencing under international human rights standards" (2004) 80 North Dakota LR 253.

88 Katherine Beckett and Steve Herbert, "Penal boundaries: Banishment and the expansion of punishment" (2010) 35 *Law & Social Inquiry* 1.

89 As Bushway remarks, "incapacitation is only problematic if it becomes the central driving force for a sentencing regime" (Shawn D. Bushway, "Incapacitation" in Luna, note 64 above).

90 Malcom M Feeley and Jonathan Simon, "The new penology: Notes on the emerging strategy of corrections and its implications" (1992) 30 *Criminology* 449.

91 Dominique Robert, "Actuarial justice" in Mary Bosworth (ed.), *Encyclopedia of Prisons & Correctional Facilities* (Sage, 2005), 11.

92 Pat O'Malley, "Volatile and contradictory punishment" (1999) 3 *Theoretical*

Much of the modern debate on incapacitation centres on the idea of imposing longer terms of imprisonment than would otherwise be deserved on persons who are predicted to re-offend. This is a troubling issue. Suppose a person being sentenced for residential burglary has 25 previous convictions for similar offences (and burglars are, in general, notorious recidivists), should a court be permitted, in the interests of public safety, to impose seven years' imprisonment even though the offence of conviction might ordinarily merit four years? The case for doing so might seem particularly strong if the offender had no apparent desire to reform or desist from further crime. Those who favour an extended sentence in this situation would argue that a person who is highly likely to reoffend should remain incarcerated for as long as possible to save members of the public from being victimised. They may accept that there is a certain injustice in imposing a longer custodial term than the offence of conviction strictly merited, but they would argue that it is an even greater injustice to expose innocent people to the experience of having their homes invaded and burglarised. They could certainly point to research showing that residential burglary often has a deep and lasting psychological impact on its victims, even where there is little material loss.[93] The same argument would doubtless be made, and even more emphatically, where the offender had a record of violent crime. As reflected in this example, nobody seriously suggests that all offenders, irrespective of their prior records and the gravity of their current offence, should be subject to sentences designed to incapacitate. Rather it is a question of whether some offenders should be singled out for prolonged incapacitation, and how this might be done. **3–45**

Selective Incapacitation

The idea and, indeed, the practice of subjecting certain offenders to longer periods of detention than would be merited by the nature and circumstances of their offence of conviction has a long history. The Prevention of Crime Act 1908, for example, which applied to Ireland as well as to England, Wales and Scotland, provided for sentences of preventive detention in certain circumstances.[94] Where a person was convicted on indictment, sentenced to penal servitude and found to be a habitual criminal, the court was authorised to pass a further sentence ordering that the person, on completing the term of penal servitude, be held in detention for an additional period of between five and ten years. That latter period was known as preventive detention. A person who had **3–46**

Criminology 175 at 177-178. Intensive supervision is discussed further in Chap 12 below.

93 Mike Maguire, "The impact of burglary upon victims" (1980) 20 *British Journal of Criminology* 261.

94 Part II of the Act which provided for such sentences was not formally abolished in its entirety in Ireland until 1997 (Criminal Law Act 1997, s 16). For detailed account of the background to the 1908 Act and its operation, until repealed in England under the Criminal Justice Act 1948,see Radzinowicz and Hood, note 84 above.

accumulated three or more previous convictions since reaching the age of 16 years and was "leading persistently a dishonest or criminal life" could be deemed a habitual criminal.[95] Sentences of preventive detention were meant to be served in a more relaxed custodial environment than an ordinary prison. Inmates would be allowed to earn small amounts of money and to associate with some degree of freedom. Lest this arrangement might prove attractive to some repeat offenders, the law insisted that they had to serve a term of penal servitude first.[96] As soon as the 1908 Act became law, courts showed themselves very willing to invoke its provisions. In *R v Jones*,[97] the applicant, on being convicted of stealing two shirts and being declared a habitual offender, was sentenced to three years' penal servitude and five years' preventive detention. The Court of Appeal upheld this sentence mainly, it seems, because the applicant had 12 previous convictions, including some for serious offences. But it stressed that a court should never increase a sentence in order to give itself jurisdiction to impose a term of preventive detention. The sentence was to be chosen strictly by reference to the nature of the offence of conviction.

3–47 The bifurcated approach to criminal punishment reflected in the Prevention of Crime Act 1908 is by no means a historical curiosity. It was bifurcated in the sense that it allowed most offenders to receive a straightforward proportionate sentence while others, because of their apparent propensity to re-offend, could be subject to harsher punishment. It was later reflected in the English Criminal Justice Act 1991 (s 2) which provided that (1) a custodial term should be commensurate with the seriousness of the offence, or the combination of the offence and other offences associated with it, and (2) in the case of a violent or sexual offence a custodial sentence should be "for such longer term (not exceeding the maximum) as in the opinion of the court is necessary to protect the public from serious harm by the offender".[98] The latter provision, literally construed, allowed courts to impose a sentence of any length, up to the maximum, considered necessary for public protection. However, the Court of Appeal insisted that an extended sentence, even when necessary, should itself be subject to some degree of proportionality, in the sense that it should bear a reasonable relationship to the offence of conviction.[99]

3–48 Selective incapacitation raises several definitional, moral and empirical questions. First, a decision must be made as to the kind of conduct it is sought to prevent. Burglars, petty thieves and persons with serious drug addictions are highly prone to re-offend. In such cases, a question

---

95 Prevention of Crime Act 1908, s 10.

96 House of Lords Debates, vol 198, cols 681-189, 10 December 1908 (speech of the Lord Stewart introducing the Bill).

97 (1911) 6 Cr App R 1. See also *R v Sweeney* (1910) 4 Cr App R 70.

98 This was re-enacted in the Powers of the Criminal Courts (Sentencing) Act 2000, s 80 which, in turn, was repealed by the Criminal Justice Act 2003

99 *R v Crow and Pennington* (1995) 16 Cr App R (S) 409. See Gavin Dingwall, "Selective incapacitation after the Criminal Justice Act 1991: A proportional response to protecting the public?" (1998) 37 *The Howard Journal* 177.

certainly arises as to whether previous convictions should be treated as an aggravating factor, an issue to be considered in Chap 5. Selective incapacitation, on the other hand, which entails imposing a longer term of detention than would be justified by the current offence, becomes an issue mainly where the predicted future conduct involves crimes of violence or other serious offences. Adoption of such a policy creates a clear conflict of rights and interests. The offender has a right (and in Ireland a constitutional right) to a penalty that is proportionate to the gravity of the current offence and his or her personal circumstances. As against this, it is arguable that potential victims, even if they cannot now be identified, have a right not to be subjected to violent attacks which would, of course, amount to a violation of *their* constitutional right to bodily integrity. The question is whether the individual's right to a fair sentence can be reconciled with the community's right to protection from serious harm. Anthony Bottoms and Roger Browsnword proposed one answer to this question, drawing on Ronald Dworkin's theory of rights.[100] They accepted that a right may be defeated by a competing right which protects an even more important social value. Are there circumstances, therefore, in which an offender's right to be released on completing a sentence which was proportionate to the offence may legitimately be required to yield to another, more compelling right? Bottoms and Brownsword proposed a "vivid danger" test according to which protective sentences would be justified only in very exceptional circumstances, "the justification lying in the anticipated depth of the offender's violation of the rights of others (discounted by the degree of uncertainty) outweighing the depth of the known violation of the offender's rights".[101] This proposal was subject to the objection that it still required a prediction (which, of the authors' own admission, could never be entirely reliable) to be made at the time of sentence as to the offender's propensity, not only to re-offend, but to do so in a serious and dangerous manner after having served the portion of the sentence merited by the offence of conviction. Assessing the probability of future offending can be difficult enough at a bail hearing where a court is usually concerned with a defendant's likely conduct during the following few weeks or months. When faced with deciding if an extended sentence should be imposed on grounds of 'dangerousness', a court must try to predict what kind and level of risk, if any, an offender will pose at a time that could be anywhere between five and ten years (and perhaps longer) after the date of sentence.[102]

---

[100] AE Bottoms and Roger Brownsword, "The dangerousness debate after the Floud Report" (1982) 22 *British Journal of Criminology* 229; Anthony Bottoms and Roger Brownsword, "Dangerousness and rights" in JW Hinton (ed), *Dangerousness: Problems of Assessment and Prediction* (George Allen & Unwin, 1983). In this part of their argument, they were drawing on Ronald Dworkin, *Taking Rights Seriously* (Duckworth, 1977).

[101] Bottoms and Brownsword, note 100 above, at 239-240. See also Anthony E Bottoms, "Reflections on the renaissance of dangerousness" (1977) 16 *Howard Journal of Criminal Justice* 70; Max de Vries and Johannes Bijlsmen, "The elusive concept of dangerousness: The state of the art in criminal legal theory and the necessity of further research" (2022) 41 *Criminal Justice Ethics* 142.

[102] Paul H Robinson, "Punishing dangerousness: Cloaking preventive detention as

3–49 The constitutional prohibition of preventive detention in Ireland is discussed in Chap 4, but there are other more empirical and policy-based difficulties as well. Decisions to incapacitate, whether by way of pre-trial detention, extended sentences or denial of parole, are typically based on predictions of dangerousness and, when used in this context, 'dangerousness' usually denotes serious re-offending of some kind.[103] Yet, our ability to predict future behaviour, criminal or otherwise, is severely limited. Research has consistently shown high rates of false positives. A false positive occurs when a person who is predicted to re-offend, whether in a specific way or more generally, within a defined period does not do so (or, at any rate, is not known to have done so). Techniques for predicting future criminal conduct may have improved, but it is widely accepted that they are still far from perfect. In the 1970s and early 1980s, it was estimated that predictions of future violent offending had a false positive rate as high as two-thirds.[104] Even if that rate is now substantially lower – and opinions differ about that – it does not follow that it is fair to deprive *individuals* of their liberty simply because they fall into a category that is actuarily assessed as posing a high risk of offending.[105] The point is well made by Andrew Ashworth and Lucia Zedner:

> "The ability to state with any confidence that there is a 40 per cent risk of future violence in a given population group is clearly better than no knowledge, but it is questionable whether it suffices to underwrite the decision to deprive an individual of liberty indefinitely. Furthermore, probabilistic assessments are impossible to refute since non-offending does not disprove the assessment because the claim is not that a given offender *will* offend but merely that there is a 40 per cent risk of someone with the offender's characteristics doing so."[106]

3–50 Andrew von Hirsch had made a rather similar argument, although in the context of defending a desert-based theory of punishment. He claimed that the fundamental moral objection to predictive restraint is that it is undeserved. A person is being punished for crimes he is considered likely to commit rather than for his past conduct. This objection, as he says, would hold true even if more reliable prediction methods became

criminal justice" (2001) 114 Harvard LR 1429 at 1452 (a particularly enlightening discussion of this topic).

[103] 'Dangerousness' is well accepted as being an elusive and slippery concept. See, for example, Jean Floud, "Dangerousness and criminal justice" (1982) 22 Brit J Criminology 213, and Jean Floud and Warren Young, *Dangerousness and Criminal Justice* (Heinemann, 1981).

[104] Morris, note 34 above; John Monahan, *The Clinical Prediction of Violent Behaviour* (National Institute of Mental Health, 1981). See generally, Michael Tonry, "Predictions of Dangerousness in Sentencing" in Tonry (ed), *American Sentencing: What Happens and Why?* Vol 48 of *Crime and Justice* (University of Chicago Press, 2019), 439.

[105] Bernard E Harcourt, *Against Prediction: Profiling, Policing, and Punishing in an Actuarial Age* (University of Chicago Press, 2007).

[106] Andrew Ashworth and Lucia Zedner, *Preventive Justice* (Oxford University Press, 2014), 133.

available.[107] He did however accept that an exception might be made for "especially fearsome cases." A related problem is that the factors on which predictions are based may result, consciously or otherwise, in discrimination on grounds such as age, gender and race.

Proponents of risk -based sentencing claim that it has two primary advantages. It is economically efficient by reserving imprisonment or, at least, long-term imprisonment for dangerous offenders. Further, it promotes public safety by incarcerating those dangerous offenders either indefinitely or for lengthy periods.[108] Yet, the presumed benefits to public safety may be undermined by replacement. Incarcerated offenders may soon be replaced by others engaging in the same criminal conduct within the community. This does not hold true of all offences, but it is almost certainly true of drug dealing and related crimes, largely because they are so profitable.[109] The same can probably be said of organised crime. Imprisoned gang members will be replaced by others. **3–51**

5. Translating Theory into Practice

Philosophers tend to argue tenaciously in favour of their preferred justification for punishment, and they are seldom willing to yield any ground to their opponents. JD Mabbott, an eminent Oxford philosopher, began his well-known essay, "Punishment", by declaring: **3–52**

> "I propose in this paper to defend a retributive theory of punishment and to reject absolutely all utilitarian considerations from its justification."[110]

This reflects the philosophical mode of inquiry which is to think deeply about fundamental questions of human existence or abstract concepts such as knowledge, truth and justice, and then argue as convincingly as possible in support of whatever conclusions seem most compelling. Philosophers have made some of the more notable contributions to punishment theory, and continue to do so, although lawyers such as HLA Hart (whose early training was in classics and philosophy) and, more recently, Andrew Ashworth, John Gardner and Andrew von Hirsch have also produced significant and highly influential theoretical work.[111] But judges and lawyers have generally tended to disavow any interest in the topic, preferring to fall back on the assertion that they are engaged **3–53**

---

[107] Andrew von Hirsch, *Doing Justice: The Choice of Punishments* (Northeastern University Press, 1986 (1976)), 125-126.

[108] Christopher Lewis, "Risk-based sentencing and the principles of punishment" (2022) 112 *Journal of Criminal Law and Criminology* 213.

[109] Bushway, note 89 above. See also Jens Ludwig and Thomas J Miles, "The silence of the lambdas: Deterring incapacitation research" (2007) 23 *Journal of Quantitative Criminology* 287.

[110] Mabbott, note 8 above, at 152.

[111] On Hart's life and work, see Nicola Lacey, *A Life of H.L.A. Hart: The Nightmare and the Noble Dream* (Oxford University Press, 2004), in particular pp 279-281, dealing with his *Punishment and Responsibility* (Clarendon Press, 1968).

in the practical business of sentencing. This, they say, requires them to concentrate on the facts of each case and to apply the governing law.

3–54 Yet the question of why the state is morally justified in punishing offenders is of great practical as well as theoretical importance. The penalty a judge considers appropriate in any case may vary significantly depending on the justification that he or she happens to support or is required by law to adopt. Suppose, for example, the offender being sentenced is a male in his late teens and a heroin addict, with no previous convictions, who has pleaded guilty to robbery. He admits to having entered a service station and forced the sales assistant at knifepoint to hand over the contents of the till which amounted to a few hundred Euro. There is credible evidence that he is making serious efforts to overcome his addiction and turn his life around. The maximum sentence for robbery is life imprisonment. The sentence imposed on this offender by a judge who was staunchly committed to a policy of just deserts or general deterrence might be considerably more severe than one imposed by a judge who believed in promoting rehabilitation whenever possible. Offences of this nature are quite common throughout the country. It is entirely possible then that two similarly situated offenders convicted of similar offences may receive markedly different penalties simply because one happens to be sentenced by a judge committed to a policy of just deserts, and the other by a judge committed to a policy of individual deterrence or rehabilitation. Of course, just deserts, deterrence and rehabilitation are all perfectly legitimate penal objectives, but is it right or just that the nature and severity of a penalty should depend so crucially on whichever objective a particular judge happens to favour? Granted, the overarching distributive principle of proportionality, as described in Chap 5, should go some way towards ensuring that nobody receives an excessively severe penalty. However, proportionality can seldom do more than point to an appropriate sentence range, and perhaps a fairly broad range at that. The precise penalty imposed may still vary with the judge's assessment of the most fitting justification for punishment in view of all the circumstances of the case.

3–55 To what extent then does punishment theory have any perceptible influence on legislation and judicial sentencing practice? It is possible to identify a few eras in fairly recent history when one or other of the traditionally rationales held sway. For a good part of the 20th century, from the 1930s to the 1970s, practically all jurisdictions in the United States, including the federal jurisdiction, had a system of indeterminate sentencing which was inspired by a policy of rehabilitation. While there were some variations from one state to another, indeterminate sentencing essentially meant that a judge would specify a minimum and maximum term of imprisonment, say three to six years, leaving it to the parole authority to determine when the offender should be released. From 1917 to 1976 California had the most indeterminate system of all. There a judge would simply indicate a maximum term (though it had to be within the maximum specified by law for the relevant offence) and the parole board then decided on the release date.[112] This was based on the assumption that the parole authority was best placed to decide when an offender was sufficiently rehabilitated to be fit for release. This system may have worked as intended in certain places, but as time when by, it became quite routine for offenders to be released after serving one-third of the term specified by the court. The reasons why indeterminate sentencing fell out of favour and was largely abandoned from the 1970s onwards have been well charted.[113] It was replaced by various measures to make sentencing determinate, in the sense that a specific sentence would be imposed by the trial court (as in our own system). It was at this time also that several states and the federal jurisdiction created sentencing commissions and introduced guidelines (discussed further in Chap 13). But what is most significant for present purposes is that rehabilitation, once abandoned, was not replaced by another sole or dominant rationale.[114]

England and Wales adopted a predominantly desert-based rationale with the Criminal Justice Act 1991. The Act itself did not expressly refer to retribution or desert, but certain of its key provisions clearly reflected a commitment to desert-based sentencing. It provided, for example, that a court should not impose imprisonment unless the offence was so serious that only a custodial sentence could be justified or else, in the case of a sexual or violent offence, that only a custodial sentence would be adequate to protect the public from serious harm by the offender. Likewise, a community sentence (such as probation, community service or a curfew order) was not to be imposed unless justified by the seriousness of the offence. Otherwise, a financial penalty would be appropriate. Further and importantly, the Act (s 2(2)) provided that a custodial sentence was to be "commensurate with the seriousness of the offence, or the combination of the offence and other offences associated with it". Even when imposing a community sentence a court had to ensure that the order was suitable for the particular offender and that any restrictions on liberty were commensurate with the seriousness of the offence as with custodial sentences (s 6). The 1991 Act was not entirely desert-based because, as noted earlier, it also provided that a custodial sentence for a violent or sexual offence should be for such longer period (not exceeding the statutory maximum) as was necessary to protect the public from serious harm by the offender. To this extent, it was giving effect to a type of bifurcated policy based on predictions of dangerousness, as described above under 'Selective Incapacitation'. Broadly speaking, however, the 1991 Act was informed by a desert-based rationale and, as such, was giving effect to the policies expressed in a Government white paper that **3–56**

[112] Kara Dansky, "Understanding California sentencing" (2008) 43 Univ San Francisco LR 45 at 60-62.

[113] Kevin Reitz, "The Disassembly and reassembly of U.S. sentencing practices" in Michael Tonry and Richard S Frase (eds), *Sentencing and Sanctions in Western Countries* (Oxford University Press, 2001), Chap 6,

[114] Albert Alschuler, "The changing purposes of criminal punishment: A retrospective on the last century and some thoughts about the next" (2003) 70 Univ Chicago LR 1.

preceded it.[115] This official conversion to desert shows what a difference a few decades can make. During the 1950s and 1960s, retribution was one policy that did *not* find favour with theorists or, as far as we know, with policy makers. Writing in 1959, JD Mabbott remarked that reform and deterrence were the theories then accepted in principle and increasingly in practice, and that no philosopher of note had defended retribution during the previous 50 years.[116]

3–57 However, the desert rationale introduced by the 1991 Act had a rather short life span. It was abandoned with the Criminal Justice Act 2003 (s 142) which provided that any court sentencing an offender must have regard to the following purposes of punishment: (a) the punishment of offenders; (b) the reduction of crime (including its reduction by deterrence); (c) the reform and rehabilitation of offenders; (d) the protection of the public; and (e) the making of reparation by offenders to persons affected by their offences.[117] The Act gives no guidance or assistance as to when one of those purposes should take precedence over the other. Its failure to do so was rather ironic considering that its sentencing provisions were largely informed by the recommendations of the *Halliday Report*, the core message of which was that a new sentencing framework should endeavour to support crime reduction and reparation while still meeting the needs of punishment. To this end, more should be done to target persistent offenders and support the crime-reduction efforts of the prison and probation services.[118] It therefore recommended that courts should no longer be constrained, as under the terms of the 1991 Act, to sentence solely or mainly according to the gravity of the offence of conviction.

3–58 England and Wales is not alone in having a menu of sentencing purposes from which courts may choose as they see fit. The Canadian Criminal Code (s 718) provides that the fundamental purpose of sentencing is to protect society and to contribute to respect for the law and the maintenance of a just, peaceful and safe society by imposing just sanctions that have one or more of the listed objectives. Those objectives are denunciation, general and specific deterrence, separating offenders from society where necessary, rehabilitation, reparation to victims and the community, and promoting a sense of responsibility in offenders as well as getting them to acknowledge the harm done by their offence. This variety of purposes, taken on its own, might result in very different sentences being imposed in similar cases, and sometimes harsh sentences at that. However, the section states that sentencing achieves its overall protective purpose through the imposition of *just* sanctions. Further, s 718.1 states as a fundamental

---

115 *Crime, Justice and Protecting the Public* (HMSO, 1990).

116 JD Mabbott, "Free will and punishment" in *Contemporary British Philosophy*, 3rd series ed by HD Lewis (Allen and Unwin, 1959), 289. See also KG Armstrong, "The Retributivist hits back" (1961) 70 *Mind* 471.

117 The current statutory provision, in identical terms, is the Sentencing Act 2020, s 57.

118 *Making Punishments Work: Report of a Review of the Sentencing Framework for England and Wales* (*Halliday Report*) (Home Office, 2001), para 1.76.

principle that a sentence must be proportionate to the gravity of the offence and the degree of responsibility of the offender. A sentence may also be increased or reduced to reflect aggravating and mitigating factors relating to the offence or the offender (s 718.2).

New Zealand's Sentencing Act 2002 (s 7) and the New South Wales Crimes (Sentencing Procedure) Act 1999 (s 3A) have similar lists of purposes, although the New Zealand Act expressly states that the order in which they are listed must not be taken to imply that any one of them is to be accorded any greater weight than the others.[119] Ireland has no similar statutory provision, but the Court of Appeal has endorsed a hybrid approach in the selection of sentencing purposes. First, in *People (DPP) v O'Brien*,[120] it held that penal objectives should be prioritised according to the circumstances of the particular case and that may involve at times prioritising rehabilitation. It elaborated on this further in *People (DPP) v W(D)*[121] where it said: **3–59**

> "There is simply no reason to think that retribution and/or deterrence are any less valid or legitimate today as penal objectives than is the penal objective of rehabilitation, even in circumstances where, as we acknowledge almost invariably occurs, a sentencing judge neither mentally addresses, nor articulates, in terms of any abstract or philosophical theory of retribution and/or deterrence what it is that he or she is trying to achieve by his or her sentence. In our judgment, the appropriate balancing of the accepted penal objectives of retribution, deterrence and rehabilitation are, in the absence of statutory guidance, uniquely matters for the exercise of judicial discretion and the required balancing exercise is fully capable of being conducted by ordinary judges on the basis of their colloquial or quotidian understanding of the concepts at issue, and without any specific need to have recourse to abstract penal theory or legal philosophy."

Notably absent from this statement is any reference to either incapacitation or denunciation. Incapacitation is sometimes seen as a taboo objective in this jurisdiction because of the constitutional prohibition on preventative detention described in the next chapter. Yet, incapacitation remains a valid sentencing purpose and it probably explains, in part at least, many lengthy prison sentences imposed by the courts. As long as those sentences are within a range that is proportionate to the offence of conviction and do not include an additional preventive element, they are perfectly acceptable. Certain non-custodial measures such as disqualification from driving are also meant to incapacitate. Censure and denunciation are also widely recognised nowadays as valid sentencing purposes. Some theorists go so far as to hold that they are the most important purposes. They are admittedly closely linked to retribution or desert in the sense that the degree of censure merited by an offence is usually reflected in **3–60**

[119] Victoria's Sentencing Act 1991 (s 1) also lists some sentencing purposes.
[120] [2018] IECA 2.
[121] [2018] IECA 143, para 78.

the severity of the punishment imposed, as has been acknowledged on many occasions by the Court of Appeal.[122]

[122] See, for example, *People (DPP) v C(R)* [2023] IECA 33; *People (DPP) v O'Connor* [2022] IECA 91.

CHAPTER 4

CONSTITUTIONAL CONSTRAINTS ON SENTENCING POWERS

4–01 Written constitutions that limit government powers, particularly through the medium of judicially enforceable rights, have been compared to an episode in Homer's *Odyssey* which tells how one man resisted temptation while, in that instance, continuing to enjoy it. During his long sea voyage from Troy back home to Ithaca, the hero, Odysseus, had to overcome many challenges, including a trap set by the Sirens. These were two ladies who, with their songs, lured passing sailors to their island in order to kill then. Odysseus, having been forewarned of this by the goddess Circe, did as she advised. He stuffed his sailors' ears with wax so that they could not hear the Sirens, and then had himself tied tightly to the mast of the ship so that he could hear the Sirens' song while being restrained from succumbing to their blandishments. It worked.[1] Similar tales abound in ancient folklore, but the Homeric account of Odysseus at the mast is regarded as the leading metaphor in classical literature for self-imposed restraint.[2] Constitutional theorists argue that when a state adopts a constitution that imposes limits on government powers, it likewise ties itself to a mast. The state is effectively declaring: "these are the rules to which we bind ourselves and, no matter how strongly we may be tempted to depart from them in the future, no matter how alluring the song of the Sirens, we will steadfastly adhere to them" Of course, the comparison is not an exact one. Modern constitutions often expressly permit departure from the rules in extreme circumstances, such as in a time of war or armed rebellion.[3] But, broadly speaking, the comparison is fairly apt.

4–02 This chapter explores the extent to which a written constitution can influence sentencing policy, whether by limiting the range and severity of permissible sentencing measures or by infusing the system with certain animating values. Essentially, we are trying to establish how strongly the different branches of government are bound to the constitutional mast when it comes to devising and administering sentencing law and policy. Modern constitutions seldom have much to say about sentencing,

1 Homer, *The Odyssey*, translated by EV Rieu and DCH Rieu (Penguin Books, 1991), Bk 12.

2 ML West, *The Making of the Odyssey* (Oxford University Press, 2014), p 120; Ludwig Radermacher, *Die Erzählungen der Odyssee* (1915).

3 Constitution of Ireland, Art 28.3.

expressly at least.[4] None of the constitutions under discussion here mandates the adoption of any overarching distributive principle such as proportionality, and none of them either endorses or prohibits the adoption of any particular penal purpose or philosophy. Most of them do, however, outlaw cruel and unusual punishment, as well as guaranteeing the right to a fair trial. Courts have had to breathe life into these proscriptions in order to carve out some fundamental sentencing principles, even of a very general nature, some of which acquire the status of constitutional imperatives. The same holds true of the major international human rights treaties adopted in the mid-20th century. All of them outlaw torture and inhuman or degrading treatment or punishment and the retrospective application of more severe penal sanctions.[5] But, like most domestic constitutions, they say nothing about the permissible purposes or distributive principles of punishment.[6] International bodies responsible for enforcing or monitoring compliance have generally been deferential to national sentencing policies and practices. Perhaps the main reason why constitutions and human rights instruments have little to say about sentencing is that they were mostly adopted at a time when sentencing was not seen as an issue of major social concern. If art 6 of the European Convention on Human Rights ('ECHR') were being drafted today rather than in 1950, it might well include, in addition to the existing catalogue of fair trial rights, a provision to the effect that a defendant, if convicted, should receive a sentence proportionate to the gravity of the offence. Indeed, it is telling that the EU Charter of Fundamental Rights, which dates from 2000, provides (at art 49(3)): "The severity of penalties must not be disproportionate to the criminal offence."

4–03 A constitution must have certain attributes before it can impose any meaningful constraints on sentencing or any other aspect of public policy. More specifically, it must guarantee certain judicially enforceable rights; it must provide for judicial review of legislation; and it must not be too easily amended. A constitution that has parliamentary sovereignty as its cornerstone or that can be amended like an ordinary statute will be largely ineffective in preventing the enactment or enforcement of harsh or discriminatory legislation. As reflected in the history of the Irish Free State Constitution (1922-1937),[7] there is little point in permitting the superior courts to review or invalidate legislation if parliament can immediately respond by amending the constitution to restore an invalidated law or introduce another that is even more repressive. The main constitutions, those of Ireland, Canada and the United States, considered in this chapter have all three of the attributes just mentioned. Each includes a catalogue

---

4 The death penalty was the only form of punishment expressly mentioned (though not required) in the Constitution of Ireland, adopted in 1937. All references to the death penalty were removed by an amendment in 2001.

5 See, for example, ECHR, arts 3 and 7.

6 Rather tellingly, however, the EU Charter of Fundamental Rights which dates from 2000 provides in Art. 49(3): "The severity of penalties must not be disproportionate to the criminal offence."

7 Leo Kohn, *The Constitution of the Irish Free State* (G Allen & Unwin Ltd, 1932).

of rights (in the form of a separate Charter of Rights and Freedoms in Canada), each permits the judicial review of legislation and none of them is easily amended.[8] In fact, the United States Constitution is well-nigh impossible to amend.

Modern constitutions, in the Western world at least, are predominantly boundary-setting instruments. At a horizontal level, they allocate powers and functions to the different branches of government, while at a vertical level, they specify zones of private autonomy (rights) into which the state may not ordinarily intrude. Granted, the institutional boundaries may be sufficiently permeable to allow for checks and balances between the different government branches.[9] In a constitutional regime of the kind under discussion here, it falls to the courts to ensure that these boundaries are observed. Constitutional rights and freedoms are often broadly defined, and a constitutional text may leave open the possibility of further, unenumerated or derived rights being judicially recognised.[10] In constitutional litigation, therefore, courts are seldom engaged in purely mechanical decision-making in the sense of having to decide if a given sub-constitutional rule or practice clearly conflicts with an express constitutional provision. Their role is usually much more interpretive than this. They must often determine the meaning and scope of a right before deciding if the litigant has suffered a violation of it. For example, Art 38.1 of the Constitution of Ireland provides: "No person shall be tried on any criminal charge save in due course of law." As reflected in the voluminous case law engendered by those 15 words, and the last four in particular, courts have had to determine the content of this right and what precisely it means for accused persons. Moreover, the concept of 'due course of law' is accepted as being dynamic rather than static; it must be interpreted according to prevailing notions of justice and fairness.[11] Sentencing is deemed to be part of the trial process and must therefore conform to the procedural and substantive values inherent in Art 38.1. **4–04**

---

8 The United States Constitution does not expressly confer a judicial power to review and invalidate legislation, but such a power exists by virtue of the Supreme Court decision in *Marbury v Madison* 5 U.S. (1 Cranch) 137 (1803). The Constitution of Canada Act 1982 (s. 52) provides that any law that is inconsistent with the Constitution is of no force or effect. The Constitution of South Africa (s. 172) has a similar provision.

9 Aileen Kavanagh, "The Constitutional Separation of Powers" in David Dyzenhaus and Malcolm Thorburn (eds), *Philosophical Foundations of Constitutional Law* (Oxford University Press, 2016), Chap 11.

10 This holds true of Irish constitutional law. See *Ryan v Attorney General* [1965] IR 294 and *Friends of the Irish Environment v Government of Ireland* [2020] IESC 49; [2021] 3 IR 1; [2020] 2 ILRM 233 (where the Supreme Court preferred the concept 'derived' rights to that of 'unenumerated' rights).

11 *Re National Irish Bank* [1999] 1 ILRM 321; *People (DPP) v E (V)* [2021] IECA 122. The most recent significant illustration of this dynamic principle is *People (DPP) v Gormley and White* [2014] IESC 17; [2014] 2 IR 591; [2014] 1 ILRM 377 regarding the entitlement of detainee to consult a solicitor before being questioned by the police.

4–05 This is not to say that every right enjoyed by suspected, accused or convicted persons comes within the ambit of constitutional due process. Some rights derive from the common law and legislation. However, in Ireland, as in Canada and the United States, criminal procedure has been progressively constitutionalised. Several fundamental rules and principles of common law or statutory origin have been judicially recognised as constitutional rights or imperatives. For instance, criminal legal aid for indigent defendants was first introduced in Ireland by statute in 1962[12] but, in 1976, the Supreme Court held that defendants who cannot afford their own legal representation have a constitutional right to state-funded legal aid and to be informed of that right.[13] The same occurred with proportionality as the primary distributive principle of sentencing (as discussed in Chap 5). Constitutionalisation has been described as "an attempt to subject all governmental actions within a designated field to the structures, processes, principles, and values of a 'constitution'".[14] It is certainly true to say that in Ireland several fundamental aspects of the criminal process have been constitutionalised in this way.

4–06 The United Kingdom provides the most obvious contrast to the constitutional arrangements under discussion here. English law (in particular) has traditionally exercised a strong influence on other common-law jurisdictions, even long after Britain ceased to have any political or legal control over the countries in question. However, its constitution, partly written and partly unwritten, has parliamentary supremacy as one of its core elements.[15] This doctrine, according to Dicey, means that parliament "has the right to make or unmake any law whatever" and that "no person or body is recognised by the law of England as having a right to override or set aside the legislation of parliament".[16] Dicey's description may no longer reflect reality, if it ever did, because of the many political and legal constraints on Westminster's law-making powers.[17] However, parliament is largely unconstrained in creating new sentencing legislation. Admittedly, it must have regard to the ECHR but, leaving aside some important Strasbourg judgments on matters such as early release from prison and voting rights for prisoners, the ECHR has not exercised much influence over the substance of English (or, for that matter, Irish) sentencing law.

---

12 Criminal Justice (Legal Aid) Act 1962.

13 *State (Healy) v Donoghue* [1976] IR 325.

14 Martin Loughlin, "What is Constitutionalisation?" in Petra Dobner and Martin Loughlin (eds), *The Twilight of Constitutionalism?* (Oxford University Press, 2010), 47.

15 Anthony King, *The British Constitution* (Oxford University Press, 2007); Vernon Bogdanor, *The New British Constitution* (Hart Publishing, 2009).

16 AV Dicey, *Introduction to the Study of the Law of the Constitution*, 10th ed by ECS Wade (Macmillan, 1959), 40.

17 Mark Elliott, "Parliamentary sovereignty in a changing political landscape" in Jeffrey Jowell and Colm Ó Cinnéide (eds), *The Changing Constitution*, 9th ed. (Oxford University Press, 2019), Chap 2. See also *R (Miller) v Prime Minister* [2019] UKSC 41; [2020] AC 373.

4–07 It is, however, worth recalling at this juncture that senior British judges are not without experience in interpreting and applying written constitutions. The Judicial Committee of the Privy Council, consisting mainly of UK Supreme Court Justices, still hears appeals from several Commonwealth countries, mostly nowadays in the Caribbean, that have adopted written constitutions.[18] Some leading Privy Council decisions have involved challenges to the constitutionality of sentencing legislation. In *Hinds v The Queen*[19] a provision of a Jamaican law conferring upon a body other than a law court the power to determine the length of prison sentences was declared void by virtue of s 2 of the country's constitution. In that case, the Privy Council drew heavily on the Irish Supreme Court judgments in *Deaton v Attorney General*[20] and *State (O) v O'Brien*[21] to bolster its conclusion. In *Reyes v The Queen*[22] the Council struck down the mandatory death penalty for murder in Belize, holding that it amounted to inhuman or degrading treatment contrary to s 7 of the country's constitution. Incidentally, the judgment in *Reyes,* delivered by Lord Bingham, has much of value to say about sentencing for murder and other important constitutional issues. Later, in *Pratt v Attorney General for Jamaica*[23] the Privy Council held that where execution of a person condemned to death is to take place more than five years after the imposition of the sentence, there will be strong grounds for holding that the delay amounts to inhuman or degrading treatment contrary to s 17(1) of the Jamaican constitution. The Council has also quashed some heavy prison sentences that Commonwealth appeal courts had imposed without affording the defendants or their counsel an opportunity to make a plea in mitigation, thus depriving them of their right to procedural fairness.[24]

4–08 A detailed analysis of all the ways in which a modern constitution might influence sentencing policy and practice would occupy a substantial volume in itself. All that can be attempted here is, first, an outline of the principal limits that the Constitution of Ireland, as judicially interpreted, has imposed on sentencing law and practice. Secondly, we shall consider, though perforce only briefly, the impact of certain core values that are either expressed or embedded in the constitutions of Ireland, the United States and Canada. What will become clear under this heading is that similarly worded constitutional provisions may produce very different outcomes, reflecting variations in the prevailing political and legal cultures of the countries in question. As we shall see, a penalty that might be condemned as grossly disproportionate in one jurisdiction may be quite acceptable in another.

---

[18] On the early history of the Privy Council, see Peter A Howell, *The Judicial Committee of the Privy Council, 1833-1876* (Cambridge University Press, 1979).

[19] [1977] AC 195.

[20] [1963] IR 170.

[21] [1973] IR 50

[22] [2002] UKPC 11; [2002] 2 AC 235.

[23] [1993] UKPC 37; [1994] 2 AC 1. See Barry Phillips, "*Pratt and Morgan v Attorney General for Jamaica*" (1994) 88 *American Journal of International Law* 775.

[24] *R v Moss* [2013] UKPC 32; [2013] 1 WLR 3884; *R v Watson* [2023] UKPC 32.

1. Formal Constitutional Constraints

Selection of Sentence is Exclusively a Judicial Function

4–09 The selection of sentence, where there is a selection to be made, is exclusively a judicial task. Trials on indictment in the Circuit Court and Central Criminal Court are held before a jury who must decide on the verdict. Once they have delivered their verdict, the jurors' task is complete. The imposition of sentence following a guilty verdict is a matter for the judge alone. Murder carries a mandatory sentence of life imprisonment which means that, once an adult is convicted of that offence, whether following a trial or a guilty plea, the judge's role is essentially a mechanical one. He or she must impose a life sentence, the sole penalty permitted by law. But in practically all other cases, the judge has a discretion as to sentence, though subject always to the applicable maximum penalty, the general distributive principles of sentencing, any guideline ranges that have been established for the offence in question and, in the District Court, the jurisdictional limits on that court's sentencing powers.

4–10 The exclusivity of the judicial sentencing function was affirmed by the Supreme Court in *Deaton v Attorney General and Revenue Commissioners*[25] where a law that allowed the Revenue Commissioners to determine the penalty to be imposed on persons convicted of certain customs offences was struck down. *Deaton* is a widely respected decision internationally and one of the few Irish cases that is routinely cited with approval elsewhere.[26] The rule it enunciates does not prohibit the legislature from specifying mandatory penalties for particular offences although, even then, any such penalties must be reasonable having regard to the nature of the offence. Mandatory penalties, the Supreme Court reasoned, are in the form of general rules applicable to everyone convicted of the offences to which they apply. However, when there is a choice of penalty available, as there almost always is, the selection of penalty in a specific case is exclusively a matter for the trial judge. It may not be conferred upon or delegated to any other authority.

4–11 Mandatory penalties remain nonetheless problematic for several reasons, some of which are discussed in Chap 13. The main question arising in the present context is whether they are compatible with the principle of proportionality which, as we shall see, enjoys constitutional status in Ireland.[27] When faced with this question in *Lynch and Whelan v Minister*

---

[25] [1963] IR 170. See also *Curtis v Attorney General and Revenue Commissioners* [1985] IR 458; *Lynch and Whelan v Minister for Justice* [2010] IESC 34; [2012] 1 IR1; *C (P) v Minister for Social Protection* [2017] IESC 63; [2017] 2 ILRM 369; *Gilligan v Ireland* [2013] IESC 45; [2014] 1 ILRM 153; [2013] 2 IR 745. For a more detailed analysis of *Deaton*, see Tom O'Malley, "The power to punish: Reflections on *Deaton v AG* (1963)" in Eoin O'Dell (ed), *Leading Cases of the Twentieth Century* (Round Hall, 2000), 196.

[26] See, for example, the Privy Council cases mentioned above.

[27] Chap 5 below.

for Justice[28] the Supreme Court circumvented it by holding that the proportionality principle applies only where statute allows for a choice of penalty – in other words where it provides for a maximum rather than a mandatory sentence.[29] The court stopped short, however, of granting the legislature *carte blanche* to prescribe any mandatory penalty it wished:

> "That is not to say that legislation which imposed a fixed penalty could not have its compatibility with the Constitution called in question if there was no rational relationship between the penalty and the requirements of justice with regard to the punishment of the offence specified."[30]

Later, in *Ellis v Minister for Justice*,[31] the Supreme Court, having referred to this statement, elaborated on it by saying: **4–12**

> "Deterrence may form part of such requirements of justice. As it is prescribed in legislation which applies generally, irrespective of the circumstances in which the offence is committed or the personal circumstances of the offender, it must be justifiable by reference to the gravity of the offence or possibly, in the *Heaney v. Ireland* [1994] 3 I.R. 593 public law sense, proportionate to the gravity of the offence, irrespective of the circumstances in which it was committed or the personal circumstances of the offender. There may be other permissible policy objectives such as deterrence which apply generally which are relevant to justification."

Therefore, it may well be that the test for determining the constitutionality of mandatory penalties is less stringent than the standard test of unreasonableness – whether the challenged rule or decision "plainly and unambiguously flies in the face of fundamental reason and common sense".[32] Further support for a more flexible test might be derived from *Meadows v Minister for Justice*,[33] difficult though it may be to identify the precise ratio of that case, as the Supreme Court later acknowledged in *Burke v Minister for Education*.[34] However, the majority judgments in *Meadows* seem to support the idea that when a person's constitutional rights are at stake, a court should have regard to proportionality when determining if a decision directly affecting those rights is reasonable. The constitutional entitlement of a convicted person to a sentence "appropriate to his degree of guilt and his relevant personal circumstances"[35] is no longer in any doubt.[36] Nor is there any question but that sentencing is an integral part of the right to trial in due course of law as guaranteed **4–13**

---

28 [2010] IESC 34; [2012] 1 IR 1.

29 [2010] IESC 34; [2012] 1 IR 1, para 55.

30 [2010] IESC 34; [2012] 1 IR 1, para 49.

31 [2019] IESC 30; [2019] 3 IR 511, para 72 (of judgment of Finlay Geoghegan J); [2019] 2 ILRM 420

32 *State (Keegan) v Stardust Compensation Tribunal* [1986] IR 642, 658; [1987] ILRM 202; *O'Keeffe v An Bord Pleanála* [1993] 1 IR 39; [1992] ILRM 237.

33 [2010] IESC 3; [2010] 2 IR 701.

34 [2022] IESC 1; [2023] 2 IR 1; [2022] 1 ILRM 73, para 90.

35 *State (Healy) v Donoghue* [1976] IR 325, 353.

36 *People (DPP) v Begley* [2013] IECCA 32; [2013] 2 IR 188; *Ellis v Minister for Justice* [2019] IESC 30; [2019] 3 IR 511, para 73; [2019] 2 ILRM 420.

by Art 38.1 of the Constitution.[37] Due course of law must indisputably include the right to proportionate punishment following conviction. A strong argument may consequently be made that proportionality should be the dominant consideration when adjudicating upon a challenge to the constitutionality of a mandatory penalty.

4–14 Murder is now in effect the only offence punishable with a purely mandatory sentence.[38] However, between 2006 and 2019, certain repeat firearms and drug offenders were subject to mandatory minimum sentences (five years in some cases, 10 years in others).[39] However, the relevant statutory provisions have been found unconstitutional. In *Ellis v Minister for Justice*[40] the Supreme Court held that one of these provisions, which applied to a firearms offence, was incompatible with the *Deaton* principle which, as noted, holds that the selection of sentence, where there is a selection to be made, is exclusively a judicial task. The court in *Ellis* confirmed this principle, while accepting that the legislature is entitled to specify a mandatory penalty provided it applies uniformly to everyone convicted of the relevant offence and provided also that it passes the test of reasonableness. However, it held that the legislature may not constitutionally "determine or prescribe by statute a penalty to which only a limited class of persons who commit a specified offence are subject by reason either of the circumstances in which the offence was committed, or the personal circumstances of the convicted person".[41] Essentially, the court's reasoning was that once the legislature specifies a mandatory or mandatory minimum penalty that is applicable only to a certain category of persons convicted of a particular offence (such as those with relevant previous convictions), it is effectively engaging in the administration of justice which is the exclusive province of the courts. Previous convictions, whether they are to be treated as affecting the gravity of the offence or as an offender-related factor, are among the circumstances that may influence sentence, and they are thus a matter which a court should be able to consider when deciding on sentence.

4–15 *Ellis* therefore sounded the death knell, not only for the statutory provision at issue, but for the other mandatory minimums applicable to drug and firearms offences, as all the relevant provisions were phrased in identical terms. Section 27(3F) of the Misuse of Drugs Act 1977, which had introduced a mandatory minimum 10-year sentence for repeat drug-dealing offenders, was soon declared unconstitutional by the High Court.[42] The remaining mandatory minimums were repealed by statute.[43] The

---

37 *C(P) v Minister for Social Protection* [2017] IESC 63; [2017] 2 ILRM 369, para 59.

38 Criminal Justice Act 1990, s 2. The same applies to treason.

39 The relevant provisions are contained in the Criminal Justice Act 2006, Pt 5 (firearms offences) and Pt 8 (drug offences).

40 [2019] IESC 30; [2019] 3 IR 511; [2019] 2 ILRM 420

41 [2019] IESC 30, para 60 of judgment of Finlay Geoghegan J; [2019] 3 IR 511, para 85; [2019] 2 ILRM 420

42 *McManus v Minister for Justice* [2021] IEHC 385.

43 Criminal Justice (Amendment) Act 2021.

decision of the Supreme Court in *Ellis* is undoubtedly welcome, but the reasoning on which it was based is not entirely convincing. It could, after all, be argued that mandatory sentences for specified repeat offenders also amount to general rules and are therefore applicable to all who come within the relevant categories. A more compelling argument would have been that the mandatory sentences in question were disproportionately severe or even unreasonable, given the range of circumstances in which they could potentially apply. As described below in the context of proportionality, when the Canadian Supreme Court is determining if a mandatory minimum sentence is grossly disproportionate, and therefore unconstitutional, it considers not only the case immediately before it, but also reasonably foreseeable or hypothetical cases. The mandatory sentence will be struck down if it would be grossly disproportionate in a reasonably hypothetical case, even if it could not be regarded as excessive in the case giving rise to the challenge. Here in Ireland, one could easily imagine cases where mandatory minimum five-year and 10-year sentences for firearms and drug offences would be disproportionately or unreasonably severe, even for repeat offenders.

Customs and excise legislation sometimes requires that specified fines be imposed, thereby limiting the jurisdiction of the courts to individualise financial penalties, but the provisions in question have so far survived constitutional challenge. In *Osmanovic v DPP*[44] the impugned legislation provided that, following conviction on indictment for illegal importation of goods, the penalty was a fine of treble the value of the goods or €12,700, whichever was the greater, a maximum term of five years' imprisonment or both the fine and imprisonment. In this instance there was an obvious option of imposing a very short prison term, a suspended sentence or community service in lieu of imprisonment. Having regard to this element of choice, the Supreme Court found that there was no breach of the separation of powers. The question arose again in *Dumitran v Ireland*[45] save that in this instance the offence, following summary conviction, was punishable with a fine of €5,000, 12 months' imprisonment or both. However, the court, if it imposed a fine, could mitigate only by 50 per cent. This meant that the District Court could not impose a fine lower than €2,500. The High Court dismissed the plaintiff's challenge to the constitutionality of the relevant statutory provision, largely on *Osmanovic* grounds – the court still had a choice of penalty, and need not impose any fine. It further held that this penalty provision was not unreasonable within the meaning of *Lynch and Whelan v Minister for Justice*,[46] as outlined above. The statutory provision unsuccessfully challenged in *Dumitran* also prohibits the application of the Probation of Offenders Act 1907 (s 1(1)) which permits a defendant to escape formal conviction even where the alleged offence is proved. This aspect of it was later challenged in **4–16**

---

44 [2006] IESC 50; [2006] 3 IR 504.
45 [2021] IEHC 567.
46 [2010] IESC 34; [2012] 1 IR 1.

Galvin v DPP[47] but the provision was upheld on the basis that it was not irrational or unreasonable in the *Lynch and Whelan* sense.

4–17 Sentencing guidelines, including those created by bodies other than courts, are unlikely to pose any constitutional problem. They can scarcely fall foul of the *Deaton* principle if all they do is offer guidance as to the appropriate sentences in specific cases, but without purporting to determine what the sentence should be in any individual case. As long as they leave courts with reasonable discretion in determining starting points or ranges and, crucially, as long as they allow for departures where the interests of justice so demand, they cannot be said to interfere with the judicial sentencing role to any appreciable or impermissible extent. Guidelines of this nature, unlike mandatory penalties, do not entail a transfer of sentencing power from the judiciary to another branch of government. Moreover, well-crafted guidelines that respect the principle of proportionality can advance other important constitutional rights and values, including fairness in the allocation of punishment and the equitable treatment of offenders convicted of similar offences.

Prohibition of Preventive Detention

4–18 Preventive detention is constitutionally prohibited, although it is probably no exaggeration to say that prohibition evolved accidentally in the sense that the foundational case was concerned with bail rather than sentencing. In *People (Attorney General) v O'Callaghan*[48] the question was whether bail could lawfully be refused because of a likelihood that the applicant would commit further offences if released. A three-judge Supreme Court answered this question resoundingly in the negative, pointing out that the expression 'further offences' was inappropriate as the applicant was still at that point entitled to be presumed innocent of the offence charged. Walsh J, while concurring with Ó Dálaigh CJ, delivered a separate judgment in which he said:

> "In this country it would be quite contrary to the concept of personal liberty enshrined in the Constitution that any person should be punished in respect of any matter upon which he has not been convicted or that in any circumstances he should be deprived of his liberty upon only the belief that he will commit offences if left at liberty, save in the most extraordinary circumstances carefully spelled out by the Oireachtas and then only to secure the preservation of public peace and order or the public safety and the preservation of the State in a time of national emergency or in some situation akin to that."[49]

4–19 Ó Dálaigh CJ likewise said that denying bail because of predicted future offending "transcends respect for the requirement that a man shall be considered innocent until he is found guilty and seeks to punish him in

---

47 [2023] IEHC 588.
48 [1966] IR 501.
49 [1966] IR 501 at 516-517.

respect of offences neither completed nor attempted".[50] The prohibition of preventive detention may have originated in connection with bail, but it is now firmly established in relation to sentencing as well. The constitutional amendment in 1996 allowing for the likelihood of future serious offending to be considered in bail decisions has not in any way diminished the relevance of the prohibition to sentencing. It was endorsed by a unanimous Supreme Court in *People (DPP) v Daniels*[51] where earlier authorities to this effect were approved. The court said:

> "All sentences of imprisonment necessarily involve an element of preventative detention in the sense that when an offender is in prison, they are not at liberty to commit other offences and in this way, a sentence of imprisonment offers protection to society from the possible commission of other offences by that individual. However, the sentence imposed should not be longer than is necessary to punish the offender for the offence or offences concerned."[52]

The appellant in *Daniels* had been sentenced to life imprisonment on pleading guilty to attempted murder. The Supreme Court (and, earlier, the Court of Criminal Appeal) rejected the claim that this amounted to preventive detention, and it upheld the sentence as appropriate having regard to the nature and circumstances of the offence. **4–20**

Whether the Supreme Court in *O'Callaghan* intended its observations about preventive detention to apply with equal force to sentencing as to bail may be a matter of debate. However, it is noteworthy that Walsh J did not discount the possibility that such detention might be appropriate in some circumstances, even if they had to be "extraordinary circumstances carefully spelled out by the Oireachtas". For reasons already discussed in Chap 3, preventive detention is deeply problematic from both a philosophical and a policy perspective. It typically involves punishing people for offences that they may, but not necessarily will, commit in the future rather than solely for offences they have committed in the past. Yet, a rare case may arise where a person with a record of violent offending is convicted of a serious violent crime, and there is strong expert evidence suggesting that he or she will continue for the foreseeable future to pose a serious risk to public safety. In such a case, it might be appropriate to impose indefinite detention (in effect, a life sentence if that is the maximum for the offence of conviction), but on the understanding that the offender can be released when it is considered safe to do so. This is **4–21**

---

50 [1966] IR 501 at 508-509.

51 [2014] 2 IR 813; [2015] 1 ILRM 99.

52 [2014] 2 IR 813 at 820. In *People (DPP) v M* [1994] 3 IR 306 at 318; [1994] 2 ILRM 541 the Supreme Court (Denham J) had said: "In contemplating the sentences is it appropriate to consider the offences and their nature and their circumstances, but this is not done for the purposes of determining whether the appellant should be incarcerated for the future so as to prevent him committing further offences; he is sentenced solely for the offences before the court." See also *People (DPP) v Carmody* [1988] ILRM 370, and *Minister for Justice v Balmer* [2016] IESC 25; [2017] 3 IR 562; [2017] 1 ILRM 1 (judgment of Dunne J).

on the assumption that the offence of conviction merited a significant prison term, irrespective of any prediction of recidivism. However, the Court of Criminal Appeal firmly rejected this approach in *People (DPP) v McMahon*[53]where the defendant committed two serious assaults on hospital personnel within months of being released from prison where he had been serving a sentence for manslaughter. There was medical evidence that, if the defendant had opted for trial, he would most likely have been found not guilty because of insanity. He had, instead, pleaded guilty and was sentenced to 10 years' imprisonment. The DPP brought an undue leniency application, arguing that in light of the defendant's propensity to re-offend, a life sentence would be more appropriate, leaving it to the parole board to determine when the defendant could safely be released. The Court of Criminal Appeal rightly interpreted this as an argument for preventive detention, and it noted the difficulties with that concept. While accepting that public protection is a legitimate sentencing factor and one that might determine where a sentence should be located within the relevant range, the court rejected the idea that it could justify preventive detention of the kind being sought by the DPP in this case. The court further noted that if the defendant continued to pose a serious risk to himself or others on the expiry of his determinate sentence, he could be the subject of an application for civil commitment to a psychiatric hospital. Preventive detention, assuming that it should be countenanced in any circumstances, raises complex issues that call for detailed research, analysis and consideration. Whether it should be introduced at all and, if so, the circumstances in which it might be imposed are clearly matters to be determined by the legislature rather than the courts. This was clearly the view of Walsh J in the passage from *O'Callaghan* quoted above. In order to survive a constitutional challenge, any statute permitting preventive detention would need to specify clearly the circumstances in which it might be an appropriate sentencing measure and provide adequate safeguards surrounding its implementation.

Non-Retroactivity Principle

4–22 A convicted person must not be sentenced to a more severe penalty than the statutory maximum that applied when the offence was committed. Both the European Convention on Human Rights ('ECHR') (art 7) and the International Covenant on Civil and Political Rights (art 15) have express provisions to this effect. The Constitution of Ireland (Art 15.5.1o) prohibits *ex post facto* criminal laws but it does not expressly provide for the principle under discussion here. However, the High Court has interpreted the Constitution (and Art 38.1 in particular) as prohibiting the imposition of a heavier penalty than applied when the offence was committed.[54] This principle becomes particularly relevant at the sentencing of sexual offences that were committed many years before being reported and prosecuted. The maximum sentences attaching to some of them

---

[53] [2011] IECCA 94; [2011] 3 IR 774.

[54] *Enright v Ireland* [2003] 2 IR 321; [2004] 1 ILRM 103.

have varied considerably over time. Indecent assault upon a female, for example, carried a maximum sentence of two years' imprisonment from 1935 to 1981, 10 years from 1981 to 1991, and five years from 1991 to 2001. Since 2001, sexual assault (as it has been known since 1990) has been punishable with up to 10 years imprisonment, or 14 years where the victim was under 17 years of age at the time of the offence.[55] This explains why individual sentences for so-called historic child abuse offences which involved indecent or sexual assault only may occasionally seem rather low by present-day standards. When a measure is expressed to apply retrospectively, the threshold question is whether it amounts to a *penalty*. The criteria employed by the courts for answering this question are discussed in Chap 7 in the context of collateral consequences.

Neither the Constitution nor the ECHR makes any reference to what is **4–23** commonly known as the *in mitius* or *lex mitior* principle. This arises where the relevant maximum sentence is reduced between offence and sentence, something that very seldom happens. According to this principle, an offender, when being sentenced, should benefit from the more lenient sentence even if a heavier one applied when the offence was committed. Article 15(1) of the International Covenant on Civil and Political Rights enshrines this principle ("If, subsequent to the commission of the offence, provision is made by law for the imposition of a lighter penalty, the offender shall benefit thereby").[56] The Charter of Fundamental Rights of the European Union (art 49(1)) has a similar provision. This formulation can, of course, give rise to problems. Does it mean, for example, that a person who was already serving a prison sentence when the applicable maximum sentence was reduced could apply to a court to be re-sentenced? Might it even provide a cause of action for persons who had already served their prison sentences but who wished to argue that, in retrospect, they were wrongly imprisoned for longer than necessary? It is unlikely that the latter claim, in particular, would succeed.

The decision of the European Court of Human Rights in *Scoppola v Italy* **4–24** *(No 2)*[57] represented a major development in this area. In that case, the Grand Chamber, though a deeply divided one, held that despite the absence of any express reference to *lex mitior* in art 7 of the ECHR, such a provision should now be read into it. The majority held that *lex mitior* had by then become "a fundamental principle of criminal law".[58] Six members of the Grand Chamber, while accepting that there had been a breach of art 6 in Scoppola's case, dissented vigorously on the art 7 point.

---

55 The relevant statutory provisions are: Criminal Law Amendment Act 1935 (s 6), Criminal Law (Rape) Act 1981 (s 10); Criminal Law (Rape) (Amendment) Act 1990 (s 2) (entered into force 18 January 1991); Sex Offenders Act 2001 (s 37) (entered into force 27 September 2001).

56 The European Charter of Fundamental Rights (s 49(1)) has a similar provision.

57 (2009) 51 EHRR 12.

58 (2009) 51 EHRR 12, para 106 (departing from the opposite conclusion reached by the European Commission on Human Rights in *X v Federal Republic of Germany* (7900/77), 6 March 1978).

They acknowledged that the ECHR is a living instrument that must be interpreted in a dynamic and evolutive manner, but they insisted that the majority were taking a step too far in reading a *lex mitior* provision into art 7. According to the dissenters, *lex mitior* was not a necessary corollary of the express provisions of art 7 and, further, the recognition of it departed from existing Strasbourg case law. In their view, it should be left to individual member states to determine if *lex mitior* should form part of their domestic law.

4–25 The matter was later considered by the United Kingdom Supreme Court in *R v Docherty*[59] which had a rather complicated legal background connected with the sentence of imprisonment for public protection (IPP). However, *Docherty*'s importance for present purposes resides in the Supreme Court's analysis of *Scoppola* and the extent to which it reflected English law. The court concluded that English legal practice recognised *lex mitior* to the extent that an offender should be sentenced according to the law and practice prevailing at the time of sentencing, though subject always to the limitation that the sentence should never exceed the maximum that applied when the offence was committed. However, it did not extend to an entitlement to have the sentence determined according to any more favourable legal provision that may have applied for a time between offence and sentence, as Docherty had claimed. Irish law is, in all probability, the same. If sentence is determined according to the law applicable at the time of sentence, it means, for example, that if the maximum sentence has been reduced since the offence was committed, the offender should be sentenced according to the lower maximum. It is seldom in the extreme that this happens. However, as already noted, under the Criminal Law (Rape) (Amendment) Act 1990, the maximum sentence for sexual assault (formerly known as indecent assault) was reduced from 10 to five years' imprisonment. The 10-year maximum had applied since 1981. This meant that a person being sentenced in 1993 for an indecent assault committed in 1989 would be given the benefit of the new five-year maximum. Admittedly, this approach would not have been free of difficulty from a policy perspective. The maximum sentence for sexual assault was reduced, not because the legislature regarded the offence as less serious than before, but because it was introducing new offences of aggravated sexual assault and rape under s 4 which covered conduct that previously came within the definition of indecent assault. If, therefore, in the example just given, the indecent assault committed in 1989 consisted of non-consensual oral or anal intercourse, it could be argued that the 10-year maximum remained appropriate. The statutory history of sexual/indecent assault also illustrates the *lex gravior* principle that a sentence should never exceed the maximum applicable when the offence was committed. In other words, an offence committed while the

---

[59] [2016] UKSC 62; [2017] 1 WLR 181; [2017] 1 Cr App R. (S.) 31. See Sebastian Walker, "Lex mitior and article 7: The Supreme Court decision in *Docherty*" [2017] 1 *Archbold News* 5, and *R v Knights* [2017] EWCA Crim 1052; [2017] 4 WLR 215; [2017] 2 Cr App R (S) 33 where the matter is further analysed by the Court of Appeal.

maximum was, say, five years' imprisonment may never be punished with a prison term exceeding five years, whatever the maximum may be today. However, under *lex mitior*, if the maximum for the offence had since been reduced and was now three years, that is the most that could now be imposed even if the offence was committed while the maximum was five years.

The prohibition on imposing a penalty exceeding the statutory maximum that applied when the offence was committed is well known and accepted. More contentious is the question of whether this principle should be extended to cover situations where the maximum sentence has remained the same, but changes to sentencing practice or parole arrangements mean that an offender will remain incarcerated for a longer term than he or she would have been required to serve under the arrangements in place when the offence was committed. This might occur where, during the interval between offence and sentence, guidelines were amended so as to require or recommend heavier sentences than had hitherto applied or where, during the currency of a prison sentence, amendments to parole legislation meant that a prisoner had to serve a longer term than anticipated before becoming eligible to release on parole. It can scarcely be denied that where such changes are made, an offender may suffer a heavier penalty than applied when the offence was committed. Yet, it seems that they do not fall foul of art 7 of the ECHR.[60] This topic is discussed further in Chap. 14. **4–26**

2. Embedded Values

The impact of a constitution on sentencing policy and practice is most visible when a statutory provision is invalidated by the courts. But a constitution may also exercise a more subtle, but nonetheless powerful, influence by infusing the criminal justice system with certain values such as proportionality, equality, dignity and procedural fairness. These values may make their presence felt at different stages of the sentencing process which, for this purpose, includes sentence implementation. **4–27**

Procedural Fairness

Sentencing decisions must be made in a procedurally fair manner. The principles of natural and constitutional justice apply to all public decision-making, and sentencing is no exception. At a minimum, sentencing judges must exercise in every case the discretion that is vested in them, something they fail to do if they insist on adhering to any inflexible rules or practices they have adopted in their own courts.[61] A convicted person has a right to be sentenced on the basis of facts that been adequately proved. All relevant factors must be considered, and all irrelevant factors excluded from consideration.[62] Above all, a convicted person has the **4–28**

---

[60] See, most recently. *Morgan v Ministry of Justice* [2023] UKSC 14; [2024] AC 130.

[61] *Pudliszewski v Coughlan* [2006] IEHC 304; *Lacatus v DPP* [2023] IEHC 328.

[62] *Whelan v Fitzpatrick* [2008] 2 IR 678. This case arose from a refusal of legal aid,

right to be heard, either personally or through a legal representative, before sentence is determined, so that all relevant and duly established mitigating factors are taken into account. Traditionally, the prosecution did not actively participate in sentencing hearings but it now has a right to be heard, especially where there is a relevant sentencing guideline and a question arises as to where on the applicable scale of punishment the offence should be located. In fact, it is now accepted, if only as a matter of good practice, that prosecuting counsel should make submissions to the sentencing judge as to the band within which the offence of conviction should be located, any sentence ranges that have been established for the offence in question and other matters such as whether consecutive rather than concurrent sentences should be imposed where several offences fall to be sentenced.[63] The prosecution should not recommend a specific sentence, and the defence may challenge any prosecution submissions on the matters just mentioned.

4–29 The principle of proportionality imposes procedural as well as substantive obligations on sentencing courts. In order to identify a proportionate sentence that reflects all the circumstances of a case, a court should methodically consider all the relevant factors so that they can be given due weight, individually and collectively. As the Supreme Court has said:

> "[A] sentencing court should conduct a systematic analysis of the facts of the case, assess the gravity of the offence, the point on the spectrum at which the particular offence or offences may lie, the circumstances and character of the offender and the mitigating factors to be taken into account – all with a view to arriving at a sentence which is both fair and proportionate."[64]

4–30 The court did qualify this by saying that the exercise need not be conducted in a formulaic or rigid manner, provided the basis for the sentence was both apparent and consistent with principle.[65] These statements were later endorsed by the Supreme Court in *Ellis v Minister for Justice.*[66]

4–31 A defendant must be sentenced solely for the offences of which he or she has been convicted or has asked to be taken into consideration. This may seem like a fundamental principle of justice, as indeed it is, but it assumes particular importance when the prosecution claims or suggests at sentencing that the defendant has engaged in a broader pattern of offending than is reflected in the offence(s) of conviction. The principles set out in the leading English case on the matter, *R v Canavan,*[67] are also accepted in Ireland. This is scarcely surprising given that the same fundamental values, including the presumption of innocence, the right

---

but the same principles apply to sentencing.

63 *People (DPP) v E (F)* [2019] IESC 85; [2021] 1 IR 217, para 40; [2020] 1 ILRM 517.

64 *People (DPP) v McC (R)* [2007] IESC 17; [2008] 2 IR 92, para 31; [2008] 1 ILRM 321.

65 [2007] IESC 47 ; [2008] 2 IR 92, para 32; [2008] 1 ILRM 321.

66 [2019] IESC 30; [2019] 3 IR 511, para 35 (of judgment of Finlay Geoghegan J); [2019] 2 ILRM 420.

67 [1998] 1 WLR 604, 607 (*sub nom. R v Kidd*); [1998]1 Cr App R (S) 243.

to contest the charges and, for serious offences, the right to trial by jury, are at stake in both jurisdictions. In *Canavan,* the English Court of Appeal stressed that a person's guilt in respect of an offence can be established only by admission or the verdict of a court, except where the person has asked for an uncharged offence to be taken into consideration. To permit a judge to conclude that a defendant is guilty of further offences would amount to depriving the defendant of the right to trial by jury. (The same would undoubtedly apply in a court of summary jurisdiction, despite the absence there of a right to jury trial.) However, it is also accepted that a sentencing judge is entitled to have regard to the surrounding circumstances of the offence(s) of conviction, even if these reveal some further misconduct on the offender's part. This can pose practical difficulties. On the one hand, the *Canavan* principle must be strictly observed while, on the other, a court "cannot act in blinkers", as the Court of Criminal Appeal said in the seminal Irish case on the matter.[68] The challenge for a court, therefore, is to stay on the right side of the divide. The essential principle, in the words of the Supreme Court, is that "[o]nce offences which have not been admitted are not used to enhance the gravity of what the accused in convicted, or pleads to, it is beyond argument that background and circumstances require consideration".[69] The more closely connected the circumstances to the offence of conviction, the more appropriate it is to take them into account for the purpose of sentencing. However, a court must be satisfied that any additional facts of this nature are adequately proved. It may never proceed on the basis of mere suspicion. As a general principle, matters adverse to the offender should be proved to the criminal standard while matters favourable to the offender need be proved only to the civil standard.

Procedural fairness also demands that courts give reasons for the sentences they impose. This may not be necessary when dealing with summary offences where the punishment is a fine, even when accompanied with a mandatory order such as disqualification from driving. In most such cases, the conviction provides an adequate explanation for the sentence. However, in more serious cases, especially where imprisonment, whether immediate or suspended, is being imposed or where community service is substituted for a term of imprisonment, courts should give reasons for sentence. A duty to give reasons is now well established as an element of natural and constitutional justice, especially in circumstances where a public body makes a decision adversely affecting an individual. As the **4–32**

68 *People (DPP) v Gilligan* [2004] 3 IR 87, 94. See also *People (DPP) v E (F)* [2019] IESC 85; [2021] 1 IR 217; [2020] 1 ILRM 517 where the Supreme Court addressed the matter in some detail.

69 *People (DPP) v E (F)* [2019] IESC 85; [2021] 1 IR 217, para 18; [2020] 1 ILRM 517. In *People (DPP) v Faulkner* [2024] IESC 16, para 9.6, the Supreme Court said: "A clear line may be enunciated as between the principle that it is wrong to punish a person for conduct in respect of which the presumption of innocence has not been displaced (no finding of guilt) and conduct which though constituting a separate crime is part of the event comprising the offence for which there is a finding of guilty, and for which, therefore, the sentence properly encompasses."

Supreme Court has said, "[t]he most obvious means of achieving fairness is for reasons to accompany the decision".[70] Reasons need not be expressed in a formulaic manner. What matters is that the person affected – the offender in a sentencing context – should be able to understand clearly and fully why the decision has been taken.

4–33 The obligation to give reasons rests, first and foremost, on the normative premise that everyone is entitled to be treated fairly by a public authority which is acting on behalf of the entire community. This general consideration becomes even more important when imposing punishment on a convicted person, with all the condemnation and censure inherent in that exercise. Offenders can legitimately be punished fairly and proportionately, but they still retain their fundamental rights (apart from those that must necessarily be suspended or curtailed as a result of the sentence), including the right to be treated with dignity. An explanation for the sentence helps to counteract the risk of degrading the offender. It affirms "the dignity of the offender as a reasoning moral agent whose suffering must be premised on legitimate goals".[71] In more instrumental terms, the provision of reasons is essential for enabling an offender to decide if he or she should challenge the sentence by way of appeal or review, and to enable the appeal or reviewing court to ascertain and evaluate the trial court's reasoning.

4–34 The date on which a prison sentence is to begin should be clearly specified. As the Court of Criminal Appeal said in *People (DPP) v Faulkner*[72] "it is a principle of the Constitution that no one should spend any time in custody – not a day or not an hour – unless it is lawfully justified". There is seldom any problem in this regard, but it may arise where a prison sentence is ordered to run consecutively to other terms of imprisonment being imposed on the offender or already being served. In such a case, a court must be careful to specify when the new consecutive sentence is to take effect. This will typically be on the expiry of the longest of the earlier ones. It will usually be sufficient for a court to state this, provided the commencement date of the new sentence can thereby be identified.

Proportionality

4–35 The origins and operation of proportionality as a distributive principle of punishment are discussed in Chap 5. The sole question being addressed

[70] *Mallak v Minister for Justice* [2012] IESC 59; [2012] 3 IR 297, para 68. See also *Connelly v An Bord Pleanála* [2018] IESC 31; [2021] 2 IR 752; *Oates v Browne* [2016] IESC 7; [2016] 1 IR 481; [2016] 2 ILRM 1; *O'Mahony v Ballagh* [2002] 2 IR 410; *Meadows v Minister for Justice* [2010] IESC 3; [2010] 2 IR 701, 732; [2011] 2 ILRM 157.

[71] Marah Stith McLeod, "Communicating punishment" (2020) 100 Boston Univ LR 2263, 2267. See also Jeremy Waldon, "How the law protects dignity" (2012) 71 Cambridge LJ 200, 218 (offenders are not to be "herded like cattle, or broken like horses or beaten like dumb animals").

[72] *Ex tempore*, Court of Criminal Appeal, 6 November 2008.

here is whether a constitutionally-derived principle of proportionality may be invoked to invalidate mandatory penalties. Ordinarily, a maximum sentence, however high, will withstand constitutional challenge, the reasoning being that it allows the courts sufficient discretion to tailor sentences to the facts and circumstances of individual cases. A very lenient penalty may still be imposed for an offence punishable with a high maximum. Fully mandatory sentences, on the other hand, deprive courts of all discretion, while mandatory minimum sentences significantly curtail discretion. Presumptive minimum sentences will probably survive constitutional challenge if they leave courts with enough leeway to take account of any offence- or offender-related factors that seem to call for a penalty below the specified minimum. This probably holds true of the presumptive minimum 10-year sentence for certain drug offences as described in Chap 10.[73] In this country, as already noted, the Supreme Court in *Ellis v Minister for Justice*[74] invalidated a mandatory minimum sentence for repeat offenders by reference to the *Deaton* principle. However, it might equally have reached the same conclusion by relying on proportionality as would have happened in Canada and (though probably with different results) in the United States. The remainder of this section will therefore concentrate on the response of the Canadian and American Supreme Courts to proportionality-based challenges to mandatory and mandatory minimum sentences.

Canada has a remarkably high number of mandatory minimum sentences, **4–36** most of them introduced since 1995. In 2021, it was estimated that there were 73 mandatory minimums on the statute books, though there has been a move of late to repeal at least some of them. They have varied in length, being as short as seven days in some cases, but more commonly four or five years for firearms and drug offences. They have also been subject to numerous constitutional challenges in the provincial courts, and some of these cases have reached the Canadian Supreme Court. Section 12 of the Charter of Rights and Freedoms which provides that "[e] veryone had the right not to be subjected to cruel and unusual treatment or punishment", has been interpreted as outlawing penalties that are 'grossly disproportionate'. Accordingly, when a mandatory minimum is constitutionally challenged, the question is whether it is grossly disproportionate. In many instances, the mandatory minimum could not be regarded as disproportionate for the offence committed by the person who has brought the constitutional challenge. In fact, a sentence above the minimum may have been appropriate in some such cases. However, when evaluating the constitutionality of a mandatory minimum, the Supreme Court considers not only if it was grossly disproportionate in the case before it, but also if it would be grossly disproportionate in a reasonably foreseeable or hypothetical case where the offending was less blameworthy or there were strong mitigating factors. It therefore applies a

---

[73] See Supreme Court's remarks in *Ellis v Minister for Justice* [2019] IESC 30; [2019] 3 IR 511, para 89; [2019] 2 ILRM 420(of judgment of Finlay Geoghegan J) which, admittedly, leave the matter rather open.

[74] [2019] IESC 30; [2019] 3 IR 511; [2019] 2 ILRM 420.

two-part test by asking: (1) what would constitute a fit and proportionate sentence, having regard to general sentencing principles?; and (2) does the impugned mandatory minimum provision require the imposition that is grossly disproportionate, having regard to what would be a fit and proportionate sentence?[75] The court has always stressed that what must be demonstrated is *gross* disproportionality.[76] However, as noted, when applying this two-part test, the court has regard not only to the case before it, but to reasonable hypothetical cases as well.

4–37 In the first such case, *R v Smith*,[77] a mandatory minimum of seven years' imprisonment for importing drugs was successfully challenged as constituting grossly disproportionate punishment. The eight-year sentence imposed on Smith himself for importing 7½ ounces of cocaine from Bolivia might not have been grossly disproportionate, but the same mandatory minimum would apply to a young person caught importing a small quantity of cannabis for personal use. It was for this reason that the mandatory minimum was struck down. The application of the reasonable hypothetical test also led to the invalidation of mandatory minimums in later cases including *R v Nur*[78] (firearms offences), *R v Lloyd*[79] (drug dealing), *R v Hills*[80] (discharging a firearm at a building) and *R v Marchand*[81] (child luring). The Supreme Court has never treated mandatory minimums as *per se* unconstitutional and it has upheld them for some offences including murder,[82] driving while prohibited[83] and criminal negligence causing death.[84]

4–38 All these Canadian decisions derive from the Charter's prohibition of cruel and unusual punishment which is also prohibited by the Eighth Amendment of the United States Constitution. Further, in both Canada and the United States federal system, the essential test for determining if a mandatory penalty is cruel and unusual is whether it is grossly disproportionate. Yet, the ways in which this test has been interpreted and applied by the highest courts of the two jurisdictions could scarcely be different. Emerging from what O'Connor J aptly described as the "thicket of Eighth Amendment jurisprudence" in the United States is the principle that a constitutional challenge to the severity of a prison sentence can succeed only if it passes the threshold test of being grossly disproportionate.[85] This was established quite conclusively in *Harmelin*

75 *R v Nur* [2015] 1 SCR 773, para. 46; *R v Bissonnette* 2022 SCC 23, para 63; *R v Hills* 2023 SCC 2, para 40.
76 *R v Smith* [1987] 1 SCR 1045.
77 [1987] 1 SCR 1045.
78 [2015] 1 SCR 773.
79 [2016] 1 SCR 130.
80 2023 SCC 2.
81 2023 SCC 26,
82 *R v Luxton* [1990] 1 SCR 711; *R v Latimer* [2001] 1 SCR 3.
83 *R v Goltz* [1991] 3 SCR 485.
84 *R v Morrisey* [2000] 2 SCR 90.
85 *Lockyer v Andrade* 538 US 63, 72 (2003) (O'Connor J delivering the opinion of the Court).

v Michigan[86] and applied in later cases, notably *Ewing v California*[87] and *Lockyer v Andrade*.[88] However, as these three cases, and the last two in particular, vividly illustrate, the test is virtually impossible to satisfy. In *Ewing*, the Supreme Court upheld a life sentence with no parole for 25 years in the case of a man (admittedly with previous convictions) who stole golf clubs worth $1,200 from a shop. In *Andrade* a man (who also had some previous convictions) was sentenced to life imprisonment with no parole for 50 years for stealing £153 worth of videotapes in two separate incidents. This sentence, which, like Ewing's, had been imposed under California's three strikes law, was also upheld by the Supreme Court. Harmelin's offence was more serious as he was caught with 672 grams of cocaine which could have produced up to 65,000 doses. His sentence of life imprisonment without parole was also upheld.

Granted, the United States Supreme Court (or, more precisely, a majority of it during the period 2005 to 2012 or thereabouts) was prepared to interpret the Eighth Amendment in a decidedly more liberal fashion when it had to decide on the constitutionality of state statutes which authorised the death penalty or life without parole for serious offences committed by persons while they were still children. These cases, beginning with *Roper v Simmons*,[89] are considered in Chap 9 below. How the court, with its present conservative majority, would now decide those cases must remain a matter of speculation. It must also be said that while the federal constitution attracts most attention in this context, some state constitutions have somewhat more liberal provisions, or else their courts are more willing to read a broad proportionality requirement into their cruel and unusual punishment clause. In Illinois, for example, as a result of an amendment adopted in 1970, the state constitution provides: "All penalties shall be determined according to the seriousness of the offence and with the objective of restoring the offender to useful citizenship".[90] **4–39**

It is scarcely credible that the sentences upheld by the United States Supreme Court in cases such as *Ewing* and *Lockyer* would have survived a challenge in the Canadian Supreme Court despite the underlying constitutional provision and the judicially developed test (gross disproportionality) being identical in both jurisdictions. What this shows is that a common standard of review, whether it be reasonableness, proportionality or gross disproportionality, is by no means guaranteed to produce similar results across national borders. Prevailing ideas about appropriate penalty levels vary from one country to another and, sometimes, as in the United States, from one part of a country to another. Those ideas, in turn, are shaped by a constellation of factors, including **4–40**

---

86 501 US 957 (1991).
87 538 US 11 (2003).
88 538 US 63 (2003).
89 543 US 551 (2005).
90 For a detailed account of the adoption of this provision, see Maria Hawilo and Laura Nirider, "Past, prologue, and constitutional limits on criminal penalties" (2024) 114 J Crim L and Criminology 51.

political ideology. Recent Eighth Amendment jurisprudence in the United States may be facially about sentencing but in truth it is about the wider and more contentious issue of constitutional interpretation. Those judges, like the late Scalia J (in his *Harmelin* judgment among many others), who favour an originalist interpretation of the Constitution by asking, in effect, what its provision were understood to mean when adopted in the late 18th century will naturally reach conclusions vastly different from those of their colleagues who see the Constitution as a living, dynamic document that should be read in the present tense.

Equality

4–41 National constitutions, especially those of recent times, almost invariably include an equality guarantee, but the language in which it is expressed (and consequently its meaning and reach) can vary considerably. Equality featured prominently in early modern declarations of rights. 'Liberty, equality, fraternity' was the clarion call of the French Revolution, while the American Declaration of Independence (1776) proclaimed: "These truths we hold to be self-evident, that all men are created equal…".[91] In 1868 it was given more concrete expression in the 14th Amendment to the United States Constitution which provides that no state shall "deny to any person within its jurisdiction the equal protection of the laws". It is nonetheless salutary to recall that the 13th Amendment, adopted about the same time, still provides that "[n]either slavery, nor involuntary servitude, except as punishment for a crime…, shall exist within the United States".[92] The Constitution of Ireland provides (at Art 40.1):

> "All citizens shall, as human persons, be held equal before the law.
>
> This shall not be held to mean that the State shall not in its enactments have due regard to differences of capacity, physical and moral, and of social function."

4–42 As explained by Walsh J in *Quinn's Supermarket v Attorney General*:[93]

> "[This] is not a guarantee of absolute equality for all citizens in all circumstances but it is a guarantee of equality as human persons… and is a guarantee related to their dignity as human beings and a guarantee against any inequalities grounded upon an assumption or indeed a belief, that some individuals or classes of individuals, by reason of their human attributes or their ethnic or racial, social or religious background, are to be treated as the inferior or superior of other individuals in the community."

4–43 Later authorities have effectively confirmed this interpretation. Differentiation based on what have been described as intrinsic human

[91] The Preamble to the Constitution of India declares that it was adopted to secure to all citizens justice, liberty, equality and fraternity.

[92] There is currently a campaign within the United States to remove this exception from the 13th Amendment.

[93] [1972] IR 1, 13-14.

qualities such as race, gender or marital status, while not inevitably unconstitutional, will always call for strict scrutiny. The same holds true where discrimination (or differentiation) particularly affects members of a group that is vulnerable to social prejudice or stereotyping.[94] More recent constitutions, including those of Canada and South Africa, have more elaborate equality provisions with an enumeration of specific grounds, such as race and religion, on which discrimination is prohibited.[95] One feature common to some of these constitutions, including Ireland's, is that they permit special measures to be adopted for those in special need or, as the Canadian Charter of Rights and Freedoms (s 15(2)) puts it, for "the amelioration of conditions of disadvantaged individuals or groups".

To treat two or more categories of person that are genuinely comparable differently will most likely amount to unconstitutional discrimination against the disadvantaged category unless there is some objective justification for the difference in treatment. The most recent manifestation of this principle occurred, as it happens, in a sentencing case. In *Musueni and Amah v Ireland*[96] the applicants were alleged to have committed a murder while under the age of 18 years. Both, however, would have reached that age by the time of trial and, if convicted, at the time of sentence. Life imprisonment is the mandatory sentence for murder and, until this decision, it had to be imposed on every adult convicted of that offence irrespective of the offender's age at the time of the offence. If a court were sentencing the applicants in this case while they were still children, it would have discretion as to the appropriate penalty, but it would be required to impose the mandatory life sentence if they had reached the age of 18 years by the time of sentence. The High Court held that this arrangement was unconstitutional as it was based on an arbitrary factor, namely, whether a person in the position of the applicants happened to have 'aged out' by the time of sentence. The State did not appeal against this decision, but instead introduced legislation disapplying the mandatory life sentence for a murder committed while the offender was under the age of 18 years.[97] **4–44**

The promotion of equality has been one of the dominant purposes of sentencing reform in many countries during the past half-century. Formal guidelines, especially those adopted in some American jurisdictions, often have equality as their avowed primary objective. However, this raises the difficult but all-important question of what exactly equality means when applied to sentencing. It could be equated with uniformity of outcome, which was the main ambition of the federal guidelines in the United States, but this raises the further question of how uniformity is to be **4–45**

---

94 *Murphy v Ireland* [2014] IESC 19; [2014] 1 IR 198; [2014] 1 ILRM 457; *Donnelly v Minister for Social Protection* [2022] IESC 31; [2023] 2 IR 415; [2022] 2 ILRM 185, in particular para 188.

95 Canadian Charter of Rights and Freedoms (s 15); Constitution of South Africa (s 9). See also Constitution of India (art 14); Basic Law of Germany (art 3).

96 [2024] IEHC 523.

97 Criminal Justice (Amendment) Act 2024, discussed further in Chap 9 below.

understood and achieved. Offence egalitarianism, to borrow a phrase from James Q Whitman, is one possibility.[98] This would demand that everyone convicted of the same offence should receive the same punishment. The emphasis is on the conduct constituting the offence, rather than on the circumstances and characteristics of the offender. Defenders of offence egalitarianism claim that it has the advantage of predictability.[99] Everyone, including potential offenders, will or should be aware of the punishment that a given offence will attract. The mandatory life sentence for murder is the principal manifestation of this approach in Ireland. It must be imposed on every adult convicted of murder, irrespective of their circumstances. Yet, offence egalitarianism is deficient in many respects. It is preoccupied with the harm caused by the offence to the exclusion, or virtual exclusion, of offender circumstances. The best it can achieve is formal equality whereas substantive equality demands consideration of the purposes of punishment, the offender's personal circumstances and the context in which the offence was committed. Incorporating these additional elements admittedly renders the exercise more complex. Once degrees of moral blameworthiness and relevant offender-related factors are taken into account, evaluating the extent to which outcomes are truly equal, or even something close to that, becomes very difficult. A recurring criticism of American sentencing guidelines, and the federal guidelines in particular, is that they prioritise equality of outcome by reference to the harm caused by the offence over other morally relevant considerations. As Albert Alschuler has argued:

> "Situational and offender characteristics are as important as social harm in assessing sentences even from a 'just deserts' perspective, but these characteristics are almost impossible to quantify and to describe in general language. In the world of sentencing guidelines, form dictates function, and guidelines have disregarded difficult-to-describe sentencing considerations. Apparently for linguistic and bureaucratic as well as criminological reasons, guidelines have focused on social harm and have dehumanized the sentencing process."[100]

4–46 When considering equality as it applies to sentencing, it is helpful to begin by noting the nine grounds on which discrimination is prohibited in Ireland under the Equal Status Act 2000.[101] As might be expected, these include gender, civil status, religious belief, race, nationality, ethnic origin,

---

[98] James Q Whitman, "Equality in criminal law: The two divergent Western roads" (2009) 1 *Journal of Legal Analysis* 119, 124.

[99] For a detailed and critical discussion, see Michael O'Hear, "The original intent of uniformity in federal sentencing" (2006) 74 Univ Cincinnati LR 749.

[100] Albert Alschuler, "The failure of sentencing guidelines: A plea for less aggregation" (1991) 58 Univ Chicago LR 901, 902-903. As he also says (at 909): "Desert and proportionality have as much to do with human beings and their circumstances as they have to do with harm". See also Richard A Bierschbach and Stephanos Bibas, "What's wrong with sentencing equality?" (2016) 102 Virginia LR 1447, 1465 (arguing that in the drafting of the federal guidelines, "math supplanted morality").

[101] A tenth ground, relating to receipt of housing and social welfare assistance, was inserted by the Equality (Miscellaneous Provisions) Act 2015, s 13.

sexual orientation and disability. Clearly, it would be wrong, and certainly unconstitutional, to sentence a person more heavily solely because of one of those characteristics or circumstances. Considering how the Supreme Court has interpreted Art 40.1 of the Constitution in *Quinn's Supermarket* and later authorities, it would scarcely be constitutional to impose a heavier than deserved sentence simply because the offender happened to profess one religion rather than another, or was married rather than single or a member of the Traveller rather than the settled community. The more difficult question is whether it is ever permissible or justifiable to treat offenders more leniently because of an intrinsic factor such as race, gender or disability. The problem with adopting a categorical approach for this purpose is that it may amount, in effect, to discrimination against those outside the favoured category. If, as a matter of law or policy, women must always be sentenced more leniently than men, it follows that men will always receive heavier sentences than women convicted of similar or identical offences. The sentences being handed down to men might be no greater than objectively deserved, but they would still be categorically more severe than those imposed on women.

Age is one characteristic that is widely accepted as justifying more lenient **4–47** punishment. Children and young persons, by virtue of their reduced culpability and other factors, usually benefit from a special sentencing regime that is designed to promote their rehabilitation and welfare.[102] At the other end of the age spectrum, elderly offenders also tend to be treated more leniently than others, though often because of factors associated with old age, such as illness or infirmity, rather than because of age itself.[103] Proportionality, as understood in Ireland, permits due consideration of other factors such as race, ethnic origin, and socio-economic background and circumstances, where they seem relevant to the assessment of an offender's culpability under the first limb of the proportionality principle or to the offender's personal circumstances under the second limb.[104] For instance, an offender who is likely to be the victim of racially-motivated abuse while in prison may be sentenced more leniently on that account. Factors of this nature do not, however, apply categorically. Membership of a particular group or category, whether based on race, gender, deprivation or anything else (apart from youth), will not automatically mitigate otherwise deserved punishment. But it may be relevant in a specific case if it helps to explain the offender's conduct, reduces culpability or is likely to render a certain kind of penalty more onerous for that individual than for others.[105] In the case of monetary sanctions, substantive equality can be advanced by ensuring that an offender's means are considered when setting the amount as, in fact, Irish law requires.[106]

---

[102] Chap 9 below.
[103] Chap 5 below, under "Mitigating Factors."
[104] Proportionality is discussed in detail in Chap 5 below.
[105] See, for example, *R v Ipeelee* [2012] 1 SCR 433 and *R v Hills* 2023 SCC 2, para 55; *R v Berkland* [2022] NZSC 143 (which is quoted at length in Chap 5 below).
[106] Chap 12 below, under "Fines."

4–48 Wealth-based discrimination can nonetheless raise difficult issues connected with sentencing equity. The idea of having one law for the rich and another for the poor is incompatible with any meaningful concept of justice. It should therefore follow that a custodial sentence should never be imposed in circumstances where the appropriate penalty would have been a fine if the offender had been in a position to pay it. Conversely, a rich offender who deserves imprisonment should not be spared it solely because of their ability to pay a heavy fine that few others could afford. Yet, courts are sometimes ready to countenance imprisonment where offenders lack the means to pay a fine. In *Osmanovic v DPP*[107] which involved an unsuccessful challenge to the constitutionality of a provision in customs legislation that mandated a specified fine or a maximum of five years' imprisonment following conviction, the essential question was whether the mandatory nature of the fine (€12,700 or treble the value of the goods whichever was greater) was constitutional. The Supreme Court rejected the argument that this arrangement was incompatible with the separation of powers. It also noted that a court need not impose any fine; it could instead impose any term of imprisonment, however short, suspended or otherwise. In this regard, the Supreme Court said:

> "In the case of an ordinary offence a judge might well be dealing with somebody who had no money and would, therefore, form the view that some kind of custodial or suspended sentence would be more appropriate as otherwise there would be no punishment. If, on the other hand, the person he is sentencing has money the fine becomes a real option. Normally, there is no element of unconstitutional discrimination in this process."[108]

4–49 Taken at face value, this is a rather troublesome statement as it appears to suggest that a person may be imprisoned in circumstances where they would escape with a fine if they were able to pay it. However, the statement was made in the context of a revenue offence and, as the court noted elsewhere in its judgment, revenue offences have "traditionally attracted a somewhat different sentencing culture".[109] Although the courts have not used this language, revenue offences may be seen as a form of unjust enrichment in the sense that they involve the retention or reception of funds to which the offenders have no lawful entitlement. These offences seem to be the only ones for which minimum fines are prescribed by law. In all other cases, a court may impose any fine up to the statutory maximum where there is one. (Some offences are punishable with an unlimited fine following conviction on indictment.) Most offenders have some means, however slight, so that even a very low fine, when properly tailored to reflect their means, as it must be, can have a punitive impact.

4–50 Treating imprisonment as a sanction of last resort is undoubtedly a worthy policy. Nobody, including a convicted offender, should be deprived of their liberty unless it is strictly necessary. Nor is excessive use of

---

107 [2006] IESC 50; [2006] 3 IR 504.
108 [2006] IESC 50; [2006] 3 IR 504, 515,
109 [2006] IESC 50; [2006] 3 IR 504, 514.

imprisonment in the public interest, not least because of its financial cost. Additionally, the stigma attached to imprisonment often renders it difficult for offenders to lead productive and law-abiding lives after release, and this too can impose a burden on the community. Consequently, imprisonment should not be imposed whenever a monetary penalty, a community sanction or a combination of the two would constitute an adequate penalty. Many so-called white-collar offenders could be punished quite severely without recourse to imprisonment. They are very seldom dangerous in the conventional sense of the word, they can afford to pay heavy fines, and they may be willing to perform community service that would be of tangible public benefit. The case against imprisoning them, unless their offences were particularly serious, may therefore seem overwhelming. The problem, however, is that this will not be a viable option for many 'ordinary' offenders convicted of similar or, perhaps, less serious crimes. Offenders in this category will seldom, if ever, be in a position to pay substantial fines and they may not always be suitable for community service. Imprisonment may therefore seem to be the only appropriate penalty for serious offences, even if purely acquisitive in nature, committed by these offenders. This creates a difficult dilemma. On the one hand, we want to avoid using imprisonment whenever there is a viable alternative. On the other, we want to ensure, as far as practicable, that the sentencing system is free of the kind of wealth- and class-based discrimination that would result from a policy of allowing white-collar offenders, but not others who engaged in broadly similar conduct, to be spared imprisonment. The answer to this dilemma is by no means apparent. Jailing more white-collar offenders, as some advocate, might be one solution, assuming we are happy for the prison population to escalate beyond its present unmanageable levels.[110]

However, it would surely be discriminatory, to the point of being unconstitutional, to imprison an indigent offender *solely* because of his or her inability to pay a fine in circumstances where, were it not for the offender's lack of means, a fine was the only appropriate penalty for the offence concerned. As the United States Supreme Court said in *Griffin v Illinois*[111] "[t]here can be no equal justice where the kind of trial a man gets depends on the amount of money he has". This was said in a case where the respondent state failed to provide the appellant with a trial transcript free of charge to enable him to prosecute an appeal, but the principle has since been applied in other criminal justice contexts.[112] **4–51**

One final possibility is to treat all or most personal characteristics as entirely irrelevant at sentencing. This was the approach adopted in the United States federal jurisdiction in the late 1980s when sentencing guidelines were introduced with the principal aim of eliminating unwarranted disparity.[113] It was believed that shifting the primary focus **4–52**

---

[110] See Chap 5, note 275 and accompanying text.
[111] 351 US 12, 19 (1956).
[112] See the Supreme Court's observations in *Bearden v Georgia* 461 US 660 (1983).
[113] Described further in Chap 13 below.

to offence gravity would reduce the levels of inconsistency that may result when courts are permitted to consider individual circumstances. The Sentencing Reform Act 1984 which created the United States Sentencing Commission therefore provided:

> "The Commission shall ensure that the guidelines and policy statements are entirely neutral as to the race, sex, national origin, creed and socioeconomic status of offenders."[114]

4–53 This might be read as a commitment to formal equality even if was primarily intended to promote consistency. It undoubtedly has a positive dimension in so far as it prohibits guidelines that discriminate *against* offenders on account of any of the characteristics in question. However, formal equality can easily mask underlying structural *inequality*, and it frequently does. This holds true of race in the United States (though in other countries also) just as it can be true of socioeconomic disadvantage almost everywhere, including Ireland. Substantive equality demands attention to differences as well to similarities in people's circumstances and life opportunities. As Martha Minow has persuasively argued, a commitment to substantive equality "requires decision makers to acknowledge and accommodate differences in people's circumstances and identities, resist attributing to personal choice the patterns and practices of society, including the different starting points and opportunities…".[115] This has clear resonance in a sentencing context where a commitment to substantive equality demands that due attention be paid to factors that impinge upon culpability or the fairness of any penalty being contemplated.

Dignity

4–54 The concept of dignity, as it applies in law generally, and human rights law in particular, has received extensive scholarly attention in recent times.[116] According to most historical accounts, dignity (and especially

[114] 28 USC §994(d). The next paragraph provides that terms of imprisonment set by the Commission shall reflect "the general inappropriateness" of considering the education, vocational training, skills, employment record, family ties and responsibilities, and community ties of defendants. The Commission's original guidelines went further (though, again, reflecting the terms of the governing statute) by providing that factors such as age, physical condition, mental or emotional condition were ordinarily irrelevant in decisions to depart from the guidelines.

[115] Martha Minow, "Equality, equity, and algorithms: Learning from Justice Rosalie Abella" (2023) 73 Univ Toronto LJ 163, 172.

[116] David Kretzmer and Eckart Klein (eds), *The Concept of Human Dignity in Human Rights Discourse* (Kluwer International, 2002); Christopher McCrudden, "Human dignity and judicial interpretation of human rights" (2008) 19 *European Journal of International Law* 655 (a particularly valuable analysis); Oliver Sensen, "Human dignity in historical perspective: The contemporary and traditional paradigms" (2011) 10 *European Journal of Political Theory* 71; Jeremy Waldron, *Thoughtfulness and the Rule of Law* (Harvard University Press, 2023), Chap 3; John Tasioulas, "Human dignity and the foundations of human rights" in

the Roman idea of *dignitas*) was originally connected with status. Only those of elevated rank, whether by virtue of heredity, being the holder of a high political or ecclesiastical office or some similar factor, were treated as possessing dignity.[117] Vestiges of that traditional view may still be detected in media references to 'all the local dignitaries' being present on some occasion. In modern times, and especially since the mid-20th century, dignity has assumed a very different meaning and more wide-ranging significance. It denotes the inherent worth of every human person irrespective of status, age, nationality or any other characteristic.[118] Most notably, it is given prominence as the source of human rights in the foundational instruments of the United Nations ('UN'). The introduction to the UN Charter (1945) refers to the "dignity and worth of the human person" while art 1 of the Universal Declaration of Human Rights (1948) proclaims: "All human beings are born free and equal in dignity and rights". Article 1 of the Charter of Fundamental Rights of the European Union provides (in terms very similar to art 1 of Germany's Basic Law): "Human dignity is inviolable. It must be respected and protected." The Constitution of Ireland, enacted almost a decade before the creation of the UN, states in its Preamble that it is being adopted "so that the dignity and freedom of the individual may be assured," among other purposes. Dignity is therefore a fundamental and animating constitutional value that informs the recognition and content of constitutional rights, irrespective of whether it can be said to exist as a freestanding right in itself.[119]

Respect for individual human dignity is a key imperative at every stage of the criminal process. For example, it should inform the manner in which the police treat suspects, defendants and, indeed, all members of the public.[120] The use of stop and search or arrest powers in ways that discriminate against racial or other groups violates the dignity of individual members of those groups.[121] In a sentencing context, excessive punishment, inhuman or degrading conditions of detention, and indefinite imprisonment without any realistic prospect of release (or, at least, a right to be objectively considered for release) all undermine individual dignity to an impermissible extent. **4–55**

Proportionality as the overarching distributive principle of sentencing is ultimately grounded on respect for human dignity.[122] A criminal conviction **4–56**

Christopher McCrudden (ed), *Understanding Human Dignity* (Oxford University Press, 2013).

[117] Sensen, note 116 above.

[118] This concept of dignity is not entirely new as it is reflected in the writings of Cicero in the 1st century BCE. In *De Officiis*, 1.10, he refers to the "superiority and dignity" of humans in contrast to animals.

[119] *Fleming v Ireland* [2013] IESC 19; [2013] 2 IR 417; [2013] 2 ILRM 73; *Simpson v Governor of Mountjoy Prison* [2019] IESC 81; [2020] 3 IR 113; [2020] 1 ILRM 81.

[120] *People (DPP) v Gormley and White* [2014] IESC 17; [2014] 2 IR 591; [2014] 1 ILRM 377 para 4 (Hardiman J on the entitlement of persons in police detention to be treated with dignity).

[121] *Utah v Strieff* 579 US 232 (2016) (Sotomayor J dissenting).

[122] See, for example, *State v Dodo* [2001] (1) SACR 594, 614 (Constitutional Court

quite legitimately leaves a person liable to punishment, but it should not undermine either their inherent personal worth or their entitlement to be treated as a responsible, rights-bearing individual, save to the extent that the sentence may necessarily curtail the exercise of some rights.[123] Excessive punishment is incompatible with human dignity because it disregards the offender's entitlement to be treated fairly, respectfully and equitably. A court that imposes excessive punishment is effectively declaring that the offender is no longer a person of sufficient dignity to deserve fair and considered treatment. Leading judicial decisions on both sides of the Atlantic have acknowledged this connection between human dignity and fair punishment. In *Trop v Dulles*[124] the United States Supreme Court held that the national government lacked the power to deprive a person of citizenship as a punishment and that, even if it had such a power, its exercise would amount to cruel and unusual punishment in this instance. Delivering the plurality opinion, Warren CJ wrote:

> "The basic concept underlying the Eighth Amendment is nothing less than the dignity of man. While the State has the power to punish, the Amendment stands to assure this power be exercised within the limits of civilized standards.... The Amendment must draw its meaning from the evolving standards of decency that mark the progress of a maturing society."[125]

4–57 The Canadian Supreme Court has held that the prohibition of cruel and unusual punishment in s 12 of the Charter of Rights and Freedoms which, as noted earlier, has been interpreted to outlaw grossly disproportionate punishment, is informed by respect for human dignity.[126] Section 12 outlaws punishments that are either by their nature incompatible with human dignity or so excessively severe as to be incompatible with human dignity.[127] Corporal punishment would fall into the first category while a term of imprisonment that was grossly disproportionate to the gravity of the offence and the offender's circumstances would fall into the second. In *R v Bissonnette*,[128] where the Supreme Court addressed at length the relationship between human dignity and just punishment, a prison

---

of South Africa), saying that a failure to enquire into proportionality between an offence and a term of imprisonment "is to ignore, if not deny, that which lies at the very heart of human dignity".

123 Jeffrie G Murphy, "Last words on retribution" in Jonathan Jacobs and Jonathan Jackson (eds), *The Routledge Handbook of Criminal Justice Ethics* (Routledge, 2016), Chap 2 at 28 (who, in defending desert-based sentencing, writes: "One of the ways that we respect the dignity of persons is through holding them responsible and sometimes resenting and even punishing them for what they do instead of insulting them by regarding them as sick or helpless victims of their fixed natures or social circumstances").

124 356 US 86 (1958). See Craig S Lerner, "Justice Scalia's Eighth Amendment jurisprudence: The failure of sake-of-argument originalism" (2019) 42 *Harvard Journal of Law and Public Policy* 91 (describing *Trop* and other leading Eighth Amendment cases in some detail).

125 356 US 86 at 100-101 (1958).

126 See discussion earlier in this Chapter under 'Proportionality'.

127 *R v Bissonnette* 2022 SCC 23, para 60.

128 2022 SCC 23.

sentence that left the offender with little or no realistic prospect of parole release was held to be "intrinsically incompatible with human dignity".[129] Such a sentence denies the possibility that the offender is capable of rehabilitation, whereas respect for dignity entails an acknowledgment that every offender has that capacity, whenever it may materialise. The offending in that case could scarcely have been worse. In 2017, Bissonnette burst into a mosque in Quebec and opened fire on those present in it, killing six people and seriously injuring five others. He pleaded guilty to 12 offences, including six counts of murder. In Canada, murder carries a mandatory life sentence without the possibility of parole for 25 years. However, under a law adopted in 2011, in a case of multiple murders, a court could impose consecutive non-parole periods. Potentially, therefore, Bissonnette could have been given a non-parole period of up to 150 years. In fact, the trial judge imposed a 40-year non-parole period. The Supreme Court struck down this law as a violation of s 12 of the Charter because it could lead to the imposition of a term of imprisonment that left the offender with no realistic prospect of release during his or her lifetime. The upshot of this decision is that Bissonnette, while remaining sentenced to life imprisonment, will be eligible for parole after 25 years.

In Germany, too, a life sentence without the possibility of parole is **4–58** considered incompatible with human dignity. Germany's Basic Law (1949) begins by affirming: "Human dignity shall be inviolable. To respect and protect it shall be the duty of all state authority."[130] In a major judgment delivered in 1977, the *Life Imprisonment Case*,[131] the Federal Constitutional Court considered a challenge to a law that mandated life imprisonment for murder and a few other offences. Under German law as it then stood, a person sentenced to life imprisonment had no entitlement to parole in the sense of being considered for release under some kind of formal, structured system. Such a person could, however, be pardoned at some point during sentence and, in practice, many life sentence prisoners were. The Constitutional Court did not find the life sentence inherently unconstitutional, but it held nonetheless that human dignity required that release on parole must be possible unless the offender is too dangerous to be set free.[132] There must be a realistic prospect, as opposed to a mere hope, of eventual release.

---

[129] 2022 SCC 23, para 8.

[130] Grundgesetz für die Bundesrepublik Deutschland, art 1(1): "Die würde des Menschen ist unantastbar. Sie zu achten und zu schützen ist Verpflichtung aller Staatlicher Gewalt." For a detailed account of how this provision has been judicially interpreted and applied, see Edward J Eberle, "Human dignity, privacy, and personality in German and American constitutional law" (1997) Utah LR 963, and the same author's "Observations on the development of human dignity and personality in German constitutional law" (2012) 33 Liverpool LR 201. See also Miriam Gur-Arye and Thomas Weigend, "Constitutional review of criminal prohibitions affecting human dignity and liberty: German and Israeli perspectives" (2011) 44 Israel LR 63.

[131] 45 BVerfGE 187 (1977).

[132] See KC Horton, "Life imprisonment and pardons in the German Federal

4–59 Whatever the length of a custodial sentence, the conditions in which it is served must also be compatible with human dignity. This is mandated by the Constitution of Ireland and international human rights law. The International Covenant on Civil and Political Rights (art 10(1)), for example, provides: "All persons deprived of their liberty shall be treated with humanity and with respect for the inherent dignity of the human person." The European Court of Human Rights has likewise interpreted the ECHR as requiring conditions of detention to be compatible with human dignity. Most notably, in *Kudla v Poland,* the court said:

> "[The state must ensure that prisoner] is detained in conditions which are compatible with respect for his human dignity, that the manner and method of the execution of the measure do not subject him to distress or hardship of an intensity exceeding the unavoidable level of suffering inherent in detention and that, given the practical demands of imprisonment, his health and well-being are adequately secured..."[133]

4–60 Prisoners detained in Ireland are constitutionally entitled to be treated with dignity. In *Simpson v Governor of Mountjoy Prison,*[134] a leading modern authority on the matter, the Supreme Court confirmed that any deprivation of liberty must not only be in accordance with law (as Art 40.4 of the Constitution requires), but "any attenuation of prisoners' fundamental rights must be proportionate: the diminution must not fall below the standards which we identify to protect human dignity". [135] This is a principle which, in the time-honoured phrase, is easy to express but difficult to apply. The state is entitled to deprive offenders of their liberty if their offences are sufficiently serious to warrant imprisonment. Moreover, it is accepted that imprisonment necessarily curtails the exercise of certain other rights and that custodial conditions will often be difficult to endure. Establishing when conditions are not merely harsh but inhuman or degrading (in which case they will be incompatible with human dignity) can be difficult, and decisions in this regard are inevitably highly fact specific.[136] In essence, the question must be whether the detainee is being held in conditions that no one should have to endure in a humane and civilised society. For this purpose, conditions must be evaluated by reference to contemporary standards, as reflected in the reference to "evolving standards of decency" in *Trop v Dulles.*[137] The Constitution of

---

Republic" (1980) 29 *International and Comparative Law Quarterly* 530; Gur-Arye and Weigend, note 130 above.

[133] (2002) 35 EHRR 11, para 94. See also *Bakhmutskiy v Russia* App No 36932/02 (European Court of Human Rights, 25 June 2009).

[134] [2019] IESC 81; [2020] 3 IR 113; [2020] 1 ILRM 81.

[135] [2019] IESC 81; [2020] 3 IR 113; [2020] 1 ILRM 81 para 98.

[136] The difficulty is reflected in a long series of cases in which prisoners have sought various remedies including, in some instances, release under Art 40 of the Constitution (so-called habeas corpus) because of the conditions in which they were being held. See, in particular, *Mulligan v Governor of Portlaoise Prison* [2010] IEHC 269; [2013] 4 IR 1 (which has a valuable survey earlier Irish and European human rights law on the matter) and *Kinsella v Governor of Mountjoy Prison* [2011] IEHC 235; [2012] 1 IR 467; [2011] 2 ILRM 509.

[137] 356 US 86 (1958).

Ireland is a living instrument that must be read and interpreted in the present tense.[138] Modes of criminal punishment that might have been tolerated in the past may no longer be compatible with the constitutional imperative to treat everyone with dignity as understood today.

Perhaps the most resounding and consequential affirmation of a state's obligation to respect and vindicate the personal dignity of prisoners came in *Brown v Plata*[139] where the United States Supreme Court upheld a lower court ruling that required a 43,000 reduction in California's prison population. At the time of trial, that state's correctional facilities held over 156,000 prisoners although it had capacity for only 80,000. Delivering the Supreme Court's opinion, Kennedy J said: **4–61**

> "As a consequence of their own actions, prisoners may be deprived of rights that are fundamental to liberty. Yet the law and the Constitution demand recognition of certain other rights. Prisoners retain the essence of human dignity inherent in all persons. Respect for that dignity animates the Eighth Amendment prohibition against cruel and unusual punishment 'The basic concept underlying the Eighth Amendment is nothing less than the dignity of man.'[140]
>
> To incarcerate, society takes from prisoners the means to provide for their own needs. Prisoners are dependent on the State for food, clothing, and necessary medical care. A prison's failure to provide sustenance for inmates 'may actually produce physical 'torture or a lingering death.' Just as a prisoner may starve if not fed, he or she may suffer or die if not provided adequate medical care. A prison that deprives prisoners of basic sustenance, including adequate medical care, is incompatible with the concept of human dignity and has no place in civilized society.
>
> If government fails to fulfil this obligation, the courts have a responsibility to remedy the resulting Eighth Amendment violation. Courts must be sensitive to the State's interest in punishment, deterrence, and rehabilitation, as well as the need for *European* dangerous task of housing large numbers of convicted criminals. Courts nevertheless must not shrink from their obligation to 'enforce the constitutional rights of all 'persons,' including prisoners.' Courts may not allow constitutional violations to continue simply because a remedy would involve intrusion into the realm of prison administration."[141]

More recently, however, the conservative majority now dominating the United States Supreme Court has seemed inclined to abandon the **4–62**

---

[138] *People (DPP) v Gormley and White* [2014] IESC 17; [2014] 2 IR 591; [2014] 1 ILRM 377, para 78, quoting *McGee v Attorney General* [1974] IR 284, 319 (Walsh J).

[139] 563 US 493 (2011).

[140] *Trop v Dulles* 356 US 86, 100 (1958).

[141] 563 US 493, 510 (2011). For an analysis of this case, see Jonathan Simon, *Mass Incarceration on Trial: A Remarkable Court Decision and the Future of Prisons in America* (New Press, 2014); On later developments, see Jonathan Simon, "Dignity and its discontents: Towards an abolitionist rethinking of dignity" (2021) 18 *European Journal of Criminology* 33. See also Note, (2011) 125 Harvard LR 261.

"evolving standards of decency" approach in favour of an originalist interpretation which, in turn, makes it virtually possible to challenge conditions of detention, however harsh, on Eighth Amendment grounds.[142]

[142] Duncan Hosie, "The hollowing of the Eighth Amendment" *New York Review of Books*, 18 June 2024.

Chapter 5

DISTRIBUTIVE PRINCIPLES

In the absence of formal guidelines, sentencing courts must depend for guidance on general principles, most of which have been judicially developed though a few are based on statute. These principles are essentially distributive in nature because they indicate, without specifying exactly, the kind and amount of punishment appropriate in a given case. Unlike a rule, which may be defined as a directive that determines the outcome of a case to which it applies, a principle operates at a higher level of abstraction. It points the way to an appropriate decision without dictating what precisely that must be. A rule is a command whereas a principle is more in the nature of a signpost. Thus, the mandatory life sentence for murder may be treated as a rule because it is the sole penalty that may legally be imposed on an adult convicted of murder. The verdict automatically dictates the penalty. A principle is a more flexible norm that resembles a rule to the extent that it is designed to give effect to some underlying policy, but it allows decision-makers more scope to consider all the relevant features of a case. It usually requires judgment on the part of those who must apply it.[1] Rules may, of course, be so framed as to allow for exceptions, but principles still delegate more authority to decision-makers to craft individualised judgments.[2] **5–01**

The legitimacy of any sentencing system depends crucially on the existence of settled principles and their consistent application in specific cases. Sentencing, no less than any other kind of legal decision-making, must comply with rule-of-law values. As Henry Hart and Albert Sachs state: **5–02**

> "Adjudication is meaningless unless the decision is reached by some rational

---

1 Jeremy Waldron, *Thoughtfulness and the Rule of Law* (Harvard University Press, 2023), 3.

2 Pierre Schlag, "Rules and Standards" (1985) 33 UCLA Law Review 379; Russell D Covey, "Rules, standards, sentencing, and the nature of law" (2016) 104 California LR 447. See also Larry Alexander, "Introduction to the Symposium on the Rationality of Rule-Following" (2005) 42 San Diego LR 53 at 54 ("rules achieve their superior ability to provide guidance by being blunt instruments, over and under-inclusive relative to the background moral goals they are meant to achieve"), and Frederick Shauer, "Rules, defeasibility, and the psychology of exceptions" in Lorand Bartels and Federica Paddeu (eds), *Exceptions in International Law* (Oxford University Press, 2020), Chap 4 (recognising that because rules are general, they may produce wrong or suboptimal outcomes when applied to particular facts).

> process... [and] if a decision is to be rational, it must be based upon some rule, principle or standard."[3]

5–03 This statement reflects the controlling precept for most judicial decision-making, and it is widely acknowledged as such. Adjudication is a reasoned process that involves identifying the relevant rules or principles and applying them impartially and consistently.[4] Yet, in the past at least, the application of this doctrinal approach to sentencing might have met with some resistance. Judges and lawyers remained attached to the idea of sentencing as a practical exercise informed by shared, though largely intuitive, notions of what the appropriate penalty for a given offence should be.[5] However, this policy of extreme pragmatism is gradually yielding to a general acceptance that sentencing, like any other kind of adjudication, should involve the consistent application of relevant rules and principles to the material facts.

5–04 Adherence to general principles is not universally accepted as a prerequisite for morally good decision-making. Moral philosophers who address this topic divide broadly into generalists and particularists. Generalists believe that morality is best understood in terms of adherence to fixed moral principles (eg, one should honour one's promises, one should not lie). Specific actions should then be evaluated according to their compatibility with the governing principles. Particularists, on the other hand, hold that good decision-making calls for a clear and honest appraisal of the particular facts, and that unrelenting adherence to pre-ordained principles, however well-intended these may have been, can lead to morally wrong decisions.[6] As explained by Ira Singer:

> "Virtuous moral agents need sensitive and accurate moral perception of particular situations, not knowledge of rigid, inflexible moral principles. Observations or intuitions of this sort are at the root of *particularism* in moral philosophy."[7]

5–05 This tension between generalism and particularism has clear resonance in sentencing. In fact, the traditional common law approach to sentencing

---

[3] Henry Hart and Albert Sachs, *The Legal Process: Basic Problems in the Making and Application of Law*. This work was prepared for publication in 1958 and was widely available in photocopied form for decades before eventually being published by Foundation Press in 1994.

[4] Philip Bobbitt, *Constitutional Fate: Theory of the Constitution* (Oxford University Press, 1982), 41.

[5] Frederick Schauer, *Playing by the Rules: A Philosophical Examination of Rule-Based Decision-Making in Law and Life* (Clarendon Press, 1991), 11 (saying that sentencing was traditionally a field of "legal decision-making that only with difficulty can be characterised as rule-based").

[6] Michael Ridge and Sean McKeever, "Moral particularism and moral generalism" in *Stanford Encyclopedia of Philosophy* (Winter 2020 edition) at <https://plato.stanford.edu> accessed 1 November 2024.

[7] Ira Singer, review of Sean McKeever and Michael Ridge, *Principled Ethics: Generalism as a Regulative Ideal* (Oxford University Press, 2006) in (2011) 42 *Metaphilosophy* 170 at 171.

amounted to particularism writ large. The orthodoxy was that, subject to the very limited constraint imposed by the statutory maximum sentence, a judge should select a penalty which, in his or her estimation, fairly reflected all the circumstances of the case. More recently, there has been a move to generalism, as reflected in the greater willingness of appeal courts to articulate, develop and apply general principles. There is merit in both approaches, and the enduring challenge is to harmonise the two. One problem with adherence to principles is that it may not always be immediately apparent which principle should govern the resolution of a given question, and the application of different principles may produce conflicting answers. Doubtless, many different principles can apply to a sentencing decision, and they may well pull in opposite directions. For instance, in a case of manslaughter committed by a young person with no previous convictions, having brought a knife to the scene of the killing will be an aggravating factor while the offender's youth and previous good character will mitigate. The essence of the judicial sentencing exercise therefore is to identify the applicable principles and to balance their relevance and impact in light of the established facts. Further, and as noted earlier, principles by their nature do not demand any specific outcome, but rather point in the direction of a morally defensible outcome.

The principles described in this chapter are essentially distributive in the **5–06** sense that they indicate, if only within broad parameters, the kind and amount of punishment appropriate for specific offences and offenders. We begin with proportionality which is the overarching distributive principle to which all others are subordinate. Having proportionality as the dominant principle ensures commensurability between the gravity of the offending conduct and the deserved penalty although, as we shall see, proportionality, as understood in Ireland, also requires that an offender's personal circumstances be taken into account. Much of the remainder of the chapter is devoted to aggravating and mitigating factors, some of which are relevant to the assessment of culpability while others relate solely to the offender's circumstances as they exist at the time of sentence. Certain other issues connected with the just distribution of punishment, such as the use of concurrent and consecutive sentences, and the sentencing of co-offenders, are discussed towards the end of the chapter.

1. Proportionality

Every sentence, unless mandatory, must be proportionate to the gravity of **5–07** the offence and the personal circumstances of the offender. This principle, though of common law origin, has gradually been elevated in Ireland to the status of a constitutional imperative. That development may be traced back to *State (Healy) v Donoghue*[8] where Henchy J said that certain key provisions of the Constitution had the combined effect of guaranteeing,

[8] [1976] IR 325 at 353.

amongst other things, that every convicted person receive "a sentence appropriate to his degree of guilt and his relevant personal circumstances." The Supreme Court's earlier decision in *Deaton v Attorney General and Revenue Commissioners,*[9] discussed in Chap 4, may also be interpreted as having endorsed proportionate sentencing as a constitutional value. At the outset, however, it should be noted that there are two separate streams of proportionality jurisprudence. One of these relates to proportionality as a sub-constitutional principle designed to operate as a fairness-based constraint.[10] Proportionality doctrine in this sense may be traced back to 19th century Prussian law but it is now well established in national and international law.[11] In the realm of constitutional law, for example, it provides a means of reconciling competing legitimate objectives. A constitution may guarantee a right to free speech, though subject to certain limitations in the interests of public order, the prevention of harm to others and so forth. The legislature may wish to introduce a law banning all forms of hate speech, defamation or some other kind of expression it deems socially harmful. If called upon to determine the constitutionality of such a law, a court will probably apply a proportionality test in order to ascertain if the legislature, in adopting this measure, can claim to be advancing a legitimate social goal and, assuming that it can, if the measure entrenches any more than strictly necessary on the fundamental right, free speech in this case, that is at stake.[12]

5–08 In a sentencing context, proportionality also acts as a restraining, fairness-enhancing principle, but it has longer and different historical roots, extending back to classical and even biblical times.[13] Thus, we find the Roman statesman, lawyer and philosopher Cicero (106-43 BC) advising:

> "We should take care also that the punishment shall not be out of proportion to the offence, and that some shall not be chastised for the same fault for which others are not even called to account. In administering punishment, it is above all necessary to allow no trace of anger. For if anyone proceeds in a passion to inflict punishment, he shall never observe that happy mean which lies between excess and defect... and it is to be desired that they who

---

9 [1963] IR 170. See observations of Supreme Court in *Gilligan v Ireland* [2013] IESC 45; [2013] 2 IR 745; [2014] 1 ILRM 153.

10 E Thomas Sullivan and Richard S Frase, *Proportionality Principles in American Law: Controlling Excessive Government Actions* (Oxford University Press, 2008); DM Beatty, *The Ultimate Rule of Law* (Oxford University Press, 2004); George Letsas, "Proportionality as fittingness: The moral dimension of proportionality" (2018) 71(1) *Current Legal Problems* 53.

11 Moshe Cohen-Eliya and Iddo Porat, "American balancing and German proportionality: The historical origins" (2010) 8 *International Journal of Constitutional Law* 263.

12 *R v Oakes* [1986] 1 SCR 103; *Heaney v Ireland* [1994] 3 IR 593; *Bank Mellat v HM Treasury* [2014] AC 700, para 20.

13 Reference is sometime made to Deuteronomy 25.2: "if the guilty man deserves to be beaten, the judge shall cause him to lie down and be beaten in his presence with a number of stripes in proportion to his offence".

> administer the government should be like the laws, which are led to inflict punishment not by wrath but by justice."[14]

Cicero, like other classical and later scholastic authors, clearly believed that the infliction of punishment, even by duly authorised officials, should never be motivated by anger or revenge. Centuries later, Hugo Grotius (1583-1645), regarded as the founder of modern international law, argued that "it is contrary to Nature for one man to be pleased and satisfied with the Pain or Trouble he brings upon another".[15] In our own time, some of the highest courts in the common law world have likewise held that sentencing must never amount to an exercise in vengeance. The Canadian Supreme Court has contrasted vengeance, which it described as "an uncalibrated act of harm upon another, frequently motivated by emotion and anger, as a reprisal for harm inflicted upon oneself" with retribution (which, for present purposes, may be equated with proportionality) which requires "an objective, reasoned and measured determination of an appropriate punishment which properly reflects the *moral culpability* of the offender".[16] The court said that retribution, unlike vengeance, incorporates a principle of restraint. **5–09**

The notion of proportionate punishment is reflected in the Magna Carta (1215) which guaranteed that a free man "shall not be amerced [fined] for a small fault, but after the manner of his fault, and for a great fault after the greatness thereof, saving to him his contenement".[17] The concluding words are taken to mean that offenders should not be fined so heavily as to deprive them of their livelihoods.[18] The English Bill of Rights (1689) provided that "excessive bail ought not to be required, nor excessive fines imposed; nor cruel and unusual punishments inflicted". This was adopted after the accession of William and Mary and was intended to curb the excesses in which some English judges, notably Chief Justice Jeffreys, had indulged during the reign of King James II.[19] The language of the English Bill of Rights was repeated in the Virginia Declaration of Rights (1776) and later in the Eighth Amendment to the United States Constitution ("Excessive bail shall not be required, nor excessive fines imposed, nor cruel and unusual punishments inflicted").[20] Proportionate punishment **5–10**

---

14 Cicero, *De Officiis* (On Duties), translated by Walter Miller, Loeb Classical Texts (Harvard University Press, 1913), 1.89.

15 Hugo Grotius, *The Rights of War and Peace*, edited by Richard Tuck (Liberty Fund, 2005) 960.

16 *R v M (CA)* [1996] 1 SCR 500, para 80. Emphasis in original. See also *People (DPP) v M* [1994] 3 IR 306 at 316 (Denham J), and Chap 3 above on the differences between retribution and revenge.

17 "Amercement" is defined as a "monetary penalty, exacted from one who had fallen into the King's mercy because of an offence": John Hudson, *The Formation of the English Common Law*, 2nd ed, (Routledge, 2018), 207.

18 William Blackstone, *Commentaries on the Laws of England*, Book 4, edited by Ruth Paley (Oxford University Press, 2016), 244-245. See also *Timbs v Indiana* 586 US 146 (2019).

19 Blackstone, note 18 above.

20 The history of the Eighth Amendment has been considered in several US

was also advocated by leading 18th century thinkers including Beccaria and William Eden who, in his pioneering treatise on criminal law, wrote:

> "The punishment should be proportionate to the flagitiousness of the crime; but the flagitiousness of the crime diminishes in proportion to the facility with which it may be committed."[21]

5–11 Significantly also, *R v Wilkes*,[22] a seminal case on consecutive prison sentences decided in 1770, Lord Wilmot, delivering the unanimous decision of the House of Lords, referred to the "first principle of distributive justice, which commands all judges to inflict that punishment, and that punishment only, which they think commensurate to the specific crime before them". He also said:

> "The punishment must be proportional to the specific offence contained in the record, upon which judgment is then to be pronounced; and must be neither longer nor shorter, wider or narrower, than that specific offence deserves."

5–12 By the beginning of the present century, many countries had adopted proportionality as their overarching distributive principle of sentencing, even if they did so by different legal means. The Canadian Criminal Code (s 718.1), for example, provides that the fundamental principle of sentencing is that a penalty "must be proportionate to the gravity of the offence and the degree of responsibility of the offender". This provision was inserted in the Code in 1996 but proportionality had been a central tenet of Canadian sentencing long before that.[23] In Australia, proportionality has been judicially adopted as the dominant principle.[24] The guidelines developed by the Sentencing Council of England and Wales also implicitly endorse proportionality. The generic guideline on offence seriousness provides that a court is required to pass a sentence that is commensurate with the seriousness of the offence[25] and, in accordance with the Sentencing Act 2020 (s 63), seriousness is to be measured by reference to both culpability and any harm the offence caused, was intended to cause or might foreseeably have caused. In Ireland, proportionality first took root as a common law principle but, as already

---

Supreme Court judgments including *Ingraham v Wright* 430 US 651 (1977); *Browning-Ferris Industries v Kelco Disposal* 492 US 257 (1989); *Solem v Helm* 463 US 277 (1983); *Harmelin v Michigan* 501 US 957 (1991).

21 William Eden, *Principles of Penal Law* (London, 1771), 8. See Anthony J Draper, "William Eden and leniency in punishment" (2001) 22(1) *History of Political Thought* 106. Eden served as Chief Secretary in Ireland from 1780 to 1782. He also wrote on prison reform and his work influenced prison reform in Ireland in the late 18th century. See Oliver MacDonagh, *The Inspector General: Sir Jeremiah Fitzpatrick and the Politics of Social Reform, 1783 to 1802* (Croom Helm,1981).

22 (1770) How St Tr 1075; (1768) 98 ER 327.

23 *R v Ipeelee* [2012] 1 SCR 433, para 36.

24 *Veen v The Queen (No 2)* (1988) 164 CLR 465 at 473; *Hoare v The Queen* (1989) 167 CLR 348 at 354.

25 Sentencing Guidelines Council, *Overarching Principles: Seriousness. Guideline* (2004).

noted, it has gradually been elevated to a constitutional imperative, at least in all cases where a court has discretion as to sentence.[26] It appears that where a mandatory penalty is constitutionally challenged, as occurred with the mandatory life sentence for murder, the test to be applied is whether there is a *reasonable*, as opposed to a proportionate, relationship between the penalty and the offence.[27]

Proportionality in sentencing has been described as "a precept of justice".[28] Its moral worth resides primarily in the firm link it establishes between punishment and blameworthiness.[29] The harm caused by an offence is undoubtedly another important factor, and so too is the more forward-looking, utilitarian consideration of crime prevention. Ireland's proportionality principle is sufficiently flexible to accommodate these and other factors, but the primary determinant of punishment must be the offender's moral blameworthiness. Adherence to a proportionality standard also enhances the legitimacy of the sentencing process. A system that routinely over-punishes offenders or treats them purely instrumentally will struggle to retain public confidence.[30] To quote again from William Eden while advocating penal reform in the late eighteenth century: **5–13**

> "Excessive correction counteracts the very intention of the law by drawing from the multitude a greater degree of compassion for the sufferer than of indignation for the offence."[31]

The advantage of prioritising proportionality in modern sentencing systems was well summarised by the Canadian Supreme Court in *R v Ipeelee*: **5–14**

> "Proportionality is the *sine qua non* of a just sanction. First, the principle ensures that a sentence reflects the gravity of the offence. This is closely tied to the objective of denunciation. It promotes justice for victims and ensures public confidence in the justice system.... Second, the principle of proportionality ensures that a sentence does not exceed what is appropriate, given the moral blameworthiness of the offender. In this sense, the principle serves a limiting or restraining function and ensures justice for the offender."[32]

---

26 *People (DPP) v M* [1994] 3 IR 306; *Gilligan v Ireland* [2013] IESC 45; [2013] 2 IR 745; [2014] 1 ILRM 153,

27 *Lynch and Whelan v Minister for Justice* [2010] IESC 34 ; [2012] 1 IR 1 (rejecting a challenge to the mandatory life sentence for murder). See discussion in Chap 4 above.

28 *Weems v United States* 217 US 349, 367 (1910).

29 *R v Martineau* [1990] 2 SCR 633 at 645; *R v M (CA)* [1996] 1 SCR 500, para 40.

30 Neal Kumar Katyal, "Deterrence's difficulty" (1997) 95 Michigan LR 2385, 2450-2451.

31 William Eden, quoted in Michael Ignatieff, *A Just Measure of Pain: The Penitentiary in the Industrial Revolution 1750-1850* (Columbia University Press, 1978), 73.

32 [2012] 1 SCR 433, para 37.

5–15 Adherence to proportionality therefore serves the instrumental purposes of appropriately denouncing the crime and acknowledging the harm suffered by the victim as well as the more intrinsic or normative purpose of pointing to a penal response that fairly reflects the offender's moral blameworthiness. Another instrumental value, as identified by Beccaria, Bentham and George Stigler, is that if crimes of unequal gravity are punishable with the same penalty, there will be no meaningful deterrent against committing the more serious of these crimes.[33]

5–16 Proportionality is a useful and morally defensible principle, but it has limited capacity to identify appropriate sentences and curb excessively severe (or unduly lenient) punishment.[34] A perfectly proportionate sentencing scheme could yield draconian penalties if the applicable maximum penalties were inordinately high. Absolute as well as proportionate limits are necessary for a moderate sentencing system.[35] Some measure of agreement may be possible as to where a specific offence should be located on the relevant penalty scale, but the resulting sentence will depend on the upper limit of the scale. An offence located halfway up a scale of zero to 30 years' imprisonment will merit a headline sentence of 15 years, whereas it would merit five years if the scale extended only to 10 years. The authors of the revised Model Penal Code sentencing provisions, as always, sum up the problem very well:

> "There are no tools in law or philosophy that can render proportionality doctrine an exact science. Indeed, different communities, and different jurisdictions, may be expected to arrive at divergent judgments about the ranges of punitive severity that will be deemed proportionate in specific cases, or across classes of cases. Short of constitutional limitations on cruel or unusual sentences, which are generally quite distant, prudential – or "sub-constitutional" – proportionality limitations in a democratic society are best derived through cooperative and collective assessments of community sentiment."[36]

---

33 Cesare Beccaria, *On Crimes and Punishments*, edited by Richard Bellamy and translated by Richard Davies (Cambridge University Press, 1995), 21; Jeremy Bentham, *An Introduction to the Principles of Morals and Legislation*, edited by JH Burns and HLA Hart (Athlone Press, 1970), 168; George J Stigler, "The optimum enforcement of laws" (1970) 78 *Journal of Political Economy* 526. See also Tracey Meares, Neal Katyal and Dan M Kahan, "Updating the study of punishment" (2004) 56 Stanford LR 1171.

34 For a thoughtful analysis of this issue, see Nicola Lacey and Hanna Pickard, "The chimera of proportionality: Institutionalising limits on punishment in contemporary social and political systems" (2015) 78 Modern LR 216. See also Jacob Bronsther, "The limits of retributivism" (2021) 24 *New Criminal Law Review* 301 , and Pamela S. Karlan, "'Pricking the lines': The due process clause, punitive damages and criminal punishment" (2004) 88 Minnesota LR 880, 882, observing that the Eighth Amendment cases decided by the United States Supreme Court show that "proportionality is both an inherently alluring and an inevitably unsatisfactory measure of constitutionality".

35 Alan H Goldman, "The paradox of punishment" (1979) 9 *Philosophy & Public Affairs* 42, 51.

36 Model Penal Code: Sentencing (Revised Final Draft, 2017), comment on §1.02(2). See also Christopher Lewis, "Risk-based sentencing and the principles of

This is an inevitable feature of ordinal proportionality, and it illustrates the importance of coherence and moderation in specifying maximum sentences which, as noted in Chap 1, is exclusively a legislative function. Cardinal proportionality, if taken seriously, may be of some assistance in this regard, as it would ensure that the scale of permissible punishment, even for the most serious offences, was kept within reasonable bounds and that maximum sentences were carefully graded according to the comparative seriousness of the offences to which they apply though the difficulties in establishing the comparative seriousness of disparate offences should not be underestimated. **5–17**

Another limitation of proportionality is that it cannot realistically claim to identify the precise or correct penalty for a specific offence. As with limiting retributivism, the best it can do is indicate a range of appropriate punishment, having regard to the statutory maximum sentence.[37] For most offences, therefore, a variety of sentencing outcomes will be justifiable and that, in turn, gives rise to the equality problem discussed previously in connection with limiting retributivism.[38] The broader the range, the greater the risk of unwarranted disparity in the treatment of similarly situated offenders convicted of similar offences. The best solution to the problem, as suggested in the earlier discussion of limiting retributivism, is to supplement the fundamental principle of proportionality with more detailed guidance on locating specific offences within the appropriate range. This might consist of formal guidelines or judicially elaborated principles specifying the factors that determine where an offence should be located within the range. **5–18**

Constructing a Proportionate Sentence

Proportionate sentencing, as understood in Ireland, demands careful consideration of two separate issues: the gravity of the offence and the personal circumstances of the offender.[39] A question therefore arises as to how a court should go about constructing a sentence that duly reflects all the relevant factors. More precisely, the question is whether a court should be obliged to identify an initial presumptive sentence based on the gravity of the offence before making any adjustments for relevant personal circumstances. This has been a contentious issue in Australia **5–19**

punishment" (2022) 112 *Journal of Criminal Law and Criminology* 213, 242, and Paul H Robinson, "Empirical desert" in Paul H Robinson, Stephen P Garvey and Kimberly Kessler Ferzan (eds), *Criminal Law Conversations* (Oxford University Press, 2009), Chap 2.

[37] Limiting retributivism is discussed in Chap 3 above. See also Kevin Reitz, "Sentencing" in James Q Wilson and Joan Petersilia (eds), *Crime and Public Policy* (Oxford University Press, 2011), 472.

[38] Chap 3 above.

[39] The same holds true in other jurisdictions. See Richard S Frase, "Excessive prison sentences, punishment goals, and the Eighth Amendment: 'Proportionality' relative to what?" (2005) 89 Minnesota LR 571, 590 (blameworthiness is assessed by reference to the harm caused or threatened by the offence and the offender's degree of culpability).

where some courts prefer the two-step or structured approach while others favour instinctive synthesis, a term that seems to have originated in *R v Williscroft*[40] where the Supreme Court of Victoria said that "every sentence represents an instinctive synthesis of all the various aspects involved in the punitive process". The matter eventually came to a head in *R v Markarian*[41] where a majority of the High Court firmly endorsed instinctive synthesis as the preferred sentencing methodology. McHugh J, one of the majority, described the difference between the two approaches as follows:

> "By two-tier sentencing, I mean the method of sentencing by which a judge first determines a sentence by reference to the "objective circumstances" of the case. This is the first tier of the process. The judge then increases or reduces this hypothetical sentence incrementally or decrementally by reference to other factors, usually, but not always, personal to the accused. This is the second tier. By instinctive synthesis I mean the method of sentencing by which the judge identifies all the factors that are relevant to the sentence, discusses their significance and then makes a value judgment as to what is the appropriate sentence given all the factors of the case. Only at the end of the process does the judge determine the sentence."[42]

5–20 In *R v Barbaro*,[43] decided in 2014, a plurality of the High Court reaffirmed its commitment to its instinctive synthesis, saying:

> "Sentencing an offender is not, and cannot be understood as, some exercise in addition or subtraction. A sentencing judge must reach a single sentence for each offence and must do so by balancing many different and conflicting features. The sentence cannot, and should not, be broken down into some set of component parts."

5–21 Instinctive synthesis commands very little academic support,[44] but within a decade of being delivered, *Markarian* had been cited more than 1,000 times thereby becoming "the most influential decision on the appropriate sentencing methodology to be utilised by Australian courts at both the primary and appellate stages".[45]

5–22 The Irish Court of Appeal is clearly familiar with this Australian jurisprudence, but it has decisively rejected the instinctive synthesis

---

40 [1975] VR 292 at 300.

41 [2005] HCA 25; (2005) 228 CLR 357.

42 [2005] HCA 25; (2005) 228 CLR 357, para 51.

43 (2014) 253 CLR 58, para 34.

44 See, for example, Mirko Bagaric, "Sentencing: From vagueness to arbitrariness: The need to abolish the stain that is instinctive synthesis" (2015) 38 Univ New South Wales LJ 76; Terry Hewton, "Instinctive synthesis, structured reasoning, and punishment guidelines: Judicial discretion in the modern sentencing process" (2010) 31 Adelaide LR 79.

45 Arie Freiberg, *Fox and Freiberg's Sentencing: State and Federal Law in Victoria*, 3rd edn (Thomson Reuters, 2014), 230. That book has a very useful analysis of the two methodologies at pp 228-233. See also Grant Hammond, "Sentencing: Intuitive synthesis or structured discretion" [2007] New Zealand LR 211.

approach. In *People (DPP) v Molloy*,[46] the court, having noted the majority decision in *Markarian*, said:

> "We have instead favoured the staged approach because it seems to us that it is likely to best focus judges at first instance on the overriding criterion of ensuring that sentences are proportionate both to the gravity of the offence and the circumstances of the offender, and in particular that the sentence *"to be imposed is not the appropriate sentence for the crime, but the appropriate sentence for the crime because it has been committed by that accused"* – see *The People (DPP) v McCormack* [2000] 4 IR 356. In addition, it has the advantage of producing better reasoned sentencing judgments, that better explain to the interested parties why a particular sentence was imposed and which are also more readily amenable to review at appellate level. Finally, we are not persuaded by the arguments against staged sentencing, namely that they do not allow sufficient individualisation of sentences, that this methodology tends to give rise to more punitive sentences, that sentencing discretion is in some way corralled or restricted if a staged approach is adopted, and that the process is in a way illusory because judicial intuition has to be applied in any event at each stage."[47]

People (DPP) v Flynn[48] is the seminal decision of the present Court of Appeal on this matter, although there had previously been Supreme Court and Court of Criminal Appeal decisions to the same effect.[49] Essentially, a court must first identify an appropriate sentence (known nowadays in Ireland as the headline sentence) by reference to the gravity of the offence of conviction, and then make appropriate adjustments to reflect the offender's relevant personal circumstances as they exist at the time of sentence. The process was described particularly clearly by the Court of Appeal in *People (DPP) v Byrne:* **5–23**

> "As we have repeatedly emphasised in numerous judgments, the exercise of sentencing generally involves a two-stage process. The first stage involves assessing the gravity of the offence, with reference to culpability (including aggravating factors tending to increase culpability and mitigating factors tending to reduce culpability), and the harm done, and determining where on the scale of available penalties the offence should be located before account is taken of any mitigating factors not already taken into account as bearing on culpability. In this way the sentencing judge determines on a headline sentence in the first instance.
>
> The second stage involves discounting from the headline sentence arrived at in the first stage for any mitigating factors not already taken into account, such as a plea, previous good character, age, remorse, cooperation, restitution, a good work record, adversities in the accused's person's life and life history, public service or positive contributions to society, good works, efforts at rehabilitation and any other relevant circumstances capable

46 [2018] IECA 37.

47 [2018] IECA 37, para 20.

48 [2015] IECA 290.

49 Notably, *People (DPP) v M* [1994] 3 IR 306 and *People (DPP) v Farrell* [2010] IECCA 116.

of going to mitigation. In this way the Court endeavours to arrive at a just and proportionate ultimate sentence."[50]

5–24 It proceeded to say that in some cases there will be a subsidiary issue as to whether a prison sentence should be suspended. If the Court of Appeal cannot discern a trial judge's rationale for imposing the sentence, having regard to the relevant principles, it may not find it possible to uphold the sentence even though there may have been perfectly good, but unarticulated, reasons for imposing it.[51] In particular, where there are significant mitigating factors, the failure to indicate a headline sentence makes it difficult for an appeal court to determine if due credit was given for those factors.[52] While insisting that this structured approach and, in particular, the initial setting of a headline sentence, is the best and most desirable practice, the Court of Appeal has stressed that a failure to abide by it will not, inevitably at least, amount to an error of principle.[53] Even if the final sentence resulted from some sort of instinctive synthesis applied by the trial judge, it may still be upheld if it appears to be correct and there is no obvious error of principle. Personal circumstances are more likely to be mitigating than aggravating, and any credit due for them must be applied to the headline sentence as opposed to the maximum sentence.[54] In an exceptionally serious case, the maximum sentence may also be the headline sentence. Even a defendant who pleads guilty may be given the maximum sentence if, in the words of the Criminal Justice Act 1999 (s 29(2)), there are "exceptional circumstances relating to the offence".[55] In fact, as a matter of common law, the circumstances of the offender, especially his or her previous record, may also justify imposing the maximum sentence, even when it is life imprisonment.[56] Normally, however, the headline sentence will be located at some point below the maximum.

5–25 As noted in Chap 1, maximum sentences both confer and limit judicial discretion. A court has discretion, to be exercised in a principled manner, to impose any sentence up to the prescribed maximum, but never beyond it, for any one offence. Proportionate penalties must be determined by reference to the maximum which is reserved for the most serious instances of the relevant offence. Less serious cases must be located at appropriate points further down the scale in order to identify a headline sentence. Due regard must always be had to changes in statutory maxima because

---

50 [2017] IECA 97, paras 26 and 27. See also *People (DPP) v Schaufler* [2020] IECA 299, para 34; *People (DPP) v Molloy* [2021] IESC 44; [2021] 2 ILRM 278, para 16.

51 *People (DPP) v Flynn* [2015] IECA 290, para 18.

52 *People (DPP) v Lynch* [2018] IECA 1.

53 *People (DPP) v Flynn* [2015] IECA 290; *People (DPP) v Molloy* [2018] IECA 37; *People (DPP) v Joyce* [2021] IECA 124; *People (DPP) v Howlin* [2022] IECA 150; *People (DPP) v H (S)* [2023] IECA 206, para 51.

54 *People (DPP) v M* [1994] 3 IR 306 at 315.

55 *People (DPP) v McC (R)* [2008] 2 IR 92. See also *People (DPP) v M (J)* [2020] IECA 285 and *People (DPP) v Coyle and Howard* [2022] IECA 114 in both of which the maximum sentence was held to be the appropriate headline sentence.

56 *People (DPP) v Duffy* [2009] IECCA 20; [2009] 2 IR 395.

these represent the current legislative (and, by implication, community) assessment of the gravity of the offences in question. Subject to the constitutional principle that an increased maximum sentence should never be applied retroactively,[57] courts must respect the legislature's prerogative by appropriately adjusting penalties for offences committed after the increase took effect. As the English Court of Appeal said in *R v Richardson*:

> "Statutory changes in sentencing levels are constant. In recent years, maximum sentences have been increased (for example, drug related offences) or reduced (for example, theft). In general, changes like these provide clear indications to sentencing courts of the seriousness with which the criminal conduct addressed by the changes is viewed by contemporary society. In our parliamentary democracy, sentencing courts should not and do not ignore the results of the legislative process, and as a matter of constitutional principle, reflecting the careful balance between the separation of powers and judicial independence, and an appropriate interface between the judiciary and the legislature, judges are required to take such legislative changes into account when deciding the appropriate sentence in each individual case, or where guidance is being offered to sentencing courts, in the formulation of the guidance."[58]

The court went on to say that the primary object of an increased maximum is to address the most serious instances of the relevant offence which may henceforth attract sentences higher than the previous maximum. But suitable adjustments should also be made for offences further down the scale of gravity. The same applies, *mutatis mutandis*, if, as very seldom happens, a maximum sentence is reduced. In that event, however, there is a view, supported by the case law of the European Court of Human Rights, that an offender should be given the benefit of the lower maximum even if the offence was committed while a higher maximum applied.[59] **5–26**

Harm

Under the first limb of the proportionality principle, a court must try to evaluate, separately at first, both harm and culpability.[60] These are the twin ingredients of offence gravity which, in turn, determines the headline sentence. Harm in this context means the harm caused or risked by the offence. In some instances, the offending conduct will have resulted in tangible harm, such as personal injury to a victim, theft or damage to property. In others, the conduct, while not intrinsically harmful, may have created a risk of future harm. This holds true of most possession offences.[61] A person who possesses drugs or firearms is not, by that conduct alone, causing any immediate harm. But such conduct is still criminalised **5–27**

---

57 *Enright v Ireland* [2003] 2 IR 321; [2004] 1 ILRM 103. See Chap 4 above.

58 [2006] EWCA Crim 3186; [2007] 2 Cr App R (S) 36, para 4. See also *R v Soto and Waite* [2023] EWCA Crim 55; [2023] 2 Cr App R (S) 19.

59 *Scoppola v Italy (No 2)* (2010) 51 EHRR 12; *R v Docherty* [2017] 1 WLR 181; [2017] 1 Cr App R (S) 31, discussed in Chap 4 above.

60 *People (DPP) v McD (J)* [2021] IECA 31, para 53.

61 Markus Dirk Dubber, "Policing possession: The War on Crime and the end of criminal law" (2001) 91 *Journal of Criminal Law and Criminology* 829.

because of the harm that would result if the drugs were distributed to others or the firearms used to inflict serious, perhaps fatal, injuries.[62]

5–28 Certain fraud, corruption and deception offences are so defined as not to require proof of any tangible resulting harm. For example, the offence of active corruption under s 5(1) of the Criminal Justice (Corruption Offences) Act 2018 is committed by a person who corruptly offers or gives a gift, consideration or advantage to another as an inducement to, or reward for, that other doing an act in relation to his or her office, employment or business. The giving or acceptance of the bribe need not harm anyone in particular. A person who bribes an official in order to get a contract may well have submitted the best tender in any event, which means that the unsuccessful bidders did not suffer any loss or harm.[63] Likewise, under the Criminal Justice (Engagement of Children in Criminal Activity) Act 2024, an adult who compels, directs or invites a child to engage in criminal activity is guilty of an offence irrespective of whether the child ever engages in that activity or intends to do so. The same holds true of some conduct amounting to deception under s 6 of the Criminal Justice (Theft and Fraud Offences) Act 2001. Conduct of this nature is not always *entirely* harmless. Rather the harm element is more remote than in 'classic' crimes such as assault, theft or robbery which almost invariably cause clear and immediate harm. Typically, the main objective of these newer offences is to counteract or reduce the risk of actual harm occurring.

5–29 Some would argue that remoteness of harm should reduce the intrinsic gravity of an offence. Others go so far as to say that remoteness should remove the relevant conduct entirely from the realm of the criminal law. In practice, remoteness seldom makes a great deal of difference, whether in relation to the setting of maximum sentences or the penalties imposed in specific cases. Some non-consummate offences, such as possession of drugs for sale or supply, carry maximum sentences as high as life imprisonment.[64] Remoteness remains nonetheless a relevant sentencing factor. Where conduct is outlawed because it poses a risk of future harm, a sentencing court must have regard to both the proximity and nature of the apprehended harm. Proximity for this purpose includes the likelihood of materialisation as well as the temporal distance between the conduct constituting the offence and the harm it may cause. Possession of drugs for sale or supply, for example, attracts heavy penalties because of the serious nature of the harm that will almost certainly result from the distribution of drugs within the community.[65] Experience shows that this harm is most likely to materialise even if the temporal question of when

---

[62] *People (DPP) v Sarsfield* [2019] IECA 260.

[63] Jeremy Horder, "Bribery as a form of criminal wrongdoing" (2011) 127 LQR 37. See also David Ormerod, "The Fraud Act 2006 – Criminalising lying?" [2007] Crim LR 193.

[64] For an enlightening discussion of non-consummate offences, see Douglas Husak, *The Philosophy of Criminal Law: Selected Essays* (Oxford University Press, 2010), Chap 5.

[65] *People (DPP) v Sarsfield* [2019] IECA 260.

the distribution and consumption will occur cannot be precisely answered. The same principle applies to all non-consummate offences. The harm element must be assessed by reference to the potential of the offending conduct to cause loss, injury or suffering to individuals (identifiable or otherwise), to the community at large or the body politic.

Inchoate offences are punishable for much the same reason. A person who attempts to commit a crime may act with a high level of culpability while causing little or no harm. But the attempt has nonetheless created a risk of harm and, for sentencing purposes, a court must have regard to the seriousness of the harm that would have resulted if the attempt had been successful. The unsuccessful pickpocket will therefore be treated more leniently than someone convicted of attempted murder. Similar considerations apply at the sentencing of conspiracy and incitement offences. The degree of risk created by conspiracy is often said to be heightened by the involvement of several participants, as conspiracy by definition consists of an agreement by two or more persons to engage in illegal activity. Obviously, the nature of the planned activity, and the harm it might cause, is another key factor in assessing seriousness. **5–30**

Harm assessment is particularly difficult where the essential gravamen of an offence resides in a person's intention to cause some future harm. We generally accept that people should not be punished solely for their thoughts, however dangerous or repugnant those thoughts may be.[66] Leading authors, including Blackstone, Stephen and Hart, have written eloquently about the injustice and futility of attempting to criminalise private thought.[67] The Treason Act 1351, still in force in the United Kingdom, might seem to be an exception because it makes it an offence to "compass or imagine the death of our Lord the King". However, it later refers to the need for an "open deed" and this has been judicially held to apply to all species of treason.[68] Yet, we are apt to forget how often criminal courts must determine what a defendant was thinking at a specific moment in the past. This holds true of the many serious offences that are so defined as to require intention as to outcome or knowledge as to circumstances. But in most such cases there will be an external act from which intention or knowledge may, with some degree of confidence, be inferred. Harm is sometimes defined, as in the English Sentencing Act **5–31**

---

66 Alan Brudner, *Punishment and Freedom: A Liberal Theory of Penal Justice* (Oxford University Press, 2009), 108; Gabriel S Mendlow, "Why is it wrong to punish thought?" (2018) 127 Yale LJ 2342.

67 Blackstone, note 18 above, 20 ("a fixed design or will to do an unlawful act is almost as heinous as the commission of it, yet, as no temporal tribunal can search the heart, or fathom the intentions of the mind, otherwise than as they are demonstrated by outward actions, it therefore cannot punish for what it cannot know"). See also James Fitzjames Stephen, *A History of the Criminal Law of England,* Vol 2 (Macmillan,1883), 78, and HLA Hart, *Punishment and Responsibility: Essays in the Philosophy of Law,* 2nd ed (Oxford University Press, 2008), 127.

68 Courtney S Kenny, *Outlines of the Criminal Law,* 15th ed by G Godfrey Phillips (Cambridge University Press, 146), 306-308.

2020 (s 63), to include *intended* harm as well as harm actually caused or reasonably foreseen. Yet, what the offender intended would logically seem relevant to culpability only. In some cases no harm may have been either caused or risked, despite the offender's clear harmful intention. In so-called 'paedophile hunter' cases, for example, offenders will have been communicating with persons they believe to be children and who they intend to sexually exploit once they meet in person. In fact, however, they are communicating with adult decoys, so there was never a child at risk of being harmed. The criminalisation of such conduct might perhaps be rationalised by treating the offender as someone who is creating a risk of harm to children generally, as there is always the possibility that he will enter into contact with an actual child.

5–32 Where actual harm has been caused, it may be immediate and short-term (as in the case of a minor theft, for example) or it may be more enduring because of its physical, psychological or material impact. In the latter event, a court must always exercise care when determining the extent to which problems or difficulties experienced by a victim can properly be attributed to the conduct for which the offender is being sentenced.[69] Some of those difficulties may derive from a previous experience or pre-existing condition. The offender's conduct may well have exacerbated an existing physical or psychological condition, and the offender can obviously be held accountable for that. Offenders must take their victims as they find them. But particular care is needed where there is evidence of a pre-existing condition, whatever its cause, and in such a case it is preferable to have professional evidence as to the impact of the current offence on the victim.

5–33 Conversely, the harm caused by an offence may extend well beyond the injury inflicted on the immediate victim. An offence, by virtue of its nature or how it was committed, may instil fear, anxiety and/or a sense of insecurity among the wider community or some section of that community. A residential burglary or, worse still, a spate of such burglaries committed against persons living alone or in remote and sparsely populated areas victimises not only those whose homes were invaded, but others living in similar circumstances who are left in fear of having a similar experience.[70] Some may feel constrained to alter their living arrangements by, for example, moving to a place where they can feel more secure. Similar considerations apply where individuals have been victimised, typically by assault, because of their race, skin colour, sexual orientation or some similar characteristic. Others in the locality who share that characteristic will naturally be fearful of being victimised in the same way.[71] To give yet another example, theft from a charity by

---

[69] *People (DPP) v C (D)* [2015] IECA 256. See also *R v PRP* [2024] EWCA Crim 1150, para 58 ("The law has recognised that psychiatric harm can be apportioned between cases").

[70] *People (DPP) v Casey and Casey* [2018] IECA 121; [2018] 2 IR 337.

[71] *People (DPP) v Lyons* [2014] IECCA 27, para 40 (attack by stranger on woman walking home at night may instil fear in other women in similar circumstances).

a trustee or employee causes harm not only to the organisation but to those who are intended to benefit from its activities. Donors may become reluctant to make financial contributions once the theft or misuse of the charity's funds becomes publicly known. Collateral harms of this nature may properly be considered at sentencing. Obviously, the full extent of the collateral harm will sometimes remain a matter of speculation, in which case a court must exercise caution in determining its permissible impact on sentence. Otherwise, it may properly do so to some degree.

Culpability

Culpability is accepted as having two meanings in criminal law. It may refer to the state of mind, commonly known as the *mens rea* or mental element, with which a defendant must have acted to be held liable for an offence. Nowadays, the required mental element is usually intention, knowledge, recklessness or (more rarely) negligence, depending on the offence.[72] But culpability, in a wider sense, can also refer to moral blameworthiness, and it is in this sense that it is primarily relevant to sentence. Blameworthiness at this point becomes scalar in nature.[73] It is no longer a question of being either blameworthy or not; rather it is question of *how* blameworthy. Conviction for a criminal offence, unless it is one of strict or absolute liability, entails a finding or admission that the defendant acted with whatever mental state the law has prescribed. The binary nature of the guilty-finding process does not allow for nuanced verdicts. The tribunal of fact, be it a judge or jury, may find the accused guilty or not guilty, but it may not return a verdict of 'a bit guilty'. A jury may, in certain circumstances, return an alternative verdict. A person tried for possessing stolen property may instead be convicted of theft, but that alternative verdict still involves a finding that the person acted with the mental state required for theft.[74] Sentencing permits, and indeed requires, a more subtle evaluation of the convicted person's culpability in the broader sense of moral blameworthiness. As Benjamin Ewing writes: **5–34**

> "Indeed, the most obvious and intuitive reason for the criminal law to leave space for aggravation and mitigation at sentencing is to enable punishments to track more fine grained judgments of defendants' moral culpability than would otherwise be possible. Aggravation and mitigation enable us to maintain simple definitions of crimes and high thresholds for affirmative defences to them while still tailoring a defendant's punishment to subtler considerations such as, for instance, coercive pressure a defendant faced that fell below the law's threshold for the excuse of duress."[75]

---

[72] As phrased in the American Model Penal Code (1962), the mental states are purpose, knowledge, recklessness and negligence.

[73] Dana Kay Nelkin, "Difficulty and degrees of moral praiseworthiness and blameworthiness" (2016) 50 *Noûs* 356.

[74] Criminal Justice (Theft and Fraud Offences) Act 2001, s 55.

[75] Benjamin Ewing, "Mitigating Factors: A Typology" in Larry Alexander and Kimberly Kessler Ferzan (eds), *The Palgrave Handbook of Applied Ethics and the Criminal Law* (Palgrave Macmillan, 2019), Chap 18 at 425-426.

5–35 Culpability in the narrow sense remains relevant for sentences purposes. A person who deliberately sets out to cause a certain harmful result is more blameworthy than one who causes the same result through recklessness or negligence.[76] In *R v Martineau*,[77] Lamer CJ of the Canadian Supreme Court quoted with approval HLA Hart's assertion that "causing harm intentionally must be punished more severely than causing the same harm unintentionally".[78] More commonly, however, assessment of culpability at sentencing involves a consideration of factors that reduce (or perhaps heighten) blameworthiness, despite the offender having acted with the legally required mental element. In practice, this involves the identification and evaluation of mitigating and aggravating factors, as described later in this chapter.

5–36 Some argue that criminal culpability should be evaluated by reference to the offender's reasons for acting and their response to those reasons, rather than according to the traditional forms of mens rea such as intention and recklessness.[79] An act may be intentional in the legal sense but its moral quality may vary greatly depending on the agent's reasons for performing it. To adapt a scenario described by Peter Strawson, sometimes seen as a progenitor of this reasons-responsiveness concept of culpability, A may intentionally shove B causing B some harm, but A may have done this (1) to protect B from suffering some greater harm; (2) with the sole purpose of inflicting an injury on B or (3) just to get B out of the way and not caring if B suffered any injury as a result.[80] In each scenario, A's action is intentional, but the reason in (1) obviously reflects a lower level of culpability (if any) than is present in either (2) or (3). Sentencing provides an opportunity to engage in more fine-grained moral evaluations of this nature, something that cannot ordinarily be done at the earlier stage of the trial when criminal liability is being determined. A key factor for this purpose at sentencing is the extent to which the offender's conduct revealed a blameworthy disregard for the safety, welfare or interests of others.[81]

---

76 In *People (DPP) v Byrne* [2018] IECA 120, para 63 (and elsewhere), the Court of Appeal noted that, in terms of "intrinsic moral culpability", the offending conduct was intentional rather than reckless or negligent, and aggravated by a degree of premeditation. See also *People (DPP) v Owens* [2024] IECA 109, para 19. Likewise, in *Tison v Arizona* 481 US 137, 156 (1987), the United States Supreme Court said: "Deeply ingrained in our legal tradition is the idea that the more purposeful is the criminal conduct, the more serious is the offence, and, therefore, the more severely it ought to be punished".

77 [1990] 2 SCR 633 at 645.

78 Hart, note 67 above, at 162.

79 Gregory Antill, "Fitting the Model Penal Code into a reasons-responsiveness picture of culpability" (2022) 131 Yale LJ 1346.

80 Peter Strawson, "Freedom and resentment" (1962) 48 *Proceedings of the British Academy* 187.

81 Larry Alexander, "Insufficient concern; A unified conception of criminal culpability" (2000) 88 California LR 931.

Combining Harm and Culpability

Having assessed both the harm caused or risked by the offence and the degree of the offender's moral blameworthiness, a court must then combine the two in order to locate the offence on the overall scale of gravity. This is quintessentially an exercise in judgment, because it is difficult to offer any prescription as to how harm and blameworthiness should be measured, at least with any degree of precision, let alone how they should be combined. The English sentencing guidelines do, however, offer some help in this respect. The Sentencing Council's definitive guidelines for particular offences generally begin by establishing three or four categories in descending levels of gravity, before listing factors that indicate greater harm and others indicating higher culpability. The degree to which those factors are present will determine the category to which the offence is allocated and this in turn will determine both the starting point and the permissible range of sentence. The domestic burglary guidelines, for example, specifies three categories of harm and three levels of culpability. For an offence with both the highest levels of harm and culpability, the starting point is three years' custody, with a range of two to six years. Lower starting points and ranges are specified for less serious cases. This guideline, like all other offence-specific guidelines, also lists factors that increase or reduce seriousness or provide further mitigation.[82] **5–37**

In some instances, harm and culpability will be fairly evenly matched. A person who goes out with the intention of inflicting serious injury on another and succeeds in doing so will have acted with a high level of culpability and caused a significant level of harm. Within any sentencing structure informed by desert or proportionality principles, this offence will rank high on the relevant penalty scale. Cases do arise, however, where the offender has caused very serious harm while acting with a low level of culpability or, conversely, has acted with a high level of culpability while causing little harm. The first of these situations may arise where a person, through careless driving, caused death or serious injury.[83] The harm caused is very grave indeed, but it may have resulted from a momentary lapse of attention or judgment by someone with an unblemished record of careful driving. Attempted murder is a classic illustration of the second situation as the offender will have acted with a very high level of culpability (intention to kill) but, by sheer fluke, may have caused little or no harm. (Some attempted murders do, of course, cause very serious physical and psychological injuries, and this will be reflected in the sentences imposed.[84]) This is one of the enduring dilemmas of sentencing policy: when there is a clear mismatch between harm and **5–38**

[82] Sentencing Council, *Burglary Offences: Revised Guideline,* effective from 1 July 2022.

[83] The current maximum sentence for this offence is two year's imprisonment, a fine of €10,000 or both (Road Traffic (No 2) Act 2011, s 4).

[84] See, for example, *People (DPP) v Daniels* [2014] IESC 64; [2014] 2 IR 813; [2015] 2 ILRM 99; *People (DPP) v Duffy* [2009] IECCA 20; [2009] 2 IR 395; *People (DPP) v Larkin* [2008] IECCA 138; [2009] 2 IR 381.

culpability, which of the two should take precedence? How much, if at all, should results matter where the offender has quite manifestly acted with a very high or a very low level of moral blameworthiness?

5–39 Philosophers have long been alive to this dilemma. Plato in his *Laws*, dating from the 4th century BC, says that "no pity should be wasted on the man who has inflicted a wound with [the intention to kill]; he should be treated with no more respect than the killer, and made to stand trial for murder".[85] However, he seems to suggest that there should be some reduction in punishment out of respect for the luck that spared the offender from succeeding in killing his victim. Adam Smith, writing in the mid-18th century, was also cognisant of the problem:

> "Our resentment against the person who only attempted to do a mischief, is seldom so strong as to bear us out in inflicting the same punishment upon him, which we should have thought due if he had actually done it. In the one case, the joy of our deliverance alleviates our sense of the atrocity of his conduct; in the other, the grief of our misfortune increases it."[86]

5–40 However, Smith immediately goes on to say that, in this respect, there is "an irregularity in the sentiments of all men" because the offender's "demerit" is undoubtedly the same in both cases. Beccaria, on the other hand, writing about the same time as Smith, accepted that attempts should be punished but not as severely as completed crimes, his reasoning being that the lower penalty might cause a would-be offender to have a change of heart and desist from committing the contemplated offence.[87]

5–41 Scholars and theorists have differed sharply on this question, although the more convincing arguments have been advanced by those who accord priority to intention over consequences.[88] Liberal theorists argue that moral blameworthiness should be the predominant, if not the sole, consideration. Offenders should not be punished for consequences which they neither intended nor foresaw. By the same token, they may be punished for consequences which they intended but which did not materialise as planned. Thus, attempted murder should be punished as severely as murder. This is essentially a subjectivist approach. Objectivists

---

[85] Plato, *The Laws*, translated by Trevor J Saunders (Penguin Books, 1975), 397.

[86] Adam Smith, *The Theory of Moral Sentiments*, edited by DD Raphael and AL MacFie (Clarendon Press, 1976), 100.

[87] Beccaria, note 33 above, at 95.

[88] Andrew Ashworth, "Taking the consequences" in Stephen Shute, John Gardner and Jeremy Horder (eds), *Action and Value in Criminal Law* (Clarendon Press, 1993) provides the best discussion of this topic. See also Andrew Ashworth, "Criminal attempts and the role of resulting harm" (1988) 19 Rutgers LJ 725; Joel Feinberg, "Equal punishment for failed attempts" (1995) 37 Arizona LR 117; Sanford H Kadish, "The criminal law and the luck of the draw" (1994) 84 J Crim Law and Criminology 679; Stephen J Schulhofer, "Harm and punishment" (1974) 122 Univ. Pennsylvania LR 1497; MJ Zimmerman, "Taking luck seriously" (2002) 99 *Journal of Philosophy* 553; Ambrose YK Lee, "Blameworthiness and the outcomes of one's actions" (2021) 17 *Criminal Law and Philosophy* 271.

argue that offenders must be prepared to 'take the consequences' which means that punishment may properly reflect the outcome of a person's actions even if that greatly exceeds, or differs from, what was intended. To a considerable extent, they rely on public perceptions and intuition. People are commonly judged according to the outcomes of their actions as opposed to what they intended.[89] However, this is a rather weak justification, especially if one accepts, as most do, that blameworthiness is a prerequisite for the legitimate infliction of punishment. As has been pointed out, just because results may matter in day-to-day activities does not mean that they should matter for the purpose of establishing moral desert.[90]

The liberal approach of prioritising culpability, while not entirely discounting consequences, seems to have won out in Ireland. In *People (DPP) v O'Shea,*[91] the defendant was convicted of careless driving causing the death of a man who was assisting in a roadworks operation. The defendant was 70 years of age at the time, and there was no question of him being under the influence of drink. Nor was there any evidence that the car, which was travelling quite slowly at the time, was defective. He claimed that his vision had been affected by the very strong sunlight at the time, and that he had slowed down for that reason. The case came before the Supreme Court on a point of law relating to the ingredients of the offence and that aspect of the case (although the central one) is immaterial for present purposes. O'Malley J, with whom all other members of the court agreed, addressed the legal point. Clarke J (as he then was) delivered a concurring judgment in which he dealt with sentencing. While accepting that consequences are an appropriate factor to consider at sentencing, he went on to say: **5–42**

> "However, it does seem to me that a primary and central feature of the criminal justice system including, importantly, the proper approach to sentencing must be the identification of the culpability or blameworthiness of the accused. Indeed, in that context, it is worth repeating one aspect of the passage from the judgment of Denham J. in *People (DPP) v O'Dwyer* [2005] 3 IR 134 cited by O'Malley J. in her judgment. Denham J. noted that 'since even a momentary inattention in the driving of a mechanically propelled vehicle can give rise to a wholly unexpected death, the court has always to define the degree of carelessness and therefore culpability of the driving.'
>
> It is, of course, the case that there are a range of factors which must be taken into account in any sentencing process. It has often been said that a proper approach to sentencing involves an analysis both of the criminal act and the circumstances of the convicted person. In respect of the criminal act it is clear that the court cannot disregard the consequences of the criminal act particularly where, and to the extent that, it might reasonably be said that

---

89 Tony Honoré, "Responsibility and luck" (1988) 104 LQR 530 (though dealing with tortious rather than criminal liability). See also Michael S Moore, *Placing Blame: A Theory of Criminal Law* (Clarendon Press, 1997), esp. Chap 5.

90 Larry Alexander and Kimberly Kessler Ferzan, "Results don't matter" in Robinson, Garvey and Kessler Ferzan, note 36 above, Chap 7 at p 150.

91 [2017] IESC 41; [2017] 3 IR 684; [2017] 1 ILRM 149 paras 17-19.

those consequences were at least potentially foreseeable. Those who take risks may often get away with them but when they do not they can hardly be heard to place undue reliance on the fact that others, who took the same risk in the past, may not have been so unlucky.

However, it remains the case, in my view, that a central and important part of that aspect of the sentencing process which requires the sentencing judge to analyse the seriousness of the criminal act must... focus on the degree of culpability.... Speaking for myself I would find it difficult to see how, everything else being equal, a person found guilty of careless driving causing death or serious bodily harm, where the bad driving concerned was at the bottom end of the spectrum encompassed by careless driving, could legitimately receive a custodial sentence at least in the absence of aggravating or other unusual factors."

5–43 O'Malley J and, by extension, the other members of the court expressly agreed with what Clarke J said about sentencing.

5–44 Assault manslaughter remains problematic in this regard. The perpetrator of an assault which causes the victim's death may be convicted of manslaughter despite the absence of an intention to kill or, indeed, foresight that the victim might die as a result of the assault.[92] This problem arises, however, from the definition of the offence as it has evolved at common law. When sentencing for manslaughter committed in these circumstances, a court is entitled to consider and, indeed, prioritise the offender's culpability, having regard to the nature of the assault or other unlawful act and the circumstances in which it was committed. A rather similar problem arises where a person is convicted of assisting a criminal organisation, knowing that its members are planning to commit an offence but not knowing what precisely that offence will be. Should the penalty for assisting be influenced by the nature of the offence that is eventually committed? In *People (DPP) v Aylmer*[93] the defendant's activity consisted of purchasing mobile phones for a criminal organisation which used them in connection with the commission of a murder.[94] The defendant claimed that he thought the phones would be used for drug dealing, and the prosecution conceded that it could not be established beyond a reasonable doubt that the defendant knew he was contributing to a murder. The Court

---

92 See, for example, *R v Mallett* [1972] Crim LR 260 (where a minor assault led to the victim falling, bumping his head against concrete and dying as a result). As the authors of a leading textbook remark: "Such a verdict can be defended only the basis that, if D engages in criminal conduct, he must take responsibility for the consequences of his criminality, whatever those consequences may be. No doubt such reasoning may have its place where D's conduct gives rise to a clear and vivid danger that serious consequences may occur." (AP Simester, JR Spencer, F Stark, GR Sullivan and GJ Virgo, *Simester and Sullivan's Criminal Law: Theory and Doctrine,* 6th ed. (Hart Publishing, 2016), 415. See also *R v Newbury* [1977] AC 500.

93 [2020] IECA 106. See also *People (DPP) v Dowdall* [2023] IECA 182.

94 He was charged with an offence contrary to the Criminal Justice Act 2006, s 72 as substituted by the Criminal Justice Amendment Act 2009, s 9 which carries a maximum sentence of 15 years' imprisonment.

of Appeal correctly identified the essential question as being whether "it is entirely *irrelevant* that a murder was committed (at least in part) by reason of the acts of assistance rendered [by the accused]?"[95] It was also correct to say that a factor may be treated as aggravating for sentencing purposes even though it is not an essential ingredient of the offence to be proved by the prosecution. More troubling, however, is the manner in which the court reasoned that the murder, although unforeseen by the defendant, was an aggravating factor in this case. Having regard to the defendant's claim that he thought the phones would be used for drug dealing, the court held that the sentencing court would have been entitled "to take judicial notice of the fact that murder is one of a range of offences frequently committed by drug trafficking gangs".[96] It was therefore not unreasonable, in the view of the Court of Appeal, to hold that a person who assists such an organisation, as this defendant had done, is taking the risk that a murder may be committed. One may question, first, if this is the kind of fact of which judicial notice may properly be taken and, secondly, if it *is* a fact. Is it factually true to say that murder is *frequently* committed by drug trafficking gangs? The Court of Appeal referred to no empirical or statistical evidence to support this conclusion, beyond referring to "several decades" of experience. On a more positive note, the court accepted that such a conclusion would not be reasonable if the murder had been committed by a gang that was typically engaged in less serious criminal conduct such as petty theft. In that instance, there would be too much of a "disconnect" between the gang's usual activities and the murder to justify treating the murder as an aggravating factor.

Irrelevance of Early Release Provisions

One further dimension of proportionality is that a court, when selecting sentence, should not take account of any remission or other form of early release to which the offender may become entitled if sentenced to imprisonment. There are two reasons for this. First, such release can never be guaranteed. In Ireland, for example, a prison is ordinarily entitled to standard remission of one-quarter (with the possibility of enhanced remission of one-third) of sentence, but such remission can be partly or entirely lost through misbehaviour while in prison. Other forms of release, such as temporary release or parole, are generally at the discretion of the executive or a designated agency such as a parole board.[97] Secondly, there is a separation of powers issue. The courts' function is to impose a sentence that is proportionate to the offence and the offender's personal circumstances. Sentence implementation, including any reduction granted in the time to be served in the case of a custodial sentence, is a matter for the executive branch of government or one of its agencies.[98] 5–45

---

95 [2020] IECA 106, para 38. Emphasis in original.
96 [2006] IECA 106, para 42.
97 Remission and parole are discussed in Chap 14 below.
98 *Hatahet v King* [2024] HCA 23, where this matter is discussed at some length by the High Court of Australia.

Cumulative Proportionality and Collateral Consequences

5–46 The collateral consequences of a conviction and their potential relevance to sentence are discussed in Chap 7. Here, it suffices to note that some of these consequences, such as disqualification from driving, can be punitive (and sometimes highly punitive) in effect, however they are legally characterised. A court may therefore take account of such consequences when determining the primary penalty which will typically consist of a fine and/or a term of imprisonment.

2. Mitigation and Aggravation

5–47 Discretionary sentencing is necessary to counterbalance the binary nature of the verdict. A finding of guilt amounts to a determination that the accused committed the act charged and did so with the mental element (typically intention, recklessness or knowledge) that must be proved to establish liability for the offence in question. What the verdict does *not* indicate is the extent of the accused's moral guilt. That is something to be judicially determined at sentencing. Certain matters that are irrelevant for the purpose of establishing criminal liability may be highly relevant in establishing moral culpability. Motive, as we shall see, is one such matter. Further, the sentence ultimately imposed in most cases is generally lower, often considerably lower, than what would have been appropriate if the sole consideration were the harm caused, threatened or risked by the offence. This is partly because the headline sentence must reflect culpability as well as harm and, for reasons already mentioned, culpability is sometimes low compared to the harm element. The headline sentence may be further reduced because of additional mitigating circumstances arising from the offender's response to the charge, his or her personal circumstances at the time of sentence, previous good character or some combination of such factors.[99] There may also be aggravating factors though most of them will be relevant to the assessment of culpability under the first limb of the proportionality principle. Relevant previous convictions, as we shall see, may be treated as aggravating, most likely as a factor increasing the gravity of the offence, though they might possibly be classified instead as a relevant personal circumstance under the second limb of the proportionality principle. Obviously, they should be considered under one limb only, so as to avoid double counting. A convicted person is always entitled to make a plea in mitigation, or to have one made on their behalf. It is considered a breach of natural justice for a court to impose sentence without affording an opportunity for such a plea to be made or to refuse to listen to a plea that is made.[100] The essential

[99] In *People (DPP) v Lynch* [2018] IECA 1, for example, the headline sentence for a fraud offence was set at five years but ultimately reduced to an effective sentence of one year because of mitigating factors.

[100] *R v Billericay Justices, ex parte Rumsey* [1978] Crim LR 305; *R v Jones* [1980] Crim LR 58; *R v Moss* [2013] UKPC 32; [2013] 1 WLR 3884; *R v Watson* [2023] UKPC 32; [2024] 2 All ER 605.

purpose of such a plea is to ensure that a court is fully aware of any factor favouring the defendant.[101]

What constitutes an aggravating or mitigating factor may depend on prevailing attitudes and social values. Circumstances which, in the past, were treated as mitigating may now be regarded as aggravating, and vice versa. Offences committed in a domestic setting are a case in point. At one time there was a tendency to treat assaults and similar offences committed against family members or intimate partners less seriously than identical offences committed against strangers. Today, courts, legislatures and guideline-setting bodies take the opposite point of view. Under the Domestic Violence Act 2018 the fact that the victim of a violent offence was the offender's spouse or partner must ordinarily be treated as an aggravating circumstance. Arguably the same should apply where the victim is a child, a dependent cohabitant or vulnerable relative of the offender, though a court is always free to increase sentence on this account in appropriate circumstances. The general justification for this policy is that victims of domestic violence are often trapped in an environment dominated by the offender on whom they may also be depending for material, financial and other support. Changing judicial attitudes are reflected in the judgment of the English Court of Appeal in *R v Bowskill*[102] where the defendant was convicted of kidnapping his partner, subjecting her to coercive control and other offences. The victim had suffered serious injuries when she jumped from the van in which she was being held while it was travelling at high speed. The court noted that in 1983, Lord Lane (then Lord Chief Justice) had stated that serious kidnapping offences should normally attract sentences of eight years' imprisonment, or substantially more where there were significant aggravating factors. However, he said that at the other end of the scale were offences that could scarcely be classified as kidnapping at all because they "very often arise as a sequel to family tiffs or lovers' disputes and they seldom require anything more than 18 months' imprisonment, and sometimes a great deal less".[103]The court in *Bowskill* pointedly distanced itself from this observation, saying that language about "family tiffs" and "lovers' disputes" was no longer appropriate. It said that where an offence such as kidnapping occurs in a domestic setting, and especially in the context of an abusive personal relationship, this will be an aggravating and, often, a seriously aggravating factor.[104] The Court of Appeal therefore increased the sentence quite substantially. **5–48**

[101] AJ Ashworth, "Prosecution and procedure in criminal justice" [1979] Crim LR 480, 485. There he quotes from David Napley, *The Technique of Persuasion*, 2nd ed (Sweet and Maxwell, 1975), 140 who claimed that the purpose of a plea in mitigation is to assist the court "to arrive at what seems to be the least punishment consistent with justice".

[102] [2022] EWCA 1358; [2022] 4 WLR 98; [2023] 1 Cr App R (S) 12 See comment by Paramjit Ahluwalia in [2024] Crim LR 153.

[103] *R v Spence and Thomas* (1983) 5 Cr App R (S) 413, 416.

[104] [2022] EWCA 1358; [2022] 4 WLR 98; [2023] 1 Cr App R (S) 12, para 20.

5–49 Sentencing statutes and guidelines often list more aggravating than mitigating factors although, in the case of statutes at least, this is often due primarily to political pressure or expediency.[105] Even in Ireland which has neither a general sentencing statute nor, as of now, formal sentencing guidelines, statutory aggravating factors have been introduced on a piecemeal basis. Examples include committing an offence while on bail[106] and committing a violent offence against one's present or former spouse or partner.[107] Normally, as in both these instances, a court may disregard this requirement in exceptional circumstances.

Motive May Aggravate or Mitigate

5–50 It has been said that there is scarcely a more settled principle of criminal law than that motive is irrelevant in establishing criminal responsibility.[108] Being well motivated does not prevent a person from forming the intention to commit a prohibited act. At sentencing, however, motive can become an important factor, though it probably aggravates more often than it mitigates.[109] Having a financial motive is an aggravating factor for some offences. The same holds true of offences committed out of hatred for some characteristic of the victim such as race, ethic origin or religion (unless that is already a definitional element of the offence). Criminal damage offences, especially in the form of arson, are all the more serious when motivated by a grudge or ill-will towards the owner, possessor or occupier. The motive may not necessarily lead to greater harm (though it could), but it can certainly increase culpability.[110] A person who commits an offence with a good motive, misguided or otherwise, is generally granted some leniency. Mercy killing is the classic example. The defendant may have believed that the fatal act was to the benefit of a seriously or terminally ill person. In fact, that person may have asked for assistance in ending their life. Obviously if the conviction is for murder, the mandatory life sentence must be imposed, but if it is for attempted murder or manslaughter, the defendant's motive may be a mitigating factor. In certain fraud cases, the offender will have been motivated by a desire to save their business from collapsing and to protect employees. This may reduce the offender's

---

105 Julian V Roberts, "Aggravating and mitigating factors at sentencing: Towards greater consistency of application" [2008] Crim LR 264 (noting that in several jurisdictions more formal guidance is provided with respect to aggravating than to mitigating factors).

106 Criminal Justice Act 1984, s 11(4) inserted by Bail Act 1997, s 10.

107 Domestic Violence Act 2018, s 40.

108 Jerome Hall, *General Principles of Criminal Law*, 2nd ed (Bobbs-Merrill, 1960), 88. For normative arguments against this principle, see Douglas Husak, "Motive and criminal liability" (1989) 8 *Criminal Justice Ethics* 3; Whitley RP Kaufman, "Motive, intention, and morality in the criminal law" (2003) 28 *Criminal Justice Review* 317.

109 Carissa Byrne-Hessick, "Motive's role in criminal punishment" (2006) 80 Southern California LR 89.

110 *People (DPP) v Doody* [2024] IECA 70, para 36; *People (DPP) v Goodchild* [2022] IECA 232; *People (DPP) v Shannon* [2023] IECA 325.

culpability, but probably only to a slight degree where the victim of the fraud has suffered a heavy loss.

Motive has become an important issue in the sentencing of environmental campaigners whose protests amounted to criminal conduct such as causing a public nuisance.[111] The participants may regard their activities as an exercise in civil disobedience and claim that they are justified in violating the law in order to advance a more important goal – in this instance to save the planet.[112] Some climate protesters, when prosecuted, have sought to rely on a defence of necessity and this has apparently been accepted by a few first instance courts in continental Europe and the United States.[113] However, the predominant (though certainly not unanimous) view is that protest activities that amount to criminal offences should be prosecuted and those convicted should be duly censured, though perhaps allowed some mitigation to reflect their motivation.[114] (There is always, of course, the possibility that a jury may acquit even in the face of compelling evidence.)[115] **5–51**

Some such protests, such as those staged by 'Just Stop Oil', have caused very considerable disruption. In *R v Trowland and Decker*,[116] for example, the appellants had scaled a bridge over the M25 carriageway in England which forced the police to close it for about 40 hours. It was estimated that more than half a million vehicles were delayed which resulted in many of their occupants missing important appointments and family **5–52**

---

[111] In England and Wales, the Police, Crime, Sentencing and Courts Act 2022 (s 78) creates an offence of intentionally or recklessly causing a public nuisance. This was introduced to deal with non-violent protest offending and it has already been used for this purpose. See, for example, *R v Trowland and Decker* [2023] EWCA Crim 919; [2024] 1 WLR 1164; [2024] 1 Cr App R (S) 13.

[112] Mathis Bönte, *Ziviler Ungehorsam in Klimanotstand* (2021) 22 *Onlinezeitschrift für Höchstrichterlich Reschtsprechung zum Strafrecht* 1671. As to whether there is always a moral duty to obey the law, there are distinguished authorities on both sides of the argument. In Plato's *Crito*, Socrates, as he awaits execution following an unjust trial, is adamant that one must always do what the law commands. On the other hand, Henry Thoreau argued (in 1849): "The only obligation which I have a right to assume is to do at any time what I think is right" (Thoreau, *Walden, Civil Disobedience and Other Writings* (LG Classics, 2016), 278). Likewise, Martin Luther King in his "Letter from Birmingham Jail" (1963) wrote: "One has not only a legal but a moral responsibility to obey just laws. Conversely, one has a moral responsibility to disobey unjust laws."

[113] Ivó Coca-Vila, "Punishing the last citizens? On the climate necessity defence" *Res Publica* (2023) <https://doi.org/10.1007/s11158-023-09642-y> accessed 23 February 2024; Michael Brogan, "The necessity defence and anthropogenic global warming protests: The times they are a-changin'" (2021) 46 Alternative LJ 268 (advocating a reconceptualised defence of necessity); Damien Gayle, Matthew Taylor and Ajit Niranjan, "Human rights experts warn against European crackdown on climate protestors" *The Guardian*, 12 November 2023.

[114] Coca-Vila, note 113 above; Christopher Bennett and Kimberley Brownlee, "Punishment and civil disobedience" in William E Scheuerman (ed), *The Cambridge Companion to Civil Disobedience* (University Press, 2021), Chap 11.

[115] JR Spencer, "Jury equity in a changing climate?" (2023) 9 *Archbold Review* 8.

[116] [2023] EWCA Crim 919; [2024] 1 WLR 1164; [2024] 1 Cr App R (S) 13.

occasions. The economic impact, in terms of lost business and so forth, was estimated at close to £1 million. The appellants, who were repeat protest offenders, were unanimously convicted by a jury of causing a public nuisance, and were sentenced to three years' imprisonment in one case and two years and seven months in the other. In dismissing their appeals against sentence, the Court of Appeal held that motive, where relevant, should be treated as a matter going to culpability, rather than as personal mitigation.[117] The court carefully confined the circumstances in which a good motive might be treated as mitigating, saying:

> "It is no part of the judicial function to evaluate (or comment on) the validity or merit of the cause(s) in support of which a protest is made. However, a conscientious motive on the part of protesters may be a relevant consideration, in particular where the offender is a law-abiding citizen apart from their protest activities. In such cases, a lesser sanction may be appropriate; a sense of proportion on the part of the offender in avoiding excessive damage or inconvenience may be matched by a relatively benign approach to sentencing.... However, the more disproportionate or extreme the action taken by the protester, the less obvious is the justification for reduced culpability or more lenient sentencing."[118]

5–53 As it happens, some limited mitigation had been accorded to the appellants in this case to acknowledge that their activities were a matter of conscience. One justification for treating this kind of motive as reducing culpability is that unlike, say, the person who commits a crime for personal gain or to inflict injury on others, the protester has (or may have) a more altruistic purpose, and may genuinely believe that their activities, however disruptive, are ultimately in the public interest.

3. Mitigation

5–54 A jurisdiction with a strong commitment to individualised sentencing is more likely than others to recognise a wide range of mitigating factors relating to the offender as well as to the offence. However, there is no list, official or otherwise, of mitigating (or aggravating) factors.[119] One empirical study of 100 speeches on mitigation in London courts in 1976-1977 identified 229 different mitigating factors.[120] More recent studies have made similar findings.[121] However, the identified factors often overlap to a considerable extent and sometimes apparently conflict. In some cases,

---

117 See comment on *Trowland and Decker* by Lyndon Harris at [2023] Crim LR 800.

118 [2023] EWCA Crim 919; [2024] 1 WLR 1164; [2024] 1 Cr App R (S) 13, para 50.

119 *R v Patel* [2021] EWCA Crim 231; [2021] 1 WLR 2997; [2021] 2 Cr App R (S) 47, para 38.

120 Joanna Shapland, *Between Conviction and Sentence: The Process of Mitigation* (Routledge & Kegan Paul, 1981).

121 See, for example, Jessica Jacobson and Mike Hough, *Mitigation: The Role of Personal Factors in Sentencing* (Prison Reform Trust, 2007), and the same authors, "Personal mitigation: An empirical analysis in England and Wales" in Julian V Roberts (ed), *Mitigation and Aggravation at Sentencing* (Cambridge University Press, 2011), Chap 8.

for example, leniency was sought because the offender had a supportive family while in others it was sought because the offender had no family or social support. This, however, may not be as contradictory as it seems. Grounds of mitigation are inevitably case-specific, and any matter that can credibly be treated as reducing the offender's culpability in committing the offence or otherwise relevant to sentence may be considered. Defence lawyers are entitled and obliged to bring all relevant factors to the court's attention. Hence in the example just given, the absence of family support might partly explain why the offender had engaged in criminal activity (and thus become relevant to culpability) whereas, in a different case, an offender with a supportive family network may be less likely to engage in further crime.

American studies of mitigation have included extensive surveys of trial judges, analyses of formal legal sources (statutes and law reports) and surveys of public attitudes to mitigation.[122] In 2010, the United States Sentencing Commission surveyed 942 federal judges in order to identify the factors to which they attributed most weight. Health-related factors, and especially mental illness and diminished capacity, were considered by most judges (79 per cent) to be ordinarily relevant. Next came voluntary disclosure of the offence and exceptional efforts at restitution followed by previous good character, employment record, prior good works, age, family ties and responsibilities.[123] Carissa Byrne Hessick and Douglas Berman undertook a major nationwide study of legal sources to identify what they described as consensus factors – those most commonly treated as mitigating.[124] They identified six: (1) imperfect defence such as provocation or duress; (2) offender's role in the offence being less than others or somewhat reduced through the conduct of others including the victim; (3) offender had compensated the victim; (4) harm caused by offender was less than that inflicted by others who committed the same offence; (5) offender's culpability less than would ordinarily be the case; and (6) reduced likelihood of recidivism. They identified two others for which there was also substantial support: (1) acceptance of responsibility or remorse, and (2) hardship to the offender or their family. Paul Robinson and colleagues conducted a study of public attitudes towards what they described as extra-legal punishment factors such as hardship, remorse and forgiveness.[125] One of their findings, also reflected in judicial surveys, was **5–55**

---

[122] For an account of these studies, see John B Meixner, "Modern sentencing mitigation" (2022) 116 Northwestern Univ LR 1395.

[123] Unites States Sentencing Commission, *Results of Survey of United States District Judges January 2010 through March 2010.*

[124] Carissa Byrne Hessick and Douglas A Berman, "Towards a theory of mitigation" (2016) 96 Boston Univ LR 161.

[125] Paul H Robinson, Sean E Jackowitz and Daniel Bartels, "Extralegal punishment factors: A study of forgiveness, hardship, good deeds, apology, remorse and other such discretionary factors in assessing criminal punishment" (2012) 65 Vanderbilt LR 737. See also Meixner, note 122 above, reporting on results of analysis of sentencing memoranda filed by defence counsel in federal felony cases.

that the extent to which people regarded a factor as mitigating depended greatly on the nature of the offence.

5–56 Ultimately, the range of recognised mitigating factors is determined by the priority accorded to the various moral justifications of state punishment. A narrow retributivist policy which treats the gravity of the offence as the sole determinant of sentence would exclude any factors unrelated to the harm caused or risked by the offence or the offender's culpability in committing it. Therefore, any post-offence conduct, however commendable or meritorious, becomes entirely irrelevant. It may deserve some reward or recognition but, according to this version of retributivism, not in the form of a reduced sentence. Later repentance or remorse would likewise be discounted. However, there is another, more inclusive form of retributivism, sometimes known as retributarianism, which holds that punishment should be determined not solely by the nature and circumstances of the offence, but partly also by the offender's' general character as it appears at the time of sentence.[126] A court should therefore take a holistic view of the offender, giving due consideration to their life history, including post-offence conduct which might involve efforts at reform, expressions of remorse or repentance and matters of that nature. In fact, as often happens in the field of criminal justice, this policy was being applied by courts long before it was given a name – retributariansim in this instance. Character and life history are well established as relevant sentencing considerations in Irish law, as reflected in the constitutional requirement that a sentence must be proportionate, not only to the offence but also to the offender's personal circumstances. The range of potentially mitigating factors is therefore quite extensive.

4. Mitigating Factors Relevant to Assessment of Gravity

5–57 Proportionality requires that the penalty ultimately chosen should reflect both the gravity of the offence and the offender's personal circumstances. This, in turn, requires a two-stage approach to sentence selection, described earlier. Mitigation may become relevant at either the first stage when the gravity of the offence is being evaluated, or at the second when the offender's present circumstances are being considered. There may well be, and often are, grounds for mitigation at both stages. We shall begin by considering what might mitigate the gravity of an offence, bearing in mind that gravity, in turn, has two ingredients: harm and culpability. The relevant mitigating factors at this point are more likely to affect culpability, in the sense of reducing the offender's moral blameworthiness. Youth, mental disability, provocation and coercion can certainly have this effect. The first two of these factors will be considered in more detail in Chap 9. Suffice it to say for now that children and persons with intellectual

[126] Hadar Dancig-Rosenberg and Netanel Dagan, "Retributarianism: A new individualization of punishment" (2019) 13 *Criminal Law and Philosophy* 129 ; Paul H Robinson and Muhammad Sarahne, "After the crime: Rewarding offenders' positive post-offence conduct" (2021) 24 *New Criminal Review* 367.

difficulties are generally regarded as less blameworthy for their harmful acts than fully competent adults.[127] Provocation often becomes an issue in assault cases. It is not a defence to an assault charge in the sense of relieving a defendant of liability (even in a murder case a successful plea of provocation merely reduces the verdict to one of manslaughter), but it may be highly relevant at sentence. A person who assaults another in response to provocation is less blameworthy than an unprovoked assailant. How much less blameworthy will depend on the circumstances. The same holds true of duress which rarely succeeds as a full defence (although it is potentially available in respect of all offences except murder) but it may reduce an offender's moral blameworthiness and thereby justify some mitigation of sentence.[128] Persons found in possession of drugs or firearms may claim, and sometimes quite credibly, that they were threatened with death or serious injury, usually by drug dealers to whom they were indebted, unless they stored the contraband in their homes or conveyed it from one place to another. A potential problem in such a case is that the offender may have caused the conditions of their own defence; their predicament arises from their own prior illegal conduct, typically using or distributing controlled drugs.[129] The English Court of Appeal has held that offenders who find themselves in this situation "must realise that that kind of excuse cannot radically affect the sentence to be passed on them", particularly if convicted of violent offences, robbery, home invasion or the like.[130] However, even in such circumstances, it has been prepared to allow some limited mitigation.[131]

Mitigation may also be applied to the harm element of an offence. Irish law does not recognise a *de minimis* defence to criminal liability. The American Model Penal Code, by contrast, recommended that a court should dismiss a prosecution if, having regard to the alleged conduct and the attendant circumstances, it finds that the defendant's conduct did not cause or threaten the prohibited harm "or did so only to an extent too trivial to warrant the condemnation of conviction".[132] This is not to say **5–58**

---

[127] *People (DPP) v R (M)* [2022] IECA 192; *People (DPP) v Donnelly* [2020] IECA 16 (mental health difficulties a relevant factor in assessing culpability).

[128] In *People (DPP) v Sarsfield* [2019] IECA 260 (a drug dealing case), the Court of Appeal said (para 13): "Duress, even at a level falling short of what would provide a defence in law, may still be relevant." It added that a factual basis to support such an assertion is required. On duress as a defence, see *People (DPP) v Gleeson* [2018] IESC 53; [2019] 2 IR 196; [2019] 1 ILRM 1; *Attorney General v Whelan* [1934] IR 518 and *People (DPP) v Dunne* [2016] IESC 24; [2017] 3 IR 1 (confirming that duress is not available as a defence to murder). Having been the victim of a pattern of coercive control may also mitigate where it appears to have contributed to the offending conduct. See Vanessa Bettinson, *Coercive Control as Mitigation at Sentencing* (Sentencing Academy, 2024).

[129] Paul H Robinson, "Causing the conditions of one's own defence: A study in the limits of theory in criminal law doctrine" (1985) 71 Virginia LR 1.

[130] *R v Mullally* [2012] EWCA Crim 687, para 22.

[131] *R v Monaghan* [2020] EWCA Crim 1785; [2021] 1 Cr App R (S) 58. See comment by Lyndon Harris at [2021] Crim LR 605.

[132] Model Penal Code, §2.12(2). See Douglas Husak, "The De Minimis 'Defence'

that *de minimis*, thus understood, is entirely irrelevant under Irish law. The fundamental consideration in deciding whether to prosecute "is whether to do so would be in the public interest".[133] Trivial violations of the criminal law need not therefore be prosecuted. Even when they are, any sentence imposed following conviction may reflect the unusually low level of the harm caused or threatened. To that extent, the low level of harm is treated as mitigating. This would hold true in a theft case where the property stolen was of very little value or an assault case where the 'force' element consisted of nothing more than touching another without their consent.[134] Bear in mind that we are concerned here solely with factors that mitigate gravity, which means that they arise under the first limb of the proportionality principle, and are thus relevant in determining a headline sentence. They bear upon either the harm caused or the offender's culpability or blameworthiness as it existed at the time of the offence. Many other mitigating factors become relevant when the offender's personal circumstances are being assessed under the second limb of the proportionality principle. Some of these are discussed below. First, however, three factors – deprivation, childhood adversity and addiction – that are primarily relevant to culpability call for some consideration.

Deprivation

5–59 The relationship between deprivation and culpability is both complex and highly contested.[135] In a theft case, for example, the defendant may claim to have stolen out of dire need. The general orthodoxy today is that need, however acute, does not excuse the offence but it may extenuate the punishment. There seems to be little support for Thomas Hobbes' contention in *Leviathan* (1651) that "no law can oblige a man to abandon his own preservation".[136] Nonetheless, it has been suggested by at least one contemporary philosopher that severe deprivation caused by a socially unjust political system undermines the state's authority to punish.[137]

to Criminal Liability" in RA Duff and Stuart P Green (eds), *Philosophical Foundations of Criminal Law* (Oxford University Press, 2011), Chap 15.

133 Director of Public Prosecutions, *Guidelines for Prosecutors,* 5th edn (2019), para 4.4.

134 This would not apply where the touching was sexual in nature.

135 The expression 'rotten social background' (RSB) or, more properly, 'severe environmental deprivation' first appeared in *United States v Alexander* 471 F 2d 923 (1973). See David L Bazelon, "The morality of the criminal law" (1976) 49 Southern California LR 385; Richard Delgado, "'Rotten social background': Should the criminal law recognize a defence of severe environmental deprivation?" (1985) 3 *Law and Inequality* 9; Steven Zeidman, "Rotten social background and mass incarceration: Who is a victim?" (2022) 87 Brooklyn LR 1299; Victor Tadros, "Poverty and criminal responsibility" (2009) 43 *Journal of Value Inquiry* 391; Barbara A Hudson, "Beyond proportionate punishment: Difficult cases and the 1991 Criminal Justice Act" (1995) 22 *Crime, Law and Social Change* 59; RA Duff, "'I might be guilty, but you can't try me': Estoppel and other bars to trial" (2003) 1 *Ohio State Journal of Criminal Law* 245 at 258.

136 Thomas Hobbes, *Leviathan,* edited by Noel Malcolm (Oxford University Press, 2012) 468.

137 RA Duff, *Punishment, Communication, and Community* (Oxford University Press,

Others claim that endemic social injustice reduces, without entirely obliterating, the obligation of a victim of that injustice to obey the law and thereby reduces the moral wrongness of their criminal conduct.[138] Most of us would probably be more inclined to agree with Kant that the responsibility of a starving person who steals food is diminished by the fact that it would have taken greater self-restraint for him or her to have resisted the temptation. According to Kant, "the more a man is driven to action by external forces, the less is his responsibility.".[139] This suggests that the thieves, assuming that they steal no more than they really need, may still be held criminally liable but deserves little, if any, punishment. A law that exempted a desperately impoverished person from all criminal liability for theft might be seen as inconsistent with the institution of private property and the personal right to own property, both of which are constitutionally protected in Ireland.[140] Much stronger objections might be made to a law that criminalised homeless persons from sleeping in public places in circumstances where they were homeless through no fault of their own. The United States Court of Appeals for the Ninth Circuit held that anti-camping ordinances, which rendered homeless persons liable to criminal penalties for camping on public property, were unconstitutional unless there were places where those persons can lawfully sleep.[141] However, the Supreme Court, by a majority, reversed this decision, holding that such a law did not violate the Eighth Amendment prohibition of cruel and unusual punishment.[142] The dissenting judgment authored by Sotomayor J (with whom two others joined) is decidedly more convincing in reaching the contrary view.

That there is a strong correlation between deprivation and crime can **5–60** scarcely be doubted, though establishing a causal connection between the two is often difficult. Many offenders, and not just white-collar offenders, come from privileged backgrounds. Most people from impoverished backgrounds never engage in crime or, at least, to no greater extent than others. Then there is the further complication that deprivation may

---

2001), 184 ("someone who... has been unjustly disadvantaged and excluded by the polity whose law it is, is not bound to regard the law as a source of authoritative requirement."). For critical responses, see Matt Matravers, "'Who's still standing?' A comment on Antony Duff's preconditions of criminal liability" (2006) 3 *Journal of Moral Philosophy* 320, and Jules Holroyd, "Punishment and justice" (2010) 36 *Social Theory and Practice* 78.

[138] Jeffrey Reiman, "The moral ambivalence of crime in an unjust society" (2007) 26 *Criminal Justice Ethics* 3. See also Tadros, note 135 above, (arguing that since economic injustice engenders criminogenic conditions, the state may be seen as being complicit in the crimes of the poor).

[139] Immanuel Kant, *Lectures on Ethics*, translated by Louis Infield (Methuen, 1979), 62.

[140] Constitution of Ireland, Arts 43 and 40.3. See Jeremy Waldron, "Why indigence is not a justification" in William C Heffernan and John Kleinig (eds), *From Social Justice to Criminal Justice: Poverty and the Administration of Criminal Law* (Oxford University Press, 2000), Chap 4.

[141] *Johnson v City of Grants Pass* 72 F4d 868 (2023). See also *Martin v City of Boise* 902 F3d 103 (9th Cir, 2018).

[142] *City of Grants Pass v Johnson* 603 US 520 (2024).

be the result of addiction and therefore to some extent self-inflicted. Addiction as a mitigating factor is considered further below. Finally, it must be recalled that crimes by the poor are not always against the rich. Victims may be just as impoverished as the offenders. However, subject to all these qualifications, the fact remains that some crime, especially acquisitive crime, is attributable to deprivation. A question then arises as to why and to what extent evidence of deprivation should mitigate punishment, assuming, contrary to what some might argue, that it should not provide a full or partial defence to criminal liability.[143] Much depends on the animating purpose of punishment. A utilitarian, especially one committed to deterrence or incapacitation, might see social disadvantage as a predictor of further offending and therefore a reason to increase punishment. A retributive approach, on the other hand, being based on the concept of deservedness, can more easily accommodate factors such as social disadvantage in assessing an offender's moral blameworthiness.[144]

5–61 Various justifications have been advanced for treating deprivation as a mitigating factor at sentencing, if not as a partial excuse (though it is seldom clear what a partial excuse might mean in these circumstances). It has been suggested that seriously deprived offenders may suffer from chronic temptation in the sense that if they are to abide by the criminal law, they must deny themselves satisfaction of some of their basic needs.[145] By way of analogy with duress, it may be argued that even persons of reasonable firmness who find themselves in this situation will find it very difficult to resist the temptation to engage in crime. A related argument is that deprived offenders have much stronger incentives than others to break the law, that this reduces their blameworthiness and, consequently, their deserved punishment.[146]

5–62 Canadian, Australian and New Zealand courts have addressed the relevance of social disadvantage more directly than their counterparts elsewhere, mainly because all three countries have large native populations that have historically been severely disadvantaged. Members of those groups tend to be disproportionately represented in the criminal justice system.[147] The Canadian Supreme Court had held that sentencing courts must take judicial notice of factors such as history of displacement, lower

---

143 For good general discussions of the topic, see Benjamin Ewing, "Recent work on punishment and criminogenic disadvantage" (2018) 37 *Law and Philosophy* 29; Stephen J Morse, "Deprivation and desert" in Heffernan and Kleinig, note 140 above.

144 Barbara Hudson, "Mitigation for socially deprived offenders" in Andrew von Hirsch and Andrew Ashworth (eds), *Principled Sentencing: Readings on Theory and Policy*, 2nd ed. (Hart Publishing, 1998), 205.

145 Richard L Lippke, "Chronic temptation, reasonable firmness and the criminal law" (2014) 34 *Oxford Journal of Legal Studies* 75,

146 Christopher Lewis, "Inequality, incentives, criminality, and blame" (2016) 22 *Legal Theory* 153.

147 Kathryn Campbell and Stephanie Wellman, "Addressing the overrepresentation of indigenous people in the criminal justice system" in Carolyn Côté-Lussier, David Moffette and Justin Piché (eds), *Contemporary Criminological Issues:*

educational attainment and higher levels of drug abuse and suicide that are particularly prevalent among aboriginal offenders. This provides the context within which the circumstances of individual cases can properly be evaluated.[148] It should be noted, however, that the Canadian Criminal Code (s 718.2(e)) requires that the circumstances of aboriginal offenders be given special attention at sentencing. However, the Canadian courts adopt a less categorical approach when dealing with other situations in which there is evidence of social disadvantage, whether as a result of systemic racism or some other factor. In those circumstances, they require some evidence of a causal connection between the factor in question and the offending. The social context will be relevant only where it helps to explain the offending or allows for a more accurate assessment of the offender's background, character and prospects.[149] Australian and New Zealand courts adopt a similar individualised approach, preferring to evaluate the possible impact of social disadvantage on a case-by-case basis. In *R v Bugmy*[150] the High Court of Australia rejected the idea of taking judicial notice of the systemic deprivation suffered by aboriginal offenders, saying it would be "antithetical to individualised justice". The New Zealand Supreme Court followed suit in *R v Berkland*,[151] where it concluded:

> "There will always be connections between the different dimensions of an offender's background and their choice to offend, although the nature and strength of those connections will vary. As the cases have said, background factors can be the 'operative' or 'proximate' cause of offending or they can make a less direct 'causative contribution'."
>
> Where it can be established that background was an operative or proximate cause of the offending it is likely to be a potent sentencing factor. Proximate afflictions such as addiction or mental illness may be examples. There may be other background factors that invite similar inferences in particular cases. As we have said, restrictive rules or heuristics that tend to exclude factors at the outset without assessing their potential relevance have no place in the making of factual assessments. They create analytical blind spots.
>
> But requiring operative or proximate cause in every case sets the bar too high. We prefer the *Carr* standard of causative contribution.[152] It captures background factors that are, as we explain below, the more diffuse drivers or the intergenerational sources of offending; factors that would be excluded as insufficiently connected under a stricter causation standard. These contributory factors are important because they can provide rational explanations for why an offender has come to offend. Contributory mental illness can still explain why an offender is living in the chaotic or conflictual circumstances that made the offending more likely. Contributory addiction can help to explain why an offender was drawn into the commercial drug

---

Moving beyond Insecurity and Exclusion (University of Ottawa Press, 2020), Chap 6.

148 *R v Ipeelee* [2012] 1 SCR 433, para 60; *R v Gladue* [1999] 1 SCR 688.

149 *R v Morris* [2021] ONCA 680 (where this topic is analysed in detail).

150 [2013] HCA 37; (2013) 249 CLR 571, para 41.

151 [2022] NZSC 143, paras 107-111. Internal references omitted. See also *R v Postlethwaite* [2023] NZCA 49.

152 Referring to *R v Carr* [2020] NZCA 357.

dealing environment. Contributory deprivation, including that precipitated by historical dispossession and sustained by poor educational and other intergenerational outcomes, can help to explain an offender's limited life options, poor coping skills or other criminogenic circumstances that made the offending more likely. Where these factors do help to explain how the offender came to offend, they will amount to causative contribution and so will be relevant for the purpose of sentencing.

Although causative contribution is a lower standard than operative or proximate cause, it must still be satisfied. There will be a point at which background factors can no longer assist in explaining the offending. For example, the link between historical deprivation and the offending can be severed. To illustrate this, not all Māori still live in circumstances of relative economic, social or cultural deprivation today. For some, the cycle of deprivation has been broken or, at least, much weakened. This too is important to understand, because any mitigatory effects of historical deprivation must be based on explanatory facts, not ethnic assumptions…

The causative contribution of background may also be displaced, in whole or in part, where the offending is particularly serious. Complex and orchestrated offending is likely to involve careful assessment of the risks of detection and therefore increased agency. The contribution of background to offending with this level of agency may therefore be significantly reduced or even negated and other sentencing goals, such as community protection, may become more important. Such assessment will depend very much on the facts, however.

Finally, it is appropriate to acknowledge that background factors will be most meaningful where the potential sentence is at the margin between imprisonment and a communitybased sentence. In commercial drug dealing the latter is more likely to be a prospect for lesser roles and the lower end of the significant role category. But that does not mean background will be irrelevant in relation to more significant roles. Where imprisonment is unavoidable, background factors that contribute causatively to an offender's degree of culpability may still mitigate sentence length."

5–63 This case, like the Canadian and Australian authorities mentioned earlier, may have been decided in a particular demographic context where a significant sub-group is classified as native or aboriginal. But the fundamental ideas, especially as reflected in *Berkland*, are nonetheless transferrable to other jurisdictions where many offenders come from backgrounds where poverty, substance abuse and other social problems are endemic. The notion of causative contribution therefore remains relevant, even if less easily assessed in circumstances where the offenders do not belong to any distinct ethnic or racial group. However, it is their individual life experience rather than their collective identity that should ultimately matter, even if, in some cases, that experience can properly be understood only by reference to broader background and environmental circumstances.

Childhood Adversity

5–64 This factor overlaps to some extent with material deprivation but it can also include parental neglect or abandonment, physical abuse (including sexual abuse), growing up in a household dominated by drug or alcohol addiction or having experienced a variety of care arrangements. Courts are usually willing to treat childhood adversity as mitigating and, while they seldom elaborate on their reasons for doing so, they obviously see it as a factor that reduces culpability. Modern psychological research supports this policy.[153] Cognitive development may be complete by the mid-teens, but psychosocial development often continues to the mid-20s.[154] The latter form of development, which includes, among other things, learning to resist peer pressure, gaining an appreciation of pro-social values and the capacity to evaluate the longer term consequences of one's actions, may be seriously inhibited by various kinds of adversity experienced during childhood and early adulthood.[155] One need not buy into control theory or any of its variants to conclude that weak internal controls and the absence of strong social (and positive) bonds may hamper this kind of development, and leave a person more prone to engage in anti-social conduct, including criminal activity.[156] Given that childhood adversity, which may produce these results, is never the fault of the child or the adult he or she becomes, it can therefore be treated as a mitigating factor at sentencing, at least where there is some evidence suggesting a link between the adversity and the offending conduct. In *People (DPP) v Owens*[157] the Court of Appeal accepted psychological evidence that childhood experience of sexual abuse provided an explanation for a sudden, unprovoked and serious assault perpetrated by the defendant against an unsuspecting victim. It concluded that the prior traumatic experience of sexual abuse had probably triggered the defendant's reaction on the occasion in question, while stressing that the victim was at no fault whatever. Here, a causal link could be established between the commission of the offence and the sexual abuse experienced during childhood. That experience could therefore be treated as a mitigating factor.

Intoxication and Addiction

Intoxication and addiction also pose difficulties. Self-induced intoxication, **5–65**
whether resulting from drink or drugs, does not ordinarily mitigate.[158]

---

[153] See Chap 9, note 33 below. See also Per-Olof H Wikstrom, Kyle Treiber and Gabriela Roman, *Character, Circumstances, and Criminal Careers* (Oxford University Press, 2024) which deals in depth with individual crime trajectories and the relationship between childhood adversity and later involvement in crime.

[154] Discussed further in Chap 9 below.

[155] This seems to have been accepted by the English Court of Appeal in *R v ZA* [2023] EWCA Crim 596; [2023] 2 Cr App R 45, para 52; [2023] Crim LR 617.

[156] On control theory, see Michael Gottfredson and Travis Hirschi (eds), *A General Theory of Crime* (Stanford University Press, 1990); Chester L Britt and Michael R Gottfredson, *Control Theories of Crime and Delinquency* (Transaction Publishers, 2003).

[157] [2024] IECA 109.

[158] *People (DPP) v Murray* [2022] IECA 314, para 59.

Courts have occasionally been prepared to make an exception where intoxication caused a person to act out of character. This might arise where a person who was completely unaccustomed to alcohol, or who had hitherto taken it only in small amounts, was unaware that he or she would act in some transgressive manner when under the influence of drink. Even in these circumstances, the degree of mitigation is likely to be modest, especially if the offence caused significant harm. Intoxication may be an aggravating factor where the offender was well aware that ingesting alcohol or drugs was likely to cause him or her to become violent or to engage in other harmful behaviour. In *People (DPP) v Murphy*[159] where the defendant attacked a taxi driver with a glass bottle in the early hours of morning, the Court of Appeal seems to have treated the defendant's drunken state as an aggravating factor. It would certainly have been justified in doing so as the defendant had numerous previous convictions for violent offences.

5–66 Addiction is a more complex matter, not least because of the varying scientific explanations for its existence.[160] The disease theory identifies similarities between addiction and infectious diseases. The 'garden path' theory developed by Herrenstein and Prelec claims that consuming addictive substances diminishes the satisfaction a person derives from other aspects of life, but the addict fails to notice this or, for some reason, chooses to ignore it.[161] Another influential theory, the visceral account developed by George Loewenstein, treats addiction as a 'drive state' like hunger and thirst. According to Loewenstein, a visceral factor generally has two central premises:

> "First, immediately experienced visceral factors have a disproportionate effect on behaviour and tend to "crowd out" virtually all goals other than that of mitigating the visceral factor. Second, people underestimate the impact on their own behaviour of visceral factors they will experience in the future."[162]

He goes on to say:

> "Like extreme hunger, thirst, pain, anger, sleeplessness, and a wide range of other visceral sensations, drug craving limits the scope for volitional control of behaviour. Once the addict is "hooked," and subject to intermittent craving, the scope for volition narrows to the point where it may not be

159 [2020] IECA 244.

160 It is accepted that the status of being an addict should not of itself be an offence. In the United States, a law that criminalised addiction to narcotics was held to violate the Eighth Amendment prohibition of cruel and unusual punishment; *Robinson v California* 370 US 660 (1962), though the status of that decision could now be in some doubt following the comments of members of the majority in *City of Grants Pass v Johnson* 603 US (2024) (28 June 2024).

161 R Herrnstein and D Prelec, "A Theory of Addiction" in G Loewenstein and J Elster (eds), *Choice Over Time* (Russell Sage Foundation, 1992).

162 George Loewenstein, "A Visceral Account of Addiction" in J Elster and OJ Skog (eds), *Getting Hooked: Rationality and Addiction* (Cambridge University Press, 1999), 235 at 236.

> useful, either theoretically or practically, to view the addict's behaviour as a matter of choice."[163]

The question therefore is whether people should be held responsible, or fully responsible, for behaviour attributable to their addiction. Note that Loewenstein says that it may not be useful to view the addict's behaviour as a matter of choice, "once the addict is 'hooked'". This qualification reflects an important and difficult reality to be confronted in a criminal law context. Almost always, addiction results from a person's own voluntary behaviour by, for example, starting to take drugs. As Gary Watson says in a leading essay on the topic, "addicts are complicit in their own impairment".[164] However, Watson, like others, recognises the pressures created by addiction and acknowledges those pressures as creating "circumstances of duress". According to Gideon Jaffe, the idea is "that addicts lack opportunities the rest of us enjoy in something like the same way as those under duress do".[165] However, Jaffe takes a slightly different view, claiming that **5–67**

> "...addicts are to be excused when they are, not because addiction disables, but because, instead, it is too much to demand that addicts should exercise their ability to comply with the norms that apply to non-addicts."[166]

Fortunately, in the present context, we can avoid the thorny question of whether addiction should ever *excuse* criminal conduct in the sense of providing a complete defence. Ordinarily, it will not, unless the accused can bring him or herself within the ambit of the insanity defence. **5–68**

Courts are nonetheless willing at times to treat drug or alcohol addiction as mitigating largely, one assumes, because it diminishes, without extinguishing, a person's capacity to control their behaviour. As such it reduces culpability. The matter was discussed at some length by the Court of Criminal Appeal in *People (DPP) v Fitzgibbon*[167]where the offence was one of causing serious harm contrary to s 4 of the Non-Fatal Offences Against the Person Act 1997. The court said: **5–69**

> "If people get drunk and commit offences while they are drunk, then they cannot be heard to use their drunkenness as a mitigating factor. However, that is not to say that, in particular, persons who suffer from a persistent problem of addiction or substance abuse should not have, in an appropriate case, that factor taken into account. There is a world of difference between a case in which a person seeks to rely on the fact that they were drunk to provide some partial mitigation for an offence and one where a person who suffers from substance abuse and, in particular, may be seeking to

---

163 Loewenstein, note 162 above,

164 Gary Watson, *Agency and Answerability; Selected Essays* (Oxford University Press, 2004), 319. The relevant chapter was originally published as "Excusing addiction" (1999) 18 *Law and Philosophy* 589

165 Gideon Yaffe, "Lowering the bar for addicts" in Jeffrey Poland and George Graham (eds), *Addiction and Responsibility* (MIT Press, 2011), Chap 5, p 116.

166 Jaffe, note 165 above, at 115.

167 [2014] IECCA 12; [2014] 2 ILRM 116.

take steps to deal with their problem, although not yet successfully, may seek to offer that as part of the general circumstances which ought to be taken into account.... [A] sentencing court is required to consider, as part of the overall circumstances, whether a persistent problem with substance abuse, most particularly if it can be said to stem from a particularly difficult upbringing, can amount to a factor which can weigh significantly in an appropriate sentencing process on the facts of a particular case. This will be so... especially if there are attempts at rehabilitation or, in the view of this court, where the accused was particularly young at the time of the offence and where there may be a realistic prospect of rehabilitation in the future."[168]

5–70 In *People (DPP) v Byrne*[169] the Court of Appeal said that in terms of mitigating factors bearing on culpability, it appeared that the defendant "was possibly acting under a degree of physical compulsion in circumstances where he is chronically addicted to alcohol and drugs and had consumed alcohol and [ecstasy] prior to committing the offence". Likewise, in *People (DPP) v Freeman*[170] the most important mitigating factor identified by the Court of Appeal was the defendant's chemical compulsion to feed their drug habit by whatever means. The impact of drug addiction on criminal responsibility was considered in greater detail by Bennett J in *United States v Hendrickson*[171] where he drew heavily on the scientific literature on the topic. He noted that addiction is defined as "a chronic, relapsing brain disease that is characterised by compulsive drug taking, seeking and use, despite harmful consequences". He said that while in the past addiction was seen as a moral failure, it is now rightly identified as a serious medical condition.[172] While accepting that the initial decision to take drugs is usually voluntary, he accepted that once drug abuse takes over, "a person's ability to exert self-control can become seriously impaired". He concluded:

"The answer, at least in most cases, is that addiction mitigates a defendant's culpability. By physically hijacking the brain, addiction diminishes the addict's capacity to evaluate and control his behaviour. Rather than rationally assessing the costs of their actions, addicts are prone to act impulsively, without adequately weighing future consequences."[173]

However, he also cautioned that addiction will not always mitigate:

"This is not to say, however, that addiction is limitlessly mitigating. For example, addiction may not be mitigating, or may be less mitigating, where

---

168 [2014] IECCA 12; [2014] 2 ILRM 116, paras 9.3 and 9.7.

169 [2018] IECA 120, para 63.

170 [2018] IECA 312, para 45.

171 25 F Supp 3d 1166 (ND Iowa, 2014). In *United States v Freeman* 992 F3d 268 (4th Cir 2021), the United States Court of Appeals acknowledged that "addiction can quickly take over a person's life". It held that a 17-year prison sentence for possessing opioids with intent to distribute was substantively unreasonable, although it was within the applicable guideline range.

172 See also Emily R Murphy, "Paved with good intentions: Sentencing alternatives from neuroscience and the policy of problem solving courts" (2013) 37 *Law and Psychology Review* 83.

173 25 F Supp 3d 1166, 1174 (ND Iowa, 2014).

> there is no nexus between the defendant's addiction and offence; or where the defendant has had numerous opportunities for treatment and has either declined drug treatment or failed to meaningfully attempt to complete drug treatment. Also, there may be some point at which a defendant no longer gets the "benefit" of addiction-based mitigation – like the defendant who, after sentencing, repeatedly violates his or her terms of supervised release by using drugs or alcohol. Addiction could even be aggravating in some situations. Each case must be carefully considered on its own and all of the [relevant statutory] factors must be balanced."[174]

In Ireland, likewise, addiction will mitigate only to a slight degree, if at all, in circumstances where the offender was well aware that the addiction posed a risk of causing him or her to engage in harmful conduct.[175] But in any case, a rehabilitative measure that may help an offender overcome addiction should be seriously considered, as this will ultimately benefit the community as well as the offender. **5–71**

What cannot be denied is the strong correlation between drug use and crime, although the precise nature of the relationship is the subject of some dispute.[176] It is commonly assumed that drug use causes crime, and acquisitive crime in particular, because addicts have to engage in crime to finance their addiction. Others claim that involvement in crime leads to drug use, in the sense that offenders often find themselves inhabiting a world where drug use is rife. A third theory is that there is no direct causal connection between the two but rather that both derive from the same circumstances. In other words, both drug use and criminal offending are explicable by the same underlying factors that may be psychological or environmental (including early life experience of deprivation). There is some support for all three hypotheses. For instance, there is some evidence that existing criminal behaviour escalates with the onset of opiate use.[177] Whatever the true explanation, the odds of offending greatly increase with drug use, and apparently opiate use in particular, except among recreational users.[178] This, in turn, points to the need for detailed research on the history and experience of both drug use and offending among known offenders who are also drug users. Such a body of knowledge is essential for developing effective policies to address drug use and the types of offending with which it is most closely associated. **5–72**

Gambling is a non-substance addictive behaviour. A recent Economic **5–73**

---

[174] 25 F Supp 3d 1166, 1175 (ND Iowa, 2014).

[175] *People (DPP) v Murray* [2022] IECA 314, para 59.

[176] Matthias Pierce et al, "Insights into the link between drug use and criminality: Lifetime offending by criminally active opiate users" (2017) 179 *Drug and Alcohol Dependence* 309; Matthias Pierce et al, "Quantifying crime associated with drug use among a large cohort of sanctioned offenders in England and Wales" (2015) 155 *Drug and Alcohol Dependence* 52; Trevor Bennett, Katy Holloway and David Farrington, "The statistical association between drug misuse and crime: A meta-analysis" (2008) 13 *Aggression and Violent Behaviour* 107.

[177] Karen Hayhurst et al, "Pathways through opiate use and offending: A systematic review" (2017) 39 *International Journal of Drug Policy* 1.

[178] Bennett , Holloway and Farrington, note 176 above.

and Social Research Institute ('ESRI') study has revealed that problem gambling is far more prevalent in Ireland than previously believed, with an estimated 3.3 per cent of the adult population being problem gamblers.[179] The American Psychiatric Association's *Diagnostic and Statistical Manual of Mental Disorders* (DSM-5) now includes gambling among substance-related and addictive disorders.[180] Federal trial courts in the United States have occasionally treated gambling addiction as a significant mitigating factor. At first sight this seems surprising because the federal sentencing guidelines expressly exclude gambling as a reason for downward departure. However, since those guidelines were declared advisory rather than mandatory in *United States v Booker*,[181] courts have been prepared to recognise a gambling addiction as mitigating, in some circumstances at least. Rather predictably, most of the cases have involved frauds, and mostly largescale frauds at that, but evidence of gambling addiction has sometimes led to remarkably lenient sentences, especially by American standards. These include *United States v Dikiara*[182] where a woman who embezzled more than $1 million from her employer was sentenced to 15 months' imprisonment, the court stating that both substance and gambling addictions "diminish the addict's capacity to evaluate and control his or her behaviours". In 2019, a New York property developer, Michael D'Alessio, was sentenced to six years' imprisonment for defrauding investors of $58 million.[183] Here in Ireland, the defendant in *People (DPP) v Hehir*[184] pleaded guilty to stealing more than €300,000 from his employer over a short time span. His addiction to gambling which the trial judge viewed as a "recognised psychological affliction" was treated as a mitigating factor (among others present in the case). He was sentenced to 240 hours community service on one count and suspended two-year sentences on all the others. The Court of Appeal declined to increase the sentence and while it did not directly comment on the gambling addiction, it commended the trial judge's sentencing statement as a model of its kind and one that comprehensively listed all the relevant factors.

---

[179] Diarmuid Ó Ceallaigh et al, *Measures of Problem Gambling, Gambling Behaviour and Perceptions of Gambling in Ireland* (Economic and Social Research Institute, 2023). The authors define problem gambling as "gambling behaviour that is disruptive or damaging for individuals".

[180] Jon E Grant and Samuel R Chamberlain, "Expanding the definition of addiction: DSM-5 v ICD-11" (2016) 21(4) *CNS Spectrums* 300; Marc N Potenza, "Non-substance addictive behaviours in the context of DSM-5" (2014) 39(1) *Addictive Behaviours* 1.

[181] 543 US 220 (2005).

[182] 50 F Supp (3d) 1029 (ED Wisconsin, 2014). On this and similar cases, see Austin W Blum and Jon E Grant, "Behavioural addictions and criminal responsibility" (2017) 45(4) *Journal of the American Academy of Psychiatry and Law* 464.

[183] See Brian A Jacobs, "A good sentencing precedent is hard to find" (2020) 32(3) *Federal Sentencing Reporter* 138. In *United States v Caspersen* (SDNY, 4 November 2016), a four-year sentence was imposed on a gambling addict who defrauded investors of $38 million and misappropriated $8 million from his employer.

[184] [2018] IECA 244.

5. Personal Mitigation

The factors considered under this heading relate primarily to the "personal circumstances of the offender" which constitute the second limb of our proportionality principle. The list of such factors is open-ended, and this holds true in many legal systems. Occasionally, the circumstances of a case will reveal a potential ground for mitigation that has never arisen before, at least in recorded case law. Yet, the overarching moral and constitutional duty of the courts to administer *justice* in every case demands that, notwithstanding the absence of precedent, any such ground be properly considered, and a determination made as to whether there is any reason in law or in principle why it should not be treated as mitigating. Personal mitigation, no matter how strong, will seldom, if ever, exempt a convicted person from all punishment. It may, however, substantially reduce the otherwise deserved penalty and justify a non-custodial sanction even if the offence, judged solely by its objective elements, has crossed the custody threshold. In *R v Foster*,[185] for example, the appellant had been sentenced to 28 months' imprisonment for administering poison with intent to procure her own miscarriage. The English Court of Appeal, while acknowledging the seriousness of the offence, substituted a fully suspended 14-month sentence because the "constellation of exceptionally strong mitigating factors" rendered it a case calling for compassion rather than punishment. In *People (DPP) v Lindsay*[186] what was described as a unique combination of mitigating factors led to a four-year reduction on a headline sentence of 10 years' imprisonment for a s 15A drug offence, with a further two years suspended. **5–74**

Guilty Plea

See Chap 6 below. **5–75**

Assisting Law Enforcement Authorities

A person who assists law enforcement authorities in some material way is entitled to additional credit on that account. A guilty plea, though common in these circumstances, is not a prerequisite for such a reduction. The degree of credit will vary with the circumstances. Occasionally, a person, once questioned about involvement in a crime, will voluntarily furnish the police with evidence that would otherwise prove difficult to obtain or assemble and that will effectively form the prosecution case. Such assistance is often particularly valuable in fraud investigations which can be difficult, complex and time-consuming if suspects are unwilling to co-operate. Those who do co-operate can expect to be rewarded with a **5–76**

---

185 [2023] EWCA Crim 1196; [2024] 1 Cr App R (S) 29, paras 47 to 49. See also *R v Griffin* [2023] EWCA Crim 1111; [2024] 1 Cr App R (S) 24 where a suspended sentence was substituted, again because of exceptionally strong mitigating factors.

186 [2024] IECA 77.

sentence discount, and sometimes a substantial one.[187] A similar principle applies where a defendant supplies information that assists in identifying others who have been engaged in criminal activities, and all the more so where those others are brought to justice as a result (or partly as a result) of the information tendered. In England and Wales, the Sentencing Act 2020 (s 74) provides for a sentence reduction in these circumstances. Ireland has no equivalent statutory provision but certain leading English cases remain useful for identifying the governing principles. At the outset, it is accepted that the justification for treating the provision of information to the police as a mitigating factor is entirely pragmatic. It typically has no bearing on the gravity of the offence of conviction and, while it might conceivably be an indication of remorse, it is more likely to be a strategic decision by an offender intent on securing a reduced sentence.[188] However, it is also widely accepted that "one of the most effective weapons in the hands of the detective is the informer"[189] and a sentence reduction is therefore "a price worth paying to achieve the overwhelming and recurring public interest that major criminals, in particular, should be caught and prosecuted to conviction".[190]

5–77 As to the factors that are relevant in determining the amount of the deserved reduction, it has been said:

> "The extent of the discount will ordinarily depend on the value of the help given and expected to be given. Value is a function of quality and quantity. If the information given is unreliable, vague, lacking in practical utility or already known to the authorities, no identifiable discount may be given or, if given, any discount will be minimal. If the information given is accurate, particularised, useful in practice, and hitherto unknown to the authorities, enabling serious criminal activity to be stopped and serious criminals brought to book, the discount may be substantial. Hence little or no credit will be given for the supply of a mass of information which is worthless or virtually so, but the greater the supply of good quality information the greater in the ordinary way the discount will be. Where, by supplying valuable information to the authorities, a defendant exposes himself or his family to personal jeopardy, it will ordinarily be recognised in the sentence passed. For all these purposes, account will be taken of help given and reasonably expected to be given in the future."[191]

5–78 Significant credit is due in those cases where the information has produced convictions for serious crimes or prevented their commission, or has led

---

187 *People (DPP) v Begley* [2013] IECCA 32; [2013] 2 IR 188.

188 *R v Royle* [2023] EWCA Crim 1311; [2024] 1 WLR 2853; [2024] 1 Cr App R (S) 41 para 9; *R v P and Blackburn* [2007] EWCA Crim 2290; [2008] 2 Cr App R (S) 5, para 22; *R v AIB* [2024] EWCA Crim 422.

189 *R v King* (1985) 7 Cr App R (S) 227, 230.

190 *R v P and Blackburn* [2007] EWCA Crim 2290; [2008] 2 Cr App R (S) 5, para 22. See also *Marks v Beyfus* (1890) 25 QBD 494.

191 *R v A and B* [1999] 1 Cr App R (S) 52, 56. See also *R v Royle* [2023] EWCA Crim 1311; [2024] 1 WLR 2853; [2024] 1 Cr App R (S) 41, para 33, where there is a further enumeration of the relevant factors.

to the breakup of criminal gangs.[192] The greater the risk to the informer in these circumstances, the greater the deserved reduction. As against this, if the information given transpires to be unreliable, vague, of little use or already known to the authorities, the sentence discount will usually be minimal.[193] Once these factors are borne in mind, the amount of the reduction is at the discretion of the trial judge who must also, of course, have primary regard to the gravity of the offence for which the informer is being sentenced. In *R v King*[194] the English Court of Appeal indicated that the appropriate reduction may be between one half and two thirds of the otherwise deserved sentence, but in any event never more than three quarters.[195] However, as was recently pointed out in *R v Royle,*[196] which includes a general review of the law in this area, the discount indicated in *King* included credit for a guilty plea. The discount for the provision of assistance was therefore about 40 per cent. It should also be recalled that the appellant in *King,* who pleaded guilty to several robberies and burglaries, had provided exceptionally helpful information that led to the conviction of at least 17 other criminals. The Court of Appeal reduced the headline sentence of 10 years and imposed a final sentence of four and a half years because of the assistance provided by the appellant. In fact, there is no general tariff for this factor. All depends on the circumstances of the case.[197] In *R v Royle,*[198] for example, the level of assistance was deemed to be quite modest and a reduction of 11 per cent appears to have been deemed appropriate.

As already noted, the justification for granting credit for the provision of information is essentially pragmatic or utilitarian in nature, and as such bears some resemblance to the guilty plea discount. The two may be intertwined in that the offender may have provided the information while indicating an intention to plead guilty. However, it is best practice to treat these two factors separately for sentencing purpose. The guilty plea merits a discount primarily because it removes the need for a trial and, in some instances, spares a victim from having to testify. These advantages accrue irrespective of whether the offender has provided information facilitating the detection or prosecution of other offences. If such information has been provided, it should be rewarded with a separate sentence reduction. An offender's motivation in providing information or assistance is largely irrelevant. After all, many offenders do so for the sole purpose of getting a reduced sentence. Yet, even in these circumstances, it is important to reward cooperation so that, for example, crime bosses and professional criminals will realise that they cannot always rely on their associates and subordinates to protect them from being identified **5–79**

---

192 *R v P and Blackburn* [2007] EWCA Crim 2290; [2008] 2 Cr App R (S) 5, para 39.
193 *R v A and B* [1999] 1 Cr App R (S) 52, 56.
194 (1985) 7 Cr App R (S) 227.
195 *R v King* (1985) 7 Cr App R (S) 227, 230; *R v P and Blackburn* [2007] EWCA Crim 2290; [2008] 2 Cr App R (S) 5, para 41.
196 [2023] EWCA Crim 1311.
197 *R v Hood* [2012] EWCA Crim 1260; [2013] 1 Cr App R (S) 49, para 20.
198 [2023] EWCA Crim 1311; [2024] 1 WLR 2853; [2024] 1 Cr App R (S) 41.

and prosecuted.[199] Failure to co-operate with the investigation or provide useful information may never be treated as an aggravating factor. Rather, it is an entirely neutral factor.[200]

Assisting Victim in Aftermath of Offence

5–80 An offender who seeks assistance for the victim by calling the emergency services or taking other steps to save the victim's life is usually entitled to some credit for doing so.[201] This typically arises in assault or homicide cases. The offender's moral culpability may be lessened by his or her immediate efforts to lessen the harm caused by the conduct constituting the offence. It may also reflect well on the offender's general character, in so far as that is a relevant consideration.[202] This factor may be particularly significant where the offender committed an assault, fatal or otherwise, in response to provocation or through the use of excessive force in self-defence, as opposed to having committed it without any obvious excuse or justification.[203]

Conduct of Defence During Trial

5–81 A defendant who, having contested the charges, is convicted following trial cannot obviously expect the customary discount granted for a guilty plea though he or she may not, of course, be in any way penalised for having gone to trial. Some credit may nonetheless be given for having conducted the defence in such a way as to minimise the inconvenience or stress to witnesses and, especially, to the complainant. A defendant might, for example, by making significant admissions, as permitted by s 22 of the Criminal Justice Act 1984, confine the defence to a legal point rather than contesting the facts or, indeed, decline to cross-examine the complainant at all.[204] *People (DPP) v Benko*[205] provides a good illustration. The appellant was tried for the attempted murder of his wife who he had attacked with a hammer.[206] He fully admitted the conduct in question and was willing to plead guilty to causing serious harm. The sole issue at trial was whether he intended to kill the victim, proof of such an intention being essential for a conviction for attempted murder. While dismissing his appeal against a sentence for 15 years' imprisonment, the Court of Appeal accepted that an accused who runs the case in a manner that causes the least use of resources or the least distress to a victim may be

---

199 *R v Hood* [2012] EWCA Crim 1260; [2013] 1 Cr App R (S) 49, para 22.

200 *People (DPP) v Owens* [2024] IECA 109, para 32.

201 *People (DPP v Millea* [2016] IECA 137.

202 Paul H Robinson and Muhammad Sarahne "After the crime: Rewarding offenders' positive post-offence conduct" (2021) 24 *New Criminal Law Review* 367, 396 ("Similarly situated offenders commonly behave differently after their offence. Those who behave better deserve to be treated better.").

203 *People (DPP) v Conway* [2019] IECA 343 seems to be one such case.

204 *People (DPP) v P (OG)* [2023] IECA 259, para 28.

205 [2022] IECA 3 (appeal against sentence).

206 See *People (DPP) v Benko* [2021] IECA 143 (appeal against conviction)

entitled to some mitigation on that account at sentencing.[207] Any discount granted under this heading will probably be considerably less than that merited by an early guilty plea.

Previous Good Character

Previous good character, particularly as evidenced by the absence of prior convictions, is widely accepted as a mitigating factor, and courts routinely grant some credit for it.[208] For this purpose, a first-time offender is usually defined as a person who had no previous convictions when the current offence was committed, rather than at the time of sentence. In fact, courts often go further and disregard previous convictions for minor offences, especially if they are dated. Convictions accumulated between the commission and sentencing of the current offence are occasionally deemed relevant, though they are unlikely to add much to the sentence that would have been imposed in their absence[209] Offenders without previous convictions may not always be persons of good character, or indeed first-time offenders, in the sense that they may have committed undetected offences or have been cautioned rather than prosecuted.[210] What provides mitigation is positive good character rather than the absence of a criminal record. A first-time offender who has hitherto led a blameless life will usually merit a reduced sentence, and all the more so if he or she has made a positive contribution to the community or the support of their family. In borderline case, this factor may tip the balance in a favour of a non-custodial or suspended sentence. Where imprisonment is inevitable, the term should be as short as possible. As the courts have consistently recognised, for many such offenders, it is the fact of imprisonment and the initial experience of it, rather than its duration, that constitutes the real punishment.[211] **5–82**

At the other end of the spectrum are those who have engaged in serial offending for a prolonged period before being reported and prosecuted. If eventually convicted, they will fall to be sentenced for a multiplicity of (usually serious) offences, committed over many years in some instances. This typically occurs in cases of child sexual abuse and occasionally in fraud cases. Quite commonly, offenders in this category have no previous **5–83**

---

[207] [2022] IECA 3, para 60.

[208] *People (DPP) v J (M)* [2022] IESC 50, para 30.

[209] In *People (DPP) v McDonagh* [2020] IECA 323, para 4, the Court of Appeal recommended that where there are several charges pending, sentencing should be adjourned so that all the charges that have resulted in conviction can be sentenced together. More controversially, the Court of Appeal expressed the view that the defence as well as the prosecution have a responsibility to bring such matters to the sentencing judge's attention.

[210] The cautioning scheme for children is described in Chap 9 below. There is also an adult cautioning scheme, introduced in 2006, which applies only to minor offences.

[211] *People (DPP) v Bates* [2020] IECA 199; *People (DPP) v Maguire* [2015] IECA 350; *People (DPP) v Doherty, ex tempore,* Court of Criminal Appeal, 31 July 2009; *People (DPP) v Egan* [2001] 2 ILRM 299; *R v Sargeant* (1974) 60 Cr App R 74.

convictions, and they may be able to point to praiseworthy contributions they have made to family or community as well. Yet, they cannot be said to be of good character. The absence of previous convictions may be due to the control or dominion they exercised over their victims who were thereby inhibited from reporting the offending conduct to the relevant authorities or, indeed, to anyone else. The question then is whether the prolonged and serial nature of the offending should cancel out any credit that might otherwise be forthcoming for any positive aspects of the offender's character or record. Arguably, some limited mitigation should still be granted for praiseworthy conduct, bearing in mind that the headline sentence in such a case is likely to be very high as, in all probability, will the ultimate sentence.[212] More importantly, a court must always fully and fairly evaluate the *person* it is now sentencing rather than concentrate exclusively on the nature of the offences and the harm caused. Due consideration must be given to the good as well as the bad aspects of the person's record. This is particularly necessary where a long interval has elapsed since the offending occurred, and where the offender now appears to be a different person from the one who committed the offences. However, an offender who used his high social standing or reputation within the community, or in a more specific setting such as a sports organisation, to facilitate the commission of the offences and cover them up is scarcely entitled to any mitigation for whatever contributions or activities earned him the reputation. In fact, the English Sentencing Council has gone so far as to say that it may be an aggravating factor for a person to use good character or exemplary conduct to facilitate the commission of the offences.[213]

5–84 Various justifications have been offered for treating previous good character or the absence of a criminal record as mitigating. It goes without saying that the harm caused by a serious offence is scarcely diminished because the perpetrator has never been known to offend before. Nor, ordinarily, will the presence of previous convictions increase or intensify the harm inflicted. One of the better known justifications for treating the absence of previous convictions as mitigating is the 'lapse' theory championed by Andrew von Hirsch. Under this theory, a reduced sentence for first offenders is a concession to human frailty.[214] There is always the possibility that a person who has thus far led a law-abiding life may 'lapse' by engaging in some kind of criminal conduct:

---

212 In *R v Ryan* [2001] HCA 21; (2001) 206 CLR 267, a bare majority of the Australian High Court held that some mitigation might be granted to a person (such as, in that case, a priest who had sexually abused many children) for being of "otherwise good character". See Ian Freckleton, "Good character, paedophilia and the purposes of sentencing: *Ryan v The Queen* [2001] HCA 21" (2001) 8 *Psychiatry, Psychology and Law* 202.

213 Sentencing Council, *Sexual Offences: Definitive Guideline* (London, 2013), Annex B.

214 See, for example, Andrew von Hirsch, "The discount approach: Progressive loss of mitigation" in Andrew von Hirsch, Andrew Ashworth and Julian Roberts (eds), *Principled Sentencing: Readings on Theory and Practice,* 3rd ed (Hart Publishing, 2009), 158.

> "The discount is, rather, a concession made to the fallibility of human nature. The scaled-down response for the first offence serves to accord some respect for the fact that the person's inhibitions functioned before, and to show some sympathy for the all-too-human weakness that can lead to a first offence. The idea is thus one of limited tolerance for human frailty."[215]

As indicated by the reference here to "limited tolerance", the absence of a criminal record will not exempt a defendant from criminal liability or justify a non-custodial sentence where the offence is sufficiently serious to warrant imprisonment. Another justification commonly suggested is that first-time offenders pose a reduced risk of re-offending. The English Sentencing Council's offence-specific guidelines usually include 'no previous convictions or no relevant/recent convictions' as a general mitigating factor. By way of explanation, they state that re-offending rates for first offenders are significantly lower than for repeat offenders. They add that first offenders are regarded as less blameworthy than repeat offenders.[216] **5–85**

Good Work Record

A good work record is routinely mentioned by courts as a mitigating factor. It is presumably regarded as an indication of good character to the extent that it shows that the offender has been self-sufficient, has supported dependent family members (where relevant) and is capable of adhering to the kind of structured lifestyle that holding down a steady job demands. If the sentencing exercise is envisaged as a kind of moral balance sheet, a good work record is therefore an item to be entered on the credit side. **5–86**

Remorse

Remorse is more contested as a mitigating factor.[217] Retributivists who hold that a sentence should be strictly commensurate with the gravity of the offence would insist that harm and culpability should be the predominant, if not the only, determinants of the appropriate punishment. Subsequent **5–87**

---

[215] Andrew von Hirsch and Andrew Ashworth, *Proportionate Sentencing: Exploring the Principles* (Oxford University Press, 2005), 151. For a critical analysis of this approach, see Julian V Roberts, "First-offender sentencing discounts: Exploring the justifications" in Julian V Roberts and Andrew von Hirsch (eds), *Previous Convictions at Sentencing: Theoretical and Applied Perspectives* (Hart Publishing, 2010), Chap 2.

[216] See, for example, the definitive guideline on dangerous driving (2023).

[217] Steven K Tudor, "Why should remorse be a mitigating factor in sentencing?" (2008) 2 *Criminal Law and Philosophy* 241; Mirko Bagaric and Kumar Amarasekara, "Feeling sorry? Tell someone who cares: The irrelevance of remorse in sentencing" (2001) 40 *Howard Journal of Criminal Justice* 364; Richard L Lippke, "Response to Tudor: Remorse-based sentence reductions in theory and practice" (2008) 2 *Criminal Law and Philosophy* 259. On the role and significance of remorse at different stages of the criminal process, see Steven Tudor, Richard Weisman, Michael Proeve and Kate Rossmanith (eds), *Remorse and Criminal Justice* (Routledge, 2022).

expressions of remorse, genuine or otherwise, by the offender cannot retrospectively reduce either the harm or culpability of the offending conduct. Viewed from this perspective, remorse, insofar as it has any relevance, is more appropriately considered by a parole authority when deciding if an imprisoned offender should be granted early or conditional release. The genuineness of the offender's remorse can be more accurately assessed at that point and, if found to be genuine, it may indicate a reduced risk of re-offending. However, this is only one perspective on the relationship between remorse and desert. Another version of desert, known as character retributivism, holds when determining punishment, a court should consider the offender holistically and not just by reference to the act constituting the offence.[218] Genuine remorse may show that the offender has become a changed or even different person.[219] According to Douglas Robbins, a proponent of this theory, "the remorseful wrongdoer separates himself not only from the bad act but from the bad actor and the character that inspired the act".[220] Indeed, Kant, although usually portrayed as an ardent retributivist, also claimed that repentance can amount to a 'new birth' through which we separate our current selves from our old selves.[221] Where a sentencing court is satisfied that the offender is so genuinely remorseful or repentant that he or she is now an ethically transformed person (to borrow another phrase from Robbins), it is justified in mitigating the sentence that would have been appropriate if selected solely by reference to the gravity of the offence. This is what separates character retributivism from strict retributivism. Mitigation for genuine remorse is equally compatible with most utilitarian penal purposes. The remorseful offender is probably more amenable to rehabilitation and less in need of specific deterrence or incapacitation. Its compatibility with general deterrence may be more troublesome. In Ireland, remorse is usually treated as a personal circumstance of the offender under the second limb of the proportionality principle. However, the reasons for regarding it as mitigating, whether under the first or second limb of that principle, are effectively the same as those suggested by character

---

218 Nick Smith, "Dialectical retributivism: Why apologetic offenders deserve reductions in punishment even under retributive theories" (2016) 44 *Philosophia* 343. See also Dancig-Rosenberg and Dagan, note 126 above, at 135-136.

219 Austin Sarat, "Remorse, responsibility, and criminal punishment: An analysis of popular culture" in Susan Bandes (ed), *The Passions of Law* (New York University Press, 2000). 168-169, describing remorse as self-punishment.

220 B Douglas Robbins, "Resurrection from a death sentence: Why capital sentences should be commuted upon the occasion of an authentic ethical transformation" (2001) 149 Univ Pennsylvania LR 1115. See also Jeffrie Murphy and Jean Hampton, *Forgiveness and Mercy* (Cambridge University Press, 1988), 26, arguing that by true repentance the offender separates himself from his past wrong, and Paul H Robinson, "The virtues of restorative processes, the vices of 'restorative justice'" (2003) Utah LR 375, 380 ("Genuine remorse, public acknowledgement of wrongdoing, and sincere apology can all, in my view, reduce an offender's blameworthiness – and, thereby, the amount of punishment deserved.").

221 Immanuel Kant, *Religion within the Limits of Reason Alone*, translated by Theodore M Greene and Hoyt H Hudson (Harper and Row, 1960).

retributivists. The remorseful or repentant offender is showing him/herself to be a different person, to some degree at least, from the person who committed the offence. This reflects the predominant modern concept of remorse as a manifestation of moral progress or personal improvement.[222]

The epistemological difficulties in identifying true remorse, however contrite an offender claims to be, are well documented and cannot be overlooked. Whether one can ever confidently know another's state of mind remains questionable.[223] Courts can only search for any concrete evidence in terms, for example, of the offender's conduct in the immediate aftermath of the offence, a pre-trial apology or offer of reparation, that may evince the authenticity of expressed remorse. Even insincere expressions of remorse can have some value, or so it has been argued. A victim may feel vindicated on hearing the offender clearly confess that what they did was wrong, and that the victim was not at fault. Moreover, this acknowledgement is being made to the public at large and not just to the victim. There is always the possibility or, at any rate, the hope that, over time, the offender may internalise an awareness of the wrongdoing as expressed in the apology.[224] Jeffrie Murphy has gone further and suggested that remorse and apology may be painfully humbling for an offender and that this, in turn, can constitute retributively deserved punishment.[225] **5–88**

In practice, genuine remorse is accepted as a mitigating factor.[226] As the Court of Appeal has observed, a truly remorseful offender can ordinarily be expected to plead guilty or indicate an intention to do so at any early stage in the proceedings.[227] We must nonetheless remain open to the possibility that genuine remorse might manifest itself at a later stage, perhaps after the offender has heard evidence about the impact of the offence. The New Zealand Court of Appeal has likewise said: **5–89**

> "It is now well established that a discrete discount for remorse will be appropriate where a "proper and robust evaluation of all the circumstances" demonstrates that an offender is remorseful. Remorse need not be extraordinary, although it must be genuine. The onus is on the defendant to

---

[222] Laurel Fulkerson, *Remorse in Classical Antiquity* (Oxford University Press, 2013) has an excellent account of the contrasting approaches to remorse in the ancient and modern worlds.

[223] Michael M O'Hear, "Remorse, cooperation, and 'acceptance of responsibility': The structure, implementation, reform of Section 3E1.1 of the federal sentencing guidelines" (1997) 91 Northwestern Univ LR 1507, 1554 ("The difficulties of *knowing* the state of mind of another – indeed, the question of whether people even possess stable, *knowable* personality attributes – have plagued modern literature and psychology").

[224] Stephanos Bibas and Richard A Bierschbach, "Integrating remorse and apology into criminal procedure" (2004) 114 Yale LJ 85, 143. See also RA Duff, *Punishment, Communication, and Community* (Oxford University Press, 2001), 94-95.

[225] Jeffrie G Murphy, *Punishment and the Moral Emotions: Essays in Law, Morality, and Religion* (Oxford University Press, 2011), Chap 7.

[226] See, for example, *People (DPP) v M (P)* [2016] IECA 49, para 27.

[227] *People (DPP) v McL (P)* [2022] IECA 234.

> show it is so. This Court has previously stated that it will look for "tangible evidence, such as engagement in restorative justice processes". Other examples include the voluntary payment of reparation, and efforts to remedy harm to the community. Where established, remorse tends to attract a discrete discount of between five and 15 per cent."[228]

5–90 Irish courts have not indicated any discount for remorse in percentage terms. It is more likely to be one of several mitigating factors (other than a guilty plea) for which a global discount will be granted.

Impact on Others

5–91 A crime can have many victims, and not just those directly harmed by its commission. A distinction has been drawn between a direct victim (eg the person assaulted or otherwise injured), a related victim (eg a person closely connected with the direct victim and who suffered to some degree as a result of the crime) and an indirect victim (who may be a member of the public who fears being victimised in a similar way or who, if only as a taxpayer, ends up bearing the cost of the crime, the punishment or both).[229] The category of indirect victims also includes persons who are somehow dependent on the offender and who will suffer as a result of the penalty that is eventually imposed.[230] Typically, these indirect victims will be young children, elderly relatives, and other dependants including, in some instances, employees. Child dependants merit particular concern if only because the United Nations Convention on the Rights of the Child (art 3(1)) provides that in all actions concerning children, including those taken by law courts, "the best interests of the child shall be a primary consideration". Regard must also be had to art 8 of the ECHR which guarantees the right to personal and family privacy. The European Court of Human Rights has repeatedly stressed that the mutual enjoyment by children and parents of each other's company is a core element of family life. Any interference with the parent-child relationship amounts to a violation of art 8 unless justified by some pressing social need, and even then any restriction should be strictly proportionate.[231] Parents of young children may therefore be imprisoned following conviction but only if that is necessary having regard to the gravity of the offence. A prison term, when imposed on such a person, should be no longer than is necessary to fulfil whatever purpose the sentence is intended to advance. Additionally, there is an abundance of research demonstrating

---

228 *R v Kohu* [2023] NZCA 343, para 40. Internal references omitted.

229 Richard L Lippke, "Retributive sentencing, multiple offenders and bulk discounts" in Mark White (ed), *Retributivism: Essays on Theory and Policy* (Oxford University Press, 2011), Chap 11.

230 For a perceptive analysis of the relationship between criminal law and family relationships generally, see Dan Markel, Jennifer M Collins and Ethan J Leib, *Privilege or Punish: Criminal Justice and the Challenge of Family Ties* (Oxford University Press, 2009).

231 *W v United Kingdom* (1987) 10 EHRR 29, para 59; *Olsson v Sweden* (1988) 11 EHRR 259; *R (P and Q) v Secretary of State for the Home Department* [2001] EWCA Civ 1151; [2001] 1 WLR 2002.

the adverse impact of parental imprisonment on children.[232] Apart from causing material hardship, it disrupts education, family relationships and other social bonds, and increases the risk of addiction with all the other problems to which that can give rise. While the emphasis here will be on responsibility for the care of young children, similar principles can apply where the offender has responsibility for other dependants, such as an elderly parent or spouse, or an older child with a disability.[233] In either event, much will depend on the circumstances including the availability or otherwise of alternative arrangements for the care of persons in question. The European Court of Human Rights has also held that "it is an essential part of the prisoner's right to respect for family life that the authorities enable him or, if need be, help him to maintain contact with his close family".[234]

Being solely or primarily responsible for the care of young children is well established as a relevant sentencing factor and, in many instances, a mitigating one. As Lord Judge CJ said in *H (H) v Deputy Prosecutor for the Italian Republic*,[235] a leading extradition case, the continuing responsibility of a sentencing court to consider the interests of children was "endorsed time without number" over the years. He cited, among other recent authorities, *R v Kayani*[236] where the Court of Appeal said that the impact on children, and particularly young children, if the person best placed to care for them was at risk of imprisonment "is a major feature for consideration in any sentencing decision". **5–92**

In New Zealand, both the Court of Appeal and the Supreme Court have likewise held that an offender's family circumstances including, where applicable, the welfare of children, is always among the personal circumstances that must be considered at sentencing.[237] Most of the guidelines produced by the English Sentencing Council specify this as a mitigating factor, irrespective of the nature of the offence. There is **5–93**

[232] Rachel Condry and Shona Minson, "Conceptualizing the effects of imprisonment on families: Collateral consequences, secondary punishment, or symbiotic harms" (2021) 25 *Theoretical Criminology* 540; Marie Hutton and Dominique Moran (eds), *The Palgrave Handbook of Prison and the Family* (Palgrave Macmillan, 2019); Sara Wakefield, "Incarceration, families, and communities: Recent developments and enduring challenges" in Michael Tonry and Sandra Bucerius (eds), *Prisons and Prisoners* (Vol. 51 of *Crime and Justice*) (University of Chicago Press, 2022), 399

[233] *People (DPP) v Conway* [2019] IECA 343. In *People (DPP) v O'N (M)* [2018] IECA 305, the Court of Appeal upheld a fully suspended sentence imposed on an 82-year-old man for sexual offences committed against his granddaughter several years earlier. The sentence was upheld mainly because the appellant was responsible for the care of his seriously ill wife who was the same age of himself. In this connection, the court referred to art 8 of the ECHR.

[234] *Guimon v France* App no 48798/14 (European Court of Human Rights, , 11 April 2019), para 37.

[235] [2012] UKSC 25; [2013] 1 AC 338, para 128.

[236] [2011] EWCA Crim 2871; [2012] 1 WLR 1927; [2012] 2 Cr App R (S) 38 para 54.

[237] *R v Harlen* [2001] NZCA 130, para 22; *R v Philip* [2022] NZSC 149; [2022] 1 NZLR 571; *R v Milne* [2023] NZCA 491.

also a remarkable consensus across common law jurisdictions as to the more specific principles that should apply when sentencing offenders who have such responsibilities.[238] They were considered in detail by the English Court of Appeal in *R v Petherick*[239] where two salient principles were confirmed:

> "[I]t will be especially where the case stands on the cusp of custody that the balance is likely to be a fine one. In that kind of case the interference with the family life of one or more entirely innocent children can sometimes tip the scales and means that a custodial sentence otherwise proportionate may become disproportionate."
>
> "[I]n a case where custody cannot proportionately be avoided, the effect on children or other family members *might* (our emphasis) afford grounds for mitigating the length of sentence, but it may not do so. If it does, it is quite clear that there can be no standard or normative adjustment or conventional reduction by way of percentage or otherwise. It is a factor which is infinitely variable in nature and must be trusted to the judgment of experienced judges."[240]

5–94 The English courts have also stressed that where immediate custody seems appropriate, a court should enquire as to whether proper arrangements have been made for the care of dependent children and, if necessary, adjourn sentence to enable this to be done.[241] This is also specified in the Sentencing Council guidelines. An Irish court would doubtless take similar steps.

5–95 Some of the authorities suggest that the offender must be the sole or primary carer of dependent children before mitigation on this account can be granted. This is probably too narrow an approach because child welfare entails more than material support. Children with a close emotional attachment to a parent may also suffer from that parent's imprisonment, even if they are otherwise being cared for. The Supreme Court of New Zealand, when referring to sentence discounts granted for this reason, has said:

> "We do not find it helpful to characterise such discounts as "rare" or to emphasise, to the exclusion of other factors, whether the defendant is the primary caregiver or the seriousness of the offending. What is required is a consideration of all of the relevant circumstances which must include the child's interests. Those interests include, as [the UN Convention on the Rights of the Child] indicates, the importance for children of growing up in a familial environment. We accept that there may be other factors in this consideration which take primacy including, by way of example,

---

238 See, for example, *M v The State* 2008 (3) SA 232 (Constitutional Court of South Africa).

239 [2012] EWCA Crim 2214; [2013] 1 WLR 1102; [2013] 1 Cr App R (S) 116. The *Petherick* principles were expressly adopted by the Northern Court of Appeal in *R v Devlin* [2023] NICA 71 which also has a useful discussion of the topic.

240 [2012] EWCA Crim 2214; [2013] 1 WLR 1102; [2013] 1 Cr App R (S) 116, paras 22 and 24.

241 *R v Rescorl* [2021] EWCA Crim 2005, para 11.

> issues of interfamilial violence; an absence of remorse and/or lack of any rehabilitative steps..."[242]

Family responsibilities seldom, if ever, have any bearing on the offender's culpability or the harm caused by the offence. They are treated as mitigating primarily to advance the interests of children. A subsidiary consideration is that the offender's continuing anxiety about the children's welfare while separated from them may exacerbate the experience of imprisonment. Further, being in a position to care for children and maintain a close bond with them may aid an offender's rehabilitation.[243] **5–96**

This principle may have limited relevance to the sentencing of serious offences where the dominant consideration is to impose a sentence that reflects the gravity of the offence.[244] Nonetheless, it is also accepted that, even in such cases, it will be in the children's interests to make the period of separation from the parent as short as possible. In *R v Rooney*,[245] for example, one of the appellants (all of whom were convicted of forced labour and related offences) had been the sole carer of his son prior to sentence, and it was accepted that imprisonment would be particularly difficult for him because of concern for the child. The (English) Court of Appeal considered that a six-year prison sentence would have been appropriate after trial but, because of this and other factors, it reduced the sentence to four years and three months. **5–97**

These principles are scarcely applicable where the offences were committed against children who were in the offender's care at the time as, for example, where a father sexually abused his own children. Parental child abduction can be a more complex matter. It is an offence, punishable with a maximum of seven years' imprisonment, for a parent to take or send a child under the age of 16 out of the state in defiance of a court order or without the consent of the parent or guardian to whom custody of the child has been judicially granted.[246]As discussed at length by the English Court of Appeal in *R v Kayani*,[247] the circumstances and impact of child abduction by a parent can vary enormously. It could possibly happen, for one reason or another, that the abducting parent was, in fact, the sole or primary carer of the children by the time the criminal proceedings were initiated or concluded. In *Kayani* itself, which was a serious case of abduction, the Court of Appeal did not consider that child abduction should be placed in a special category when applying the principle that responsibility for young children has little relevance when sentencing for **5–98**

---

[242] *R v Philip* [2022] NZSC 149; [2022] 1 NZLR 571, para 56.

[243] *R v Philip* [2022] NZSC 149; [2022] 1 NZLR 571, para 54.

[244] *R v Kayani* [2012] EWCA Crim. 2871; [2012] 1 WLR 1927; [2012] 2 Cr App R (S) 38; *R v Rescorl* [2021] EWCA Crim 2005, para 17 ("Caring responsibilities are not, of course, an automatic passport to a non-custodial sentence or to a suspended sentence").

[245] [2019] EWCA Crim 681, para 96; [2019] 4 WLR 89; [2019] 2 CR App R 32.

[246] Non-Fatal Offences Against the Person Act 1997, s 16.

[247] [2012] EWCA Crim. 2871; [2012] 1 WLR 1927; [2012] 2 Cr App R (S) 38.

serious offences. It therefore upheld prison sentences of five years and three years imposed on the two unrelated appellants in that case (the applicable maximum being seven years). This may have been reasonable in the circumstances, but an exceptional case could still arise where the offending parent, despite having unlawfully abducted the children, had become their sole carer and was, by all credible accounts, discharging that role conscientiously. In that event, the two *Pertherick* principles, as set out above, might apply.

5–99 Treating responsibility for young children as a mitigating factor is often linked with the role of gender at sentencing. In practical and empirical terms, the connection is quite apt because women are considerably more likely than men to be the sole or primary carers of young children.[248] This is one reason – though there are others as well – why some advocate a special sentencing regime for women offenders. It is not proposed to deal here with the broader issue of gender, except to note the acknowledged importance of maintaining meaningful links between mothers and their young children, even where the mothers have offended.[249] Women who must be imprisoned should be enabled to care for their recently born children, where possible, and older children should have adequate opportunities to visit their mothers in prison.[250] However, the general principle concerning responsibility for young children as a relevant sentencing factor must apply irrespective of gender. To make the concession available to women (or men) only would amount to unwarranted discrimination. After all, the children's interests are the most important consideration and furnish the primary justification for the principle.

5–100 A more general issue of parity also arises in this context. If two or more offenders commit similar offences with similar levels of culpability, or perhaps participate in the same offence, is it defensible to give one a significantly more lenient sentence than the others simply because they are responsible for the care of young children or other dependants? If the

---

[248] Shona Minson, "Sentencing and dependents: Motherhood as mitigation" in Julian V Roberts (ed), *Exploring Sentencing Practice in England and Wales* (Palgrave Macmillan, 2015), Chap 8

[249] These is an extensive international literature on the sentencing of women. See, for example, Pat Carlen and Anne Worrall, *Analysing Women's Imprisonment* (Willan, 2004); Lorraine Gelsthorpe and Gillian Sharpe, "Women and Sentencing: Challenges and choices" in Roberts, note 248 above, Chap 7; Julian V Roberts and Gabrielle Watson, "Reducing female admissions to custody: Exploring the options at sentencing" (2017) 17 *Criminology and Criminal Justice* 546; Baroness Corston, *Report of a Review of Women with Particular Vulnerabilities in the Criminal Justice System* (Home Office, 2007). Erin Collins, "Punishing gender" (2024) 71 UCLA LR 316 (which has an extensive exploration of issues relating to the imprisonment of women and covers much of the (mainly American) modern literature on the topic). For an up-to-date survey of research (mainly American) on women in prison, see Sandra Bucerius and Sveinung Sandberg, "Women in prisons" in Tonry and Bucerius, note 232 above, at 137.

[250] *R (P and Q) v Secretary of the State for the Home Department* [2011] EWCA Civ 1151; [2001] 1 WLR 2002.

predominant consideration is to achieve parity for offenders with equal or similar levels of culpability, the reduction is probably not defensible. However, as already noted, the reduction is granted primarily in the interests of children, even if it is an undeserved windfall of sorts for the offender. By way of mitigating any such disparity, the reduction granted for this reason is unlikely to be very significant in the sentencing of serious offences. Secondly, under the general principles governing the sentencing of co-offenders, discussed further below, the person who receives the more severe sentence may secure some reduction if an appeal court is satisfied that he or she has a justifiable sense of grievance as a result of the disparity.

Factors Rendering Imprisonment More Onerous Than Usual

The duration of a custodial sentence is only one factor, albeit an important one, when assessing its likely punitive impact. Elderly, infirm, disabled or chronically ill persons will probably find incarceration more onerous than the average, able-bodied person. The experience of imprisonment is, to this extent, subjective.[251] A given unit of custodial punishment can be more severe in its effect for some than for others. Courts generally recognise this by treating old age, disability and serious or chronic illness as mitigating factors, thereby reducing the custodial term to be served.[252] In a cusp case, such a factor, if present to a sufficient degree, may tip the balance in favour of a non-custodial measure. Courts are also influenced by the extent to which the prison in which the offender is likely to be held is equipped to deal with his or her medical or other needs.[253] The English Court of Appeal once said that the imprisonment of an extremely ill or disabled person could, of itself, amount to inhuman or degrading treatment or punishment as prohibited by art 3 of the European Convention on Human Rights, though it hastened to add that such a case would be extremely rare.[254] A significant reduction in the otherwise deserved term is usually the most appropriate response in these circumstances.[255] **5–101**

Some argue that sentencing courts need not concern themselves with the likely impact of imprisonment on seriously ill or disabled offenders because the prison authorities must ensure that they are provided with adequate treatment while in custody. Moreover, the executive branch of government is always empowered to release a prisoner on compassionate **5–102**

---

[251] Adam Kolber, "The subjective experience of punishment" (2009) 109 Columbia LR 182; Skylar Albertson, "Do prison conditions change how much punishment a sentence carries out? Lessons from federal sentence reduction rulings during the Covid-19 pandemic" (2022) 18 *Northwestern Journal of Law and Social Policy* 1; Richard A Posner, "An economic theory of the criminal law" (1985) 85 Columbia LR 1193, 1212; Julia L Torti, "Accounting for punishment in proportionality review" (2013) 88 New York Univ LR 1908, 1945-1949.

[252] *People (DPP) v O'Brien* [2015] IECA 1, paras 32 to 37.

[253] *People (DPP) v O'Brien* [2015] IECA 1.

[254] *R v Qazi and Hussain* [2010] EWCA Crim 2579; [2011] 2 Cr App R (S) 8.

[255] *R v Hall* [2013] EWCA Crim 82; [2013] 2 Cr App R (S) 68; *R v Bernard* [1997] 1 Cr App R (S) 135.

grounds.[256] In *R v Bernard*[257] the English Court of Appeal, when dealing with a drug offender who suffered from multiple illnesses, emphasised the executive power to grant clemency to such a prisoner, but it said that a court could still grant some reduction in sentence "as an act of mercy in the exceptional circumstances of a particular case, rather than by virtue of any general principle". Later, in *R v Hall*[258] the court said that mitigation on account of serious illness could be granted either because of the greater impact of imprisonment on the offender or as an act of mercy. Likewise, in *People (DPP) v Wallace,*[259] the Irish Court of Appeal upheld a fully suspended sentence for a drug dealing offence that would ordinarily have attracted a substantial prison sentence in the case of a defendant who had serious health problems and who was dependent on the use of a wheelchair. This approach is entirely defensible, though the extent to which it will save a person from immediate imprisonment will depend on factors such as the gravity of the offence and the availability or otherwise of appropriate facilities within the prison system. Equivalence of impact, though incapable of precise measurement, is an important consideration when crafting a proportionate sentence, bearing in mind that proportionality includes the notion of similar punishment for similar offences. Two penalties might be quantitatively equal (as in identical terms of imprisonment). Yet, they are not truly equal if one will have a significantly more severe impact on a particular offender than on others. The Canadian Supreme Court has expressly linked this consideration with the principle of proportionality which it has interpreted to imply that "where the impact of imprisonment is greater on a particular offender, a reduction in sentence may be appropriate".[260] The English Court of Appeal has also accepted as a possible mitigating factor that custody may have a particularly harsh impact on the offender.[261]

5–103 An offender's previous occupation may also be relevant in this context. Former members of the police or the prison service, for example, may encounter hostility from fellow prisoners and this, in turn, may necessitate restrictions on their freedom of movement within prison. This consideration will seldom, if ever, save an offender from imprisonment where the offence is sufficiently serious, but it may justify a shorter term than would otherwise be imposed. In some cases, there may be a countervailing argument that the offence was all the more serious because it was committed by, say, a serving member of the police. Some trade off between these competing considerations, one mitigating and

---

256 In Ireland, the Government has a constitutional power to commute or remit any punishment imposed by a criminal court. See Chap 14 below.

257 [1997] 1 Cr App R (S) 135.

258 [2013] EWCA Crim 82; [2013] 2 Cr App R (S) 68.

259 [2016] IECA 57, para 22. See also *People (DPP) v Creighton,* unreported, Court of Criminal Appeal, 15 April 2002.

260 *R v Hills* [2023] SCC 2, para 135, referring to Benjamin L Berger, "Proportionality and the experience of punishment" in David Cole and Julian Roberts (eds), *Sentencing in Canada: Essays in Law, Policy, and Practice* (Irwin Law, 2020), 368.

261 *R v Patel* [2021] EWCA Crim 231; [2021] 1 WLR 2997; [2021] 2 Cr App R(S) 47, para 38. See also *Bernard* and *Hall* described above.

the other aggravating, will then be necessary. In *People (DPP) v Doherty*[262] the appellant had been sentenced to three years' imprisonment for harassment committed while she was a serving member of the Gardaí. The Court of Appeal accepted "as a point of substance" that her experience of imprisonment was more onerous because she was a former Garda. However, it also said that "there is something particularly reprehensible about a serving member of An Garda Síochána, from whom much better should be expected, engaging in such conduct".[263] Nonetheless, having regard to all the mitigating factors and the need to encourage desistance from further offending, the court suspended the balance of the sentence.

At one time, it was generally assumed that a foreign national would find imprisonment more burdensome because of language difficulties, being unable to maintain meaningful contact with family and friends, the lack of a support network within the country and similar considerations. This categorical approach has gradually been abandoned in favour of a more individualised assessment. Nowadays, a court will consider the circumstances of each foreign offender to determine if they will, in fact, find imprisonment more onerous than an Irish national serving a similar sentence.[264] Courts do not however hesitate to grant some mitigation when satisfied that a foreign offender is likely to find imprisonment more difficult for any of the reasons just mentioned. The Court of Appeal was so satisfied in *People (DPP) v Witkowski and Sowa*,[265] involving two Polish nationals, although it ultimately increased their sentences because of the gravity of the offence. In *People (DPP) v P(C)*[266] the defendant, a Romanian national who had been living in Ireland for a short time, was convicted of three counts of rape and one of false imprisonment, all committed against the same victim. He had a limited command of English and, during the four years he had been imprisoned prior to trial, had no visitors apart from his solicitor. The trial judge imposed 10 years' imprisonment but suspended the last three and a half years on the basis that, in terms of hardship, each day served by the defendant was equivalent to one and a half days served by a local prisoner. The Court of Appeal, while agreeing with the trial judge that the defendant would find imprisonment more difficult because of language difficulties, held that the judge erred in granting a discount of this order. It therefore found the sentence to be unduly lenient and substituted a 10-year sentence with the last one and a half years suspended. **5–104**

Transgender persons may also find imprisonment exceptionally difficult. This has been judicially recognised in England, most recently **5–105**

---

262 [2019] IECA 350.
263 [2019] IECA 350, para 8.
264 *People (DPP) v Daly* [2011] IECCA 104; [2012] 1 IR 476, para 41.
265 [2020] IECA 10, para 11. Earlier decisions to the same effect include *People (DPP) v Belousova*, unreported, Court of Criminal Appeal, 24 April 2009 and *People (DPP) v Stratan* [2015] IECA 362, para 5.
266 [2023] IECA 9.

in *R v Simmonds*[267] where the Court of Appeal, in reducing the sentence imposed on a transgender woman, noted that imprisonment would be more arduous for her as a result of having to serve it (at least initially and probably for the entire term) in a male prison. As has been pointed out, there has been much comment on the dangers that transgender prisoners might pose for other inmates, but far less attention to the real risk that they themselves may be victimised in various ways while in custody.[268]

Prison Conditions

5–106 Conditions of detention, in so far as they can be identified or predicted at the time of sentence, may render imprisonment more (or perhaps less) difficult than normal. For instance, a sentence to be served mostly or entirely in solitary confinement or in an overcrowded or primitive custodial environment will clearly be more onerous than one served in ordinary prison conditions, difficult though these may be at the best of times. In *People (DPP) v Lynch*[269] it had been indicated to the trial judge that the custodial regime in Dublin's women's prison varied depending on whether the sentence was for more or less than a year. This does not seem to have been elaborated upon, but the judgment of the Court of Appeal suggests that the court might have afforded some mitigation on this ground if it had been presented with evidence on the matter.

5–107 Courts cannot, however, ignore clear evidence of circumstances that may exacerbate the prison experience for all or most inmates. The restrictions necessitated by the Covid-19 pandemic made imprisonment considerably more onerous than usual and this was recognised by the English Court of Appeal in *R v Manning*.[270] There, the court held that the additional hardships caused to prisoners by Covid-19-related restrictions could properly be taken into account in deciding if a prison sentence should be suspended. (Under English law, a sentence of two years or less may be suspended). The court said:

> "In accordance with established principles, any court will take into account the likely impact of a custodial sentence upon an offender and, where appropriate, upon others as well. Judges and magistrates can, therefore, and in our judgment should, keep in mind that the impact of a custodial sentence is likely to be heavier during the current emergency than it would otherwise be. Those in custody are, for example, confined to their cells for much longer periods than would otherwise be the case—currently, 23 hours a day. They are unable to receive visits. Both they and their families are likely to be anxious about the risk of the transmission of Covid-19."[271]

---

[267] [2023] EWCA Crim 1063; [2024] 1 Cr App R (S) 22, para 26.

[268] See comment by Sebastian Walker on *Simmonds* in *Criminal Law Week*, Issue 10 of 2024, and Caroline Gorden et al, "A literature review of transgender people in prison: An 'invisible' population in in England and Wales" (2017) 233 *Prison Service Journal* 11.

[269] [2018] IECA 1.

[270] [2020] EWCA Crim 592; [2020] 4 WLR 77; [2020] 2 Cr App R (S) 46.

[271] [2020] EWCA Crim 592; [2020] 4 WLR 77; [2020] 2 Cr App R (S) 46, para 41.

In that case, which arose from an undue leniency application in respect of a 12-month suspended sentence for certain sexual offences, the Court of Appeal increased the sentence to 24 months, but suspended that also, while leaving various ancillary orders in place. **5–108**

The Covid-19 emergency may have been *sui generis*, and hopefully will not recur. Prison overcrowding is a different matter because this can occur periodically and may last for quite some time. Throughout much of 2023 and 2024, the Irish prison system was operating in excess of 100 per cent capacity. For instance, in mid-June 2024, it was operating at 111 per cent capacity. There were almost 5,000 people in custody (including 924 on remand) at a time when bed capacity was 4,514. The women's prisons in Dublin and Limerick seem to suffer from chronic overcrowding. A new women's prison with a capacity of 56 was opened in Limerick in autumn 2023. Yet, by mid-June 2024, it had 73 inmates, which left it operating at 130 per cent capacity while the women's prison in Dublin, with 180 inmates, was operating at 123 per cent capacity. **5–109**

Prison overcrowding has long been recognised by the English courts as a factor that may properly influence both the choice of penalty and the duration of custodial sentences.[272] There is a consistent line of authority to the effect that imprisonment, while at all times the sanction of last resort, should be used particularly sparingly at times of prison overcrowding. It should not be imposed at all unless strictly necessary and, where necessary, it should be for the shortest term possible. This was stressed most recently by the English Court of Appeal in *R v Ali*,[273] decided at a time when there could be no ambiguity about the extent of prison overcrowding because the government had just requested the use of 400 police cells to hold persons who would otherwise have been committed to prison on remand or under sentence. In *Ali*, the Court of Appeal substituted a suspended sentence for a six-month term of immediate imprisonment, partly because of prison overcrowding. It said that this factor "will principally apply to shorter sentences because a significant proportion of such sentences is likely to be served when the prison population is very high".[274] It was to apply only to sentences passed during such a time. There is no reason why a similar principle should not apply in Ireland, especially when the extent of prison overcrowding is confirmed by official prison statistics.[275] Overcrowded conditions undoubtedly make the prison experience more onerous. The English Court of Appeal was right to say that this factor is especially relevant to short sentences, the reasoning presumably being **5–110**

---

272 See, for example, *R v Bibi* [1980] 1 WLR 1193; [1980] 2 Cr App R (S) 177; *R v Seed and Stark* [2007] EWCA Crim 254; [2007] 2 Cr App R (S) 69; *R v Kefford* [2002] EWCA Crim 519; [2002] 2 Cr App R (S) 106.

273 [2023] EWCA Crim 232; [2023] 2 Cr App R (S) 25. See comment and analysis by Lyndon Harris at [2023] Crim LR 431.

274 [2023] EWCA Crim 232; [2023] 2 Cr App R (S) 25, para 22.

275 The Irish Prison Service publishes statistics on the prison population for each weekday. See, for example, <https://www.irishprisons.ie/wp-content/uploads/documents_pdf/31-October-2024.pdf> accessed 1 November 2024.

that short-term prisoners will have to endure overcrowded conditions throughout all or most of their sentences. However, it may be equally relevant when imposing longer sentences, particularly where all the available information indicates that a significant portion of those sentences will probably be served in overcrowded conditions.

Lapse of Time Since Commission of the Offence

5–111 Every accused person has a constitutional right to be tried with reasonable expedition. Time for this purpose begins to run when the person is first formally confronted with the allegation. A breach of this right may justify prohibition of the trial, although it is only in very rare circumstances nowadays that the superior courts will prohibit a trial because of delay, the general policy being that any claims of resulting prejudice are best left to the trial court to address.[276] Otherwise, delay may be a mitigating factor at sentencing. In effect, a sentence reduction functions as a remedy for blameworthy delay in the investigation, prosecution or trial of the offence.[277] The degree of mitigation will depend primarily on the length of the unwarranted delay and its impact on the accused.[278] A person who faces a real possibility of imprisonment if convicted will obviously experience stress and worry in the leadup to the trial, and the experience will be exacerbated by unwarranted delay.[279] This holds true of first-time offenders in particular, though it can apply to others as well.

5–112 More difficult questions arise when there has been a significant lapse of time between the commission of the offence and the point at which it was detected by or formally reported to the police. In the event of a conviction, the interval between the commission of the offence and the initiation of the proceedings may be a relevant factor at sentencing. The law's response to so-called historic offences of this nature (and they are almost invariably sex offences) depends on the dominant conception of responsibility and blameworthiness, though this is something that is seldom made explicit. Should we assess a person's blameworthiness solely by reference to the time at which the offence was committed or the time at which the person is being sentenced? In the philosophical literature, these times are often referred to as t_1 and t_2, respectively. As already noted in Chap 3, strict desert theorists hold that blameworthiness should be measured solely by reference to t_1 (synchronic responsibility) rather than to t_2 (diachronic

[276] *T(A) v DPP* [2020] IECA 6; *People (DPP) v CC* [2019] IESC 94.

[277] See Chap 8 below, discussing the remedies for breach of the right to a reasonably expeditious trial.

[278] The impact of blameworthy prosecution delay on sentence was discussed by the English Court of Appeal in *R v Timpson* [2023] EWCA Crim 453, para 23; *R v Mboma* [2024] EWCA Crim 110; *R v Ambrose* [2024] EWCA Crim 632.

[279] See, for example, *People (DPP) v McGinty* [2019] IECA 27 , para 19 (where the child pornography offences in question were detected in October 2013 but the matter was not finally disposed of until March 2018 when sentence was imposed). This is not an uncommon situation in child pornography cases because of delays in analysing the material.

responsibility).[280] This, of course, assumes that the offender is the same person at t_2 as he or she was at t_1. Yet, in *Reasons and Persons*,[281] Derek Parfit, widely regarded as the leading moral philosopher of our times, says this:

> "Suppose that a man aged ninety, one of the few rightful holders of the Nobel Peace Prize, confesses that it was he who, at the age of 20, injured a policeman in a drunken brawl. Though this was a serious crime, this man may not now deserve to be punished."

Parfit was primarily interested in notions of personal identity and personality, rather than punishment theory, but others have been inspired to develop these concepts in the context of blameworthiness and punishment for criminal conduct. In very simple terms, the essential question is: does each of us remain the same person throughout life? In physical terms we do, allowing for ageing and so forth. But whether we retain the same personality throughout our lives is a more complex question. Personality has been defined as "an individual's characteristic patterns of thought, emotion, and behaviour, together with the psychological mechanisms – hidden or not – behind those patterns".[282] **5–113**

At a philosophical level, there are competing arguments as to whether an offence committed years or decades before being reported should be prosecuted at all and, if it is, whether it should attract the same punishment as an identical offence committed very recently. According to one line of argument, it is unjust to prosecute, say, a 70-year-old for an offence he committed at the age of 20, the reasoning being that the 70-year-old is a different person from the 20-year-old he once was. There is a diminished psychological connectedness between the younger and the older self, to the extent that to punish the 70-year-old in our example is tantamount to punishing one person for the crimes of another.[283] The plausibility of this argument depends, first, on whether one accepts the concept of psychological connectedness, at least to this extent (and many do not) and, further, on what one regards as the fundamental purpose of the criminal process. If that purpose were specific deterrence, rehabilitation or incapacitation, the case for prosecuting our 70-year-old could be very weak. Retribution or general deterrence, by contrast, might militate in favour of prosecution. Further, neither the harm caused by the offence nor the offender's culpability at the time of its commission is diminished by the passage of time. This can be especially true where the offence involves the sexual abuse of a child by an adult.[284] **5–114**

---

280 Andrew C Khoury, "Synchronic and diachronic responsibility" (2013) 165 *Philosophical Studies* 735. See also, Antje du Bois-Pedain, "Penal desert and the passage of time" in Antje du Bois-Pedain and Anthony E Bottoms, *Penal Censure: Engagements Within and Beyond Desert Theory* (Hart, 2019), Chap 12.

281 Derek Parfit, *Reasons and Persons* (Clarendon Press, 1984), 326.

282 David C Funder, *The Personality Puzzle*, 6th ed (W.W. Norton, 2012), 5.

283 For a discussion of the concept of psychological connectedness, see Thomas Douglas, "Punishing wrongs from the distant past" (2019) 38 *Law and Philosophy* 335.

284 *R v Ambrose* [2024] EWCA Crim 632, para 37.

5–115 However, under Irish law, a proportionate sentence must reflect the offender's personal circumstances as well as the gravity of the offence. It is principally in that context that a long interval between offence and sentence may benefit an offender who has stayed out of trouble during that period. Evidence of such desistance may indicate a genuine effort to reform which, in turn, points to a low risk of re-offending.[285] It may also reflect well on the offender's general character as it now stands. This has been judicially recognised on many occasions. In *People (DPP) v H (P)*,[286] Charleton J while imposing sentence for sexual offences committed about 25 years before the date of conviction, said:

> "The court might then usefully look at the date on which the offences were committed. A sentencing court, in structuring any sentence, is obliged to have regard to the subsequent life circumstances of the victim. In terms of settling on the final tariff of sentence, the offender's conduct in the intervening years will be of particular importance. If there was evidence of genuine repentance of the offending; if the offender had led a good life of family, or friendship, and work; or if the offender had sought in some meaningful way to make up for his abuse of the victims, this should be taken into account. The reason that I mentioned these factors is that part of the settled sentencing principles operated by the Superior Courts emphasise that while punishment must be meted out to an offender in order to ensure the social stability of the community, and that deterrence is a necessary aspect of sentencing policy, one of the ultimate goals of the sentencing processes is the rehabilitation of the offender. If he has managed to effect that purpose, in the intervening years between offending and sentence, by his own efforts, then, it seems to me, a discount, perhaps substantial in appropriate cases, of the relevant sentence might be contemplated."

5–116 This statement has since been quoted with approval by other courts, including the Supreme Court.[287] English courts occasionally adopt the same approach.[288]

5–117 Lapse of time may operate to the offender's disadvantage where victim impact is a significant factor at sentencing. This is most likely to occur in a case of child sexual abuse where the victim is well into adulthood by the time the criminal proceedings are initiated. Evidence tendered at sentencing as to the impact of the offending will naturally include an account of its long-term consequences and, in many cases, these will be severe. A sentence is likely to be influenced by a victim's claim that their entire life has been adversely affected, perhaps very badly damaged, by the abuse experienced during childhood. The accumulated experience of the courts over the past few decades undoubtedly confirms that children subjected to sexual abuse may suffer its consequences throughout much

---

285 *People (DPP) v Elders* [2014] IECA 6, an assault case where almost six years elapsed between offence and sentence.

286 [2007] IEHC 335, para 26.

287 See, for example, *People (DPP) v J (M)* [2022] IESC 50 and *People (DPP) v H (S)* [2023] IECA 206. There was a statement to the same effect by the New Zealand Court of Appeal in *R v Tutty* [1998] 3 NZLR 165, 169.

288 *R v Trundle* [2024] EWCA Crim 588.

of their lives. However, courts must always be alert to the possibility of over-attribution. Many people who have never been victims of sexual abuse encounter problems such as addiction, depression and relationship difficulties as they go through life. Cogent expert evidence is desirable before a court can reliably conclude that problems of this nature experienced by a victim are solely or substantially attributable to the offender's conduct.

The sentence imposed for any offence must be proportionate having regard to the maximum penalty that applied when the offence was committed. The constitutional and human rights underpinnings of this rule, which are well accepted, have already been discussed in Chap 4. It means, for example, that a person now being sentenced for a single offence of sexual assault committed between 1990 and 2001 may not receive sentence in excess of five years' imprisonment, the maximum applicable during that era. The more difficult question is whether a court should go further and try to select a sentence equivalent to what the offender would probably have received if convicted shortly after the offence was committed.[289] There is, of course, the factual or empirical difficulty of establishing what that sentence might have been. Until the early 1990s prosecutions for sexual offences were relatively rare, at least when compared to recent decades. Regard must also be had to the reasons for the delayed reporting and prosecution. An offender whose own conduct has caused the delay can scarcely complain if punished according to the standards and principles generally applicable at the time of sentence. However, where the offender was still young at the time of the offending, regard must be had to his or her level of maturity at that time, an important factor in assessing culpability. An offender's degree of moral responsibility or culpability is not increased by the passage of time.[290] Regard must obviously be had also to any other factors mitigating culpability, as well as to the offender's conduct and life course since the offending ended, and his or her future prospects. The sentencing of adults for offences committed while children is discussed further in Chap 9 below. **5–118**

Old Age

Old age typically becomes an issue at the sentencing of sexual abuse offences committed in the past, and often in the distant past. The issues discussed under the previous heading therefore become relevant. This will not invariably be the case. An elderly person convicted of a recently committed murder must be sentenced to life imprisonment, though there may be strong grounds for early release through some form of executive clemency. Any other offence committed in old age must also be punished **5–119**

[289] On the approach adopted by the English courts, see *R v Forbes* [2016] EWCA Crim 1388; [2016] 2 Cr App R (S) 44; [2017] 1 WLR 53; *R v Ahmed* [2023] EWCA Crim 281 ; [2023] 1 WLR 1858; [2023] 2 Cr App R (S) 32.

[290] *R v Limon* [2022] EWCA Crim 39; [2022] 4 WLR 37; [2022] 2 Cr App R (S) 21 para 30; *R v Ahmed* [2023] EWCA Crim 281 ; [2023] 1 WLR 1858; [2023] 2 Cr App R (S) 32.

proportionately, though age may be a significant mitigating factor.[291] In the typical case, however, where there has been a long interval since the offences were committed, the approach to sentencing is determined largely by the priority accorded to the various purposes of punishment. Some utilitarian purposes such as incapacitation, rehabilitation and individual deterrence may point to little or no punishment, simply because the offender, by virtue of advanced age, no longer needs to be incapacitated, rehabilitated or deterred. Desert and general deterrence, where they are allowed to predominate, usually point in the opposite direction. Unless the offender is now treated as a different person from the one who committed the offences,[292] he or she deserves to be punished for the morally blameworthy harm inflicted on the victim, however long ago. The interests of general deterrence are likewise served by showing that those who engage in serious criminal conduct will eventually be called to account, even if in their extreme old age.

5–120 Courts nowadays are more likely to prioritise desert, while making some allowance for age. This holds true of the English Court of Appeal which, in 2017, upheld a 13-year prison sentence imposed on a 101-year-old man for sexually abusing children between 1974 and 1981. In a conjoined case a three-year prison sentence was upheld in the case of a 96-year-old man for similar offences committed between 1985 and 1992.[293] The five-judge Court of Appeal acknowledged that, under existing precedents, courts were entitled to show "a limited degree of mercy" to elderly offenders.[294] But it held that the "primary drivers" of a sentencing decision must be the harm caused or intended by the offence and the offender's culpability in committing it, as required by s 143(1) of the Criminal Justice Act 2003. (This is effectively equivalent to the first limb of the proportionality principle in Ireland.) While accepting that old age, even in the absence of associated health issues, was a mitigating factor, the Court of Appeal said that regard must also be had to the reasons why it can take so long for child sexual abuse to come to light:

> "[A]s frequently happens in cases of this sort, the vulnerable young victims' contemporaneous complaints were rejected in the face of the offender's denials. Matters often do not reach the stage of complaint because of threats or bribes made by offenders. By these means offenders often avoid investigation and prosecution for many years, thus denying their victims justice and helping to perpetuate the harmful effects of their actions. It seems to us therefore that the matter cannot wholly be viewed in these cases from

---

[291] In *R v Trundle* [2024] EWCA Crim 588, the appellant, when 82 years of age, had attempted to engage in sexual communication with a child. He was 85 at the time of sentence. He was sentenced to 10 months' imprisonment which was suspended by the Court of Appeal a short time later.

[292] Notes 280-283 above and accompanying text.

[293] *R v Clarke and Cooper* [2017] EWCA Crim 393; [2017] 1 WLR 3851; [2017] 2 Cr App R (S) 18.

[294] *R v Millberry* [2002] EWCA Crim 2891; [2003] 1 WLR 546; [2003] 2 Cr App R (S) 31, para 17.

> the standpoint of the offender, who has either by his inaction or by positive steps avoided justice and been enabled to enjoy life into old age."[295]

This may not be true of every such case but, as the court also stressed, the facts of each case, including the offender's state of health and other personal circumstances must be carefully examined in order to determine the appropriate level of mitigation. **5–121**

In Ireland, the Court of Appeal has likewise prioritised desert, while being willing to make allowance, where appropriate, for age-related factors that will make imprisonment more onerous than usual. In *People (DPP) v C(R)*[296] the court said: **5–122**

> "An imperative to impose a sentence involving significant censure, denunciation and justly deserved hard treatment involving deprivation of liberty for a considerable period, may remain notwithstanding the age of the offender."

In the same case, the court said:

> "Where advanced age is put forward as a mitigating factor it is not the offender's age *per se* that is potentially relevant but the fact that it may be (and frequently is) accompanied by other sentencing considerations, particularly concurrent ill-health, reduced life expectancy, reduced risk of re-offending, the fact that incarceration may be more onerous for the elderly due to physical challenges or cognitive issues or mental health issues, vulnerability, risk of intimidation/fears of intimidation by younger stronger prisoners, and sometimes concern about an elderly partner for whom the offender might have been the primary carer."[297]

Despite the court's initial assertion that old age is not *per se* a relevant factor, the specific matters it then proceeds to enumerate are most likely to arise in the case of elderly offenders. **5–123**

One critical factor in the sentencing of elderly offenders, especially those suffering from ill-health or infirmity, is whether the prison in which they are likely to be held is equipped to provide for their basic health and other needs. If no such facility is available, it may be inappropriate to impose any term of immediate custody. Nobody should be held in conditions that violate their fundamental human rights. Otherwise, a reduced term of imprisonment may be imposed where the conditions are likely to be particularly onerous, even if they do not fall below a standard that fails to respect the rights and dignity of the person concerned. The growth in the number of elderly offenders convicted of serious offences, predominantly sexual offences, has resulted in at least some prisons being specially adapted to cater for their needs. However, a court should always enquire **5–124**

---

[295] *R v Clarke and Cooper* [2017] EWCA Crim 393; [2017] 1 WLR 3851; [2017] 2 Cr App R (S) 18, para 20.
[296] [2023] IECA 33 , para 96.
[297] [2023] IECA 33 , para 83.

as to the availability of appropriate facilities when sentencing persons, elderly or otherwise, who have special health needs.

Efforts to Address Factors Contributing to Offending

5–125 A person who, by the time of sentencing, has already taken steps to address problems or issues that caused or contributed to their offending is usually entitled to some mitigation on that account. This is especially true where the offender has voluntarily taken such steps as part of a genuine resolve to desist from further criminal conduct. Efforts to overcome addiction are usually treated as mitigating. A recent large-scale study of personal mitigation in sentencing for assault and burglary in England and Wales found that for both offences, addressing addiction was a particularly strong mitigating factor.[298] The same would apply to participation in an anger management programme or altering living arrangements so as to avoid situations or encounters that might lead to a recurrence of the offending conduct. Genuine efforts of this nature reflect well on an offender's character and outlook as they appear at the time of sentence, and they may also point to a reduced risk of re-offending. A sentencing measure designed to encourage the offender to persevere with self-rehabilitation will often be appropriate in these circumstances. Depending on the gravity of the offence, a probation order or a fully or partly suspended sentence may be the most efficient way of incentivising the offender to desist from further crime.

Where Offence Amounts to a Restriction of a Fundamental Right

5–126 The conduct element of an offence may constitute a limitation, though usually an entirely legitimate one, of a fundamental right. Any offence committed through speech, such as a threat to kill, hate speech, incitement to crime or (in some countries) defamation clearly restricts the right to freedom of expression which is widely protected under state constitutions and international human rights law.[299] Likewise, the criminalisation of public protest would limit, if not contravene, the right to peaceful assembly. The general policy, at European level and elsewhere, is that conduct of this nature, if it is to be criminalised at all, should not be punished so severely as to have a chilling effect on the legitimate exercise of the right in question. However, much depends on the nature of the conduct involved. For instance, if punishing threats to kill has a chilling effect on such utterances, that is scarcely to be lamented. Different considerations apply where there is a fine line between protected and prohibited speech, and the same applies to public assemblies and protests. In those instances, the possibility of the criminal law having a chilling

[298] Ian K Belton and Mandeep K Dhami, "The role of character-based personal mitigation in sentencing judgments" (2024) 21 *Journal of Empirical Legal Studies* 208.

[299] Constitution of Ireland, Art 40.6.1°(i); ECHR, art 10.

effect must be seriously considered and, where appropriate, reflected in sentencing practice.

In *Taranenko v Russia*[300] the applicant, who had participated in what was essentially a non-violent protest against Russian President Putin, had been held in pre-trial detention for a year and then given a three-year suspended sentence. The European Court of Human Rights found a violation of art 10 of the ECHR (which protects freedom of expression) as interpreted in light of art11 (which protects the right to peaceful assembly). In so doing, the court said: **5–127**

> "The Court must exercise the utmost caution where the measures taken or sanctions imposed by national authorities are such as to dissuade the applicants and other person from imparting information or ideas contesting the established order of things."[301]

It was precisely because of the potentially chilling effect of the penalties imposed in *Taranenko* that a violation of the ECHR was found. The Strasbourg court has been more tolerant of penalties imposed for violent or seriously disruptive conduct. For instance, it found no violation of art 11 of the ECHR in *Kudrevičius v Lithuania*[302] where a 60-day suspended sentence had been imposed for participation in a protest that had blocked three main highways, causing significant disruption. The court stressed that what art 11 protects is the right to *peaceful* assembly, and it said that seriously disruptive activities were "not at the core" of the freedom protected by art 11. Recent English jurisprudence on the sentencing of environmental protesters has been considered earlier in this chapter.[303] **5–128**

6. Aggravating Factors

While numerous circumstances are treated as aggravating for sentencing purposes, there is surprisingly little jurisprudence on the essential nature of an aggravating factor. Broadly speaking, it is some special factor that takes the offence out of the ordinary because of the nature or extent of the harm inflicted or because of the offender's moral blameworthiness for the offence in question. This might suffice as a working definition though it probably leaves some questions unanswered, such as when, if ever, post-offence conduct should aggravate the offence. If murder were punishable with a maximum rather than a mandatory sentence, should the fact that the offender dismembered or otherwise violated the body of the deceased after the killing be treated as aggravating?[304] Such post-offence **5–129**

---

[300] European Court of Human Rights, 15 May 2014.

[301] Para 81 of judgment.

[302] (2016) 62 EHRR 34.

[303] Notes 111 to 118 above and accompanying text.

[304] See Richard Edney and Mirko Bagaric, *Australian Sentencing: Principles and Practice* (Cambridge University Press, 2007), 111-116, which has an illuminating discussion of this general question. Under English law, concealment, destruction or dismemberment of a body is an aggravating factor for both

conduct can scarcely be said to affect the gravity of the offence which had already been completed. Or, to take a more common situation, when sentencing for an assault, should a court treat as aggravating the fact that the offender left the scene without seeking any assistance for the seriously injured victim? In the latter case, it might be argued that there was, in a sense, a continuing course of conduct and that the offender's failure to assist the victim reflected heightened moral culpability. Many aggravating factors are offence-specific, at least in respect of the harm element. For instance, ransacking a dwelling is an aggravating factor in residential burglary, intrusion into the victim's dwelling is an aggravating factor in rape and other offences involving sexual violence, having a leading or directing role in a drug trafficking enterprise is an aggravating factor in drug dealing offences. Others are more generally applicable. Careful planning, premeditation or targeting vulnerable victims will aggravate many different offences.[305]

5–130 A factor may never be treated as aggravating if it is an essential ingredient of the offence. It would be wrong, for example, to treat unlawful entry of a building as an aggravating factor in burglary which is defined as entering a building as a trespasser with intent to commit an arrestable offence.[306] Likewise, being intoxicated should not be treated as an aggravating factor when the offence consists of alcohol-impaired driving.[307] To engage in such double counting would amount to an error of principle. On the other hand, it is perfectly acceptable to treat unlawful entry into the victim's dwelling as an aggravating factor for rape, as this is not a definitional element of the offence. The fact that the parties were in an intimate relationship may be treated as an aggravating factor when sentencing for assault, but not for the offence of coercive control since the existence of an intimate relationship is a constituent element of that offence.[308] Courts must be careful to avoid the possibility of double counting in other contexts as well. For instance, the impact of an offence on the victim may be an aggravating factor, especially since the introduction of victim impact evidence under the Criminal Justice Act 1993. Yet, where the harm inflicted by the offence has already been considered, as it should be, when assessing gravity under the first limb of the proportionality principle, it would be wrong to treat that same harm as a further aggravating factor because of its impact on the victim. Some additional weight may, however, be attributed to victim impact where the offence has had particularly adverse consequences for the victim, over and above the harm that would normally be inflicted by the offence in question. Similar considerations apply to treating breach of trust as an aggravating factor, as discussed under that heading below.

---

murder and manslaughter: Sentencing Act 2020, Sch 21; *R v Kelly* [2019] EWCA Crim 668.

305 The English Sentencing Council's *General Guideline: Overarching Principles* (2019) has a useful list of general aggravating and mitigating factors.

306 Criminal Justice (Theft and Fraud Offences) Act 2001, s 12.

307 *R v Lacasse* [2015] 3 SCR 1089, para 83.

308 Domestic Violence Act 2018; *People (DPP) v Kane* [2023] IECA 86, para 31.

A person who, having been convicted following a contested trial, accepts the verdict may be entitled to some mitigation on that account, especially where the acknowledgement of guilt affords some sense of vindication or other benefit to the victim. Failure to accept the verdict or even continuing to assert one's innocence should not be treated as an aggravating factor. After all, the defendant may be right and the tribunal of fact, be it a judge or jury, may have got it wrong. However strongly we believe in the wisdom and integrity of juries, we would never go so far as to claim that they are infallible. Miscarriages of justice may be rare, but they can and do occur. Failure to accept the verdict more commonly arises in parole decision-making, and it may well be a decisive factor in refusing parole. However, this too may result in serious injustice, as illustrated by *R v Malkinson*,[309] described further in Chap 14 below, where a person wrongly convicted of rape spent many years longer than necessary in prison because he refused to accept that he was guilty of the offence. In fact, he should never have been in prison. Refusal to accept the jury's verdict and a consequent unwillingness to engage with any rehabilitative service on offer may, of course, justify the withholding of any additional leniency in the form, for example, of a part suspended sentence designed to incentivise rehabilitation.[310] **5–131**

A statutory aggravating factor should always be considered and given due weight in any case where it is relevant. A court should not seek to neutralise its impact by artificially reducing a sentence so as to avoid the consequences which the application of the statutory provision might have.[311] Legislation seldom imposes an absolute obligation to treat a factor as aggravating, More commonly, it qualifies the requirement by specifying that a court need not treat the matter in question as aggravating if satisfied that there are exceptional circumstances to justify adopting this course of action.[312] In addition to the aggravating factors discussed below, the following are also accepted as aggravating in most cases: (1) targeting a vulnerable victim; (2) committing offence as part of a group; (3) offence committed in the presence of children; (4) having wrongfully blamed others; (5) significant level of planning and premeditation; or (6) high level of profit derived or intended to be derived from offence.[313] **5–132**

Another possible aggravating factor, though a strongly contested one, is a low probability of detection. Leading 18th-century penologists, notably Beccaria and Bentham, argued that punishment should "be increased, in **5–133**

---

309 [2023] EWCA Crim 954.

310 *People (DPP) v H (D)* [2023] IECA 203.

311 *People (DPP) v Doyle* [2004] IECCA 5.

312 See, for example, Criminal Justice Act 1984, s 11(4), inserted by Bail Act 1997, s 10; Domestic Violence Act 2018, s 40; Criminal Law (Human Trafficking) Act 2008, s 4A, inserted by Criminal Law (Human Trafficking) (Amendment) Act 2013, s 2.

313 The English Sentencing Council's *General Guideline: Overarching Principles* (2019) has a useful list of generally applicable aggravating and mitigating factors.

point of magnitude, in proportion as it falls short in point of certainty".[314] The underlying idea is that a heavier than normal penalty is needed to deter those who believe they can escape detection. However, it is questionable if this should even be treated as an *aggravating* factor because it does not, ordinarily at least, make the offence more serious than usual. Further, it is scarcely compatible with desert principles which require that offenders be punished according to their degree of blameworthiness. A low probability of detection should therefore be irrelevant unless, perhaps, it is proved to have been a factor that motivated the offender to engage in the criminal conduct in question. It would also have to be shown that there is, in fact, a low detection rate for that type of offence.

Offence Motivated by Hatred or Prejudice

5–134 A crime is treated as more serious if it was motivated by hatred or prejudice towards the victim on account of their race, ethnic or national origin, disability, religion, sexual orientation or some similar personal characteristic. The harm or injury inflicted on the victim may be no greater than that resulting from similar conduct that was not so motivated, but the hatred or prejudice increases the offender's moral blameworthiness. It is also, however, possible that a victim will suffer additional psychological or emotional harm from knowing that he or she was targeted because of the relevant characteristic. Such knowledge can leave a victim feeling degraded and devalued as a human being. Statements made or language used by the offender towards the victim before, during or after the commission of the offence will usually provide evidence of the motivation. In other cases, the motivation may be inferred from a pattern of behaviour by the offender or their associates towards the victim or a category of person to which the victim belongs. This principle is well accepted as part of the common law. In *People (DPP) v Donnelly*,[315] the appellant was convicted of three threats to kill or cause serious injury. The trial judge set a headline sentence of three years' imprisonment, eventually mitigated to two-and-a-half years. Dismissing the appeal against sentence, the Court of Appeal said that, were it not for the appellant's mental health difficulties, a headline sentence of at least five years' imprisonment would have been appropriate because of racially motivated comments made by the appellant to the victim. The offence in *People (DPP) v Elders*[316] was not racially motivated, but a racially offensive remark had been directed at a group of people associated with the victim. This was held to be an aggravating factor.

5–135 The Criminal Justice (Hate Offences) Act 2024, which came into force on

[314] Jeremy Bentham, *Introduction to the Principles of Morals and Legislation* (Blackwell Publishers, 1948), Chap 14, s XVIII (first published 1843); Cesare Beccaria, *On Crimes and Punishments*, edited by Richard Bellamy (Cambridge University Press, 1995). See also Jonathan Baron and Ilana Ritov, "The role of probability of detection in judgments of punishment" (2009) 1 *Journal of Legal Analysis* 553.

[315] [2020] IECA 16, para 36.

[316] [2014] IECA 6.

31 December 2024, makes significant changes in this area. First, it specifies higher maximum sentences for certain offences when they are found to have been aggravated by hatred. It achieves this by creating new variants of several existing offences under the Criminal Damage Act 1991, the Criminal Justice (Public Order) Act 1994 and the Non-Fatal Offences Against the Person Act 1997. These parallel offences are defined in the same way as their existing equivalents but with the additional element of being aggravated by hatred on account of a protected characteristic of the victim or, in some instances, of a group of persons. The term 'protected characteristic' is given a wide definition in s 3 of the 2024 Act, and includes race, nationality, gender, religion, sexual orientation and national or ethnic origin (including membership of the Traveller community). By way of example, s 2 of the Non-Fatal Offences Against the Person Act 1997 creates a summary offence of assault punishable with a fine up to £1,500, a prison term not exceeding six months or both. The 2024 Act has inserted a new s 2A which creates an offence of 'Assault Aggravated by Hatred' which carries a maximum penalty of a class B fine (current maximum €4,000), a prison term not exceeding nine months or both. This pattern is repeated in respect of other specified offences. Courts obviously retain their sentencing discretion, but the higher maximum sentences for the new offences must, in accordance with established principle, be taken into account when sentencing for specific instances of those offences. A sentencing court must always begin by anchoring the specific offence on the overall penalty scale. The higher the statutory maximum, the higher will be the headline sentence before allowance is made for any relevant offender-related factors.

Secondly, the 2024 Act has a more general provision applicable to the **5–136** sentencing of all offences other than the new offences mentioned in the previous paragraph or an offence contrary to the Prohibition of Incitement to Hatred Act 1989. Under s 8 of the 2024 Act, a court must treat as an aggravating factor hatred against a person or group of persons on account of a protected characteristic. A heavier sentence must be imposed than would be appropriate in the absence of this factor. This does not apply where the sentence for the offence is one of life imprisonment (presumably meaning a mandatory life sentence) or where the court considers that there are exceptional circumstances to justify it not imposing the enhanced punishment. In any case, the penalty may not exceed the prescribed statutory maximum, and a court, when it applies this provision, must state and record that it has done so, and specify the protected characteristic involved. As noted, this general provision does not apply to the sentencing of the new aggravated offences. To apply it when sentencing for any of those offences would amount to double counting.

Violent Offence Committed Within an Intimate Relationship

When imposing sentence for a violent offence, a court must, in the absence **5–137** of exceptional circumstances, treat the fact that the offence was committed within an intimate personal relationship as an aggravating factor and impose a more severe sentence, no higher than the statutory maximum, than would ordinarily be appropriate for the offence in question.[317] This requirement applies where the offence was committed against the offender's spouse or civil partner or somebody with whom the offender was, at the time of the offence or previously, in an intimate relationship. The relevant offences for this purpose include any offence created by ss 2 to 15 of the Non-Fatal Offences against the Person Act 1997, any offence involving violence or the threat of violence to any person, and certain sexual offences including rape, sexual assault and aggravated sexual assault. The sentencing of domestic violence is considered further in Chap 10.

Offence Committed While on Bail

5–138 When imposing sentence for an offence committed while on bail and in circumstances where the imposition of consecutive prison sentences is legally required, a court must treat the fact of the offence being committed while on bail as an aggravating factor. This does not apply where the sentence for the previous offence is one of life imprisonment or where the court is satisfied that there are exceptional circumstances to justify a departure from the general rule.[318] However, failure to have due regard to this factor amounts to an error of principle.[319]

Offence Committed During the Currency of a Suspended Sentence or Other Criminal Court Order

5–139 Commission of a further offence during the currency of a criminal court order such as a suspended sentence or probation order may be treated as an aggravating factor or, in any event, as militating against granting further leniency by way, for example, of part-suspension of a prison sentence for the current offence.[320] The offender's failure to take advantage of the opportunity offered by the earlier order and their defiance of that order may be said to heighten their culpability for the later offence. Even then, regard must always be had to the offender's circumstances when the later offence was committed and, if those circumstances were extenuating, it may be unfair to increase the sentence for that offence to any appreciable extent, if at all. If the earlier suspended sentence is activated as a result of the commission of the current offence, this is a factor to be considered when deciding if the breach should be treated as aggravating the current offence. However, the case for treating the commission of an offence during the currency of a suspended sentence or similar order as an aggravating factor will be stronger where the later offence was rationally and deliberately committed for gain, or where there were no obvious excusing circumstances.

---

[317] Domestic Violence Act 2018, s 40. The entire Act entered into force on 1 January 2019.

[318] Criminal Justice Act 1984, s 11(4) inserted by the Bail Act 1997, s 10.

[319] *People (DPP) v Alcorn and Graham*, unreported, Court of Criminal Appeal, 11 March 2011.

[320] *People (DPP) v Carew* [2019] IECA 77. See also *People (DPP) v Curtis* [2022] IECA 184, *People (DPP) v Kinsella* [2022] IECA 143 and *People (DPP) v McGauley* [2022] IECA 16.

Attention should also be paid to the portion of the suspended sentence or other order the offender served before re-offending. Where the offence was committed towards the end of a long operational period of a suspended sentence which had otherwise been fully observed, a court may ignore the fact that the sentence was still in operation at the time.[321]

Previous Convictions

Most jurisdictions either require or permit previous convictions to be treated as an aggravating factor. This is essentially a policy choice, though not one that follows inexorably from any fundamental principle. One clear alternative, and an entirely defensible one, is flat-rate sentencing whereby a penalty is determined solely by reference to the nature and circumstances of the offence(s) of conviction, without regard to the offender's previous record. As a variation on this, some mitigation might be granted for previous good record, but there would be no so-called recidivist premium for previous convictions. Flat-rate penalty systems are not unknown in Ireland or elsewhere. Administrative penalties, such as parking fines, usually operate in this way. However, when it comes to judicial sentencing, there is, in many jurisdictions at least, a presumption in favour of escalating penalties for repeat offenders.[322] Public opinion is often cited as one justification for such a policy, and research conducted elsewhere suggests that it has significant public support.[323] A public opinion survey conducted in connection with the Halliday review of sentencing in England and Wales in 2000-2001 showed that an offender's previous convictions were regarded as by far the most significant factor that should "have a great deal of influence on sentence".[324] There never seems to have been any great public clamour for escalated sentencing in Ireland, though most people, if casually asked during an opinion survey, would probably agree that repeat offenders should be punished more severely than first offenders. But their main concern would be that offenders should be punished appropriately for their current offences, however good or bad their previous records may be. Empirical studies of sentencing practice have consistently shown that, after the offence of conviction, the offender's previous record is treated as the next most important factor in determining sentence. **5–140**

Rules and principles governing the treatment of previous convictions at **5–141**

---

321 The English Sentencing Council's *General Guideline: Overarching Principles* (2019) has a provision to this effect ("The extent to which the offender has completed the conditions of a licence or order (including the time that has elapsed since its commission) will be a relevant consideration").

322 Richard L Lippke, "The ethics of recidivist premiums" in Jonathan Jacobs and Jonathan Jackson (eds), *The Routledge Handbook of Criminal Justice Ethics* (Routledge, 2017), Chap 1.

323 Julian V Roberts, *Punishing Persistent Offenders: Exploring Community and Offender Perspectives* (Oxford University Press, 2008).

324 *Making Punishments Work: Report of a Review of the Sentencing Framework for England and Wales* (the Halliday Report) (Home Office, 2001), p. 111.

sentencing have important practical consequences not only for offenders but also for the criminal justice system. A very significant proportion of those who come up for sentence, including for serious offences, have previous convictions for offences of some description. Some categories of offender tend to have worse criminal records than others. Burglars, for example, are often persistent recidivists. A survey of 60 cases of burglary that came before the Court of Appeal between 2014 and late 2023 showed that of the 70 offenders involved, all but four had previous convictions of some kind.[325] The highest total number of previous convictions was 341, including 112 for burglary.[326] Another offender had 115 previous burglary convictions.[327] Many sex offenders, on the other hand, will be recorded as having no previous convictions but, as noted earlier in the context of previous good character, this can be somewhat artificial in cases of serial child abuse where there has been persistent, though unreported, offending over a prolonged period. A consistent practice of imposing significantly more severe sentences on repeat offenders, apart from the impact on the individuals concerned, would therefore have important consequences for the criminal justice system, notably by increasing the prison population with all the costs that entails.

5–142 Habitual offender statutes have a long history but, in modern times, other legal strategies have been adopted throughout the common law world to deal with repeat offenders.[328] The United States has introduced the most severe measures in this regard, including 'three strikes and you're out' laws enacted in California and several other states in the early 1990s.[329] As reflected in certain cases decided by the United States Supreme Court, some of these laws have operated very harshly. Sentences running to decades of imprisonment have been upheld for relatively minor offences, solely on account of the offender's previous record.[330] Under the grid-centred guidelines operating in several United States jurisdictions, sentence is determined partly by the score attributed to the offence but partly also, and sometimes significantly, by the offender's

[325] The survey was undertaken by the present writer in connection with a case under appeal to the Supreme Court.

[326] *People (DPP) v Redmond* [2022] IECA 44, para 35.

[327] *People (DPP) v Matthews* [2019] IECA 365.

[328] On habitual offender statutes, see Chap 3 above under "Incapacitation". On the use of recidivist premiums throughout history, see Sarah French Russell, "Rethinking recidivist enhancements: The role of prior drug convictions in federal sentencing" (2010) 43 UC Davis LR 1135, 1149.

[329] Franklin Zimring, Gordon Hawkins and Sam Kamin, *Punishment and Democracy: Three Strikes and You're Out in California* (Oxford University Press, 2001). See also John B Meixner, "Shocking sentences", (2024) 100 Indiana LJ (forthcoming), available at <https://papers.ssrn.com/so13/papers.cfm?abstract_id=4759836> accessed 1 November 2024]. (on the range of recidivist premium provisions in various American states), and *Wells-Yates v Colorado* 454 P3d 191 (2019) on Colorado's recidivist statute (which led to an aggregate sentence of 72 years' imprisonment at first instance in that case).

[330] See, for example, *Ewing v California* 538 US 11 (2003); *Lockyer v Andrade* 538 US 63 (2003); *Harmelin v Michigan* 501 US 957 (1991), described in Chap 4 above.

criminal history. Under both the federal and Minnesota guidelines, for example, presumptive sentences increase quite dramatically with criminal history.[331] A federal defendant with an offence score of 20 and a criminal history score of one is liable to 33 to 41 months' imprisonment, but this increases to 70 to 87 months if he or she has, say, 14 previous convictions (a criminal history score of 6, which is the highest). The same applies under the Minnesota guidelines which have seven criminal history categories. Under such schemes, the past is decidedly more important than the present in the sense that the sentence imposed on a person with several previous convictions is determined more by criminal record than by the current offence. This is one reason why American guidelines have found no imitators elsewhere. In England and Wales, courts are statutorily obliged to treat each previous conviction as an aggravating factor if it is reasonable to do so having regard to the nature of the previous offence and its relevance to the current offence, and the time that has elapsed since the earlier conviction.[332] This was largely inspired by a recommendation in the Halliday Report that "the severity of punishment should reflect the seriousness of the offence and the offender's criminal history".[333] In its summary of recommendations, the Report further specified that sentence should increase "when an offender has sufficiently recent and relevant previous convictions".

The present Irish law on the relevance of previous convictions may be reduced to four general principles: (1) absence of previous convictions, especially when this equates with previous good character, is a mitigating factor, as already outlined; (2) a small number of previous convictions for minor offences, especially if unrelated to the current offence and accumulated some time in the past, will usually be ignored, thereby allowing the offender to be treated in effect as a first-time offender; (3) previous convictions for more serious offences that were different in nature from the current offence will not aggravate punishment but they may lead to a progressive loss of mitigation; and (4) previous convictions for 'related' serious offences, meaning offences that are broadly similar in nature to the current offence, may be treated as an aggravating factor. Progressive loss of mitigation means that while the absence of previous convictions is generally a mitigating factor, their presence, unless perhaps for trivial or minor offences, will gradually reduce the degree of mitigation an offender may deserve for previous good record. Repeated convictions will eventually exhaust all entitlement to mitigation.[334] Obviously, this principle cannot be applied in a purely mathematical fashion. A court must have regard to factors such as the nature and seriousness of the previous offences, and the period of time that has elapsed since they were committed. Even one previous conviction for a serious offence might be sufficient to obliterate any entitlement to character-based mitigation, **5–143**

[331] These guidelines are further described in Chap 13 below.
[332] Sentencing Act 2020, s 65 (previously Criminal Justice Act 2003, s 143).
[333] Halliday Report, note 324 above, para 2.8.
[334] Andrew von Hirsch, "Record-enhanced sentencing in England and Wales" (2002) 4 *Punishment and Society* 443, 444-445.

especially if the current offence was committed shortly after the sentence for the previous one was served or, *a fortiori,* while it was being served. On the other hand, an offender might be entitled to some mitigation under this heading despite having some previous convictions for offences of a low to medium level of gravity, especially if there was an appreciable interval since the last of them was committed. The concept of progressive loss of mitigation is not free of difficulty. It has been argued, for example, that if first-time offenders are treated more leniently by reference to the 'lapse' theory (described above in the context of previous good character), it does not seem very logical to grant credit to offenders who have repeatedly lapsed.[335]

5–144 Previous convictions for offences similar in nature to the instant offence may, however, be treated as aggravating, particularly if they were serious in nature. The elapse of a long interval since the last such offence may counterbalance the recidivist premium to some degree, especially if the offender has not re-offended in the meantime. Although relevant previous convictions may increase the otherwise deserved punishment for the instant offence, they may not do so to a degree that is wholly disproportionate to the gravity of that offence. Irish law differs greatly in this respect from American statutes and guidelines that prescribe heavy recidivist premiums. In Ireland, the additional punishment, if any, to be imposed for relevant previous convictions is always a matter of judicial discretion, and it should never amount to more than a modest enhancement of the penalty considered appropriate for the offence(s) being sentenced. For instance, in *People (DPP) v Kinsella,*[336] the Court of Appeal held that the appellant's substantial number of relevant previous convictions did not justify a headline sentence of three years' imprisonment for possessing a stolen item worth €500, the maximum sentence being five years.[337] In other words, the recidivist premium was disproportionate having regard to the nature of the current offence. As illustrated by a later case, also called *People (DPP) v Kinsella,*[338]relevant previous convictions are not invariably treated as aggravating. The appellant, who was being sentenced for endangerment and assault causing harm, had 174 previous convictions including several for violent offences. Yet both the trial court and the Court of Appeal seem to have regarded this record as justifying progressive loss of mitigation rather than enhanced punishment. A court may always take account of circumstances, such as chronic addiction or severe deprivation, that have contributed to the persistent offending. As noted in Chap 4, statutory provisions introduced in 2006 requiring mandatory minimum prison sentences for certain drug and firearms offences where the offender had a previous conviction for a similar offence, were struck down as unconstitutional in 2019.[339]

---

[335] Richard S Frase and Julian V Roberts, *Paying for the Past: The Case Against Prior Record Sentence Enhancements* (Oxford University Press, 2019), 32.
[336] [2022] IECA 143.
[337] Criminal Justice (Theft and Fraud Offences) Act 2001, s 18.
[338] [2024] IECA 20.
[339] *Ellis v Minister for Justice* [2019] IESC 30; [2019] 3 IR 511; [2019] 2 ILRM 420.

5–145 An increase in sentence to reflect previous convictions is difficult to justify in principle, although a few standard justifications are offered in its defence.[340] One is that a criminal record reflects bad character, but this raises a fundamental question of whether character, as opposed to the conduct constituting the offence, should have any impact on sentence. Further, people cannot always be held responsible for their character which is often shaped by circumstances and experiences beyond their control. A second justification revolves around the concept of notice. A person already convicted of an offence has been given clear notice of the wrongfulness and unacceptability of their conduct. Blatant disregard of such notice increases their culpability for a later offence, although this should only hold true, if at all, where both offences were similar in nature. Yet another justification, and connected with the idea of notice, is that repeat offending represents continued disobedience of the law and, to this extent, the repeat offender is openly defying accepted social norms. It has been argued that a criminal conviction imposes an obligation on the offender to rearrange their life so as to avoid further wrongdoing, and the later offence reflects a failure in this regard.[341] Common to all these supposed justifications is the assumption that the offender has had a fair opportunity to desist from criminal activities. Yet, in many cases, an offender's life history, living conditions (which may include homelessness), mental health issues or chronic addiction may go a considerable way towards explaining, if not excusing, their repeat offending. This reality has led to occasional suggestions that recidivism should be treated as a mitigating rather than an aggravating factor, given that it can reflect social deprivation or some such factor. Certainly, any factors that appear to be contributing to recidivism should always be carefully considered before a sentence is increased on account of previous convictions.

5–146 Viewed through the prism of punishment theory, recidivist premiums might possibly be defended by reference to retribution, risk or some combination of the two. According to the retributive argument, the recidivist would be more culpable, in the sense of being more morally blameworthy, for having offended despite having been previously convicted. This is essentially the assumption underpinning the various justifications outlined in the previous paragraph. The harm element of the current offence is seldom affected by the offender's record, whether it be good or bad. This might not invariably be true because, for example, a victim of domestic violence or persistent sexual abuse may be said to suffer more, emotionally and otherwise, on account of the offender's repetitive misconduct. This is certainly an important factor where, as often happens, the early offences (or all of them) remained unreported for some

---

340 For a critical analysis of these justifications, see Guha Krishnamurthi, "Against the recidivist premium" (2024) 98 Tulane LR 411; Michael Tonry, *Doing Justice, Preventing Crime* (Oxford University Press, 2020), 102-113.

341 Youngjae Lee, "Repeat offenders and the question of desert" in Julian V Roberts and Andrew von Hirsch (eds), *Previous Convictions at Sentencing: Theoretical and Applied Perspectives* (Hart Publishing, 2010), Chap 4.

time and the offender is eventually being sentenced for several offences committed against one or more victims over a long period. In that event, the main issue is whether any prison terms imposed should be concurrent or consecutive, a topic addressed later in this chapter. But where an offender continues to assault or abuse a victim, despite having previous convictions for similar offences against that same victim, the repetition may be viewed as increasing harm. As far as risk is concerned, it must be accepted that an offender's previous record is often the best predictor of future conduct. However, while this may hold true in broad actuarial terms, it cannot reliably support the conclusion that any individual with a criminal record will continue to offend or, at any rate, to reoffend in a particular way.

5–147 The major objection to recidivist premiums is that they amount to double punishment for previous offences. Suppose an offender was sentenced in 2018 to four years' imprisonment for a serious assault, and that this was a proper and proportionate penalty at the time. He commits a similar assault in 2024 for which the appropriate penalty is also deemed to be four years, but he is sentenced to five years because of his previous conviction. In a sense, he is being resentenced to an additional year for the earlier offence, despite that offence having been sentenced proportionately at the time. This problem with recidivist premiums was acknowledged by the Supreme Court in *Ellis v Minister for Justice*[342] and, while the court did not go so far as to condemn the practice of increasing sentence because of previous convictions, it did note that this practice was open to criticism. Defenders of the practice will argue that it does not really amount to additional punishment for the earlier offence(s) but is rather a reflection of the offender's enhanced culpability in respect of the current offence. However, as already noted, all the various justifications for attributing such enhanced culpability on account of previous convictions are themselves open to criticism.

Prevalence

5–148 Courts sometimes treat the increased prevalence of an offence in a locality as a basis for increasing sentence.[343] As with other potentially aggravating factors, the first question is whether prevalence, even if reliably established, can be said to affect either harm or culpability, the two constituent elements of gravity. In many cases, it affects neither. The harm inflicted on the victim of an assault or a robbery is probably the same irrespective of whether assaults or robberies are becoming more or less frequent in the relevant locality.[344] This, of course, is on the assumption

---

342 [2019] IESC 30; [2019] 3 IR 511; [2019] 1 ILRM 420 para 80.

343 See, for example, *R v Anderson* [1972] 1 QB 304, 317; (1972) 56 Cr App R 115, 130 (*sub nom R v Neville*) where the English Court of Appeal said that when an offence becomes more prevalent, the only course to be taken is to increase sentences "to readjust for the increase in the incidence of the offence".

344 Lord Justice Asquith, "The problem of punishment" (11 May 1950) 43 *The Listener* 821, argued that an exemplary sentence to reflect prevalence "may be

that we think of harm solely in terms of the impact on the person against whom the offence was committed. The harm caused by some offences is arguably more diffuse. People other than the immediate victim may be adversely affected by knowledge that a certain offence has been committed and even more so if offences of that kind are actually becoming more prevalent. Residential burglary in rural areas is a case in point. When a spate of such burglaries occurs (not an uncommon experience in Ireland), those whose homes are invaded are clearly the primary victims. But others living in similar circumstances will experience ongoing fear that they will be the next victims. Some may feel compelled to make life-changing decisions by, for example, selling or abandoning their homes and moving into a more sheltered residential setting. The same applies where there has been a series of sexual assaults committed against women by strangers in public places. This may well create a widespread fear in the locality and may, for example, cause other women to refrain from walking home alone, something they should be perfectly entitled to do without fear of being molested. In such cases, offenders could also be deemed more culpable if they are, or should be, aware of the more widespread harm caused by the prevalence of the offence they are committing, a prevalence to which they are contributing.

The first question is whether, as a matter of principle, prevalence should ever be treated as an aggravating factor. The Canadian Supreme Court has said that offence prevalence is not, of itself, an aggravating factor, though courts may consider it when balancing the various sentencing objectives. It might, for example, be influential in deciding if priority should be accorded to deterrence. Even then it should never lead to a demonstrably unfit sentence.[345] The English Court of Appeal, as we shall see, has been prepared to treat it as an aggravating factor in certain, carefully defined circumstances. Perhaps the better view is that it may influence the location of a sentence within the applicable range, provided the offender was aware, or should reasonably have been aware, that he or she was contributing to the prevalence of the criminal conduct in question, and that this prevalence could have the kind of harmful impact already described. **5–149**

In any case, care must be exercised before increasing a sentence on account of prevalence. A court must be satisfied that the offence is, in fact, becoming more prevalent. It cannot just act on a hunch. An increase in the number of persons being charged with a given offence may well reflect changes in policing or prosecution practices as opposed to a growing incidence of the conduct in question. As the English Court of Appeal said in *R v Bondzie*[346] a judge should not increase sentence solely because **5–150**

---

expedient; it may even be imperative. But one thing it is not: it is not just. The guilt of a man who commits a crime which happens to be on the increase is no greater than that of another who commits the same crime when it is on the wane".

345 *R v Lacasse* [2015] 3 SCR 1089, para 90.

346 [2016] 1 WLR 3004; [2016] 2 Cr App R (S) 28.

of a personal view that 'there is too much of this sort of thing going on in the area'.[347] Reliable evidence from a responsible authority should be presented to the court to support any claim of increased prevalence, and all parties should have an opportunity to make submissions in respect of that evidence.[348] In *Bondzie*, which involved supplying class A drugs, the court said:

> "Even if such material is provided, a judge will only be entitled to treat prevalence as an aggravating factor if: (a) he is satisfied that the level of harm caused in a particular locality is significantly higher than that caused elsewhere (and thus already inherent in the guideline levels); (b) that the circumstances can properly be described as exceptional; and (c) that it is just and proportionate to increase the sentence for such a factor in the particular case before him. It is clear, therefore, that a court should be hesitant before aggravating sentence by reason of prevalence. Judges will only be too well aware of the types of harm which are caused by drug dealing and will not be assisted by statements of the obvious. Only if the evidence placed before the court demonstrates a level of harm which clearly exceeds the well understood consequences of drug dealing by a significant margin should courts be prepared to reflect this in sentence. If judges do so, they must clearly state when sentencing that they are doing that."[349]

5–151 This was said in respect of an offence for which there was a definitive sentencing guideline, but the same logic should apply in a jurisdiction without guidelines which treats proportionality as the overarching distributive principle. Ordinarily, when assessing harm, courts will have regard to the broader social impact of the relevant criminal conduct. In fact, this is usually the sole consideration in respect of offences such as drug dealing where there is seldom, if ever, an identifiable victim. This is not to say (and the court in *Bondzie was* not saying) that prevalence is never relevant. Rather it is the case that, as a matter of fundamental justice, increased prevalence, where it is claimed to exist, should be properly established and a court should be satisfied that the sentence that would ordinarily be appropriate for the relevant offence inadequately reflects the greater or wider harm resulting from that prevalence. Even where increased prevalence is adequately established, it must never be more than one factor influencing the sentencing decision. It should not be treated as a controlling factor that can trump other important considerations such as providing young or first-time offenders with an incentive to desist from further crime.[350] In *People (DPP) v Larkin*[351] the trial judge was held to have been justified in accepting police evidence on the prevalence of gun crime in the locality where the offence was committed (and the evidence in question seems to have been quite reliable). However, the Court of Criminal Appeal went on to say that a court must also have due regard

[347] This is also to be inferred from *R v Priest* (1996) 30 OR3d 538; (1996) 110 CCC (3d) 289 (Ontario CA).

[348] *R v Lacasse* [2015] 3 SCR 1089, para 94.

[349] [2016] 1 WLR 3004; [2016] 2 Cr App R (S) 28, p 261, para 11.

[350] *R v Priest* (1996) 30 OR (3d) 538; 110 CCC (3d) 289 (Ontario CA); *R v Vandale* (1974) 21 CCC (2d) 250 (Ontario CA).

[351] [2008] IECCA 138; [2009] 2 IR 381.

to the principle of proportionality, the offender's personal circumstances and the possibility of rehabilitation.

Breach of Trust

Breach of trust is often treated as an aggravating factor, especially in child sexual abuse and fraud cases. The reasons are obvious. Many child abuse offences are committed by persons who are responsible for the care of their victims or who, for one reason or another, have privileged access to them. In fact, it may be argued that any adult who abuses a child, even in the absence of any special relationship, is guilty of a breach of trust on account of the child's intrinsic vulnerability and their general powerlessness when confronted by an adult intent on exploiting them. Likewise, the commission of a fraud offence may have been possible only because of the trust that had been reposed in the offender by an employer, investor or whoever the victim happened to be. Breach of trust is primarily a factor affecting culpability. An offender may be said to be more morally blameworthy for having exploited a situation in which he or she was expected to act with care and integrity, and was well aware of that, but instead took advantage of it to gain personal gratification or profit. In a child sexual abuse case, breach of trust may also be relevant to harm. The victim's suffering may be exacerbated by the feeling of betrayal that results from being abused by a person to whom he or she could normally look for care or protection. **5–152**

Having said this, a court must be careful to avoid double counting or over-counting when considering breach of trust. Where the exploitative nature of the conduct has already been considered when assessing the gravity of the offence, it should not be treated as an additional aggravating factor under the separate heading of breach of trust. Further, as the English Court of Appeal pointed out in *R v Forbes*[352] a sentencing judge should always investigate if the relationship between the offender and victim can properly be treated as one of trust. There must always be, as was said in *Forbes,* "a close examination of the facts and clear justification given if breach of trust is to be found". However, the court also accepted that breach of trust may occur in what it described as an "ad hoc situation" such as where a late-night taxi driver assaults a lone passenger. Double counting would also occur if, for example, a court treated the location of the offence as a separate aggravating factor where the breach of trust consisted essentially of committing the offence in that location. For example, the offender may have abused a child while living, or being allowed to live, in the child's family home, an arrangement that allowed him to be alone with the child.[353] **5–153**

352 [2016] EWCA Crim 1388; [2017] 1 WLR 53; [2017] 2 Cr App R (S) 44, para 18.
353 *R v Singh* [2024] EWCA Crim 259; [2024] 2 Cr App R(S) 17.

7. Cultural Differences

5–154 Ireland, like every other Western country, has become an increasingly multi-ethnic and multicultural society. Cultural diversity enriches any society, but it can also give rise to difficult questions about the extent to which members of national, religious, ethnic and racial minorities should be expected to integrate into the dominant culture.[354] Never does this dilemma become more acute than when someone charged with a criminal offence claims that their conduct was excusable or even justified because it is acceptable or perhaps required within the minority culture to which they belong. Much of the extensive literature on this topic deals with cultural beliefs or commitments as exculpatory factors which, if successfully invoked, could relieve a defendant of all criminal liability. Here we are dealing solely with the impact of cultural difference on sentence, but some of the issues relating to culture as a complete defence to liability remain relevant to our discussion. Continental European literature tends to deal with 'cultural offences' while in common law countries the emphasis tends to be on 'cultural defences'.[355] Jeroen Van Broeck defines a cultural offence as:

> "[A]n act by a member of a minority culture which is considered an offence by the legal system of the dominant culture. That same act is nevertheless, within the cultural group of the offender, condoned, accepted as normal behaviour and approved or even endorsed and promoted in the given situation."[356]

5–155 The extent to which cultural difference may excuse or mitigate depends partly on the nature of the conduct and also, at times, on whether it engages the exercise of a fundamental right. Some leading American cases in this area have resulted from claims that a particular criminal prohibition conflicted with the right to free exercise of religion as protected by the First Amendment to the United States Constitution. In *Yoder v Wisconsin*[357] the Supreme Court held that the rights of Amish parents to the free exercise of their religion was violated by a state law that compelled them under pain of penalty to send their children to school until they reached the age of 16 years, whereas the Amish community believed that children should be withdrawn from school at about 14 years. There have also been cases, with mixed results, concerning the use of prohibited drugs such as peyote for the purposes of traditional religious rituals by certain groups.[358] Conduct of this nature may be tolerable where it causes little harm, if any, to the individuals involved or to the broader community.

---

[354] The dominant culture might not necessarily be the majority culture but rather the one that has determined or shaped the law applicable within the jurisdiction.

[355] Jeroen Van Broeck, "Cultural defence and culturally motivated crimes (cultural offences)" (2001) 9 *European Journal of Crime, Criminal Law and Criminal Justice* 1 (which includes references to a wide range of other writing on the topic).

[356] Van Broeck, note 355, at 5.

[357] 406 US 205 (1972).

[358] *Gonzales v O Centro Espírita Beneficente União do Vegetal* 546 US 418 (2006);

However, there is a general consensus that cultural difference should have no impact on the sentencing of violent offences. Any obligation which a state may have to respect the traditions, customs or beliefs of an offender is outweighed by the obligation to protect everyone, whether native or foreigner, within its jurisdiction from violent conduct at the hands of others. This is one situation where a state is entitled to insist that anyone who chooses to reside in or visit a country should be required to acquaint themselves with that country's laws as it applies to any kind of interpersonal violence. The right of every inhabitant of a country to be free from subjection to violence, including non-consensual sexual activity, must outweigh any claim by an offender for leniency on account of cultural differences.[359] Female genital mutilation is a case in point. It is practised in at least 30 countries, and an estimated 200 million women and girls have been subjected to it. Yet, it is strongly and rightly condemned at the highest international level as a serious human rights violation.[360] In 2020, the UN Human Rights Council adopted a resolution on the elimination of female genital mutilation. It was criminalised in Ireland in 2012, and the relevant statute expressly provides that it is not a defence that the accused believed that the act was "required or permitted for customary or ritual reasons".[361] Even if never specifically outlawed, it would constitute an assault under the pre-existing law. **5–156**

8. Consecutive and Concurrent Prison Sentences

Sentencing a multiple offender (meaning a person being sentenced at the same time of several offences) poses one of the more intractable problems faced by the criminal courts. If some or all of the offences call for prison sentences, should those sentences be ordered to run concurrently or consecutively? A judge who makes all the sentences concurrent might be accused of granting a discount for bulk offending. In that event, the offender may spend no longer in prison than a person convicted of any one of the offences of conviction. Entirely consecutive sentences, on the other hand, may result in an aggregate prison term greatly exceeding the most severe determinate sentence that would ordinarily be deemed appropriate for any one of the offences, however serious. Two very tragic cases, each involving the deaths of dozens of people being smuggled into Britain on cargo containers, illustrate the point. In *R v Wacker*[362] the appellant **5–157**

Employment Division v Smith 494 US 872 (1990).

[359] Katie L Zaunbrecher, "When culture hurts: Dispelling the myth of cultural justification for gender-based human rights violations" (2011) 33 *Houston Journal of International Law* 679.

[360] World Health Organisation, *Female Genital Mutilation: Key Facts* (2023) at <https://www/who.int/news-room/fact-sheets/detail/female-genital-mutilation> accessed 29 February 2024.

[361] Criminal Justice (Female Genital Mutilation) Act 2012, s 2. See also *R v Noor* [2024] EWCA Crim 714; [2024] 4 WLR 62; [2024] 2 Cr App R(S) 42 on sentencing for female genital mutilation, and especially para 66 which touches on the cultural issue.

[362] [2002] EWCA Crim 1944; [2003] QB 1207; [2003] 1 Cr App R (S) 92.

was convicted on 58 counts of manslaughter by gross negligence, all the victims, who were of Chinese origin, having been found dead on arrival at Dover. He was sentenced to six years for each of the 58 manslaughters, all sentences to run concurrently but consecutively to an eight-year sentence for a related conspiracy. The Court of Appeal left the cumulative 14-year sentence intact, but increased each manslaughter sentence to 14 years, all of them as well as the conspiracy sentence to run concurrently. In *R v Nica and Hughes*[363] four defendants were convicted (two on guilty pleas) on 39 counts of manslaughter, the victims being Vietnamese nationals who died in transit from Belgium to Britain. They were sentenced to terms varying from 13 years and four months to 27 years, all the individual sentences being concurrent in each case. Two-thirds of these sentences would have to be served in prison before release. If a consecutive sentence had been imposed in respect of each death (which would not be illogical), the cumulative terms would have ranged from 520 years to 1,053 years. Sentences of this length, or even longer, are not uncommon in parts of the United States, but they are unknown in these islands and, indeed, throughout much of the rest of the world. Obviously, it makes little sense, except perhaps for purely rhetorical or declaratory purposes, to impose a sentence that will extend well beyond an offender's natural life span. Admittedly, the two cases just mentioned are highly exceptional, and entirely consecutive sentences would effectively have amounted to whole-life orders for the offenders. More realistically, one might ask if there is anything objectionable about imposing, say, seven consecutive five-year prison terms on a 25-year-old offender convicted of seven serious robberies committed on different occasions and against different victims over a six-month period. The answer ultimately depends on the moral and cultural values underpinning the sentencing system. The general preference for concurrent sentences and for the avoidance of very severe or 'crushing' sentences is often defended on proportionality grounds. Just as an individual sentence should be proportionate to the gravity of the offence, so a combination of sentences should be proportionate to the totality of the offending, or so the argument goes. The problem with this line of argument is that proportionality, despite its critical importance as a sentencing value, cannot readily tell us what *is* appropriate for the overall offending. Values such as moderation and the opportunity for redemption must therefore come into play as well and, in practice, they usually do, even if not expressly mentioned.

5–158 The common law power to order prison sentences to run consecutively was put beyond doubt as early as 1770 in *R v Wilkes*[364] where the House of Lords held that a court, when sentencing for two or more misdemeanours, could devise a fair punishment by "tacking one imprisonment to the other", as Lord Wilmot put it. That case dealt with misdemeanours only, although the same would probably have been said about felonies.[365] In

[363] [2021] EWCA Crim 1790.
[364] (1770) 19 How St Tr 1075; (1768) 98 ER 327.
[365] For a detailed analysis of *Wilkes* and its historical context, see *R v Paul* [1982] 1 SCR 621, 635-642. See also *R v Castro* (1881) 6 AC 229.

fact, some years later, the power to impose consecutive sentences for felonies was introduced by statute in both England and Ireland.[366] The English Court of Appeal has more recently held that the Crown Court may order a prison sentence imposed following a criminal conviction to run consecutively to a sentence imposed by another court for contempt of court, just as imprisonment for contempt may be ordered to run consecutively to other prison sentences.[367]

There is often a stark contrast between the treatment of repeat offenders (meaning those who have previously been convicted of offences) and those who are being sentenced simultaneously for several offences. Many countries nowadays require (or at least permit) previous convictions to be treated as an aggravating factor. As noted above in the context of previous convictions, American sentencing guideline systems often impose heavy recidivist premiums. Yet, if all the offences were being dealt with at the same time, some or all the sentences would probably be made concurrent. Kevin Reitz, in particular, has drawn attention to the disparity that can result when, to use his example, two robbers are sentenced, one as a repeat offender and the other having been simultaneously convicted of two robberies. The total prison term served by the first may greatly exceed that served by the second. Yet the totality of the harm they have inflicted may be very similar.[368] **5–159**

One might begin by asking why concurrent sentences are ever justified. Why should a person who commits several offences receive the same punishment as if he or she had committed only one of them? How can it be right that A who has been convicted of burglary, assault upon an occupant of the premises and damaging the premises in order to gain entry (all the offences having formed part of the same transaction) should receive the same sentence as B who committed a similar burglary but no other accompanying offence? From a purely retributive perspective, it is difficult to justify such an arrangement. Of course, A in this example need not receive the same sentence as B, even if all A's sentences are concurrent, as the burglary sentence could be increased to reflect his other criminal conduct, a point to which we shall return. Concurrent sentences can operate as a corrective to over-charging by the prosecution. Charge stacking is a troublesome practice in many United States jurisdictions where one criminal transgression can lead to numerous charges.[369] That may not be much of a problem in Ireland, but even here it can happen that two or more charges are brought in respect of what was essentially **5–160**

---

[366] Criminal Law Act 1827 (s 10); Criminal Law (Ireland) Act 1828 (s 20).

[367] *R v Anomo* [1998] 2 Cr App R (S) 269; [1998] Crim LR 356; *R v Stredder* [1997] 1 Cr App R (S) 209.

[368] Kevin R Reitz, "The Illusion of Proportionality: Desert and Repeat Offenders" in Julian V Roberts and Andrew von Hirsch, *Previous Convictions at Sentencing: Theoretical and Applied Perspectives* (Hart Publishing, 2010), Chap 8.

[369] John F Stinneford, "Dividing crime, multiplying punishments" (2015) 48 Univ College Davis LR 1955; Note, "Stacked: Where criminal charge stacking happens – and where it doesn't" (2023) 136 Harvard LR 1390.

a single course of criminal conduct. As discussed further below, this may occur in respect of drug dealing and associated money laundering. Concurrent sentences are normally appropriate in those circumstances.[370]

5–161 In Ireland, the formal law on consecutive and concurrent sentences is clear. There are some situations in which consecutive sentences must be imposed. Any sentence of imprisonment passed on a person for an offence committed while on bail must be consecutive to any sentence passed on him or her for a previous offence.[371] Likewise, any sentence of imprisonment for an offence committed while serving a prison sentence must be made consecutive to the sentence being served.[372] A mandatory consecutive sentence may be suspended, absent any statutory prohibition on doing so, but, save in exceptional circumstances, it should not be fully suspended.[373] These few exceptions aside, the general orthodoxy is that a judge has discretion as to whether multiple prison sentences should be ordered to run concurrently or consecutively.[374] Discretion should, as always, be exercised in accordance with settled principles but the question in this instance is whether any such principles can be identified.

5–162 There is, in fact, one well-known principle – the one-transaction principle – though its general utility is questionable. David Thomas in his *Principles of Sentencing*, which was based on an analysis of hundreds of English Court of Appeal sentencing decisions up the late 1970s, stated the principle in these terms:

> "The essence of the one-transaction rule appears to be that consecutive sentences are inappropriate when all the offences taken together constitute a single invasion of the same legally protected interest."[375]

He goes on to say:

> "The concept of a 'single transaction' may be held to cover a sequence of offences involving a repetition of the same behaviour towards the same victim, such as a series of sexual offences with the same partner, a number of frauds on the same victim or several perjured statements made in the course of the same trial, provided the offences are committed within a relatively short space of time. The concept will not normally apply to a series of offences involving different victims, even though the offences are of a similar nature."

5–163 The one-transaction principle nonetheless retains some value, at least

---

370 See, for example, *People (DPP) v Curtis* [2021] IECA 184.

371 Criminal Justice Act 1984, s 11(1) as substituted by Criminal Justice Act 2007, s 22.

372 Criminal Law Act 1976, s 13. The constitutionality of this section was upheld by the Supreme Court in *Gilligan v Ireland* [2013] IESC 45; [2013] 2 IR 745; [2014] 1 ILRM 153.

373 *People (DPP) v Culhane* [2017] IECA 59, para 30

374 *People (DPP) v E (F)* [2019] IESC 85; [2021] 1 IR 217; [2020] 1 ILRM 517 (which has a detailed account of concurrent and consecutive sentencing).

375 David Thomas, *Principles of Sentencing*, 2nd ed. (Heinemann, 1979), 53-54.

to the extent that it points to concurrent sentences for offences that were genuinely part of one continuous transaction. Thus, in *People (DPP) v Conroy*[376] the Court of Appeal held that the sentence imposed for the unlawful seizure of a vehicle should have been ordered to run concurrently with that for a related endangerment offence. Admittedly, it so decided mainly because the aggregate sentence imposed by the trial court, which had ordered the sentences to run consecutively, was excessive in the circumstances. The same applies *à fortiori* where several charges are brought, and convictions obtained, in respect of what is effectively a single criminal act. For instance, it is not uncommon for a person found in possession of drugs with a market value of €13,000 or more to be charged not only with a s 15A offence, but also with a s 15 offence (possession of drugs for sale or supply) and a s 3 offence (possession of drugs simpliciter).[377] Clearly, any prison sentences imposed in such a case should run concurrently. Nor is it uncommon nowadays for money laundering to be charged in conjunction with the underlying offence from which the criminal proceeds were derived. In a drug trafficking case, for example, the defendant may have been found in possession of a substantial quantity of cash as well as drugs. If convicted of both offences, the defendant should ordinarily receive concurrent sentences unless the money laundering offence involved conduct that went beyond that directly connected with the underlying offence, in which case some element of consecutive sentencing or an uplift on the sentence for the underlying offence might be appropriate. In *R v Cooper*[378] the English Court of Appeal provided some useful guidance on sentencing offenders in these circumstances, saying:

> "[T]here is a broad spectrum of cases involving the combination of [money laundering] offences and other underlying, primary, offending. At one end of the spectrum, the [money laundering] offence does not involve any additional culpability or harm and does not aggravate the seriousness of the primary offence. At the other end, the [money laundering] offending... is markedly distinct from the primary offending and involves significant additional culpability and harm, aggravating the primary offence to an extent that would not otherwise be reflected in the sentence for that offence if considered in isolation."

It then identified two primary principles:

> "(1) Where the [money laundering] offence adds nothing to the culpability and harm involved in the primary offence then there should be no additional penalty ... In such a case it is appropriate to impose concurrent sentences, with no upward adjustment.
>
> (2) Where the [money laundering] offence involves additional criminality (whether increasing the culpability or harm, or both) beyond that involved in the other offences for which sentences are imposed, an additional penalty

[376] [2019] IECA 313.

[377] These offences are described in Chap 10 below under 'Drug Offences'.

[378] [2023] EWCA Crim 945; [2024] 1 WLR 1433; [2024] 1 Cr App R (S) 14; [2023] Crim LR 751.

> should be imposed ... The seriousness of the additional criminality is to be assessed by reference to the culpability of the offender and the harm caused by the [money laundering] offending. In such a case the sentencing judge may either impose concurrent sentences with an appropriate upward adjustment, or consecutive sentences, often with a downward adjustment."[379]

5–164 The court also listed certain factors that might indicate additional culpability or harm, such as where the money laundering involved additional or different criminal property, beyond the proceeds of the primary offending. In Ireland, likewise, the Court of Appeal has held that a concurrent sentence is appropriate where the money laundering was "a significant and integral part" of the drug dealing.[380] This principle applies in most situations where all the charges arose from the same, or substantially the same, course of conduct. In *R v Westguard*,[381] for example, the appellant pleaded guilty to breaches of a restraining order and stalking, all committed against the same victim. He was sentenced to 16 months' imprisonment for the breaches and two months consecutive for the stalking. The English Court of Appeal, while upholding the overall sentence (by increasing the 16 months to 18 months), held that the sentences should have been concurrent because there were "no elements of the [stalking] offending that were not already covered by the breaches of the restraining order".[382] Likewise, when sentencing for a serious road traffic offence, such as causing death by dangerous or careless driving, a court will usually impose concurrent sentences for any related offences, though the sentence for the most serious offence may be increased to reflect the others.

5–165 Aside from relatively straightforward situations like these, there are no clear and unequivocal criteria for trial courts to apply when sentencing multiple offenders. Identifying all-embracing criteria for this purpose might well be impossible. It has often been said that, in this country, concurrent sentences are the norm and consecutive sentences rare or exceptional, but this does not preclude their imposition in appropriate circumstances. Statements to this effect, even if statistically true, fail to identify the rationale for preferring concurrent sentences and, more to the point from a practical perspective, they fail to indicate when exactly consecutive sentences are appropriate. The one-transaction principle, especially as described by David Thomas (above), is scarcely more helpful. It may seem intuitively acceptable when applied to several offences committed during the same criminal transaction. However, Thomas's formulation also allows for concurrent sentences where there has been a series of offences of a similar nature or committed against the same victim at different times. He does, however, add the important proviso that this

---

[379] [2023] EWCA Crim 945; [2024] 1 WLR 1433; [2024] 1 Cr App R (S) 14 para 10.

[380] *People (DPP) v McInerney* [2023] IECA 221, para 13.

[381] [2024] EWCA Crim 378. See also *R v O'Reilly* [2023] EWCA Crim 1615; [2024] 1 Cr App R (S) 50, and *R v Ali* [2023] EWCA Crim 1464; [2024] 1 Cr App R (S) 48 to the same effect.

[382] [2024] EWCA Crim 378, para 27.

applies (only, one may surmise) where the offences were committed within a short timeframe. But he then says this will not normally apply where the offences, even if similar in nature, were committed against different victims. Yet, it cannot be right that A who committed 100 sexual assaults against one of his children should be sentenced more leniently than B who committed one such assault of the same level of gravity against each of three different children. By any standards, the seriousness of A's overall offending greatly exceeds that of B. The same would apply where A repeatedly stole substantial sums of money from one employer while B stole much smaller sums from different clients.

Perhaps the best that can be said is that there are certain fact situations which, when they arise, should cause a court to consider carefully whether consecutive or concurrent sentences, as the case may be, are appropriate. Consecutive sentences must obviously be considered when two entirely separate offences are being dealt with, eg a robbery committed on one occasion and an unrelated burglary on another. A consecutive sentence is also appropriate where the offender is already serving a prison sentence for an unrelated offence and would undergo no additional punishment if the sentence for the current offence were made entirely concurrent with the earlier one.[383] A series of offences, whether different or similar in nature committed against different victims, even within a short time span, will usually attract consecutive sentences or, at least, some element of consecutive sentencing.[384] As already noted, some courts follow a practice of imposing consecutive sentences for similar offences committed against different victims. In fact, the Court of Appeal has said that the point has now been reached where it is an error of principle not to at least consider imposing consecutive sentences in these circumstances, especially where the victims were children.[385] A consecutive sentence should not be imposed for an offence the conduct element of which has already been treated as an aggravating factor for another offence for which sentence is being, or has been, passed.[386] Concurrent sentences are most appropriate where there is a close nexus between the offences.[387] However, the case law clearly shows that concurrent sentences are imposed in a much wider range of circumstances than 'one-transaction' scenarios. In fact, they are often imposed in respect of offences that were entirely unconnected and that had little in common apart from being committed by the same person. This approach is not necessarily to be criticised as long as the ultimate sentence fairly reflects the totality of the offending and the offender's personal circumstances. To accomplish this objective, the longest sentence may be increased to reflect the other offences for which concurrent sentences are being imposed. **5–166**

383 *People (DPP) v Donoghue* [2023] IECA 303.
384 *People (DPP) v Crowley* [2021] IECA 178.
385 *People (DPP) v PP* [2019] IECA 246; *People (DPP) v C(S)* [2019] IECA 348.
386 *People (DPP) v Purcil* [2020] IECA 328, para 31.
387 See, for example, *People (DPP) v Jones* [2019] IECA 51.

5–167 In *People (DPP) v McGauley*[388] the Court of Appeal said:

> "A judge may impose a higher sentence than that which might otherwise be appropriate on a single freestanding offence in order to take account of a multiplicity of offences. An alternative is to impose consecutive sentences."

5–168 This principle is reflected in other cases such as *People (DPP) v Munteanu*[389] where the appellant had pleaded guilty to 28 offences including participating in a criminal organisation (one count), theft (11 counts) and possessing a false instrument (16 counts). All related to ATM fraud by means of 'skimming' which resulted in a total of €120,000 being stolen from machines throughout the country. The trial judge identified headline sentences of 11 years for involvement in a criminal organisation (the maximum being 15 years), 10 years for each false instrument offence (the maximum being 10 years) and nine and a half years for each theft offence (the maximum being 10 years). The sentence ultimately imposed was seven years' imprisonment with the last six months suspended. It is to be inferred from the judgment that all the sentences were ordered to run concurrently. On appeal it was argued that the trial judge erred in adopting headline sentences that were at or near the maximum for most of the offences. However, the Court of Appeal held that the maximum sentence is the maximum for a single offence. In this case, there were many offences and, in any event, significant mitigation had been granted. The appeal was therefore dismissed. In effect, the court accepted that, when concurrent sentences are being imposed for several offences, the longest of them may be increased to a level beyond what would otherwise be proportionate (subject to the statutory maximum) to reflect the additional criminality. There are many English authorities to the same effect. In *R v Kelly*,[390] for example, concurrent sentences were imposed for manslaughter and the false imprisonment of the victim prior to the killing. However, it was accepted that, in these circumstances, the false imprisonment justified increasing the manslaughter sentence.

5–169 In this connection, it is noteworthy that the current English Council guideline on concurrent and consecutive sentencing is entitled 'Totality'.[391] The underlying policy is that the aggregate sentence for multiple offending should be just and proportionate, irrespective of whether resort is had to concurrent or consecutive sentencing, or some combination of the two. The guideline states:

> "When sentencing for more than one offence, the overriding principle of totality is that the overall sentence should:
>
> - reflect all of the offending behaviour with reference to overall harm and culpability, together with the aggravating and mitigating

[388] [2022] IECA 16, para 32. See also *People (DPP) v PP (No.2)* [2015] IECA 316, para 14.
[389] [2022] IECA 62.
[390] [2019] EWCA Crim 668.
[391] The guidelines became effective on 1 July 2023.

- factors relating to the offences and those personal to the offender; and
- be just and proportionate."

It then offers more specific guidance for sentencers: **5–170**

> "1. Consider the sentence for each individual offence, referring to the relevant sentencing guidelines.
> 2. Determine whether the case calls for concurrent or consecutive sentences. When sentencing three or more offences a combination of concurrent and consecutive sentences may be appropriate.
> 3. Test the overall sentence against the requirement that the total sentence is just and proportionate to the offending as a whole.
> 4. Consider and explain how the sentence is structured in a way that will be best understood by all concerned."

This broadly reflects the present Irish approach. For instance, in *People (DPP) v U(M)*[392] the Court of Appeal said, in relation to the sentencing of two sexual assaults in that case, that if consecutive sentences were passed the totality principle would have to be applied, whereas if the sentences were made concurrent, it would be necessary to impose a sentence that reflected the overall offending. In effect, therefore, the important consideration is to sentence for the totality of the offending, whichever route is chosen to arrive at the appropriate penalty.[393] **5–171**

Where a person is convicted of multiple 'fungible' offences, as may occur in cases of drug dealing, fraud or revenue offences, a single sentence representing the total quantity of drugs or money, as the case may be, is usually appropriate. In effect, all the individual offences, of which there may be many, are treated as if they were a single transaction. A sentence chosen to reflect the aggregate of the amount is usually sufficient to punish all the individual offences, and may even obviate the need to specify a sentence for each of those offences (though it is still best practice to do so). In *People (DPP) v Gargan*,[394] for example, the defendant had been charged with 84 VAT-related offences, committed over a seven-year period, with the total unpaid VAT amounting to more than €180,000. By the time of sentence, he had paid all the outstanding VAT and interest. While the Court of Appeal varied the entirely suspended sentence imposed by the trial judge to an effective sentence of one year's imprisonment, it seems to have treated the offending as if it amounted, in effect, to one transaction, and it determined the sentence accordingly. **5–172**

Courts sometimes invoke what might be described as the 'gap principle' – the idea being that consecutive sentences are appropriate where there were two or more periods of offending with an interval of some length between them. In those circumstances, the sentences for the offences committed **5–173**

---

392 [2021] IECA 357, para 25. See also *People (DPP) v C(L)* [2023] IECA 30 and *People (DPP) v PP* [2023] IECA 169.

393 *People (DPP) v C(S)* [2019] IECA 348.

394 [2024] IECA 156.

during each period would be concurrent *inter se* but consecutive to those imposed in respect of the other period(s). This idea seems to derive from *People (DPP) v McKenna (No 2)*[395] in which the DPP brought an undue leniency application in respect of 31 concurrent sentences of three years' imprisonment imposed on the defendant for sexual offences committed against his young daughter between 1985 and 1993. While all the charges were ones of indecent assault and sexual assault, the conduct appears to have been of a particularly serious nature. The defendant was out of the country between autumn 1989 and spring 1990, but he resumed the offending after his return. The Court of Criminal Appeal found it "particularly reprehensible" that he should have resumed the offending given the opportunity that he had while abroad to reflect on his conduct. The court increased the overall sentence to six years by making the concurrent three-year sentences imposed for the later set of offences consecutive to those imposed for the other set. Yet, it is important not to read too much into *McKenna* as far as the 'gap principle' is concerned. Undoubtedly, it was one factor that influenced the court in that case but equally significant, if not more so, was the particularly depraved nature of the offending conduct, as the court made clear.[396] It is reasonable to surmise that, even if there had been no gap in the offending, the court would still have found the overall three-year sentence unduly lenient. Granted, it may be argued that, in some circumstances at least, a person who resumes offending against the same victim(s) after a period of desistance or separation is somewhat more culpable on that account. However, what must ultimately matter and determine the overall sentence is the totality of the offending conduct, irrespective of whether it has been continuous or episodic or, as in *McKenna*, interrupted because of the offender being temporarily separated from the victim(s). It would obviously be perverse if a person who continuously abused a victim for a given period received a lower sentence than someone who engaged in the same conduct against another victim for a similar period, save that in the latter case there was a gap, as in *McKenna*. This could occur if all the sentences in the first case were concurrent, but some of those in the second case were made consecutive. The disparity would be unjustified if there was no material difference between the two cases in terms of the gravity of the offending conduct, viewed in its totality.

5–174 Finally, it may be noted that one possible strategy for dealing with repeat sexual offending against the same victim is to have an offence of maintaining a sexual relationship with a child, as exists in some Australian jurisdictions. This typically requires proof that that the defendant engaged in two or more sexual acts with or towards a child during a given period. The title of the offence has recently been changed to 'repeated sexual conduct with a child' in Queensland and 'persistent sexual abuse of a child' in New South Wales, the changes being a response to concern that the expression 'maintaining a sexual relationship with a child' might fail

---

395 [2002] 2 IR 345.

396 [2002] 2 IR 345, 349-350.

to reflect the exploitative nature of the conduct. In both jurisdictions the maximum sentence is life imprisonment.[397] A survey of sentencing for this offence in Queensland for the period 2005 to 2020 showed that there were 801 cases in which this offence was the principal offence, that 100 per cent of offenders sentenced received custodial sentences, and that the average term of imprisonment was 7.4 years. However, the present Irish system of charging multiple specific offences may be preferable as a means of reflecting the overall conduct of the offender, even if the sentences are eventually concurrent.

Totality Principle

This principle, which applies where two or more consecutive prison sentences are passed, is intended to ensure that the aggregate sentence is reasonably proportionate to the totality of the offending. It is also applicable where several fines are simultaneously imposed. According to David Thomas: **5–175**

> "The effect of the totality principle is to require a sentencer who has passed a series of sentences, each properly calculated in relation to the offence for which it is imposed and each properly made consecutive in accordance with the principles governing consecutive sentences, to review the aggregate sentence and consider whether the aggregate is 'just and appropriate.'"[398]

Courts throughout the common law world have expressed the principle in substantially similar terms. In *People (DPP) v Casey and Casey*,[399] the Court of Appeal said: **5–176**

> "The totality principle is potentially engaged whenever a court is seeking to reflect the overall gravity of two or more offences for which an accused faces sentencing, either by means of overlapping sentences, or wholly consecutive sentences. It permits a court to adjust the final sentence, and some or all of its individual components, as required to reach an overall figure that is proportionate both to the gravity of the offending, but also to the circumstances of the individual offender.
>
> It is most frequently seen to operate where a court approaches sentencing on the basis of first determining in the normal way the appropriate post-mitigation sentence for each individual offence, and whether and to what extent those sentences should be consecutive or concurrent *inter se*, without reference to any considerations of what cumulative figure it may result in. The court is then required to step back and give consideration to the resultant cumulative figure and if necessary adjust it downwards, with appropriate *pro rata* adjustments to the individual component sentences, so as to avoid the imposition of a "crushing" sentence on the offender."

The Canadian Supreme Court has likewise said: **5–177**

---

[397] Queensland, Criminal Code, s 229B; New South Wales Crimes Act, s 66EA. See *Xerri v The King* [2024] HCA 5.

[398] Thomas, note 375 above, at 56, citing *R v Smith* [1972] Crim LR 124.

[399] [2018] IECA 121; [2018] 2 IR 337, paras 20-21.

> "The totality principle, in short, requires a sentencing judge who orders an offender to serve consecutive sentences for multiple offences to ensure that the cumulative sentence does not exceed the overall culpability of the offender."[400]

5–178 The totality principle is conventionally justified by reference to proportionality. Just as the sentence for each individual offence should be proportionate, so too should the aggregate sentence for the totality of the offending. That is why a judge who has imposed consecutive prison sentences should 'stand back' and consider if the aggregate sentence needs adjusting before finalising the matter. Such an adjustment will be unnecessary if the aggregate seems fair and proportionate, but if it is needed, it may be given effect in various ways.[401] A court may deem it appropriate to impose consecutive sentences for offences committed against different victims but this does not relieve it of the responsibility to consider the totality principle and, if necessary, make a suitable adjustment to the aggregate sentence.[402]

5–179 Totality may be achieved by, for example, making one of the sentences concurrent with another, rather than having them all consecutive,[403] or by making a suitable reduction from the aggregate and then adjusting one or more of the individual sentences accordingly.[404] Part-suspension is another possible strategy though, for reasons outlined in Chap 12 in connection with suspended sentences, a straight reduction rather than part-suspension is the preferable means of extending leniency, unless there is also a desire to incentivise rehabilitation or desistance. As always, a sentence should be identified for each offence of conviction, irrespective of whether the sentences are being ordered to run concurrently, consecutively or partly concurrently.

9. Sentencing Co-Offenders

5–180 Two or more offenders who participate in the commission of the same offence should receive identical or similar sentences unless there is some rational basis for treating them differently.[405] This principle is grounded primarily on considerations of fairness; it would be unjust to impose different punishments on equally culpable offenders. Public confidence in the sentencing system would also be eroded if there was no obvious

---

400 *R v M (CA)* [1996] 1 SCR 500, para 42.

401 *People (DPP) v Crowley* [2021] IECA 178, para 60.

402 *People (DPP) v Crowley* [2021] IECA 178. See also *People (DPP) v Kenneally* [2018] IECA 274 where, although the totality principle does not seem to have been expressly considered by the trial judge, the aggregate sentence ultimately imposed was upheld on appeal.

403 *People (DPP) v Shannon* [2023] IECA 325.

404 *People (DPP) v Keogh* [2023] IECA 322.

405 The many authorities for this proposition include *People (Attorney General) v Poyning* [1974] IR 402; *People (DPP) v O'Driscoll* [2019] IECA 315; *People (DPP) v Norton* [2015] IECA 276.

justification for the disparity.[406] In practice, there usually is some basis for differential treatment.[407] The offenders may have had different levels of involvement in the commission of the offence. One may have inflicted more damage or injury than another; one may have been acting under the influence of another; or one may have reduced culpability because of youth, mental disorder or some similar factor. Their previous records may also vary, with one having many previous convictions for similar offences while another has few such convictions or none. One may have pleaded guilty while another was convicted following trial. There may also be differences in their degree of cooperation during the investigation of the offence, and in their personal circumstances at the time of sentence. The presence of one or more of these factors undoubtedly justifies the imposition of different penalties. Even in cases of joint enterprise account must be taken of differences in culpability where they exist.[408] In truth, the question is more often one of relativity than of parity. Occasionally, though probably rarely, two or more co-offenders will deserve equal punishment. More often, it will be a case of ensuring that the penalties they receive fairly reflect their respective levels of culpability. In a classic statement of the principle, Gibbs CJ of the High Court of Australia said:

> "The true position in my opinion may be briefly stated as follows. It is obviously desirable that persons who have been parties to the commission of the same offence should, if other things are equal, receive the same sentences, but other things are not always equal, and such matters as the age, background, previous criminal history and general character of the offender, and the part he or she played in the commission of the offence, have to be taken into consideration."[409]

Parity aims at substantive equality, as opposed to producing identical outcomes.[410] If each sentence is proportionate, having been determined according to the same distributive principles or guidelines, there is unlikely to be disparity in the sense of substantive inequality. Conversely, **5–181**

---

[406] *People (DPP) v Conroy (No 2)* [1989] IR 160; [1989] ILRM 139; *People (DPP) v Duffy* [2003] 2 IR 192. Recent examples of where the Court of Appeal adjusted sentences somewhat because of disparity include *People (DPP) v Kelly* [2023] IECA 37 and *People (DPP) v Davis* [2022] IECA 57.

[407] *R v Kim* [2023] NZCA 332, para 39 ("The circumstances of one offender can rarely be closely compared with those of another, even where they have been involved in similar offending").

[408] In *People (DPP) v Wall, Walsh, O'Connor and Tynan* [2020] IECA 48, different sentences were justified although all four accused had participated in the armed robbery of a post office. See also *People (DPP) v Byrne and others* [2017] IECA 136 involving an aggravated burglary committed by a gang of seven men, and *People (DPP) v Fitzgerald and O'Driscoll* [2018] IECA 15 involving a serious assault perpetrated by three men; *People (DPP) v McDonnell* [2022] IECA 200; *People (DPP) v Norton* [2015] IECA 276; *People (DPP) v Dowdall* [2023] IECA 182.

[409] *Lowe v The Queen* [1984] HCA 46, para 3; (1984) 154 CLR 606, 609. See also *Green v The Queen* [2011] HCA 49; 244 CLR 462.

[410] *R v Morris* [2021] ONCA 680, para 108. See also *R v Friesen* [2020] 1 SCR 424, para 32 (true parity is an expression of proportionality) and *R v Ipeelee* [2012] 1 SCR 433 (disparity in sanctions for apparently similar offences must be justified).

disparity may arise where identical sentences are imposed on offenders with different levels of culpability. For instance, in *People (DPP) v B (M)*[411] the imposition of identical sentences on two offenders was held to be an error of principle because of a difference, albeit a marginal one, in their degrees of culpability. In *People (DPP) v Byrne and others,*[412] a particularly serious case of aggravated burglary committed by a gang, the Court of Appeal reduced somewhat the heaviest sentences imposed on the basis that they diverged excessively from the other sentences.

5–182 When sentencing co-offenders, a court should begin by considering each individual separately in order to identify an appropriate sentence, having regard to the gravity of the offence, including the individual's culpability in committing it, and his or her relevant personal circumstances. As the Court of Criminal Appeal said in *People (DPP) v Daly,*[413] "[t]he foremost consideration in sentencing is to ensure the imposition of an appropriate sentence". However, a court must then consider any sentence already imposed or about to be imposed on a co-offender, to ensure that there is appropriate degree of parity or relativity between them. A suitable adjustment can then be made, but only if necessary, having regard to the relative culpability of the offenders.

5–183 Essentially, a court must observe two fundamental principles which, in fact, are quite compatible, even if they may not appear so at first sight. First, each offender must receive a proportionate sentence, namely, one that is neither excessively severe nor unduly lenient, having regard to all the relevant circumstances. Secondly, the sentences imposed on co-offenders should not be so disparate as to leave the recipient of the more severe sentence with a justifiable sense of grievance. The key word here is 'justifiable'. Anyone who receives a heavier sentence than other participants in the same crime will probably feel some sense of grievance, but that reaction will be justified only there was no principled or legitimate basis for the difference..[414] As already noted, the imposition of identical sentences may also be a source of justifiable grievance if they fail to reflect different levels of culpability. Some reduction in the penalty imposed on the less culpable offender may therefore be appropriate.[415] The test in Northern Ireland is whether there is a 'very marked' disparity and the difference in treatment is "so glaring that the court considered that a real sense of grievance was engendered".[416]

5–184 The greatest difficulty arises when one co-offender (A) has received a

---

411 [2023] IECA 215.

412 [2017] IECA 136.

413 [2011] IECCA 104; [2012] 1 IR 476, para 77.

414 In *People (DPP) v Kelly* [2023] IECA 37, for example, it was held that the appellant could have a justifiable sense of grievance. His sentence was therefore reduced by a year to make it equal to that imposed on his co-accused.

415 *People (DPP) v B (M)* [2023] IECA 215; *People (DPP) v Robinson* [2022] IECA 311.

416 *R v Delaney* [1994] NIJB 31, 33, approved in *R v Stewart* [2009] NICA 4 and *R v Coulter* [2023] NICA 8.

considerably more severe sentence than another (B), despite the absence of any obvious grounds for differentiating between them (either at all or to any significant degree), but the sentence imposed on B was, by any standards, too lenient. Here, the two principles just mentioned can come into conflict. It may be argued that A's sentence should be upheld if it is proportionate, or else varied to whatever extent necessary to render it proportionate, but that A cannot have a justifiable sense of grievance just because B was treated too leniently. As the Court of Criminal Appeal once said, when an appeal court is adjusting sentence to remove an unwarranted disparity, it should not substitute a sentence that is itself unduly lenient. To do so "would be to displace one potentially unjustified approach with another equally unjustified sentence".[417] The matter was analysed in greater detail in *People (DPP) v Daly*[418]where the Court of Criminal Appeal, having considered numerous Irish and Commonwealth authorities, concluded that there is no obligation to apply the parity principle (meaning, presumably, to impose identical sentences) where the earlier sentence was manifestly inadequate or where there were relevant differences between the offenders. The Northern Ireland Court of Appeal has likewise said that it is "not unfair to an appellant who receives a perfectly proper sentence that a co-accused is punished less severely".[419] The sole question, according to this line of argument, is whether A was treated too harshly for the offence that he or she committed. As against this, principles of fairness and the need to avoid any public perception of arbitrariness in the sentencing process may militate in favour of reducing, if not removing, the disparity. In these circumstances, where there seem to have been no obvious grounds for differentiating between the offenders, an appeal court should pay particular attention to the heavier sentence to ensure that it is not disproportionately severe. If it can be reduced somewhat, without sacrificing the proportionality principle, this may alleviate the sense of grievance but it cannot, of course, be reduced to a point where it becomes unduly lenient.

10. Credit for Time Spent on Remand

When imposing a sentence of imprisonment, a court normally grants **5–185** credit for any time the offender has spent on remand in respect of the offence being sentenced. The Court of Appeal once said that judges have a discretion to decline to give any credit or only limited credit for the remand period "in appropriate cases, and with regard to the totality principle".[420] However, it is difficult to envisage circumstances in which such credit might justly be withheld, assuming the custodial remand was solely for the offence being sentenced. Different considerations may apply where the offender was on remand in respect of several unrelated charges,

417 *People (DPP) v Cunningham* [2015] IECCA 2, para 2.16.
418 [2011] IECCA 104; [2012] 1 IR 476, paras 54 to 77.
419 *R v Stewart* [2009] NICA 4, para 25. See also *R v Coulter* [2023] NICA 8 (where an appeal on this ground was dismissed).
420 *People (DPP) v Flaherty* [2015] IECA 161.

some of which might be more serious than the offence for which sentence is being imposed. Limited rather than full credit might sometimes be appropriate, such as where the offender had been remanded in custody having breached conditions of bail that had originally been granted. A judge undoubtedly has discretion as to the manner in which the remand period is factored into the sentence.[421] The sentence may be ordered to run from the date on which the offender was taken into custody, or from the date of sentence with a reduction to reflect the period already spent on custodial remand. A court adopting the latter approach usually allows for the fact that the period spent on remand is not exactly equivalent to an identical period of post-sentence imprisonment, because of the standard remission (currently one-quarter) to which sentenced prisoners are ordinarily entitled. Additional credit may be given where the custodial conditions during remand were particularly harsh or restrictive.

5–186 Canada happens to have an extensive jurisprudence on credit for time spent on remand, not only in custody but also, in some instances, while on bail.[422] The Canadian Criminal Code (s 719(3)) permits a court to grant credit for any time spent in custody as a result of the offence (as does Irish common law), but it specifies, in the first instance, that credit shall be limited to one day per day in pre-sentence custody. However, this is immediately qualified by a provision permitting a day-and-a-half per day on remand "if the circumstances justify it". Additionally, there is what is known as *Duncan* mitigation, named after a decision of the Ontario Court of Appeal,[423] which may be granted where the offender has been held in particularly harsh pre-sentence incarceration. This is treated as a mitigating factor as distinct from credit for time spent on remand, the idea being that the experience of harsh custodial conditions prior to sentence is a personal mitigating factor that is to be considered in conjunction with other mitigating and aggravating factors present in a case. Canadian courts are also willing to grant credit for time spent on bail where the conditions were particularly onerous. This might apply where the offender had been subject to prolonged house arrest, a stringent curfew requirement or other conditions that severely affected his or her ability to engage in normal activities.[424]

---

[421] *People (DPP) v Delaney* [2021] IECA 201.

[422] For a detailed analysis, see Allan Manson, "Pre-sentence custody and the determination of sentence (or how to make a mole hill out of a mountain)" (2004) 49 *Criminal Law Quarterly* 292. See also *R v Arrance* [2000] 1 SCR 488.

[423] *R v Duncan* [2016] ONCA 754. See also *R v Marshall* [2021] ONCA 344.

[424] *R v Downes* [2006] CanLII 3957 (ONCA); 205 CCC(3d) 488.

Chapter 6

PLEADING GUILTY

In the public imagination, as in a great deal of legal scholarship, the criminal trial is assumed to be the standard method of determining guilt or innocence. A hotly contested trial, real or fictional, always makes for compulsive television viewing. Guilty pleas, by contrast, seldom provoke any high drama. Hence the general impression that most guilty verdicts result from trials. Law students might be forgiven for labouring under the same misapprehension. Their criminal law, criminal procedure and evidence courses are chiefly devoted to topics that are solely relevant to contested trials. Yet, this is one area where "law in books and law in action" clearly diverge.[1] In most common law jurisdictions, as outlined below, a very high percentage of convictions, close to 100 per cent in some instances, result from guilty pleas rather than trials. None of this renders criminal law and evidence irrelevant as subjects of academic study or areas of practice. After all, criminal trials still take place, even if far less frequently than guilty pleas, and some result in acquittals. The outcome of many of these trials (and later appeals) depends on how offence definitions, principles of criminal liability and rules governing the admissibility of evidence are judicially interpreted. Aside from that, the prevalence of guilty pleas is partly determined by the content of the criminal law and the rules of evidence. The more broadly offences are defined, in terms of both conduct and mental elements, the more likely it is that alleged misconduct will come within their definition, a consideration that is surely conducive to pleading guilty. Offences of strict or absolute liability which have proliferated in many jurisdictions in recent times, as well as offences that are so defined as to impose a reverse burden of proof on the accused, are difficult to contest once the prosecution manages to establish certain basic facts.[2] Persons charged with such offences may have little choice but to plead guilty, especially with the incentive of a reduced sentence for doing so. Rules of evidence may be equally influential. Those rules may be predominantly inclusionary or exclusionary and, as such, can influence plea decisions. A defendant who foresees a strong likelihood that key prosecution evidence will be excluded (perhaps because it was illegally obtained) is less likely to plead guilty. Research conducted by the 6–01

1 Roscoe Pound, "Law in books and law in action" (1910) 44 American L Rev 12.

2 Andrew Ashworth and Meredith Blake, "The presumption of innocence in English criminal law" [1996] Crim LR 306 (revealing the high percentage of indictable offence offences triable in the English Crown Court that have a reverse onus of proof or impose some form of strict liability).

English Sentencing Council showed that the likelihood of being convicted at trial is the main factor influencing plea decisions, and that the weight of the evidence is critical for this purpose.[3]

6–02 High guilty plea rates also have implications for the integrity of the overall criminal process. The more pleas, the fewer trials. A contested trial serves important purposes beyond determinations of guilt or the absence of it. The primary purpose may be to hold the accused to account, but the ancillary purpose of holding agents of the state to account is no less vital. A trial permits the conduct of police, prosecutors and other law enforcement personnel to be held up to effective scrutiny.[4] Where a guilty plea is entered, any shortcomings or illegality associated with the investigation of the offence will usually remain unexposed and unexplored.[5] One important function of the criminal law is to affirm and, where necessary, vindicate, fundamental principles of justice.[6] Similar observations have been made about settlement in civil litigation, especially when it engages fundamental rights.[7] The decline in jury trials which can, of course, be attributed to the rise in summary proceedings and bench trials as well as to guilty pleas, has also been lamented because jury service can strengthen participatory democracy and reaffirm commitment to shared communal and ethical values.[8] Guilty pleas are commonly said to benefit victims who are thereby spared the experience of having to testify and undergo cross-examination at trial. There is certainly some truth in this, but sometimes victims would wish for a trial where they could testify about their experience, and have the defendant's conduct and the circumstances in which it occurred examined in detail. This has led some to question

---

3 Sentencing Council, *Attitudes to guilty plea sentence reductions* (2011).

4 Sarah A Seo, "Reimagining the public defender" *New York Review of Books*, 2 December 2021.

5 There are occasional exceptions as in the appropriately named Post Office Scandal in England where dozens of former post office employees had their convictions for dishonesty offences quashed by the Court of Appeal, though many of them had pleaded guilty. See, for example, *Hamilton v Post Office* [2021] EWCA Crim 577. Unusually, a statute was later passed, the Post Office (Horizon System) Offences Act 2024, which quashed the convictions of hundreds of postmasters, provided certain criteria were met.

6 Kate Stith and José Cabranes, *Fear of Judging: Sentencing Guidelines in the Federal Courts* (University of Chicago Press, 1998), 78 (the criminal justice system "exists not only to protect society in a reasonably efficient and humane way, but also to defend, affirm and, when necessary, to clarify the moral principles embodied in the law"). See also Sean Doran, John D Jackson and Michael L Siegel, "Rethinking adversariness in nonjury criminal trials" (1995) 23 American J Crim L 1, and Albert W Alschuler, "The defence attorney's role in plea bargaining" (1975) 84 Yale LJ 1179.

7 Owen M Fiss, "Against settlement" (1984) 93 Yale LJ 1073 (a classic piece of writing on the topic). See also the same author's "The history of an idea" (2009) 78 Fordham LR 1273.

8 Daniel S McConkie, Jr, "Criminal justice citizenship" (2020) 72 Florida LR 1023; Jenny Carroll, "The jury as democracy" (2015) 66 Alabama LR 825; John D King, "Juries, democracy, and petty crime" (2022) 24 *Journal of Constitutional Law* 817.

whether 'sparing the victim' is really such a convincing justification for guilty plea discounts.[9] Further, criticism of plea negotiations and guilty plea discounts usually proceeds from the assumption that a contested trial is the best way of achieving justice. Yet, this holds true only if the trial system is fair and tribunals of fact are scrupulously impartial and objective in deciding on the criminal responsibility of accused persons.[10]

While guilty pleas have long been accepted in common law jurisdictions, they were traditionally unknown in inquisitorial systems such as those of continental Europe. As Mirjan Damaška explained in his seminal work on comparative criminal justice, rules of legal procedure are closely connected with prevailing concepts of state power.[11] In inquisitorial systems of justice, the criminal process is treated "as an official investigation, done by one or more impartial officials, to determine the truth".[12] Judges are therefore expected to participate actively in criminal investigations and the interrogation of witnesses. The procedural objective is to discover if the suspected offence was committed by the accused and, if so, to determine, in accordance with the facts so found, what the penalty should be. Even if the accused confesses to the charge, the court must proceed with the inquiry to satisfy itself of the relevant facts.[13] **6–03**

In common law adversarial systems, on the other hand, the legal process, civil and criminal, is viewed as an exercise in conflict resolution. A criminal prosecution entails a conflict between the state and the accused, but if the accused pleads guilty, there is no longer a conflict to be resolved.[14] Stipulations (agreement that certain facts need not be proved) are similarly explicable.[15] Indeed, a guilty plea must ordinarily be accepted even if **6–04**

---

9 Fiona Leverick, "Tensions and balances, costs and rewards: The sentence discount in Scotland" (2004) 8 Edinburgh LR 360 at 373.

10 Thea Johnson, "Trial ambivalence" (2023) 20 Ohio State J Crim L 269.

11 Mirjan Damaška, *The Faces of Justice and State Authority: A Comparative Approach to the Legal Process* (Yale University Press, 1986); Mirjan Damaška, "Negotiated justice in international criminal courts" (2004) 2 *Journal of international Criminal Justice* 1018.

12 Máximo Langer, "Legal transplants to legal translations: The globalization of plea bargaining and the Americanization thesis in criminal procedure" (2004) 45 Harvard International LJ 1 (which has an excellent analysis of this entire topic).

13 Mirjan Damaška, "Evidential barriers to conviction and two models of criminal procedure: A comparative study" (1973) 121 Univ Pennsylvania LR 506 at 564. See also Abraham S Goldstein, "Reflections on two models: Inquisitorial themes in American criminal procedure" (1974) 26 Stanford LR 1009, noting that in inquisitorial systems, the dominant mode is state control of the trial. The state has an affirmative obligation to implement fully its own substantive and procedural policies, and the judiciary has primary responsibility for ensuring this is done.

14 Mirjan Damaška, "Negotiated justice in international criminal courts" (2004) 2 *Journal of International Criminal Justice* 1018 at 1021. See also *R v Grafton* [1993] QB 101 at 104; (1993) 96 Cr App R 156 where Lord Taylor CJ describes the essence of an adversarial criminal trial.

15 Criminal Justice Act 1984 s 22 provides for proof of facts by formal admission

the trial judge has reason to believe that the accused might qualify for a defence of insanity which would lead to an acquittal but also, possibly, to a lengthy term of non-penal detention which the accused wishes to avoid. A guilty plea in these circumstances will often be tactical, but nonetheless valid provided the accused is fit to plead.[16] In adversarial proceedings, therefore, the contours of the dispute are determined by the parties, and the court's role is to resolve the conflict presented to it. If, because of a guilty plea, there is no longer any conflict as to criminal liability, the court is confined to determining the sentence, though again based on the facts presented to it. The same holds true of tort actions, relatively few of which end up in court but, when they do, the sole issue for resolution is likely to be the quantum of damages rather than any question of liability.

6–05 Some forms of plea recognised in the United States are difficult to reconcile with any process that has the avowed aim of discovering the truth. One of these is the Alford plea whereby a defendant enters a guilty plea while protesting his innocence. This typically occurs where the defendant is seeking to avoid the heavy penalty – possibly even the death penalty – that would result from conviction following trial.[17] The United States Supreme Court has been prepared to endorse this arrangement provided there is a strong evidential basis for the charge to which the plea is entered.[18] Another is the plea of *nolo contendere* where the defendant does not expressly admit guilt, but waives his right to trial and effectively authorises the court to sentence him as if he were guilty.[19] This plea has its roots in medieval English law, but no example of its use by the English courts has been found since the beginning of the 18th century.[20]

6–06 Guilty pleas may traditionally have been unknown in inquisitorial systems, but this has changed in recent decades. In fact, plea bargaining and other trial-avoiding mechanisms have been spreading rapidly throughout the world.[21] Some continental European countries now accept confessions which, while not exactly the same as guilty pleas, have a broadly similar

---

by either prosecution or defence.

16 *People (DPP) v Redmond* [2006] IESC 25; [2006] 3 IR 188; [2006] 2 ILRM 182. See also *Connors v Governor of Limerick Prison* [2017] IECA 218, para 54. A similar issue arose in *Lynch v Overholser* 369 US 705 (1962).

17 Stephanos Bibas, "Harmonizing substantive-criminal-law values and criminal procedure: The case of Alford and nolo contendere pleas" (2003) 88 Cornell LR 1361 (arguing for the abolition of both pleas).

18 *North Carolina v Alford* 400 US 25 (1970).

19 *Hudson v United States* 272 US 451 (1926). See also Bibas, note 17 above.

20 *Queen v Templeman* (1702) 1 Salk 55; 91 Eng Rep 54. On the history of the plea, see William L Mills Jr, "Criminal law – Pleas and defences – Nolo Contendere" (1952) 30 North Carolina LR 407; *North Carolina v Alford* 400 US 25 at 35 (1970).

21 Máximo Langer, "Plea bargaining, conviction without trial, and the global administratization of criminal convictions" (2021) 4 *Annual Review of Criminology* 377. On the spread of plea bargaining and other hallmarks of adversarial criminal justice in Latin America, see Máximo Langer, "Revolution in Latin American criminal procedure: Diffusion of legal ideas from the periphery" (2007) 55 *American Journal of Comparative Law* 617.

effect by greatly abbreviating, though not entirely replacing, criminal trials. This holds true of the *Absprache* which has gradually become an accepted part of German criminal procedure.[22] In Italy, where the criminal process has become progressively more adversarial, the *pattegiamento* (literally a bargain) resembles common law plea negotiations quite closely. The defence and prosecution can reach an agreement on the sentence which the judge will be asked to impose. If accepted, the plea can lead to a sentence reduction of up to one-third, but only where the reduced sentence will not exceed five years' imprisonment.[23]

International criminal tribunals make for an interesting study in this **6–07**
context because their constitutions and procedural rules have been drawn up by bodies comprised of representatives from different legal traditions. Article 65 of the Rome Statute of the International Criminal Court (ICC) sets out the procedure to be followed where an accused makes an admission of guilt.[24] The trial chamber must determine if the admission is voluntary, if the accused understands its nature and consequences and if the admission is supported by the charges and the materials furnished by the prosecutor. Once satisfied in respect of these matters, the trial chamber "shall consider the admission of guilt, together with any additional evidence presented, as establishing all the essential facts that are required to prove the crime to which the admission of guilt relates, and may convict the accused of that crime".[25] However, the chamber is always entitled to seek additional evidence or even to order the trial to continue (before another chamber) as if the admission of guilt had not been made. So far, there has been only one guilty plea before the ICC, and this was in the case of *Al Mahdi* involving a prosecution for attacks against religious and cultural buildings in Mali. The defendant's sentence was later reduced from nine to seven years' imprisonment, in part at least because of the guilty plea.[26] Article 65 therefore seems to reflect both adversarial and inquisitorial traditions. Admissions of guilt are acceptable, but the court must still satisfy itself as to the material facts in each case.

---

[22] Regina E. Rauxloh, "Formalization of plea bargaining in Germany: Will the new legislation be able to square the circle?" (2011) 34 Fordham International LJ 296; Thomas Weigend, "The decay of the inquisitorial ideal: Plea bargaining invades German criminal procedure" in John Jackson, Máximo Langer and Peter Tillers (eds), *Crime, Procedure and Evidence in a Comparative and International Context: Essays in Honour of Professor Mirjan Damaška* (Hart Publishing, 2008), Chap 3.

[23] Mariangelo Impieri, *Il Patteggiamento: Un Procedimento Penale Speciale* (2021) <www.dirittoconsenso.it/2021/06/01/patteggiamento-procedimento-penale-speciale/> accessed 4 July 2024; Paolo Tonini, *Manuale de Procedura Penale,* 20th edn (Giuffrè, 2019).

[24] For a detailed account, see Office of the Prosecutor of the ICC, *Guidelines for Agreement Regarding Admission of Guilt* (October 2020) and Fabricio Guariglia and Gudran Hochmayr, "Article 65 – Proceedings on an admission of guilt" in Kai Ambos (ed), *Rome Statute of the International Criminal Court. Article-by-Article Commentary,* 4th ed. (Beck, Hart, Nomos, 2021).

[25] art 65(2).

[26] *The Prosecutor v Al Mahdi,* Judgment of Appeal Chamber, No ICC-01/12-01/15 (25 November 2021).

1. Plea Negotiation

6–08 Plea bargaining is often said to be unknown in Ireland and in these islands generally. This claim is usually based on the assumption that 'plea bargaining' refers to a practice, widespread in the United States, whereby defence and prosecution lawyers engage in pre-trial negotiations which, if successful, will lead to some charges being dropped or replaced with less serious ones and, in many instances, a commitment by the prosecutor to recommend to the court a more lenient sentence than the defendant would face if convicted on the original charges. While practices vary across the United States, judges will often impose the recommended sentence or something close to it. This, however, is only one form of plea negotiation which may be explicit, as in the example just given, or implicit as when a defendant pleads guilty with the expectation of receiving a reduced sentence, though without getting an express assurance to that effect. The common denominator is that a defendant foregoes the right to trial in exchange for a more lenient penalty.[27] Asher Flynn and Arie Freiberg have identified 14 different kinds of plea negotiation in the Australian state of Victoria.[28] These include substituting less serious charges for those originally preferred, reducing the number of charges, proceeding with a limited number of representative counts, an agreement as to what the prosecution will say in its submissions to the sentencing court and consent to deal with the charges in a lower court with more limited sentencing powers. Most of these are familiar to us in one form or another.

6–09 Charge bargaining occurs when the prosecution agrees to accept a plea to a lesser charge, such as manslaughter instead of murder.[29] Life imprisonment may be the maximum sentence for manslaughter, just as it is the mandatory sentence for murder, but a plea to manslaughter will most likely result in a determinate prison sentence, and possibly a moderate one at that. The key characteristic of this arrangement is that it entails some engagement or negotiation between defence and prosecution, and it is not unusual for the prosecution to decline the offer of a plea to a lesser offence. Nowadays, in Ireland at least, the prosecution generally consults with the victim before accepting a plea to a less serious sexual offence such as sexual assault instead of rape. Many offences are triable either way in the sense that they may be disposed of summarily in the District Court or tried on indictment in a higher court. The choice of forum usually rests

---

27 Milton Heumann, "A note on plea bargaining and case pressure" (1975) 9 *Law and Society Review* 515 ("Plea bargaining may be defined as the process whereby the defendant relinquishes his right to go to trial in exchange for a reduction in charge and/or sentence".) Likewise, Albert W Alschuler, "An exchange of concessions" (1992) 142 *New Law Journal* 937 describes as "implicit bargaining" the practice whereby a defendant pleads guilty in anticipation of a less severe sentence, even in the absence of any express 'bargain' to that effect.

28 Asher Flynn and Arie Freiberg, *Plea Negotiations: Pragmatic Justice in an Imperfect World* (Palgrave Macmillan, 2018).

29 Examples of cases where this occurred include *People (DPP) v Millea* [2016] IECA 137; *People (DPP) v Burke* [2019] IECA 167 and *People (DPP) v Shanley* [2017] IECA 340.

with the prosecution though for some offences, such as those created by the Criminal Justice (Theft and Fraud Offences) Act 2001, the accused must also consent to summary trial. More relevant for present purposes, s 13 of Criminal Procedure Act 1967 permits the District Court, with the consent of the prosecutor, to deal with any indictable offence (apart from a few very serious ones) to which the defendant is willing to plead guilty. The maximum sentence the court may impose in these circumstances is a class A fine (currently €5,000), a 12-month prison term or both. Prosecutorial consent to summary disposal under this provision can be a significant advantage for a defendant who is thereby assured that, even in a worst-case scenario, the sentence will not exceed one year's imprisonment (or two years for a combination of offences). The prosecution, for its part, is assured of a conviction, assuming the defendant agrees to plead guilty in the District Court. Prosecutors should refrain from applying any pressure on defendants to plead in the District Court by threatening to proceed on indictment if they do not. Like all other strong incentives, this creates a risk of innocent defendants pleading guilty.

Plea deals that result in the defendant pleading to less serious charges than those originally preferred are sometimes criticised as running counter to the desert principle. The defendant ends up receiving less punishment than he or she deserves, or so the critics would argue. This, of course, rests on the assumption, always a dubious one, that the defendant would have been convicted of the original offence if the matter had gone to trial. Plea agreements, of whatever kind, are essentially risk-management exercises. The prosecution is guaranteed a conviction without having to run the risks inherent in a contested trial, while the defendant is all but guaranteed a more lenient sentence than would have been imposed following conviction on the original charge. The defendant eventually receives a penalty that is commensurate with the offence of conviction, albeit a conviction resulting from a plea, and to that extent the desert principle is observed. At a more practical level, charge bargaining where it becomes prevalent often leads to overcharging, as happens in the United States in particular. Prosecutors 'load on' charges in the knowledge that defendants will be willing to plead guilty to some of them in order to avoid the heavy penalties, including mandatory minimums, that would result from being found guilty of the others. This has led some to propose that charge bargaining should be severely restricted, and that trial penalties, as described below,[30] should be prohibited.[31] **6–10**

Plea negotiation, unless subject to some formal constraint or judicial supervision, as it seldom is, may also undermine the impact of guidelines that are designed to eradicate unwarranted disparities in judicial sentencing. Such guidelines may be successful to some degree in ensuring that similarly situated offenders convicted of similar offences receive similar, if not identical, sentences. But where there has been a **6–11**

---

[30] Note 45 below and accompanying text.

[31] Richard L Lippke, *The Ethics of Plea Bargaining* (Oxford University Press, 2011).

guilty plea, whether resulting from an explicit bargain or otherwise, the offence of conviction may not reflect the offence that was committed. To borrow an example given by Ilene Nagel and Stephen Schulhofer, persons *convicted* of bank robberies committed in similar circumstances may receive similar sentences under guidelines such as those operating in the United States federal jurisdiction. But persons who *commit* bank robberies in similar circumstances may receive quite different sentences because of bargains that allowed some of them to plead guilty to less serious charges.[32] When drawing up the federal guidelines, the United States Sentencing Commission was conscious of this problem which it sought to address by providing for 'real offence' sentencing. This means that a court, when calculating the offence score under the guidelines, must take account of all the offender's conduct in committing the relevant offence. Thus, for example, it must determine the sentence according to the nature and quantity of drugs involved, the amount of money stolen or whether a weapon was used, irrespective of the charge to which the offender has pleaded guilty. This practice creates its own problems, not least because acquitted conduct may also be considered for this purpose.[33] The rationale of this rather surprising and highly contentious practice is that a person is acquitted if the jury is unconvinced of his or her guilt beyond a reasonable doubt, whereas fact-finding at sentencing is on the preponderance of the evidence. A sentence may therefore be enhanced, sometimes substantially, because of judicial fact-finding even if some of the facts found clearly conflict with an earlier jury verdict. In *McClinton v United States,*[34] for example, the defendant was convicted by a jury of two robberies but acquitted of murder. The guideline sentence for the robbery offences would have been about six years, but the trial judge, having considered the circumstances of the alleged murder, imposed a 19-year sentence which was upheld on appeal. In 2023, the United States Supreme Court declined to hear the case, though four justices made a point of saying that this was being done on the understanding that the Sentencing Commission would be addressing the issues. They expressly left open the possibility that the court would take up the issue in another case if the Commission did not act.[35] At least one state Supreme Court has been willing to strike down such a law as incompatible with the

---

[32] Ilene Nagel and Stephen J Schulhofer, "A tale of three cities: An empirical study of charging and bargaining practices under the federal sentencing guidelines" (1992) 66 Southern California LR 501, 502.

[33] At least one member of the present US Supreme Court, Kavanaugh J has expressed serious reservations about allowing acquitted conduct to enhance sentence for an offence of conviction. See, for example, *United States v Brown* 892 F3d 385, 415 (DC Cir 2018) (Kavanaugh J dissenting in part). For a defence of real offence sentencing, see Julie R O'Sullivan, "In defence of the US sentencing guidelines' modified real-offence system " (1997) 91 Northwestern Univ LR 1342, with a critical response from David Yellen, "Just deserts and lenient prosecutors: The flawed case for real offence sentencing" (1997) 91 Northwestern Univ. LR 1434.

[34] 23 F4th 732 (7th Cir 2022).

[35] *McClinton v United States* 600 US – (2023) .

state's constitution.[36] Granted, this seems to be a peculiarly American phenomenon and is clearly at odds with the constitutional right to trial by jury. But, leaving aside the acquitted conduct issues, the American experience indicates how any consistency it is hoped to generate through sentencing guidelines may be subverted by unrestrained prosecutorial power to engage in plea negotiations.[37]

2. Plea Deals as Incentives

Plea negotiation, whatever form it takes, has been staunchly defended and vigorously criticised.[38] It has been defended as a form of contractual bargaining with both parties freely agreeing to forfeit some of their rights in exchange for a guaranteed or expected benefit.[39] From a law and economics perspective, criminal justice is essentially a market system in which people can sell some of their rights in exchange for advantages.[40] Frank Easterbrook, for example, claims that a defendant 'buys' his or her plea "by surrendering his right to impose costs on the prosecutor by demanding trial and by surrendering his chance of acquittal at trial".[41] On the other hand, it cannot be denied that, irrespective of whether they are the product of bargaining or otherwise, sentence discounts for guilty pleas amount to incentives. An incentive is intended to influence the choice a person makes. It may not compel the offeree to act in a particular way, but it does make one course of action more attractive than another.[42] Incentives might therefore be viewed as manifestations of 'nudge theory' which has attracted much attention in recent times.[43] From a purely economic perspective, incentives seem unobjectionable because they entail 6–12

36 In *People v Beck* 504 Mich 605; 939 NW2d 213 (2019), the Michigan Supreme Court held that an equivalent state law violated the defendant's constitutional due process rights.

37 Prosecution decisions are, for the most part, immune from judicial review under American law (or federal law, at least), unless there is evidence of bias on account of race, religion or some similar factor. See Rachel Barkow, "Separation of powers and the criminal law" (2006) 58 Stanford LR 989 at 1025, referring to leading authorities such as *Wayne v United States* 470 US 598 (1985).

38 Even the discount for the guilty plea, as in Ireland, which is probably the simplest form of plea negotiation, has been subject to academic criticism. See, for example, Kathy Mack and Sharyn Roach Anleu, "Sentence discount for a guilty plea: Time for a new look" (1997) 1 *Flinders Journal of Law Reform* 123.

39 Robert E Scott and William J Stuntz, "Plea bargaining as contract" (1992) 101 Yale LJ 1909.

40 Bibas, note 17 above.

41 Frank H Easterbrook, "Criminal procedure as a market system" (1983) 12 *Journal of Legal Studies* 289, 309.

42 Ruth W Grant, "The ethics of incentives: Historical origins and contemporary understandings" (2002) 18:1 *Economics and Philosophy* 111; Ruth W Grant, "Ethics and incentives: A political approach" (2006) 100(1) *American Political Science Review* 29.

43 See Cass R Sunstein and Richard Thaler, *Nudge: Improving Decisions about Health, Wealth and Happiness* (Yale University Press, 2008), and Cass R Sunstein, *The Ethics of Influence: Government in the Age of Behavioural Science* (Cambridge University Press, 2016).

an exchange of benefits. Both parties stand to gain from the transaction. However, if they are treated as a form of power, like force or persuasion, as Ruth Grant argues they should be, incentives raise important ethical issues. Their purpose is to get one person to act as another wants them to act, and that may not always be in the interests of the individual or society. Specifically, in relation to plea bargaining, Grant maintains that it subverts the proper purpose of the criminal justice system which is to establish guilt or innocence and punish those found guilty. These objectives cannot, she argues, be served by a bargaining process.[44] This, of course, is a highly contestable proposition because many, probably most, guilty pleas, even if bargained, are genuine in the sense that defendants are actually guilty of the offences to which they plead. Moreover, their conduct may well come within the definition of a more serious offence, but the original charge has been bargained down.

6–13 Grant's argument nonetheless merits some reflection. If the overriding objective of the criminal process were to discover the truth, as in the inquisitorial systems described earlier, guilty pleas, especially if to less serious charges than the alleged conduct might have justified, could seriously impede the attainment of that objective. Further, even within an adversarial system, with its emphasis on conflict resolution, incentives to plead guilty may be so strong as to exert unfair pressure on defendants to waive their right to trial. This is a particularly important consideration where, as in many American jurisdictions, there is a heavy 'trial penalty", meaning that the likely penalty following a contested trial is vastly greater than what would follow guilty plea.[45] Where that applies, there is certainly a danger of some innocent persons pleading guilty or factually guilty persons accepting harsh deals.

6–14 Courts in other jurisdictions have occasionally acknowledged this possibility, though it seems that a trial penalty must be very severe before being condemned as impermissibly oppressive or an abuse of process. In *McKinnon v United States*[46] the appellant was resisting extradition to the United States where he faced charges connected with the deletion of data from government computers to which he had gained unlawful access. Under a plea deal offered by the American prosecutor, if he consented to extradition and then pleaded guilty, he would qualify for a prison sentence of three to four years with repatriation to the UK after serving six to 12 months. Once repatriated, he might qualify for release at the halfway point of the nominal sentence. However, if he refused to

---

[44] Ruth W Grant, *Strings Attached: Untangling the Ethics of Incentives* (Princeton University Press, 2011), Chap 6.

[45] In 2019, the *Federal Sentencing Reporter* devoted a full issue to this problem of the trial penalty. See, especially the editors' observations: Norman L Reimer and Martin Antonio Sabelli, "The tyranny of the trial penalty: The consensus that coercive plea practices must end" (2019) 31 (4-5) *Federal Sentencing Reporter* 215. See also Jeffrey Bellin, "Plea bargaining's uncertainty problem" (2023) 101 Texas LR 539.

[46] [2008] UKHL 59; [2008] 1 WLR 1739.

cooperate and was convicted of the charges, he could expect a sentence of eight to 10 years without the possibility of repatriation. He argued that his extradition would amount to an abuse of process because of the sentence differential in the proffered deal. The House of Lords dismissed his appeal, holding that the deal offered did not fall into the extreme category that would warrant a refusal of extradition. Lord Brown, with whom all the other Law Lords agreed, noted that even under English law, a guilty plea could attract a discount of up to one-third, and additional credit may be granted for other mitigating factors. He did, however, proceed to say:

> "In one sense all discounts for pleas of guilty could be said to subject the defendant to pressure, and the greater the discount the greater the pressure. But the discount would have to be very substantially more generous than anything promised here (as to the way the case would be put and the likely outcome) before it constituted unlawful pressure such as to vitiate the process. So too would the predicted consequences of non-cooperation need to go significantly beyond what could properly be regarded as the defendant's just deserts on conviction for that to constitute unlawful pressure."[47]

The court did not therefore rule out the possibility that a heavy trial penalty might influence an extradition decision, but in this case the penalty had not reached the requisite threshold of severity. **6–15**

The potentially coercive nature of plea deals was more directly acknowledged by the Alberta Court of Appeal in *R v Naslund,*[48]a high-profile case in which a woman who killed her husband after having been abused by him for almost 30 years was initially charged with murder. However, the defence and prosecution made a joint submission to the trial judge recommending a sentence of 18 years' imprisonment in return for the defendant's plea to manslaughter.[49] The judge imposed the recommended 18 years. The defendant appealed against the severity of this sentence (a rare occurrence when the recommended sentence is imposed). A majority of the Court of Appeal found the sentence manifestly excessive and reduced it to nine years' imprisonment. The most relevant aspect of the judgment for present purposes is its acknowledgement that where, as in this instance, a defendant is charged with murder and therefore facing the possibility of a life sentence with no chance of parole for 25 years, there is a significant power imbalance between defence and prosecution when it comes to negotiating the terms of a plea. As the court said: **6–16**

> "It is within the discretion of the prosecutor to accept a guilty plea to a lesser-included offence, and that power risks leading to a coercive bargain

---

47 [2008] UKHL 59; [2008] 1 WLR 1739, para 38.

48 [2022] ABCA 6.

49 Joint submissions of this nature are quite common in Canada. They are typically accepted, though a judge may in certain circumstances reject the recommendation and impose a different sentence. See discussion in *R v Anthony-Cook* [2016] 2 SCR 204 and in *Naslund* itself.

> where the alternative involves the accused having to gamble at trial with a possible mandatory life sentence."[50]

6–17 The court later reiterated the point, referring to "the unique power imbalance at play ...where battered women are charged with murder for killing their abusive partners".[51] The European Court of Human Rights has also found that negotiated plea deal which was "tainted by constraint" violated a defendant's right to a fair trial under art 6 of the European Convention on Human Rights ('ECHR').[52]

6–18 Particular care is needed when dealing with suspects and defendants who are vulnerable because of youth, mental disability, learning difficulties, living conditions or some other factor. How such persons are dealt with, especially by the police, at the early stages of a criminal investigation can be crucially important. Admissions made at that point will usually form a significant part of the prosecution case and may therefore place a suspect under pressure to plead guilty when the time comes. Yet, one must remain alive to the possibility that the admissions were attributable to vulnerability rather than to a truly voluntary and well-informed decision to answer questions in a particular way. As John Taggart has written:

> "Research has shown how suspects with learning disabilities and mental health disorders are over-represented in custody and that many suffer heightened levels of suggestibility, compliance and acquiescence. Indeed, suspects in police interview may be at higher risk of not fully understanding the questions put to them or the implications of their answers."[53]

6–19 This in turn underscores the need for special measures for vulnerable persons at all stages of the criminal process, and not just at trial. The right to consult a solicitor before being questioned (and to be informed of that right) is now well established,[54] but it is also important that lawyers engaging in such work should be trained to recognise vulnerability and how it may affect a suspect's conduct and responses while being questioned, whether in police custody or elsewhere. Intermediaries also have a vital role whenever a suspect has communication difficulties. Incentives to plead guilty must always be critically assessed and monitored to ensure that they do not have the effect of inducing pleas

---

50 [2022] ABCA 6, para 124. The Supreme Court of Canada made a rather similar point in *R v Anthony-Cook* [2016] 2 SCR 204, para 52.

51 [2022] ABCA 6, para 170.

52 *Deweer v Belgium* (1979-1980) 2 EHRR 439 See also *Navalnyy and Ofitserov v Russia* (2019) 68 EHRR 25, and Pavlo Pushkar, "The right to a fair trial and use of unlawfully obtained evidence and guilty pleas in the case-law of the European Court of Human Rights" (2010) 2 Constitutional LR 38;

53 John Taggart, "Vulnerable defendants and the HMCTS court appointed intermediary services" [2022] Crim LR 432, 440 (internal references omitted).

54 *People (DPP) v Gormley and White* [2014] IESC 17; [2014] 2 IR 591; [2014] 1 ILRM 377.

from vulnerable persons who may be innocent of the charge or have a valid defence.[55]

The potential strength of incentives to plead guilty have led some to question the compatibility of guilty plea discounts and various forms of plea bargaining with the presumption of innocence which is protected expressly by art 6 of the ECHR and implicitly by the Constitution of Ireland.[56] The obvious concern is that an innocent person may feel compelled or pressurised to plead guilty in return for the promise or prospect of a lenient sentence in circumstances in which he or she is apprehensive about contesting the charge lest the trial results in a guilty verdict, or perhaps because of a wish to avoid the difficult experience of undergoing trial at all. This is one reason why continental lawyers have been generally opposed to guilty pleas and plea bargaining.[57] It is undoubtedly true that, while the discount is a reward for those who cooperate for pleading guilty, it means that those who are convicted following a contested trial are, in a sense, penalised for having exercised their right to trial. This consideration once led the Scottish Court of Appeal to observe that, in light of the presumption of innocence, it would be wrong "that an accused person should be put in the position of realising that if he pleads guilty early enough he will receive a lower sentence than he would otherwise receive for the offence".[58] Significant discounts for guilty pleas have also been subject to academic criticism, again because they may discourage defendants from exercising their right to trial. Andrew Ashworth and Mike Redmayne, for example, while not opposed to allowing some discount for a plea, argued that it should not exceed 10 per cent as it should "[aim] at preserving the freedom of choice of someone who maintains innocence and at ensuring that the exercise of the right to be presumed innocent until proved guilty does not have a significant cost".[59] **6–20**

3. Rationale for Guilty Plea Discount

The justifications for rewarding a guilty plea with a reduced sentence are essentially utilitarian or pragmatic in nature. A plea facilitates the smooth operation of the criminal justice system which would probably come under severe strain if every accused person insisted on exercising their right to trial, or so it is commonly assumed. As such, it saves the state a good deal of time and money. Further, it can benefit victims by sparing them the experience of having to testify at trial and undergo cross- **6–21**

---

[55] Jill Peay and Elaine Player, "Pleading guilty: Why vulnerability matters" (2018) 81 Modern LR 929; Rebecca K. Helm, "Conviction by consent? Vulnerability, autonomy and conviction by plea" (2019) 83 *Journal of Criminal Law* 161.

[56] *O'Leary v Attorney General* [1995] 1 IR 254; [1995] 2 ILRM 259.

[57] Jean Pradel, *Droit penal comparé*, 2nd ed (Dalloz, 2002), 611.

[58] *Strawhorn v McLeod* [1987] SCCR 413. See Leverick, note 9 above.

[59] Andrew Ashworth and Mike Redmayne, *The Criminal Process*, 4th ed (Oxford University Press, 2010), 317.

examination which, in many cases, can be very stressful. The assumptions underpinning both of these justifications have been challenged, but it is undoubtedly true that many, though perhaps not all, victims of sexual and other violent offences welcome early admissions of guilt followed by a guilty plea on arraignment.[60] A plea can certainly benefit witnesses other than the victim who would have been required to testify at a trial, perhaps at a good deal of inconvenience to themselves.

6–22 The English Sentencing Council's definitive guideline on discounts for guilty pleas states that an acceptance of guilt by an accused:

> "a) normally reduces the impact of the crime upon victims;
> b) saves victims and witnesses from having to testify; and
> c) is in the public interest in that it saves public time and money on investigations and trials."[61]

6–23 Importantly, the guideline also states that these benefits apply irrespective of the strength of the case against the accused, and that the strength of the evidence should *not* be taken into account when determining the level of discount. This is consistent with the benefits specified in the guideline, or in any system in which the plea is justified solely on utilitarian grounds. Courts have often treated guilty pleas as evidence of remorse and, for that reason alone, worthy of a discount. However, the more prevalent view nowadays and, it is suggested, the better one, is that remorse, where genuine, is a separate mitigating factor that may warrant a further sentence reduction[62]. Nor would there be much support for the view expressed by some members of the High Court of Australia in *R v Cameron*[63] that the discount can be justified on the basis that a guilty plea reflects a willingness by the offender to facilitate the administration of justice. In a separate and more compelling judgment in that case, Kirby J said that the true foundation for the discount is an acceptance that it is in the public interest and this, in turn, is essentially utilitarian.[64] Guilty pleas save time and money and facilitate the efficient administration of justice (whatever the desires or attitudes of offenders in that regard), and this is the main public benefit they confer. Scottish courts have likewise treated administrative efficiency as the primary justification for the discount.[65]

---

60 *People (DPP) v Tiernan* [1988] IR 250; [1989] ILRM 149 (regarding rape offences). But see also *People (DPP) v McAuliffe* [2018] IECA 100, para 9, where it was noted that the guilty plea to theft and robbery offences "avoided the necessity for the severely traumatised elderly victim to attend court and give evidence".

61 Sentencing Council, *Reduction in Sentence for a Guilty Plea; Definitive Guideline* (2017), 4. For an analysis of this guideline, see Jay Gormley, Julian V Roberts, Jonathan Bild and Lyndon Harris, *Sentence Reductions for Guilty Pleas* (Sentencing Academy, 2020).

62 Remorse as a mitigating factor is discussed in Chap 5 above.

63 [2002] HCA 6; (2002) 209 CLR 339.

64 [2002] HCA 6; (2002) 209 CLR 339, para 66.

65 *Du Plooy v HM Advocate* [2003] SCCR 640; *Gemmell v HM Advocate* [2011] HCJAC 129. See Jay Gormley, "The inefficiency of plea bargaining" (2022) 49 *Journal of Law and Society* 277.

Judicial consensus on the rationale for guilty plea discounts is essential, especially in the absence of any formal guideline or statutory provision on the matter. Without such a consensus, the levels of discount granted to offenders who have committed similar offences with similar degrees of culpability may vary considerably and to an unwarranted extent. One judge may decide that a discount is deserved solely where a plea reflects remorse. Another may decide that the discount should be negligible where the prosecution evidence is overwhelming, and yet another may decide that neither of these factors is relevant, and that it is the practical benefits to witnesses and the legal system that should count. These questions are addressed later in this chapter in the context of setting and applying the discount. In short, however, it is suggested that the sole rationale for the discount should be utilitarian (without regard to remorse or the general attitude of the offender), that the point at which the plea is indicated or entered should ordinarily determine the amount of discount but that a downward adjustment of that amount may be appropriate where the prosecution case is very strong. **6–24**

4. Requirements for a Valid Guilty Plea

A guilty plea amounts, in effect, to an acknowledgement that the prosecution has proved the charge beyond a reasonable doubt just as if there had been a valid conviction following trial.[66] Numerous judicial statements reflect this understanding of a plea. In *R v Asiedu*, for example, the English Court of Appeal said: **6–25**

> "A defendant who pleads guilty is making a formal admission in open court that he is guilty of the offence.... But ordinarily, once he has admitted such facts by an unambiguous and deliberately intended plea of guilty, there cannot be an appeal against conviction, for the simple reason that there is nothing unsafe about a conviction based on the defendant's own voluntary admission in open court."[67]

The court acknowledged that in exceptional circumstances, such as where the plea was equivocal or unintended, an appeal against conviction might **6–26**

---

66 *Boykin v Alabama* 395 US 238 at 242 (1969) ("A plea of guilty is more than a confession which admits that the accused did various acts; it is itself a conviction; nothing remains but to give judgment and determine sentence"); *People (DPP) v Hughes* [2012] IECCA 69, para 27 (a guilty plea is an acknowledgement that the defendant is guilty of the offence); *R(E) v DPP* [2019] IESC 86, para 34 ("By pleading guilty, the accused accepts responsibility for the facts and mental element relevant to the count on the indictment which he or she admits").

67 [2015] EWCA Crim 714; [2015] 2 Cr App R 8, para 19. See also *S v Recorder of Manchester* [1971] AC 481 at 501 per Lord Morris ("Guilt may be proved by evidence. But also it may be confessed"), *R v Rimmer* (1972) 56 Cr App R 196 at 200 (a guilty plea "is a confession of fact; secondly, it is such a confession that without further evidence the court is entitled to and indeed in all proper circumstances will so act upon it that it results in a conviction"); *Healy v HM Advocate* [1990] SCCR 110 (a guilty plea is "a full admission of the [charge] in all its particulars"); *R v BRP* [2023] EWCA Crim 40, para 53.

still lie.[68] However, the fundamental assumption is that a plea constitutes a full and voluntary confession of guilt. In substance, therefore, it equates with a guilty verdict following trial, but the differences between these two ways of establishing guilt are quite profound. Those who opt for trial are entitled to an array of procedural protections flowing from the presumption of innocence and the more general entitlement to a fair trial. These include the privilege against self-incrimination, the right to challenge the admissibility of prosecution evidence on various grounds and, above all, the onus resting on the prosecution to satisfy the court to the criminal standard of proof (beyond a reasonable doubt) of each element of the offence charged. Irrespective of the mode of trial, the judge bears the ultimate responsibility for ensuring that the accused gets a fair trial. A guilty plea is, of course, formally entered in court on arraignment, but the circumstances and considerations that motivated it are very seldom subject to judicial supervision or scrutiny.[69] A decision to plead occasionally results from negotiation between defence and prosecution but, in most cases, it is taken by the defendant him/herself, though usually following receipt of legal advice. Either way, the essence of a guilty plea is that it emanates from one or both parties to the case rather than from the court.[70]

6–27 Defendants who plead guilty are therefore waiving their legal and (in Ireland) constitutional right to a trial in due course of law with all the protections that entails. Waiver of any constitutional right must always be knowing, voluntary and intelligent (in the sense that the accused is adequately aware of the consequences). The Supreme Court has held that the waiver of a constitutional right (to be legally represented in criminal proceedings in that instance) must be the result of a knowing and freely made choice and it is not lightly to be inferred that this occurred. The burden of asserting that a constitutional right has been waived rests with the party asserting waiver.[71] The United States Supreme Court has likewise said:

> "Waivers of constitutional rights not only must be voluntary but must be knowing, intelligent acts done with sufficient awareness of the relevant circumstances and likely consequences."[72]

---

68 This possibility has been more fully addressed in *R v Tredget* [2022] EWCA Crim 108; [2022] 4 WLR 62; [2022] 2 Cr App R 1 where the Court of Appeal identified three categories of cases where a conviction may be set aside notwithstanding a guilty plea, including where the plea was equivocal or unintended, or where it was vitiated by improper pressure. See comment on *R v Tredget* by Umar Azmeh in [2022] Crim LR 407.

69 Jeremy Horder, *Ashworth's Principles of Criminal Law,* 8th ed. (Oxford University Press, 2016), 11 ("A guilty plea is not automatically subject to vigorous testing for its veracity, in the way that a not guilty plea is tested.")

70 Jacqueline Hodgson, "Plea bargaining; A comparative analysis" in James D Wright (ed) *International Encyclopedia of the Social & Behavioural Sciences,* 2nd ed (Elsevier, 2015), Vol 18, pp 226 at 230.

71 *People (DPP) v Sheehan* [2021] IESC 49; [2021] 1 IR 33; *People (DPP) v M (K)* [2018] IESC 21; [2018] 1 IR 810.

72 *Brady v United States* 397 US 742 at 748 (1970).

Somewhat earlier, the same court had said, "[i]gnorance, incomprehension, coercion, terror, inducements, subtle or blatant threats might be a perfect cover-up of unconstitutionality ".[73] The European Court of Human Rights has likewise held that defendants may waive their rights under art 6 of the ECHR provided the waiver is "established in an unequivocal manner and [is] attended by minimum safeguards commensurate with its importance.... [and it] must not run counter to any public interest".[74] In *Natsvlishvili and Togonidze v Georgia*[75] the court had to decide if a plea agreement which entailed the waiver of the right to trial and to ordinary appellate review was compatible with art 6 of the ECHR. On the facts, the court found no violation of art 6, as the plea had not resulted from duress or false promises and there were sufficient safeguards against abuse of process. The European Union Directive on the presumption of innocence and the right to be present at trial also countenances waivers, whether tacit or express, provided they are unequivocal.[76] These principles are reflected in English (and probably Irish) law in circumstances in which a conviction may be quashed despite the appellant having pleaded guilty.[77] For instance, in *R v Inns*[78] the English Court of Appeal said that a plea cannot be treated as genuine if it resulted from pressure or threats. It has further held that a court should not accept an equivocal guilty plea, especially from an unrepresented defendant, but it has a discretion in the matter where a defendant later seeks to change an unequivocal plea to one of not guilty.[79] **6–28**

A decision to plead guilty must always be taken by the accused personally. It must never be the product of pressure or coercion exercised by the accused's legal representative or anyone else. Of course, a legal representative may and, indeed, should give appropriate advice to the accused as to the strength of the prosecution case and the likelihood that **6–29**

---

73 *Boykin v Alabama* 395 US 238 at 242 (1969). See also *Machibroda v United States* 368 US 487 at 493 (1962) ("A guilty plea, if induced by promises or threats which deprive it of the character of a voluntary act, is void. A conviction based upon such a plea is open to collateral attack."), and *Santobello v New York* 404 US 257 (1971), to the same effect.

74 *Hermi v Italy* (2008) 46 EHRR 46, para 73. See also *Sejdovic v Italy* (2006) 42 EHRR 17, para 33.

75 European Court of Human Rights, 29 April 2014. For critical analyses, see Rebecca K Helm. "Constrained waiver of trial rights? Incentives to plead guilty and the right to a fair trial" (2019) 46 *Journal of Law and Society* 423; Lorena Bachmaier, "The European Court of Human Rights on negotiated justice and coercion" (2018) 26 *European Journal of Crime, Criminal Law and Criminal Justice* 236.

76 Directive (EU) 2016/343 of the European Parliament and of the Council of 9 March 2016 on the strengthening of certain aspects of the presumption of innocence and of the right to be present at trial in criminal proceedings, Recital 35.

77 Discussed further below.

78 (1974) 60 Cr App R 231 at 233. See also *R v Swain* [1986] Crim LR 480 where a conviction was quashed because the defendant may have been affected by a delusion caused by drug consumption when he pleaded guilty.

79 *R v NJ* [2022] EWCA Crim 790; [2022] 2 Cr App R 13.

a guilty plea will be rewarded with a reduction in sentence. However, a legal representative must also ensure that the accused is made fully aware of the meaning and consequences of a plea and, in particular, that it amounts in effect to an acceptance that the prosecution has proved the relevant charge beyond a reasonable doubt. The Code of Conduct for the Bar of Ireland (para 10.12) has clear provisions to this effect.

5. Change of Plea

6–30 A court should not, in the absence of exceptional circumstances, prevent an accused person from changing their plea from not guilty to guilty[80]. However, a person who has pleaded guilty has no automatic entitlement to change that plea to one of not guilty, though an application may be made to the trial court to permit this to be done. The application may be made at any time before the conclusion of the proceedings, and that will usually be the point at which sentence is imposed. The grant of permission to change a plea to not guilty is at the trial court's discretion,[81] but it is not a discretion lightly exercised in favour of the accused, especially where the court is satisfied that the accused fully understood what he or she was doing in pleading guilty. The dominant consideration is to ensure that the accused's constitutional right to a fair trial is protected.[82] A change of plea, if allowed, may have a disruptive effect on court proceedings. Other cases may have to be adjourned in order to cater for an unanticipated trial. Witnesses who had assumed that they would not be required to testify must now be prepared to do so, and in some instances this may be stressful. Obviously, the constitutional right to a fair trial must always prevail, whatever the inconvenience to others. However, a trial judge must carefully consider the question of whether permission to change a plea is really necessary to protect an accused's constitutional rights, and the decision will necessarily be fact-specific. *People (DPP) v O'Loughlin*[83]is one example of a case where the trial judge was held to be justified in refusing to permit a change of plea. On the other hand, in *Byrne v McDonnell*[84] it was held that leave to change a plea to not guilty should have been permitted so that the defendant, who happened to be a child, could be legally represented from the beginning of the trial. He had no representation when he pleaded guilty and was remanded in custody. In *People (DPP) v B*[85] the appellant had pleaded guilty to certain sexual offences at a time when neither he nor his counsel was aware of certain statements that were not included in the book of evidence and of a diary kept by the complainant. This was an appeal against conviction which was set aside, with a re-trial ordered, on the basis that counsel might have

[80] *Connors v Governor of Limerick Prison* [2017] IECA 218, para 54.

[81] *R (E) v DPP* [2019] IESC 86.

[82] *Dunne v McMahon* [2007] 4 IR 471, 477; *People (DPP) v O'Loughlin* [2022] IECA 18; *People (DPP) v Judge* [2018] IECA 242.

[83] [2022] IECA 18.

[84] [1997] 1 IR 392; [1996] 1 ILRM 543.

[85] [2002] 2 IR 246 .

advised against pleading guilty if he was aware of the material in question and the appellant might have accepted the advice. When a problem of this nature comes to light before the conclusion of the proceedings in the trial court, it would strongly favour allowing a change of plea.

An accused might also seek to resile from a guilty plea by claiming to have been put under undue pressure to plead guilty or given incorrect or misleading legal advice. When the application is made on this ground, the accused bears the burden of demonstrating undue pressure or erroneous advice, as the case may be.[86] There must have been an impermissible degree of pressure. Strong professional advice to plead guilty is insufficient for this purpose although, admittedly, there may sometimes be a fine line between the two. A person who, having been charged with an indictable offence, pleads guilty to and is sentenced for that offence in the District Court pursuant to s 13 of the Criminal Procedure Act 1967 may not change their plea to one of not guilty in a subsequent appeal to the Circuit Court. Any appeal to the latter court in those circumstances must be confined to sentence only.[87] **6–31**

6. Challenging a Conviction Following a Guilty Plea

A genuine guilty plea amounts to an acceptance that the prosecution has proved its case to the requisite standard of proof.[88] Ordinarily, therefore, a person who pleads guilty cannot later challenge a conviction entered following the plea. However, there are some circumstances in which such an appeal may be entertained.[89] As already noted, a conviction may be quashed where the plea was involuntary, unintended or equivocal. A plea would also be treated as a nullity if it resulted from improper pressure being applied to the accused, especially if the pressure emanated from the trial judge.[90] The same might occur if "the plea was compelled as a matter of law by an adverse ruling from the trial judge which left no arguable defence to be put before the jury".[91] Needless to say, the ruling, in addition to being adverse, must also have been wrong in law. In those circumstances, the accused may have no realistic option but to plead guilty at trial but should not be prevented from later challenging the ruling on appeal. Thirdly, though it very seldom arises in practice, there may be an appeal against conviction if the accused should not have been prosecuted or tried for the offence. This would occur where the prosecution or trial **6–32**

---

86 *R (E) v DPP* [2019] IESC 86, para 35.

87 *People (DPP) v Czelusniak* [2023] IECA 159.

88 See note 66 and 67 above.

89 The current English law on the matter is set out in *R v Tredget* [2022] EWCA Crim 108; [2022] 4 WLR 62; [2022] 2 Cr App R 1, and *AAD v R* [2022] EWCA Crim 106; [2022] 1 WLR 4042; [2022] 1 Cr App R 19. See also *R v Boal* [1992] QB 591; (1992) 95 Cr App R 272 at 278. Irish courts would probably adopt a similar approach.

90 *R v Inns* (1974) 60 Cr App R 231; *R v Nightingale* [2013] EWCA Crim 405; [2013] 2 Cr App R 7.

91 *R v Asiedu* [2015] EWCA Crim 714; [2015] 2 Cr App R 8, para 20.

was deemed to be an abuse of process. It might, for example, be an abuse of process to prosecute a person who appeared to be a victim of human trafficking for an offence committed as a result of the trafficking,[92] or where for some other reason, such as patently flawed evidence, the prosecution should never have been brought in the first place.[93] A person might plead guilty as a result of receiving wrong or misleading legal advice. For instance, he or she might have been advised that the alleged conduct came within the definition of a criminal offence when, in fact, it did not. This can also lead to the conviction being quashed, though the English Court of Appeal has held that the advice "must go to the heart of the plea, so that… the plea would not be a free plea and what followed would be a nullity".[94] More recently, however, the same court has said that a plea may be vitiated by erroneous legal advice or failure to advise as to the availability of a defence that would probably have succeeded, "even where the advice may not have been so fundamental as to have rendered the plea a nullity".[95]

6–33 Otherwise, an appeal against a conviction resulting from a guilty plea will rarely succeed. In *People (DPP) v Walsh*[96] where, unusually, the appellant, who had pleaded guilty, was seeking to challenge her conviction despite not having sought to change her plea in the trial court, the Court of Appeal said:

> "It is not possible to exhaustively indicate the type of exceptional circumstances which, if supported by sufficiently cogent evidence, would justify an appellate court in exercising its discretion to set aside a guilty plea, but we believe that the case law to date suggests that matters such as being unfit to plead at the time, pleading on an insufficiently informed basis (eg in circumstances of vulnerability and without having had the benefit of legal advice, or having received manifestly incorrect legal advice), or pleading under genuine duress, could (depending on the exact circumstances) potentially qualify."[97]

6–34 It is significant that the court stressed that an appellant who seeks to rely on any of these grounds must be able to point to 'sufficiently cogent evidence.' A bare claim or assertion that he or she was, for example, under duress or given erroneous legal advice will seldom, if ever, be enough to convince an appeal court to set aside a conviction resulting from a guilty plea.

---

[92] *R v AGM* [2022] EWCA Crim 920.

[93] See, for example, *White v Post Office Ltd* [2022] EWCA Crim 435 and the comment by Umar Azmeh in [2022] Crim LR 685.

[94] *R v Saik* [2004] EWCA Crim 2936, para 57.

[95] *R v BRP* [2023] EWCA Crim 40, para 55.

[96] [2023] IECA 314.

[97] [2023] IECA 314, para 51.

7. Setting and Applying the Discount

Within the common law world at least, a guilty plea is the most securely established and widely accepted of all mitigating factors. It has therefore long been accepted that a guilty plea ordinarily merits some reduction in sentence,[98] but it is also firmly established that a defendant convicted following trial may never be penalised for not having pleaded guilty.[99] This distinction may be "not without its subtleties"[100] but it is nonetheless well recognised. Appeal courts never hesitate to quash a sentence if there is reason to believe that the trial judge treated the defendant's decision to contest the charge as an aggravating factor. This is as it should be. Every accused person has a constitutional right to trial in due course of law which, in turn, includes the right to require the prosecution to prove the charge beyond a reasonable doubt.[101] A person who foregoes that right, with all the procedural safeguards afforded to the defence during a contested trial, deserves a reward for doing so. A judge may indicate that, but for the guilty plea, the sentence would have been higher or, where there has been a conviction following trial, that the defendant cannot expect any discount that would have been awarded for a guilty plea. What is absolutely forbidden is to treat the absence of a guilty plea as an aggravating factor. This has been repeatedly stressed by the highest judicial authorities in Ireland and elsewhere. For example, it was addressed at some length by the Court of Appeal in *People (DPP) v Daly*.[102]Moreover, the manner in which the defendant conducted the case, even if vigorous and stressful for other participants and, even indeed, if he or she tendered perjured testimony (a separate offence in itself) should not be treated as aggravating. As the Supreme Court summarised the matter in *People (DPP) v Wharrie*: **6–35**

> "An accused person is entitled to contest a case. While he or she may be given credit appropriate to an early admission of guilt, a plea of guilty, or, to a lesser extent, an approach to the trial process which saves time and money, no trial judge is entitled to aggravate the appropriate sentence because the accused gave perjured evidence in his own defence or in defence of others. Perjury is a separate crime and it is not a factor of aggravation of an existing offence."[103]

Earlier in the same judgment, the court said: "nothing should be taken into account at sentencing which would inhibit the full entitlement of an **6–36**

---

98 *R v Boyd* (1980) 2 Cr App R (S) 234 at 235; *R v Hollington and Emmens* (1985) 7 Cr App R (S) 364.

99 *People (DPP) v Counihan* [2015] IECA 76 (among many other authorities). In *R v Shannon* (1971) 21 SASR 442 at 445, a leading Australian authority on the matter, it was said: "It is impermissible to increase what is the proper sentence for the offence committed in order to mark the court's disapproval of the accused's having put the issue to proof or having presented a time-wasting or even scurrilous defence."

100 *R v Cameron* [2002] HCA 6; 209 CLR 339, para 12.

101 Constitution of Ireland, Art 38.1.

102 [2011] IECCA 104; [2012] 1 IR 476, paras 79 to 82.

103 [2017] IESC 47; [2017] 2 IR 743, para 33.

accused person to contest the case and make whatever contrary case he or she regards as appropriate".[104]

6–37 Granted, in a discretionary sentencing system with little or no guidance on appropriate penalties, the distinction between reducing a sentence where there has been a plea and not increasing sentence where there has been a trial can be difficult to enforce or supervise.[105] For example, a judge who says that the sentence would be one of nine years' imprisonment were it not for the guilty plea which brings it down to six years, might well have imposed six years even if the offender had been convicted following trial. This underscores the importance of sentencing guidance, judicially developed or otherwise, on headline sentences and, equally, of judges adhering to the practice of specifying a headline sentence in each case before adjusting for relevant factors including a guilty plea. A person who indicated a willingness at the outset to plead guilty to a lesser offence, such as manslaughter instead of murder, is ordinarily entitled to a discount if eventually convicted of that lesser offence.[106] Despite the references being made here to a 'discount', in Ireland a guilty plea is simply one of many potentially mitigating factors, though usually an important one. Under the English sentencing guidelines, on the other hand, credit for a plea is classified as a reduction to be considered in isolation from other mitigating factors.

6–38 It is only in more recent times that appropriate levels of discount have been specified or indicated in various legal instruments. South Australia is unusual, if not unique, in specifying by statute the maximum reductions for a guilty plea, up to 40 per cent for an early plea with lesser reductions in other circumstances.[107] Elsewhere, discounts are indicated in guidelines or appeal court judgments. The English Sentencing Council's definitive guideline provides for a sliding scale of sentence discounts depending primarily on when the plea as was indicated. The maximum reduction is one-third which may be granted where the plea is indicated at the first stage of the proceedings, reducing to one-quarter where it is entered after that, to one-tenth where it is entered on the first day of the trial, and even less where it is entered after the trial has begun.[108] In United States federal courts before the adoption of the federal sentencing guidelines

---

[104] [2017] IESC 47; [2017] 2 IR 743, para 26, referring to *R v Siganto* [1998] HCA 74; 194 CLR 656 and *R v Harper* [1968] 2 QB 108.

[105] As Bray CJ said in *R v Reiner* (1974) 8 SASR 102 at 105, "the distinction between refraining from taking something off and adding something on when there is no fixed normal penalty may seem, in some cases, to approach the metaphysical…".

[106] *People (DPP) v Kelly* [2004] IECCA 14; [2005] 2 IR 321; [2005] 1 ILRM 19; *R v Cardoso* [2003] NSWCCA 15.

[107] Criminal Law (Sentencing) Act 1988, ss 39 and 40 (as amended).

[108] Sentencing Council, note 61 above. For analysis, see Gormley *et al*, note 61 above; Andrew Ashworth and Rory Kelly, *Sentencing and Criminal Justice*, 7th ed (Hart, 2021), 170-182.

in 1987, guilty pleas were generally rewarded with a reduction of 30 to 40 per cent.[109]

In Ireland, the s 29 of the Criminal Justice Act 1999 (the '1999 Act') provides that a court, when sentencing a person who has pleaded guilty, shall, "if it considers it appropriate to do so" take into account (a) the stage in the proceedings at which the defendant indicated an intention to plead guilty, and (b) the circumstances in which the indication was given. This is a rather weak provision because, to begin with, it is effectively optional; a court need only apply it when it considers it appropriate to do so. Secondly, it does not expressly say that more generous discounts should be granted for early pleas, though this is to be implied. Finally, it gives no indication whatever as to the appropriate levels of discount. Although clearly based, apart from the discretionary element, on s 48 of the UK Criminal Justice and Public Order Act 1994, s 29 of the 1999 Act merely reflects the pre-existing law.[110] For instance, in *People (DPP) v Tiernan*[111] the Supreme Court made clear that in sentencing for rape (and presumably for most other offences), an early admission of responsibility followed by a guilty plea is a significant mitigating factor. That remains the law. The Court of Appeal has occasionally indicated appropriate discount ranges for guilty pleas, typically 10 to 30 per cent, depending largely on when the plea was first indicated.[112] However, where a plea is entered at an early stage and it has clear utilitarian value, it should normally attract a discount of at least 25 percent and possibly as high as 30 per cent.[113] In fact, a discount of up to one-third seems to have been the accepted norm by Irish and English courts before there was ever any guidance on the matter.[114] A defendant who enters a signed plea of guilty to an indictable offence in the District Court and consents to being sent forward for sentence to the appropriate higher court (pursuant to the Criminal Procedure Act 1967 (s 13)) is ordinarily entitled to a more substantial reduction, assuming, of course, that he or she adheres to the guilty plea.[115] This holds true even where there was strong evidence, such as CCTV footage, that the defendant committed the offence.[116] A signed **6–39**

---

109 Michael M O'Hear, "Remorse, cooperation, and 'acceptance of responsibility': The structure, implementation, and reform of Section 3E1.1 of the Federal Sentencing Guidelines" (1997) 91 Northwestern Univ LR 1507.

110 The relevant English provision is now s 73 of the Sentencing Act 2020 which is phrased in mandatory terms: a court *must* take into account the stage at which there was a plea indication and the circumstances in which it was given. The idea of having such a statutory provision may be traced back to the *Report of the Royal Commission on Criminal Justice*, Cm 2236 (HMSO, 1993), Chap 7, para 48 which was concerned with encouraging early guilty pleas.

111 [1988] IR 250; [1989] ILRM 149.

112 *People (DPP) v Molloy* [2016] IECA 239; *People (DPP) v D (T)* [2021] IECA 289.

113 *People (DPP) v Whelan* [2018] IECA 142, para 9.

114 *R v Buffrey* (1993) 14 Cr App R (S) 511, 515.

115 *People (DPP) v Cambridge* [2019] IECA 133, para 8; *People (DPP) v Stubbins* [2021] IECA 229, para 24 (saying that any such reduction is not "a result of any mathematical calculation").

116 *People (DPP) v O'Callaghan* [2020] IECA 172.

plea normally obviates the need to prepare a book of evidence and gives an early indication to the victim, where there is one, that no trial will take place.[117] It may well merit a discount in excess of 30 per cent, especially if it has clearly benefited a victim or obviated the need for what might have been a long or complex trial (with all the preparation that would have entailed). The Court of Appeal once said that a signed plea, because of its systemic value, should generally earn a one-third reduction, irrespective of the strength of the prosecution case.[118] A significant reduction will also be merited where the offending, or some of it, came to light only because the defendant voluntarily admitted it.[119] The same applies where a prosecution would have been difficult, if not impossible, were it not for the defendant's admissions and co-operation.[120] A late plea, on the other hand, may merit only a slight reduction. In *People (DPP) v McDonnell*[121] the trial court was held to be correct in granting only a one-year reduction on a 10-year sentence imposed on defendant who pleaded guilty to a firearms offence on the fifth day of his trial at the close of the prosecution case.

6–40 A guilty plea may occasionally determine the nature as well as the amount of penalty. It may, for example, bring a prison sentence down to a point at which it can be suspended, thereby marking the gravity of the offence while at the same time recognising the offender's acceptance of responsibility or some exceptional circumstances existing at the time of either the offence or the sentence. Concern has, however, been expressed that the promise or prospect of a non-custodial penalty in return for a plea may unfairly induce innocent defendants to plead guilty rather than risk a trial.[122] This, of course, is a relevant consideration irrespective of the nature of the anticipated reward (which will often be a reduced prison sentence), but it has particular salience where defendants are reasonably confident, if not assured, they will be spared custody if they admit guilt. The possibility that innocent persons may plead guilty in any circumstances underscores the need to ensure that any waiver of the right to trial is voluntary and made on a fully informed basis, and that defendants have access to competent legal advice for this purpose.

6–41 One recurring question is whether the strength of the prosecution evidence should influence the level of reduction for a guilty plea. Defendants will sometimes have been caught red-handed or there may be a good quality video recording showing the offence being committed. Those who video

---

117 *People (DPP) v Malone* [2022] IECA 262.

118 *People (DPP) v O'Callaghan* [2020] IECA 172, para 20.

119 *People (DPP) v H (S)* [2023] IECA 206.

120 *People (DPP) v Doolan* [2014] IECA 22; *People (DPP) v Begley* [2013] IECCA 32; [2013] 2 IR 188.

121 [2022] IECA 200 . See also *Cameron v The Queen* [2002] HCA 6; (2002) 209 CLR 339, para 66 (Kirby J), indicating that, even in these circumstances, a guilty plea may have some utilitarian value. It may, for example, reduce the overall costs of the proceedings.

122 Andrew Ashworth, "Sentencing" in Mike Maguire, Rodney Morgan and Robert Reiner (eds), *The Oxford Handbook of Criminology*, 4th ed (Oxford University Press, 2007), 990, 1012.

record themselves committing sexual offences, as sometimes happens, are, for all practical purposes, convicting themselves.[123] Whether any of this should affect the level of discount depends on the underlying rationale of the discount itself. If it is justified on purely pragmatic or utilitarian grounds, it should not vary with either the strength of the evidence or the defendant's motive in entering the plea. A contested trial will still have been avoided, with all the benefits that confers, or is assumed to confer, on the justice system. Further, a conviction can never be guaranteed, however strong the evidence appears to be. A court must always be wary of assuming that the case against a defendant is 'overwhelming' solely on the basis of untested prosecution evidence.[124] As Megarry J famously said, although in a different context:

> "As anyone who has anything to do with the law well knows, the path of the law is strewn with examples of open and shut cases which, somehow, were not; of unanswerable charges which, in the event, were completely answered; of inexplicable conduct which was fully explained, of fixed and unalterable determinations that, by discussion, suffered a change."[125]

Additionally, a procedural hitch may lead to a trial being aborted thereby necessitating a re-trial if it is decided to persevere with the prosecution. All this was acknowledged by the Court of Appeal in *People (DPP) v Howlin* where it said: **6–42**

> "Every plea has some value even where an accused has been caught red handed, or where the State's case is otherwise very strong. Even in such a case, if an accused pleaded not guilty there would be court resources taken up for the duration of the trial, there would be expense involved and there would be risk involved. Even strong cases may fail due to unanticipated events such as a key witness becoming suddenly unavailable due to death or illness, or the development of some other problem. Moreover, juries can be unpredictable. There is no such thing as a certainty of conviction. What a plea does, even in a strong case, is that it removes that uncertainty. Accordingly, every plea has a value. That said, it is accepted that some pleas are more valuable than others."[126]

Having said this, defendants *are* sometimes caught red-handed in circumstances that would leave them with little or no realistic prospect of acquittal. As just noted, some effectively convict themselves by recording the commission of the offence. This should not deprive them of all credit for a guilty plea, as courts now accept, but it may reduce the amount of credit to which they are entitled.[127] All depends on whether the rules or guidelines within the relevant jurisdiction limit the factors **6–43**

---

[123] *People (DPP) v McD (J)* [2021] IECA 31, para 93. The same occurred in *R v Webster and French* [2006] EWCA Crim 1335; [2007] 2 Cr App R (S) 40 where the offenders had taken photographs of the abusive conduct.

[124] *R v Caley* [2012] EWCA Crim 2821; [2013] 2 Cr App R (S) 47, para 24.

[125] *John v Rees* [1970] Ch 345, 402.

[126] [2022] IECA 150, para 65.

[127] *R v Wilson* [2012] EWCA Crim 386; [2012] 2 Cr App R (S) 77; [2012] Crim LR 560, discussed further below.

a court may consider when deciding on the level of discount. As noted earlier, the present English Sentencing Council guideline treats the stage at which an intention to plead guilty was indicated as the dominant, if not the sole, consideration. However, there is nothing to prevent other jurisdictions adopting a more flexible or multi-factored approach, with the strength of the prosecution case as one relevant factor. In fact, English law itself has undergone quite a few changes in this regard. Before the introduction of guidelines, the Court of Appeal took the view that credit for a guilty plea could be denied where to do so was necessary for public protection or where the defendant was caught red-handed.[128] The first guideline on the matter produced by the Sentencing Guidelines Council in 2004 recommended that the strength of the prosecution case should be irrelevant. A revised version of that guideline in 2007 qualified this by providing that there was a presumption that full credit should be given where a plea was indicated at the earliest opportunity but there might be a departure from this presumption where the case against the defendant was overwhelming. In that event, a smaller reduction might be granted, and it was indicated that this might be in the region of 20 per cent.[129] The present guideline, dating from 2017, provides that the strength of the prosecution case is irrelevant. However, there is nothing inherently right or inevitable about that approach, as reflected in a judgment of the United Kingdom Supreme Court which held that Northern Ireland courts were perfectly entitled to treat the strength of the prosecution case as a relevant factor in deciding on the level of discount for a guilty plea.[130] Even where the stage at which a plea is indicated is a decisive factor, it is accepted that a defendant may need professional advice before deciding how to plead, particularly where the charge is a serious one and the defendant may possibly have a defence. This is a factor to be considered when determining if the plea was entered at the first reasonable opportunity, and all the more so if the defendant is young or has a mental illness or learning difficulties.[131] A defendant need not have been caught red-handed for the value of the plea to be diminished. There may have been independent witnesses or the defendant may have been made admissions.[132]

6–44 Irish law continues to recognise the strength of the prosecution evidence as a relevant and, sometimes, vital factor in determining the level of discount.[133] This is particularly relevant to possession-based offences which are difficult to defend. Being found in possession of prohibited material, such as drugs, firearms or child pornography, is usually sufficient to establish guilt unless, perhaps, the defendant can succeed in convincing the court that he or she was unaware of the nature of the material. A guilty plea in those circumstances may not be of great value though it obviously has some because the defendant always retains the

---

128 *R v Costen* (1989) 11 Cr App R (S) 182; *R v Morris* (1988) 10 Cr App R (S) 216.
129 *R v Simpson* [2009] EWCA Crim 423; [2009] 2 Cr App R (S) 69.
130 *R v Maughan (Appellant) (Northern Ireland)* [2022] UKSC 13; [2022] 1 WLR 2820.
131 *R v Peters* [2005] EWCA Crim 605; [2005] 2 Cr App R (S) 101, paras 17-19.
132 *People (DPP) v Malone* [2022] IECA 262.
133 See, for example, *People (DPP) v O'Driscoll* [2019] IECA 315, para 16.

right to contest the case, however strong it may be. The special sentencing regime for s 15A drug offences, described in Chap 10, includes a guilty plea as one of the exceptional and specific circumstances to which a court may have regard when deciding whether to grant a downward departure from the presumptive minimum 10-year sentence. In interpreting this provision, the Court of Appeal has noted that guilty pleas to this offence are typically entered against a backdrop of strong and overwhelming evidence. As such it is unlikely of itself to bring the ultimate sentence below the 10-year minimum in a very serious case[134] The court has treated the fact that the defendant was caught re-handed as a "highly relevant circumstance" which reduced the amount of deserved mitigation.[135] As against this, where contraband, such as drugs or firearms, are found in a location where there are several people present, it may be difficult for the prosecution to establish possession on the part of any one of them. A defendant who was among those present and who pleads guilty will certainly be entitled to reasonable credit for that.[136]

Drawing the various authorities together, it seems that Irish law on the matter may be summarised as follows. In circumstances where the prosecution case is not particularly strong or overwhelming, the stage at which a guilty plea is first indicated is the dominant consideration in determining the appropriate discount. It must be recalled that s 29 of the Criminal Justice Act 1999 refers to the stage at which an intention to plead guilty is 'indicated' rather than the point at which it is formally entered. Further, what constitutes the first reasonable opportunity to indicate an intention to plead, or to enter a plea, may depend on case-specific factors such as access to legal advice or the point at which disclosure is made by the prosecution. Where the prosecution evidence is particularly strong because, for example, the defendant was caught red-handed or there is video evidence of the offence being committed, a court must consider if the normal discount should be reduced for this reason.[137] Credit for a guilty plea should never be denied altogether, however strong the prosecution case, for the reasons set out by the Court of Appeal in *People (DPP) v Howlin*[138] (quoted above). It may still have a utilitarian value if, for example, it spared a victim or other witness the experience of a contested trial where distressing evidence might have to be adduced, analysed and possibly contested. In *R v Wilson*[139]the defendant pleaded guilty to raping and sexually abusing several children. Moreover, he had photographed and, in some instances, video recorded the abusive conduct, and this material was found on his computer. The trial judge refused to give any **6–45**

[134] *People (DPP) v Sarsfield* [2019] IECA 260.

[135] *People (DPP) v O'Dwyer* [2020] IECA 353, para 47. See also *People (DPP) v Kenny* [2011] IECCA 16, and *People (DPP) v Curtis* [2022] IECA 184.

[136] *People (DPP) v Hanney* [2017] IECA 209, para 11,

[137] In *People (DPP) v Duffy* [2022] IECA 307, a 20 per cent discount where the plea was not an early one and the offender had been caught red-handed at the scene of the crime was held to be appropriate.

[138] [2022] IECA 150, para 65.

[139] [2012] EWCA Crim 386; [2012] 2 Cr App R (S) 77; [2012] Crim LR 560.

credit for his guilty plea to the two rape charges (against a three-year-old child) because they had been recorded. The recordings identified the child but not the defendant. The English Court of Appeal disagreed with this approach, saying the plea still had two significant advantages. First, it meant that the movie involving the child would never be shown in public and, secondly, the jury would be spared the traumatic experience of having to watch it. Therefore, the court, while upholding a sentence of life custody, granted a modest reduction in the minimum term to be served. Under Irish law, it seems that in the absence of some special feature such as this, a strong prosecution case justifies reducing the discount to some extent, even in a case where the offender had entered a signed plea of guilty in the District Court and adhered to it, although the authorities do not seem entirely consistent on this point.[140]

6–46 A person charged with a criminal offence may institute judicial review proceedings for an order restraining the trial or bring a so-called s 4E application (a procedure whereby, after being sent forward for trial, an accused may apply to the trial court to dismiss a charge).[141] If unsuccessful with such an application, the person may then quickly plead guilty. This in turn raises a question about the level of discount, if any, merited by a plea entered in those circumstances. Credit for a guilty plea should not be denied to a person who has exercised a legal right at the pre-trial stage. In fact, the judicial review proceedings may have been taken to vindicate a constitutional right, such as the right to trial with reasonable expedition. Ordinarily, therefore, any such proceedings should be ignored when determining if the plea was indicated as early as was reasonably possible. However, a defendant cannot, in these circumstances, claim any credit over and above the standard amount, unlike, for example, a person who entered a signed plea of guilty in the District Court.[142]

6–47 Turning to the normative question of how much discount, if any, a guilty plea *should* merit, irrespective of prevailing principles, we find quite a diversity of opinions. If systemic efficiency is the dominant consideration, it will favour generous reductions for admissions of guilt. The objective, after all, will be to avoid expensive and time-consuming trials to the greatest extent possible, thereby permitting cases to be processed more quickly, and to encourage those who intend to plead guilty to do so as early as possible. This, in turn, will benefit victims, witnesses, defendants (in some instances) and criminal justice system more generally. In fact, a Council of Europe recommendation dating from 1987 recommends "out-of-court settlements", though admittedly in relation to "minor and mass offences".[143] The greater the reduction on offer, the more defendants are likely to plead guilty, or so it is assumed. In 2010, the English Ministry

[140] Compare *People (DPP) v Hayes* [2020] IECA 257, para 9 with *People (DPP) v O'Callaghan* [2020] IECA 172, para 20.

[141] Criminal Procedure Act 1967, s 4E inserted by Criminal Justice Act 1999, s 9.

[142] *People (DPP) v Dowdall* [2023] IECA 182, para 24.

[143] Recommendation No R(87) 18 of the Committee of Ministers to member states concerning the simplification of criminal justice (1987).

of Justice published a Green Paper proposing to increase the maximum discount for a guilty plea from one-third to one-half.[144] It was estimated that this would result in a reduction of 3,400 prisoners by 2014/2015 and financial savings of £130 million, as well as reducing the burden on the various criminal justice agencies. However, the proposal encountered considerable opposition from politicians and sections of the media, largely because it might result in excessively lenient sentences for serious offences such as rape. It was therefore quickly and quietly dropped.[145] Substantial sentence reductions for guilty pleas also give rise to ethical concerns. The discount may result from some sort of plea bargain or, as in Ireland, it may simply apply routinely as a reward for pleading guilty. Either way, it amounts to an incentive and, as noted earlier, incentives can operate unfairly unless carefully monitored and scrutinised. The promise or prospect of a substantial sentence reduction may induce innocent defendants to plead guilty. This danger is particularly acute in jurisdictions where suspects are identified, arrested and charged largely because they have criminal records and where the rules of evidence facilitate the disclosure of previous convictions at trial.[146]

8. Prevalence of Guilty Pleas

The United States is often singled out, and indeed criticised, for its high **6–48** rate of guilty pleas. Approximately 97 per cent of federal convictions result from guilty pleas, with a similar rate in state courts.[147] As Justice Kennedy remarked when delivering the opinion in *Missouri v Frye*,[148] the negotiation of a guilty plea rather than the unfolding of a trial is today "almost always the critical point for a defendant". Yet, many other common law jurisdictions, including Ireland, are not far behind in this respect. In Canada, about 90 percent of criminal cases are resolved through guilty pleas.[149] In Ireland, according to statistics published by the Director of Public Prosecutions, of the cases prosecuted on indictment in 2017

---

144 Ministry of Justice, *Breaking the Cycle: Effective Punishment, Rehabilitation and Sentencing of Offenders*, Cm 7972 (2010).

145 Jacqueline Beard, *Reduction in Sentence for a Guilty Plea*, House of Commons Library Briefing Paper No. 5974 (2017).

146 Josh Bowers, "Punishing the innocent" (2008) 156 Univ Pennsylvania LR 1117 (dealing with this phenomenon in the United States). He notes (p 1124): "There is no longer any serious question that innocent people are charged with and convicted of crimes".

147 Jed S Rakoff, "Why prosecutors rule the criminal justice system – and what can be done about it" (2017) 111 Northwestern Univ LR 1429, noting that in 2015, only 2.9 per cent of federal defendants went to trial and that in the states the figure may be as low as two percent. In 2023, 97.2 per cent of those sentenced in the federal system pleaded guilty (United States Sentencing Commission, *Annual Report 2023*).

148 566 US 134 (2012). See also special issue of *Federal Sentencing Reporter*, note 45 above.

149 Government of Canada, *Victim Participation in the Plea Negotiation Process in Canada*, at <www.justice.gc.ca/eng/rp-pr/cj-jp/victim/rr02_5/p3.html> accessed 10 January 2022.

(excluding those yet to be heard when the relevant annual reports were published), 94% resulted in conviction and 6 percent in acquittal. About 95 per cent of the convictions resulted from guilty pleas. The rate of guilty pleas varies with the offence, being of the order of 85 to 90 percent for drug and property offences, but lower for sexual offences.[150] In England and Wales, almost 80 per cent of cases concluded in the magistrates' courts in 2019-2020 were resolved though guilty pleas. The equivalent figure for the Crown Court was 73 per cent.[151] As in Ireland, the rate varied with the offence, that for sexual offences being much lower than for theft and drug offences.[152] In Scotland, the guilty plea rate varies from 63 per cent to 97 per cent, depending on the charge. In the lower courts, it can be as high as 90 per cent.[153]

6–49 Research in England and Wales, the United States and elsewhere has shown that members of ethnic minorities are considerably less likely to plead guilty than majority population defendants.[154] Particularly strong evidence has emerged in England and Wales to support this conclusion. In his landmark study on race and sentencing, Roger Hood found that defendants with an Afro-Caribbean background were less likely than others to plead guilty and, when convicted, tended to receive heavier sentences, partly of course because they did not have the benefit of a guilty plea discount.[155] More recently, a major study by Cheryl Thomas of all Crown Court cases in England and Wales concluded between 2006 and 2014 found that a larger proportion of BAME (Black, Asian and Minority Ethnic) defendants pleaded not guilty (40 per cent) than White defendants (31 per cent). This applied across virtually all offence categories, but the difference was especially striking in sexual offences (where 38 per cent of White defendants and 67 percent of BAME defendants pleaded not guilty) and homicide offences where the equivalent figures were 32 per cent for White defendants and 82 per cent for BAME defendants.[156] In 2022, 79 per cent of White offenders pleaded guilty, compared with 66 per cent of Black offenders.[157] Research conducted for the Lammy Review showed

---

[150] Director of Public Prosecutions, *Annual Report 2020* (2021), 23.

[151] Crown Prosecution Service, *Annual Report and Accounts 2019-2020* (2020).

[152] Ministry of Justice, *Criminal Courts Statistics Quarterly, England and Wales, January to March 2019* (2019). It notes the rate of guilty pleas in the Crown Court had remained fairly stable over the previous four years.

[153] Gormley, note 65 above.

[154] Celesta A Albonetti, "Race and the probability of pleading guilty" (1990) 6 *Journal of Quantitative Criminology* 315, analysing American data and concluding (p 329): "These data suggest that controlling for offence severity, prior record, presence of physical evidence, eyewitness identification, pretrial release, type of counsel, and whether the defendant confessed, black defendants are less willing to accept the seemingly routine process of case disposition through a guilty plea".

[155] Roger Hood, *Race and Sentencing: A Study in the Crown Court* (Oxford University Press, 1992).

[156] Cheryl Thomas, "Ethnicity and the fairness of jury trials in England and Wales 2006-2014" [2017] Crim LR 860.

[157] Julian V Roberts and Andrew Ashworth, *Sentencing Guidance, the Sentencing Council, and Black and Ethnic Minority Offenders* (Sentencing Academy 2022) who

that Black and Asian men were more than one and a half times more likely than White men to plead not guilty, while women from minority racial backgrounds were also more likely to contest the charges.[158] The author, David Lammy MP, attributes this difference to a "trust deficit" in many BAME communities. He concluded that many BAME defendants trusted neither the advice of solicitors paid for by the government nor the promise of the criminal justice system to treat less punitively those who plead guilty.[159] Other studies have also identified lack of trust as a reason for lower rates of guilty pleas among racial minorities.

Much more contentious has been the question of why so many defendants plead guilty.[160] The best known and most controversial study is Baldwin and McConville's *Negotiated Justice* which claimed that many defendants pleaded guilty because of pressure from their own counsel, a claim that was staunchly contested by members of the legal profession.[161] As has been pointed out, lawyers generally benefit more when cases go to trial rather than when they end with a guilty plea.[162] There seems to be little or no empirical research on this matter in Ireland, though it is a matter worthy of investigation, especially in light of research conducted on behalf of the Royal Commission on Criminal Justice in England and Wales which showed that some innocent persons do plead guilty, a finding about which, alarmingly, the Commission seemed largely unconcerned.[163] **6–50**

9. Advance Indications of Sentence

Defendants who are uncertain as to how they should plead would doubtless welcome a firm advance indication from the trial court as to the sentence they could expect if they pleaded guilty or what it might be if they were convicted following trial. English law permits such indications to be given, although in Ireland the practice is strongly discouraged. In England and Wales, prior to the Court of Appeal decision in *R v Turner*[164] it **6–51**

---

also note that while ethnic minority defendants are less likely to plead guilty, BAME defendants are also acquitted at a higher rate than White defendants.

158 *The Lammy Review: An independent review into the treatment of, and outcomes for, Black, Asian and Minority Ethnic individuals in the criminal justice system* (2017).

159 *The Lammy Review,* note 158 at 29.

160 For a good survey of research on this topic, see Kevin Kwok-yin Cheng, "Pressures to plead guilty: Factors affecting plea decisions in Hong Kong's magistrates' courts" (2013) 53 Brit J Criminology 257.

161 John Baldwin and Michael McConville, *Negotiated Justice: Pressures on Defendants to Plead Guilty* (Martin Robertson, 1977). A flavour of the controversy it engendered may be had from the review by J.E. Adams in (1978) 41(3) MLR 358.

162 Peter W Tague, "Barristers' selfish incentives in counselling defendants over the choice of plea" [2007] Crim LR 3.

163 Royal Commission on Criminal Justice, note 110 above, para 7.42 (where the Commission, ironically in light of its remit, simply remarks, "it would be naïve to suppose that innocent persons never plead guilty because of the prospect of a sentence discount").

164 [1970] 2 QB 321; (1970) 54 Cr App R 352.

was quite common for counsel to approach the trial judge for a sentence indication. However, *Turner* effectively condemned this practice. The court held that a judge should never state that he or she would impose one sentence following a guilty plea and another on conviction following trial. The one permitted exception was that a judge could indicate that whatever happened, and irrespective of the nature of the plea, the sentence would or would not take a particular form, e.g., a fine or term of custody. From the early 1990s onwards, pressure grew for more flexibility in this regard. The Royal Commission on Criminal Justice recommended that defendants should be able to receive a reliable early indication of the highest sentence they would face if convicted.[165] The Auld Report made a similar recommendation.[166] Further, the Criminal Justice Act 2003 (Sch 3) provided that in the case of 'either way' offences, an accused, when deciding on trial venue, could seek an indication from the magistrates' court as to whether a custodial or non-custodial sentence would be more likely if he were to be dealt with summarily and plead guilty.

6–52 These developments eventually led the Court of Appeal in *R v Goodyear*[167] to depart from *Turner* to the extent of holding that a trial judge should be permitted to give an advance indication of sentence. But this should normally be confined to indicating the maximum that would be imposed if a plea of guilty were tendered at the stage at which the indication is sought. The court in *Goodyear* stressed, first of all, as it had previously done in *Turner*, that defendants are personally and exclusively responsible for their pleas. The court described this as the fundamental starting point. Secondly, it stressed that a trial judge has an unfettered discretion to refuse to give an indication or to reserve his or her position until it becomes feasible to give one. Further, the court set out guidelines specifying the duties and responsibilities of all the actors involved in seeking and granting sentence indications.[168] A judge should adhere to the indication given if there has been no change of any significance by the time of sentence.[169] However, a judge may depart from an indication if it transpires to have been based on incorrect information or incompatible with an applicable guideline.[170] In that event, a defendant should be given an opportunity to vacate his or her plea, and there can ordinarily be no ground for complaint if he or she passes up on the opportunity to do so. The all-important consideration is that a legal and proportionate sentence should be imposed in each case. A sentence indication never precludes the possibility of an undue leniency application.

---

165 Royal Commission on Criminal Justice, note 110 above, paras 7.48–7 55.

166 Robin Auld, *Review of the Criminal Courts of England and Wales* (Stationery Office, 2001).

167 [2005] 1 WLR 2532; [2006] 1 Cr App R (S) 6; [2005] Crim LR 659.

168 For a detailed description and analysis of *Goodyear* and its current operation, see Lyndon Harris and Sebastian Walker, *Sentencing Principles, Procedure and Practice 2021* (Sweet and Maxwell, 2021), 122-136.

169 *R v Davies* [2015] EWCA Crim 930; [2015] 2 Cr App R 57.

170 *R v Newman* [2010] EWCA 1566; [2011] 1 Cr App R (S) 68.

The position in Ireland seems to be that consultations with a judge in chambers are not absolutely prohibited provided they do not entail any kind of sentence bargaining.[171] For example, if a defendant were suffering from a terminal illness (and perhaps unaware of its terminal nature), that is a matter that could properly be mentioned confidentially to the trial judge in chambers. However, *Goodyear*-type sentence indications are effectively prohibited. As far back as 1998, the DPP issued a direction that any such discussions in chambers should be discontinued, and the Supreme Court in *People (DPP) v Heeney*[172] agreed. While it accepted that the discussions in that case did not amount to plea bargaining, it held that chambers discussions as to sentence were undesirable and should be discontinued. The same approach may be inferred from the more recent Supreme Court judgment in *R (E) v DPP*.[173] In that case, where the defendants were charged with assaulting a young child, the trial judge had stated in open court, prior to cross-examination of the injured party, that if the defendants pleaded guilty, they might be dealt with by way of a non-custodial measure but that custodial sentences could scarcely be avoided if they were convicted following trial. As the Supreme Court accepted, the judge was well motivated in making this statement, as he was anxious to spare a young child from being cross-examined, possibly twice in the circumstances. However, the court also stated quite categorically: **6–53**

> "Whether in open court, or worse still, in secrecy of chambers, discussions with the court as to sentence have no place in the constitutional order of a trial in due course of law under Article 38.1 of the Constitution."[174]

R (E) did not have to address squarely the advantages and drawbacks of chambers discussions about sentence. The principal issue for resolution was whether the appellant should have been allowed to change her plea back to one of not guilty, and there was a further question of whether the judicial review proceedings should have been initiated before the conclusion of the trial court proceedings. The Supreme Court dismissed the appellant's appeal. Yet, the merits of a *Goodyear*-type process, with all its limitations and qualifications as outlined earlier, remain worthy of consideration. The need to encourage more early guilty pleas may not be as pressing here as it was perceived to be in England and Wales when the Royal Commission on Criminal Justice reported and, later, when *Goodyear* was decided. Yet, there may be other reasons why, out of fairness to accused persons, some limited provision for allowing advance indications of sentence should be considered. **6–54**

---

[171] *People (DPP) v Heeney* [2001] 1 IR 736.
[172] [2001] 1 IR 736.
[173] [2019] IESC 86.
[174] [2019] IESC 86, para 32.

CHAPTER 7

COLLATERAL CONSEQUENCES

Proportionality demands that a sentence must be commensurate with the gravity of the offence and the offender's personal circumstances. As this principle is customarily expressed, it seems to apply solely to *sentences*, meaning penalties judicially imposed following conviction. But if it were expressed in terms of commensurate *punishment*, as arguably it should be, judicial penalties might need adjusting to reflect other punitive consequences suffered by offenders for their crimes.[1] These collateral consequences include loss of employment, adverse publicity, social ostracisation and even so-called punishment beatings. Others apply by operation of law, as exemplified by disqualification from driving following conviction for certain road traffic offences, disqualification from exercising a profession or holding public office as in the case of corruption offences,[2] being subject to a notification requirement following conviction for a sexual offence or becoming ineligible for jury service (in so far as that is seen as punishment).[3] In some jurisdictions, conviction for a serious offence may lead to long-term deprivation of basic civil and political rights. Most notably, in the United States a person convicted of a felony may lose the right to vote (temporarily or permanently), become ineligible for housing and other welfare benefits and be barred from many kinds of employment.[4] According to some estimates, as many as 45,000 **7–01**

1 The distinction is well-recognised in Canadian jurisprudence. In *R v Basque* [2023] SCC 18, for example, the Supreme Court, having referred to the report of the Canadian Sentencing Commission (1987) and *R v Wust* [2000] 1 SCR 455, said (para 56): "It can therefore be said that the concept of punishment is fundamentally different from that sentence, since the former reflects the global punishment imposed on an offender, whereas the latter concerns only the portion of the punishment that the offender must serve after judgment is tendered". (This was said in respect of circumstances where an offender had already served part of the punishment, eg, by having served pre-trial detention, before being sentenced.)

2 Criminal Justice (Corruption Offences) Act 2018, s 17.

3 Juries Act 1976, s 8. On jury disqualification following conviction in the United States, see James M Binnall, *Twenty Million Angry Men: The Case for Including Convicted Felons in Our Jury System* (University of California Press, 2021).

4 There is a vast literature on collateral consequences in the United States, especially in relation to felony disenfranchisement laws and impediments to securing employment. See, for example, United States Commission on Civil Rights, *Collateral Consequences: The Crossroads of Punishment, Redemption, and the Effects on Communities* (2019) available at <www.usccr.gov> accessed 18

federal, state and local ordinances impose various kinds of restrictions on persons convicted of criminal offences in the United States.[5] Many of those restrictions endure long after the judicially imposed sentence has been served; some will last throughout the offender's entire life. As Reuben Jonathan Miller argues, incarceration has an "afterlife" because of the severe constraints to which many former prisoners are subject. They are therefore condemned to what he calls an "alternative form of citizenship".[6] In Ireland, at least, there is no question of being disenfranchised. Serving prisoners as well as ex-prisoners have the right to vote.[7]

November 2024 (a detailed briefing document describing and analysing the various collateral consequences operating in the United States); Michael Pinard, "Collateral consequences of criminal convictions: Confronting issues of race and dignity" (2010) 85 New York Univ LR 457; Michael Pinard, "An integrated perspective on the collateral consequences of criminal convictions and re-entry issues faced by formerly incarcerated individuals" (2006) 86 Boston Univ LR 623; Margaret Colgate Love, Jenny Roberts and Wayne A. Logan, *Collateral Consequences of Criminal Conviction: Law, Policy and Practice* (Thomson Reuters, 2018); Nora V Demleitner, "Collateral sanctions and American exceptionalism" in Kevin R Reitz (ed), *American Exceptionalism in Crime and Punishment* (Oxford University Press, 2018); Wayne A Logan, "Informal collateral consequences" (2013) 88 Washington LR 1103; John Hagan and Ronit Dinovitzer, "Collateral consequences of imprisonment for children, communities, and prisoners" (1999) 26 *Crime and Justice* 121; Alessandro Corda, "The collateral consequence conundrum: Comparative genealogy, current trends and future scenarios" (2019) 77 *Studies in Law, Politics and Society* 69; James B Jacobs, *The Eternal Criminal Record* (Harvard University Press, 2015); Marc Mauer, "Confronting felony disenfranchisement: Toward a movement for full citizenship" (2018) 45(1) *Social Justice* 13; Marc Mauer and Meda Chesney-Lind (eds), *Invisible Punishment: The Collateral Consequences of Mass Imprisonment* (New Press, 2003); Beth M Huebner and Natasha A Frost (eds), *Handbook on the Consequences of Sentencing and Punishment Decisions* (Routledge, 2019). For a more extensive and highly perceptive analysis of collateral consequences, see Zachary Hoskins, *Beyond Punishment? A Normative Account of the Collateral Legal Consequences of Conviction* (Oxford University Press, 2019).

5 Cameron Kimble and Ames Grawert, *Collateral Consequences and the Enduring Nature of Punishment* (Brennan Centre for Justice, 2021) < www.brennancenter.org> accessed 18 November 2024.

6 Reuben Jonathan Miller, *Halfway Home: Race, Punishment, and the Afterlife of Mass Incarceration* (Little, Brown & Company, 2020). See also Michael D Mayfield, "Revisiting expungement; Concealing information in the information age" [1997] Utah LR 1057 (referring to how ex-prisoners often face public ostracism "as confining as prison bars and an equally formidable obstacle to reintegration into society"), and *United States v Morgan* 346 US 502, 519 (1954) (Minton J dissenting).

7 Electoral (Amendment) Act 2006. See Cormac Behan, *Citizen Convicts: Prisoners, Politics and the Vote* (Manchester University Press, 2014). In *Hirst v United Kingdom (No.2)* (2006) 42 EHRR 41, the European Court of Human Rights held that the blanket ban on prisoner voting in England and Wales violated Protocol No 1 of the ECHR. Under a compromise reached in 2017, prisoners on temporary release may now vote in England. Some prisoners in Scotland and Wales are allowed to vote while in custody. See Colin RG Murphy, "Prisoner voting and devolution: New dimensions to an old dispute" (2021) 25(3) Edinburgh LR 291. In *Sauvé v Canada* [2002] 3 SCR 519, the Canadian Supreme Court invalidated a law that denied the right to vote to prisoners serving two

7–02 This chapter is principally concerned with collateral consequences as a form of punishment and, more specifically, with the question of whether they should influence the nature and severity of judicially imposed penalties in a sentencing system where proportionality is the overarching distributive principle. Most of the consequences under discussion flow from conviction, but some can result from the commission of the offence. This holds true, for example, of 'natural punishment' and civil penalties incurred for the offending conduct. Both are discussed further below. One important question is whether ancillary measures that are expressed or interpreted to be preventive in nature or purpose are nonetheless punitive in effect and therefore relevant factors at sentencing. The narrow focus of this chapter on collateral consequences as punishment means that other important dimensions of those consequences are not addressed. Some ancillary measures, including various kinds of disqualification and exclusion from certain occupations can seriously hinder the social reintegration of offenders.[8] They may also have the effect of discriminating unfairly against racial minorities or persons from disadvantaged backgrounds. There is a significant body of scholarship on these issues,[9] though somewhat less on the issue being addressed here.

7–03 Before proceeding further, two preliminary points should be noted. First, an acquittal, no less than a conviction, may have collateral consequences, though they are usually less severe than those flowing from a conviction. Exceptionally, certain orders such as a bind over or non-molestation order may be made against an acquitted person, though these seldom do more than require desistance from objectionable or impermissible conduct.[10] More pertinently, an acquitted person, unless granted criminal legal aid, may have to pay substantial defence costs, and possibly face financial ruin as a result. Only in limited circumstances will the prosecution be ordered to pay an acquitted person's costs.[11] Having to stand trial and await a verdict is obviously stressful and can have a lasting psychological

---

years or longer. On prisoner disenfranchisement more generally, see Mandeep K Dhami and Paula A Cruise, "Prisoner disenfranchisement: Prisoner and public views of an invisible punishment" (2013) 13(1) *Analyses of Social Issues and Public Policy* 211; Robert Jones and Gregory Davies, "Prisoner voting in the United Kingdom: An empirical study of a contested prisoner right" (2023) 86 MLR 900.

8 Joy Radice, "The reintegrative state" (2017) 66 Emory LJ 1315; George P Fletcher, "Disenfranchisement as punishment: Reflections on the racial uses of *infamia*" (1999) 46 UCLA LR 1895.

9 They are addressed in many of the works cited in note 4 above. On the collective impact of disenfranchisement, see Pamela S Karlan, "Convictions and doubts: Retribution, representation, and the debate over felon disenfranchisement" (2004) 56 Stanford LR 1147, and Michelle Alexander, *The New Jim Crow: Mass Incarceration in the Age of Colorblindness* (Penguin Books, 2019).

10 On binding over, see Thomas O'Malley, *Sentencing Law and Practice,* 3rd ed (Round Hall, 2016), Chap 26.

11 *People (DPP) v Bourke Waste Removal Ltd.* [2010] IECC 122; [2012] IECCA 66; [2013] 2 IR 94; [2012] 2 ILRM 496; *People (DPP) v Ryan* [2014] IECC 1; *People (DPP) v O' Donoghue* [2024] IECA 179.

impact.[12] Further, an acquittal can never be guaranteed to restore a defendant to their pre-charge standing in the eyes of the community. The prosecution's failure to satisfy the trial court of a defendant's guilt will not always convince acquaintances, employers and others of his or her innocence. Indeed, the very fact of having been charged with a sexual offence may effectively disqualify a person from securing certain kinds of employment.[13] In the United States, an arrest record, without more, may have seriously negative consequences for a person's immigration status, access to housing or education and child custody.[14]

7–04 Secondly, while our primary concern here is with collateral consequences of conviction, the conduct constituting the offence may be subject to multiple penalties. As reflected in a working definition adopted by the Canadian Supreme Court, a collateral consequence is "any consequence arising from the commission of the offence, the conviction for an offence, or the sentence imposed for an offence, that impacts the offender".[15] Violations of revenue law, for example, are usually dealt with by way of civil penalties and interest payments imposed and collected by the revenue authorities without recourse to court proceedings. Where the violation is considered particularly serious, the taxpayer may also be prosecuted and, if convicted, fined or imprisoned. Ordinarily, however, in these circumstances, sentencing courts take account of the civil penalties already incurred.[16]

7–05 Collateral consequences have only recently begun to receive serious scholarly attention, but the practice of subjecting wrongdoers to sustained public condemnation or disapproval has a long history.[17] In ancient Greece, loss of honour (*atimia*) exposed a wrongdoer to many civil disabilities. In the archaic period it left him liable to be assaulted or even killed with impunity. By the classical period, it meant, among other things, being prohibited from participating in political affairs, serving as a juror, giving evidence in court or holding a magistracy.[18] *Infamia* had a rather similar impact in ancient Rome where it meant a decline in social standing as well as disqualification from exercising certain legal functions such as prosecuting in a criminal case or representing another in court.[19] Other

---

[12] Samantha K Brooks and Neil Greenberg, "Psychological impact of being wrongly accused of criminal offences: A systematic literature review" (2021) 6 *Medicine, Science and the Law* 44.

[13] For a more detailed treatment of this topic, see Jill Peay and Elaine Player, "'Not a stain on your character?': The finality of acquittals and the search for just outcomes" [2021] Crim LR 921.

[14] Eisha Jain, "Arrests as regulation" (2015) 67 Stanford LR 809, 826-844.

[15] *R v Suter* [2018] 2 SCR 496, para 47.

[16] *People (DPP) v Redmond* [2001] 3 IR 390; *People (DPP) v Gargan* [2024] IECA 156.

[17] Katherine I Pettrus, *Felony Disenfranchisement in America: Historical Origins, Institutional Racism, and Modern Consequences,* 2nd ed. (State University of New York Press, 2013), Chap 1.

[18] Brook Manville, "Solon's law of stasis and *atimia* in archaic Athens" (1980) 110 *Transactions of the American Philological Association* 213.

[19] Tiziana J Chiusi, "'*Fama*' and '*Infamia*' in the Roman legal system: The cases

ancient legal systems had similar punitive measures, including outlawry.[20] Some of these practices may have been the sole penalties imposed for certain kinds of wrongdoing, but they illustrate the enduring tendency to subject wrongdoers to prolonged social censure, whether formally authorised by law or otherwise.

One need not hark back to the ancient world to find examples of multi-layered punishments. Conviction for a serious offence may no longer entail 'civil death' but it can still result in an array of restrictions on the offender's freedom and autonomy over and above the primary punishment.[21] One of the first cases to come before the European Court of Human Rights, *De Becker v Belgium*,[22] provides an extreme example of legally mandated collateral consequences of conviction. The applicant, who had been editor of a Belgian newspaper, was convicted in 1946 of collaborating with German occupying forces. He was sentenced to death, but this sentence was commuted to life imprisonment and later to 17 years' imprisonment. Moreover, under the prevailing Belgian law anyone sentenced to more than five years' imprisonment for this offence was automatically deprived for life of a long list of rights including the right to vote, the right to practice law, to teach, to have any role whatever in the editing or production of any newspaper or other publication, in administering cultural activities, or managing a company or commercial organisation. De Becker later claimed that this law violated his rights under various articles of the European Convention on Human Rights ('ECHR'), and especially Art 10 which guarantees the right to freedom of expression. The European Commission on Human Rights agreed that there had been a violation of art 10, and it referred the case to the court. In the meantime, however, the offending parts of the Belgian law were amended, and the case was struck out on consent. Belgium was by no means unique in imposing disqualifications of this nature. In Germany, so-called *Berufsverbot* resulted in many persons being disqualified from holding certain positions following a criminal conviction or because of their political activity.[23] Closer to home, s 34 of the Offences Against the State Act 1939 provided that a person convicted by the Special Criminal Court of a scheduled offence was disqualified from holding public sector employment for a period of seven years. In *Cox v Ireland*,[24] this was 7–06

of Afrania and Lucretia" in Andrew Burrows, David Johnson and Reinhard Zimmermann (eds), *Judge and Jurist: Essays in Honour of Lord Rodger of Earlsferry* (Oxford University Press, 2013), Chap 15, p 147. See also Demleitner, note 4 above.

[20] Mirjan Damaška, "Adverse legal consequences of conviction and their removal: A comparative study" (1969) 59 J Crim Law, Criminology and Police Science 347 and 542.

[21] Gabriel J Chin, "The new civil death: Rethinking punishment in the era of mass incarceration" (2012) 160 Univ Pennsylvania LR 1789 at 1793-1799.

[22] (1979-80) 1 EHRR 43.

[23] See, for example, *Vogt v Germany* (1996) 21 EHRR 205 involving a teacher who was dismissed because of her membership of the Communist Party. This was held to constitute a violation of arts 10 and 11 of the ECHR.

[24] [1992] 2 IR 503. See also *Lovett v Minister for Education* [1997] 1 ILRM 89 and

declared unconstitutional on the ground that it was impermissibly wide and indiscriminate. As will become apparent from the remainder of this chapter, many other collateral consequences still persist.

7–07 The decision of the United States Supreme Court in *Padilla v Kentucky*[25] brought the issue of collateral consequences firmly to the fore in that jurisdiction and elsewhere. The petitioner, a native of Honduras, pleaded guilty to drug charges which meant that he faced deportation, despite having lawfully resided in the United States for over 40 years and having served with the American army in Vietnam. His defence lawyer had failed to advise him that his guilty plea would leave him liable to deportation and, in fact, had told him that he need not worry about his immigration status because he had been in the United States for so long. The question for the Supreme Court was whether this amounted to ineffective assistance of counsel as defined in *Strickland v Washington,*[26] and a majority of the court held that it did. In so deciding, the court recognised the punitive impact of deportation even if it was not part of the formal penalty for the offence. The court's observations in this regard will be noted later in this chapter.

1. Classification of Collateral Consequences

7–08 Collateral consequences may be categorised in various ways. Taking a lead from Mirjan Damaška, one might classify them according to the right or interest they affect, eg, citizenship and political rights, personal freedom, entitlement to pursue an occupation or profession and so forth.[27] Alternatively, they might be broadly divided in the first instance into legal and incidental consequences. Some, such as disqualification from driving and sex offender notification requirements, are prescribed by law. They may be mandatory or discretionary but, either way, they are based on statute. Others – what we shall call incidental consequences – follow, mostly as a matter of fact rather than law, from the commission of the offence, the conviction or sentence. They include loss of employment, disbarment from a profession,[28] loss of social standing and being the subject of sustained unfavourable public comment. Burdens of this nature may, of course, affect not only the offender but his or her family, dependants and, sometimes, employees as well. Actual consequences could also consist of patently unlawful acts such as subjecting the offender to a punishment beating. Nigel Walker adopted the term "obiter punishment" to describe the punishment unintentionally inflicted on others, such as an offender's

---

C(P) v Minister for Social Protection [2017] IESC 63; [2017] 2 ILRM 369.

25 559 US 356 (2010). See Margaret Colgate Love, "Collateral consequences after *Padilla v Kentucky*: From punishment to regulation" (2011) 31 St Louis Univ Public LR 87.

26 466 US 668 (1984).

27 Damaška, note 20 above.

28 In many instances, disbarment or disqualification from exercising an occupation will be required or permitted by statute.

family members, as the by-product of sentence. As he noted, imprisonment almost always inflicts obiter punishment on someone. He used the term "incidental punishment" to describe the additional punitive consequences of a sentence, such as loss of employment, for the offender personally.[29] The two can, of course, overlap. Dependent family members will suffer if the sole breadwinner becomes unemployed following conviction or sentence. In such a case there will have been both incidental and obiter punishment.

Legal consequences typically flow from the nature of the offence rather than the personal characteristics or circumstances of the offender. In some instances, the precise nature of the offence is immaterial as long as it reaches a certain threshold of seriousness. A law might provide, for example, that a non-citizen convicted on indictment is subject to deportation, or that a person sentenced to imprisonment for a specified period or longer is to be disqualified from doing certain things such as serving on a jury. More commonly, however, the nature of the offence will be decisive. Driving offences, sexual offences, drug offences and firearms offences, to name but some, will often entail specific collateral consequences. Most consequences in this category apply indiscriminately upon conviction regardless of the personal history, character, circumstances or prospects of individual offenders. Mandatory driving bans and sex offender notification provisions can be especially problematic in this regard. Their duration is typically set by statute, and they become automatically applicable upon conviction for the relevant offence, without permitting any judicial adjustment to reflect the degree of risk posed by the offender, even when such measures have public protection as their avowed purpose or rationale. Further, a collateral consequence, however punitive, may automatically attach to a conviction, irrespective of the relative gravity of the particular offence. This can have the rather perverse result that persons convicted of less serious offences may suffer more than those convicted of very serious offences. A professional person sentenced to a long term of imprisonment for, say, fraud, can scarcely expect to resume professional practice upon release. Yet, another member of the same profession, convicted of a much less serious offence, and perhaps spared immediate imprisonment, may also suffer perpetual or long-term disqualification from exercising that or any other profession.[30] As recognised by the American Bar Association, among other authorities, the indiscriminate application of collateral consequences may frustrate the successful reintegration of offenders and therefore lead to recidivism.[31] **7–09**

---

[29] Nigel Walker, *Why Punish: Theories of Punishment Reassessed* (Oxford University Press, 1991), Chap 13.

[30] This point is well made by Chin, note 21 above, at 1806.

[31] ABA Standards for Criminal Justice, Collateral Sanctions and Discretionary Disqualification of Convicted Persons (3rd ed, 2004), 8-10. In *Doe v United States* 110 F Supp 3d 448 (2015), Judge Gleeson granted expungement of a conviction to a woman who was finding it extremely difficult to secure employment because of an offence committed 17 years earlier, stating: "I sentenced her to five years of probation supervision, not a lifetime of unemployment."

7–10 The formal classification of collateral consequences is not particularly important for the purpose of the argument being advanced in this Chapter. Rather what matters is their impact on the offender. It is not being suggested here that all collateral consequences are undeserved. Many are deserved, if only in the sense of being necessary to protect the public from further offending of a similar nature by the offender. This holds true, for example, of certain disqualification orders. Others, such as privately inflicted punishments, are undeserved. Either way, and to adopt the language of the Canadian Supreme Court, they may form part of the global punishment imposed on the offender.[32] Finally, it is acknowledged that not every collateral consequence will have a punitive impact. All depends on the offender's particular circumstances and how they will be affected by the order in question. In some instances, the collateral consequence may be the most severe aspect of the overall punishment; in others it may simply require abstention from conduct in which the offender could not lawfully engage in any event.

2. What is Criminal Punishment?

7–11 If it is correct to say that what the law requires is a *punishment* proportionate to the gravity of the offence and the offender's personal circumstances, one must then ask what 'punishment' should mean. Which penalties, burdens or hardships suffered by an offender as a consequence of the offence or conviction should qualify as punishment for this purpose? A person may suffer, perhaps severely, by committing the offence, apart altogether from any legal proceedings that follow. The term 'natural punishment' generally refers to some negative consequence suffered by an offender from the conduct constituting the offence, though not because of any official intervention.[33] This concept has a long history.[34] Kant, for example, distinguished between 'natural punishment' and 'forensic punishment'. Natural punishment occurs where "vice punishes itself and [it is something] which the legislator does not take into account".[35] Kant's definition – vice, in the sense of wrongdoing, punishing itself –

Unfortunately, the Court of Appeals reversed this decision holding that the District Court lacked the necessary jurisdiction: *Doe v United States* 833 F3d 192 (2016). See also Richard D Schwartz and Jerome H Skolnick, "Two studies of legal stigma" (1962) 10(2) *Social Problems* 133, 136 referring to the "status degradation" of a conviction and the consequent barriers to securing employment and achieving social reintegration.

32 note 1 above.

33 Raff Donelson, "Natural punishment" (2022) 100 North Carolina LR 557. He defines natural punishment as "any sufficiently serious adversity resulting from a wrongdoer's misconduct without the intervention of anyone intending to cause retributive harm to the wrongdoer" (p 563).

34 There are two excellent articles in Spanish on the topic: Carlos Bobabilla Barra, "La 'pena natural': fundamentos, límites y posible aplicación en el derecho chileno" (2016) 11, No 22 *Política Criminal* 548; Enzo Finocchiaro, "La pena natural: Breves consideraciones" (2012) No 5 *Revista de derecho penal y criminología* 68.

35 Kant, *The Metaphysics of Morals* in Immanuel Kant, *Practical Philosophy,*

captures the essence of natural punishment. It typically occurs when an offender sustains a serious injury through committing the offence. A driver who causes death by dangerous driving may also sustain life-changing injuries himself.[36] Some would include genuine anguish and remorse on the offender's part as another form of natural punishment, and this may well have been intended by Kant also.[37] This too can arise in a dangerous driving case where the offender has caused the death of a close friend or family member. Opinions vary as to whether a court should mitigate sentence because of an injury suffered while committing the offence. Some argue that since the injury is a burden directly resulting from the offence, it should be accorded some weight, even if not very much, when determining sentence. Others claim that it should be no different than if the offender had later suffered a similar injury or loss in circumstances completely unrelated to the offence. In that event the injury would be irrelevant at sentencing unless perhaps it left the offender in a condition that rendered imprisonment exceptionally burdensome.[38]

Criminal punishment, or forensic punishment in Kant's terms, is imposed **7–12** through a legal process on a convicted person. It clearly includes a judicially imposed penalty, and some might define it to include no more than that. However, an offender can suffer further punishment through the operation of a general law, though it forms no part of the sentencing judgment. After all, an Irish judge imposing sentence for a serious offence never tells the offender that he or she will be ineligible for jury service for a defined period,[39] any more than American judges (typically at least) tell offenders that they will be disenfranchised for the duration of the sentence, and perhaps well beyond that. Yet, disqualifications of this nature are part of the overall punitive burden an offender must bear as a consequence of conviction.

The Punitive Nature of Preventive Measures

Many collateral consequences consist of ancillary orders that may or must **7–13**

---

translated and edited by Mary Gregor (Cambridge University Press, 1996), 473.

[36] Donelson, note 33 above mentions the case of a man who robbed a hot dog stand in Chicago while having a pistol in his waistband. As he was running away with the proceeds, he accidentally triggered the pistol and shot himself in the penis. This provoked some debate as to whether he had 'suffered enough'.

[37] Michael Naas, "Kant with Freud: Derrida's analysis of the ancient dream of self-punishment" (2016) 27 *Law and Critique* 151 at 154 ("if an evil-doer is sometimes punished by some non-juridical means in nature; that is (we might speculate since Kant does not), by the natural consequences of his actions or else by remorse, or by what others might call fate or 'poetic justice', then this is something that Kant simply asserts that the 'legislator does not take into account'"). See also Fiacha Heneghan, "Philosophy's persuasiveness of death: Kant in Derrida's death penalty seminars" (2022) 66 *Philosophy Today* 149.

[38] Mirko Bagaric, Lidia Xynas and Victoria Lambropoulos, "The irrelevance to sentencing of (most) incidental hardships suffered by offenders" (2016) 39 University of New South Wales LJ 47.

[39] Juries Act 1976, s 8.

be imposed following conviction. Disqualifications of various kinds as well as registration and notification requirements are typical of such orders. Many of these orders are formally justified on preventive grounds. This holds true, for example, of sex offender notification requirements. Irish and American courts, as well as the European Court of Human Rights, have occasionally had to decide if those notification requirements and similar provisions should be treated as 'penalties' for the purpose of the *nulla poena sine lege* principle which is protected by the Irish and United States constitutions and under the ECHR.[40] This principle (also known as *ex post facto)* prohibits the imposition of a more severe penalty than applied when the offence was committed.[41] If, therefore, a sex offender notification order were a penalty, it could not lawfully be applied to a person who committed a sex offence before the statute that introduced such orders entered into force.

7–14 The United States Supreme Court has adopted a two-part test for establishing if a measure such as a sex offender notification order or compulsory confinement in a psychiatric hospital following release from prison is a punishment (in which case the rule against retroactive application applies) or a civil measure that is preventive or protective in nature. First, a court must ask if the legislature intended the measure to be a punishment. If it did, that decides the matter and the measure is deemed to be punitive. But if a court concludes that the measure was not intended to be punitive, it must determine if the measure is nevertheless punitive in effect. However, it can answer the latter question in the affirmative only where there is the "clearest proof" to justify so doing.[42] In *Smith v Doe*[43] a majority of the Supreme Court, applying this test, held that Alaska's sex offender registration law was non-punitive in nature. Ireland has, for all practical purposes, followed suit. In *Enright v Ireland*[44]the High Court applied the American test to establish if the sex offender notification requirement introduced by the Sex Offenders Act 2001 amounted to a penalty. If it did, it could not constitutionally apply retroactively. The court found that the statute did not manifest an intent to treat this requirement as punitive, and it further declined to find that it

---

[40] Leading Strasbourg decisions on this issue include *Welch v United Kingdom* (1995) 20 EHRR 247; *Ibbotson v United Kingdom* (1998) 27 EHRR CD 332; *Adamson v United Kingdom* (1999) 28 EHRR CD 209. See generally O'Malley, note 10 above, Chap 3.

[41] Wayne A Logan, *The Ex-Post Facto Clause: Its History and Role in a Punitive Society* (Oxford University Press, 2022).

[42] In *Kennedy v Mendoza-Martinez* 372 US 144 (1963), the Supreme Court listed seven factors to be considered when determining if a statute is punitive in effect.

[43] 538 US 84 (2003). For critical analysis of this line of case law see David A Singleton, "What is punishment: The case for considering public opinion under *Mendoza-Martinez*" (2015) 45 Seton Hall LR 435; Aaron Xavier Fellmeth, "Civil and criminal sanctions in the Constitution and courts" (2005) 94 Georgetown LJ 1; Wayne A Logan, "The ex post facto clause and the jurisprudence of punishment" (1998) 35 American Crim LR 1261.

[44] [2003] 2 IR 321; [2004] 1 ILRM 103.

was "so punitive either in purpose or effect" that it should be considered to constitute punishment.[45]

However, the classification of a measure such as a sex offender notification order as something other than a 'penalty' for the purpose of an *ex post facto* rule like that enshrined in art 7 of the ECHR, should not preclude a court from treating the measure as still being punitive to some degree in effect. An ancillary measure of this nature may impose a considerable burden on an offender, depending on his or her personal circumstances, and courts have been willing to recognise this. For instance, in *CC v Ireland*,[46] the Supreme Court said that the stigma attached to the sexual offence under consideration (sexual intercourse with a female under the age of consent) was compounded by the sex offender notification requirement. It then referred, with apparent approval, to *People (DPP) v Redmond*[47] where the Court of Criminal Appeal held that the totality of punitive consequences should be considered in selecting sentence. *CC* itself was not a sentencing case – it dealt with the constitutionality of a statutory provision that effectively made it a strict liability offence for a male to have sexual intercourse with a female under 15 years of age – but the Supreme Court's view on the relevance to sentence of a measure such as a mandatory notification order is nonetheless clear. If the measure has a clear punitive impact on the offender, it becomes relevant. This approach is quite compatible with the *Enright* line of cases on the test to be applied when deciding if a measure is a 'penalty' for the purpose of the non-retroactivity rule. What those cases hold is that, to qualify as a 'penalty' in this sense, a measure must be inherently so punitive in purpose or effect that it could not properly be treated as anything else. But, as reflected in *CC*, any collateral consequence, whether formally a penalty or not, may have such a punitive impact in a specific case that it may legitimately be treated as part of the overall punishment an offender will suffer. **7–15**

3. Collateral Consequences and Proportionate Punishment

Should a criminal court that is legally or constitutionally obliged to impose proportionate penalties take account of collateral consequences when deciding on sentence? It will be argued here that it should, at least to some degree, provided the consequence in question has a genuinely punitive impact. To suggest otherwise would imply that punishment should be equated with primary penalties such as a fine or term of imprisonment. However, as explained in the previous section, this is too narrow an understanding of criminal punishment and one finds little support in modern authorities. There is nothing inherent in the concept of punishment to suggest that it should take any particular form of hard treatment. Thus, intense stigmatisation may amount to punishment just as much as, say, incarceration, though one may be more severe than **7–16**

[45] See also *H(P) v Ireland* [2006] 2 IR 540; *F(J) v Ireland* [2015] IEHC 468.
[46] [2006] 4 IR 1, 76.
[47] [2001] 3 IR 390.

the other. To the objection that the offender has brought the collateral consequences upon himself, as courts have occasionally said, it may be replied that the same holds true of primary penalties.[48] Those who commit serious offences become liable to imprisonment (and may thus be said to have brought it upon themselves) but that does not disentitle them to proportionate custodial sentences. They may also suffer additional, genuinely punitive consequences (which they will also, for the most part, have brought upon themselves), but they should also be entitled to have these taken into account. It must, of course, be stressed that it is not a question of *exempting* an offender from primary punishment because of collateral consequences, but rather of *adjusting* the primary punishment to reflect those consequences. The degree of adjustment should reflect the severity of the consequences.

7–17 The version of proportionality favoured in Ireland further supports the practice of taking account of genuinely punitive collateral consequences. Rather than holding that a punishment should be proportionate to the gravity of the offence, and that alone, Irish law requires that punishment must be proportionate to the gravity of the offence and the offender's personal circumstances. In the oft-quoted words of the Court of Criminal Appeal, "[t]he sentence to be imposed is not the appropriate sentence for the crime, but the appropriate sentence for the crime because it has been committed by that accused".[49] The personal circumstances of an offender, as they exist at the time of sentence, may provide further grounds for considering collateral consequences. Those circumstances might, for example, have significantly deteriorated since the commission of the offence through loss of employment or being subjected to sustained adverse public comment or harassment. Being liable to deportation, a matter considered further below, is another obvious example of a collateral consequence that will be particularly severe for a long-time resident in the State. Some claim that collateral consequences cannot logically be taken into account in a system that adheres to a strict desert-based policy whereby punishment is determined solely by the gravity of the offence. But this does not necessarily follow. Even if punishment is determined by offence gravity alone, it need not consist solely of primary penalties. It might also incorporate other hardships suffered by the offender.

7–18 Two Canadian cases support this conclusion.[50] To appreciate their potential relevance to Ireland, it should be noted that under the Canadian Criminal Code (s 718.1), a sentence must be proportionate to the gravity of the offence and the degree of responsibility of the offender. This effectively corresponds to the first limb of our proportionality principle.

---

[48] *R v Buffrey* (1993) 14 Cr App R (S) 511, 514 (a fraud case in which the English Court of Appeal said that those who commit such offences must bargain with the possibility that their careers and family life will be adversely affected by a conviction but this is something they should consider before committing an offence).

[49] *People (DPP) v McCormack* [2000] 4 IR 356 at 359.

[50] *R v Pham* [2013] 1 SCR 739 and *R v Suter* [2018] 2 SCR 496.

However, the Canadian Code also provides (s 718.2) that "a sentence should be increased or reduced to account for any relevant aggravating or mitigating circumstances relating to the offence or the offender". Additionally, the Canadian Supreme Court has repeatedly stressed the importance of individualisation and parity in sentencing which, in turn, means that account must be taken of an offender's personal circumstances.[51] Fundamentally, therefore, Ireland and Canada share the same understanding of a just sentence. They reach the same destination by slightly different routes.

In *R v Pham*[52] the appellant had been sentenced to two years' imprisonment following conviction for drug offences. This meant that he was disqualified from appealing against any removal order made against him, because under the relevant immigration laws, a non-citizen sentenced to at least two years' imprisonment lost such a right of appeal. In his appeal against sentence, he argued that he should have been sentenced to two years less a day in view of the collateral consequence he would suffer if the two-year sentence were allowed to stand. He succeeded before the Canadian Supreme Court which varied the sentence to two years less a day. Delivering the court's judgment, Wagner J said that the relevance of collateral consequences flows partly from the principles of individualisation and parity but partly also from the objective of assisting the rehabilitation of offenders.[53] **7–19**

While offender rehabilitation is undoubtedly an important consideration in this context, a more fundamental reason for taking account of certain collateral consequence is that they amount to punishment in themselves, though not part of the prescribed legal punishment. Sometimes, as in the case of punishment beatings, they may be downright illegal. Yet they are part of the burden the offender must bear or has already borne as a result of committing the offence. In *Pham*, Wagner J concluded: **7–20**

> "The general rule continues to be that a sentence must be fit having regard to the particular crime and the particular offender. In other words, a sentencing judge may exercise his or her discretion to take collateral immigration consequences into account, provided that the sentence ultimately imposed is proportionate to the gravity of the offence and the degree of responsibility of the offender."

In *R v Suter*[54] the appellant, accompanied by his wife, drove to a **7–21**

---

51 *R v Ipeelee* [2012] 1 SCR 433, para 39; *R v Wust* [2000] 1 SCR 455, para 21; *R v M (CA)* [1996] 1 SCR 500, para 92; *R v Pham* [2013] 1 SCR 739, para 8.

52 [2013] 1 SCR 739.

53 In this connection, Wagner J quoted with approval from Allan Manson, *The Law of Sentencing* (Toronto: Irwin Law, 2001), 136-137 where it was argued that burdens and hardships flowing from conviction are relevant "if they make the rehabilitation path harder to travel" and that indirect consequences resulting from stigmatisation cannot be ignored at sentencing "if they will have a bearing on the offender's ability to live productively in the community".

54 [2018] 2 SCR 496.

restaurant and pulled up outside a glass partition that separated the patio of the restaurant from the parking area. Because he accidentally hit the accelerator rather than the brake, the car crashed through the glass partition and into an area where people were dining. Unfortunately, a two-year-old child who was there with his family died as a result of being hit by the car. The appellant was eventually charged with refusing to provide a breath sample knowing that he had caused an accident resulting in death, an offence to which he pleaded guilty. This is a serious offence in Canada where it carries a maximum of life imprisonment with a typical sentence in the range of two to ten years. Between offence and sentence, the appellant had been subjected to a severe punishment beating. As described by the Supreme Court:

> "Sometime after being charged, Mr Suter was abducted by vigilantes. Three hooded men took him from his home in the middle of the night, handcuffed him, and placed a canvas bag over his head. His attackers then drove him to a secluded area, cut off his thumb with pruning shears and left him unconscious in the snow. Mrs Suter was also attacked by vigilantes in a shopping mall parking lot. Both incidents were linked to Mr and Mrs Suter's role in [the child's] death."[55]

7–22 The appellant, having pleaded guilty to the aforementioned charge, was sentenced to four months' imprisonment with a 30-month driving prohibition. The Alberta Court of Appeal increased the custodial sentence to 26 months. The Supreme Court found fault with the reasoning of both courts, and substituted a sentence of time served which, in this instance, amounted to 10⅓ months. One member of the court, dissenting in part, would have restored the original four-month sentence. Essentially, however, Supreme Court treated the vigilante attack on the appellant as an element of his personal circumstances and therefore a factor to be considered when determining an appropriate sentence.[56] There was no requirement that collateral consequences should emanate from the state in order to qualify as mitigating factors.[57] However, the court cautioned that collateral consequences should not be given such weight as to lead to a disproportionately lenient sentence, having regard to the gravity of the offence and the offender's culpability. It is reasonable to assume that Irish courts would adopt a similar approach.

4. Privately Inflicted Punishment

7–23 Punishment beatings, whether administered by vigilantes, victims or relatives of a victim, are paradigmatic of privately inflicted punishment. But offenders may also be subject to social stigmatisation, ostracism, boycotting, adverse public comment or other non-violent action imposed

---

55 [2018] 2 SCR 496, para 14.

56 The court noted that the Federal Court of Australia had adopted a similar approach in *R v Mamarika* [1982] FCA 94 where the offender was subjected to violence by members of his community as a result of killing another person.

57 [2018] 2 SCR 496, para 56.

or orchestrated by private individuals. These too are real punishments because of their social, psychological and, sometimes, financial impact. American studies have shown that 'reputational penalties' imposed on corporate wrongdoers can have a significant impact on the value of a company's common stock and its general profitability. Moreover, this effect manifested itself once the allegations and investigations, as opposed to any later convictions, were publicised.[58] Companies were most likely to suffer in this regard where they defrauded customers or suppliers, but less so where the victims were third parties, as in the case of environmental offences. However, with increasing public commitment to environmental protection, this is likely to change. Even in the early years of this century, it was found, again in the United States, that firms investigated or charged in connection with environmental crime suffered significant decreases in common share values, though the overall impact was seldom greater than the judicially imposed penalties.[59] The authors of these studies were mainly concerned with identifying optimal penalties, namely penalties sufficient to deter rational actors from engaging in illegal conduct. If reputational or other privately inflicted penalties are sufficient for this purpose, they arguably obviate the need for criminal or civil sanctions.[60] This conclusion holds good only if one adopts a utilitarian view of the law as a vehicle for maximising efficiency. Yet, it also helps to define the question that concerns us here: should privately inflicted penalties, whether effectuated through the operation of the market or otherwise, influence sentences judicially imposed following conviction? Both past and recent experience shows that privately inflicted physical punishment tends to be excessive, bearing little relationship to the gravity of the alleged or suspected conduct.[61]

Fundamental to any discussion of this topic is the question of whether **7–24**

---

[58] Jonathan M Karpoff and John R Lott, "The reputational penalty firms bear from committing criminal fraud " (1993) 36 *Journal of Law and Economics* 757. Having examined 132 cases of alleged or actual corporate fraud dating from 1978 to 1987, they found that the affected companies suffered a decrease of 1.34 percent, or $60.8 million, in the value of their common stock. For frauds against government agencies, the corresponding loss was 5.05 percent, or $40 million. See also Cindy R Alexander, "On the nature of reputational penalty for corporate crime: Evidence" (1999) 42 *Journal of Law and Economics* 489 ("Criminal and civil sanctions are imposed through the courts. 'Reputational' penalties are imposed through the market").

[59] Jonathan Karpoff, John R Lott and Eric W Wehrly, "The reputational penalties for environmental violations: Empirical evidence" (2005) 48 *Journal of Law and Economics* 653.

[60] Richard A Bierschbach and Alex Stein, "Overenforcement" (2003) 93 Georgetown LJ 1743 at 1752 ("Market spillovers occur when the invocation of the legal process and the ultimate imposition of a legal penalty combine with extralegal sanctions to bring the total harm to a defendant above the total optimal amount for deterrence").

[61] David Garland, "Penal excess and surplus meaning: Public torture lynchings in twentieth-century America" (2005) 39 *Law and Society Review* 793; Dany Franck A Tiwa, "Killing is just the solution: Lynching as informal incapacitation" (2022) 62 Brit J Criminology 699.

the state has, or should have, a monopoly on the right to impose criminal punishment. In thus narrowing the discussion, we are omitting two matters that are undoubtedly related to this general question though not for present purposes. One concerns the legitimacy of parental punishment of children[62] and the other the use of private parties to implement judicially imposed punishment. The latter issue is undoubtedly important as it deals with the use of private prisons, privately operated probation services and, some would argue, shaming sanctions.[63] However, our present preoccupation is with the judicial sentencing decision, rather than its aftermath. We shall assume that the state legitimately exists and that its society is not so divided that some segments of it have lost all trust in official law enforcement agencies. Where that trust is lacking, vigilantism may well flourish.[64] Several leading philosophers and theorists seem to assume the state's monopoly on the right to punish criminal offenders, without dwelling on the basis of the monopoly. Kant, for example, describes the right to punish as "a right a ruler has against a subject to inflict pain upon him because of his having committed an offence".[65]

7–25 John Locke provided a more elaborate defence of the state's monopoly on the infliction of criminal punishment as part of his social contract theory. In pre-political society, the so-called state of nature, everyone had an equal right to punish offenders (though, interestingly, according to Locke, in a proportionate manner). Yet, because individuals could not always be trusted to exercise this natural right properly and fairly, they somehow collectively decided to cede it to a political sovereign in return for an ordered society affording greater protection for personal security and private property. Locke argued that "every man who has entered into civil society, and is become a member of any commonwealth, has thereby quitted his power to punish offences, against the law of nature, in prosecution of his own private judgment".[66] He also wrote that

---

62 See, for example, Shachar Eldar, "Criminal law, parental authority, and the state" (2018) 12 *Criminal Law and Philosophy* 695.

63 Malcom M Feely, "The unconvincing case against private prisons" (2014) 89 Indiana LJ 1401; Paul Moyle, "Separating the allocation of punishment from its administration: Theoretical and empirical observations" (2001) 41 Brit J Criminology 77; Alon Harel, "Why only the state may inflict criminal sanctions: The case against privately inflicted sanctions" (2018) 14 *Legal Theory* 113. On shaming sanctions, see James Q Whitman, "What is wrong with inflicting shaming sanctions?" (1998) 107 Yale LJ 1055; Dan Kahan, "What's really wrong with shaming sanctions?" (2006) 84 Texas LR 2075, rowing back on his earlier defence of such sanctions in "What do alternative sanctions mean?" (1996) 63 Univ Chicago LR 591.

64 Kieran McEvoy and Harry Mika, "Punishment, policing and praxis: Restorative justice and non-violent alternatives to paramilitary punishments in Northern Ireland" (2001) 11 *Policing and Society* 359.

65 Immanuel Kant, *The Metaphysics of Morals* (1797), in Immanuel Kant, *Practical Philosophy*, translated and edited by Mary J Gregor (Cambridge University Press, 1996), 472.

66 John Locke, *Second Treatise of Government* in *Two Treatises of Government*, edited by Peter Laslett (Cambridge University Press, 1988), §88 (pp 324-325). See also A John Simmons, "Locke and the right to punish" (1991) 20 *Philosophy and Public*

nobody is justified in punishing another unless he "has commission and power to do so".[67] Locke's precepts in this regard have been adopted by leading American judges and jurists, which is scarcely surprising as he has been described as "still intractably America's philosopher".[68] They were invoked by Roberts CJ (dissenting) in *Robertson v United States*[69] to support the view that "[a] basic step in organising a civilised society is to take [the sword] out of private hands and turn it over to an organised government, acting on behalf of all the people". About the same time, Stevens J (dissenting) in *McDonald v City of Chicago*[70] said that "it is a fundamental premise of modern government that the State holds a monopoly on legitimate violence". Even those who do not accept Lockean social contract theory would probably agree with these sentiments.

Others deploy an instrumentalist argument to justify the state's monopoly on criminal punishment. The state is uniquely equipped with the necessary institutions such as courts to administer punishment, and it can (ideally at least) be relied upon to act fairly and impartially to a degree that might not, for example, be expected of crime victims. However, this explanation suggests that if some private party had that same institutional capacity and adopted that same ethical approach, it too could legitimately punish offenders. It therefore fails to explain why the state should have a monopoly in the matter.[71] Another approach is to assume that a legitimately constituted state has a right to rule, and the exclusive power to punish offenders is one of the privileges flowing from this right.[72] The more convincing explanations seem to hinge on the state's duty to protect individual rights. Christopher Wellman argues that a state is legitimate to the extent that it protects the human rights of all its constituents, and it cannot successfully fulfil this critical function unless vested with the exclusive authority to punish all wrongdoers within its jurisdiction.[73] Andrew Ashworth offers rather similar justifications: **7–26**

> "Two arguments are that criminal justice should be administered "in the public interest", and that it should ensure respect for human rights. Since…

Affairs 311; James Tully, "Political freedom" (1990) 87 *Journal of Philosophy* 517. A concept of the state somewhat similar to Locke's may be identified in Plato's *Crito* in Plato, *The Last Days of Socrates,* translated by Hugh Tredennick and Harold Tarrant (Penguin Books, 2003).

[67] John Locke, *A Second Letter Concerning Toleration,* quoted in Alex Tuckness, "Retribution and restitution in Locke's theory of punishment" (2010) 72 *The Journal of Politics* 720 , 726.

[68] John Dunn, "Measuring Locke's shadow" in Ian Shapiro (ed), *Two Treatises on Government and A Letter Concerning Toleration by John Locke* (Yale University Press, 2003), 260.

[69] 560 US 272, 282-283 (2010).

[70] 561 US 742, 892 (2010).

[71] Christopher H Wellman, "Rights and state punishment" (2009) 106 *Journal of Philosophy* 419, 429.

[72] This seems to be implied by Dudley Knowles, *Political Obligation: A Critical Introduction* (Routledge, 2010).

[73] Christopher H Wellman, *Rights Forfeiture and Punishment* (Oxford University Press, 2017), Chap 3.

a defining feature of criminal offences is that they are offences against the state or collectivity, it is right that the state should ensure that the response is based on general principles duly established and applicable throughout the jurisdiction. This connects closely with the second argument about respect for human rights. The state surely owes it to offenders to exercise its power according to settled principles that uphold citizens' rights to equal respect and equality of treatment. Decisions on sentence should be taken by independent and impartial tribunals... operating on principle and transparency, within a legal framework."[74]

7–27 Some leading works on punishment philosophy have also assumed that punishment, by definition, must be imposed by an official authority. HLA Hart, for example, identifies as one of the definitional elements of punishment that it "must be imposed and administered by an authority constituted by a legal system against which the offence is committed".[75] Acceptance of the state's exclusive right to punish criminal offenders does not entail the conclusion that all privately inflicted punishments or sanctions are illegal. Punishment beatings clearly are, but the same cannot be said, for example, of ceasing to do business with a company that has defrauded its customers or suppliers.

7–28 Irrespective of its nature, privately inflicted punishment, provided it results directly from the offence, may be taken into consideration at sentencing. To do so is consistent with the principle of proportionality as understood in Ireland. A privately inflicted punishment, whatever form it takes, is almost invariably irrelevant to the assessment of offence gravity. It will have affected neither the harm caused by the offence nor the offender's culpability in committing it. However, it can properly be included among the offender's personal circumstances under the second limb of the proportionality principle.[76] This was the clear view of the Canadian Supreme Court in *R v Pham*[77] and *R v Suter*,[78] considered earlier in this chapter. *Pham* admittedly dealt with a statutory collateral consequence as opposed to privately inflicted punishment, but the rationale for treating such consequences as mitigating was largely the same in both cases. Australian courts have been less than unanimous on this issue.[79] In *R v Gooley*[80] where there had been a revenge attack on a man who had sexual intercourse with a 14-year-old girl, Doyle CJ held that such conduct should not be permitted to influence sentence as to do so would

---

74 Andrew Ashworth, "Responsibilities, rights and restorative justice" (2002) 42 Brit J Criminology 578, 571. See also Andrew Ashworth and Lucia Zedner, "Just prevention: Preventive rationales and the limits of the criminal law" in RA Duff and Stuart Green (eds), *Philosophical Foundations of Criminal Law* (Oxford University Press, 2011), Chap 8.

75 HLA Hart, *Punishment and Responsibility: Essays in the Philosophy of Law*, 2nd ed (Oxford University Press, 2008), 5.

76 Chap 5 above.

77 [2013] 1 SCR 739.

78 [2018] 2 SCR 496.

79 James Duffy, "Roll the dice, rational agent: Should extra-curial punishment mitigate an offender's sentence?" (2012) 31 Univ Queensland LJ 115.

80 (1996) 87 A Crim R 209.

be tantamount to allowing private punishment to influence punishment by the state. He said that courts that were willing to treat privately inflicted punishment as a mitigating factor were sending out mixed messages. On the one hand, they were condemning such punishment while on the other they were allowing it to mitigate the judicial sentence. This is a fair point, but it is equally important to convey to those who engage in punishment beatings that their actions will have consequences, including at sentencing. However, as stated by the Canadian Supreme Court held in *Suter* (above), mitigation granted for this reason should be limited. Privately inflicted punishment should not result in the offender's own conduct being treated with impunity.

5. Deportation

Deportation may not usually be classified as a criminal sanction, but it can undoubtedly be punitive, and sometimes extremely punitive, in nature. It is not proposed here to describe the laws of any jurisdiction governing deportation following conviction. Rather, the question is whether, as a general principle, deportation should be treated as part of the punishment for an offence. An offender who has been resident in the jurisdiction for only a short time may not suffer greatly from being deported, especially if the exclusion is for a defined period. However, in many countries long-term residents can be deported back to their 'native' countries although they may have no connection with the place to which they are being deported, apart possibly from having been born there. In fact, in some continental European countries, such as the Netherlands, where citizenship is based on *ius sanguinis* rather than *ius soli*, second-generation immigrants, although born within the country, may be deported following conviction to the country of which they are presumed to be citizens, despite having little or no personal connection with it. **7–29**

The punitive impact of deportation has been acknowledged by many courts around the world, including the United States Supreme Court. A century ago, that court said that deportation can deprive a person of liberty, property, the opportunity to pursue a career and "all that makes life worth living".[81] It can be equivalent of banishment or exile.[82] As noted earlier, the court returned to the topic more recently in *Padilla v Kentucky*[83] where it held that defence counsel must advise an accused person if a guilty plea will carry the risk of deportation. Counsel's failure to do so in that case meant that the petitioner had ineffective legal assistance. The conviction was therefore reversed, and the case remanded to the state courts. Central to the court's reasoning was a recognition that the number of offences for which non-citizens may be deported had grown exponentially over the years. This, in turn, had "dramatically raised the **7–30**

---

[81] *Ng Fung Ho v White* 259 US 276 (1922). See also *Bridges v Wixon* 326 US 135 (1945).

[82] *Delgadillo v Carmichael* 332 US 388 (1947).

[83] 559 US 356 (2010).

stakes of a noncitizen's criminal conviction". Further, recent statutory changes had made deportation a virtual certainty for a broad class of non-citizen offenders. The court reiterated what had been said in earlier cases about the punitive impact of deportation which it described as a severe 'penalty' even if not a formal criminal sanction. In that case, a native of Honduras faced deportation despite having lived and worked in the United States for more than 40 years.

7–31 The European Court of Human Rights has dealt with the deportation of convicted offenders on many occasions, although in most cases the question has been if deportation would violate the applicant's rights to family life under art 8 of the ECHR.[84] Recently, for example, in *Azerkane v The Netherlands*[85] the court upheld the deportation of an offender who had been born and lived all his life in the Netherlands though, legally, he was a Moroccan national who held temporary renewable residence permits in The Netherlands. He had a rather bad criminal record but, disappointingly, the Strasbourg court focused exclusively on his art 8 rights without giving any meaningful consideration to the extraordinary punitive impact of deportation in those circumstances. Individual members of the court have, however, acknowledged the punitive dimension. In a particularly strong dissent in *Uner v The Netherlands*[86] three judges said that foreign nationals, especially those legally resident in the country, should be treated just as fairly as nationals, and accorded a legal status as close as possible to that of nationals. Regarding deportation, they said:

> "The principle is that of "double punishment", or rather the discriminatory punishment imposed on a foreign national in addition to what would have been imposed on a national for the same offence. We do not agree with the assertion [of the majority] that the applicant's expulsion was to be seen as preventive rather than punitive in nature. Whether the decision is taken by means of an administrative measure, as in this case, or by a criminal court, it is our view that a measure of this kind, which can shatter a life or lives—even where, as in this case, it is valid, at least in theory, for only ten years (quite a long time, incidentally)—constitutes as severe a penalty as a term of imprisonment, if not more severe. This is true even where the prison sentence is longer but is not accompanied by an exclusion order or expulsion. That is why some states do not have penalties of this kind specific to foreign nationals, while others have largely abolished them in recent times..."[87]

7–32 There were dissents to similar effect in *Boujlifa v France.*[88] This surely represents the better and more defensible view of deportation as a punitive measure. Obviously, the extent to which it is punitive will depend on factors such as the duration and strength of the offender's ties

---

84 Leading cases include *Boultif v Switzerland* (2001) 33 EHRR 50 (where the court set out criteria for determining such applications) and *Uner v The Netherlands* (2007) 45 EHRR 14.

85 European Court of Human Rights, , 2 June 2020.

86 (2007) 45 EHRR 14.

87 (2007) 45 EHRR 14, para O-II17.

88 (2000) 30 EHRR 419.

to their country of residence and to the country in which they are likely to live following deportation. This is discussed further in Chap 12 in the context of requiring an offender to leave the jurisdiction as a condition of a suspended sentence.

6. Public Opprobrium

Being charged with or convicted of a serious offence almost invariably leaves one open to adverse comment. Those who commit serious offences must bargain with the strong possibility that their reputation will be severely damaged as a result, and this in turn will lead to a decline in their social standing. However, an offender may also have been subjected to sustained adverse publicity or, together perhaps with family members, have been the target of insulting, abusive or intimidatory conduct from others. This is a species of privately inflicted punishment. Offenders deserve punishment, but only of the kind and amount duly specified by a court of law. Members of the public, however strongly they may feel, have no right to take the law into their own hands and subject offenders, or suspected offenders, to additional punishment of their own choosing, even if that punishment is non-violent in nature (unlike the situation in *R v Suter*[89] and other cases considered earlier). As with all species of privately inflicted punishment, this poses a dilemma for sentencing policy makers and judges. On the one hand, they may wish to acknowledge that public opprobrium is part of the overall punishment suffered by the offender, and therefore a factor to be considered in the selection of sentence. On the other, they must be careful not to validate privately inflicted punishment, whether it takes the form of physical violence or derogatory conduct, verbal or otherwise, directed at the offender. They must be vigilant to ensure that offenders do not orchestrate any such conduct against themselves in order to secure more lenient sentences. Assuming they are satisfied on this score, courts usually take some account of public opprobrium especially, though not exclusively, where it has had identifiable material consequences. It may, for example, have resulted in the offender being put out of business or dismissed from his or her employment, and left with little hope of being able to rebuild a career anytime in the near future, if ever. In *People (DPP) v Sutton,*[90] for example, the appellant, a self-employed accountant with no previous criminal history, was convicted of assaulting his then partner and given an effective sentence of one year's imprisonment. The Court of Appeal, while it increased the sentence to two years and four months, said: 7–33

> "We accept that he is a professional man whose reputation is severely damaged and whose business has been, and will continue to be, badly affected in consequence of the penalties that have had to be applied to him, and that this represents an element of inevitable additional hardship that he must endure. We have been apprised of his bleak financial situation

[89] [2018] 2 SCR 496.
[90] [2020] IECA 280.

> and of the fact that, at least for the moment, he no longer has access to his children. We have also been told that he found prison difficult, and that he is anxious and apprehensive at the prospect of having to return to prison and we are prepared to take that into account."

7–34 It may be inferred from this that the court gave some credit for the reputational damage suffered by the appellant. However, it seems to have been very limited credit because the court fixed the headline sentence at four years and then granted a 20-month reduction to reflect all the mitigating circumstances, including the "disappointment factor" associated with successful undue leniency applications.[91] A similar argument was made in *People (DPP) v Boles*[92] but the Court of Appeal did not directly address it. In *People (DPP) v Lyons*[93] the degree of opprobrium and harassment directed at the offender and his family was particularly acute. While the Court of Criminal Appeal evinced little sympathy for him, saying that he had brought it upon himself through his offending, it still seems to have to have allowed him some mitigation on this account.

7–35 As with other forms of privately inflicted punishment, the relevance of adverse public comment on sentence depends on the animating rationale and the primary distributive principle of state punishment. Under a strict desert-based policy which holds that the penalty should be determined solely by the gravity of the offence, anything that happened after the offence (apart perhaps from a guilty plea) would be irrelevant for sentencing purposes. Privately inflicted punishment would therefore be irrelevant, though it might be addressed in some other way. In this regard, it must be recalled that while a punishment beating or criminal damage to the suspected offender's property could be the subject of criminal proceedings against the perpetrator, adverse public comment, however sustained, will seldom, if ever, amount to an offence. Nor, in most cases, is it likely to be defamatory under civil law. A sentence reduction may therefore be the only viable response, if there is to be any. However, most versions of desert theory are sufficiently inclusive to include at least some factors that have materialised after the offence, including conduct directed against the offender. Public stigmatisation is therefore a matter that may be taken into account in determining the primary penalty although, save in the most exceptional circumstances, it is unlikely to be considered a sufficient penalty in itself.

7–36 Treating adverse public comment and social stigmatisation as mitigating can, admittedly, give rise to an awkward ethical dilemma when it is owing to the high public profile or status of the offender. On the one hand, an otherwise privileged offender may have endured real punishment as a result of public opprobrium, and possibly harassment, experienced prior to sentence. On the other, equality considerations militate against treating such a person more leniently than a less privileged individual who

---

[91] Chap 2 above.
[92] [2023] IECA 211.
[93] [2014] IECCA 27, para 72.

committed a similar offence but who, being largely unknown, has escaped criticism, in any public forum at least. Even in these circumstances, the impact of adverse or abusive comment cannot be ignored. Douglas Husak, for example, argues:

> "No person deserves an extraordinary amount of disdain simply because she is a public figure who has been convicted of a crime. The state has good reason to limit this ridicule, as it has good reason to restrict the unofficial impositions of hard treatment and deprivations imposed by [vigilantes]."[94]

One qualification to be entered in this connection is that those who have taken advantage of their status, whether economic or social, to commit the offences for which they are being sentenced can scarcely complain if they are publicly denounced for having done so, and especially if their conduct has harmed society generally or some sector of it. Otherwise, social stigmatisation is a factor to which some weight should be given at sentencing. In many cases, it may not mitigate to any significant extent, but a case could still arise where the public opprobrium was so prolonged and intense that a court would be justified in concluding that the offender had already, in effect, served some of the punishment that the offence would otherwise deserve. **7–37**

7. Disqualification

A formal disqualification, whether imposed by a court or another state agency in response to a criminal conviction or proven wrongdoing, prohibits the offender from engaging in an otherwise lawful activity. Apart from disqualification from driving, which is the main focus of this section, there are numerous other examples including disqualification from exercising a profession such as that of solicitor or disqualification from holding public offence following conviction for a corruption offence.[95] The Companies Act 2014 specifies numerous grounds on which a person may or must be disqualified from acting as a company director. Section 839, which is most relevant for present purposes, provides that anyone convicted on indictment of an offence under companies legislation or any offence involving fraud or dishonesty is automatically disqualified from acting as director or other officer, statutory auditor, receiver, liquidator or examiner, or being in any way involved in setting up or managing a company. The standard disqualification period is five years from the date of conviction, though the court may specify a longer or shorter period.[96] **7–38**

Under road traffic legislation, a distinction is drawn between a consequential and an ancillary disqualification from driving.[97] In **7–39**

---

94 Douglas Husak, "Already punished enough" in Douglas Husak, *The Philosophy of Criminal Law: Selected Essays* (Oxford University Press, 2010), Chap 17, p 442.

95 Criminal Justice (Corruption Offences) Act 2018, s 17.

96 Companies Act 2014, ss 838 and 839.

97 Road Traffic Act 1961, s 26 (consequential disqualification), s 27 (ancillary

simple terms, the first of these is mandatory because it is an automatic consequence of conviction for an offence to which it applies, whereas the second may be imposed at the discretion of the court. The offences carrying consequential disqualification orders are listed in Sch 2 of the Road Traffic Act 1961. In the case of drink driving, for example, which is now governed by s 4 of the Road Traffic Act 2010, the maximum primary penalty is a fine of €5,000, six months' imprisonment or both. Additionally, a person convicted of an offence contrary to s 4(1) of that Act (driving while being intoxicated to such an extent as being incapable of having proper control over the vehicle) is subject to a consequential disqualification order of at least four years on a first conviction and at least six years on a second or subsequent conviction. For other drink driving offences, the mandatory disqualification period depends on the level of alcohol in the person's system. It ranges from six months to three years on first conviction, and from one year to six years on a second or subsequent conviction. Many other offences also carry significant disqualification periods, eg four years on a conviction for dangerous driving, and also for careless driving (but only for a repeat offender).[98]

7–40 Under s 27 of the 1961 Act, a court may (but need not) make a disqualification order where a person is convicted of a road traffic offence (other than one attracting a consequential order) or an offence in the commission of which a mechanically propelled vehicle was used. This is known as an ancillary disqualification order, and it may be for such period as is specified by the court.[99] A court should not make such an order without giving the defence an opportunity to address it on the matter and, in particular, to outline any reasons why such an order would cause hardship on the offender. It was so held by the English Court of Appeal in *R v Ireland*[100] but the same doubtless applies in Ireland because of the underlying principle common to both jurisdictions that an offender, on being sentenced, should not be taken by surprise by being given an unanticipated penalty or other restrictive measure.

7–41 The question that concerns us here, in keeping with the general theme of the chapter, is whether disqualification orders of this nature should be treated as punishments. If so, they should be calibrated to the seriousness of the particular offence, including the offender's degree of culpability

---

disqualification), s 28 (special disqualification). This Act has been extensively amended during the 60 years and more since its enactment and badly needs to be replaced with a modern statutory code of road traffic law. However, a revised version of the Act, updated to May 2024 (at the time of writing), has been produced by the Law Reform Commission, < www.lawreform.ie> accessed 18 November 2024, under 'Revised Acts'.

98 *People (DPP) v McCann* [2022] IECA 302.

99 See *People (DPP) v Osagie* [2021] IECA 356 where a four-year disqualification period was upheld in respect of an offence of possessing drugs, the offender having been caught driving a vehicle containing the drugs, and *People (DPP) v Sweeney* [2014] IECA 5, where it was held that such an order should not have been imposed because of the nature of the offence.

100 (1988) 10 Cr App R(S) 474, 476; [1989] Crim LR 458.

and, secondly, they should be taken into account when determining the overall punishment.[101] What might be termed the official view of disqualification from driving is that it is essentially a finding of unfitness and that the order itself is primarily preventive in nature. This view may be traced back to *Conroy v Attorney General*[102] where the question was whether the offence of drink driving, created by s 49 of the Road Traffic Act 1961, should be treated as a minor offence and therefore fit to be tried summarily in the District Court. (Art 38.2 of the Constitution confines the criminal jurisdiction of the District Court to 'minor offences'.)[103] At the time, a s 49 offence was punishable with a maximum of six months' imprisonment, a fine of £100 or both. Were these the sole consequences of a conviction, there could be no doubt about the minor nature of the offence. However, a person convicted of this offence also had to be disqualified from driving for at least 12 months on a first conviction and at least three years on a second or subsequent conviction. These disqualification periods could later be reduced, but not below six months. The Supreme Court found that there was nothing unconstitutional about making this a minor offence, despite the significant punitive impact which a driving ban might have for an individual. It drew a distinction between primary and secondary penalties, primary penalties being typically in the nature of a fine or imprisonment, and secondary penalties including such matters as disqualification from driving. Only primary penalties, according to the court, counted for the purpose of deciding if an offence was minor for the purpose of the Constitution. It further held that a disqualification is essentially a finding of unfitness to hold a driving licence. A person, having been found so unfit, may therefore lose the right to drive for a specified period. The court therefore concluded that "[s]uch disqualification is not a punishment notwithstanding that the consequence of such finding of unfitness might be both socially and economically serious for the person concerned".[104]

This reasoning is not entirely convincing. Of the court's own admission, disqualification can have a highly punitive impact, much more so than a fine or possibly even more than a short term of imprisonment. The distinction drawn between primary and secondary penalties was a convenient strategy for ensuring that drink driving offences remained within the jurisdiction of the District Court rather than attracting the right to jury trial. But that does not detract from the reality, effectively accepted by the Supreme Court, that disqualification is punitive in effect. The policy reasons underpinning *Conroy* were quite candidly acknowledged and apparently endorsed by the Court of Appeal in *People (DPP) v Sweeney*[105] where it said: **7–42**

---

[101] For an enlightening analysis of this general topic, see Andrew von Hirsch and Martin Wasik, "Civil disqualification attending conviction: A suggested conceptual framework" (1997) 56 Cambridge LJ 599.

[102] [1965] IR 411.

[103] Chap 2 above.

[104] [1965] IR 411, 442.

[105] [2014] IECA 5, para 13.

> "If the power to disqualify could be exercised in any wider fashion, then it would cease to retain the essential quality of a determination of fitness to drive. Such a broader interpretation would alter the general character of the disqualification power so that it would thereby evolve from a regulation of the fitness to drive into a form of primary punishment. This would have significant implications throughout the wider criminal justice system and would once again call into question the constitutionality of legislation providing for the summary disposition of drunk driving offences. As we have just pointed out, the constitutionality of s 49 of the 1961 Act was upheld in Conroy on the basis that provisions of this nature were not in their nature primary punishments, even if they had unwelcome and inconvenient consequences for those affected by the making of such disqualification orders. It seems necessarily implicit in the reasoning of Walsh J. in Conroy that if such a disqualification order could be regarded as a primary punishment this would have led to a finding of unconstitutionality in that case inasmuch as s 49 of the 1961 Act would thereby have sanctioned the summary trial of a non-minor offence, contrary to Article 38.2 and Article 38.5 of the Constitution. This point was also made in *The People (Attorney General) v. Poyning* [1972] IR 402, 411 where Walsh J. said that such "disqualifications are not primarily punishments and are not to be so regarded by trial judges.""

7–43 These authorities reflect a clear anxiety to keep drink driving and related offences within the jurisdiction of the District Court at all costs. Whether this is for reasons of efficiency or out of a mistrust of juries must remain a matter of speculation. But the reality is that mandatory disqualification periods (like mandatory prison sentences) are blunt instruments to the extent that they remove the possibility of adjusting their duration to reflect the circumstances of a particular case. Even if they are reflections of unfitness, they fail to explain why a particular offender should be deemed unfit to drive for, say, three years as opposed to six months (depending on the concentration of alcohol found in the person's system).

7–44 In practice, disqualification from driving is a punitive measure, and it is often by far the most punitive consequence of conviction for a road traffic offence. In fact, in some jurisdictions it can operate solely as a form of penalty. Under the English Sentencing Act 2020, s 163, for example, a court may order that a person convicted of any offence be disqualified from holding or obtaining a driving licence for such period as the court thinks fit. This power is exercisable in respect of any offence, although there is also a more specific provision in s 147 of the same Act for making a disqualification order where a vehicle was used to facilitate the commission of an offence. The English Court of Appeal has stated categorically that the power conferred by s 146 is "an additional punitive power" and part of the overall punitive element of a sentence.[106] It may be used as either a standalone or an ancillary penalty. This provision was first

[106] *R v Sofekun* [2008] EWCA Crim 2035; [2009] 1 Cr App R(S) 78, paras 9-10; *R v Cliff* [2004] EWCA Crim 3139; [2005] 2 Cr App R(S) 22. See comment by David Thomas on *Cliff* at [2005] Crim LR 250, and Lyndon Harris and Sebastian Walker, *Sentencing Principles, Procedure and Practice 2021* (Sweet and Maxwell, 2021), 407-411.

introduced in England and Wales in 1997[107] and there is nothing in the text to suggest that it is intended as a preventive measure. As David Thomas noted, an affluent offender might not find a fine very onerous, but might suffer far more from being disqualified from driving.[108] Disqualification under this provision is therefore quite unambiguously punitive in both purpose and effect.

On the other hand, there are situations where disqualification quite properly has a preventive function and rationale. A solicitor who has engaged in a pattern of grossly dishonest conduct by, for example, raiding client accounts should be disqualified to protect future clients from being victimised in this manner. Later reinstatement of such a person as a practising solicitor should be countenanced, if at all, only where there are compelling reasons to believe that the offending conduct will not be repeated. The same holds true of other kinds of professional malpractice that has inflicted harm or injury on others. Likewise, under animal welfare legislation, a person convicted of certain offences involving cruelty to or neglect of animals may be disqualified from owing, controlling or working with animals for such period as the court thinks fit, and that may be for the rest of the offender's life.[109] Such a preventive measure is clearly justifiable to prevent further cruelty to animals. **7–45**

Irish courts have, in fact, recognised the punitive impact of driving disqualification when dealing with cases where the trial judge imposed a consequential order for a period exceeding the mandatory minimum or where an ancillary order was imposed. For instance, in *People (DPP) v Coen*[110] (which involved dangerous driving causing serious bodily harm), the Court of Appeal reduced the disqualification period from 10 to seven years, noting that it would have "significant consequences for the appellant and his family in terms of employment". Likewise in *People (DPP) v O'Flaherty*,[111] the Court of Appeal refused to increase the disqualification period above the statutory minimum, saying: **7–46**

> "Insofar as the period of disqualification is concerned, being that of the minimum period of four years, we have considered whether this is appropriate in the circumstances. We are aware that the respondent is a man in his mid-sixties, his occupation was that of professional driver, he is a widower and he lives in a remote rural area with limited public transport. We are informed that due to Covid-19, he cannot avail of lifts from friends or neighbours and is therefore somewhat isolated. The effect of any disqualification from driving, must have a significant impact on the respondent and indeed will impact more on him than on other individuals

---

[107] Crime (Sentences) Act 1997, s 39.
[108] Thomas, note 106 above.
[109] Animal Health and Welfare Act 2013, s 58.
[110] [2022] IECA 308.
[111] [2021] IECA 43, para 27. See also *People (DPP) v Kazinski* [2016] IECA 305 where a disqualification period was reduced from 10 to three years in recognition of the hardship it would cause.

> in different circumstances. We have therefore decided not to interfere with the period of disqualification."

7–47 In *People (DPP) v O'Dowd*[112] which involved careless driving causing death and related offences, the trial judge had imposed a four-year disqualification period on the erroneous assumption (which seems to have been widely shared at the time) that this was the mandatory minimum for the offence in question.[113] However, when the Court of Appeal came to resentence, it had no hesitation in making an ancillary disqualification order, also for four years. It did so on the basis that the nature of the offence was, in its view, particularly egregious and, further, the appellant had two previous convictions for drink driving and had been disqualified in respect of both. The court explained its decision in these terms:

> "We think that what is required in this case is a significant period of disqualification from holding a driving licence, in the hope that the appellant may reflect on the manner of his driving heretofore, and his failure to take appropriate care and to respect the road traffic laws in diverse respects, and that it might engender a resolve on his part to do better on that account in the future. Until he has reached that point, and is personally prepared to truly embrace road safety culture, we adjudge that he is not fit to be on the road and it is appropriate that he be temporarily disqualified....We appreciate the adversities that he has experienced in his life and that his circumstances are somewhat difficult. However, it is relevant that he has been given chances before, and clearly shorter periods of disqualification have not been adequate to bring about a sufficient change of attitude on his part involving an appropriate appreciation of what is required in terms of road safety and respecting other road users. The appalling consequences of his want of care in the present case are also something that we are entitled to take into account in this context."[114]

7–48 While the court justified its decision by reference to unfitness, it quite clearly selected the disqualification period by reference to the particular circumstances of the offence and the offender, and that is how it should be. The case was also one where unfitness, about which there could be little doubt, and the prevention of serious risk to others were important considerations.

---

112 [2023] IECA 157.
113 The matter was clarified in *People (DPP) v McCann* [2022] IECA 302.
114 [2023] IECA 157, paras 38-39.

CHAPTER 8

REMEDIAL SENTENCING

Where judges have extensive sentencing discretion, they are free to take account of any factor they reasonably consider relevant to the determination of the ultimate penalty. Sentencing statutes, where they exist, often specify certain factors that may or must be treated as aggravating or mitigating but they almost invariably permit other factors to be considered as well.[1] The common law, on which Ireland relies, is even more flexible in this regard. Judges may not be free to create new aggravating or mitigating factors at will; any such factor, novel or otherwise, must be rationally connected with the nature of the offence or the offender's personal circumstances. But judges are not constrained by any exhaustive list of factors constituting the sole permissible grounds for increasing or reducing an otherwise deserved penalty. The more common mitigating and aggravating factors have already been discussed in Chap 5. Here, we turn to the more contentious question of whether an offender whose rights have been violated during the investigation, prosecution or trial of the offence may claim some penalty reduction on that account. This could arise where, for example, the offender had been assaulted or otherwise seriously mistreated by the police at the time of arrest. The problem here is that the police misconduct does not affect the gravity of the preceding offence, and opinions differ as to whether it should be treated as a personal circumstance of the offender (under the second limb of the proportionality principle in Ireland). **8–01**

System failures resulting in rights violations can take many forms. Police violence, as in the example just given, is hopefully now a rarity. More commonly, the failure will consist of a non-violent infringement of the offender's rights during the pre-trial process. Evidence may have been obtained through a breach of the offender's legal or constitutional rights, the accused may have been wrongly denied the right to be present at trial,[2] the court may have lacked impartiality[3] or there may have been unwarranted delay in the prosecution or trial of the offence.[4] Assuming the offender is entitled to some redress for such a rights violation (an assumption that is not universally shared where the violation caused **8–02**

---

1 See, for example, New Zealand's Sentencing Act 2002, s 9.

2 *Hermi v Italy* (2008) 46 EHRR 46; *Poitrimol v France* (1994) 18 EHRR 130.

3 *Piersack v Belgium* (1983) 5 EHRR 169.

4 In *R v Nasogaluak* [2010] SCC 6; [2010] 1 SCR 206 at paras 47 to 55, the Canadian Supreme Court considers several earlier cases where sentence discounts were granted for rights violations of this nature.

no obvious harm or injustice), the question is whether sentencing is the appropriate means of providing that redress. Should sentencing, in addition to imposing a just penalty for the offence, have a remedial function in the sense of compensating the offender for an injustice that has no bearing on the harm caused by the offence, the offender's culpability in committing it or, perhaps, on the offender's personal circumstances as they are conventionally understood? Needless to say, some system failures and misconduct by state officials can cause real harm or detriment to accused persons, in which case remedial sentencing is easier to defend.

8–03 The notion of remedial sentencing might, of course, be interpreted more broadly to include a policy of treating sentencing as an opportunity to acknowledge, or even compensate for, an offender's deprived or disadvantaged background. An argument can undoubtedly be made that deprivation, especially where it is the product of social injustice, is a contributing factor to the commission of certain kinds of crime.[5] There is some truth in Alan Norrie's claim that "[w]e hold the offender responsible for what he has done to society when, in reality, his crime is the product of what society has done to him".[6] However, factors of this nature are likely to become relevant, in some circumstances at least, when assessing the offender's culpability and are therefore best considered in that context. They have already been discussed in Chap 5 in connection with the impact of social deprivation on personal culpability.

8–04 Additionally, sentencing has long been used to address or even avoid awkward questions of criminal liability.[7] The law generally prefers to keep defences, whether justifications or excuses, within clear and sometimes narrow bounds. Mistake of law, for example, might occasionally seem to be excusing from a moral perspective, but the law refuses to recognise it as a defence to a criminal charge.[8] It may, however, be an important consideration at sentencing, especially if the mistake was genuine or the defendant had relied on mistaken official or legal advice. Likewise, when the English Law Commission recommended abolishing the defence of necessity, if it ever existed, it offered the consolation that "[t]he need to plead necessity as a defence is frequently bypassed by sentencing policy and related factors".[9] The Commission concluded that the wide discretion vested in sentencing courts to grant an absolute or conditional discharge would adequately deal with any case where necessity seemed to be a factor. Claims of self-defence or provocation in circumstances

---

5 See Chap 5 above under 'Deprivation'.

6 Alan Norrie, *Crime, Reason and History*, 3rd ed (Cambridge University Press, 2014), 348.

7 Martin Wasik, "Excuses at the sentencing stage", [1983] Crim LR 450.

8 For a critique of this 'ignorance of law' doctrine, see Andrew Ashworth, "Ignorance of the criminal law, and duties to avoid it" (2011) 74 Modern LR 1, and reprinted in Andrew Ashworth, *Positive Obligations in Criminal Law* (Hart Publishing, 2013), Chap 3.

9 Law Commission, *Criminal Law. Report on Defences of General Application,* Law Com No 83 (London, 1977), para 4.8.

where neither provides a full or partial defence may also be addressed at sentencing. These issues too have earlier been discussed in Chap 5. Suffice it to say here that the practice of adjusting a penalty to reflect the presence of an incomplete defence might also be viewed as a form of remedial sentencing.

This chapter is solely concerned with rights violations committed by officials or agencies of the state, and it seems clear that any such violation calls for a remedy. In some instances, the violation may be so serious in nature or so prejudicial to the accused that nothing short of prohibiting a trial or excluding evidence will adequately eliminate the risk of an unfair trial or mark the egregiousness of official misconduct. Evidence obtained through torture, to take an extreme example, should be excluded.[10] Unwarranted delay in prosecuting an offence may justify restraint of trial where the delay has seriously prejudiced the accused.[11] Entrapment, when it amounts to abuse of process, may lead to a stay of prosecution, in England at least,[12] and the same now apparently applies to officially-induced error in Ireland.[13] However, a significant degree of encouragement to commit a crime, though falling short of entrapment, may justify a reduction in sentence.[14] What these remedies, apart from sentence reduction, have in common is that they are 'all or nothing' in nature. They may also, from some perspectives at least, amount to an undeserved windfall for a factually guilty defendant.[15] If a prosecution is stayed or a trial prohibited, the accused walks free. Exclusion of vital evidence may necessitate a directed acquittal. If, on the other hand, a **8–05**

---

[10] This is required under the United Nations Convention Against Torture and Other Cruel, Inhuman or Degrading Treatment or Punishment, art 15.

[11] Kristin Saetveit, "Beyond *Pollard*: Applying the Sixth Amendment's speedy trial right to sentencing" (2016) 68 Stanford LR 481 at 504 ("a speedy trial right violation effectively requires the government to forfeit its case to remedy the harm done to the defendant. At sentencing, forfeiture by the government results only in a lower sentence, not discharge of the conviction."). Inexcusable delay may also, in some systems, justify quashing a conviction. See, for example, *Darmalingum v The State* [2000] UKPC 30; [2000] 1 WLR 2303; [2000] 2 Cr App R 445. On the Irish principles governing prohibition of trial because of prosecutorial or systemic delay, see *M (P) v DPP* [2006] IESC 22; [2006] 3 IR 172.

[12] *R v Loosely* [2001] UKHL 53; [2001] 1 WLR 2060; [2002] 1 Cr App R 29. See Andrew Ashworth, "Re-drawing the boundaries of entrapment" [2002] Crim LR 161. A stay may also be appropriate where a defendant is prosecuted despite having been given a clear and unequivocal assurance that there would be no prosecution or that it would not proceed: *R v Killick* [2011] EWCA Crim 1608; [2012] 1 Cr App R 10.

[13] *People (DPP) v Casey* [2019] IESC 7; [2019] 3 IR 482.

[14] *R v Birtles* (1969) 53 Cr App R 469 at 472; *R v McCann* (1972) 56 Cr App R 359; *R v Mealey and Sheridan* (1974) 60 Cr App R 59; *R v Sang* [1980] AC 402 at 423; (1979) 69 Cr App R 282.

[15] See, for example, Akhil Reed Amar, *The Constitution and Criminal Procedure: First Principles* (Yale University Press, 1997), in particular Chap 1, and a review of that book by Louis Michael Seidman, "Akhil Amar and the (premature?) demise of criminal procedure liberalism" (1998) 107 Yale LJ 2281.

trial proceeds and culminates in a guilty verdict, sentencing provides an opportunity to grant a more nuanced remedy that is proportionate to any rights violation that has occurred. Before proceeding further, we need to consider the relationship between rights and remedies in more general terms.

1. Rights and Remedies

8–06 Rights and remedies are inseparable, even if rights tend to attract far more judicial and scholarly attention than remedies. Possessing a right is of little value without a concomitant entitlement to a remedy for its violation.[16] The common law principle *ubi ius ibi remedium* (where there is a right there is a remedy) finds expression in modern constitutional and international human rights law. According to Blackstone, it is "a general and indisputable rule, that where there is a legal right, there is also a legal remedy, by suit or action at law, whenever that right is invaded".[17]In another well-known statement, Marshall CJ of the United States Supreme Court said that the government of that country would no longer deserve to be described as a government of laws and not of men "if the laws furnish no remedy for the violation of a vested legal right".[18] These sentiments are now reflected in major international human rights instruments including the Universal Declaration of Human Rights, the International Covenant on Civil and Political Rights ('ICCPR') and the European Convention on Human Rights ('ECHR').[19] Art 13 of the ECHR provides:

> "Everyone whose rights and freedoms as set forth in this Convention are violated shall have an effective remedy before a national authority notwithstanding that the violation has been committed by persons acting in an official capacity."

8–07 Article 2(3) of the ICCPR is similarly phrased, save that it also requires

---

16 Paul Gewirtz, "Remedies and resistance" (1983) 92 Yale LJ 585 at 587 ("The function of a remedy is to 'realize' a legal norm, to make it a 'living truth'", referring to *Cooper v Aaron* 358 US 1, 20 (1958)); Karl Llewllyn, *The Bramble Bush* (Oceana Publications, 1960), 83 ("Absence of remedy is absence of right. Defect of remedy is defect of right. A right is as big, precisely, as what the courts will do"); Richard H Fallon, "Constitutional remedies: In one era and out the other" (2023) 136 Harvard LR 1300.

17 William Blackstone, *Commentaries on the Laws of England,* Book III, edited by Thomas P Gallanis (Oxford University Press, 2016), 22. See also John Austin, *Lectures on Jurisprudence,* edited by Robert Campbell (Henry Holt & Co, 1875), Lecture XLV, and *Ashby v White* (1703) 92 Eng Rep 126 . On the right to a remedy in a constitutional context, see Tracy A Thomas, "*Ubi Jus, Ibi Remedium:* The fundamental right to a remedy under due process" (2004) 41 San Diego LR 1633.

18 *Marbury v Madison* 5 US (1 Cranch) 137, 163 (1803).

19 For detailed analysis, see Dinah Shelton, *Remedies in International Human Rights Law,* 3rd ed (Oxford University Press, 2015); Amal Clooney and Philippa Webb, *The Right to a Fair Trial in International Law* (Oxford University Press, 2021), Chap 14.

that any claim to a remedy for a rights violation be determined by a competent authority and that the relevant authority must enforce a remedy where granted.[20] Three aspects of art 13 of the ECHR are worthy of note. First, a remedy must be effective. Secondly it should be available from a national authority; states may not simply rely on international tribunals to grant effective remedies. Thirdly, remedies must be available in respect of violations committed by state actors as well as by others.[21] The European Court of Human Rights has occasionally found a violation of art 13 in addition to a violation of one of the fundamental Convention rights where the respondent state was unable or unwilling to provide an adequate remedy for the latter. Indeed, such a finding has been made against Ireland in cases where there was a breach of the right to trial within a reasonable time and there was no effective remedy at domestic level.[22] It has said that the effect of the article is "to require the provision of a domestic remedy to deal with the substance of an 'arguable complaint' under the Convention and to grant the appropriate relief".[23] Further, a state is legally obliged "to make reparation for [the consequences of a violation] in such a way as to restore as far as possible the situation existing before the breach".[24] This reflects the *Chorzow* principle, so-called after a decision of the Permanent Court of International Justice where it was said that a remedy should, as far as possible, wipe out all the consequences of the illegal act and restore the situation that would probably have existed if the act had not been committed.[25]

International human rights bodies and criminal tribunals have ordered or recommended, depending on their powers, a variety of remedies for violations of the right to a fair trial. But they, too, have encountered some of the difficulties already mentioned. Certain remedies will often seem too drastic because of their consequences for other parties, including victims of the relevant offences. Scholars have remarked on the tendency of international bodies to avoid these consequences by narrowly defining the right at stake or interpreting the facts in such a way as to avoid the conclusion that a rights violation, or one of any significance, has occurred.[26] Findings of harmless error, familiar from American constitutional jurisprudence, are one manifestation of this phenomenon. In theory, the stronger the available remedy for a rights violation and the more willing the relevant authorities are to grant it, the rarer the violation in question should become. This is sometimes known as remedial deterrence.[27] Yet, a **8–08**

---

[20] art 8 of the Universal Declaration of Human Rights is to the same effect.

[21] For an elaboration on the requirements imposed by art 13, see *Keaney v Ireland* (2020) 71 EHRR 22, paras 107-111.

[22] *McFarlane v Ireland* (2011) 52 EHRR 20; *Keaney v Ireland* (2020) 71 EHRR 22. See also *Kudla v Poland* (2002) 35 EHRR 11.

[23] *Kudla v Poland* (2002) 35 EHRR 11, para 156.

[24] *Lustig-Prean and Beckett v United Kingdom (Art 41)* (2001) 31 EHRR 23.

[25] *Factory at Chorzow* (Judgment No 13) [1928] PCIJ, Series A, No 17, 22 at 47.

[26] Sonja Starr, "Rethinking 'effective' remedies: Remedial deterrence in international courts" (2008) 83 New York Univ LR 693.

[27] Daryl J Levinson, "Rights essentialism and remedial equilibration" (1999) 99 Columbia LR 857.

strong remedy such as reversing a conviction or ordering the immediate release of a person serving a prison sentence for an egregious crime, however apparently justified or whatever its deterrent capacity, may seem too unpalatable or costly to be granted. For instance, in 2007 the average cost of trying a defendant at the International Crimes Tribunal for Former Yugoslavia (ICTY) was estimated at US$10.9 million and possibly as high as US$15 million.[28] This factor alone provided a strong disincentive against ordering retrials. Considerations such as these have prompted scholars of both international law and domestic constitutional law to reflect on the contrast between the abstract, elevated nature of rights discourse and the more mundane practical realities that must be confronted when deciding on remedies.[29] In one highly influential article, Paul Gewirtz identified two different approaches to remedies: "rights maximisation" and "interest balancing".[30] Under the first of these, a court is concerned solely with providing an effective remedy for the victim of a rights violation, whatever the direct or collaterals costs of that remedy may be. An interest balancing approach, on the other hand, treats victim interests as just one relevant consideration and those interests must sometimes be sacrificed, in part at least, to accommodate wider social interests and concerns.

8–09 Gewirtz was primarily concerned with equitable remedies granted by United States courts to bring racially segregated schooling to an end, but the binary distinction he developed has much wider relevance. In a criminal justice context, the quashing of a conviction as a remedy for a rights violation during the trial or pre-trial phases may affect persons other than the offender. Someone who has suffered serious injury or harm as a result of the offence may understandably feel that justice has not been done, and all the more so if there seems to be little doubt about the offender's responsibility for the injury or harm in question. In such circumstances, the interest balancing approach may be the more appropriate (though all depends on the gravity of the rights violation). Sentence reduction is one obvious solution, as it leaves the conviction intact while providing some redress for the offender.

8–10 Remedies can have an expressive function, especially when granted in response to wrongdoing by state actors. Even if official wrongdoing is not of a very serious nature – not sufficiently serious, for example, to justify prohibiting a trial or quashing a conviction – it still conveys a message, however indirectly or implicitly, that the person harmed or affected by it is less deserving of respect than others. It can send "demeaning messages about human worth".[31] An expressive remedy recognises the wrong that

---

28 Sonja Starr, "Extraordinary crimes at ordinary times: International justice beyond crisis situations" (2007) 101 Northwestern Univ LR 1257 at 1276.

29 Owen Fiss, "Foreword: The forms of justice" (1979) 93 Harvard LR 1, 52; Peter Schuck, *Suing Government: Citizen Remedies for Official Wrongs* (Yale University Press, 1983), 28.

30 Gewirtz, note 16 above.

31 Andrew E Taslitz, "The expressive Fourth Amendment: Rethinking the good faith exception to the exclusionary rule" (2006) 76 Mississippi LJ 483, 564. See

has been done and reaffirms the right of the affected person to be treated with dignity and respect. It confirms that person's status as a full member of the community.[32] By way of example, a suspect who is detained for questioning for longer than the law permits or whose dwelling is searched on foot of an expired or flawed warrant has suffered a breach of his or her constitutional right to liberty or privacy, as the case may be. The responsible state actors, assuming they are acting deliberately, or even negligently, are effectively signalling that the suspect matters less than other members of the community. If the rights breach was minor in nature, it may not call for a very strong corrective response (such as quashing a conviction), but it remains nonetheless a rights violation that should not have occurred and it therefore calls for an expressive response. A modest sentence reduction will often be the most appropriate remedy in these circumstances. As discussed later in this chapter, some other remedy may have to be crafted if the person is eventually acquitted for some reason other than the rights violation.

2. Sentence Reduction as a Remedy

A sentence reduction cannot adequately compensate for every rights **8–11**
violation. Courts are obliged to protect not only the rights of the accused, but also the integrity of the judicial process. There will be times when neither obligation can be fulfilled without staying the trial, excluding evidence or quashing a conviction. Criteria for restraining criminal trials, whether by way of prohibition or stay, are now well settled in most common law jurisdictions. In Ireland, the essential question is whether there is a real and unavoidable risk of an unfair trial. In Canada, abuse of process will warrant a stay only where the prejudice caused by the abuse will be manifested, perpetuated or aggravated through the conduct of the trial or by its outcome and no other remedy is capable of removing that prejudice.[33] Criteria for excluding unconstitutionally obtained evidence tend to be more intricate, but the general judicial tendency of late has been to reject rigid exclusionary rules.[34] Our concern here is with those cases where a rights violation has occurred but not to an extent that would justify restraining a trial or excluding evidence.[35]

---

also Elizabeth E Anderson and Richard H Pildes, "Expressive theories of law" (2000) 148 Univ Pennsylvania LR 1503.

32 Sonja B Starr, "Sentence reduction as a remedy for prosecutorial misconduct" (2009) 97 Georgetown LJ 1509, 1534-1537. See also Charles J Ogletree, Jr, "*Arizona v Fulminante*: The harm of applying harmless error to coerced confessions" (1991) 105 Harvard LR 152, 162, arguing that criminal procedure is designed in part to protect the human dignity of the accused.

33 *R v O'Connor* [1995] 4 SCR 411, para 75; *R v Regan* [2002] SCC 12; [2002] 1 SCR 297, para 54.

34 In Ireland, the Supreme Court in *People (DPP) v C(J)* [2015] IESC 31; [2017] 1 IR 417 introduced a balancing test to replace the more rigid exclusionary rule established in *People (DPP) v Kenny* [1990] 2 IR 110.

35 For an excellent discussion of this topic, though mainly from an American perspective, see Starr, note 32 above.

8–12 The judgment of the Canadian Supreme Court in *R v Nasogaluak*[36] provides a useful starting point for any discussion of this question. The defendant, who was driving at high speed, was being pursued by police who tried to remove him from his car when they caught up with him. When he resisted, he was hit several times on the head by one police officer and, after being removed from the car, he was pinned to the ground and punched by another officer. As a result of this attack, he suffered broken ribs and a collapsed lung. He was brought to a police station to provide breath samples, but no effort was made to get him medical assistance. It was only when he checked himself into hospital the following morning that the extent of his injuries came to light.

8–13 Nasogaluak pleaded guilty to charges of impaired driving and flight from the police, having failed in his bid to secure a stay of the proceedings. Those offences normally attracted prison terms in the range of six to 18 months' imprisonment, but in this instance the trial judge held that the police conduct was "so egregious as to justify taking Mr Nasogaluak from the realm of cases that require incarceration". He therefore imposed a 12-month conditional discharge on both counts. The provincial appeal court agreed that a sentence reduction was available as a remedy in these circumstances but held that the penalty still could not fall below a statutorily mandated minimum sentence, as applied to the impaired driving offence in this case.[37] It therefore substituted a conviction and the minimum fine in respect of this charge, a decision later upheld by the Supreme Court of Canada. When the case came before the Supreme Court, the main question was whether the sentences were lawfully reduced as a remedy for excessive force used by the police. The police action in this case unquestionably amounted to a violation of s 7 of the Charter of Rights and Freedoms which guarantees the right to life, liberty and security of the person. The Supreme Court therefore had to address certain arguments about the relevance of s 24 of the Charter which entitles anyone whose Charter rights or freedoms have been infringed to a judicial remedy. That aspect of the judgment need not concern us because the court's primary holding was that the general law of sentencing provided an adequate remedy in these circumstances. Section 718 of the Canadian Criminal Code sets out certain fundamental sentencing principles, with particular emphasis on proportionality. Moreover, it describes the fundamental purpose of sentencing as being to contribute to "respect for the law and the maintenance of a just, peaceful and safe society". Having regard to this provision, the Supreme Court said:

> "This function must be understood as providing scope for sentencing judges to consider not only the actions of the offender, but also those of state actors. Provided that the impugned conduct relates to the individual offender and the circumstances of his or her offence, the sentencing process includes consideration of society's collective interest in ensuring that law

---

[36] [2010] SCC 6; [2010] 1 SCR 206.

[37] This principle had already been established in *R v Ferguson* [2008] SCC 6; [2008] 1 SCR 96.

> enforcement agents respect the rule of law and the shared values of our society."[38]

The court noted several earlier provincial court decisions to the same effect, including *R v Pigeon*[39] which also involved police violence.[40] Essentially, therefore, a sentence reduction is available in Canada as a remedy for official misconduct, whether amounting to a Charter violation or otherwise, provided the matter complained of relates to the circumstances of the offence or the offender.[41] **8–14**

The decision in *Nasogaluak* was strongly influenced by an express Criminal Code provision to the effect that the overriding purpose of sentencing is to contribute to respect for the law and maintain a just, peaceful and safe society. Ireland has no equivalent statutory provision, but its sentencing system arguably has that same animating purpose. After all, the ultimate purpose of the criminal law is to articulate the standards of conduct expected of those to whom it applies. Sanctions imposed for breaches of that law serve not only to punish offenders but also to re-affirm society's commitment to the values underpinning the prescribed behavioural norms.[42] This routine, public re-affirmation of communal values promotes respect for the law, and it is intended to do so. Sentencing also helps to maintain a just, peaceful and safe society by deterring socially injurious conduct and censuring those who engage in it. The ideals of promoting respect for the law and maintaining a just society could scarcely be realised if sentencing courts were prohibited from taking account of rights violations suffered by offenders during the process leading to their conviction. Where those violations result from official misconduct or institutional failure, they call for some remedy, if only to promote respect for the law. Wilful (or, at times, negligent) violation of a defendant's rights by a state official or institution is a wrong, maybe not as serious as the crime alleged or proved against the defendant, but still a wrong. It would surely run counter to our collective sense of justice, not to mention the rule of law, if one of those wrongs (that committed by the defendant) were punished while the other was ignored. A sentence reduction may not always be the only possible remedy, but it will often be the most effective means of acknowledging a rights violation and its impact on the offender.[43] Just as a sentence must be proportionate to the **8–15**

38 [2010] SCC 6; [2010] 1 SCR 206, para 49.

39 (1992) 73 CCC (3d) 337.

40 For further and more recent examples of such cases, see Kent Roach, *Remedies for Human Rights Violations* (Cambridge University Press, 2021), 323-324.

41 This has been recognised in later cases, notably *R v Morris* [2021] ONCA 680, para 174.

42 This idea may be traced back to Durkheim's claim in *The Division of Labour* that penal sanctioning reinforces the 'collective conscience' and re-affirms society's values. For a critical account of this theory, see David Garland, *Punishment and Modern Society: A Study in Social Theory* (Clarendon Press, 1990), Chap 2.

43 As the European Court of Human Rights has said, "[d]ifferent remedies may redress the violation appropriately" (*Scordino v Italy (No.1)* (2007) 45 EHRR 7, para 186).

gravity of the offence and the offender's circumstances, so any reduction for a rights violation should be proportionate to the nature and gravity of the conduct constituting the violation.[44]

8–16 International courts and human rights bodies have often applied or recommended sentence reductions as a remedy for rights violations. The European Court of Human Rights has held that a sentence reduction may be an adequate remedy for unwarranted delay in the criminal process or some other violation of art 6 of the ECHR.[45] The United Nations Human Rights Committee has repeatedly recommended such a remedy where, for example, applicants had been denied the right to counsel or where their trials had been unduly delayed.[46] The Appeals Chamber of the International Criminal Tribunal for Rwanda (ICTR) has likewise held that where an accused persons rights have been violated, but not to an egregious extent, the sentence should be reduced if the accused is found guilty.[47] It has held, in particular, that this may be an appropriate remedy where the accused has been detained for longer than necessary.[48] Financial compensation may be appropriate where a person whose rights have been violated is eventually acquitted.[49]

3. Remedial Sentencing and Proportionality

8–17 Official misconduct and system failures are seldom relevant to the assessment of offence seriousness. Entrapment is exceptional in this regard as it may have been at least partly responsible for persuading or motivating the offender to engage in criminal conduct. However, police mistreatment of the offender after arrest, delay in prosecuting or trying the offence, or invasion of rights during the investigation do not affect either the harm caused or risked by the offence or the offender's culpability in committing it. A further distinction must be drawn between official misconduct or system failures that caused some tangible harm, detriment or disadvantage to the offender, and those that did not. A police assault on the offender, as in *Nasogaluak*, or unwarranted prosecution delay that prejudiced the defence in some material way will have caused tangible harm. A violation of legal or constitutional rights during the investigation, on the other hand, may not always have such impact, though sometimes it does. Detention of a suspect for significantly longer than the law permits

---

44 For further, theoretical perspectives on this general question, see Marie Manikis, "Recognising state blame in sentencing: A communicative and relational framework" (2022) 81 Cambridge LJ 294.

45 *Beck v Norway* App no 26390/95 (European Court of Human Rights, , 26 June 2001); *Scordino v Italy (No. 1)* (2007) 45 EHRR 7, para 186.

46 Clooney and Webb, note 19 above, at 874.

47 *Kajelijeli v Prosecutor*, Appeals Chamber, ICTR-98-44A-4 (23 May 2005), §255.

48 *Nyiramasuhuko v Prosecutor*, Appeals Chamber, ICTR-98-42-A (14 December 2015), §395.

49 *Barayagwiza v Prosecutor*, Appeals Chamber, ICTR-97-19-AR72 (31 March 2000), §75.

amounts to an inherently detrimental deprivation of liberty.[50] By contrast, the search of a dwelling on foot of a warrant that is just marginally out of date may not cause any tangible harm, though it is undoubtedly illegal and unconstitutional.

With these considerations and variables in mind, we must ask if sentence reductions for the kinds of factors discussed here are compatible with the proportionality principle. The answer depends on now proportionality is defined. The Canadian Criminal Code, for example, provides that a sentence must be "proportionate to the gravity of the offence and the degree of responsibility of the offender".[51] Read in isolation, this suggests that a sentence should be determined solely by reference to the circumstances existing at the time of the offence. Neither the gravity of the offence nor the offender's responsibility is likely to be affected by anything that happened afterwards. However, this provision cannot be read in isolation because the Code has a suite of further provisions augmenting the basic proportionality principle. It provides, for example, that a sentence should be increased or reduced to account for any relevant aggravating or mitigating factors relating to the offence or the offender. Also, as noted earlier in the discussion on *Nasogaluak*, it provides that the fundamental purpose of sentencing is "to protect society and to contribute to respect for the law and the maintenance of a just, peaceful and safe society" by imposing just sentences that will advance certain specified objectives.[52] Proportionality could potentially be defined so as to exclude from consideration anything other than the gravity of the offence, though gravity would include the offender's degree of culpability when committing the offence. On the other hand, proportionality might be more broadly defined to permit consideration of certain factors postdating the offence. **8–18**

In Ireland, the constitutionally grounded principle of proportionality provides that a sentence must be proportionate to the gravity of the offence and the personal circumstances of the offender.[53] This reflects a defining characteristic of Irish sentencing law. An offender's personal circumstances, including those existing at the time of sentence though not necessarily at the time of the offence, constitute part of the proportionality matrix. They are not merely additional factors to be considered once a proportionate sentence has been determined. The gravity of the offence is usually all that counts in identifying a headline sentence, but the ultimate, proportionate sentence must also reflect personal circumstances. A rights violation suffered by the offender at some point during the process leading up the final disposition of the case may undoubtedly be treated as a personal circumstance that is worthy of consideration at sentencing. **8–19**

---

50 Deliberate detention for *any* longer than legally permitted is, of course, illegal and unconstitutional, but the longer the illegal detention, the more detrimental it becomes.

51 s 718.1.

52 s 718.

53 Chap 5 above.

The same would apply at any re-sentencing following a successful appeal or undue leniency application. The extent to which it should mitigate is an entirely different matter. A minor (what some might call a technical) violation would justify no more than a slight reduction, if any. A more serious violation such as prolonged and unwarranted delay in processing a case would ordinarily merit a more substantial reduction, and for at least three reasons. First, a rights violation perpetrated by a state agent diminishes, without necessarily obliterating, the legitimacy of the state's power to pursue a conviction and extract a punishment from the alleged offender. It no longer has the same moral authority in this regard as if it would enjoy if the violation had not occurred. Secondly, it communicatees to state officials that violating the rights of a suspect or accused has consequences, even where the violation resulted from negligence or incompetence as opposed to deliberate wrongdoing. Thirdly, the remedy, whether in the form of a sentence reduction or otherwise, compensates the victim of the violation for the disregard of his or her rights.[54]

4. Remedial Sentencing as Moral Accounting

8–20 Remedial sentencing might be viewed as a kind of moral accounting in the sense that the wrongs committed by and against the offender are entered on the debit and credit sides of the metaphorical balance sheet before offsetting one against the other.[55] The term 'moral accounting' is used rather loosely here because in philosophical discourse it usually refers to how individuals perform good deeds to compensate for their harmful deeds.[56] It is sometimes used of sentencing more generally to reflect the common practice of giving credit to offenders for commendable post-offence conduct which might include acceptance of responsibility, efforts at self-rehabilitation or offering assistance to victims. However, it is suggested that this question of remedial sentencing is best viewed through the lens of proportionality which governs all discretionary sentencing decisions. Of course, one can argue that proportionality, especially as it applies in Ireland, is an exercise in moral accounting to the extent that a court is balancing positive aspects of the offender's character and, in some instances, commendable post-offence conduct against his or her culpable misconduct and, where relevant, previous bad character. But

---

54 Adiel Zimran and Netanel Dagan, "Retributivism, state misconduct, and the criminal process" (2023) 42 *Criminal Justice Ethics* 20.

55 George Lakoff and Mark Johnson, *Philosophy in the Flesh: The Embodied Mind and its Challenge to Western Thought* (Basic Books, 1999), 293 ("Justice is when the moral books are balanced. Just as literal bookkeeping is vital to economic functioning, so moral bookkeeping is vital to social functioning"). For further discussion in a sentencing context, see Thomas O'Malley, "Remedial sentencing: Penalty adjustments for human rights violations" (2016) 26 *Irish Criminal Law Journal* 100.

56 Samuel GB Johnson and Jaye Ahn, "Principles of moral accounting: How our intuitive moral sense balances rights and wrongs" (2021) 206 *Cognition* 104467, describing moral accounting as "how our intuitive morality balances harmful acts against beneficial acts".

proportionality, however it is metaphorically expressed, remains the lodestar of sentencing practice.

5. Delay

Delay in criminal proceedings has been a particularly contentious issue from a remedial perspective. The right to a speedy trial (in American parlance), a trial with reasonable expedition (the preferred formula in Ireland) or trial within a reasonable time (under art 6 of the ECHR) is well-established under many state constitutions and international human rights instruments.[57] It is equally well accepted that a violation of that right entitles the accused person to a remedy. What that remedy should be has been the source of considerable disagreement, especially since delay, unlike other fair trial violations, cannot be remedied by, for example, ordering a retrial.[58] One possibility is to prohibit the trial from taking place. At one time, for roughly a decade beginning in the mid-1990s, Irish courts were willing to grant this remedy by way of judicial review proceedings if satisfied that there was a real and unavoidable risk of an unfair trial.[59] While this is still possible, it has become extremely rare, the predominant view of the superior courts now being that the trial should proceed and that any issues relating to delay are best addressed by the trial court.[60] In other jurisdictions, a plea in bar of trial might be made on the basis that allowing the trial to proceed would constitute an abuse of process. A convicted person might seek to have the conviction quashed because of unwarranted delay in the proceedings, Such an appeal is unlikely to succeed unless it is shown that, whether on account of delay or some other factor, the trial was unfair. One reason why courts are reluctant to grant an 'all or nothing' remedy, such as prohibition, is that criminal proceedings affect persons other than the accused. Victims will feel that they have been denied justice if the trial is prohibited or the conviction quashed solely on account of delay. The community also has a direct interest in having criminal offences prosecuted and punished. Of course, the fundamental principle remains that the defendant's right to a fair trial takes precedence over the rights and interests of all others, and if a fair trial cannot be had, it should not proceed.[61] But in many instances, unwarranted delay, although it violates the defendant's rights and may cause him or her added stress, will not affect the fairness of the trial. All the prosecution evidence may still be available and the defendant, despite the lapse of time, may still be able to mount an effective defence. **8–21**

[57] Among the many authorities on this right under Irish constitutional law in respect of civil as well as criminal matters, see *O'Callaghan v Ireland* [2021] IESC 68; [2021] 2 ILRM 397; *Nash v DPP* [2016] IESC 60; [2017] 3 IR 320; *C (G) v DPP* [2012] IEHC 430.

[58] See comment by Lord Rodger in *Attorney General's Reference No 2 of 2001* [2003] UKHL 68; [2004] 2 AC 72; [2004] 1 Cr App R 25.

[59] *H (S) v DPP* [2006] IESC 55; [2006] 3 IR 575; [2007] 1 ILRM 401.

[60] *People (DPP) v CC* [2019] IESC 94; *People (DPP) v K (B)* [2022] IECA 119; *S (M) v DPP* [2021] IECA 193; *T (J) v DPP* [2023] IEHC 724.

[61] *D v DPP* [1994] 2 IR 465, 474.

8–22 Damages are in principle available as a remedy for breach of a constitutional right, including the right to a timely criminal trial. Where awarded, they must be commensurate with the nature and gravity of the breach.[62] Further, under the European Convention on Human Rights Act 2003 (s 3(2)), a person who suffers loss, injury or damage as a result of a failure by an organ of the state to perform its functions in a manner that is compatible with the ECHR may, if no other remedy in damages is available, institute proceedings to recover damages in respect of the contravention. Delay in legal proceedings has been an ongoing problem in many member states of the Council of Europe. Ireland is no exception in this regard, and it has been found to be in breach of art 6 of the ECHR (and usually of art 13 as well for failure to provide an adequate domestic remedy) on account of unwarranted delay in criminal and civil proceedings.[63] The Government finally responded to this problem with the Court Proceedings (Delays) Act 2024 which confers a statutory right on persons who are parties to legal proceedings to have those proceedings concluded within a reasonable time.[64] Anyone claiming to have suffered a breach of that right will be entitled to make an application to an officer known as the Chief Assessor for a declaration to that effect and, in certain circumstances, for compensation for the breach. The aim is to provide an efficient and speedy process for such applications to be assessed and for compensation to be awarded where appropriate. It will also be possible in certain circumstances to make an application to the Circuit Court. When fully operational, this scheme may provide an adequate remedy for delay in many cases but sentence reduction may remain as a further option. It is, after all, well recognised in the jurisprudence of the European Court of Human Rights and in the domestic law of several countries as a viable remedy for prosecutorial or system delay.

8–23 In *Attorney General's Reference No 2 of 2001*,[65] the House of Lords held that a breach of the right to trial within a reasonable time as guaranteed by art 6 of the ECHR always calls for some remedy. However, save in extreme cases, this should not consist of an order restraining the trial or quashing a conviction. Rather, if the breach has been established retrospectively, "the appropriate remedy may be a public acknowledgement of the breach, a reduction in the penalty imposed on a convicted defendant or the payment of compensation to an acquitted defendant".[66] More recently, the Northern Ireland Court of Appeal in *R v Dunlop*[67] (which has a useful survey of ECHR and UK precedents) noted that it had become judicial practice to grant some sentence reduction where there had been delay in breach of

---

62 *O'Callaghan v Ireland* [2021] IESC 68; [2021] 2 ILRM 397, para 113.

63 The more notable cases include *McFarlane v Ireland* (2011) 52 EHRR 20 and *Keaney v Ireland* (2020) 71 EHRR 22.

64 For an account of the background to this Act and its contents, see Rebecca Halpin, *Court Proceedings (Delays) Bill 2023. Bill Digest* (Houses of the Oireachtas Library and Research Service, 2023).

65 [2003] UKHL 68; [2004] 2 AC 72; [2004] 1 Cr App R 25.

66 [2003] UKHL 68; [2004] 2 AC 72; [2004] 1 Cr App R 25, para 24.

67 [2019] NICA 72, para 34.

art 6 of the ECHR, even if this is not invariably the appropriate response. The court distilled eight general principles from the jurisprudence of the House of Lords and the UK Supreme Court, including the following:

> "(1) The appropriate remedy (or 'just satisfaction') will depend upon the nature of the breach, considered in conjunction with all relevant circumstances, including particularly the stage of the proceedings at which the breach is established. Other case sensitive facts and factors may feature.
>
> (2) Remedy options *include* a public acknowledgement of the breach, steps to expedite completion of the trial process and the release of the accused on bail.
>
> (3) Specifically, one of the remedy options is 'a reduction in the penalty imposed on a convicted Defendant'."[68]

The Privy Council has likewise held that in some instances a sentence reduction will adequately compensate for delay, whereas in others nothing short of quashing a conviction will suffice. In the case in question, where there had been inordinate delay (13 and a half years in total) between arrest and trial, and subsequently between conviction and the final determination of the appeal, it said: **8–24**

> "[Their Lordships] do not suggest that there may not be circumstances in which it might arguably be appropriate to affirm the conviction but substitute a non-custodial sentence, e.g. in a case where there had been a guilty plea or where the inexcusable delay affected the convictions on some counts but not others. But their Lordships are quite satisfied that the only disposal which will properly vindicate the constitutional rights of the appellant in the present case would be quashing of the convictions."[69]

American courts have also occasionally treated sentence reductions as an appropriate remedy for rights violations or prosecutorial misconduct. In *United States v Dicus*,[70] a federal district court granted a sentence reduction in response to the prosecution's failure to honour a plea agreement and, in so doing, discussed the merits of sentence reductions as a remedy. **8–25**

6. Possible Counter Arguments

The arguments made thus far may be summarised as follows. Some rights violations suffered by suspects or defendants may be so egregious, fundamental and prejudicial that nothing less than a drastic remedy such as prohibition of trial or a directed acquittal may suffice. Less serious violations also call for some kind of remedy but in many cases a sentence reduction will be adequate and appropriate. Further, it has been argued that mitigation of sentence in these circumstances is compatible with the **8–26**

---

[68] [2019] NICA 72, para 29

[69] *Darmalingum v The State* [2000] UKPC 30, para 22; [2000] 1 WLR 2303, 2310; [2000] 2 Cr App R 445.

[70] 579 F Supp 2d, 1142 (ND, Iowa, 2008).

principle of proportionality as it is understood in Ireland. However, we must now consider two counter arguments. First, there is the elementary point that a person cannot be sentenced unless convicted. A defendant who suffered a rights violation of the kind being discussed here and who is later acquitted following a full trial cannot be compensated with a sentence reduction. This point has been recognised by the courts. The best answer to this objection, it is suggested, is that a sentence reduction remains an appropriate remedy for a convicted offender, but that some other remedy may have to be considered for acquitted persons. In some instances, the acquittal itself may be the remedy, as where key evidence was excluded because of the manner in which it was obtained. In other circumstances, the acquitted person may have to seek a civil remedy.

8–27 The second counter argument centres on deterrence. As anyone familiar with debates on the exclusionary rule will be aware, the most common argument in its defence is that it deters police misconduct. Police often become heavily invested, even in a personal way, in the investigation of serious offences, and they do not like 'losing' a prosecution (in the sense of it resulting in an acquittal). The possibility that key evidence may be excluded because it was obtained in breach of a person's constitutional rights therefore provides a strong incentive to conduct investigations in a manner that scrupulously respects those rights. However, police are mostly preoccupied with securing convictions. They may not be very concerned about sentence, and certainly not about a minor penalty reduction to compensate for a rights violation. This line of argument might therefore suggest that the only effective (in the sense of deterrent) remedy for a rights violation perpetrated by police or prosecutors is to bar a conviction, whether by prohibiting the trial, excluding evidence or some other measure. Yet, arguments based on deterrence must always be treated with caution.[71] Drastic remedies such as prohibiting trials may not have quite the deterrent impact that is sometimes imagined, though they probably have some, and it is accepted here that drastic remedies *are* sometimes appropriate. Even if it were accepted that rights violations further down the scale of gravity would also be more effectively deterred by, for example, prohibiting a trial or excluding evidence, regard must still be had to the interest balancing approach identified by Gewirtz.[72]

8–28 The effectiveness of sentence reductions as a deterrent to police misconduct was the subject of contrasting views by two eminent American lawyers, Guido Calabresi and Yale Kasimar, in articles published about 20 years ago.[73] Calabresi argued in favour of sentence reductions, though combined with fining the police as an additional deterrent. Kasimar claimed that the police do not care "one whit" about sentencing, and that exclusion of evidence was the most effective deterrent. Perhaps the solution, as

[71] See Chap 3 above, discussing deterrence as a justification for punishment.

[72] Gewirtz, note 16 above.

[73] Guido Calabresi, "The exclusionary rule" (2003) 26 *Harvard Journal of Law and Public Policy* 111; Yale Kasimar, "In defence of the search and seizure exclusionary rule" (2003) 26 *Harvard Journal of Law and Public Policy* 119.

already suggested, is that both kinds of remedy should be available. Egregious rights breaches call for a firm response and that may well be an 'all or nothing' remedy such as excluding evidence, restraining a trial or quashing a conviction. However, less serious breaches must also be suitably acknowledged and remedied, and it is in this context that sentence reductions are most appropriate.

CHAPTER 9

SPECIAL CATEGORIES OF OFFENDER: CHILDREN AND PERSONS WITH MENTAL DISORDER

The rules and principles of sentencing considered so far are predominantly based on the assumption that offenders are rational beings of full age and capacity who have freely chosen to engage in criminal conduct. Granted, there has been a longstanding debate among criminologists and others about the extent to which people in general can properly be regarded as free agents and fully responsible for their behaviour. Positivist criminology rejects the classical notion that crime, like other human behaviour, is the product of free will, and asserts instead that human behaviour is either predetermined by physical or psychological characteristics or shaped by social and environmental factors over which individuals have little or no control.[1] Be that as it may, the criminal law proceeds on the assumption that human beings, once they reach a certain age, are able to exercise self-restraint, and that they can properly be blamed and punished when their failure to do so results in them committing an offence. But it also recognises that children and persons with certain mental disorders cannot be presumed capable of exercising the level of judgment and restraint we expect from fully competent adults. **9–01**

1. YOUTH

Most legal systems, ancient and modern, have accepted that children below a certain age should not be held criminally responsible. What that age should be is a different question. At common law, a child below the age of seven years was conclusively presumed incapable of committing a crime. Those between the ages of seven and 14 years had the benefit of a rebuttable presumption of criminal incapacity (*doli incapax*) which meant, in effect, that the prosecution, in addition to proving all the ingredients of the offence charged, had to prove at the outset that the child knew that what he or she was doing was seriously wrong.[2] On reaching the age of **9–02**

---

1 Thomas J Bernard, Jeffrey B Snipes and Alexander L Gerould, *Vold's Theoretical Criminology*, 6th ed (Oxford University Press, 2010).

2 *C (A Minor) v DPP* [1996] AC 1; [1995] 2 WLR 383. The judgments in this case include detailed accounts of the *doli incapax* presumption as it operated in

14 years, a child was treated as an adult for the purposes of establishing criminal liability. As will be apparent from this brief description, what mattered was chronological age. Blackstone, writing in the mid-18th century, noted: "Under seven years of age indeed an infant cannot be guilty of felony; for then a felonious discretion is almost an impossibility in nature, but at eight years old he may be guilty of felony".[3] This, as he explained, derived from Roman law which treated the period from birth to seven years as infancy (*infantia*), and that from seven to 14 years as childhood (*pueritia*).[4] Chronological cut-off points of this nature are still endemic in our law, civil and criminal. For almost all civil purposes, 18 years is now the age of majority in most European countries, including Ireland.[5] This is the age at which people can vote, enter into valid contracts and marry. No such uniformity is to be found in the criminal law which is based on a policy of variable competence.[6] Children may be held criminally responsible at a fairly young age, but they remain ineligible for certain penalties until they reach a higher age. The age(s) at which they are deemed legally capable of consenting to sexual acts may be different yet again.[7] Chronological age limits are by no means ideal for establishing capacity in any context, as they may fail to reflect the true extent of an individual's cognitive or emotional development.[8] But they have the advantage of neatness and precision and are therefore unlikely to be dislodged as the basis for key decisions in the juvenile justice system.

9–03 Our main concern here is with the treatment of children convicted of criminal offences. As far as the age of criminal responsibility is concerned, the present Irish law may be summarised as follows. There is no longer an express statutory age of criminal responsibility. Instead, the Children Act 2001 (s 52 as amended by s 129 of the Criminal Justice Act 2006) provides that no child under the age of 12 years shall be charged with an offence, unless it is one of murder, manslaughter, rape, rape contrary to s 4 of the Criminal Law (Rape) (Amendment) Act 1990 or aggravated sexual assault, in which case a child of 10 years or older may be charged. The rebuttable

England and Wales for children aged between 10 and 14 years. It operated similarly in Ireland, save that it applied to children aged between seven and 14 years. The presumption was abolished in England and Wales by the Crime and Disorder Act 1998, s 34.

3 William Blackstone, *Commentaries on the Laws of England*, Bk IV edited by Ruth Paley (Oxford University Press, 2016), 14. The *Commentaries* were first published in 1765-69.

4 William Smith (ed), *A Dictionary of Greek and Roman Antiquities* (Taylor and Walton, 1842), s.v. "Infans".

5 Age of Majority Act 1985.

6 The term 'variable competence' is used here to denote the different age limits applicable for certain purposes, such as being held fully criminally responsible. It is sometimes used also to indicate that individuals may mature at different rates which would mean that some could be held fully responsible earlier than others.

7 In Ireland, the age of consent for most sexual acts is 17 years, though for some it is 15 years: Criminal Law (Sexual Offences) Act 2017.

8 See the observations of Kennedy J delivering the opinion of the United States Supreme Court in *Roper v Simmons* 543 US 551, 574 (2005).

presumption of incapacity for children aged between seven and 14 years has been abolished. However, where a child under 14 years is charged with an offence, the trial court may dismiss the charge if it determines that, having regard to the child's age and level of maturity, he or she did not fully understand what was involved in the commission of the offence.[9] In most European countries, the age of criminal responsibility is 14 or 15 years, though it remains at 10 years in England and Wales. Such cross-national variations show that the age of responsibility is more a reflection of political values and preoccupations than of current knowledge about child and adolescent development. As Lucia Zedner wrote at a time when the age of responsibility in Ireland was seven years but 15 years in Sweden:

> "Given that it is unlikely that children mature at such widely differing rates in near neighbouring countries, these differences would seem to confirm that the age of criminal responsibility is a social construct determined more by differences in legal, social, and political culture, by differential attitudes to juvenile delinquency, and the use of criminal sanctions, than differential rates of juvenile development."[10]

Until the reforms of the 19th century, the law showed little mercy to child offenders provided they were seven years or older. In England, during the era of the Bloody Code (from the late 17th to the early 19th century) more than 200 felonies were capital offences. Children convicted of such offences were liable to be sentenced to death, though very few were executed.[11] Blackstone mentions a few instances of children, in one case as young as eight years, being executed.[12] Young children were occasionally executed in America also. In 1828, a 12-year-old black slave, James Guild, was put to death in New Jersey for the murder of a white woman who belonged to a prominent family.[13] Young offenders were also subject to deportation and imprisonment. Almost 1,000 offenders, male and female, **9–04**

---

9 Children Act 2001, s 76C inserted by Criminal Justice Act 2006, s 134.

10 Lucia Zedner, "Sentencing young offenders" in Andrew Ashworth and Martin Wasik (eds), *Fundamentals of Sentencing Theory* (Clarendon Press, 1998), 165, 170. See also Elizabeth Scott, "The legal construction of childhood" in Margaret K Rosenheim, Franklin Zimring, David S Tanenhaus and Bernardine Dohrn (eds), *A Century of Juvenile Justice* (University of Chicago Press, 2002), Chap 4.

11 BEF Kroll, "Capital punishment: Its administration in relation to juvenile offenders in the 19th century and its possible administration in the eighteenth" (1965) 5 Brit J Criminology 198 (showing that between 1801 and 1836 at the Old Bailey in London 103 children were sentenced death, almost all for theft, but none of them was executed). Admittedly, similar patterns of clemency existed in respect of adult offenders.

12 Blackstone, note 3 above, at 15. He also mentions the case of 10-year-old William York who was sentenced to death in 1748 for the murder of his young foster sister. York was later pardoned on condition that he entered the navy.

13 *State v Guild* 5 Halst, 163 (1828) (NJ Sup Ct). Victor L Streib, *Death Penalty for Juveniles* (Indiana University Press, 1987) records that during the previous 350 years 281 minors were executed for crimes committed while they were under 18 years of age. Their ages at the time of execution ranged from 12 to 28 years. See also Victor L Streib, "Juveniles' attitudes toward their pending executions" in Michael L Radelet (ed) *Facing the Death Penalty: Essays on a Cruel and Unusual Punishment* (Temple University Press, 1989), Chap 4.

under the age of 21 were transported from these islands to Australia between 1812 and 1817 alone.[14] A major shift in thinking occurred in the mid-19th century, largely through the efforts of campaigners such as Mary Carpenter and Matthew Davenport Hill in England. Similar efforts were being spearheaded by philanthropists in the United States. The establishment of reformatory and industrial schools in England and Ireland in the 1850s represented an acknowledgment that children who engaged in criminal activity needed and deserved special treatment.[15] It further acknowledged the special needs of deprived children who were at risk of becoming involved in crime. Broadly speaking, industrial schools were for deprived children while reformatories were for those convicted of criminal offences.

2. Children's Diminished Culpability

9–05 It has long been recognised that children, because of their immaturity, are less culpable than adults who engage in similar wrongdoing.[16] Recent research in developmental psychology and neuroscience provides empirical support for this intuition.[17] Modern judicial approaches to the sentencing of children have, in turn, been influenced by this research. It was relied upon, as we shall see, by the United States Supreme Court in a series of decisions prohibiting the imposition of the death penalty and life imprisonment without parole on those who committed serious offences while under the age of 18 years. The differential treatment of children can scarcely be justified by reference to the harm element of an offence. A street robbery is no less harmful just because it is committed by a teenager rather than an adult. Culpability, the other ingredient of offence gravity, may however vary with age and mental capacity. This was recognised by the (American) Twentieth Century Fund in a report on sentencing children:

> "[A]dolescents, particularly in the early and middle teen years, are more vulnerable, more impulsive, and less self-disciplined than adults. Crimes committed by youths may be just as harmful to victims as those committed by older persons, but they deserve less punishment because adolescents may

---

14 Margaret May, "Innocence and experience: The evolution of the concept of juvenile delinquency in the mid-nineteenth century" (1973) 17(1) *Victorian Studies* 7 at 9.

15 In England, these institutions were established by the Reformatory Schools Act 1854 and Industrial Schools Act 1857, and in Ireland by the Reformatory Schools (Ireland) Act 1858 and the Industrial Schools (Ireland) Act 1868. See Jane Barnes, *Irish Industrial Schools 1868-1908* (Irish Academic Press, 1989).

16 In *Eddings v Oklahoma* 455 US 104 at 116 (1982), Powell J, delivering the opinion of the Supreme Court, said: "Our history is replete with laws and judicial recognition that minors, especially in their earlier years, generally are less mature and responsible than adults".

17 A convenient summary of this research is included in the amicus brief submitted to the United States Supreme Court by the American Psychological Association and others in *Miller v Alabama* 567 US 460 (2012), <https://www.apa.org/about/offices/ogc/amicus/miller-hobbs.pdf> accessed 26 February 2024.

> have less capacity to control their conduct and to think in long-range terms than adults. Moreover, youth crime, as such, is not exclusively the offender's fault; offences by the young also represent a failure of family, school, and the social system, which share responsibility for the development of America's youth."[18]

Behavioural psychologists and neuroscientists have identified two stages of adolescent development: cognitive and psychosocial. Cognitive development occurs mainly between late childhood and middle adolescence, so that by the time they reach the age of 16 years or so, most adolescents are capable of information processing, deductive reasoning and hypothetical thinking to a degree quite similar to that of an adult.[19] Psychosocial development occurs more slowly. Research on brain development and functioning has corroborated existing behavioural research showing continued maturation in certain capacities beyond mid-adolescence into early adulthood.[20] These capacities include the ability to resist peer pressure, to consider the long-term consequences of one's actions, to evaluate objectively the risks and rewards associated with a particular activity, and to control impulsive behaviour.[21] What all this scientific research confirms is that adolescence represents a distinct stage in cognitive and emotional development.[22] It explains why children should be treated as less culpable than adults who commit similar offences. As far back as classical Greece, a distinction has been drawn between responsibility and culpability. Responsibility signifies the relationship between an agent and his or her acts – acts are one's own unless entirely involuntary or performed by someone else. Culpability, on the other hand, signifies blameworthiness.[23] Responsibility is necessary, but not always sufficient, for the attribution of culpability. Various factors may either eliminate or reduce legal or moral blameworthiness. The scientific findings relating to adolescent development, as just outlined, may not eliminate culpability, but they reduce it to the extent that children and young adults deserve less punishment than older adults who engage in the same criminal conduct. This was recently acknowledged by the English Court **9–06**

---

18 *Confronting Youth Crime: Report of the Twentieth Century Fund Taskforce on Sentencing Policy Toward Young Offenders* (Holmes and Meier Publishers Inc., 1978), 7.

19 Elizabeth Cauffman and Laurence Steinberg, "Emerging findings from research on adolescent development and juvenile justice" (2012) 7 *Victims and Offenders* 428, 432-434; D Kuhn, "Adolescent thinking" in Richard M Lerner and Laurence Steinberg (eds), *Handbook of Adolescent Psychology*, 3rd ed (Wiley, 2009), 151.

20 Kathryn Monahan, Laurence Steinberg and Alex R Piquero, "Juvenile justice policy and practice: A developmental perspective" (2015) 44 *Crime and Justice* 577, 590.

21 Cauffman and Steinberg, note 19 above; Grace Icenogle et al, "Adolescents' cognitive capacity reaches adult levels prior to their psychosocial maturity: Evidence for a 'maturity gap' in a multinational, cross-national sample" (2019) 43 *Law and Human Behaviour* 69.

22 Elizabeth S Scott and Laurence Steinberg, *Rethinking Juvenile Justice* (Harvard University Press, 2008).

23 Mary Margaret Mackenzie, *Plato on Punishment* (University of California Press, 1981), 82-83.

of Appeal in *R v ZA*[24] where it noted that brain development continues up to the age of 25 years or thereabouts. This is one major reason why, according the court, children and young persons should not be treated for sentencing purposes as if they were 'mini adults'.

9–07 In *Roper v Simmons*[25] the United States Supreme Court drew on this research to identify three reasons why juveniles under the age of 18 "cannot with reliability be classified among the worst offenders". First, persons in this age group generally lack maturity and have an underdeveloped sense of responsibility, and this in turn can result in impetuous and ill-considered actions and decisions. Secondly, juveniles are more vulnerable and susceptible to negative influences and outside pressures, including peer pressure. Thirdly, the character of a juvenile is not as well-formed as that of an adult, and the personality traits of a juvenile are more transitory.[26] In light of these and other considerations, a majority of the court concluded that to execute a person for a capital crime committed while under the age of 18 would violate the Eighth Amendment which prohibits cruel and unusual punishment. The court reiterated these observations in *Graham v Florida*[27] where it outlawed the imposition of life imprisonment without parole for non-homicide offences committed by a juvenile. Indeed, it noted that ongoing developments in psychology and brain science continued to show differences between juvenile and adult minds. Later, in *Miller v Alabama*[28]a majority of the court applied the same reasoning when it held that a sentencing scheme that mandated, without exception, life imprisonment without parole for juvenile homicide offenders violated the Eighth Amendment (though it did not discount the possibility that such a sentence might be constitutional in some instances). Similar observations, though without reference to the scientific literature, have been made by the Irish courts.[29]

9–08 Gideon Yaffe, an American philosopher of law, suggests a different reason for treating child offenders more leniently than adults.[30] He accepts, as

---

24 [2023] EWCA Crim 596; [2023] 2 Cr App R (S) 45; [2023] Crim LR 617.

25 543 US 551 (2005).

26 543 US 551 at 569-570 (2005). In support of the third of these differences the Court referred to Eric H. Ericson, *Identity: Youth and Crisis* (W.W. Norton & Company, 1968), a seminal work on identity formation.

27 560 US 48 (2010).

28 567 US 460 (2012). By this time, there yet more scientific research available on adolescent brain development. See Monahan, Steinberg and Piquero, note 20 above, at 598.

29 *G v DPP* [2014] IEHC 33, paras 92-95; *B v Director of Oberstown Children Detention Centre* [2020] IESC 18; [2020] 1 ILRM 469, paras 68-69. In *R (Smith) v Secretary of State for Home Department* [2006] 1 AC 159; [2005] 3 WLR 410, Baroness Hale quoted with approval from *Roper v Simmons* 543 US 551 (2005), decided a short time earlier, on why juvenile homicide offenders deserve special consideration. See, more recently, *R v ZA* [2023] EWCA Crim 596;[2023] 2 Cr App R (S) 45 para 52; [2023] Crim LR 617.

30 Gideon Yaffe, *The Age of Culpability: Children and the Nature of Criminal Responsibility* (Oxford University Press, 2018). The book is reviewed at length by Cynthia V Wood, "Criminal culpability and the political meaning of age" (2019)

do most others, that children convicted of criminal offences 'deserve a break', but not because of the psychological and neurobiological factors that swayed the Supreme Court in *Roper v Simmons*.[31] Yaffe claims instead that child offenders should be treated more leniently because they do not have a right to vote. He argues that those who are in a position to influence the criminal law are more "complicit with the punishment" it inflicts than those who have no such influence. By virtue of their "diminished citizenship", children should be punished less than adults convicted of identical offences. Yaffe is not saying that children should, for this reason, be treated with impunity, but rather that they should be treated more leniently. While his book has been well received for its analysis of criminal culpability, punishment theory and other matters, it is less than convincing in its central argument about the justification for according special treatment to child offenders. Very few of us, after all, have any meaningful say over the content of the criminal law, much of which may have been enacted long before we were born. One might, of course, draw on various strands of democratic theory to argue that enfranchised adults are in a position to exercise some influence over the law's content. In reality, they seldom are, unless there is an organised campaign to change some aspect of it. Further, children are not alone in being denied an opportunity to shape the law of the country in which they live. The same could be said of people, whether adults or children, who have recently come to live in it. If Yaffe's argument were taken to its logical conclusion, some children could be punished to the same degree as adults if the voting age were lowered, perhaps to 15 or 16 years. Yet most of us would probably baulk, and with good reason, at the notion of denying special treatment to young teenage offenders merely because they had the right to vote.

3. The Age-Crime Curve

Another factor to which policy makers and decision makers must have regard is the so-called age-crime curve which shows that most young people grow out of crime. Several longitudinal studies conducted over various time periods and in different countries have shown that criminal and delinquent activity increases from early adolescence, but usually peaks at about the age of 17 years and declines further thereafter. This pattern may vary with the nature of the crime. The peak age for non-violent crimes tends to be somewhat lower than 17 years, but somewhat higher in the case of violent crime.[32] Some of these studies suggest that as few as five to 10 per cent of child offenders go on to become persistent offenders. This, in turn, strongly suggests that criminal justice policy, **9–09**

38(2) *Criminal Justice Ethics* 123, and Jeffrey W Howard, "Yaffe on democratic citizenship and juvenile justice" (2019) 14 *Criminal Law and Philosophy* 241.

31 543 US 551.

32 A Piquero, David Farrington and A Blumstein, "The criminal career paradigm: Background and recent developments" (2003) 30 *Crime and Justice* 359; Cauffman and Steinberg, note 19 above, at 442.

and sentencing policy in particular, should be designed to maximise the chances that child offenders will grow out of crime, and that as few as possible become chronic offenders. A sentencing regime oriented towards welfare, education and rehabilitation will be far more effective in achieving this objective than a predominantly punitive one. It is self-evidently in the public interest that all children, including those who have offended, even seriously, should grow up to become socially integrated adults and productive members of society. Many, not necessarily all, children who engage in criminal activity will have experienced poverty, neglect, intra-familial violence, homelessness or some combination of these disadvantages which, in turn, may have led to their early introduction to drugs. Research has shown that adverse childhood experiences (ACEs) are a key risk factor for a number of negative outcomes including later involvement in crime and recidivism.[33] Children should not, of course, be subject to more severe penalties than they deserve solely to advance their welfare, a principle reflected in the Children Act 2001.[34] But within the bounds of permissible sanctions, child offenders should be treated in a manner that will promote their personal development and help them to desist from further offending.

4. Intergenerational Transmission of Offending

9–10 Research findings on the intergenerational transmission of offending have important policy implications. The most significant study for this purpose is the Cambridge Study in Delinquent Development (CSDD), one of the leading criminological research projects conducted anywhere since the mid-20th century. This prospective longitudinal study began in 1961 with the selection of a sample of 411 boys, then aged eight to nine years and attending schools in a predominantly working-class area of London.. Over the next 40 years, indeed longer, the progress of these boys was periodically surveyed, mainly to identify how many had become involved or persisted in crime. The results have been published in numerous books and articles, principally by Professor David Farrington and the originator the study, Professor Donald West.[35] By the time they reached the age of 50, 41 per cent of those in the sample had been convicted of at least

[33] Michael T Baglivio et al, "The prevalence of adverse childhood experiences (ACEs) in the lives of juvenile offenders" (2014) 3 *Journal of Juvenile Justice* 1; Kevin T Wolff, Michael T Baglivio and Alex R Piquero, "The relationship between adverse childhood experiences and recidivism in a sample of juvenile offenders in community-based treatment" (2017) 61 *International Journal of Offender Therapy and Comparative Criminology* 1210.

[34] s 96(1)(b) refers to "the principle that criminal proceedings should not be used solely to provide any assistance or service needed to care for or protect a child".

[35] See David P Farrington, Jeremy W Coid and Joseph Murray, "Family factors in the intergenerational transmission of offending" (2009) 19 *Criminal Behaviour and Mental Health* 109 (which has an extensive bibliography); David P Farrington et al, *Criminal Careers up to Age 50 and Life Success up to Age 48: New Findings from the Cambridge Study in Delinquent Development*, Home Office Research Study No 299 (Home Office, 2006).

a moderately serious offence; motoring and other minor offences were excluded.[36] For present purposes, the most relevant finding to emerge from later stages of the study was that there was significant intergenerational transmission of convictions from fathers and mothers to sons and from those sons to their own biological sons and daughters. Having a convicted parent or older sibling by the 10th birthday was among the best predictors of later offending and anti-social behaviour. As the authors acknowledge, other socio-economic and individual risk factors, including various kinds of disadvantage, reduced the predictive value of parental conviction but, even controlling for those factors, parental offending was still a reasonably reliable predictor. Earlier studies by other researchers had identified similar patterns of intergenerational offending, as did the Pittsburgh Youth Study which, like the CSDD, was a prospective longitudinal study, which began in 1987 with an initial sample of about 1500 boys. The Pittsburgh study found that arrested persons were highly concentrated in families, and that an arrested father was the best predictor of a boy's delinquency.[37] A constant recommendation in the various publications emerging from the CSDD is that steps be taken to reduce intergenerational offending.[38] What this research illustrates is the need to target the risk factors associated with offending. Family support, improved material living conditions and help for those with learning difficulties are obviously important. But no less important are measures to ensure, as far as possible, that those who do offend during childhood and early adulthood do not persist in criminal activity, so that their children will not directly experience parental conviction or imprisonment. This should be an important consideration in devising sentencing policy for children and young adults.

5. Justice and Welfare

The tension between justice and welfare has been an enduring theme in **9–11**
juvenile justice discourse and policy making. In simple terms, a justice approach entails granting to children who are suspected, accused or convicted of crime the same rights as those enjoyed by adults. These include the entire range of procedural rights flowing from the constitutional entitlement to trial in due course of law.[39] Arguably, it would also require that convicted children should receive proportionate sentences which may be severe or lenient depending on the nature and circumstances of their offences. A welfare approach is less concerned with procedural propriety and equality of treatment, and more with taking steps to respond to problems which the child's wrongful conduct may have brought to light. There are arguments to be made in favour of both approaches. Children are going through an important developmental

---

36 Farrington et al, note 35 above.

37 David P Farrington et al, "The concentration of offenders in families, and family criminality in the prediction of boys' delinquency" (2001) 24 *Journal of Adolescence* 579 (dealing with Pittsburgh study).

38 Farrington, Coid and Murray, note 35 above, at 123.

39 Constitution of Ireland, Art 38.1.

phase in their lives and their offending behaviour may be attributable to disadvantage, neglect or deprivation. They may, for example, have been deprived of adequate parental support or guidance, or have grown up in a criminogenic environment. In such circumstances, it may seem only sensible to view their offending as a product of circumstances that were largely, or entirely, beyond their control, and to craft responses that will help or benefit rather than punish them. As against this, a child should not be convicted of an offence, with all the adverse consequences this entails, without being afforded the same due process rights as are enjoyed by adults. Nobody of any age should be convicted unless their guilt has been established beyond a reasonable doubt, whether following a properly conducted trial or on foot of a plea that has been voluntarily entered with full knowledge of the possible consequences.[40]

9–12 An exclusively welfare-based approach could be quite repressive, though it need not be. A court or other agency might decide that a child's interests were best served by removing him or her from their immediate family or locality for a considerable period of time, even if the offending behaviour was minor in nature. On the other hand, it is undeniable that many children accused or convicted of criminal offences can benefit from education, training, supervision and other measures that will help them to desist from further criminal or anti-social behaviour. But care must be taken to ensure that such measures, however well intentioned, are not disproportionately punitive in effect, a particularly important consideration when children are being deprived of their liberty. Justice-based models have their own potential drawbacks. A system that concentrates on providing child defendants with procedural justice may well advance important values such as rationality, non-discrimination and due process of law.[41] Yet, it may fail to recognise the particular needs of children who come into conflict with the law and the desirability of allowing courts and other agencies to respond constructively to those needs. As Robert J Harris has written:

> "[In a system that prioritises procedural justice] offenders may be treated equally but they may be treated equally harshly as well as equally leniently, and a philosophy of justice which jettisons a range of humanising values such as compassion, tolerance, altruism and a quest for social justice – however complex, nebulous and problematic in practice they may be – is removing from its scope the capacity to act with wisdom as well as justice."

9–13 A study by Stanton Wheeler and colleagues in the United States in the 1960s showed, rather paradoxically, that juvenile court judges who were 'progressive' in the sense that they were well read on the causes of delinquency and the treatment of offenders were more likely to commit

---

40 As Douglas J said in *Haley v Ohio* 332 US 596 at 601 (1948), "Neither man nor child can be allowed to stand condemned by methods which flout constitutional requirements of due process of law".

41 Robert J Harris, "Towards just welfare: A consideration of a current controversy in the theory of juvenile justice" (1985) 25 Brit J Criminology 31 at 37.

young delinquents to institutions, and sometimes for lengthy periods, even where the offending conduct was not particularly serious.[42] By contrast, 'conservative' judges adopted a more straightforward punitive approach but this, in turn, meant that they reserved institutionalisation for cases involving serious misconduct. In less serious cases, they generally chose less intrusive measures. Judges in the former category were clearly welfare oriented. They regarded institutions such as industrial schools as a social good and believed that young delinquents could benefit, in the long term at least, from being committed to them.

The juvenile court systems established in Britain, Ireland and the United States in the late 19th and early 20th centuries illustrate the contrast between the justice and welfare approaches. In these islands, a juvenile court was established by the Children Act 1908 (the '1908 Act'), one of several progressive measures enacted at Westminster while the Liberal Party was in power between 1906 and 1914.[43] Apart from consolidating most of the existing law on reformatory and industrial schools, it contained a range of measures dealing with child protection. Most significantly for present purposes, it established what it called a 'juvenile court', but this was, in effect, a court of summary jurisdiction dealing with children who were charged with criminal offences. The 1908 Act provided (s 111) that such a court, when hearing a charge against a child, should sit in a different building or room from that in which ordinary sittings were held or, failing that, sit on different days or at different times.[44] However, it remained a criminal court with jurisdiction over children (then defined as persons under 14 years) and young persons (then defined as persons aged between 14 and 16 years).[45] The 1908 Act included important measures designed to ease the plight of children accused or convicted of criminal offences. It prohibited the imposition of the death penalty on a child or young person and provided for a range of sentencing options including conditional discharge, probation and committal to the care of a relative or other fit person.[46] It prohibited the imprisonment of children and young persons, but with the caveat that a young person could be imprisoned if so unruly a character that he or she could not be detained in a place of **9–14**

42 Stanton Wheeler et al, , "Agents of delinquency control" in Stanton Wheeler (ed), *Controlling Delinquency* (Routledge 2017), Chap 3. First published 1968.

43 Francis H Herrick, "British liberalism and the idea of social justice" (1944) 4(1) *American Journal of Economics and Sociology* 67. Other legislation enacted during this era included the Probation of Offenders Act 1907, the Prevention of Crime Act 1908 (which introduced Borstal training) and the Criminal Appeal Act 1907.

44 The Courts of Justice Act 1924, s 80 provided for the establishment of a children's court (in effect a special weekly sitting of the District Court) in Dublin, Cork, Limerick and Waterford. But the Dublin Metropolitan Children's Court was the only one ever established.

45 Under the Children Act 1941, a child was redefined as a person under 15 years and a young person as someone aged between 15 and 17 years.

46 Children Act 1908, s 107.

detention or was so depraved that he or she was not a fit person to be so detained.[47]

9–15 In the United States, as in these islands, various initiatives were undertaken throughout the 19th century to assist deprived children and to provide more humane treatment for those accused or convicted of criminal offences.[48] At the turn of the 20th century, these efforts culminated in the creation of a juvenile court system that was radically different from that established by the Children Act 1908. The juvenile court for Cook County, Illinois which opened in Chicago in 1899 is believed to have been the first of its kind. Another was soon established in Colorado and, within a decade, similar courts existed in more than 30 American jurisdictions.[49] Eventually, virtually every state had a juvenile court of some description. What distinguished most American juvenile courts from their counterparts in these islands is that they were not criminal courts. Instead, they exercised a *parens patriae* jurisdiction, a concept borrowed from chancery law which signified that the state was, in a sense, the ultimate parent that could, and should, step in to safeguard the interests of certain vulnerable persons. It had traditionally been assumed to apply only where the property of such persons required protection. But those who promoted the establishment of the juvenile court system in the United States believed that it should be extended to allow courts, as agents of the state, to protect deprived and delinquent children, irrespective of any property-related considerations.[50] The philosophy of the juvenile court was well summarised by Judge Julian Mack, a judge in Cook County about the time the first court was established there:

> "Why is it not the duty of the state, instead of asking merely whether a boy or a girl has committed a specific offence, to find out what he is, physically, mentally, morally, and then if it learns he is treading the path that leads to criminality, to take him in charge, not so much to punish as to reform, not to degrade but to uplift, not to crush but to develop, not to make him a criminal but a worthy citizen?"[51]

9–16 Typically, a juvenile court dealt with children up to a prescribed age, which was mostly in the 16- to 18-year range, who were accused of being delinquent. Delinquency, in turn, could consist of engaging in conduct that would constitute a crime if done by an adult, but it also included other

---

47 Children Act 1908, s 102. See *State (Holland) v Kennedy* [1977] IR 193.

48 Phyllida Parsloe, *Juvenile Justice in Britain and the United States: The Balance of Needs and Rights* (Routledge & K. Paul, 1978), Chap 2.

49 Julian W Mack, "The Juvenile Court" (1909) 23 Harvard LR 104.

50 Janet Friedman Stansby, "*In re Gault*: Children are people" (1967) 65 California LR 1204 at 1207 (The doctrine of *parens patriae* meant that "[b]ecause the child who engages in delinquent conduct needs care, the state, as a loving parent, intervenes to care for him. It is obviously in the child's best interests that the state care for him and cure him of the problems that resulted in his delinquency. Therefore, procedural formality should not block a finding of delinquency").

51 Mack, note 49 above, at 107.

vaguely defined activities such as truancy, incorrigibility, being beyond control and "habitually involved in immoral matters".[52]

It is scarcely surprising that this system came under attack in the 1960s, an era in which the United States Supreme Court was strongly emphasising the rights of suspects and defendants under the due process clause of the Fourteenth Amendment to the federal constitution. Yet, the juvenile court was empowered to imprison children, in the sense of committing them for long periods to institutions usually known as industrial schools or 'receiving homes' without affording them a criminal trial or any of the procedural safeguards a criminal defendant would enjoy. Eventually, the case of Gerald Gault provided the ideal opportunity for such a challenge. When Gault was 15 years old, he was alleged to have made a lewd telephone call to a neighbour, which was a criminal offence.[53] He was immediately brought before a juvenile court where he was adjudged to be a delinquent and, at a subsequent hearing, committed to an industrial school for the remainder of his minority, unless lawfully released earlier. This was in Arizona where the age of majority was then 21 years. Gault therefore found himself committed to detention for a maximum of six years whereas an adult convicted of the same offence would be liable to no more than two months' imprisonment or a $50 dollar fine. **9–17**

A delinquency hearing in the juvenile court typically consisted of three phases: the pre-judicial phase, the adjudicatory phase and the dispositional phase. Gault's challenge centred exclusively on the adjudicatory phase at which he had been declared a delinquent without being afforded the procedural safeguards constitutionally guaranteed to criminal defendants. Upholding the challenge by a majority of eight to one, the United States Supreme Court stopped short of saying that all of the elements of a fair trial guaranteed by the Fourteenth Amendment applied to delinquency hearings. However, it held that the essentials of due process and fair treatment did apply.[54] A child charged with delinquency, and his parents or guardian, were entitled to timely notice of the precise charge and the alleged facts. The child was also entitled to the assistance of counsel (paid for by the state where necessary) as well as the rights to confront and examine adverse witnesses and to be advised of the privilege against self-incrimination.[55] The court was highly critical of the absence of such protections in the Arizona juvenile court, although other states had already made some improvements in this regard. It rejected outright the contention that because delinquency status was not a crime and the proceedings were not criminal in nature, due **9–18**

[52] Norman Dorsen and Daniel A Rezneck , "*In re Gault* and the future of the Juvenile Court" (1967) 1(4) *Family Law Quarterly* 1 at 16.

[53] *Re Gault* 387 US 1 (1967).

[54] The Court said that a proceeding "where the issue is whether a child will be found to be 'delinquent' and subjected to the loss of his liberty for years is comparable in seriousness to a felony prosecution" (387 US 1 at 36).

[55] For a detailed analysis of *Gault*, see Dorsen and Rezneck, note 52 above. The authors represented Gault in the Supreme Court.

process need not apply. Justice Fortas, who delivered the court's opinion in *Gault*, famously declared that "the condition of being a boy does not justify a kangaroo court".[56] Later, in *re Winship*[57] the court held that the constitutional requirement of proof beyond a reasonable doubt applied to fact-finding at delinquency hearings, and it was just as important as the safeguards listed in *Gault*.

9–19 In both *Gault* and *Winship*, the Supreme Court was keen to stress that adherence to due process and fair procedures need not displace or diminish the substantive benefits of the juvenile court system. Those properly adjudged to be delinquent could still be given individualised treatment, as the guiding philosophy of the system demanded. Therefore, while insisting on justice at the adjudicatory stage, the court was by no means discouraging the adoption of welfare-enhancing measures at the dispositional stage. This has now, in effect, become the orthodoxy, as reflected in the international instruments discussed immediately below. A child accused of an offence should be entitled to the entire range of due process rights, favourably adjusted where necessary to reflect their needs and level of understanding, up to the moment of verdict.[58] If convicted, a child should be dealt with in a manner most likely to advance their welfare and promote their personal development. Any penalty should be, at most, proportionate to the gravity of the offence and should not be made more onerous solely to advance what are perceived to be the child's best interests. This is a particularly important consideration when the penalty entails loss of liberty.

6. International Norms

9–20 During the 1980s, the United Nations became active in promoting children's rights and setting standards for the administration of juvenile justice. The General Assembly adopted three important, though non-binding, instruments: Minimum Rules for the Administration of Juvenile Justice (the Beijing Rules 1985), Guidelines for the Prevention of Juvenile Delinquency (the Riyadh Guidelines 1990) and Rules for the Protection of Juveniles Deprived of their Liberty (the Havana Rules 1990). By far the most significant development was the adoption in November 1989 of the Convention on the Rights of the Child which had been more than a decade in the making. It entered into force in September 1990 and remains the most widely ratified international human rights treaty.[59] It contains an extensive catalogue of children's rights, but the key provisions on juvenile justice are contained in art 37 dealing with deprivation of liberty

---

[56] 387 US 1 at 28 (1967).

[57] 397 US 358 (1970).

[58] *T and V v United Kingdom* (2000) 30 EHRR 121.

[59] John Tobin (ed), *The UN Convention on the Rights of the Child: A Commentary* (Oxford University Press, 2019) has a detailed commentary on each article of the Convention, and the opening chapter describes earlier instruments on children's rights adopted by the League of Nations and the United Nations.

(as well as outlawing torture and other inhuman or degrading treatment or punishment) and art 40 which sets out the rights of children suspected, accused or convicted of criminal offences. These articles encapsulate the essence of the earlier non-binding instruments, and the Beijing Rules in particular, though they are not so detailed. Article 40(1) proclaims the fundamental values that should inform the juvenile justice process:

> "States parties recognize the right of every child alleged as, accused of, or recognized as having infringed the penal law to be treated in a manner consistent with the promotion of the child's sense of dignity and worth, which reinforces the child's respect for the human rights and fundamental freedoms of others and which takes into account the child's age and the desirability of promoting the child's reintegration and the child's assuming a constructive role in society."

This is followed by a catalogue of familiar due process rights, including the presumption of innocence, the right to legal representation, the right to confront adverse witnesses and the right to appeal or review. Article 40 may therefore be interpreted as endorsing a justice model at the investigation, prosecution and trial stages of the process. Welfare considerations are expected to predominate at sentencing, as reflected in art 40(4): **9–21**

> "A variety of dispositions such as care, guidance and supervision orders; counselling; probation; foster care; education and vocational training programmes and other alternatives to institutional care shall be available to ensure that children are dealt with in a manner appropriate to their wellbeing and proportionate both to their circumstances and to the offence."

This provision reflects a commitment to *just* welfare. All of the measures listed are to be encouraged, but the response in each case must still be proportionate to the circumstances of the offence and the offender. The drafters of the Convention were clearly aware of the need to ensure that states parties did not resort to the kind of repressive welfarism described earlier. **9–22**

Article 37 further underscores the importance of moderation in the use of punitive sanctions. The arrest, detention and imprisonment of children must be in conformity with law "and shall be used only as a measure of last resort and for the shortest appropriate period of time". Conditions of detention, where such a measure is necessary, must be conducive to the child's welfare and development. Article 37(c) provides: **9–23**

> "Every child deprived of liberty shall be treated with humanity and respect for the inherent dignity of the human person, and in a manner which takes into account the needs of persons of his or her age. In particular, every child deprived of liberty shall be separated from adults unless it is considered in the child's best interests not to do so and shall have the right to maintain contact with his or her family through correspondence and visits, save in exceptional circumstances."

9–24 The terms of art 37 are reflected in the Children Act 2001 which provides (s 96) that any penalty imposed on a child should cause as little interference as possible in the child's life and be the least restrictive measure that is appropriate in the circumstances, with detention reserved as the penalty of last resort.

7. Diversion and Expungement

9–25 A criminal conviction, even if accompanied by a lenient punishment, may have enduring consequences and carry a stigma that is difficult to dislodge. This holds true for all offenders, but those convicted during their childhood arguably have most to lose because their life chances as they grow into adulthood may be seriously diminished. Pre-trial diversion and the expungement of criminal records are the two main strategies that have been adopted to address this problem. The policy of diverting young offenders from the criminal justice system (or, at least, from the criminal trial process) was widely supported in the mid- to late 20th century. In the United States, the President's Task Force on Juvenile Delinquency recommended in 1967:

> "The formal sanctioning system in prevention of delinquency should be used only as a last resort. In place of the formal system, dispositional alternatives to adjudication must be developed for dealing with juveniles including agencies to provide and coordinate services and procedures to achieve necessary control without unnecessary stigma."[60]

9–26 Viewed through the lens of criminological theory, diversion may be seen as a policy consequence of labelling theory which is most closely associated with Howard Becker, Edwin Lemert and Aaron Cicourel.[61] According to this theory, many, if not most, young people engage in some kind of delinquency, but whether they persist in criminal or other anti-social conduct depends on society's reaction to the first delinquent act (the 'primary deviance'). A person who is labelled as delinquent or offender as a result, for example, of a criminal conviction, will afterwards be regarded as such by society. More importantly, the application of the label may also determine the person's own self-image and self-definition. In other words, their 'master status' becomes that of delinquent or criminal.[62] This was quite a revolutionary theory. Criminologists had hitherto assumed that it was the commission of a deviant act that shaped society's perception of the actor. Labelling theorists, on the contrary, claimed that it was

---

60 President's Commission on Law Enforcement and Administration of Justice, *Juvenile Delinquency and Youth Crime* (Government Printing Office, 1967), 21.

61 Tim Newburn, *Criminology*, 3rd ed (Routledge, 2017), 231.

62 This concept was most notably developed by Edwin Lemert in two books, *Social Pathology: A Systematic Approach to the Theory of Sociopathic Behaviour* (McGraw-Hill, 1951) and *Human Deviance, Social Problems, and Social Control* (Prentice Hall, 1967). See Michael J Rosenberg, "Lemert, Edwin M.: Primary and secondary deviance" in Francis T Cullen and Pamela Wilcox (eds), *Encyclopedia of Criminological Theory* (SAGE publications, 2010).

society's reaction that caused individuals to become deviant.[63] As one of those theorists, Howard Becker, wrote:

> "[S]ocial groups create deviance by making the rules whose infraction constitutes deviance, and by applying those rules to particular people and labelling them as outsiders. From this point of view, deviance is not a quality of the act the person commits, but rather a consequence of the application by others of rules and sanctions to an "offender." The deviant is one to whom the label has successfully been applied; deviant behaviour is behaviour that people so label." [64]

For Becker, the central fact about deviant behaviour is that it is created by society. Labelling, as might be expected, has had its critics, some of whom have condemned it for assuming that people passively adopt whatever label society attaches to them. Moreover, it seems to ignore the reality that certain kinds of behaviour, most notably serious crimes, are well known to be deviant and morally unacceptable, whatever the social response may be. In terms of its policy consequences for young offenders, labelling theory supports non-intervention or, at most, limited intervention by the criminal justice system.[65] In those cases where some response is needed, diversion should be preferred to prosecution. This, at least, will save the young person from being labelled a criminal. **9–27**

Ireland has had a diversion system, which used to be known as the juvenile liaison scheme, since the early 1960s.[66] It was placed on a statutory basis by Pt 4 of the Children Act 2001 (the '2001 Act') which created a diversion programme.[67] The programme's stated objective is "to divert any child who accepts responsibility for his or her criminal or anti-social behaviour from committing further offences or engaging in further anti-social behaviour".[68] This is to be achieved by administering a caution to the child and, where appropriate, placing him or her under the supervision of a juvenile liaison officer and by convening a conference to be attended by the child, family members and other concerned persons. The general legislative policy seems to be that, where possible, a caution should be **9–28**

---

63 Chris Cunneen and Rob White, *Juvenile Justice: Youth and Crime in Australia* (Oxford University Press, 2002), 45-48. In fact, the insight of labelling theory was not entirely new. A Select Parliamentary Committee on Prison Discipline that reported in 1850 noted that one result of treating children as adult criminals was that a boy, once labelled a criminal "regards himself as belonging to the criminal classes" (quoted in May, note 14 above, at 12).

64 Howard Becker, *Outsiders: Studies in the Sociology of Deviance* (Free Press of Glencoe, 1963), 8-9.

65 Edwin Schur, *Radical Non-Intervention: Rethinking the Delinquency Problem* (Prentice-Hall, 1973).

66 Helen Burke, Claire Carney and Geoffrey Cooke (eds), *Youth and Justice: Young Offenders in Ireland* (Turoe Press, 1981), 67-68.

67 For a detailed account of programme and its operation, see the *Annual Report of the Committee Appointed to Monitor the Effectiveness of the Diversion Programme* (produced by An Garda Síochána) and *M (J) v Commissioner of An Garda Síochána* [2022] IEHC 149.

68 Children Act 2001, s 19(1) as substituted by Criminal Justice Act 2006, s 124.

preferred to a prosecution. Section 18 of the 2001 Act[69] states that "[u]nless the interests of society otherwise require", any child who has committed an offence or behaved anti-socially and who accepts responsibility for the offence or the behaviour, as the case may be, shall be considered for admission to the programme. A child who has reached the age of 10 years and is under the age of 18 years may be admitted.[70] In fact, every child in that age group who engages in criminal behaviour must be considered for admission to the programme; that seems clear from s 22 of the 2001 Act (although, under s 47, the Minister may specify by regulation any criminal behaviour of a serious nature by virtue of which admission to the programme is excluded). To qualify for admission, the child must accept responsibility for his or her criminal behaviour, having had a reasonable opportunity to consult with parents or guardians and having obtained any legal advice sought. Further, the child must consent to being cautioned and, where appropriate, to being supervised by a juvenile liaison officer. The age for admission shall be the child's age on the date the offence was committed.[71]A caution may be formal or informal, the main difference being that a formal caution must normally be administered in a Garda station by a senior Garda officer or a juvenile liaison officer who has been trained in mediation skills and in the presence of the parents or guardians. There is also provision for the presence of the victim at a formal caution, and the Garda administering the caution may invite the child to apologise to the victim or to make financial or other reparation to him or her.[72]

9–29 The Director of the diversion programme, a senior Garda officer, occupies quite a powerful position in the criminal justice system. A child may not be prosecuted for any criminal behaviour, or any related behaviour, in respect of which he or she has been admitted to the programme.[73] Admission bars any later prosecution. The role of the Director of Public Prosecutions ('DPP') in prosecuting offences committed by children is therefore restricted to the extent that a prosecution is possible only in those cases where admission to the programme has been refused. In this connection it must be borne in mind that admission may be granted in respect of any offence no matter how serious, though the Minister has the power, as yet unused, to exclude offences of a serious nature.[74] In recent years, the annual number of referrals has been in the region of 20,000, involving about 10,000 children. In 2019, there were 18,567 referrals involving 9,482 children of whom 1,605 (accounting for over 6,000 referrals) were deemed unsuitable for admission. The offences in respect of which referrals were made covered almost the entire spectrum of criminal behaviour. Most came under the headings of theft, public order, drugs, assault and criminal damage. But there were also 447 sexual offences, including 115 rapes and 56 child pornography offences. Admission may, of course, have been

---

69 As substituted by Criminal Justice Act 2006, s 123,
70 Children Act 2001, s 23 as amended by Criminal Justice Act 2006, s 125.
71 Children Act 2001, s 23(5).
72 Children Act 2001, ss 25 and 26.
73 Children Act 2001, s 49, as substituted by Criminal Justice Act 2006, s 127.
74 Children Act 2001, s 47.

refused in some of these cases.[75] A decision by the Programme Director not to admit a child to the diversion programme is amenable to judicial review, and does not attract the attenuated standard of review applicable to decisions by the DPP. Further, the Director is obliged to provide reasons for denying a child admission to the programme, if requested to do so.[76]

A criminal conviction may have enduring, even life-long, consequences that are greatly disproportionate to the offence to which it relates. It may adversely affect the offender's employment opportunities, access to housing or other benefits, despite strong evidence that having a legitimate job reduces the risk of recidivism.[77] A system for expunging criminal records is therefore essential to prevent a past conviction unfairly inhibiting a person's life chances, and especially when the offence was committed during childhood. The same consideration applies to adult offenders.[78] Many countries now have legislation which, at a minimum, saves people from having to reveal past convictions when seeking employment or applying for insurance cover and in other specified circumstances.[79] A criminal record is part of a person's private life and the disclosure of such a record therefore engages the right to privacy under art 8 of the European Convention on Human Rights ('ECHR'). Because that right is not absolute, it allows for the compulsory disclosure of criminal records in some circumstances provided the disclosure regime is in accordance with law and necessary in a democratic society. It follows that "a fair balance must be struck between the general aim of public protection, the specific aims of employer selection processes and the individual's right to respect for privacy as well as criminal justice interests in rehabilitation and reintegration".[80] **9–30**

---

75 All these figures are derived from the *Annual Report of the Committee Appointed to Monitor the Effectiveness of the Diversion Programme 2019.*

76 *S (Identity Protected) v Director of the Garda Juvenile Diversion Programme* [2019] IEHC 796.

77 Jessica S Henry and James B Jacobs, "Ban the box to promote ex-offender employment" (2007) 6 *Criminology and Public Policy* 755; Steven Raphael, "The intended and unintended consequences of ban the box" (2021) 4 *Annual Review of Criminology* 191. ('Ban the box' refers to a practice adopted in parts of the United States prohibiting employers from requiring job applicants to state if they have criminal convictions.)

78 The Criminal Justice (Spent Convictions and Certain Disclosures) Act 2016 applies to adults, but its scope is severely limited in several respects.

79 The literature on this topic includes James B Jacobs, *The Eternal Criminal Record* (Harvard University Press, 2015); Alexander L Burton et al,, "Beyond the eternal criminal record: Public support for expungement" (2020) 20 *Criminology and Public Policy* 123; JJ Prescott and Sonja Starr, "Expungement of criminal convictions: An empirical study" (2021) 133 Harvard LR 2460. Elena Larrauri, "Conviction records in Spain: Obstacles to reintegration of offenders?" (2011) 3 *European Journal of Probation* 50; James B Jacobs and Elena Larrauri, "Are criminal convictions a public matter?" (2012) 14 *Punishment and Society* 3.

80 Elena Larrauri Pijoan, "Criminal record disclosure and the right to privacy" [2014] Crim LR 723, 735, commenting on *MM v United Kingdom* [2012] ECHR 1906 (13 November 2012) where the European Court of Human Rights held that the disclosure of a caution in a police record in Northern Ireland breached

9–31 The Children Act 2001 provides for the "non-disclosure of certain findings of guilt" in respect of a child. Section 258(1) provides:

> "Where a person has been found guilty of an offence, whether before or after the commencement of this section, and
> (a) the offence was committed before the person attained the age of 18 years,
> (b) the offence is not an offence required to be tried by the Central Criminal Court,
> (c) a period of not less than 3 years has elapsed since the finding of guilt, and
> (d) the person has not been dealt with for an offence in that 3-year period
>
> then, after the end of the 3-year period or, where the period ended before the commencement of this section, after the commencement of this section, the provisions of subsection (4) shall apply to the finding of guilt."

9–32 By virtue of s 258(4), a person to whom this provision applies shall be treated for all legal purposes as a person who has not committed, been charged with, prosecuted for, found guilty of or otherwise dealt with in respect of offences covered by subs (1). As is clear from the latter subsection, non-disclosure does not apply to an offence triable in the Central Criminal Court– effectively murder, rape and aggravated sexual assault. Overall, this is an enlightened provision as it permits those who committed offences, apart from a few very serious ones, during childhood to wipe the slate clean and thereby avail themselves of the opportunity to start their lives afresh without the burden of having to disclose those offences for most purposes, including access to employment.

8. The Children Act 2001

9–33 For most of the 20th century, the Irish juvenile justice system was based on the Children Act 1908 which was undoubtedly an enlightened measure by the standards of its time.[81] However, as noted earlier, it did allow for the imprisonment of young persons (15- to 17-year olds) in certain circumstances. It was entirely repealed in England and Wales in 1958 (and many of its individual provisions had been repealed earlier),[82] but it had a much longer shelf life in Ireland where it was amended periodically throughout the 20th century. By the end of that century, it was clear that an entirely new approach was needed. The Children Act 2001 represented the culmination of a legislative process that began with the Children Bill

---

art 8 of the ECHR. This finding, however, was largely based on the absence of an appropriate statutory framework.

81 Kate Bradley, Anne Logan and Simon Shaw, "Youth and Crime: Centennial Reflections on the Children Act 1908" (2009) 3(2) *Crimes and Misdemeanours: Deviance and the Law in Historical Perspective* 1 (later editions of this online journal appeared under the title *Law, Crime and History*).

82 Children Act 1958. It was fully repealed in Northern Ireland by the Children and Young Persons Act (Northern Ireland) 1950.

1996 which fell with the general election of 1997. A new Children Bill introduced in 1999 eventually led to the 2001 Act. But this was not to be the end of the road. The 2001 Act was brought into force episodically between 2002 and 2007, and only after substantial amendment by the Criminal Justice Act 2006 (the '2006 Act'). Almost 40 sections of the 2006 Act are devoted to amending the 2001 Act.[83] During the period 2001 to 2006 the Government clearly had second thoughts about some of the 2001 Act's key provisions. Section 52 had originally set the age of criminal responsibility at 12 years in all cases. The substituted version (in s 129 of the 2006 Act) makes no reference to an age of criminal responsibility but provides instead that no child under 12 years shall be charged with an offence unless it is murder, manslaughter, rape or aggravated sexual assault in which case a child aged 10 or 11 years may be charged. Also, the 2001 Act originally provided for children detention schools for offenders under 16 years and children detention centres for offenders aged between 16 and 18 years. As a result of the 2006 amendments, all children under 18 years being sentenced to detention must be sent to a children detention school. One thing that did not change was the clear prohibition on sentencing or committing a child to prison.[84] Findings of unruliness and depravity were at last consigned to history.[85]

Guiding Sentencing Principles

The principles and values that should animate criminal proceedings against children are set out in s 96 of the 2001 Act which reads: **9–34**

> (1) Any court when dealing with children charged with offences shall have regard to –
> (a) the principle that children have rights and freedom before the law equal to those enjoyed by adults and, in particular, a right to be heard and to participate in any proceedings of the court that can affect them, and
> (b) the principle that criminal proceedings shall not be used solely to provide any assistance or service needed to care for or protect a child.
>
> (2) Because it is desirable whenever possible –
> (a) to allow the education, training or employment of children to proceed without interruption,
> (b) to preserve and strengthen the relationship between children and their parents and other family members,
> (c) to foster the ability of families to develop their own means of dealing with offending by their children, and
> (d) to allow children to reside in their own homes,
>
> any penalty imposed on a child for an offence should cause as little interference as possible with the child's legitimate activities and

---

83 A revised version of the Children Act 2001 incorporating all amendments up to May 2023 has been produced by the Law Reform Commission and is available at <www.lawreform.ie> accessed 10 July 2024 under 'Revised Acts'.

84 Children Act 2001, s 156 ("No court shall pass a sentence of imprisonment on a child or commit a child to prison").

85 See text accompanying note 47 above.

pursuits, should take the form most likely to maintain and promote the development of the child and should take the least restrictive form that is appropriate in the circumstances; in particular a period of detention should be imposed only as a measure of last resort.

(3) A court may take into consideration as mitigating factors a child's age and level of maturity in determining the nature of any penalty imposed, unless the penalty is fixed by law.

(4) The penalty imposed on a child for an offence should be no greater than that which is appropriate in the case of an adult who commits an offence of the same kind, and may be less, where so provided for in this Part.

(5) When dealing with a child charged with an offence, a court shall have due regard to the child's best interests, the interests of the victim of the offence and the protection of society.[86]

Sentencing Options

9–35 The sentencing options for children convicted of criminal offences range from a reprimand to a period of detention.[87] Section 98 provides:

> "Where a court is satisfied of the guilt of a child charged with an offence it may, without prejudice to its general powers and in accordance with this Part, reprimand the child or deal with the case by making one or more than one of the following orders:
> (a) a conditional discharge order;
> (b) an order that the child pay a fine or costs;
> (c) an order that the parent or guardian be bound over;
> (d) a compensation order;
> (e) a parental supervision order;
> (f) an order that the parent or guardian pay compensation;
> (g) an order imposing a community sanction;
> (h) an order (the making of which may be deferred pursuant to section 144) that the child be detained in a children detention school, including an order under section 155 (1);[88]
> (i) a detention and supervision order."

9–36 When read in conjunction with s 96, this section seems to require that a court should begin by considering if one of the less restrictive measures such as a conditional discharge or a fine is adequate in any given case. Only if these are eliminated as suitable responses should a court move to consider a community sanction (of which there are 10 different varieties under s 115) or, as a last resort, either detention or detention and supervision. A court may make one or more of the orders listed in s 98. Where a court is considering imposing either a community order or detention, it must adjourn proceedings and remand the child to allow for the preparation of a probation report (and a victim impact report if it considers this would be helpful). These reports must be prepared

---

86 subs (5) was substituted by the Criminal Justice Act 2006, s 136.

87 Children Act 2001, Pt 9.

88 s 144 provides for the deferment of a detention order. s 155 (as amended) deals with the detention of children convicted on indictment. Both are discussed further below.

expeditiously. The remand period should not exceed 28 days or, where the child is on bail, 42 days.

Section 98 permits certain orders to be made against the child's parent or guardian as well as against the child. However, the 2001 Act provides elsewhere (s 111) that a parental supervision order may be made where a court "is satisfied that a wilful failure to take care of or control the child contributed to the child's criminal behaviour". It does not expressly say that this is the sole circumstance in which such an order may be made, but that seems implicit, given that it would generally be unfair to make an order against blameless parents. Parental supervision orders are intended to be constructive rather than punitive. They may, for example, require a parent to undergo treatment for drug or alcohol abuse or participate in a course for the improvement of parenting skills. A probation officer may be appointed to supervise the parent(s) and monitor their compliance with the programme. However, a failure to comply with a supervision order may be treated as contempt in the face of the court. A parent or guardian may also be required to pay compensation but solely in circumstances where the court is satisfied that a wilful failure to take care of or control the child contributed to the child's criminal behaviour (s 113). The parent or guardian has a right to be heard before such an order is made, and the court must have regard to the present and future means and financial commitments of the parent or guardian in question. A parent or guardian may also be bound over (s 114) in the sense that he or she may be ordered, on consent, to enter into a recognisance to exercise proper and adequate control over the child. An unreasonable refusal to consent to such an order may amount to contempt of court. The maximum amount of the recognisance is quite modest (the Euro equivalent of £250) and may be forfeited only if the child commits a further offence during the relevant period and parental failure to exercise proper and adequate control contributed to the commission of that later offence. **9–37**

Community Sanctions

The 2001 Act (s 115) provides for 10 different forms of community sanction including community service (where the child is aged 16 or 17 years), various kinds of probation orders, a day centre order, a care and supervision order and a restriction on movement order. Subsequent sections of the 2001 Act set out in detail the nature of each of these sanctions and the rules governing their operation. A court may impose any one of them when, having considered a probation or other report, it determines that it would be the most suitable way of dealing with the child. Certain general conditions, specified in s 117, may be attached to any such order. These include requiring the child to attend school regularly, limiting the child's attendance at certain premises or his or her association with specified persons, or prohibiting the consumption of alcohol. A court must always explain to the child why a community sanction is being imposed, what it entails and what is expected of the child and his or her parents or guardian in order to comply with it. Detention is not to be **9–38** treated as the automatic default option if the child fails to comply with the terms of a community sanction or where such a sanction is revoked. Before imposing detention in these circumstances, a court must be satisfied that it is the only suitable way of dealing with the child (s 116(4)).

Detention

9–39 A child may not be sentenced to imprisonment or otherwise committed to prison in any circumstances.[89] Detention in a children detention school is the most severe penalty that may be imposed on a child offender, and it should be used only as a measure of last resort.[90] The primary mission of a children detention school is to educate, rehabilitate and prepare the child for social rehabilitation. As s 158 of the 2001 Act states:

> "It shall be the principal object of children detention schools to provide appropriate education and training programmes and facilities for children referred to them by a court and, by
> (a) having regard to their health, safety, welfare and interests, including their physical, psychological and emotional wellbeing;
> (b) providing proper care, guidance and supervision for them;
> (c) preserving and developing satisfactory relationships between them and their families;
> (d) exercising proper moral and disciplinary influences on them; and
> (e) recognising the personal cultural and linguistic identity of each of them,
>
> to promote their reintegration into society and prepare them to take their place in the community as persons who observe the law and are capable of making a positive and productive contribution to society."

9–40 A child sentenced to detention is entitled to the standard one-quarter remission applicable to adult prison sentences,[91] but there is no legally enforceable entitlement to be considered for enhanced remission.[92] Detention may have a predominantly educational and therapeutic purpose, as reflected in the terms of s 158, but it is undoubtedly punitive as well. Children are deprived of their liberty and confined in a closely monitored environment. They, no less than adult prisoners, retain all their constitutional rights apart from those necessarily suspended or curtailed by the fact of incarceration.[93] They may be sanctioned for misbehaviour within the school and, if necessary, subject to separation or solitary confinement where this is judged necessary for the maintenance of order

89 Children Act 2001, s 156.
90 Children Act 2001, ss 96(2) and 143.
91 *Byrne (A Minor) v Director of Oberstown Children Detention Centre* [2013] IEHC 562; [2020] 2 IR 338; [2014] 1 ILRM 346. Here the High Court (Hogan J) decided that children serving sentences of detention were entitled to the same standard remission as adult prisoners and this decision was accepted by the Government.
92 *B v Director of Oberstown Children Detention Centre* [2020] IESC 18; [2023] 2 IR 191; [2020] 1 ILRM 469.
93 *F (S) v Director of Oberstown Children Detention Centre* [2017] IEHC 829; [2018] 3 IR 466; [2018] 1 ILRM 459.

and to prevent damage to property or injury to persons. However, a measure of this nature must be attended by procedural safeguards and be proportionate in terms of both its duration and conditions.[94] The 2001 Act (s 201) confers a general power on the school Director to discipline a child in a way that is both reasonable and within the prescribed limits. Any disciplinary measure must never involve (a) corporal punishment or any kind of physical violence; (b) deprivation of food or drink; (c) treatment that could reasonably be expected to be detrimental to physical, psychological or emotional wellbeing; or (d) treatment that is cruel, inhuman or degrading.

The Director also has significant powers, set out in ss 202 to 207 of the 2001 Act, to permit a child to be absent from the school for specified purposes. Short absences may be permitted for a purpose such as attending a funeral or visiting a relative who is seriously ill (s 202). A child may also be absent, on either a one-off or recurring basis, for the purpose of seeking or engaging in employment, receiving education or training or participating in sport (s 203). Children may also be allowed to take part in mobility trips designed to promote their social and personal reintegration, their awareness and appreciation in matters of culture, education and recreation, and, where appropriate, the implementation of any necessary treatment or counselling directions (s 204). The Director must also formulate a temporary leave programme for each child, although no such leave may be granted during the first month of detention (s 205). A child on temporary leave shall be in the care of his or her parents or guardian or of a responsible person who shall undertake to the Director to supervise the child during the leave. Various sanctions are available where a child contravenes the conditions of leave or fails to return to the school at the appointed time (s 206). Most significantly, the Director may also authorise the placing out of a child under probationary supervision to reside with his or her parents or guardian or a responsible person willing to receive and take charge of the child. Such a placing out shall be in force until it is revoked or until the period of detention imposed by the court has expired, whichever is the sooner. The Director may revoke the placing out if it is necessary to do so for the protection of the child's welfare, if the child, without reasonable excuse, fails to abide by the conditions, or the child is not receiving appropriate education or training (s 207). A child aged 18 years or over who is still in detention may also be placed out. In such a case, there is no requirement that he or she should live with a specified person but there must instead be a requirement to reside at a specified place.[95] The placing out provisions in s 207 effectively amount to a form of supervised parole. The Director of the school may make such an order "at any time" after consultation with the Director of the Probation Service and, as noted, the child may remain under supervision in the community until the sentence has expired, unless the order has to be revoked earlier. **9–41**

[94] *F (S) v Director of Oberstown Children Detention Centre* [2017] IEHC 829; [2018] 3 IR 466; [2018] 1 ILRM 459.

[95] Children Act 2001, s 207(1A) inserted by Children (Amendment) Act 2015, s 22.

Finally, the Minister for Education may at any time order a child's release from a detention school on compassionate grounds if satisfied, on the basis of a report from the Director and after consultation with the Director of the Probation Service, "that exceptional circumstances exist which justify the release" (s 209).

Deferred Detention

9–42 Where a court, having considered a probation report and any other evidence it considers appropriate, determines that a detention order would be appropriate, it may defer making that order if no place is available in a children detention school or "for any other sufficient reason".[96] A court shall make such an order only if satisfied that, "having regard to the nature of the offence, and the age, level of understanding, character and circumstances of the child" it would be in the interests of justice to do so. The reference to the nature of the offence suggests that deferred detention may not be appropriate following conviction for a very serious offence. If detention is deferred for want of a place in a detention school, the court shall order the Director of the school to apply to the court to make a detention order once a place becomes available. Section 144(10) states that where a court "proposes to make a children detention order" following such an application from the Director, it may summon the child to appear before it. This suggests that is not obliged to make a detention order in these circumstances.

9–43 A court, as already noted, may defer making a detention order "for any other sufficient reason". In that event, the court shall openly state the period of detention that is being deferred, the date of the resumed hearing and that the court shall take into account at that hearing a probation report on the child's conduct in the meantime and any other relevant matters. All this must be clearly explained to the child. The resumed hearing must take place within a year at most from the date of what is described as the "adjourned hearing", and it may take place notwithstanding that the child has reached the age of 18 years. At that hearing, the court, having considered the probation report and any evidence from the probation officer, may (1) impose the period of detention which it had deferred or any shorter period; (2) suspend in whole or in part any period of detention so imposed; or (3) impose a community sanction appropriate to the age of the child concerned. It is difficult to reconcile the provision that the resumed hearing may take place even where the child has reached the age of 18 years with the options available to the court, apart possibly from some of the community sanctions. A detention order, suspended or otherwise, is no longer possible at that point, and the section does not permit the imposition of a prison sentence where the offender has reached the age of 18 on the resumed hearing date. In *People (DPP) v O'Leary*[97]the Court of Appeal, in answering a consultative case stated on this point,

[96] Children Act 2001, s 144.

[97] [2023] IECA 48,

held there was no authority under the 2001 Act or otherwise for making a detention order in respect of an adult, and that it was not possible to read into s 144(9) an implied power to impose a prison sentence. A community order could be imposed on a person who had come an adult by the time of the resumed hearing but, in effect, the only such order that could be imposed was one pursuant to s 2 of the Probation of Offenders Act 1907. All the remaining community orders listed in s 115 seem to apply to child offenders only. As discussed further below, a deferred detention order is, for all practical purposes, a suspended sentence. It will typically be appropriate where the offence is so serious that nothing less than a period of detention, although a measure of last resort, would adequately express the deserved degree of censure, but where there are countervailing factors that justify giving the child an opportunity to avoid detention by remaining well behaved during the deferment period.

Detention and Supervision

Where a court is satisfied that detention is the only suitable way of dealing with a chid offender, it may, instead of imposing a straightforward sentence of detention, make a detention and supervision order.[98] This means that the child will spend half the specified period in detention and the other half under probation supervision in the community. Where the child is released before the specified detention period has expired, supervision shall begin immediately upon release. When making such an order, a court may specify such of the conditions listed in s 117 of the 2001 Act as it considers necessary to ensure the child will be of good behaviour and to reduce the likelihood of further offending. These are the same conditions that may be attached to a community sanction and include, for example, requiring the child to attend school or undergo counselling or medical treatment, to desist from consuming alcohol or from associating with specified persons. Where a child fails to comply with a detention and supervision order or to fulfil a condition attached to the supervision, he or she may be dealt with in accordance with s 130 of Act. This means that the court may order the child to comply with the order or revoke the order and replace it with one under s 129 of the 2001 Act or another community sanction. A s 129 order involves assigning the child to the care of a suitable person. It is unclear if a detention and supervision order may be made where the child will reach adulthood before the supervision element is fulfilled. There is a view that it should not because the kind of conditions that may be attached to the supervision and the orders that may be made in the event of non-compliance are mostly applicable to children only.[99] If this is the correct interpretation, there is a strong case to be made for reforming the law, as detention followed by supervision is a valuable option for dealing with children convicted of serious offences. Many such children will be in the mid to late teenage years which means that they **9–44**

---

98 Children Act 2001, s 151.

99 See *People (DPP) v S (M)* [2020] IECA 178, para 7 (2 July 2020).

will be 18 years or more by the time the order fully expires. Section 151 could easily be amended to provide for this eventuality.

Suspension of a Detention Order

9–45 The Children Act 2001 makes no provision for the full or part suspension of a detention order at the point of imposition. The Court of Appeal has held that s 99 of the Criminal Justice Act 2006 provides solely for the suspension of prison sentences, and child detention does not come within the definition of imprisonment in s 98 of the 2006 Act. Nor could the court identify any other legal basis, in either the 2001 Act or the common law, for suspending a period of detention in a children detention school.[100] Later, in *B v Director of Oberstown Children Detention Centre* the Supreme Court mentioned this decision and, while not disagreeing with it, did not exactly endorse it either.[101] However, the 2001 Act does provide for suspension where a deferred detention order has been made. As noted immediately above, at the resumed hearing, the court may, among other things, suspend in whole or in part the period of detention that had been specified at the outset. The inclusion of this option shows that the drafters of the 2001 Act had no principled objection to a term of detention being suspended, even if in these circumstances suspension is being ordered some time after the original sentencing hearing. In fact, as noted, a deferred detention order, by its nature, bears a close resemblance to a suspended sentence. A court will have decided at the outset that detention is appropriate, and it will have specified the term of detention that is being deferred. The child is then effectively placed on probation until the resumed hearing at which point a final decision on sentence is made. Admittedly, when a prison sentence is suspended, no further court hearing is necessary if the offender abides by the conditions throughout the operational period. However, the so-called 'Damocles sword' element of a suspended sentence is equally present in a deferred detention order in the sense that a child who misbehaves or commits a further offence before the resumed hearing date is clearly at risk of custody or, at least, a community sanction.

9–46 Viewed from a policy perspective, there are arguments for and against permitting the suspension of a detention order. Those who oppose it typically argue that when dealing with child offenders, it is vitally important that the penalty should be imposed and served as soon as possible after the offence so that the child will associate the punishment with the wrongdoing constituting the offence, something that may not happen if there is a significant interval between offence and sentence. This is undoubtedly a valid argument. A child, depending on age and circumstances, may have difficulty understanding why he or she is being committed to detention some years after the offence (if the sentence

---

[100] *S (A) v DPP* [2017] IECA 310. See also Law Reform Commission, *Suspended Sentences* (2020), Chap 7.

[101] [2020] IESC 18; [2023] 2 IR 191; [2020] 1 ILRM 469, para 60.

was activated). As against this, it may be argued that since the Children Act 2001 emphatically treats detention as a sanction of last resort, suspended detention would be another useful strategy for avoiding custody, especially where it appeared that such a measure would help or encourage the child to desist from further offending. Being subject to probationary supervision would almost certainly be a condition of suspension. Secondly, in response to the argument that suspension of detention would prolong the interval between offence and sentence (if the sentence were later activated), it must be said that a suspended sentence is a punishment in itself. This has been repeatedly acknowledged by the courts in relation to suspension of prison sentences, and it would undoubtedly apply to suspended detention as well. The risk of having to undergo detention in the future, being subject to supervision, having (in most cases) to abide by conditions that may involve engaging in or refraining from specified activities all combine to constitute the punitive bite of a suspended custodial sentence of whatever kind. Finally, it may be observed that if detention is considered appropriate, the offence is likely to have been a serious one which, in turn, means that the child is unlikely to have forgotten it in a way that less serious matters like public order offences or shoplifting might be fairly quickly forgotten. However, the concern about having a prolonged interval between the offence and committal to detention, where that happens, remains valid. It might, however, be addressed by imposing a statutory limit, not more than 12 months, on the operational period of a suspended detention order.

One way of avoiding the difficulty caused by the absence of a power to suspend a term of detention from the outset might be to defer a final sentencing decision until the child reached the age of 18 years. At that point, he or she will be sentenced as an adult which means that a fully or partly suspended prison sentence may be imposed. However, this would be appropriate only where the child was very close to the age of 18 years at the time of sentence and, importantly, where the court was satisfied that such a course of action would be beneficial to the child. After all, it is normally more advantageous to be sentenced as a child for offences committed as a child. A court might, however, consider it important that the child should be subject to some period of probationary supervision following release from custody, in which case a part-suspended prison sentence might be the most appropriate penalty. Needless to say, the prison term should be no longer than what would have been an appropriate period of detention, and it might well be shorter given the difference in custodial regimes. The Court of Appeal approved this approach in *People (DPP) v McD (D)*[102]where a child was being sentenced a few weeks before his 18th birthday and it appeared that he would benefit from probationary supervision following release. The court therefore quashed the sentence of four years' detention and substituted four years' imprisonment with the last eight months suspended. More recently, however, the court has **9–47**

[102] [2020] IECA 149.

cast doubt on its own decision in this regard.[103] The difficulty it seems to have identified derives from s 3 of the Criminal Procedure Act 1993 which provides that when the Court of Appeal quashes a sentence it may replace it with one which the trial court could have imposed. In *McD* it arguably erred by imposing a sentence of imprisonment, something the trial court could not have done because the appellant was still a child when sentenced. However, this difficulty would not arise if the offender were sentenced as an adult in circumstances where the trial court had deferred finalisation of sentence until the offender reached the age of 18 years.

Reviewable Detention Order

9–48 When imposing a long period of detention, including a life term for murder, judges occasionally include a review date on which the child will be brought back before court so that the sentence can be reviewed. The review hearing will typically be some years into the sentence, and the expectation is that the court will consider suspending the balance of the sentence if the child appears to have made good progress while in custody and is unlikely to pose a risk to the public. Obviously, there is no promise or guarantee of suspension but the possibility of getting released on the review date or shortly thereafter should provide the child with an incentive to make good use of their time in custody. In *People (DPP) v S (M)* the Court of Appeal said:

> "We see merit in the review mechanism. The existence of a review date means that there is a target date for the young respondent to work towards. On that review date, there will be a number of options open to the judge conducting the review. One possibility is that the review might not result in the release of the respondent. Another possibility is that the judge might decide to suspend the balance of the sentence then unserved, either from that point, or from some date in the future. The option would also be available to the judge to provide that the balance of the sentence would be suspended for a period in excess of the sentence remaining to be served, so, by way of example, if there was to be a review at a time when two years of the sentence was unserved, the judge might decide to suspend the balance of the sentence, either from that day, or, perhaps, from a date six months later, and to stipulate that the sentence would be suspended for a period of, say four or five years, on condition that he would specify including that the respondent be of good behaviour during any remaining period custody and for the specified period post-release."[104]

9–49 In that case, the court found the sentence imposed by the trial judge to be unduly lenient, but only on account of the review date that had been set. The child had been sentenced to 11 years' imprisonment with effect from late December 2017 with a review to commence on 1 February 2023. The Court of Appeal substituted 1 January 2025 as the review date. Review

---

[103] *People (DPP) v L (R)* [2023] IECA 47, para 6.

[104] [2020] IECA 178, para 8. The Court of Appeal delivered two judgments delivered in this case, and both bear the same neutral citation. The passage quoted is from the judgment of 29 July 2020 (on the resentencing of the respondent).

dates are commonly set when sentencing children convicted of murder. For example, in one high-profile case, two teenagers, known as Boy A and Boy B, were found guilty of the murder of a 14-year-old girl. Both were 13 years at the time of the offence. Boy A was sentenced to life detention with review after 12 years (and given a concurrent sentence for a sexual offence committed against the same victim), while Boy B was sentenced to 15 years with review after 8 years.[105]

The legality of this practice has recently been called into question. The Children Act 2001 does not expressly provide for it, and the statutory provision on which courts previously relied, as in *People (DPP) v G*,[106] has been repealed. The problem essentially derives from *People (DPP) v Finn*[107] where the Supreme Court, having considered all the previous case law on the matter, concluded that reviewable prison sentences were "undesirable" and should not be imposed, principally because they could be said to conflict with the power to commute or remit judicially imposed sentences which is constitutionally allocated to the executive branch of government. The court did stress that everything it said in this respect was *obiter* and it seems that this point was not argued before it. However, the unanimous court seemed certain that the practice followed by many judges at the time of including a review date when imposing a prison sentence was, to say the least, constitutionally problematic. It did not appear to have any problem with review powers being conferred by legislation, including any law empowering a parole authority to release prisoners before the expiry of their sentences. Nor, did it seem to have any problem with the review power conferred on judges by s 27 of the Misuse of Drugs Act 1977 (as amended) when imposing the presumptive 10-year sentence on certain offenders convicted of s 15A offences. In an earlier judgment, *People (DPP) v Sheedy*[108] the Supreme Court had indicated that a reviewable sentence, in so far as it had a rehabilitative purpose, could be suitable for young offenders, though it also said that the general question about the legality of such sentences had not been fully argued. The matter was recently ventilated at some length before the Central Criminal Court in a case involving a 17-year-old child convicted of a murder committed when he was 14 years. The trial judge was rightly critical of the gaps in the Children Act 2001 in so far as it related to the sentencing of children for serious offences such as this. In particular he noted the absence of any provision for part suspension of the sentence.[109] The Minister for Justice has indicated that the 2001 Act will be reviewed in light of the issues that arose in this and other similar cases. 9–50

---

105 *Irish Times*, 5 November 2019.

106 [2005] IECCA 75.

107 [2001] 2 IR 25; [2001] 2 ILRM 211.

108 [2000] 2 IR 184, 194.

109 For an account of the case, see Eoin Reynolds, "Teenager sentenced to life for murder of Urantsetseg Tserendorj", *Irish Times*, 20 February 2023. The judge imposed a life sentence with review after 13 years, while noting that the defendant would be eligible for parole after 12 years. The defendant's appeal against conviction was dismissed: *People (DPP) v CC* [2023] IECA 295.

9–51 The problem has already been solved to a limited degree by the Parole Act 2019 (s 24) which provides that prisoners serving life sentences are eligible for parole when they have served at least 12 years. For this purpose, a sentenced prisoner includes a person who was sentenced to detention as a child but subsequently transferred to prison.[110] It would seem, therefore, that pending any statutory amendment, a court imposing a sentence of life detention should no longer include a review date as this could conflict with the statutory parole provision. The same will apply to lengthy determine sentences (of at least eight years) when the necessary regulations are made enabling the Parole Board to consider granting parole to prisoners serving such sentences.[111] However, the Children Act 2001 should still be amended to specify exactly the powers of the courts when sentencing children convicted of murder and other serious offences. Formal provisions should be made for both the part suspension and review of sentences. This may entail consequential amendments to the Parole Act 2019 in respect of prisoners who were initially sentenced to detention in a children detention school. Attention would also have to be paid to s 207 of the 2001 Act which, as noted above, permits the Director of a children detention school to "place out" a child at any time for supervision in the community and this may last until the sentence has expired or the placing out order revoked. The compatibility of this power with a reviewable detention order may require consideration.

Undue Leniency Applications and Appeals Against Severity Involving Child Offenders

9–52 The power vested in the DPP to apply to the Court of Appeal to review an unduly lenient sentence is described in Chap 2 above. This undoubtedly applies to sentences imposed on child offenders because a 'sentence' is defined in the Criminal Justice Act 1993 (the '1993 Act') (s 1) as including a sentence of imprisonment "or any other order made by a court dealing with a convicted person" (with two exceptions that are irrelevant for present purposes). However, the 1993 Act provides that the Court of Appeal, having heard such an application, may refuse it or "quash the sentence and in place of it impose on the convicted person such sentence as it considers appropriate, being a sentence which would have been imposed on him by the sentencing court concerned".[112] This clearly posed a problem where a respondent, having been sentenced to detention as a child, had reached adulthood by the time the undue leniency application was heard. The Court of Appeal could not impose a prison sentence because that was not an option available to the trial court, and it could not substitute a longer period of detention because child detention cannot be imposed on adult. In *People (DPP) v McC (P)*,[113] for example, the Court of Appeal, although satisfied that the sentence was unduly lenient, could not interfere with it because the respondent had reached the age of 18

[110] Parole Act 2019, s 2(3).
[111] See Chap 14 below.
[112] Criminal Justice Act 1993, s 2(3).
[113] [2018] IECA 309.

years. This problem has now been addressed by the addition the following subsections to s 2 of the Criminal Justice Act 1993:

> "(5) Where the convicted person in relation to whom an application under this section is made is a person who was under the age of 18 years when the sentence was imposed on him by the sentencing court concerned and he has attained the age of 18 years or before the date on which the application is determined by the court, the reference in subsection 3(a) to a sentence which could have been imposed on him by the sentencing court concerned shall be construed as a reference to a sentence which could have been imposed on him by the sentencing court concerned had he attained that age at the time when the sentence was so imposed.
>
> (6) Where subsection (5) applies and the application under this section is in respect of a sentence imposed on a person convicted of treason or murder before the person has attained the age of 18 years, the court may, notwithstanding section 2 of the Criminal Justice Act 1990, impose such sentence as it considers appropriate."[114]

Consequently, the Court of Appeal, if satisfied that that a sentence of child detention was unduly lenient, may now increase it to a term of imprisonment. Obviously, any period of detention already served will count towards the service of the prison sentence. However, if the respondent was convicted of murder while still a child, and the sentence of detention imposed by the trial court is found to be unduly lenient, he or she need not be sentenced to life imprisonment (the mandatory penalty for an adult convicted of murder). Rather, the Court of Appeal has discretion as to the term of imprisonment to be substituted. **9–53**

The same difficulty arose in defence appeals against severity of sentences of detention imposed on child offenders. The Criminal Procedure Act 1993 (s 3(2)) provides: **9–54**

> "On the hearing of an appeal against sentence for an offence the court may quash the sentence and in place of it impose such sentence or make such order as it considers appropriate, being a sentence or order which could have been imposed on the convicted person for the offence at the court of trial."

Taken on its own, this provision requires that any sentence substituted by the Court of Appeal following the quashing of the original sentence must be one that could have been imposed by the trial court.[115] Consequently, as in the case of an undue leniency application, the Court of Appeal could not substitute imprisonment for detention if the appellant had reached adulthood by the time the appeal was decided.[116] It was therefore confined to upholding the original sentence or quashing it and making no further order. This problem too has now been addressed by the addition of the following subsection to s 3 of the Criminal Procedure Act 1993: **9–55**

---

[114] Inserted by Criminal Justice (Miscellaneous Provisions) 2023, s 61, effective from 1 August 2023.

[115] Criminal Procedure Act 1993, s 3.

[116] *People (DPP) v L (R)* [2023] IECA 47.

"(10) For the purposes of subsection (2), where a convicted person in relation to whom an appeal against sentence is brought is a person who was under the age of 18 years when the sentence was imposed on them by the court of trial and the person has attained the age of 18 years on or before the date on which the appeal is determined by the Court, the reference in that subsection to a sentence or order which could have been imposed on the convicted person for the offence at the court of trial shall be construed as a reference to a sentence or order which could have been imposed on the convicted person for the offence at the court of trial had he attained that age at the time when the sentence or order was so imposed."[117]

9–56 The Court of Appeal may substitute a term of imprisonment for a sentence of detention which it quashes as a result of a defence appeal. Where the appellant was convicted of murder while still a child, but is an adult when the appeal is decided, the Court of Appeal has discretion as to the term of imprisonment to be substituted. It need not impose the mandatory life sentence applicable to adults convicted of murder.[118]

9. Children Convicted of Serious Offences

9–57 When a child is convicted of a serious offence, especially one of a violent nature, a court may conclude that detention, although the measure of last resort, is the only suitable penalty. Detention is never, of course, mandatory even in these circumstances. The Children Act 2001 does not specify what is meant by "last resort" in s 96, nor does it indicate in s 143 the factors a court should consider in order to be satisfied that detention "is the only suitable way of dealing with the child". However, judicial sentencing practice and appeal court decisions strongly suggest that the inherent gravity of an offence, without more, may justify a term of detention, even if the child has no previous convictions. A court may still wish to consider some related measure such as deferred detention or detention followed by supervision (assuming that they are available in the circumstances). The length of sentence is largely at the discretion of the court, though it may never exceed the maximum sentence of imprisonment for the relevant offence. The 2001 Act, s 149[119] provides that any term of detention imposed following conviction in the Children Court "shall not be for a period longer than the term of detention or imprisonment which the court could impose on an adult who commits such an offence". The Children (Amendment) Act 2015 (s 9) substitutes the following section for s 149 of the 2001 Act:

"(1) Where a child is convicted of an offence and a period of detention is imposed on the child by a court, the period of detention shall not exceed

[117] Inserted by Criminal Justice (Miscellaneous Provisions) Act 2023, s 62, effective from 1 August 2023.

[118] Criminal Procedure Act 1993, s 3(11), inserted by Criminal Justice (Miscellaneous Provisions) Act 2023, s 62.

[119] As amended by Criminal Justice Act 2006, s 141

> the term of detention or imprisonment that the court could have imposed on a person of full age and capacity who is convicted of such an offence.
>
> (2) Where a court imposes a period of detention exceeding 3 years on a child, it shall give its reasons for doing so in open court in language that is appropriate to the age and level of understanding of the child."

Inexplicably, however, this section, which would apply to children convicted on indictment as well as those convicted in the Children Court, has still not been brought into force almost a decade after its enactment. These various sections, in their past, present and future formulations, all refer to the custodial term a court "could" impose on an adult. This presumably refers to the maximum sentence for the offence although it also means that the Children Court may not exceed the jurisdictional limit of the District Court (12 months' imprisonment for one offence or two years for a combination of offences). These provisions must also be read in conjunction with s 96(4) of the 2001 Act which provides: **9–58**

> "The penalty imposed on a child for an offence should be no greater than that which would be appropriate in the case of an adult who commits an offence of the same kind and may be less, where so provided for in this Part."

Section 96(3) further permits a court to consider as mitigating factors a child's age and level of maturity when deciding on the nature of any penalty, unless the penalty is fixed by law. **9–59**

Essentially, therefore, a court sentencing a child may impose a more lenient penalty than would be appropriate for an adult convicted of the same offence, but it may never impose a more severe penalty than the adult would deserve.[120] Almost invariably, the penalty will be more lenient because of the diminished culpability of children generally, and because there may be additional extenuating circumstances particular to the child being sentenced. Judicially developed sentencing guidelines now exist for several offences, but they are usually crafted with adult offenders in mind.[121] When sentencing anyone, whether a child or an adult, a court must have regard to any guideline applicable to the offence of conviction. However, where the offence was committed by a child, the guideline is merely a starting point, albeit an important one, and this holds true even if the offender is an adult by the time of sentence. Having identified the appropriate range, a court must then adjust the headline sentence that would be appropriate for an adult to reflect the reduced culpability or moral blameworthiness of the child. In some instances, this may call for a substantial downward adjustment and result in a headline sentence falling within a lower range. Credit must then be given for any additional mitigating factors coming within the second limb of the proportionality principle. If the child's diminished culpability is not taken into account when determining the headline sentence (as is the preferable approach), **9–60**

---

[120] *People (DPP) v S (M)* [2020] IECA 178, para 7 (2 July 2020).

[121] The main guidelines developed to date are described in Chaps 10 and 13 below.

it should be considered as a mitigating factor under the second limb.[122] Further, if the offender is an adult by the time of sentence, it will normally be appropriate to consider if any portion of a prison sentence being imposed should be suspended to incentivise rehabilitation. For young adults as for children, rehabilitation is obviously an important consideration, but this is not to discount the possibility that it may also be relevant when sentencing older offenders for offences committed during childhood. All this is on the assumption that the child is being sentenced to detention, but even where the offence is a serious one, a court must still have regard to the transcendent principle that detention is to be treated as the sanction of last resort. It must therefore be satisfied that no other measure would be an adequate penalty in the circumstances.

9–61 Several Court of Appeal judgments illustrate the application of these principles. In *People (DPP) v O'F (A)*[123] the offender had pleaded guilty to numerous counts of rape, sexual assault and other sexual offences committed against his niece while she was aged between eight and 11 years and he was aged between 14 and 17 years. The trial judge imposed a fully suspended five-year prison sentence, the offender having reached adulthood by the time of sentence. The Court of Appeal found this to be unduly lenient and substituted an effective sentence of 2 and a half years' imprisonment (five years with the last 2 and a half years suspended). What is significant for present purposes is the way in which the Court of Appeal arrived at this revised sentence. It was accepted that the offending fell into the 'more serious' category identified by the Supreme Court in *People (DPP) v E (F)*[124] for which the guideline range is 10 to 15 years. The trial judge, while recognising this, said that a sentence in the range of 10 to 12 years would be appropriate if the offender had been an adult, but identified a headline sentence of five years in this case to reflect the defendant's age and emotional immaturity, and she then suspended this sentence in its entirety. The Court of Appeal took the view that the appropriate sentence, were the offender an adult, would be in the range of 12 to 14 years. Having regard to this offender's age and emotional immaturity at the time of the offending, it identified a headline sentence of 7 and a half years' which it further reduced to five years to account for other mitigating factors. It then suspended the last 2 and a half years to incentivise rehabilitation. In this case, therefore, the headline sentence was set at almost half the level that would have been appropriate for an adult. As the court said, a child's reduced culpability is a factor that relates to the gravity of the offence and should therefore be considered when determining the headline sentence.[125]

9–62 While adult headline sentences should undoubtedly be discounted for child offenders, there is no settled reduction in the way for example, that an early guilty plea with a significant utilitarian value ordinarily attracts

122 *People (DPP) v McD (J)* [2021] IECA 31.
123 [2022] IECA 122.
124 [2019] IESC 85; [2021] 1 IR 217; [2020] 1 ILRM 517.
125 [2022] IECA 122, para 45.

a discount of about one-third. This is scarcely surprising in light of the extent to which the culpability of child offenders can vary depending on their age (which could be anywhere between 10 and 18 years), their level of intellectual and emotional development, their appreciation of the wrongfulness of their offending conduct and its impact on the victim, and the nature and duration of the conduct itself. In *People (DPP) v D (T)*[126]the Court of Appeal noted the English Sentencing Council's recommendation that for offenders in the age group 15 to 17 years, a custodial sentence in the region of half to two-thirds of that applicable to an adult offender may be appropriate. The Council's guideline (which has a great deal of interest to say on the sentencing of children generally) states in this regard:

> "When considering the relevant adult guideline, the court may feel it appropriate to apply a sentence broadly within the region of half to two thirds of the adult sentence for those aged 15 – 17 and allow a greater reduction for those aged under 15. This is only a rough guide and must not be applied mechanistically. In most cases when considering the appropriate reduction from the adult sentence the emotional and developmental age and maturity of the child or young person is of at least equal importance as their chronological age."[127]

However, the English Court of Appeal has rightly cautioned against adopting this element of the guideline as a starting point. The earlier, more general provisions regarding the sentencing of children should carefully be considered first.[128] **9–63**

The court in *D (T)*, while acknowledging differences in the applicable laws and sentencing schemes between Ireland and England and Wales, said it regarded the recommended reduction as being "at least a helpful indication as to the potential significance of the fact of minority in any assessment of an offender's culpability".[129] Greater reductions have been made in some cases. In *People (DPP) v H (J)*,[130] for example, the appellant, on pleading guilty to two counts of sexual assault and two of s 4 rape, was **9–64**

---

[126] [2021] IECA 289. In *People (DPP) v W(M)* [2020] IECA 272 the Court of Appeal reduced a sentence for sexual assaults because the trial judge had not given adequate credit for the appellant's young age (17 to 18 or 19 years) at the time of the offending. As the court observed (at para 33), the level of discount necessarily depends on several case-specific factors, some of which may be aggravating as well as mitigating. In *People (DPP) v G(A)* [2024] IECA 284, an undue leniency application, the respondent was being resentenced for 6 counts of s 4 rape committed during the period 1998 to 2002 when he was aged 15 to 19 years and the victim was aged 8 to 12 years. The Court of Appeal adopted a headline sentence of 12 years' imprisonment reduced to 8 years because of the respondent's age at the time, with a further one-year reduction to reflect other mitigation.

[127] Sentencing Council, *Sentencing Children and Young People: Overarching Principles and Offence Specific Guidelines for Sexual Offences and Robbery. Definitive Guideline* (2017), para 6.46.

[128] *R v ZA* [2023] EWCA Crim 596; [2023] 2 Cr App R (S) 45, para 55; [2023] Crim LR 617.

[129] [2021] IECA 289, para 33.

[130] [2017] IECA 206.

sentenced to a total of four years' imprisonment with the last two years suspended. At the time of the offending, he was aged 15 years while the victim of 11 years. The Court of Appeal agreed with the trial judge that for an adult offender the headline sentence would have been eight years. However, in light of the appellant's youth and circumstances, it held that the appropriate sentence in this case was 2 and a half years which it reduced to 18 months in light of other mitigating factors, with the last six months suspended. In *People (DPP) v S (M)*[131] a case involving attempted murder with several aggravating factors, the trial judge indicated that the appropriate sentence for an adult would have been life imprisonment or, if a determinate sentence were being imposed, approximately 17 and a half years. However, he identified a headline sentence of 11 years in this case where the defendant was 15 and a half years of age at the time of the offence. The Court of Appeal did not find fault with this approach although it increased the period which the defendant had to serve being eligible for a sentence review.[132] More recently, in *People (DPP) v W (A)*[133] where the sexual offending had occurred while the defendant was aged between 15 and 18 years, the Court of Appeal decided that the headline sentence for the most serious offence, if committed by an adult, would have been 10 years. However, it reduced this to six years on account of the defendant's young age at the time of the offending, with a further two-year reduction for other mitigating factors.

9–65 Problematically, the Children Act 2001 fails to specify how child murderers should be sentenced. An adult convicted of murder must be sentenced to life imprisonment, but a person under the age of 18 years may not, in any circumstances, be committed to prison. A convicted murderer who is still a child at the time of sentence must therefore be sentenced to detention. Arguably, even in these circumstances, detention is not mandatory, but the circumstances in which a court could properly conclude that a murder did not call for the penalty of last resort would be very rare indeed. Cases of this kind have become more prevalent in Ireland during the past few years, having been extremely rare throughout most of the history of the state. Both trial courts and the Court of Appeal have proceeded on the basis that the maximum as opposed to the mandatory penalty for murder committed by a child is detention for life. As already noted, they have also accepted that a trial court, when imposing detention either for life or for a determinate period, may specify a date on which the sentence will be reviewed. By that date, the offender will almost certainly be in prison, having been transferred there on reaching the age of 18 years, and the court, having conducted the review, may suspend the balance of the sentence or order continued detention, perhaps with a further

131 [2020] IECA 178.

132 Discussed above under 'Reviewable detention order'.

133 [2023] IECA 204. This was an undue leniency application and, while the court found the sentence imposed by the trial judge to be unduly lenient, it decided, in all the circumstances, not to return the defendant to prison. See also *People (DPP) v Cotter* [2014] IECA 40 and *People (DPP) v PP* [2023] IECA 169.

review date.[134] However, as noted earlier under the heading 'Reviewable detention order', there are now some doubts about the legality of this practice. Any review of the sentencing provisions of the Children Act 2001 should also include consideration of the penalty to which an adult should be liable when being sentenced for a murder committed as a child. At present it seems such a person must be sentenced to life imprisonment, but this is scarcely just given that a more lenient penalty would have been available at the time of the offence.

In recognition of the disadvantages associated with being sentenced as an adult for offences committed as a child, the courts have insisted that the prosecution of child defendants should proceed as quickly as possible. Everyone has a constitutional right to trial with reasonable expedition, but the obligation to proceed expeditiously is heightened when a child is facing trial.[135] The disadvantages of being tried as an adult are: (1) the District Court may not have the same jurisdiction to deal summarily with an indictable offence as it has under s 75 of the Children Act 2001 when the defendant is a child; (2) the restrictions on publicly identifying the defendant under s 93 of the 2001 Act no longer apply; (3) the obligation to obtain a probation report prior to imposing certain kinds of penalties, pursuant to s 99 of the 2001 Act, no longer applies; and (4) the defendant is no longer eligible for the special sentencing measures provided for in the 2001 Act and, in particular, the requirement that detention should be a measure of last resort. (Arguably, of course, imprisonment should also be a measure of last resort, not least when sentencing a person for offences committed during childhood.) Aside from these considerations, there is another more general reason why criminal proceedings against children should not be delayed to an unwarranted or unnecessary extent. Childhood is an important developmental phase, and sometimes a vulnerable one, in a person's life which explains why responses to criminal offending should be designed to promote the child's welfare, providing opportunities and incentives for him or her to become socially integrated and law abiding. The more quickly the criminal process unfolds the better its chance of fulfilling these objectives.[136] **9–66**

The superior courts are willing to consider prohibiting a trial where the defendant is a child, and it is claimed that there has been an unwarranted or unexplained delay in the investigation or prosecution of the alleged **9–67**

[134] See, for example, *People (DPP) v H(B)* [2021] IECA 129 (life detention for murder, with a review after 10 years): *People (DPP) v S(M) (A Minor)* [2020] IECA 178 (11 years detention for attempted murder, with a review after seven years in custody).

[135] *F (B) v DPP* [2001] 1 IR 656; *Donoghue v DPP* [2014] IESC 56; [2014] 2 IR 762; [2015] 1 ILRM 112. In its determination in *Furlong v DPP* [2023] IESCDET 8, the Supreme Court said that no further elucidation was required of the principles set forth in *Donoghue*.

[136] See the observations of Quirke J in *Jackson v DPP* [2004] IEHC 380, cited with approval by the Supreme Court in *Donoghue v DPP* [2014] IESC 56; [2014] 2 IR 762; [2015] 1 ILRM 112, paras 47-49.

offence. As in the case of delay applications generally, the courts apply a two-part test.[137] First, they must determine if there has been prolonged and blameworthy delay. If satisfied that there has been, they then undertake a balancing exercise to identify if, apart from the delay, there is some additional factor that outweighs the public interest in the prosecution of serious offences. Regarding that balancing exercise, the Supreme Court has said:

> "Thus, in a case involving a very serious charge, the fact that the person to be tried was a child at the time of the commission of the alleged offence and as a consequence of the delay will be tried as an adult, may not be sufficient to outweigh the public interest in having such a charge proceed to trial. In carrying out the balancing exercise, one could attach little or no weight to the fact that someone would be tried as an adult in respect of an offence alleged to have been committed whilst a child if the alleged offence occurred shortly before their 18th birthday. Therefore, in any given case a balancing exercise has to be carried out in which a number of factors will have to be put into the melting pot, including the length of delay itself, the age of the person to be tried at the time of the alleged offence, the seriousness of the charge, the complexity of the case, the nature of any prejudice relied on and any other relevant facts and circumstances. It is not enough to rely on the special duty on the state authorities to ensure a speedy trial of the child to prohibit a trial. An applicant must show something more as a consequence of the delay in order to prohibit the trial."[138]

9–68 The application of this balancing test means that it is rare enough for a trial to be prohibited. Very often the seriousness of the alleged offence will outweigh other considerations, and the trial will be allowed to proceed.[139]

10. Sentencing Adults for Offences Committed as Children

9–69 On reaching the age of 18 years, a person is liable to sentenced as an adult even for offences committed during childhood. The terms of the Children Act 2001 no longer apply. However, culpability must still be assessed by reference to the time at which the offence was committed and, for the reasons outlined earlier, children are categorically treated as less culpable than adults. Equally importantly, if not more so, regard must always be had to the individual offender's personal circumstances at the time of the offence. A court must carefully consider any evidence of mental illness, learning difficulties, parental neglect, experience of physical or emotional

---

137 *M (P) v DPP* [2006] IESC 22; [2006] 3 IR 172; [2006] 2 ILRM 361.

138 *Donoghue v DPP* [2014] IESC 56; [2014] 2 IR 762; [2015] 1 ILRM 112 para 52.

139 See *Bernotas v Commissioner of An Garda Síochána* [2019] IEHC 296 where the High Court (Noonan J) sets out the principles and refers to earlier decisions in which they were applied. In *Bernotas* it was held that there was no culpable delay but that, even if there had been, it would still be in the public interest for the trial to proceed. *S (M) v DPP* [2018] IEHC 285 is an example of case where the trial was ordered to proceed even though there had been unwarranted and inexcusable delay. There are several more recent cases, including *McCann v DPP* [2024] IEHC 314 where the law is discussed in detail, and *Oscar v DPP* [2024] IEHC 279.

abuse, living in a household or environment dominated by alcohol or drug abuse and any other factor present during the offender's childhood that may have a bearing on his or her culpability. This is well accepted and reflects the various judgments considered under the previous heading where several of the defendants were over 18 years when sentenced. As noted, the sentences considered appropriate for those defendants were considerably more lenient than what would have been appropriate for adults who committed similar offences.

When sentencing adults for offences committed as children, two different scenarios must be contemplated. One is where the offences were committed in the recent past but shortly before the offender reached adulthood. The other is where the offences were committed in the distant past, but during the offender's childhood. Cases falling into the first of these categories are the more straightforward because a court may be able to assess what the sentence would have been if the offender had been sentenced as a child.[140] In making this assessment, a court must carefully consider the offender's age, level of maturity and degree of moral blameworthiness at the time of the offence. The penalty imposed should reflect, as far as reasonably possible, that which would have been imposed if the offender were still a child when sentenced. Obviously, there will be some differences. Several measures for child offenders under the Children Act 2001 will no longer be available and, if a custodial penalty is deemed necessary, it will have to be imprisonment rather than detention. However, the last resort principle should still be observed even where the offender has reached adulthood by the time of sentence. **9–70**

The second scenario is most likely to arise when an adult is being sentenced for sexual offences committed during childhood, typically against a younger sibling or other relative. In these circumstances there may well be an interval of years or decades between offence and sentence. However, the passage of time should not deflect a court from assessing the offender's culpability and circumstances as they existed when the offences were committed. In *R v Limon*[141]the English Court of Appeal quoted with approval a submission by defence counsel that "[t]he passage of time does not imbue the appellant with greater culpability or moral responsibility than he had at the time of the offence". Irish courts would undoubtedly agree as they have consistently held that culpability is an ingredient of offence gravity, and that must be assessed by reference to the time of the offence. Some additional factors must nonetheless be considered when sentencing offenders in this category. First, the sentence should be determined by reference to the maximum that applied when the offence **9–71**

---

[140] In *People (DPP) v H (J)* [2017] IECA 206, for example, the Court of Appeal estimated that if the appellant had been sentenced at the time of the offences (when he was 15 years of age), he would probably have received 12 months' detention, possibly followed by a period of supervision under the Children Act 2001, s 151. He was sentenced in 2016 for offences committed in 2008.

[141] [2022] EWCA Crim 39; [2022] 4 WLR 37; [2022] 2 Cr App R(S) 21, para 30. See comment by Lyndon Harris and Vincent Scully at [2022] Crim LR 419.

was committed. This is an element of the broader principle of legality. Secondly, the offender's good behaviour since the commission of the offences may be a significant mitigating factor. It must be borne in mind that the overarching principle of proportionality as it applies in Ireland has two limbs – the gravity of the offence which must be determined by reference to the circumstances in which it was committed, and the offender's personal circumstances as they exist at the time of sentence. It is undoubtedly a relevant personal circumstance that the offender has desisted from further offending (or offending of any serious nature) during the years or decades since the commission of the offences being sentenced.[142]

9–72 The more difficult question is the extent to which sentences imposed in these circumstances should approximate to those that would have been imposed when the offences were committed. In many cases it may be impossible to establish with any certainty what those sentences would have been, given the rarity of prosecutions for child sexual abuse until the 1990s and, even then, most defendants were well into adulthood when prosecuted. But it will always be possible to identify the nature and maximum level of the penalty or penalties that applied at the time. The English Court of Appeal has addressed this question in several leading judgments of which the most relevant, from an Irish perspective, is *R v Ghafoor*[143] as it was decided before the enactment of the Criminal Justice Act 2003 and the adoption of the Sentencing Council's definitive guideline on sentencing children, both of which influenced the decisions in later cases.[144] In *Ghafoor*, the court said:

> "The approach to be adopted where a defendant crosses a relevant age threshold between the date of the commission of the offence and the date of conviction should now be clear. The starting point is the sentence that the defendant would have been likely to receive if he had been sentenced at the date of the commission of the offence. It has been described as "a powerful factor". That is for the obvious reason that... the philosophy of restricting sentencing powers in relation to young persons reflects both (a) society's acceptance that young offenders are less responsible for their actions and therefore less culpable than adults, and (b) the recognition that, in consequence, sentencing them should place greater emphasis on rehabilitation, and less on retribution and deterrence than in the case of adults. It should be noted that the "starting point" is not the *maximum* sentence that could lawfully have been imposed, but the sentence that the offender would have been likely to receive.
>
> So the sentence that would have been passed at the date of the commission

---

[142] See, for example, *People (DPP) v Hegarty* [2013] IECCA 67, para 27; *People (DPP) v C* [2015] IECA 76; *People (DPP) v B(P)* [2015] IECA 315.

[143] [2002] EWCA Crim 1857; [2003] 1 Cr App R (S) 84; [2002] Crim LR 739.

[144] *R v Bowker* [2007] EWCA Crim 1608; [2008]1 Cr App R (S) 72; *R v Y* [2013] EWCA Crim 1175; [2014] 1 Cr App R (S) 39; *R v Scothern* [2020] EWCA Crim 1540; [2021] 1 WLR 1735; [2021] 2 Cr App R (S) 4; *R v Amin* [2019] EWCA Crim 1583; [2020] 1 Cr App R (S) 36; *R v Limon* [2022] EWCA Crim 39; [2022] 4 WLR 37; [2022] 2 Cr App R (S) 21.

> of the offence is a "powerful factor". It is the starting point, and other factors may have to be considered. But in our judgment, there have to be good reasons for departing from the starting point. An examination of the authorities to which we have been referred shows that, although the court has looked at other factors to see whether there should be a departure from the starting point, it is not obvious that there has in fact been a departure in any of them. This serves to demonstrate how powerful a factor the starting point is. That is because justice requires there to be good reason to pass a sentence higher than would have been passed at the date of the commission of the offence.
>
> That is not to say that the starting point may not be tempered somewhat in certain cases. We have in mind in particular cases where there is a long interval between the date of commission of the offence and the date of conviction. By the date of conviction, circumstances may have changed significantly. The offender may now have been revealed as a dangerous criminal, whereas at the date of the offence that was not so. By the date of conviction, the tariff for the offence in question may have increased. These are factors that can be taken into account, and can, in an appropriate case, properly lead to the passing of a sentence somewhat higher than the sentence that would have been passed at the date of the commission of the offence. It will rarely be necessary for a court even to consider passing a sentence that is more severe than the maximum that it would have had jurisdiction to pass at the date of commission of the offence."[145]

Most of this seems to accord with principle. If the dominant consideration is the gravity of the offence, of which the offender's culpability and moral blameworthiness is a key ingredient, then the penalty that would have been imposed at the time of the offence should be a 'powerful factor', as the court said. It need not be the only factor because, as already mentioned, the offender's desistance from further crime and positive good character during the interval between offence and sentence may justify further mitigation. The more contentious question is whether there are any circumstances that would justify imposing a heavier sentence. An increase might well be justified where the victim was inhibited from reporting the offending conduct when it occurred, and perhaps for a considerable time thereafter, because he or she was subject to control or domination by the offender. In those circumstances, a court might well conclude that the offender should be subject to the level of penalty considered appropriate at the time of sentencing for the offences in question, or something close to that level. Some would argue that, even in the absence of this factor, a more severe sentence may be justified on deterrent grounds. Deterrence remains a valid sentencing purpose but only to the extent that it may justify imposing a sentence at a higher rather than a lower point within the relevant range. A court may therefore impose the highest sentence to which, in its estimation, the offender would have been liable if sentenced at the time of the offence. However, anything more severe than that would involve treating the offender instrumentally in order to deter others, and that, as noted in Chap 3, is morally dubious. **9–73**

---

[145] [2002] EWCA Crim 1857; [2003] 1 Cr App R (S) 84, paras 31-33.

9–74 Until recently, a person who committed murder while still a child but who had reached the age of 18 years by the time of sentence was subject, like very other adult, to the mandatory sentence of life imprisonment. The manifest injustice of this arrangement was recognised by the High Court in *Musueni and Amah v Ireland*[146] where it held that it amounted to unconstitutional discrimination for one category of child murderers (those sentenced while still children) to have the benefit of a discretionary sentencing regime while another (those who happened to have reached the age of 18 years by the time of sentence) to be subject to a mandatory life sentence. The State did not appeal against this decision but introduced amending legislation in the form of the Criminal Justice (Amendment) Act 2024. This Act amends s 2 of the Criminal Justice Act 1990 which states that every person convicted of treason or murder shall be sentenced to imprisonment for life. The 2024 Act renumbers s 2 of the 1990 Act as s 2(1) and adds a new subsection (s 2(2)) which states:

> "Subsection (1) shall not apply to the sentencing of a person convicted of murder who was under the age of 18 years when he or she committed the murder but has attained that age on or before the date of such sentencing."

9–75 A potentially problematic aspect of this new subsection is that while it clearly disapplies the mandatory life sentence to anyone who committed a murder while a child, irrespective of their age at sentence, it fails to state what a court *may* do. It is to be implied the legislative intent was to confer discretion upon a court sentencing an adult for a murder committed during childhood, but it would have been helpful if it clarified that a court in such a case could impose such sentence as it considered appropriate subject to a maximum of life imprisonment. The 1924 Act applies retrospectively and it also applies to the sentencing of murders to which s 4 of the 1990 Act applies (formerly capital murders).

11. Young Adult Offenders

9–76 Under the previous heading, we were concerned with sentencing adults for offences committed during childhood. Here we are dealing with the sentencing of offences committed in early adulthood.[147] Crossing a chronological age barrier, such as 18 years, is never accompanied by any dramatic transformation in an individual's character, personality or capacity. This is a human and social fact to which the law must have regard when devising sentencing rules and principles for young adults – those who were aged between 18 and 21 years (at least) when they offended. Their culpability may be only marginally greater, if at all, than that of a person who was still legally a child at the time of the offence. Appeal

---

[146] [2024] IEHC 523.

[147] For valuable analyses of this issue, see David Emanuel, Claire Mawer and Laura Janes, "The sentencing of young adults: A distinct group requiring a distinct approach" (2021) Crim LR 203, and Howard League for Penal Reform, *Sentencing Principles for Young Adults* (2019).

courts have cautioned against a "sudden shift in the sentencing regime" applicable to children to that applicable to adults, simply because the offence was committed by somebody who was slightly older than 18 years.[148] As the English Court of Appeal said in *R v Clarke*:

> "Reaching the age of 18 has many legal consequences, but it does not present a cliff edge for the purposes of sentencing. So much has long been clear.... Full maturity and all the attributes of adulthood are not magically conferred on young people on their 18th birthdays. Experience of life reflected in scientific research... is that young people continue to mature, albeit at different rates, for some time beyond their 18th birthdays. The youth and maturity of an offender will be factors that inform any sentencing decision, even if an offender has passed his or her 18th birthday."[149]

The same court has held that when sentencing young persons, including young adults, for serious offences, trial courts should ensure that they have all relevant information, preferably in the form of professional reports, about the offender. Reports should cover any issues relating to mental health, learning difficulties, brain injury, traumatic life experience, communication difficulties, experience of abuse or neglect, vulnerability to self-harm and similar matters.[150] Reliable information on these matters is particularly important when the offender is still a child as it may relate directly to his or her welfare and development which are always key considerations when sentencing children. But it is also highly desirable at the sentencing of young adults who may have experienced similar difficulties in the recent past or who may, indeed, continue to experience them. **9–77**

In what may well come to be regarded as a landmark decision in this area, the Supreme Judicial Court of Massachusetts has recently held that a sentence of life without parole amounted to cruel or unusual punishment when imposed on an "emerging adult" which, for this purpose, meant a person aged 18, 19 or 20 years (though the court recognised that some would include persons up to 24 years in this category).[151] In so holding, the court relied heavily on scientific evidence showing that while people may reach cognitive maturity at about 16 years, their psychosocial development often continues well beyond 18 years.[152] Young adults in the **9–78**

---

148 *R v Meanley* [2022] EWCA Crim 1065; [2022] 4 WLR 85, para 53.

149 [2018] EWCA Crim 185; [2018] 1 Cr App R (S) 52, para 5. See also *R v Peters* [2005] 2 Cr App R (S) 101, para 11 ("Although the passage of an 18th or 21st birthday represents a significant moment in the life of each individual, it does not necessarily tell us very much about the individual's true level of maturity, insight and understanding. These levels are not postponed until nor suddenly accelerated by an 18th or 21st birthday.").

150 *R v PS* [2019] EWCA Crim 2286; [2020] 2 Cr App R (S) 9; *R v Meanley* [2022] EWCA Crim. 1065; [2022] 4 WLR 85, para 63. These factors are listed as relevant to a child's welfare in the Sentencing Council's Definitive Guideline on Sentencing and Young Persons (2017), para 1.12.

151 *Commonwealth v Mattis,* Supreme Judicial Court of Massachusetts, 11 January 2024.

152 The distinction between these two kinds of personal development is described

18 to 20-year category therefore tend to (1) lack impulse control; (2) be more prone to risk taking; (3) be more susceptible to peer pressure; and (4) have a greater capacity for change than older adults. In other words, as the court concluded, emerging adults have the same core neurological characteristics as juveniles under the age of 18 years. That case was concerned with life without parole for a person who committed murder while aged 18 years, but the court's reasoning, especially if adopted elsewhere, provides a powerful argument for a special sentencing regime for young adults.[153] Irish courts have so far shown little inclination to follow suit. In *People (DPP) v Dullaghan*[154] the defendant was convicted of causing serious harm and aggravated burglary committed when he was 20 years of age. The trial judge, who imposed an effective sentence of four years' imprisonment, stated that he was adopting a lower headline sentence because of the defendant's youth. The Court of Appeal found this to be an error of principle, saying:

> "While the [defendant] was undoubtedly a young adult, he was 20 years old at the time of the offences and not a minor. He was of normal intelligence. Therefore, the headline sentence should have been selected on the basis that he was an adult to reflect the culpability of an adult and the harm done, in the normal way."[155]

9–79 The court did, however, appear to concede that some credit might be given for the defendant's young age, provided it was considered under the second limb of the proportionality principle as a potentially relevant personal circumstance. But it seems to have ruled out the idea that young adults were categorically entitled to mitigation on account of age. The Court of Appeal increased the effective sentence to one of six years' imprisonment.

9–80 Having an appropriate custodial regime for young adults who must be sentenced to custody, or who are transferred to prison institutions once they reach an age at which they must leave a children detention school, is vitally important. The ideas that inspired the introduction of Borstal training at the beginning of the 20th century were fundamentally sound. Borstal institutions were intended to provide training for offenders who were in their late teens and early 20s.[156] The Irish Borstal, originally located in Clonmel, became St Patrick's Institution in Dublin in 1960,

---

above under 'Children's Diminished Culpability'.

153 For reviews of the modern scientific literature on young adult development, see Elizabeth E Scott, Richard J Bonnie and Laurence Steinberg, "Young adulthood as a transitional legal category: Science, social change, and justice policy" (2016) 85 Fordham LR 641; Kelsey B Shust , "Extending sentencing mitigation for deserving young adults" (2014) 104 *Journal of Criminal Law and Criminology* 667; Aliza Hochman Bloom, "Reviving rehabilitation as a decarceral tool" (2024) 101 Washington Univ LR 1989.

154 [2024] IECA 115.

155 [2024] IECA 115, para. 21.

156 Roger Hood, *Borstal Re-assessed* (Heinemann, 1965); Nial Osborough, *Borstal in Ireland: Custodial Provision for the Young Adult Offender 1906-1974* (Institute

but that has recently been closed. Unfortunately, the reality of life in these young offender institutions seldom reflected the goals they were intended to achieve. St Patrick's Institution, for example, was part of the Mountjoy Prison complex. Rehabilitation and social reintegration should predominate among sentencing goals for young adult offenders as well as for children. Where a custodial penalty is deemed necessary, it should be served in an institution that is dedicated to advancing these goals, and the typical adult prison is seldom suitable for this purpose. Not all young adult offenders might be suitable for detention in a special facility of this nature, but those who are assessed as having a realistic prospect of rehabilitation should be spared ordinary adult imprisonment if they have to be incarcerated at all.

12. Mental Disorder

The term 'mental disorder' is used here, as in modern mental health legislation, to encompass both mental illness and significant intellectual disability.[157] An accused person may, at the time of committing the alleged offence, have been suffering from such a degree of mental disorder as to qualify for the insanity defence. However, the disorder must have been such that the person did not know the nature or quality of the act, did not know that what he or she was doing was wrong, or was unable to refrain from committing the act.[158] This defence, if successful, leads to an acquittal although the person may be subject to some period of therapeutic detention. If, in the course of criminal proceedings, an accused person is deemed unfit to be tried, meaning that, by reason of mental disorder, he or she is unable to understand the nature or course of the proceedings, the court must adjourn the proceedings until further order.[159] Our concern here, however, is with those persons who have properly been convicted of criminal offences but who are suffering from some degree of diminished mental capacity.[160] Such a condition is widely accepted as a mitigating factor, and largely for the reasons identified by the United States Supreme Court in *Atkins v Virginia*[161] where it said: **9–81**

> "[Intellectually disabled] persons frequently know the difference between

---

of Public Administration, 1975); Conor Reidy, *Ireland's "Moral Hospital": The Irish Borstal System 1906-1956* (Irish Academic Press, 2009).

[157] Mental Health Act 2001, s 3.

[158] Criminal Law (Insanity) Act 2006, s 5.

[159] Criminal Law (Insanity) Act 2006, s 4 as amended by Criminal Law (Insanity) Act 2010, s 4. See also Ronnie Mackay and Warren Brookbanks (eds), *Fitness to Plead: International and Comparative Perspectives* (Oxford University Press, 2018).

[160] The English Sentencing Council Definitive Guideline on Sentencing Offenders with Mental Disorders, Developmental Disorders, or Neurobiological Impairments has a useful plain-language description of the main classes of mental disorders and presenting features.

[161] 536 US 304, 318 (2002). The court refers throughout to 'mental retardation' whereas we would now refer to 'intellectual disability'.

> right and wrong and are competent to stand trial. Because of their impairments, however, by definition they have diminished capacity to understand and process information, to communicate, to abstract from mistakes and learn from experience, to engage in logical reasoning, to control impulses, and to understand the reactions of others. There is no evidence that they are more likely to engage in criminal conduct than others, but there is abundant evidence that they often act on impulse rather than pursuant to a premeditated plan, and that in group settings they are followers rather than leaders. Their deficiencies do not warrant an exemption from criminal sanctions, but they do diminish their personal culpability."

9–82 If the diminished capacity existed at the time of the offence, it may reduce culpability and fall to be considered under the first limb of the proportionality principle (as described in Chap 5). Otherwise, it will count among the personal circumstances of the offender under the second limb of that principle. When dealing with the first of these situations, it is important to recall that we are dealing with diminished culpability rather than absence of culpability. The offender is still to some extent blameworthy for the criminal conduct, and the challenge at sentencing is to determine the degree, if any, to which the disability has reduced culpability. Quite commonly, the disorder will have been present both when the offence was committed and at the time of sentencing. In that event, the disorder may reduce culpability and, additionally, become a relevant personal circumstance under the second limb of the proportionality principle. At the latter stage, it is relevant if it is likely to make the experience of imprisonment more difficult for the offender.[162] Research has shown that while imprisonment can be traumatic for most inmates, it is even more so for persons with a mental disability.[163]

9–83 Some have argued that diminished mental capacity should be categorically treated as a mitigating factor in the same way as youth.[164] The alternative approach might be described as one of causality and calibration, the question being whether the offending was connected with the diminished capacity and, if so, to what extent. The latter seems to be the more favoured approach. Courts in most common law jurisdictions insist that, before an offender's mental disorder can be treated as mitigating, there must be some causal link between the disorder and the offence.[165] Canada happens to have a rich jurisprudence in this area, and most of it would

---

162 This seems to have been the case in *People (DPP) v Donnelly* [2020] IECA 16 where the Court of Appeal said that the trial judge was entitled to treat the appellant's mental health problems as a mitigating factor when assessing moral culpability. Later in the judgment, the court noted that those same problems would make imprisonment more onerous for the appellant.

163 Mika'il DeVaux, "The trauma of the incarceration experience" (2013) 48 Harvard Civil Rights-Civil Liberties LR 257 ; Katie Kronick, "Intellectual disability, mitigation and punishment" (2024) 65 Boston College LR 1561.

164 Kronick, note 163 above makes a strong argument to this effect.

165 *R v McSweeney* [2023] EWCA Crim 1250; [2024] 1 Cr App R (S) 39, para 58 ("there must be a sufficient connection between the offender's impairment or disorder and the offending behaviour").

probably find favour in Ireland as well. In *R v Ellis*[166] the Ontario Court of Appeal confirmed both the necessity for a causal connection and the importance of determining the extent to which the illness contributed to the offending conduct. In that case a member of a refugee claims tribunal was convicted of a breach of trust in public offence by suggesting to a South Korean woman who was seeking refugee status that he would treat her application favourably if she was willing to engage in intimate relations with him. Medical evidence showed that he had bipolar disorder, a factor which the trial judge took into account in sentencing him to 18 months' imprisonment. The sentence was upheld by the Court of Appeal which said that the central issue was whether the appellant's culpability was sufficiently attenuated by his mental illness to tilt the balance in favour of rehabilitation as opposed to denunciation and deterrence. Having regard to the particular facts, including the absence of evidence that the appellant had acted impulsively, the court held that the sentence of immediate imprisonment, although shorter than might have been appropriate in the absence of the illness, was justified. The English Court of Appeal has interpreted the relevant Sentencing Council Guideline as mandating a similar approach, saying:

> "As to sentencing mentally disordered defendants, the Sentencing Council guideline establishes that the fact that a defendant has an impairment or disorder should always be considered by the court, but will not necessarily have an impact on sentencing. In assessing whether the impairment has any impact, the approach should be individualistic and focused on the issues in the case. Culpability will only be reduced if there is sufficient connection between the defendant's impairment or disorder and the offending behaviour. A careful analysis of all the circumstances of the case and all relevant materials is required. The court may wish to focus on the following question as a useful starting point: did the defendant's disorder impair their ability to exercise appropriate judgment, to make rational choices or to understand the nature and consequences of their actions?"[167]

In *R v WHD*[168] the same court said that "the critical question" in that case was whether the appellant's culpability for the sex offences of which he was convicted was reduced by the post-traumatic stress disorder which he experienced and which seemed to be connected with his army service. **9–84**

---

[166] (2013) 312 OAC 328; 303 CCC(3d) 228.

[167] *R v Johnstone* [2021] EWCA Crim 1683; [2022] 2 Cr App R (S) 7, para 33, referring to the Definitive Guideline on Sentencing Offenders with Mental Disorders, Developmental Disorders, or Neurobiological Impairments (2020) which includes the following provisions: "(11) Culpability will only be reduced if there is sufficient connection between the offender's impairment or disorder and the offending behaviour. (12) In some cases, the impairment or disorder may mean that culpability is significantly reduced. In other cases, the impairment or disorder may have no relevance to culpability. A careful analysis of all the circumstances of the case and all relevant materials is therefore required." See also *R v McSweeney* [2023] EWCA Crim 1250, [2024] 1 Cr App R (S) 39, para 58 (on the need for a causal connection between the impairment and disorder and the offending conduct).

[168] [2024] EWCA Crim 99, para 38.

The court was satisfied on the facts that his culpability was not reduced for this reason. By contrast, in *R v Calocane*[169] the defendant, on pleading guilty to three counts of manslaughter and three of attempted murder, was made subject to a hospital restriction order, without any term of imprisonment. This disposition was upheld by the Court of Appeal on the basis that the defendant's level of retained responsibility was low and that the offending would not have occurred but for his schizophrenia.

9–85 Canadian courts have nonetheless advocated flexibility when it comes to identifying a causal link where the offender suffers from a serious and chronic condition such as schizophrenia. In *R v Ayorech*[170] the Alberta Court of Appeal held that conditions of this nature can significantly mitigate sentence, even in the absence of a causal connection or of evidence that the offence was committed during a period of delusion, hallucinations or something similar. As the same court said more recently, such a person is less blameworthy than "someone operating with an unimpaired view of the world". Rarely, said the court, in cases of this kind do the offence and the mental illness stand entirely apart.[171]

9–86 The impact of mental disorder on criminal liability was also the subject of some leading judgments by the Victoria Court of Appeal. In *R v Tsiaris*[172] the court said:

> "Serious psychiatric illness not amounting to insanity is relevant to sentencing in at least five ways. First, it may reduce the moral culpability of the offence, as distinct from the prisoner's legal culpability. Where that is so, it affects the punishment that is just in all the circumstances and denunciation of the type of conduct in which the offender engaged is less likely to be a relevant sentencing objective. Second, the prisoner's illness may have a bearing on the kind of sentence that is imposed and the conditions in which it should be served. Third, a prisoner suffering from a serious psychiatric illness is not an appropriate vehicle for general deterrence, whether or not the illness played a part in the commission of the offence. The illness may have supervened since that time. Fourth, specific deterrence may be more difficult to achieve and is often not worth pursuing as such. Finally, psychiatric illness may mean that a given sentence will weigh more heavily on a prisoner than it would on a person in normal health."

9–87 The first consideration mentioned by the court relates to the offender's culpability when committing the offence, and it would therefore become relevant under the first limb of the proportionality principle in Ireland. The remaining considerations are more relevant to circumstances existing at the time of sentence and, as the court rightly observes, the mental illness may have developed during the interval between offence and sentence. The court was also surely right to say that individual or specific deterrence has little relevance where the offender is suffering from a

---

169 [2024] EWCA Crim 490; [2024] Crim LR 667
170 2012 ABCA 82, para 10.
171 *R v Shevchenko* [2018] ABCA 31, para 28.
172 [1996] 1 VR 398 at 400.

mental disorder that diminishes the capacity for rational thinking and evaluation, a capacity that is generally presumed by deterrent theories of punishment. General deterrence is also customarily said, as in *Tsiaris* and *Verdins* (to be considered presently), to have little or no relevance when sentencing mentally disordered offenders. The Alberta Court of Appeal has likewise said: "Little would be achieved by making an example of an offender whose acts are committed at the time of mental illness, and specific deterrence has little impact on the mentally ill".[173] This, however, requires some elaboration. General deterrence is about dissuading others from engaging in the kind of conduct for which the offender is being sentenced. A severe sentence imposed on a mentally disordered offender might have such a dissuasive impact on persons of full mental capacity – always bearing in mind that severe sentences do not deter to anything like the same extent as is commonly assumed.[174] However, it is suggested that general deterrence should not be a factor in sentencing a mentally disordered offender simply because it would be unfair, even unethical, to make an example of a person who has to cope with a mental illness or disability. As discussed in Chap 3, deterrent sentences are morally dubious in any case because they treat an offender instrumentally, at least when they result in more severe punishment than the offender deserves for the offence of conviction. The injustice would surely be compounded if the offender were mentally ill or had an intellectual disability.

The Victoria Court of Appeal revisited the question of sentencing offences with 'impaired mental functioning' in *R v Verdins*.[175] There it held that mental illness or disability could be relevant to sentence in six different ways which are largely similar to those indicated in *Tsiaris*, save for the addition of one further consideration, namely, that where there is a serious risk that imprisonment will have a significant adverse impact on the offender's mental health, this will be a factor tending to mitigate punishment. It also added that denunciation is unlikely to be a relevant sentencing factor. This seems logical given the offender's diminished moral blameworthiness. **9–88**

It is clearly established in Irish law that mental illness or disability is a factor that may diminish culpability.[176] The leading authority on the matter is now *People (DPP) v R (M)*[177] where the Court of Appeal analysed the impact of mental disorder on criminal responsibility in greater detail than had been done in any previous judgment. Having considered various authorities including the two Australian judgments described above, the court recommended a general approach to be adopted when sentencing **9–89**

173 *R v Resler* [2011] ABCA 167. See also *R v Tremblay* [2006] ABCA 252;
174 Chap 3 above.
175 [2007] VSCA 102.
176 *People (DPP) v R (M)* [2022] IECA 192; *People (DPP) v Redmond* [2006] 3 IR 188; [2006] 2 ILRM 182; *People (DPP) v C* [2013] IECCA 91; *People (DPP) v Kilmartin* [2015] IECA 54; *People (DPP) v Donnelly* [2020] IECA 16.
177 [2022] IECA 192.

"a significantly cognitively impaired or mentally ill offender".[178] A court should first determine the headline sentence that would be appropriate were it not for the presence of the mental condition in question. The Court of Appeal made a point of saying that at this stage, as in all cases, a provisional decision should be made as to whether the custody threshold has been passed, bearing in mind the parsimony principle and the various purposes of punishment. At the second stage, the sentencing judge should "take account of the offender's cognitive issue or mental health disorder, and consider to what extent, in light of that factor, there may need to be an adjustment to his/her culpability as provisionally assessed [at the first stage] in order to arrive at the headline sentence" in the particular case.[179] A court should have all relevant information, including an expert evidence, available to it for this purpose. If, at this stage,

> "[a] court determines that by virtue of the mental impairment or disorder at issue the offender's culpability is diminished (or, in what we think is likely to be a rare case, perhaps even eliminated), then the court's provisional assessment as to what would have been the appropriate headline sentence, will require adjustment based on the now re-assessed gravity of the offending conduct, following the taking into account of the influence on the offender's culpability of that mental impairment or disorder."[180]

9–90 This may bring the case below the custody threshold or, alternatively, justify a shorter prison term that would otherwise be deserved. There is also an important third stage because, as in all cases, consideration must be given to any other mitigating factors relating to the offender's personal circumstances. The offender's mental condition may also be relevant at this point if it is likely to make the experience of custody more onerous or if custody might even worsen that condition. The sentence ultimately selected must reflect all these factors.

9–91 Mentally disordered offenders can nonetheless pose a serious dilemma for sentencing courts. The disorder typically reduces the offender's blameworthiness, but it may also strongly indicate that he or she, if left at liberty, will pose a danger to the community. To complicate matters further, there may be evidence that incarceration, in a prison at any rate, would be harmful to the offender. As already noted, courts have little difficulty in accepting that mental disorder ordinarily reduces culpability. There is further international consensus, as already noted, that

---

[178] [2022] IECA 192, para 84 onwards. For this purpose, the Court derived considerable assistance from the English Sentencing Council's guideline, *Sentencing Offenders with mental disorders, developmental disorders, or neurobiological impairments* (2020), and also from Ailbhe O'Loughlin, Jay Gormley, Lucy Willmott, Jonathan Bild, Julian Roberts and Anne Draper, *Mental Health and Sentencing: Literature Review*, Report prepared by the Sentencing Academy for the Scottish Sentencing Council (2022). See also Ailbhe O'Loughlin, *Mental Disorder, Disability and Sentencing: A Review of Policy, Law and Research* (Sentencing Academy, 2022).

[179] [2022] IECA 192, para 97.

[180] [2022] IECA 192, para 97.

deterrence, whether general or specific, has little relevance in such cases. But there remains the morally difficult question of whether a mentally disordered offender who is assessed as being at risk of re-offending, and perhaps in a serious way, should be subject to some form of prolonged or indefinite detention in the interests of social protection. The arguments for and against preventive detention and selective incapacitation based on predictions of dangerousness were considered in Chap 3, and many of them also apply here. In the case of mentally disordered offenders, predictions of re-offending may sometimes be more confidently made because of the nature of the disorder, the individual offender's track record or both. But here too the same tension arises between the offender's right to a just and proportionate sentence and the undoubted public interest in protecting society from the harm or injury which the offender, once released from custody, may inflict on its members. Where the disorder is accepted as reducing culpability, it seems even more unjust, from the offender's perspective at least, to treat the disorder as a justification for prolonged or, perhaps, any detention. Ultimately, however, a mentally disordered offender is as entitled as any other to a proportionate sentence, as the Constitution requires. The disorder is a factor to be considered in determining a proportionate sentence, as the case law confirms. Any custodial sentence, whatever its underlying rationale, has an incapacitative effect. A court may take account of a mentally disordered offender's likelihood of re-offending, but only within the parameters of a proportionate sentence. It is a factor that may influence the location of the offence within the applicable range, but no more than that. There can be no question of preventive detention being the primary purpose of the sentence[181] Social protection remains an important consideration, but it is probably best achieved through the invocation of civil commitment procedures where necessary. A person who, on the completion of his or her deserved term of imprisonment, is deemed to pose a danger to others may be committed to a psychiatric facility under the terms of the Mental Health Act 2001.[182] This too will entail deprivation of liberty but it will be for treatment rather than punishment.

Mental illness may also become an issue during detention, whether before or after conviction. There is now a substantial body of case law under art 3 of the ECHR to the effect that conditions of detention may amount to inhuman or degrading treatment or punishment if they fail to accommodate the essential needs of a detainee who is suffering from an illness, disability or infirmity. To amount to a violation of art 3, ill-treatment will usually involve physical injury or suffering, but it may also consist of treatment that "humiliates or debases an individual, showing a lack of respect for or diminishing his or her human dignity, or arouses feelings of fear, anguish or inferiority capable of breaking an individual's psychological or physical resistance".[183] Imprisonment **9–92**

[181] *People (DPP) v R (M)* [2022] IECA 192, para 97.

[182] *People (DPP) v McMahon* [2011] IECCA 94; [2011] 3 IR 774.

[183] *Butrin v Russia* App no 16179/14 (European Court of Human Rights, 22 March 2016), para 47.

following conviction is presumed to be a legitimate restriction on the right to personal liberty conferred by art 5 but it may violate art 3 if it undermines a detainee's dignity and entails "particularly acute hardship that [causes] suffering beyond that inevitably associated with a prison sentence and treatment for cancer" (which was the issue in that case).[184] This consideration is highly relevant where a detainee is suffering from a serious physical illness, but it applies equally to mental illness, as recognised by the Grand Chamber of the European Court of Human Rights in *Rooman v Belgium* where it said:

> "[D]etainees with mental disorders are more vulnerable than ordinary detainees, and certain requirements of prison life pose a greater risk that their health will suffer, exacerbating the risk that they suffer from a feeling of inferiority, and are necessarily a source of stress and anxiety. [The Court] considers that such a situation calls for increased vigilance in reviewing if the Convention has been complied with (....). In addition to their vulnerability, the assessment of the situation of these particular individuals has to take into consideration, in certain cases, the vulnerability of such persons and, in some cases, their inability to complain coherently or at all about how they are being affected by any particular treatment. (...)"[185]

9–93 As the court also said in that case, among others, it is insufficient for such detainees to be medically examined and a diagnosis made. Proper treatment for the problem diagnosed must also be provided. Article 3 does not impose any general obligation to release a detainee on health grounds, but it requires that he or she be held in appropriate conditions and given any necessary treatment.[186]

---

[184] *Mouisel v France* (2004) 38 EHRR 34, para 48. See also *A v UK* (2009) 49 EHRR 29, para 127. For an excellent analysis of all the relevant case law, see Natasa Mavronicola, *Torture, Inhumanity and Degradation under Article 3 of the ECHR: Absolute Rights and Absolute Wrongs* (Hart Publishing, 2021), in particular pp 113-126.

[185] App no 18052/11 (ECHR, 31 January 2019), para 145. Internal references omitted.

[186] *Butrin v Russia* App no 16179/14 (ECHR, 22 March 2016), para 48,

Chapter 10

SENTENCING PARTICULAR OFFENCES

The general principles described in Chap 5 apply to all offences carrying discretionary penalties. This chapter deals with the sentencing of some commonly prosecuted serious offences, with particular emphasis on those for which formal or informal guidelines have been issued by the superior courts. **10–01**

1. Homicide

Murder

Murder, which consists of causing the death of another person while intending to kill or cause serious injury, carries a mandatory sentence of life imprisonment. Until the entry into force of the Criminal Justice Act 1964 (the '1964 Act'), all murders carried the death penalty although, as discussed further in Chap 14, it was frequently commuted to some term of imprisonment. The 1964 Act abolished the death penalty for most murders but retained it for some, including the murder of a member of the Gardaí or a prison officer acting in the course of their duty. The Criminal Justice Act 1990 (the '1990 Act') abolished the death penalty completely, but it made special sentencing provisions for most of the murders that had remained capital under the 1964 Act.[1] As the law now stands under the 1990 Act, every murder committed by an adult carries a mandatory life sentence, but when sentencing an adult for the murder of a garda or a prison officer and for certain other murders, a court must specify at least 40 years' imprisonment as the minimum term to be served. For attempted murder falling into this category, a minimum of 20 years must be specified. The constitutionality of the mandatory life sentence for murder was upheld by the Supreme Court in *Lynch and Whelan v Minister for Justice.*[2] A person serving a life sentence, including one for murder, is eligible for parole once he or she has served at least 12 years of that sentence.[3] Where parole is refused on a first or subsequent application, the Parole Board must **10–02**

[1] In 2001, the Constitution was amended to prohibit the death penalty. Art 15.5.2o now reads: "The Oireachtas shall not enact any law providing for the imposition of the death penalty". The amendment was supported by 62 per cent of those who voted.

[2] [2010] IESC 34; [2012] 1 1R 1.

[3] Parole Act 2019, s 24. On parole generally, see Chap 14 below.

inform the applicant of the reasons for the refusal and specify a date, not later than two years from the date of the decision, when the applicant will again be eligible to apply.[4] On 30 November 2022, there were 367 prisoners (approximately 11 per cent of the sentenced prisoner population) serving life sentences.[5] It may be assumed that almost all of these were convicted of murder. (Life sentences are also occasionally, though rarely, imposed for manslaughter and serious sexual offences). The average time spent in custody by life sentence prisoners before release has trebled over the past 50 years. From 1975 to 1984, it was seven and a half years. It then increased significantly over the following decades, so that since 2019 it has been 21.25 years. In 2023, eight life sentence prisoners were released, and they had served an average of 24 years in custody.[6]

10–03 The mandatory life sentence for murder is not readily defensible.[7] Murder is self-evidently a crime of the utmost gravity. Short of genocide, it is the most serious offence known to our law. Yet, not all murders are equally serious in terms of culpability. Intention to cause serious injury, which suffices for a murder conviction, is less blameworthy than intention to kill. The offender's motive is also irrelevant under the present law. A so-called mercy killing amounts to murder just as much as a well-planned assassination, but a court has no discretion as to penalty. Life imprisonment is the automatic consequence of a murder conviction, whatever the circumstances of the killing. In any murder case there may be mitigating factors such as provocation or mental disorder although not present to such a degree as would warrant an acquittal or a manslaughter verdict.[8] A guilty plea may have great utilitarian value in a murder case, as in any other, but yet it cannot be acknowledged at sentencing, whatever about at later parole proceedings.[9] Furthermore, the offender may also have provided valuable information or assistance to the law enforcement

---

4 Parole Act 2019, s 30.

5 <https://www.irishprisons.ie/information-centre/statistics-information/snapshot-statistics/> accessed 31 August 2024.

6 These figures are drawn from a press release dated 6 August 2024 and entitled "Taoiseach and Minister McEntee announce cabinet approval for Bill allowing judges recommend minimum prison terms for life sentences" (available at www.gov.ie).

7 There have been many recommendations for the abolition of the mandatory life sentence in England and elsewhere in the United Kingdom. See, for example, Advisory Council on the Penal System, *Sentences of Imprisonment: A Review of Maximum Sentences* (HMSO, 1978); House of Lords, *Report of the Select Committee on Murder and Life Imprisonment* (HMSO, 1989); Howard League for Penal Reform, *Murder and Life Imprisonment* (submission to House of Lords Select Committee) (London, 1989); JC Smith, "The penalty for murder" (1988) 19 Cambrian LR 5. In the England and Wales, the mandatory life sentence remains but a court, when sentencing for murder, must make a whole life order or else specify a minimum term to be served before qualifying for early release (Sentencing Act 2020, ss 275, 321, 322 and Sch 21).

8 See mitigating factors listed in (English) Sentencing Act 2020, Sch 21.

9 *R v Last* [2005] EWCA Crim 106; [2005] 2 Cr App R(S) 64 (on the impact of a guilty plea on the determination of the minimum term to be served for murder under English law).

authorities, another factor that could be taken into account if a court had discretion in determining the sentence or recommending the minimum term to be served.[10] At the other end of the spectrum multiple murders are, in effect, punished the same as a single murder. A life sentence will be imposed for each but several life sentences must be ordered to run concurrently. It would be pointless to make them consecutive because each sentence, in theory at least, lasts for the rest of the offender's life. Prisoners serving multiple life sentences may not be granted parole or temporary release as early as others, but that is a matter of executive discretion. A court cannot predetermine how long such a person will actually remain in prison. A life sentence may be ordered to begin on the expiry of a determinate sentence, but not vice versa.[11]

Various reform options have been canvassed over the years, but there is currently no political appetite for interfering with the mandatory life sentence. One possibility would be to make murder punishable with a maximum rather than a mandatory sentence of life imprisonment, thereby allowing courts to tailor sentences to the circumstances of individual cases. As a variation on this model, there could be a presumption of life imprisonment, while allowing for a lower penalty in an exceptional case. Another alternative would be to retain the mandatory life sentence, while permitting or requiring the court to specify a minimum term to be served before the offender became eligible for parole. This is essentially the arrangement in England and Wales save that a court, unless it makes a whole life order, must apply certain starting points (eg 30 years or 15 years) specified by legislation, depending on the circumstances of the offence.[12] In Zealand, murder is punishable with a life sentence unless, given the circumstances of the offender and the offender, it would be manifestly unjust. Where a life sentence is imposed, a court must order a minimum term, not less than 10 years, to be served. The governing legislation sets out certain circumstances in which a minimum of 17 years must be specified unless it would be manifestly unjust to do so.[13] In August 2024 the Irish Government published the heads of the Life Sentences Bill 2024. This proposes that a court, when imposing a life sentence for murder, shall specify a recommended minimum custodial term which must be not less than 12 years (the current minimum to be served by a life sentence prisoner before being eligible for parole). This is intended to reflect the court's view of the minimum term that should be served before parole is granted, and it is a factor to which the Parole Board will be required to have regard **10–04**

[10] *R v Hood* [2012] EWCA Crim 1260; [2013] 1 Cr App R (S) 49 where this factor led to a reduction in the minimum term which, in turn, had been influenced by the presence of certain aggravating factors.

[11] *People (DPP) v Whelan* [2003] 4 IR 355.

[12] Sentencing Act 2020, Sch 21 (originally introduced by the Criminal Justice Act 2003). For an excellent analysis of this legislation and its application, see Richard Martin, *Sentencing for Murder: A Review of Policy and Practice* (Sentencing Academy, 2024). It is also described in some detail in *R v Barrow* [2024] EWCA Crim 509; [2024] 2 Cr App R(S) 31; [2024] Crim LR 824.

[13] Sentencing Act 2002, ss 102-104. See *R v Frost* [2023] NZCA 294 which has a useful discussion on the topic.

when deciding on an application from a prisoner in respect of whom such a recommendation has been made. It will not affect existing constitutional or statutory powers to grant commutation, special remission, parole or temporary release. Recommended minimum sentences will be subject to appeal and review. The key word in the proposed legislation appears to be 'recommended'. The court will not be specifying the minimum custodial term that *must* be served, but rather the term that, in its estimation, having regard to the nature and circumstances of the offence, *should* be served prior to release on parole. Mitigating factors, including a guilty plea, will presumably influence such recommendations, but so too will aggravating factors. This arrangement broadly reflects the Law Reform Commission's recommendation in 2013 that the mandatory life sentence for murder should be retained but that the sentencing judge or court should be able to recommend a minimum custodial term to be served.[14]

Attempted Murder

10–05 Attempted murder is punishable with a maximum sentence of life imprisonment. The penalty is therefore discretionary, unless the case is one of those mentioned earlier where a minimum of 20 years' imprisonment must be imposed. The sole *mens rea* of attempted murder is intention to kill; intention to cause serious injury or recklessness as to the result will not suffice.[15] The harm caused by attempted murder can vary considerably, unlike murder and manslaughter where the harm (death) is always the same. At one end of the spectrum the intended victim might suffer no harm, of a physical nature at least, if, say, the offender discharged a firearm directly at the victim, but by sheer fluke, happened to miss. More commonly, however, the victim will have suffered significant physical injuries, the nature, extent and consequences of which will be key factors in determining sentence. Harm and culpability are often closely linked in this context. The greater the injuries inflicted, the more suffering the offender probably intended to visit upon the victim, even if the ultimate objective of killing the victim was not realised. Other factors pointing to increased culpability include premeditation and planning,[16] the victim being particularly vulnerable because of age, medical condition, disability or some other factor, or the victim having been targeted because of a personal characteristic such as race, ethnic origin or sexual orientation. Obviously, any mitigating factors personal to the offender must also be placed in the balance.

10–06 Heavy custodial sentences, up to and including life imprisonment, have been imposed and upheld for attempted murder where serious injuries were inflicted on the victim.[17] Sentences of 15 years' imprisonment were

---

14 Law Reform Commission, *Mandatory Sentences* (2013).

15 *People (DPP) v Benko* [2021] IECA 143.

16 *R v Valle-Quintero* (2002) 169 CCC(3d) 140 (Ontario Court of Appeal).

17 In *People (DPP) v Daniels* [2014] IESC 64; [2014] 2 IR 813; [2015] 1 ILRM 99, the Supreme Court upheld a life sentence for the attempted murder of a child. The Court of Criminal Appeal upheld a life sentence in *People (DPP) v Duffy* [2009]

upheld or substituted in *People (DPP) v Larkin*,[18] *People (DPP) v Whelan*,[19] *People (DPP) v Belousova*[20] and *People (DPP) v Benko*[21] all of which had significant aggravating factors, though in the particular circumstances of *Benko* that sentence might seem somewhat excessive. Lower sentences may, of course, be justified to reflect mitigating factors, though the fact that the offender will always have intended to kill generally reduces the scope for leniency. However, an exceptional case might arise where, for example, the offender attempted a so-called mercy killing though death did not result. This was the background to *R v Hough*[22] which was effectively a case of assisted suicide (and death did result in that case) where the English Court of Appeal upheld a nine-month prison sentence. The offender's age may also be a mitigating factor, as reflected in *People (DPP) v S (M)*[23] where the injuries inflicted on the victim can only be described as horrific. Had the offender been an adult, the headline sentence would probably have been life imprisonment, as the trial judge indicated. However, because the offender was only 15 years at the time of the offence, he was sentenced as a child, and he also had some mental health issues. A sentence of 11 years' detention was imposed, though with a review date which the Court of Appeal subsequently extended somewhat.

Conspiracy to Commit Murder

Conspiracy to commit murder and soliciting another to commit murder are offences contrary to s 4 of the Offences Against the Person Act 1861. Each offence created by that section used to carry a maximum sentence of 10 years' imprisonment, but this was increased to a maximum of life imprisonment by s 3 of the Criminal Justice (Miscellaneous Provisions) Act 2023 which entered into force on 1 November 2023. **10–07**

Manslaughter

Manslaughter carries a maximum sentence of life imprisonment, and it may also be punished with a fine.[24] As courts have repeatedly acknowledged, manslaughter can vary enormously in gravity. In some instances, it may be close to murder while in others it may be bordering on accident. The harm is invariably the same: one or more people will have lost their lives as a result of the defendant's action. Culpability, however, can vary considerably and this is the key factor when identifying an appropriate headline sentence. Manslaughter is conventionally divided into two broad categories: voluntary manslaughter which is committed by a person who **10–08**

IECCA 20; [2009] 2 IR 395, largely because of the offender's previous record which included a conviction for murder.

[18] [2008] IECCA 138; [2009] 2 IR 381.

[19] [2003] 4 IR 355.

[20] [2009] IECCA 49.

[21] [2021] IECA 143.

[22] (1984) 6 Cr App R (S) 406.

[23] [2020] IECA 178.

[24] Offences Against the Person Act 1861, s 5.

had the *mens rea* for murder but who can rely on a partial defence such as provocation; and involuntary manslaughter where one person wrongfully causes the death of another, though without intending to kill or cause serious injuries. Most manslaughter offences fall into the latter category and result from an assault or the commission of some other unlawful and dangerous act. Manslaughter may also be committed through gross negligence, as might occur in the course of medical treatment or through particularly dangerous driving.

10–09 Assault manslaughter is the subject of a sentencing guideline provided by the Supreme Court in *People (DPP) v Mahon.*[25] Having considered available statistical data and numerous earlier appeal court decisions, the court adopted a four-fold categorisation of assault manslaughters: (1) worst cases: (2) cases with high culpability; (3) cases with medium culpability; and (4) cases with lower culpability. It noted that cases in category (1) generally attract sentences of 15 to 20 years, with the possibility of life imprisonment, those in category (2) sentences ranging from 10 to 15 years, those in category (3) sentences ranging from four to 10 years, and those in category (4) sentences up to four years, with fully suspended sentences in exceptional cases. This part of the *Mahon* judgment is cast in descriptive rather than explicitly prescriptive terms. It concentrates on describing the earlier cases falling into the various categories. However, the court's adoption of the four-fold classification, coupled with its more general observations on the desirability of consistency, strongly suggests that this was intended as a formal guideline and it has been so treated by other courts in the meantime.

10–10 Manslaughter through gross negligence may be committed in a variety of circumstances including highly negligent or reckless driving that resulted in one or more fatalities. According to *People (Attorney General) v Dunleavy,*[26] still the leading authority on the matter, the negligence must be "of a very high degree and such as to be reckless or to amount to reckless disregard for the life and safety of others". The *Mahon* guidelines are of limited relevance for this form of manslaughter which can probably be divided into the standard low, middle and high ranges with a notional upper limit of 15 years' imprisonment, with the possibility of anything up to life imprisonment in an exceptionally serious case. The number of deaths caused is certainly a relevant factor in assessing gravity, but the conduct of the offender before, during and after the fatal collision is usually the predominant consideration. Evidence of a high degree of recklessness, especially if manifest over a prolonged period, and not just at the moment of the collision, will place the offence in the upper reaches of the scale of gravity. In one such case, which resulted in three deaths, a headline sentence of 14 years' imprisonment was identified by the trial judge who ultimately imposed concurrent sentences of 10 years with one

---

[25] [2019] IESC 24; [2019] 3 IR 151.

[26] [1948] IR 95. See also *People (DPP) v O'Shea* [2017] IESC 41; [2017] 3 IR 684; [2017] 1 ILRM 149.

year suspended. The Court of Appeal, while recognising that this was a severe sentence for someone without previous convictions, dismissed the appeal against severity.[27]

Both the English and Northern Ireland Courts of Appeal have made clear that in sentencing for motor manslaughter the relevant maximum sentence is life imprisonment, and that a court should not proceed on the basis that the effective maximum is that for dangerous driving causing death (currently 10 years' imprisonment in Ireland, though recently increased to life imprisonment in England and Wales).[28] Irish courts would doubtless agree, as some manslaughter cases can involve a very high degree of culpability in addition to having catastrophic consequences. **10–11**

Manslaughter Resulting from Diminished Responsibility

Diminished responsibility provides a partial defence to murder. Under the Criminal Law (Insanity) Act 2006 (s 6), where a person is on trial for murder and the jury (or other tribunal of fact) finds that the accused did the alleged act while suffering from a mental disorder which, while not sufficient to justify a finding of insanity, "was such as to diminish substantially" the accused's responsibility for the act, the accused may be found not guilty of murder but guilty of manslaughter.[29] The key question at sentencing will usually concern the extent to which the offender's responsibility was diminished. It will seldom be entirely extinguished – if it were, a finding of insanity might be appropriate. In *People (DPP) v Anderson*,[30] now the leading Irish authority, the Court of Appeal held that in sentencing for manslaughter resulting from diminished responsibility, a court should follow the approach set out in *People (DPP) v R(M)*[31] for sentencing persons with mental disorders. A court should begin by identifying the headline sentence that would be appropriate were it not for the presence of the mental disorder. It should then make an appropriate discount for the diminished responsibility resulting from that disorder. Finally, it should consider if there are any other mitigating factors and, if so, grant a further reduction for those. In *Anderson* itself, the offender had stabbed to death a man who parked his car without permission outside her home at a time when, according to medical evidence, she was suffering from a psychotic relapse of bipolar affective disorder. She also had a long history of mental illness. The trial judge identified a headline sentence of 20 years, reduced to 13 years because of the mental disorder, and then to 11 years to reflect other mitigating factors. Further, the last three years of the 11-year sentence were suspended with four years. The **10–12**

---

27 *People (DPP) v Lennon* [2022] IECA 97.

28 *R v Gault* (1995) 16 Cr App R(S) 1013; *R v Dudley* [2006] 2 Cr App R(S) 77; *R v Phair and Togher* [2023] NICA 18.

29 A literal reading of s 6 suggests that this verdict is permissible only following a trial for murder. However, in several cases, the prosecution has accepted a plea of guilty to manslaughter because of diminished responsibility.

30 [2024] IECA 50.

31 [2022] IECA 192, discussed in more detail in Chap 9 above.

Court of Appeal approved the approach adopted by the trial judge and dismissed the appeal against severity of sentence.

10–13 The degree of retained responsibility together with the manner and circumstances in which the killing occurred are therefore the predominant considerations. Another potentially relevant factor is the extent to which offender's own actions, such as abusing alcohol or drugs or voluntarily failing to seek or follow medical advice, contributed to the mental disorder as it existed at the time of the offence.[32] In some instances, responsibility may be so diminished as to bring the offence within the lower sentencing ranges for manslaughter as identified in *People (DPP) v Mahon*.[33] In others, such as the English case of *R v Wood*,[34] responsibility may be "just, but only just sufficiently diminished". In *Wood*, the Court of Appeal upheld a life sentence with a minimum term of 13 years. Likewise, in *People (DPP) v Crowe*[35] the Court of Criminal Appeal imposed a 20-year sentence (in substitution for the life sentence imposed by the trial court) for manslaughter resulting from diminished responsibility to which the appellant had pleaded guilty. The offence was particularly serious, the appellant having attempted to murder another person on the same occasion, and it was difficult to see how his responsibility was diminished to any significant extent. At the other end of the spectrum, in *R v Calocane*,[36] a very tragic case in which the defendant stabbed three people to death and attempted to murder three others, a hospital with restrictions order (as described below) was upheld by the English Court of Appeal. In that case, it was accepted that the offences were entirely due to the paranoid schizophrenia from which the defendant was suffering. An offender who has a mental disorder at the time of sentencing may, for that reason, find imprisonment more difficult than others, and this is a factor a court may take into account.[37] Two guidelines issued by the English Sentencing Council, one on manslaughter by reason of diminished responsibility and the other on sentencing mentally disordered offenders, are valuable for indicating factors affecting culpability and as well as other aggravating and mitigating factors.[38]

10–14 Irish courts do not have the option of making a direct hospital order by way of sentence where a person is convicted of an offence (as opposed to being acquitted on the ground of insanity). In England and Wales, a hospital order may be imposed on a person convicted of an imprisonable offence (other than murder) where there is medical evidence that the

---

32 See English Sentencing Council Guideline, *Manslaughter by Reason of Diminished Responsibility* (2018).
33 [2019] IESC 24; [2019] 3 IR 151.
34 [2009] EWCA Crim 651; [2010] 1 Cr App R(S) 2
35 [2009] IECCA 57; [2010] 1 IR 129; [2009] 2 ILRM 225.
36 [2024] EWCA Crim 490; [2024] Crim LR 667.
37 *People (DPP) v Anderson* [2024] IECA 50, para 76.
38 Sentencing Council, *Manslaughter by Reason of Diminished Responsibility* (2018) and *Sentencing Offenders with Mental Disorders, Developmental Disorders, or Neurological Impairments* (2020).

offender is suffering from a mental disorder of a nature or degree which makes it appropriate that he or she should be detained in a hospital for mental treatment and that appropriate treatment is available.[39] Where a hospital order is imposed with restrictions, the offender may not be discharged or granted temporary release without the consent of the relevant Secretary of State. A court may also make a hybrid order which consists of a hospital order followed by a term of imprisonment.[40] In Ireland, a prisoner may be transferred to the Central Mental Hospital if assessed as needing in-patient treatment.[41] The hospital orders available in England have the advantage of permitting an offender to be held in a therapeutic setting until such time as he or she can safely be released.

2. Assault Offences

The Non-Fatal Offences Against the Person Act 1997, as amended (the '1997 Act'), effectively codifies the substantive law on assault and related offences. Most prosecutions under the 1997 Act are for assault (s 2), assault causing harm (s 3) and causing serious harm (s 4). Assault contrary to s 2 is a summary offence punishable with a maximum of six months' imprisonment, a £1,500 fine or both. Assault causing harm has carried a maximum sentence of 10 years' imprisonment since s 20 of the Criminal Justice (Miscellaneous Provisions) Act 2023 entered into force on 1 November 2023. Prior to that it was five years' imprisonment. The maximum sentence following summary conviction is 12 months' imprisonment, a £1,500 fine or both. Causing serious harm is punishable with a maximum of life imprisonment and is subject to a guideline issued by the Court of Criminal Appeal in *People (DPP) v Fitzgibbon*.[42] There, the court held that in the absence of any unusual factor (such as a significant mismatch between the harm intended and the harm caused by the perpetrator), a sentence between two to four years was appropriate for offences in the lowest range, a sentence between four and seven and a half years for offences in the middle range, and a sentence between seven and a half and 12 and a half years for offences in the highest range, with the qualification that, in exceptionally serious cases, a sentence in excess of 12 and a half years and up to life imprisonment might be appropriate. *Fitzgibbon* must now be read in conjunction with 10–15

---

[39] Mental Health Act 1983, s 37.

[40] These orders are clearly described and explained in *R v Calocane* [2024] EWCA Crim 490. For a more detailed account, see Lyndon Harris and Sebastian Walker, *Sentencing Principles, Procedure and Practice 2021* (Thomson Reuters, 2021), 1014-1025.

[41] Art O'Connor and Helen O'Neill, "Male prison transfers to the Central Mental Hospital, a special hospital (1983-1988)" (1990) 7 *Irish Journal of Psychological Medicine* 118 (reporting on 627 transfers during that era); Brian Hutton, "Mentally ill prisoners waiting up to two years for Central Mental Hospital transfer", *Irish Times*, 9 September 2019 (indicating that 16 male and three female prisoners were transferred to the Central Mental Hospital in 2018.

[42] [2014] IECCA 12; [2014] 2 ILRM 116.

People (DPP) v O'Sullivan[43]where the upper limit of the mid-range band was increased to 10 years and the upper limit of the highest range band to 15 years. The court said:

> "The experience of the courts operating under *Fitzgibbon* is that an upper limit of seven and a half years for a mid-range is too low and a figure of ten years would be more appropriate. Likewise, we are inclined to the view that a figure of twelve and a half years as a pre-mitigation for high-end offences is too low and should be increased to fifteen years with exceptional cases higher again. We stress, and it is our impression that this is not always fully appreciated, that the guidance was offered in respect of pre-mitigation sentences. In many cases there will of course be factors present by way of mitigation so that the ultimate sentence imposed will be less than the sentence identified as a headline or starting pre-mitigation sentence. In some cases, there may be very powerful mitigation present in which case the ultimate sentence imposed will, in all likelihood, diverge very considerably indeed from the starting pre-mitigation headline sentence". [44]

10–16 As foreseen in *Fitzgibbon,* cases have arisen where sentences considerably longer than 15 years were deemed appropriate. In *People (DPP) v Harte, O'Brien and Redmond*[45] the defendants were found guilty of assaulting a victim with what the Special Criminal Court described as "premeditated brutality" and "calculated savagery" executed to serve the ends of organised criminals. Harte (known as 'YZ' during the trial), who was held to have inflicted the most serious injuries, was sentenced to 30 years imprisonment. He had 180 previous convictions, including several for serious offences. O'Brien was sentenced to 25 years and Redmond to 18 years with the last three years suspended.

10–17 At the other end of the spectrum, a s 4 offence may not always merit an immediate custodial sentence or anything more than a reasonably short prison term. While the injury suffered by the victim will, by definition, have been severe, the offender's culpability may be lessened by the circumstances in which assault occurred including, in some instances, the actions of the victim or somebody associated with the victim. However, for a fully suspended sentence to be upheld there must generally be strong personal mitigation as well.[46] Factors such as youth or evidence of determination to deal with addiction (where that contributed to the offending) and the general desirability of promoting and incentivising rehabilitation where that seems a realistic possibility may tip the balance in favour of full or part suspension. As with all violent offences, society is best served by penal measures that will reduce the risk of similar re-offending.

---

43 [2019] IECA 250.

44 [2019] IECA 250, para 8. See also *People (DPP) v Dullaghan* [2024] IECA 115 (10-year headline sentence appropriate for causing serious harm and aggravated burglary).

45 Special Criminal Court, 20 December 2021.

46 *People (DPP) v Byrne* [2017] IECA 97; *People (DPP) v Smith* [2019] IECA 1. Entirely suspended sentences were upheld in both.

There is sometimes a fine dividing line between assault causing harm (s 3) and assault causing serious harm (s 4). The key distinguishing factor is the nature of the harm inflicted. 'Harm' is defined in s 1 (the general interpretation clause) as "harm to body or mind and includes pain and unconsciousness". 'Serious harm' is defined as "injury which creates a substantial risk of death or which causes serious disfigurement or substantial loss or impairment of the mobility of the body as a whole or of the function of any particular bodily member or organ". This definition is clearly meant to include injuries that were life-threatening or that resulted in a serious physical impairment, although 'serious harm' does not require proof of an injury "with protracted or long-term consequences".[47] However, it covers more than this, as reflected in the reference to serious disfigurement, a term that is not further defined. Many assaults committing with knives or broken glass leave their victims with permanent scars on the face or neck, even with medical treatment. It is certainly arguable that this amounts to serious disfigurement but the charge in many such cases is assault causing harm rather than causing serious harm. In *People (DPP) v McGrath, Dolan and Brazil*[48](a set of undue leniency applications in respect of sentences for unrelated cases of assault causing harm), the first respondent had attacked a pregnant woman in a car park, inflicting four stab wounds to her face and torso and leaving her with permanent facial scarring. An effective sentence of 18 months' imprisonment imposed by the trial judge was found to be unduly lenient and increased to four years with the last six months suspended to incentivise rehabilitation. An effective sentence of six months' imprisonment imposed on the respondent Dolan who had attacked the victim in a nightclub by smashing a glass in his face, leaving him with a permanent scar, was also found to be unduly lenient. The Court of Appeal substituted three and a half years but suspended it entirely, largely because the respondent had by then served the original term and was, by all accounts, making serious efforts to turn his life around. The respondent, Brazil, had seriously assaulted the victim with a metal bar or golf club, leaving him with a fractured cheekbone, nasal bone and skull base. The two-year prison sentence imposed by the trial judge was found to be unduly lenient and increased ultimately to three years. **10–18**

In *McGrath, Dolan and Brazil*[49] the Court of Appeal offered further guidance on sentencing assault causing harm. Noting there was often a fine dividing line between this offence and the offence of assault causing serious harm, the court held that the maximum of five years **10–19**

---

[47] *People (DPP) v Kirwan* [2005] IECCA 136 where the Court of Criminal Appeal said that "where 'substantial impairment of the mobility of the body as a whole or of the function of any particular bodily member or organ' is concerned, a jury should be told that no requirement of permanent or protracted impairment…. is required provided they are satisfied that such impairment was or is 'substantial'". It also said, however, that when dealing with disfigurement, the outcome of any medical treatment must also be considered.

[48] [2020] IECA 50.

[49] [2020] IECA 50.

would sometimes be appropriate the headline sentence for more serious manifestations of this offence. This principle will be largely irrelevant in any case of assault causing harm where the new maximum of 10 years' imprisonment applies. In those cases the sentence ranges will probably be zero to three years, three to six years and six to nine years, with the proviso that an exceptionally serious instance of the offence might merit the maximum of 10 years. This will provide more scope for selecting a sentence that properly reflects the conduct constituting the offence. In some instances, that conduct and its consequences can be very serious even if falling outside the definition of causing serious harm contrary to s 4 of the 1997 Act.

10–20 Irrespective of whether an assault falls within the definition of ss 2, 3 or 4 of the 1997 Act, an assessment must still be made of its relative seriousness for the purpose of locating it on the appropriate scale of gravity. This can be a complicated task. Opinions vary as to whether the primary concern should be the actual injury inflicted, the longer-term impact on the victim or the circumstances in which the offence was committed. When assessing culpability, relevant factors include any provocation from the victim, which will tend to reduce culpability, or the attack being entirely unprovoked or, worse still, motivated by the victim's nationality, skin colour, gender, sexual orientation or some similar characteristic, factors that will tend to increase culpability.[50] In practice, a court must weigh all of these factors to the extent that they are present, and then form a view as to overall seriousness. In one research study, Clarkson and colleagues identified the following relevant factors:

> "(i) actual physical injury; (ii) potential for more serious injury or, conversely, a recognition that the severity of the injury was in some part a matter of chance, or ill-fortune; (iii) degree of threat, taking into account the relative strengths of victim and attacker; (iv) use of a weapon; (v) emotional or psychological harm; (vi) duration of attack; and (vii) provocation by the victim."[51]

10–21 In *People (DPP) v Conway*[52] where the appellant had pleaded guilty to a s. 3 assault that caused significant injuries to the victim, the Court of Appeal said that when determining a sentence for this offence, the relevant factors included "the context of the assault, the surrounding circumstances and in particular the immediate proximate events which led to it, the severity and nature of the assault and the degree of injury suffered".[53] In that case, the assault appeared to arise from an unanticipated altercation between two strangers, with some degree of provocation, which resulted in a

---

50 The Criminal Justice (Hate Offences) Act 2024 creates new offences of assaults aggravated by hatred and, in respect of other offences, requires hatred against a person or group of persons to be treated as an aggravating factor. See paras 5–135 and 5–136 above.

51 Chris Clarkson et al, "Assaults: The relationship between seriousness, criminalisation and punishment" [1994] Crim LR 4, 7.

52 [2019] IECA 343.

53 [2019] IECA 343, para 32.

single punch being thrown. The appellant had been sentenced to three years' imprisonment with the last year suspended. The Court of Appeal varied this to two years' imprisonment with the balance suspended. However, there were exceptionally strong personal mitigating factors and the appellant had been in prison for about six months before the appeal was decided.

Assaults committed against members of the emergency services and other front-line workers are generally punished more severely than similar assaults committed against other victims. Enhanced sentences for such offences are justified on grounds of both harm and culpability. The harm element consists not only on the injury immediately inflicted but also in the danger that as a result of the assault, the injured party will be prevented from protecting the public, providing medical assistance or providing other vital services. The offender is also more culpable for having targeted such a person while knowing, or failing to consider, that front-line workers are inherently vulnerable because of the events and situations with which they must deal, and that the attack may result in others being deprived of the protection, assistance or medical treatment that they need, and perhaps as a matter of urgency. The maximum sentence for assaulting a police officer while acting in the course of his or her duty or who assaults a person acting in aid of a police officer has recently been increased to 12 years.[54] **10–22**

The Criminal Justice (Hate Offences) Act 2024, effective since 31 December 2024, has created a new set of parallel offences for those already existing under ss 2, 3, 4, 5, 9, 10 and 13 of the Non-Fatal Offences Against the Person Act 1997. As already described (paras 5-135 – 5-136 above), each of these new offences retains the same definition as the corresponding existing offence but with the additional ingredient of being aggravated by hatred on account of a protected characteristic, such as race, religion, gender or sexual orientation.[55] To give one example, a threat to kill or cause serious harm aggravated by hatred contrary to the new s 5A of the 1997 Act carries a maximum prison sentence of 12 years, in contrast to the 10-year maximum for an ordinary s 5 offence. The main purpose of the new provisions is to prescribe higher maximum sentences for offences aggravated by hatred. The legislature is therefore implicitly directing the courts to consider imposing higher sentences for those offences than for their existing equivalents.[56] **10–23**

Strangulation, Suffocation, Harassment and Stalking

The Criminal Justice (Miscellaneous Provisions) Act 2023 (the '2023 Act') creates new offences of non-fatal strangulation or suffocation which **10–24**

---

[54] Criminal Justice (Public Order) Act 1994, s 19(2) as amended by Criminal Justice (Miscellaneous Provisions) Act 2023, s 63.

[55] The complete list of protected characteristics is set out in s 3 of the Criminal Justice (Hate Offences) Act 2024.

[56] See paras 5–135—5–136 above.

carries a maximum sentence of 10 years' imprisonment (though it may also be prosecuted summarily) and non-fatal strangulation or suffocation causing serous harm which is triable on indictment only and punishable with a maximum of life imprisonment.[57] The necessity for these offences is debatable as all the conduct elements seem to fall within the definitions of existing assault offences. However, there may be some value in what Jeremy Horder has called "moral nominalism", the idea that the titles as well as the definitions of offences should capture "the moral essence of the wrong involved".[58] Representative labelling of this kind serves to convey the true nature and comparative gravity of the offending conduct, even if the ultimate penalty is the same as might have been imposed for the relevant generic offence (such as causing serious harm). The English Court of Appeal has indicated some relevant general principles on the sentencing of strangulation offences, including an enumeration of some aggravating factors.[59]

10–25 The 2023 Act also substitutes a new definition of harassment for that contained in the Non-Fatal Offences Against the Person Act 1997 (s 10), and also creates a new offence of stalking. Each of these offences may be prosecuted summarily or on indictment, and following conviction on indictment, carries a maximum sentence of 10 years' imprisonment.[60] The fact that the offender has previously been convicted of an offence (including a criminal damage offence) against the victim or a person connected with the victim must be treated as an aggravating factor. A court may, however, disapply this provision if there are exceptional circumstances to justify it doing so. In any case, the maximum sentence for the offence of conviction may never be exceeded. Further, s 10(4) of the 1997 Act (as substituted by s 23 of the 2023 Act) provides:

> "Where a person is guilty of [a harassment or stalking offence], the court may, in addition to or as an alternative to any other penalty, order that the person shall not, for such period as the court may specify, communicate by any means with or about the other person or that the person shall not approach within such distance as the court shall specify of the place of residence, education or employment of the other person."

10–26 Although such an order may be made as an alternative to any other

---

[57] These are created by ss 21 and 22 of the 2023, inserting new provisions in the Non-Fatal Offences Against the Person Act 1997.

[58] Jeremy Horder, "Rethinking Non-Fatal Offences Against the Person" (1994) 14 *Oxford Journal of Legal Studies* 335. For analysis of this article and its significance, see Rachel C Tolley, "Jeremy Horder, 'Rethinking Non-Fatal Offences Against the Person' (1994)" in Chloë Kennedy and Lindsay Farmer (eds), *Leading Works in Criminal Law* (Routledge, 2023), Chap 12.

[59] *R v Cook* [2023] EWCA Crim 452; [2023] 2 Cr App R (S) 34; *R v Butler* [2023] EWCA Crim 800; [2023] 2 Cr App R (S) 50.

[60] The maximum sentence for harassment under s 10 of the 1997 Act was originally seven years, but this was increased to 10 years by the Harassment, Harmful Communications and Related Offences Act 2020 (s 10), effective from 10 February 2021.

penalty for any harassment or stalking offence, it will rarely be adequate in itself where the conduct was of a serious nature or had a severe impact on the victim. It may well be appropriate in less serious cases, especially where there is reason to believe that the offender is likely to desist from repeating the offending conduct. Failure to comply with such an order is an offence punishable with up to 10 years' imprisonment following conviction on indictment or 12 months following summary conviction. Any such order must be reasonable and clearly expressed. An offender should be informed by the court of what precisely he is required to refrain from doing. Further, a restriction must be reasonable. Protecting the victim from further harassment or harm is, of course, a paramount consideration, but the burden imposed on the offender should be no more than is strictly necessary to achieve this purpose. In *Mooney v DPP*[61] the High Court quashed a District Court sentence which included as a condition of a restraining order that the defendant would not live within eight kilometres of the injured party. This order, which was apparently to last indefinitely, would effectively have prevented the defendant from living in his native town where his family also lived. The High Court found this condition to be disproportionate, presumably in the sense of unreasonable, and quashed the entire sentence with the case later remitted to the District Court.[62]

The Harassment, Harmful Communications and Related Offences Act 2020 created new offences of distributing or publishing intimate images of another person without their consent and with intent to cause harm or being reckless in that regard (punishable with up to seven years' imprisonment, though it may also be prosecuted summarily) and of recording, distributing or publishing intimate images of another person without their consent (a summary offence punishable with up to 12 months' imprisonment). It also creates an offence of distributing, publishing or sending a threatening or grossly offensive communication with intent to cause harm (punishable with up to two years' imprisonment, though it may also be prosecuted summarily). **10–27**

Because it may take many different forms, especially with the expanded definitions of the relevant offences under recent legislation, harassment can be difficult to sentence. In fact, the conduct may also come within the definition of other offences such as demanding with menaces, blackmail or threatening to kill or cause serious injury, and be charged as such.[63] If committed in the context of a family or domestic relationship, it may involve, among other things, breach of a safety or barring order.[64] What victims will often want most is reassurance that the conduct will not be repeated. This is invariably a matter of concern to the courts as well, but courts must also consider and assess the nature of the offender's **10–28**

---

61 [2019] IEHC 625.

62 *Mooney v DPP* [2019] IEHC 647.

63 *People (DPP) v Molloy* [2021] IESC 44; [2021] 3 IR 494; [2021] 2 ILRM 278 includes a description of some such cases.

64 Domestic Violence Act 2018, s 33.

conduct and culpability as well as his or her personal circumstances at the time of sentence. Conduct intended to maximise fear or distress, or persistent and prolonged harassment will normally bring an offence into the highest level of gravity.[65] A history of disobeying court orders may also be treated as aggravating. The Supreme Court issued guidelines on sentencing for harassment in *People (DPP) v Molloy*.[66] By the time of judgment, the maximum sentence had increased to 10 years (though it was still seven years when the offences in that case were committed), and it is by reference to the higher maximum that the guidelines were devised. The court adopted a threefold categorisation. It described offences in the worst category as harassment, menaces or blackmail involving "structured and thought-through planning that aims to cause real distress to the victim, most especially where what is involved is not an aberration brought about by severe emotional distress, but a prolonged campaign." A headline sentence of seven years is appropriate in such a case, but "worse cases involving gang action for cynical gain may tend towards the maximum".[67]

10–29 Cases in the middle category were described by the court as ones where the offender is driven by personal obsession or emotion, rather than careful planning, but where one or more victims are deeply hurt by the conduct. A sentence of four years' imprisonment was recommended as a starting point for offences in this category and it may be assumed that the range should be four to seven years. Cases in the lowest category were described as ones where "less distress is caused to the victim, where the campaign can hardly be so characterised because of lack of thought and planning, where the timespan is especially limited and where personal attributes the victim are not sought out and exploited, perhaps silly lies or fantasies being invented and projected on to him or her instead ...".[68] Where additionally, there has been failure to desist and repetition of the conduct, a headline sentence of two and a half years may be appropriate, although a combination of such factors may bring the sentence up towards the middle category.[69] In *People (DPP) v Hannan*,[70] the Court of Appeal upheld an aggregate sentence of four years' imprisonment for three harassment offences, two of which were committed while on bail, and all were committed while the maximum sentence was seven years' imprisonment. It was accepted that the offences were non-violent in nature but there was the aggravating factor that the appellant had persisted in contacting the victims despite warnings from the Gardaí.

65 English Sentencing Council, *Intimidatory Offences: Definitive Guideline* (2018). See also *R v Evans* [2023] EWCA Crim 1520.

66 [2021] IESC 44; [2021] 3 IR 494; [2021] 2 ILRM 278.

67 [2021] IESC 44; [2021] 3 IR 494; [2021] 2 ILRM 278, para 37.

68 [2021] IESC 44, [2021] 3 IR 494; [2021] 2 ILRM 278, para 39.

69 Apart from *Molloy*, other cases in which sentencing for harassment is discussed include *People (DPP) v Doherty* [2019] IECA 350; [2020] IESC 45 (appeal against conviction dismissed); *People (DPP) v Doolin* [2020] IECA 231; *People (DPP) v Carraher (No 2)* [2018] IECA 170.

70 [2024] IECA 203.

Strangely enough, however, the judgment makes no reference to *Molloy* or the sentence ranges it recommended.

As the Supreme Court stated, these are all headline sentences that may be reduced to account for any relevant mitigating factors, though subject always to the consideration that harassment, because of its impact on victims, is an inherently serious matter. The *Molloy* guidelines are obviously intended to apply following conviction on indictment. Harassment and stalking may also be prosecuted summarily in which case the maximum sentence is 12 months' imprisonment. A non-custodial or suspended sentence may be appropriate where the conduct was not particularly serious and if the offender has undertaken not to repeat it. Concrete steps taken by the offender, such as moving away from the locality where the harassment occurred or the victim resides, may provide evidence of his or her resolution to desist from the offending conduct. This could also function as a mitigating factor following conviction on indictment. **10–30**

Domestic Violence

Domestic violence typically consists of an assault of some kind, and it will therefore be sentenced primarily according to the principles governing the various assault offences as described above. It may also involve threats to kill or cause serious injury, or damage to property. However, the Domestic Violence Act 2018 has supplemented this law in some important ways. First, it creates an offence of coercive control which consists of controlling or coercive behaviour that has a serious effect on the person against whom it is directed. That person must be the spouse or civil partner of the defendant, or a person with whom the defendant is or was in an intimate relationship. This offence may be prosecuted summarily or on indictment and, following conviction on indictment, it carries a maximum sentence of five years' imprisonment.[71] As with most other offences, courts are likely to adopt a tripartite range extending in this instance from, perhaps, zero to 20 months, 20 to 40 months and 40 to 60 months. Typically, however, this offence will be charged in conjunction with related offences such as assault. If sentences are ordered to run concurrently, the sentence for the most serious offence may be increased to reflect the overall conduct reflected in the offences of conviction. Subject to the application of the totality principle, consecutive sentences would be permissible where the offences were separated in time, though committed against the same victim.[72] **10–31**

Factors to be considered when evaluating the gravity of a coercive control offence (and any associated offences) include the nature of the defendant's conduct and, in particular, the extent to which it was of a violent nature, its duration, its impact on the victim and whether the offender had taken **10–32**

---

[71] Domestic Violence Act 2018, s 39.
[72] *People (DPP) v Kane* [2023] IECA 86.

advantage of any vulnerability on the victim's part.[73] The conduct will be all the more serious if it was perpetrated against somebody who, by reason of age, disability, emotional or financial dependency or social isolation, was or felt constrained to remain under the offender's control and was thereby inhibited from seeking protection. At a time of a severe accommodation shortage, for example, people may become trapped in abusive relationships simply because they have nowhere else to go. Delay on the part of the victim in seeking needed medical assistance may indicate that she or he was subject to a high level of control or domination by the offender. The presence of a child while the violent or abusive conduct was occurring is undoubtedly an aggravating factor.[74] In those circumstances, the child is also a victim of the offence even if the offending conduct was directed at somebody else. Steps taken to prevent the victim from seeking assistance or reporting the offence will also be treated as aggravating.[75]

10–33 In terms of mitigation, a court must have regard to any factors that may explain or have contributed to the offender's conduct. These might include experience of violence during childhood, addiction or having to cope with serious adversity of some kind. Such factors can never, of course, excuse abusive or coercive behaviour but they may provide a basis for fashioning a penalty or response that will help the offender to reflect upon and acknowledge the harm caused to the victim and to take meaningful steps to address the underlying causes of their behaviour. Evidence that the offender is already making progress in that regard may point to a short prison sentence or suspended sentence coupled with treatment or supervision as the most productive response. In *People (DPP) v Farnan*,[76] which arose from an undue leniency application, the defendant's violent conduct towards his partner would ordinarily have merited a substantial custodial sentence. However, having considered the significant progress towards rehabilitation made by the defendant and other mitigating factors, the Court of Appeal ultimately decided not to interfere with the fully suspended sentence imposed by the trial judge. As in the case of sexual offences, a plea of guilty may be of significant value if it spares the victim from having to testify, and especially if there is reason to believe that the victim would have found that experience particularly stressful. In both *Farnan* and *People (DPP) v Connor*,[77] decided on the same day, the Court of Appeal said that domestic violence of this nature should normally attract a sentence that includes some term of immediate custody, in order to mark society's condemnation of such conduct and to act as a deterrent. It is only in exceptional circumstances that the sentence for such an offence should be fully suspended. In *Connor* itself, a fully suspended sentence was varied to an effective term of 18 months' imprisonment.

---

73 *People (DPP) v Boles* [2023] IECA 211, para 87.

74 See, for example, *People (DPP) v Kelly* [2019] IECA 11 and *People (DPP) v Keogh* [2024] IECA 132.

75 This factor is included in the English Sentencing Council's definitive guideline, *Overarching Principles – Domestic Abuse* (2018).

76 [2020] IECA 256.

77 [2020] IECA 255.

In *People (DPP) v Boles*[78] the defendant pleaded guilty to one count of coercive control, five counts of assault causing harm and two counts of criminal damage, all committed against the same victim. He was sentenced to two years' imprisonment, entirely suspended. The Court of Appeal agreed with the trial judge that three years' imprisonment was the appropriate headline sentence for the coercive control offence, but it held that the headline sentence for at least some of the assault offences should have been five years. It found the ultimate sentence to be unduly lenient. Bearing in mind the various mitigating factors, including the perceptible progress towards rehabilitation made by the defendant, it substituted a net sentence of two years' imprisonment with the last year suspended for the coercive control offence, and for each of the assault offences a net sentence of three years with the last two years suspended. As all the sentences were ordered to run concurrently, the ultimate sentence to be served in custody was one year. This was also the sentence ultimately imposed, again following an undue leniency application, in *People (DPP) v Kelly*[79] which involved one violent incident. **10–34**

At the other end of the spectrum, a sentence of 12 and a half years' imprisonment with the last two years suspended was upheld in *People (DPP) v Kane.*[80] There, however, the appellant had been convicted of one count of coercive control, 12 counts of assault causing harm and one count each of assault, intimidation and attempting to pervert the course of justice. The offending, which occurred over a 20-month period, was characterised by the Court of Appeal in these terms: **10–35**

> "It is clear on the evidence adduced that the appellant subjected the injured party to a campaign of fear, emotional suffering, subjugation, threats of violence, violence plus humiliation, leading to her being fearful, meek, submissive and on edge. The fact that she did not attend hospital for a couple of days with a comminuted fracture of her arm is telling in itself of the atmosphere in the home. His behaviour was prolonged, oppressive, domineering, manipulative and frequently brutal, psychologically and physically, designed to humiliate and degrade her, and place her in constant fear. He used different methods of controlling and coercive conduct; violence, threats of violence, humiliation and verbal and emotional abuse. In the circumstances, his moral culpability was high and correctly found to be so by the sentencing judge, the harm done to the injured party was significant and as a consequence, we do not find any error with the judge placing the offending in the mid to upper range of penalties available and her resulting nomination of the notional headline sentence."[81]

Heavier sentences have been imposed where the conduct included rape or serious sexual assault in addition to other offences.[82] **10–36**

---

78 [2023] IECA 211.
79 [2019] IECA 11.
80 [2023] IECA 86.
81 [2023] IECA 86, para 32.
82 In *People (DPP) v Ward,* Central Criminal Court, 28 July 2022, a sentence of 18 years' imprisonment with the last year suspended was imposed on a man convicted of several offences of assault, false imprisonment, rape and coercive

10–37 A series of assaults committed over a period of time against the same victim in a domestic setting, even if not amounting to coercive control, may attract a more severe sentence than would otherwise be appropriate for those assaults, either individually or collectively. The repetition of the violent conduct is an aggravating factor.[83] Additionally, the Domestic Violence Act 2018 (the '2018 Act') (s 40) provides that, when sentencing for certain violent and sexual offences as listed in that section, a court must treat as an aggravating factor the fact that the victim was the offender's spouse or civil partner or a person with whom the offender was or had been in an intimate relationship. In these circumstances, a court must impose a sentence greater than would otherwise be appropriate, but it may disapply this provision if it considers that there are exceptional circumstances to justify so doing. Obviously, this provision does not apply to the sentencing of coercive control because the existence of such a relationship is an ingredient of the offence. In *People (DPP) v S(A)*[84] the Court of Appeal stressed the importance of trial courts having due regard to this provision and the duty of counsel to draw it to a court's attention if necessary. In this case, which arose from an undue leniency application, the Court of Appeal decided that, despite the presence of mitigating factors, there had to be some increase in the sentence to give effect to s 40 of the 2018 Act. It seems to have been principally for this reason that the court found the sentence to be unduly lenient and it increased the effective custodial term (for aggravated sexual assault) from 40 months to 48 months.

10–38 The current law, in terms of both legislation and sentencing practice, reflects the growing social awareness of the prevalence of domestic violence, the many forms it can take and its impact on victims and, in some cases, their dependants. This is reflected in a statement of the Northern Ireland Court of Appeal In *R v Hughes*[85] where it upheld a cumulative sentence of 50 months' imprisonment (half of which was to be served in custody) following a guilty plea to 15 offences, mostly common assault but including one count of assault occasioning actual bodily harm, committed against the appellant's partner. The court said:

> "It will be apparent from what we have said that in future perpetrators of sustained domestic violence such as this can expect to obtain higher sentences for this type of offending. Such sentences are a reflection of the growing appreciation of the seriousness of this type of offending, the frequency of it within our society, the repetitive nature of it and the effects on victims. Higher sentencing reflects society's need to deter this type of behaviour and mark an abhorrence of it. There is also a need for the education of society in general, to understand that this behaviour is

---

control committed against the victim during a six-week period in 2019. He had previously received a four-year sentence for the assault and false imprisonment of a young woman.

83 *People (DPP) v Keogh* [2024] IECA 132.

84 [2023] IECA 171.

85 [2022] NICA 12.

> not normal, it should not be tolerated, and if it does occur it will result in significant sentences."[86]

The same holds true in this jurisdiction as reflected in the various judgments considered above. **10–39**

The European Court of Human Rights has been willing to find a violation of the European Convention on Human Rights ('ECHR') where a state party failed to discharge its positive obligation to adopt and implement measures to protect people from violent conduct and to respond effectively to such conduct when it occurred. This obligation applies to actions by private parties as well as by public authorities. A state is therefore duty-bound to afford effective protection against domestic violence which means that complaints of such violence must be properly investigated, prosecuted where there is a basis for doing so, and punished appropriately in the event of a conviction.[87] The European Court has, for example, found a violation of art 3 of the ECHR (which outlaws torture and inhuman or degrading treatment or punishment) where a victim was badly assaulted on five occasions by her partner and the state failed to prosecute.[88] In so doing, the court said: **10–40**

> "Article 3 requires states to put in place effective criminal law provisions to deter the commission of offences against personal integrity, backed up by law enforcement machinery for the prevention, suppression and punishment of breaches of such provisions, and this requirement also extends to ill treatment administered by private individuals."[89]

In a concurring opinion, Judge Pino de Albuquerque stressed both the gendered nature of domestic violence and its inherently degrading nature:

> "[I]t is self-evident that the very act of domestic violence has an inherently humiliating and debasing character for the victim, which is exactly what the offender aimed at. Physical pain is but one of the intended effects. A kick, a slap or a spit is also aimed at belittling the dignity of the partner, conveying a message of humiliation and degradation."

Conduct constituting domestic violence may also violate arts 2, 8 or 14 of the ECHR. **10–41**

---

86 [2022] NICA 12, para 51.

87 *Levchuk v Ukraine,* European Court of Human Rights, 3 September 2020. In *Kurt v Austria* (2022) 74 EHRR 6 the court analysed in detail a state's obligation under art 2 of the ECHR to prevent domestic violence. See Ronagh McQuigg, "Domestic abuse and Article 2 of the European Convention on Human Rights: Applying the Grand Chamber judgment in *Kurt v Austria*" (2023) European Human Rights LR 564.

88 *Valiuliene v Lithuania,* European Court of Human Rights, 26 March 2013. See Ronagh McQuigg, "The European Court of Human Rights and domestic violence: *Valiuliene v Lithuania*" (2014) 18 *International Journal of Human Rights* 756.

89 *Valiuliene v Lithuania,* European Court of Human Rights, 26 March 2013, para 75.

10–42 The Istanbul Convention, which Ireland ratified in 2019, requires states parties to take all necessary steps to protect women from all forms of violence, and to prevent, prosecute and punish violence against women and domestic violence.[90] Article 5(2), which is particularly in the present context, provides:

> "Parties shall take the necessary legislative and other measures to exercise due diligence to prevent, investigate, punish and provide reparation for acts of violence covered by the scope of this Convention that are perpetrated by non-State actors."

10–43 In both this Convention and the jurisprudence of the European Court, the emphasis is on violence against women because they are the victims in most cases but, as the court has acknowledged, men may also be victims, while children are often casualties as well, whether directly or indirectly.[91]

3. Sexual Offences

10–44 The number of sexual offences known to Irish law has grown significantly in recent years, especially with the enactment of the Criminal Law (Sexual Offences) Act 2017 which created several new child abuse and exploitation offences.[92] So far, there is little by way of sentencing guidance for those offences but, in accordance what is now standard practice, courts are likely to proceed by dividing the relevant penalty scale into three equal bands and then determining if the offence falls into the low, middle or high category. This will indicate an appropriate headline sentence before any necessary adjustments are made for the offender's personal circumstances. Here we shall deal with four offences only: rape, sexual assault, aggravated sexual assault and defilement. The principles and guidelines applicable to those offences are also helpful for the sentencing of other sexual offences. The sentencing of prolonged or serial child abuse will also be considered.

10–45 As will be evident from any survey of the modern case law in this area, some offenders come up to for sentence in respect of a single sex offence while many others must be sentenced for a series of such offences. The major challenge in these circumstances is to maintain some semblance of ordinal proportionality. At one level, this is easily accomplished; the more inherently serious the offence, the heavier the deserved punishment. Rape, therefore, will ordinarily be punished more severely than sexual assault. Calibrating the penalties appropriate for single and multiple instances of a sexual offence is a much more difficult task. If, for example, seven years' imprisonment is deemed a proportionate penalty for one rape offence, how can 14 years be proportionate for a pattern of child abuse

---

90 Council of Europe Convention on Preventing and Combating Violence against Women and Domestic Violence (CETS No 210).

91 *Levchuk v Ukraine*, European Court of Human Rights, 3 September 2020, para 78.

92 Criminal Law (Sexual Offences) Act 2017, ss 3 to 8.

involving the repeated rape and sexual assault of one or more victims over a period of several years? One might contrast, for this purpose, the headline sentences approved in *People (DPP) v H(D)*[93] where one adult male sexually assaulted another while the latter was asleep, and *People (DPP) v A(S)*[94] where the appellant was convicted following a lengthy trial on three counts of rape and 20 counts of sexual assault committed against two sisters aged 10 and 12 years during the period December 2010 to March 2011. The appropriate headline sentence in *H(D)*, according to the Court of Appeal, was 4 and a half years (ultimately reduced to an effective custodial term of 18 months). In *A(S)*, a sentence of 14 years' imprisonment, which was presumably the headline sentence, with the last two years suspended was upheld, subject to some amendment of the conditions of suspension and the addition of a post-release supervision order. Yet the offending in *A(S)* was surely more than three times more serious than that in *H(D)*. The headline sentence in *H(D)* is even more difficult to square with the nine-year prison term substituted by the Court of Appeal, following an undue leniency application, in *People (DPP) v L(M)*[95] where the defendant was convicted following trial of 60 sexual assaults committed against six young sisters during the period 1994 to 2005, 23 of the assaults having been committed while the maximum sentence was 14 years' imprisonment.

10–46 There is no easy answer to this problem which ultimately derives from the deeper dilemma associated with sentencing the multiple offender, as discussed earlier in Chap 5. On the one hand, a court sentencing for a single offence must be guided by the statutory maximum when selecting a proportionate penalty. Thus, in *H(D)*, the Court of Appeal was entitled to conclude that the offence was in the middle range and should be sentenced accordingly. On the other, when sentencing a multiple offender, no matter how numerous the offences, a court generally tries to avoid imposing a crushing sentence that will deprive the offender of all hope of rejoining society (though in some cases an indeterminate life sentence will be necessary). In these circumstances, there is inevitably some discount for bulk offending. Perhaps there are two lessons to be learned from this conundrum. First, when sentencing for a single offence, a court should at least have regard to sentences that have previously been approved at appeal court level in cases involving multiple instances of that offence (and probably of others as well) and the circumstances in which those offences were committed. This might help in maintaining some degree of ordinal proportionality. Secondly, it points to the need for more formal guidelines than currently exist in this area, those guidelines being based on a thorough investigation and analysis of past sentencing practice. This information and analysis should provide the basis for considered recommendations on the sentence levels or ranges appropriate for different categories of sex offender.

---

93 [2024] IECA 71.

94 [2020] IECA 311.

95 [2015] IECA 144.

Rape

10–47 Rape is punishable with a maximum sentence of life imprisonment, as is rape contrary to s 4 of the Criminal Law (Rape) (Amendment) Act 1990 and attempted rape. The Supreme Court has held that, in the absence of wholly exceptional circumstances, rape should attract "a substantial immediate custodial sentence".[96] This principle is reflected in current sentencing practice, and it is virtually unknown for anything other than an immediate custodial sentence to be imposed for rape, though part-suspended sentences are reasonably common. The sentencing of rape was the subject of a detailed Supreme Court judgment in *People (DPP) v E(F)*[97] which is now treated, in effect, as a formal guideline. Having surveyed and analysed a large number of previous appeal court decisions, the Supreme Court identified the following bands as being appropriate in rape cases, though they are not presented here in the sequence adopted by the court.

10–48 Seven years' imprisonment was identified by the court as the ordinary headline sentence. Since offences at the next highest level were said to merit a sentence range of 10 to 15 years, it may be inferred that seven to 10 years is the appropriate penalty range for offences in this "ordinary" category, described by the court as "ones where coercion or force or other aggravating circumstances were not at a level that would require a more serious sentence". The next highest category is described as "more serious cases" calling for a headline sentence of 10 to 15 years. These are cases where there is "a more than usual level of degradation of the victim or the use of violence or intimidation beyond that associated with the offence, or the abuse of trust". Two of the previous cases cited by the court as having fallen into this category, *People (DPP) v Hearne*[98] and *People (DPP) v Keogh,*[99] certainly illustrate factors and circumstances that warrant treating a case as "more serious". Both involved the infliction of serious harm in addition to that inherent in the rape offences (of which there was more than one in each case). The court concluded its observations on this category by stating:

> "[A] series of offences is not an ordinary rape and, on the headline sentence, is not to be punished as if such offences were in that lower band of seriousness. Where there is unusual violence or cynical planning, the ordinary category of rape cases is passed and consideration of this higher band should be where the sentencing court starts."[100]

10–49 The point about placing a series of offences in one of the higher categories certainly holds good where concurrent sentences being imposed. In that event, the repetition of the offending may properly aggravate the seriousness of whichever offence is selected as the primary one. If consecutive sentences were being imposed, each offence should be

96 *People (DPP) v Tiernan* [1988] IR 250 at 253; [1989] ILRM 149.
97 [2019] IESC 85; [2021] 1 IR 217; [2020] 1 ILRM 517.
98 [2019] IECA 137.
99 [2017] IECA 210.
100 [2019] IESC 85; [2021] 1 IR 217; [2020] 1 ILRM 517, para 64.

assessed separately and sentenced according to its seriousness which might, of course, place any one of the offences or all of them in a higher rather than a lower category. As always, the totality principle would then have to be applied to arrive at any appropriate aggregate sentence.

The highest range identified in *E(F)* is described as "cases requiting up to life imprisonment". Here the range is 15 years to life, with the possibility of lengthy determinate sentences in between. Offences in this category will obviously have one or more seriously aggravating factors. A leading example, as cited in *E(F),* would be *People (DPP) v Tiernan*[101] which involved the gang rape of a young woman who was sitting in a car with her boyfriend when she was set upon by three men and subjected to repeated and extreme sexual violence. One of them, Tiernan, was sentenced to 21 years, though this was reduced by the Supreme Court to 17 years. Most cases falling into this category today will have involved the serial sexual abuse of a child (and described below under 'Prolonged sexual abuse of one or more children'). However, a *Tiernan*-type case involving an adult victim would still attract a headline sentence in the 15 years to life range. **10–50**

At the lower end of the scale, there have been cases, as the Supreme Court recognised in *E(F),* where sentences lower than seven years have been imposed, sometimes four years or less. These were almost invariably cases where the offender was a young person at the time of the offence or there was some significant mitigating factor arising from the offender's current personal circumstances. However, when considering these cases, it must be recalled that in many of them the appropriate headline sentence would have been considerably higher than that ultimately imposed. (The practice of identifying headline sentences had not been established when some of these cases were decided.) The ultimate sentence would often have reflected some significant mitigating factor such as the offender's youth. A fully suspended sentence for rape is now virtually unknown. As stated by the Supreme Court in *People (DPP) v Tiernan,*[102]only truly exceptional circumstances would justify such a sentence. Part-suspended sentences for rape are not uncommon but the offender will almost invariably be required to spend a significant portion of the overall sentence in custody. In England and Wales, the sentencing of sexual offences is governed by a comprehensive guideline first adopted in 2014.[103] This includes a useful list of aggravating and mitigating factors for rape as for all other sexual offences. *R v Millberry,*[104] the leading pre-guideline judgment on sentencing for rape, which was delivered by the Court of Appeal with advice from the Sentencing Advisory Panel, is also valuable for this purpose. **10–51**

---

[101] [1988] IR 250; [1989] ILRM 149.
[102] [1988] IR 250; [1989] ILRM 149.
[103] Sentencing Council, *Sexual Offences Definitive Guideline* (2014).
[104] [2002] EWCA Crim 2891; [2003] 1 WLR 546; [2004] 2 Cr App R(S) 31.

Sexual Assault

10–52 A sexual assault consists of an assault committed in circumstances of indecency.[105] An assault for this purpose need not involve the actual application of force to the person of another; it may also consist of conduct that intentionally or recklessly causes another to apprehend the application of unlawful force.[106] The maximum sentence for sexual assault, formerly known as indecent assault, has varied considerably over time.[107] A convicted person may never be subject to a higher maximum than applied when the offence was committed. It is therefore important to be familiar with the history of maximum sentences for sexual assault, especially as it is often among the offences charged in so-called historic child sexual abuse cases. Under the Criminal Law Amendment Act 1935 (s 6) a person guilty of indecent assault upon a female was subject to a maximum sentence of two years' imprisonment on a first conviction and a maximum of five years on a second or subsequent conviction. This was repealed by the Criminal Law (Rape) Act 1981 (s 10) which specified a maximum of 10 years' imprisonment for indecent assault upon a female, irrespective of whether it was a first or subsequent conviction. Unusually, under the Criminal Law (Rape) (Amendment) Act 1990, the maximum sentence for sexual assault, as the offence had then become known, was reduced to five years, irrespective of the gender of either the perpetrator or the victim. To compensate, a new offence of aggravated sexual assault, punishable with a maximum of life imprisonment, was introduced by the same Act. A decade later, however, the Sex Offenders Act 2001 (s 37) increased the maximum sentence for sexual assault back up to 10 years and to 14 years where the victim was under the age of 17 years when the offence was committed. This remains the law. The sentencing regime for sexual assaults upon a male was problematic for a time owing to the fact that under the Offences Against the Person Act 1861, indecent assault of a male carried a maximum 10-year sentence while the maximum for indecently assaulting a female was two years.[108] However, the maximum sentence is now the same irrespective of the gender of either the offender or the victim.

10–53 As with rape, a distinction must be drawn between sentencing for a single offence of sexual assault committed against a child or adult, and a series of such assaults which in most cases will have been committed against a child. In either case, the offence can vary enormously in gravity. It may consist of unwanted touching of a sexual nature or it may involve serious sexual violence bordering on rape or s 4 rape. Needless to say, a sexual assault of any kind amounts to a violation of the victim's constitutional

[105] The meaning of sexual assault is analysed in detail in *People (DPP) v N(F)* [2022] IESC 22; [2022] 1 ILRM 279.
[106] *Director of Military Prosecutions v Donaghy* [2016] IECA 191.
[107] The Criminal Law (Rape) (Amendment) Act 1990, s 2 renamed indecent assault as sexual assault but did not alter the definition of the offence.
[108] See *M(S) v Ireland (No 2)* [2007] IEHC 280; [2007] 4 IR 369 and *People (DPP) v Maher* [2016] IESC 31; [2016] 2 IR 634.

right to bodily integrity and of their moral right to personal autonomy. When committed against a person aged 17 years or older, a sexual assault is now punishable with a maximum of 10 years' imprisonment which means that a court will usually proceed on the basis that there are three sentence bands (approximately 0 to three years, four to six years and seven to nine or 10 years), depending on the gravity of the particular offence.[109] The bands will be commensurately higher where the 14-year maximum applies. When setting a headline sentence, the court will have regard primarily to the nature of the conduct and the physical or psychological injury suffered by the victim. The use of additional violence, including non-sexual assault, the deployment of a weapon, subjecting the victim to particularly degrading treatment, taking advantage of a victim who was asleep or heavily intoxicated,[110] or attacking a victim who was alone in an isolated area or late at night[111] are all factors that point to a sentence in the upper bands. So too is the conscious exploitation of a victim's physical, emotional, psychological or financial vulnerability.[112]

Multiple sexual assaults are most likely to occur as part of a pattern of child sexual abuse. Here we shall concentrate on those cases where the abuse consisted solely of indecent or sexual assaults (depending on the dates of commission), although many such cases also involve rape, defilement or exploitation. When considering the sentences imposed for offending of this nature, regard must always be had to the maximum that applied when the offences were committed. For instance, the three-year sentence upheld in *People (DPP) v F(N)*[113] where the appellant had pleaded guilty to multiple sexual assaults committed against his young step-daughter over a seven-year period may seem low, but the applicable maximum was five years. Further, the perpetrators of the abuse may have been children themselves at the time, and this too will be reflected in the **10–54**

---

[109] *People (DPP) v S(C)* [2022] IECA 282, para 50; *People (DPP) v Haig* [2023] IECA 299, para 25.

[110] *People (DPP) v H(D)* [2024] IECA 71. Here the headline sentence for one sexual assault committed against a sleeping victim but which lacked some of aggravating features of other such assaults was reduced to four and a half years, and further reduced to an effective custodial term of 18 months. See also *People (DPP) v S(C)* [2022] IECA 282 where an 18-month prison sentence with the last three months suspended was upheld for the sexual assault of a sleeping woman. In *People (DPP) v Haig* [2023] IECA 299, which arose from an undue leniency application, the Court of Appeal held that a headline sentence of five years was appropriate, reduced to three and a half years with the last year suspended. The defendant had sexually assaulted a sleeping woman but he had cut her undergarments with a sharp object, a factor which the court regarded as significantly aggravating.

[111] *People (DPP) v Lyons* [2014] IECCA 27 (sentence of six years with four years suspended substituted for an effective custodial sentence of six months)

[112] *People (DPP) v D(J)* [2023] IECA 314 (headline sentence of six years substituted by Court of Appeal for five offences of indecent assault committed against a victim in these circumstances during the year 1989).

[113] [2024] IECA 131.

ultimate sentences.[114] The aggregate penalty for a series of sexual assaults committed against a child (or an adult, for that matter) is unlikely to fall into the lowest band of the relevant sentence range, unless perhaps the assaults were minor in nature, few in number and committed over a short time span. The overall sentence range may extend from zero to five years, 10 years or 14 years, depending on when the offences were committed and the victim's age at the time of the offence.

Aggravated Sexual Assault

10–55 Aggravated sexual assault is defined as a sexual assault "that involves serious violence or the threat of serious violence or is such as to cause injury, humiliation or degradation of a grave nature to the person assaulted".[115] It is punishable with a maximum sentence of life imprisonment. The sentencing bands are therefore likely to be 0 to five years, six to 10 years and 11 to 15 years, with the possibility of a higher sentence up to and including life in an exceptionally serious case.[116] Because of the inherent gravity of the offence, a headline sentence for aggravated sexual assault is unlikely to fall into the lower band (as that would render it equivalent to a sexual assault) although the presence of strong mitigating factors might result in a final sentence within that band. In *People (DPP) v A(S)*,[117] for example, the offence was committed in circumstances where the victim was subject to considerable violence beforehand, and the offender tried to sexually penetrate her. The Court of Appeal nominated a headline sentence of eight and a half years, reduced ultimately to five years and eight months with the last 20 months suspended. In this case, two sexual assault charges were taken into consideration, but the aggravated sexual assault itself fell within the mid-range.

Defilement

10–56 "Defilement" refers to an offence under ss 2 or s. 3 of the Criminal Law (Sexual Offences) Act 2006, as substituted by ss 16 and 17 of the Criminal Law (Sexual Offences) Act 2017. It consists of a sexual act (meaning, for this purpose, sexual intercourse, buggery, aggravated sexual assault or rape contrary to s 4 of the Criminal Law (Rape) (Amendment) Act 1990) with a person under the age of consent.[118] Where the young person was under 15 years at the time of the offence, the maximum sentence is life imprisonment. Where he or she was under 17 years, the maximum sentence is seven years' imprisonment, but 15 years where the defendant

[114] See, for example, *People (DPP) v D(G)* [2024] IECA 25, although the offences in this case included rape as well as sexual assault.

[115] Criminal Law (Rape) (Amendment) Act 1990, s 3.

[116] *People (DPP) v A(S)* [2023] IECA 171.

[117] [2023] IECA 171.

[118] The age of consent for this purpose is 17 years although it increases to 18 years where the offence was committed by a person in authority (Criminal Law (Sexual Offences) Act 2006, s 3A as inserted by Criminal Law (Sexual Offences) Act 2017, s 18).

was then or had been in the past a person in authority in relation to the young person.[119]

Defilement offences vary in gravity. After all, it is an offence for a person of any age to engage in any of the specified sexual conduct with a child under 17 years of age. At the lower end of the scale, it may consist of sexual intercourse between two consenting teenagers who are in a relationship. The law now provides for a "young person's defence" to the extent that consent may be a defence where the child was aged between 15 and 17 and the defendant was either younger or less than two years older than the child. This addresses some of the more awkward situations that arose in the past where, say, two 16-year-olds engaged in consensual sexual intercourse, but only the male was criminally liable. However, consent would still provide no defence to a 19-year-old who had sexual intercourse with a 16-year-partner. Absent any evidence of coercion or exploitation, such an offence would probably be sentenced leniently. A suspended or non-custodial sentence would not be unreasonable in those circumstances. As a rule, the greater the age gap between the parties, the more seriously the offence will be regarded. A defendant who was significantly older than the child is usually more blameworthy if, as is often the case, he took advantage of the child's immaturity or vulnerability, even though he was not a person in authority (in the legal sense) or in a position of trust (in the sense of being under some legal or moral obligation to safeguard the child).[120] **10–57**

Defilement charges are sometimes brought even where the evidence suggests that the child did not consent to the sexual activity.[121] In those circumstances, a conviction for rape or sexual assault might well have resulted if such a charge had been brought. However, consent or the apparent absence of it always remains relevant when sentencing for defilement.[122] Irrespective of the ages of the parties, evidence of any kind of coercion or of knowledge on the part of the defendant that the child was not consenting will generally bring the case above the custody threshold, with the obvious caveat that there may be strong mitigating factors or exceptional circumstances to justify a more lenient response. A countervailing factor in some such cases is that the defendant will have been under 18 years when he committed the offence. If still under that age at the time of sentence, he must be dealt with in accordance with the **10–58**

---

[119] 'Person in authority' is defined in the Criminal Law (Sexual Offences) Act 2006, s 1 as amended by the Criminal Law (Sexual Offences) Act 2017, s 15.

[120] *People (DPP) v McD(J)* [2021] IECA 31, para 64; *People (DPP) v V(A)* [2021] IECA 230, para 26.

[121] In *People (DPP) v McD(J)* [2021] IECA 31, for example, the indictment included counts of rape contrary to s 4 of the Criminal Law (Rape) (Amendment) Act 1990 which apparently related to the same conduct giving rise to the defilement charges.

[122] *People (DPP) v T(V)* [2021] IECA 117, paras 33-35, stating that knowledge that the victim was not consenting or recklessness in that regard "involves significantly greater culpability".

Children Act 2001 which means, among other things, that detention must be treated as a sanction of last resort.[123] If he has reached the age of 18 by then, due regard must be had to his young age at the time of the offence. In *People (DPP) v T(V)*[124] the Court of Appeal upheld 18 months' detention in the case of a male who pleaded guilty to one count of defilement (though in circumstances where there seems to have been absence of consent) committed when he was 15 years against a female of the same age. He was sentenced on the day before his 18th birthday. There were aggravating factors mainly connected with the victim's vulnerability owing to intoxication, though there was no evidence of additional physical violence or abuse.

10–59 However, a defilement offence becomes considerably more serious when it is accompanied by a significant degree of exploitation, manipulation, control or oppression, where there has been prolonged abuse or where the defendant was considerably older than the victim. In *People (DPP) v Vickers,*[125] one of the worst defilement cases to come before the Irish courts, the defendant regularly engaged in sexual intercourse with the first complainant over a two-year period. The sexual activity began when she was 14 years and he was about 25 years. She became pregnant by him and gave birth to a child. He also exercised extreme control over her and assaulted her on a number of occasions. He also had sexual intercourse on two occasions with the first complainant's cousin. He introduced both complainants to heroin, and he had also plied the first complainant with alcohol. The trial judge described the defendant's behaviour as "manipulative, controlling, violent, narcissistic, and pure evil". The Court of Appeal agreed that the case was of the utmost seriousness and said that the defendant's conduct in making the complainants take heroin (and alcohol in the case of the first complainant) put the case right at the upper end of the spectrum. The headline sentences identified by the trial judge were: 10 years' imprisonment for defilement of the first complainant, three years for defilement of the second complainant, and two years for assault causing harm to the first complainant. This aggregate of 15 years was then reduced to 11 years to reflect mitigating factors. Finally, the judge suspended the last two years, leaving an effective sentence of nine years. The DPP referred the case to the Court of Appeal, arguing that the final sentence was unduly lenient. The Court agreed that the sentence was very lenient and expressed the view that a two-year reduction for the guilty plea would have been adequate. Ultimately, however, it decided that the sentence was not so unduly lenient as to justify quashing it and resentencing the defendant. *People (DPP) v V(A)*[126] also fell into the most serious category. Again, there were two complainants, one aged 14 years and the other 16 years at the time of the offending. The appellant had sexual intercourse on numerous occasions with the first complainant who he also plied with drugs. The trial judge identified a global sentence

---

[123] See Chap 9 above.
[124] [2021] IECA 117.
[125] [2020] IECA 66.
[126] [2021] IECA 230.

of 14 years, reduced to 12 years with the final two years suspended. The appeal against severity of sentence was decided after the judgment in *McD* (below) was delivered. The Court of Appeal located the case between the upper end of the mid-range and the lower end of the high range, thus yielding an 11-year sentence. This was reduced to nine years, to reflect mitigating factors, and with the last two years suspended on terms.

The Court of Appeal offered some general guidance on sentencing for defilement in *People (DPP) v McD(J)*[127] though this is an informal guideline in the sense identified in *People (DPP) v O'Sullivan.*[128] The court said that, assuming an effective 15-year maximum in most defilement cases, three sentence ranges could be identified: a low range extending from a non-custodial measure up to five years' imprisonment; a mid-range of five to 10 years, and an upper range of 10 to 15 years. Sentences exceeding 15 years and up to life imprisonment may be appropriate in particularly egregious cases. The court felt that this sentencing arrangement was broadly in line with the Supreme Court judgment in *People (DPP) v E(F)*[129] on sentencing for rape. The presence of strong mitigating or aggravating factors bearing on culpability may justify moving an offence from one range to another. The court in *McD* further said: **10–60**

> "[W]e feel we can safely say that a s 2(1) defilement offences [where the child was under 15 years] not involving force, coercion or seriously aggravating factors would in general merit the nomination of a headline sentence in the low range, the precise appropriate starting point necessarily depending on the circumstances of the case. By the same token, if the offending behaviour has involved force or coercion (including blackmailing behaviour, abuse of a dominant position or exploitation of an inequality of power) or other seriously aggravating circumstances (e.g. multiple instances of the offending behaviour over a prolonged period; the causing of significant harm or suffering beyond that intrinsic to the basic violation; degradation or humiliation of the victim beyond that intrinsic to the basic violation; exploitation of a known vulnerability; a gross breach of trust, recording the crime and/or dissemination of a recording of the crime, to name but some possibilities), it will merit a headline sentence starting in the mid-range, or possibly above particularly where there are multiple such aggravating circumstances of them and depending on the egregiousness of them."[130]

The court held that the offences in *McD* should be located in the upper half of the mid-range because there were several serious aggravating factors including the videorecording of the first offence, and the age disparity between the parties. The defendant was 16 and a half years at the time while the victim was 12 and a half years though she had led him to believe she was 14. The headline sentence of eight years' imprisonment nominated by the trial judge, discounted to four years to reflect mitigating factors, was therefore appropriate and the appeal against severity of sentence was dismissed. **10–61**

---

[127] [2021] IECA 31.
[128] [2020] IECA 331, discussed further in Chap 13 below.
[129] [2019] IESC 85; [2021] 1 IR 217; [2020] 1 ILRM 517.
[130] [2021] IECA 31, para 59.

10–62 *McD* may not be a formal guideline for reasons the Court of Appeal itself identified, but pending any further guidelines offered by the court or the Judicial Council, it provides useful guidance for trial courts on sentencing defilement offences, It may therefore be accorded the status granted to *People (DPP) v Byrne*[131] on sentencing for robbery as discussed below under that heading. As already noted, the Court of Appeal followed *McD* when assessing the appropriateness of the sentence imposed in *People (DPP) v V(A).*[132] The maximum sentence for defilement depends on whether the child was under or over the age of 15 years, and the difference is quite significant. Where the child was under the age of 15 years, the maximum is life imprisonment whereas it is ordinarily seven years where the child was under 17 years (though a 15-year maximum applies if the offender was a person in authority). However, if the child is close to 15 years, it will usually be appropriate to adopt a headline sentence of, at most, seven years because, were it not for a difference of a few months, that is the maximum to which the offender (unless a person in authority) would have been subject. This was the view of the Court of Appeal in *People (DPP) v Conroy*[133] where the victim was 14 and a half years and the offender 19 years at the time of the offence. The court held that a headline sentence of five years (then the maximum for defilement of a child under 17 years) or even four years would have been appropriate. It substituted two years for the effective sentence of three years that had originally been imposed. Further in this regard, it should be noted that the offence to which the lower maximum applies is not defined as the defilement of a person aged between 15 and 17 years, but rather the defilement of a person under 17 years. The effect of this formulation is that the prosecution has discretion to charge the less serious offence even where the child was under 15 years at the time. While a court must obviously impose a sentence that reflects the offence of conviction, it is entitled in a case like *Conroy* to consider the possibility that the less serious offence might have been charged in which case the lower maximum would apply.

Prolonged Sexual Abuse of one or more Children

10–63 It is difficult to provide guidance, of a specific nature at least, on the sentencing of offenders who have sexually abused one or more children over a lengthy period, short of saying that such offending usually calls for a severe headline sentence. This may be significantly reduced where there are strong extenuating circumstances such as old age, ill-health or infirmity on the part of the offender. Even then, some term of immediate imprisonment is likely to be imposed unless it would be manifestly inhumane to do so. For this purpose, regard will be had to the capacity of the prison system to cater for any mobility or health-related problems being experienced by the offender. While it is always good practice to impose a separate sentence for each offence of conviction, the reality in

[131] [2018] IECA 120.
[132] [2021] IECA 230.
[133] [2018] IECA 350.

most cases of this nature is that a court must begin by standing back and deciding on a global sentence that fairly reflects the totality of the offending. The key determinants of this sentence will be the nature, duration, intensity and context of the abuse, taking account also of any additional conduct that, deliberately or otherwise, entailed further degradation, humiliation, isolation or domination of the victim(s). The age of the children when they were abused and the extent to which they were dependent upon or under the control of the abuser are critically important factors as well. The younger the victim and the greater their degree of vulnerability and dependency, the greater the moral culpability of the offender. Conduct involving sexual penetration, especially if repeated, will normally place the overall offending high on the scale of gravity, and all the more so if it left a victim at risk of pregnancy or contracting a sexually transmitted disease. Sentences towards the lower end of the scale are generally appropriate where conduct consisted solely of non-penetrative exploitation such as repeatedly touching the victim in an indecent or sexual manner.[134] However, prolonged sexual abuse of this kind may still also have a serious and enduring impact on a victim, a factor that must be reflected in a global sentence.

Where the offending includes rape, s 4 rape, aggravated sexual assault, defilement of a person under the age of 15 years or child sexual exploitation[135] the available penalty range extends up to life imprisonment. Cases in the most serious category have occasionally attracted life sentences, even in response to a guilty plea, as occurred in *People (DPP) v McC(R)*,[136] decided by the Supreme Court. Otherwise, a lengthy determinate sentence is usually appropriate. In *People (DPP) v X*,[137] for example, the Court of Appeal upheld an overall sentence of 18 years' imprisonment with the last three years suspended in the case of a man who had sexually abused his daughter over a 12-year period while she was aged between four or five years and 16 years. He had pleaded guilty to multiple charges including rape, s 4 rape, sexual assault and assault causing harm. The court agreed with the trial judge that life imprisonment was the appropriate headline sentence before credit was given for mitigating factors. The duration of the offending need not be a decisive factor. Persistent abuse of a serious nature, even if perpetrated over a relatively short time span, may still attract a severe sentence. In *People (DPP) v CC*[138] the defendant was convicted of numerous offences of child sexual exploitation, sexual assault and child neglect committed against five of her six young children during a period **10–64**

---

[134] *People (DPP) v C(M)* [2022] IECA 252.

[135] The offence of child sexual exploitation was created by Child Trafficking and Pornography Act 1998, s 3, as amended by Criminal Law (Human Trafficking) Act 2008, s 3.

[136] [2007] IESC 47; [2008] 2 IR 92; [2008] 1 ILRM 321. See also *People (DPP) v DD* [2024] IECA 224 where the sentence imposed on a man convicted of serious sexual and other offences committed against several of his children was increased by the Court of Appeal from 15 years to life imprisonment.

[137] [2021] IECA 168.

[138] [2024] IECA 223.

of less than two years. The sexual offences were committed against three of those children and there were other adult family members involved in some of the abusive acts.[139] The child sexual exploitation offences were described by the Court of Appeal as particularly egregious in nature, and for those offences the trial judge had set a headline sentence of 12 years' imprisonment, mitigated to nine years. Having found this to be unduly lenient, the Court of Appeal increased the headline sentence to 15 years, this being the top of the second highest range identified in *People (DPP) v E(F)*,[140] and reduced it to 12 years to reflect certain mitigating factors.

10–65 Many complicating factors can arise in cases of this nature. For instance, the offender may have been a child himself when the abuse was committed or, at least, when it began. His reduced culpability by virtue of youth must therefore be reflected in the headline sentence.[141] The same applies where the offender had a mental disability or learning difficulty that limited his capacity to understand the full implications of his conduct and the harm it was causing.[142] A choice must often be made between consecutive and concurrent sentences, especially where there has been more than one victim or where, as in *People (DPP) v H(S)*,[143] there were two separate periods of offending with a significant interval between the two. Courts sometimes favour consecutive sentences in cases with multiple victims in order to acknowledge the harm inflicted on each. However, as noted earlier, the important consideration is that the aggregate sentence, whether consisting of concurrent or consecutive terms of imprisonment, should reflect the totality of the offending. How this is best achieved is largely a matter of judicial discretion.

4. Drug Offences

10–66 Most existing drug offences have been created by the Misuse of Drugs Act 1977 (the '1977 Act'), as substantially amended.[144] Here, we shall concentrate on the possession, supply and cultivation of controlled drugs. The 1977 Act is structured so that the sentencing provisions in respect of all offences are contained in s 27. Simple possession of drugs is outlawed by s 3. This section makes no reference to the possession

[139] In *People (DPP) v AA* [2024] IECA 225, the Court of Appeal increased to 20 years the headline sentence imposed on an uncle of the children in respect of this offending, but reduced it to 18 and a half years to reflect the limited mitigation present. The sentence imposed on the children's father was increased to life imprisonment by the Court of Appeal: *People (DPP) v DD* [2024] IECA 224. The court described the offending in his case as "grave, systematic, prolonged and depraved" and at the top of the scale of gravity.

[140] [2019] IESC 85; [2021] 1 IR 217; [2020] 1 ILRM 517.

[141] *People (DPP) v R(C)* [2023] IECA 136.

[142] *People (DPP) v L(J)* [2024] IECA 87.

[143] [2023] IECA 206.

[144] A revised version of 1977 Act, incorporating all amendments to date, has been produced by the Law Reform Commission and is available at www.lawreform.ie, under 'Revised Statutes'.

being for personal use only, but that is to be inferred from s 15(2) which creates a rebuttable presumption to the effect that a person is deemed to possess drugs for sale or supply if, having regard to the quantity of drugs found in his or her possession and other relevant matters, a court is satisfied that they were "not intended for the immediate personal use of the person". The maximum sentence for a s 3 offence depends on the nature of the drug and the presence or absence of previous convictions. Where the drug is cannabis, and the court is satisfied that it was for the defendant's personal use, the possession offence is punishable solely with a fine irrespective of whether the offence is dealt with summarily or on indictment. A third conviction carries the possibility of imprisonment (up to 12 months following summary conviction and up to three years following conviction on indictment), although a fine may be imposed either instead of or together with imprisonment. In the case of any other drug and irrespective of whether it is a first or subsequent conviction, the maximum sentence is a fine and/or imprisonment (12 months on summary conviction and seven years on indictment).

Under s 15 of the 1977 Act, a person convicted of possessing a controlled **10–67** drug for sale or supply is liable, following conviction on indictment, to a maximum of life imprisonment, or 12 months on summary conviction. In either event, a fine may be imposed in addition to or instead of imprisonment. No indication is given of the type or precise quantity of drug that a person must possess to be guilty of this offence. As already noted, a court is entitled to presume that the drugs were intended for sale or supply unless it is satisfied that the quantity was such as to be for immediate personal use only. In principle, therefore, possession of any quantity of drugs exceeding that amount may lead to a prosecution for a s 15 offence. However, since 1999, there has existed an additional, more specific offence, widely known as a s 15A offence, which outlaws the possession by a person aged 18 years or over of controlled drugs for sale or supply where the drugs have a market value of €13,000 or more.[145] The significance of this offence is that, while it is punishable with a maximum of life imprisonment, it is also subject to a presumptive minimum sentence of 10 years' imprisonment. This is not, as is sometimes claimed, a *mandatory* minimum sentence. It is presumptive in the sense that a court must impose at least 10 years' imprisonment (or, in the words of the statute, "specify a term of not less than 10 years as the minimum term of imprisonment to be served"), unless it determines that, by reason of exceptional and specific circumstances relating to the offence or the offender, it would be unjust in all the circumstances to do so. For this purpose, a court may have regard to any matters it considers appropriate including whether the offender pleaded guilty, the stage at which the plea was entered, the circumstances in which an indication to plead was given, and whether the offender materially assisted in the investigation of the offence. As a result of further amendments by the Criminal Justice Act 2006 (s 84), considerable emphasis is placed on the

[145] This offence was first introduced by the Criminal Justice Act 1999, s 4.

presence or absence of previous convictions for similar offences. When imposing sentence for a s 15A offence, a court must, in the first instance, have regard to whether the offender has previous convictions for a drug trafficking offence.[146] Further, when deciding if it would be unjust in all the circumstances to impose the presumptive 10-year minimum, a court may "in particular" have regard to whether the offender has previously been convicted of a drug trafficking offence and whether the public interest in preventing drug trafficking would be served by the imposition of a lesser sentence.[147] "Drug trafficking" is defined in the Criminal Justice Act 1994 (s 4) as including possession of drugs for sale or supply. A consolidated version of these subsections of s 27 of the 1977 Act on the sentencing of s 15A offences is conveniently provided in s 33 of the Criminal Justice Act 2007.[148] Section 15B, introduced by the Criminal Justice Act 2006 (s 82), outlaws the importation of controlled drugs with an aggregate market value of €13,000 or more. The sentencing provisions applicable to this offence are essentially the same as those for s 15A. Section 27(3F), which provided for a mandatory (as opposed to a presumptive) minimum 10-year sentence for repeat ss 15A or 15B offences, no longer applies as it was declared unconstitutional in *McManus v Minister for Justice*.[149] A previous conviction for drug dealing remains an aggravating factor, save that it no longer automatically triggers a minimum 10-year sentence.

10–68 The proper approach to sentencing a s 15A offence is now well settled and was authoritatively summarised in *People (DPP) v Sarsfield:*

> "It has long been recognised that the proper approach to sentencing is for a judge to identify the appropriate sentence without reference to the presumptive minimum. If the appropriate sentence is at or in excess of the statutory minimum, nothing further is required. If the sentence under contemplation is below the presumptive minimum, the court will have to address the presumptive minimum and consider whether the imposition of the mandatory presumptive minimum would, in all the circumstances of the case, be unjust. Where the offence involves significant involvement in a very high-level drug offence, the headline or pre-mitigation sentence is likely to well in excess of the statutory presumptive minimum. In the case of high-level commercial drug dealing involving very large quantities of drugs, we would expect that the headline or pre-mitigation sentence is likely to be of the order of fourteen or fifteen years, and in some exceptional cases, significantly higher."[150]

10–69 Therefore, in any case where the appropriate sentence seems to fall below the presumptive 10-year minimum, a court must still be satisfied of the existence of factors relating to the offence, the offender or both that would

[146] Misuse of Drugs Act 1977, s 27(3B).
[147] Misuse of Drugs Act 1977, s 27(3D)(c).
[148] See also the updated version of the entire Misuse of Drugs Act 1977 produced by the Law Reform Commission (note 144 above).
[149] [2021] IEHC 385, following the Supreme Court decision in *Ellis v Minister for Justice* [2019] IESC 30; [2019] 3 IR 511; [2019] 2 ILRM 420.
[150] [2019] IECA 260, para 18. See also *People (DPP) v Renald,* Court of Criminal Appeal, 23 November 2001.

render it unjust to impose the minimum. Even if so satisfied, it must also, when selecting sentence, have due regard to the fact that the legislature has deemed a minimum of 10 years to be ordinarily appropriate for the possession of drugs worth €13,000 or more for sale or supply. *Sarsfield* is a guideline judgment that deals, mainly in general terms, with the sentencing of s 15A offences and the circumstances in which departure from the presumptive minimum may be appropriate. The Court of Appeal had sought additional submissions on those matters before proceeding to deliver judgment. In terms of sentence ranges, it said that in a case of high-level drug dealing involving a large quantity of drugs the headline sentence is likely to be 14 or 15 years, or even significantly higher. Even a plea of guilty is unlikely to bring the ultimate sentence below 10 years in such a case, especially if the prosecution case was strong. The court nonetheless acknowledged that the offender's role in the overall enterprise remains an important factor, whatever the quantity or value of the drugs.[151] Mitigating factors include duress which can arise where the offender handled, stored or transported drugs as a result of threats received, typically, from someone to whom the offender was indebted.[152] However, as the appeal courts have often stressed, the presumptive 10-year minimum should never be regarded as the maximum sentence for a s 15A offence. The maximum is life imprisonment.

In setting an initial headline sentence, a court must, as in all cases, assess the gravity of the offence, taking account of both harm and culpability. The principal factors to be considered for this purpose were set out by the Court of Appeal in *People (DPP) v Sloyan*:[153] **10–70**

> "In the case of s.15A offending there are many different circumstances in which the offending may be committed. Culpability will depend on the individual offender's role in the matter; and if he/she was part of a common design it must be assessed with reference to their place in the organisational hierarchy if there was one, the overall degree of pre-planning and sophistication involved, the scale of the enterprise, their actual contribution to the enterprise, their state of knowledge and the extent to which they had actually benefitted or stood to benefit. Moreover, the circumstances of the individual's involvement might require additional aggravating or mitigating factors bearing on culpability to be taken into account.
>
> In assessing the harm caused, or potentially to be caused, the principal considerations are likely to be nature of the controlled drug, it's addictive propensity and other dangers associated with it, and the quantity involved."

In that case, an effective sentence of seven years was reduced on appeal to an effective sentence of 3 and a half years (five years with 18 months suspended to incentivise further the appellant's efforts at rehabilitation). **10–71**

---

151 See also *People (DPP) v Lindsay* [2024] IECA 77, para 32.

152 See also *People (DPP) v O'Toole*, unreported, Court of Criminal Appeal, 26 March 2003 (which involved the importation €41.5 million worth of drugs) a 20-year sentence was reduced to 16 years for this reason.

153 [2019] IECA 242, paras 36-37.

The Court of Appeal also had regard to the limited scale of the operation and the total value of the drugs involved (about €51,000 worth of cocaine). Section 15A draws no distinction between different kinds of drug; the offence is committed once a person possesses for sale or supply any type of controlled drug with a market value of €13,000 or more. The appeal courts have nonetheless held that the nature as well as the amount of the drugs is a relevant factor at sentencing.[154]

10–72 As reflected in *Sarsfield,* the heaviest sentences, often extending well beyond 10 years, are typically reserved for cases where there was a large quantity of drugs, coupled with a high level of involvement by the offender in a sophisticated or well-organised operation. Largescale importation may attract sentences measured in decades rather than years. In *People (DPP) v Gilligan,*[155]where s 15A and its associated sentencing provisions did not apply because of the time at which the offences were committed, a sentence of 28 years' imprisonment was reduced on appeal to 20 years for dealing in large quantities of cannabis. A concurrent 12-year sentence for importation was left intact. The most severe sentences so far imposed seem to be those arising from the discovery off the Cork coast in 2007 of cocaine estimated to be worth at least €100 million and possibly more than €400 million. Following a lengthy trial, three men were convicted, a fourth having pleaded guilty and received a 10-year sentence. Of those convicted, Daly was sentenced to 25 years' imprisonment which was upheld on appeal.[156] Wharrie and Wanden were each sentenced to 30 years, although Wharrie's sentence was reduced on appeal to 17 and a half years.[157] The Supreme Court subsequently held that the Court of Criminal Appeal had erred in treating a particular factor as mitigating in Wharrie's case.[158] But as the appeal (by the DPP) to the Supreme Court was taken "without prejudice", the reduced sentence remained undisturbed.

10–73 At the other end of the spectrum, a wholly suspended sentence, though certainly exceptional, may be appropriate where the offender had a low level of involvement in the overall enterprise and received, or was promised, little by way of financial reward, and where there was strong personal mitigation. As the Court of Criminal Appeal said in *People (DPP) v McGinty,*[159] the foundational case on the matter, "where there are special reasons of a substantial nature and wholly exceptional circumstances, it may be that the imposition of a suspended sentence is correct and in

[154] *People (DPP) v Daly* [2011] IECCA 104; [2012] 1 I.R. 476; *People (DPP) v Long* [2006] IECCA 49; *People (DPP) v Wharrie* [2017] IESC 47; [2017] 2 IR 743; *People (DPP) v Sloyan* [2019] IECA 242.

[155] [2004] 3 IR 87.

[156] *People (DPP) v Daly* [2011] IECCA 104; [2012] 1 IR 476.

[157] *People (DPP) v Wharrie* [2016] IECCA 1.

[158] *People (DPP) v Wharrie* [2017] IESC 47; [2017] 2 IR 743. The error consisted in treating as mitigating the fact that Wharrie had not given perjured evidence at his trial.

[159] [2006] IECCA 37. See also *People (DPP) v Jervis and Doyle* [2014] IECCA 14.

the interests of justice". Or, as the Court of Appeal explained further in *People (DPP) v Flanagan*:

> "[Several earlier authorities considered by the Court] clearly illustrate that in the overwhelming majority of cases, a s.15A offence will attract and require the imposition of an immediate, and frequently significant, custodial sentence. In acknowledging that, however, it is important not to lose sight of the requirement that a sentencing judge is not sentencing for the offence *per se*, but for the offence as committed by the particular offender in the particular circumstances of the individual case. While it is clear that a custodial sentence will be the norm in s. 15A cases, having regard to the position taken by the legislature in especially deprecating the harm caused to society by drug trafficking, and in setting a presumptive mandatory minimum sentence of ten years for such offences that is only to be departed from where exceptional circumstances exist, it cannot be the case that the legislature intended to so emasculate the discretion of a sentencing judge as to preclude him from ever imposing a non-custodial sentence in a wholly exceptional but nonetheless appropriate case. It is accepted, however, that such cases are likely to be rare and infrequent."[160]

In that case, arising from an undue leniency application, the respondent's personal circumstances were found to be sufficiently exceptional to justify upholding the fully suspended sentence imposed by the trial court. In *People (DPP) v Bowen*[161] (the respondent being a co-accused of Flanagan), the Court of Appeal held that there were insufficiently exceptional circumstances to justify a fully suspended sentence when it was imposed by the trial court, but that such circumstances had come into being by the time the undue leniency application was decided. The court therefore imposed a fully suspended two-year sentence. The total value of the drugs involved in *Flanagan* and *Bowen* seems to have been about €80,000 and almost €28,000 in cash was discovered as well. What cases such as these and others like *People (DPP) v Zinck*[162] (considered below in relation to cannabis cultivation) illustrate is the need for caution in treating the sentences ultimately imposed or upheld in undue leniency cases as guidelines or even as useful comparators. Those sentences often reflect factors that have materialised since sentence was imposed and almost always include the "disappointment" factor as well. But they are not necessarily, or even predominantly, the sentences that would have been appropriate at first instance. The Court of Appeal will often, however, state what the appropriate headline sentence should have been. This can be a useful indicator of appropriate penalty levels for similar offences. **10–74**

Most s 15A cases fall somewhere between these two extremes. Because the nature and quantity of the drugs bear a direct relationship to the degree of harm their distribution will cause to individuals and communities, sentences in excess of 10 years are presumptively appropriate in high-value cases. What constitutes 'high value' is difficult to identify but it may **10–75**

---

[160] [2015] IECA 94, para 30.
[161] [2015] IECA 95 and [2015] IECA 177.
[162] [2016] IECA 368 and [2017] IECA 33.

safely be said that cases where the drugs are worth €1 million or more fall into this category, without excluding the possibility that the same may apply where the drugs were valued at hundreds of thousands of Euro. In *People (DPP) v Sarsfield,*[163] considered earlier, where the drugs were valued at €4.1 million, the Court of Appeal held that the appropriate headline sentence was 15 years which, in light of certain mitigating factors, it reduced to the presumptive minimum of 10 years. Later, in *People (DPP) v O'Dwyer*[164](the respondent being a co-defendant of Sarsfield), the Court of Appeal again identified a headline sentence of 14 or 15 years, ultimately reduced because of exceptional mitigating circumstances to nine years. In *People (DPP) v Mahony and Brennan*[165] which involved cocaine and heroin valued at €3.5 million, a headline sentence of 13 years, ultimately reduced to 10 years, was upheld. In *People (DPP) v Devlin and Devlin*[166]sentences of 12 years' imprisonment with four years suspended in the case of one appellant and two years suspended in the case of the other were upheld on appeal. This involved a sophisticated operation and cannabis with an estimated value of €1.3 million.

10–76 Unless the value of drugs is particularly high, or the offender had a key role in the drug dealing enterprise or had a previous conviction for a similar offence, or some combination of these factors is present, the headline sentence will probably be somewhat lower than 10 years, with the possibility of a further reduction for personal mitigation. Courts are sometimes criticised for failing, or being reluctant, to impose the statutory presumptive minimum. Yet, as stated in the passage from *Flanagan* quoted above, the legislation expressly allows for the imposition of a lower sentence and, in effect, confers considerable discretion on the courts in this regard. Granted, there must be exceptional and specific circumstances, but courts are not confined to considering the factors expressly mentioned in s 27(3D). They may, for this purpose, consider any other factors they consider appropriate. Another point critics often ignore is that in many, perhaps most cases, where the presumptive minimum is not imposed, the sentences are still quite severe. Headline sentences are likely to be somewhere between five and 10 years which means that offenders serve significant custodial terms. To take one random example, in *People (DPP) v Flynn,*[167] an effective sentence of four years' imprisonment was upheld for the possession of €87,612 worth of diamorphine. The statistics quoted in *Sarsfield* bear this out, as do prison statistics. On 30 November 2022, there were more drug offenders (110) serving sentences in the five-to 10-year bracket than any other group of prisoners except sex offenders (180). On the same date there were 98 drug offenders serving sentences of three to five years, and 17 serving sentences longer than 10 years. The total number in prison for drug offences on that date was 386.[168] Further, the

---

163 [2019] IECA 260.
164 [2020] IECA 353.
165 [2014] IECA 57.
166 [2016] IECA 125.
167 [2022] IECA 140.
168 Irish Prison Service *Annual Report 2022* (2023), 74.

Court of Appeal has not hesitated to increase sentences for s 15A offences to 10 years or more where there was no justification for departing from the presumptive minimum.[169]

From a policy perspective, the statutory scheme for sentencing s 15A offences is difficult to defend. Its application depends on the drugs having a specified market value which can only be estimated at best. This 'cliff edge' was originally set at £10,000 but converted to €13,000 with the introduction of the Euro. There has been no real adjustment to the minimum value during the past quarter of a century, even though the market value of certain drugs may have increased in the meantime. Opinions differ as to whether this happened, but if the street price of drugs has risen, it means that some offenders now find themselves liable to be prosecuted for a s 15A offence despite having a smaller quantity of drugs than would have brought them within the scope of that offence when it was first introduced in 1999. This is one unsatisfactory consequence of defining the offence by reference to estimated market value rather than the nature and amount of the drugs. Secondly, it must be recalled that the presumptive 10-year minimum applies even on a first conviction for a s 15A (or s 15B) offence. It is therefore a case of 'one strike and you're out'. In England and Wales, on the other hand, a seven-year sentence must be imposed for a third Class A drug trafficking offence, *unless* there are particular circumstances making it unjust to do so.[170] There, the focus is on repeat offenders whereas here even a first-time offender becomes liable to the presumptive 10-year minimum. Here, as already noted, the Criminal Justice Act 2006 provided for a mandatory 10-year minimum for repeat s 15A and s 15B offences, but that provision was declared unconstitutional in 2021.[171] Now that the Court of Appeal and Supreme Court are developing offence-specific sentencing guidelines, and with the Judicial Council Act 2019 providing for the creation of more formal guidelines, there is a strong case for abolishing presumptive minimum sentences altogether. A set of more nuanced guidelines would provide a better framework, in terms of both fairness and effectiveness, for sentencing the offences in question. **10–77**

In the federal jurisdiction of the United States, possession of controlled substances also attracts mandatory minimum prison sentences, provided they exceed a statutorily prescribed weight which varies from one kind of drug to another.[172] For instance, a person caught with 500g of cocaine is liable to a minimum five-year sentence but to a minimum of 10 years if the amount is 5kg or more. For heroin, the equivalent amounts are 100g and 1kg. The heaviest sentences are reserved for methamphetamine (which now accounts for about half of all drug trafficking offences sentenced federally). For that drug, 5g attracts a minimum of five years while 50g **10–78**

---

169 Apart from *People (DPP) v Sarsfield* [2019] IECA 260, considered above, see also *People (DPP) v Curtis* [2022] IECA 184.

170 Sentencing Act 2020, s 313; *R v Woofe* [2019] EWCA Crim 2249; [2020] 2 Cr App R (S) 6; *R v Yeates* [2023] EWCA Crim 719; [2023] 2 Cr App R (S) 43.

171 *McManus v Minister for Justice* [2021] IEHC 385.

172 21 USC 841(b)(1) and 960(b).

attracts a minimum of 10 years.[173] Sentences for some drugs also depend in part on purity levels. According to a recent report, it takes 10 times less pure methamphetamine to trigger the same penalty than a mixture containing a detectable amount of that drug.[174] Establishing the weight and purity levels of drugs may present some logistical difficulties, but these are more defensible criteria than the estimated monetary value applicable in Ireland. Estimating the street value of drugs at any given moment is far from being an exact science, but that estimate remains an important factor in the determination of sentence. Weight can, of course, pose its problems if adopted as the decisive factor. A so-called drugs mule could be caught importing or transporting as much drugs as might be found in the possession of a serious dealer. Yet any payment given or promised to the mule might be infinitesimal compared with the profit made by the dealer.[175] This underscores the importance of treating the offender's level of involvement, bearing in mind what they gained from it and any pressure or coercion to which they were subject, as a major consideration at sentencing, even though the quantity or value of drugs and the harm that would result from their distribution, must be another important consideration.

Cannabis Cultivation

10–79 Under s 17 of the Misuse of Drugs Act 1977, as amended, it is an offence to cultivate opium poppy for the production of opium or any cannabis or erythroxylon plant (the latter being a source of cocaine). This offence may be prosecuted either summarily or on indictment. Following conviction on indictment, it carries a maximum sentence of 14 years' imprisonment.[176] Most prosecutions are for the cultivation of cannabis. This can range from an individual growing a few plants for their own recreational or medicinal use to largescale cultivation in a cannabis farm or factory. Cases at the lower end are likely to be dealt with summarily and result in a fine, suspended sentence or, where there was a fairly large quantity involved or there had been repeat offending, a short custodial sentence. More serious cases prosecuted on indictment can be difficult to sentence because of a frequent mismatch between harm and culpability. The cannabis-growing operation may be a well-planned, sophisticated operation and therefore capable of producing a large quantity of the drug for sale within the community. In some decided cases, the ultimate street value of the cannabis being cultivated was estimated at more than €1 million. However, the persons who are prosecuted are often merely minders (often called 'gardeners') rather than owners, managers or others with a significant stake in the operation. They are sometimes, though not always, impoverished economic migrants who may have had little choice

---

173 United States Sentencing Commission, *Methamphetamine Trafficking Offences in the Federal Criminal Justice System* (2024), 13.

174 United States Sentencing Commission, note 173 above, at 14.

175 Mark William Osler, "The Weight" at <https://papers.ssrn.com/so13/papers.cfm?abstract_id=4958105> accessed 26 September 2024.

176 Misuse of Drugs Act 1977, s 27(2).

but to accept the work in question and, more often than not, in return for a paltry wage. In fact, a question has occasionally arisen as to whether defendants were victims of human trafficking. While their circumstances, short perhaps of being trafficked, do not extinguish their culpability, they significantly diminish it. This is a relevant factor when evaluating the gravity of the offence for the purpose of identifying a headline sentence or, if not, it becomes a relevant personal circumstance under the second limb of the proportionality principle. What matters is that it be given due weight at either of those stages. Even if the extent and nature of the operation, including the value of the drug, points to a severe headline sentence, the ultimate sentence may have to be very much lower. This would hold true where, for example, the defendant was a victim of exploitation or was for all practical purposes being coerced to work for the owners of the cannabis-growing operation. Some defendants, because of language difficulties, lack of education or skills, or some similar problem, would have had little hope of securing any other employment.

Considerably heavier sentences will ordinarily be imposed on defendants **10–80** who had a controlling or intermediate role in the operation, as opposed to being so-called gardeners, especially where a significant quantity of cannabis was being produced. The sentences eventually imposed on five persons involved in a major cannabis growing operation in Piltown, County Kilkenny in 2012 illustrate the point. This was largest such operation hitherto discovered in the State, with the total value of the drug estimated as being close to €3 million. Three Asian defendants who were tending the plants were each sentenced to seven years' imprisonment with the last six years suspended on condition that they leave the State immediately. (They had already spent more than a year in custody when sentenced.)[177] However, a fourth, Mr Kilkenny, who pleaded guilty to a s 15A offence, was found to have had a more central role. He had, for example, leased the premises and been involved in sourcing the machinery. He was sentenced to 10 years' imprisonment with the last six years suspended (and to a concurrent four-year sentence for another s 15A offence). Following an undue leniency application by the DPP, the Court of Appeal increased this sentence to 12 years but, taking account of the "disappointment factor" and other matters, suspended the last four years.[178] The court said that, absent these factors, the ultimate sentence could not have been less than 10 years. The fifth defendant, Mr Zinck, who also pleaded guilty to a s 15A offence, was found not to be at the lowest level but somewhere above that. He had been promised €5,000 for his involvement. He was given an entirely suspended nine-year prison sentence. This, too, was the subject of an undue leniency application. The Court of Appeal increased this to 10 years but, in light of wholly exceptional circumstances, including the progress made by the defendant

---

[177] *People (DPP) v Kilkenny* [2016] IECA 348, para 2.
[178] *People (DPP) v Kilkenny* [2016] IECA 348, para 14.

since his arrest some years earlier, decided to suspend that sentence in its entirely.[179]

5. Property Offences

Robbery

10–81 Robbery consists of stealing accompanied by the use of force on any person (or putting any person in fear of being there and then subjected to force).[180] It is punishable with a maximum sentence of life imprisonment, although it may also be dealt with summarily in the District Court in which case it is punishable with a maximum of 12 months' imprisonment, a class A fine or both.[181] Robbery is thus a composite offence consisting, in effect, of theft and assault, a characteristic that is reflected in sentencing practice. Severe sentences may be imposed where the victim suffered serious injury or trauma even if the value of the property stolen was relatively low. The same would apply where the value of the stolen property was very high (as might be true of bank robbery) even if nobody suffered any significant personal injury in the process. Bank robberies are now quite rare, at least when compared with their prevalence between the 1960s and early 1990s. Increased security (so-called target hardening) and the fact that many branches have become largely cashless because of electronic banking are among the standard explanations for the decline.[182] This may have a displacement effect in the sense that other businesses such as retail shops, pharmacies and service stations are more vulnerable to being robbed, and there is some evidence of such an effect.[183] Armed robberies of post offices and cash in transit vehicles still occur and they usually attract heavy sentences.

10–82 The English Sentencing Council's definitive guideline on robbery provides useful guidance on the factors that are most relevant when assessing the gravity of a robbery.[184] England and Wales, like Ireland, has a single robbery offence which is defined in identical terms in both jurisdictions.[185]

---

179 *People (DPP) v Zinck* [2016] IECA 368 and [2017] IECA 33.

180 Criminal Justice (Theft and Fraud Offences) Act 2001, s 14.

181 Criminal Justice (Theft and Fraud Offences) Act 2001, s 53, as amended by Fines Act 2010, s 10.

182 Jay L Zagorsky, "Why bank robbing has gone out of style" at <https://nypost.com/2022/10/12/why-bank-robbing-has-gone-out-of-style/> accessed 12 December 2023; Ronald V Clarke, Simon Field and G McGrath, "Target hardening of banks in Australia and displacement of robberies" (1991) 2 *Security Journal* 84. It has been reported that Denmark had no bank robbery in 2022. There were 26 bank robberies in London in 2012 compared with 291 in 1992. See Duncan Campbell, "Where did all the bank robbers go?", *The Guardian*, 4 July 2014.

183 Clarke, Field and McGrath, note 182 above; Thomas Gabor, "The crime displacement hypothesis: An empirical examination" (1981) 27 *Crime and Delinquency* 390.

184 Sentencing Council, *Robbery: Definitive Guideline* (2016).

185 Theft Act 1968, s 8 (England and Wales); Criminal Justice (Theft and Fraud

For sentencing purposes, however, the guideline divides robberies into three broad categories: street and less sophisticated commercial robberies, professionally planned commercial robberies and robbery in a dwelling. Robberies in the first category are probably the most prevalent, and the heaviest sentences are generally reserved for those that cause serious physical and/or psychological harm to a victim or have a serious detrimental impact on a business, coupled with the use of a weapon to inflict violence or intimidate, or the use of a significant amount of force. At the other end of the spectrum, more lenient sentences are appropriate where only minimal force was used or threatened, the value of the property stolen was low and victim impact was not particularly severe. Other more general aggravating factors also, of course, apply. For instance, a robbery offence will be more serious where a victim was targeted because of actual or perceived vulnerability, where the offender played a leading role, or where there was significant planning or a prolonged attack. The criteria for assessing the seriousness of the second and third categories of robbery identified by the Sentencing Council are broadly similar to those for the first, save that the recommended sentence ranges are higher.

In *People (DPP) v Byrne*[186] the Court of Appeal offered the following general guidance on sentencing for robbery: **10–83**

> "On the basis that a life sentence is likely to be reserved for only the very worst and most egregious offences of this type, the practical reality is that the effective range of custodial penalties caps out at fifteen years, or thereabouts, for all but the most exceptional cases. An effective fifteen-year range allows for a low range of zero to five years, a mid-range of six to ten years and a higher range of eleven to fifteen years."

These ranges relate to headline sentences; the ultimate sentence may well be lower if adjustments must be made for mitigating factors, as occurred in *Byrne* itself. As the Court acknowledges, exceptionally serious cases may call for prison sentences longer than 15 years. This might hold true, for example, of a major bank robbery as in the English case of *R v Turner.*[187] However, the vast majority of cases will fall within one of the three *Byrne* ranges. The seriousness of a robbery offence for the purpose of identifying a headline sentence must be assessed by reference to harm and culpability (as is true of all offences). As already noted, robbery is a composite offence including both theft and assault. The heaviest sentences are likely to be imposed for planned robberies, involving a group of offenders, which resulted in the loss of a considerable amount of money or other property and where victims suffered physical or psychological harm. Thus, in *People (DPP) v Wall, Walsh, O'Connor and Tynan*[188] a group of men committed an armed robbery at a post office while there were both staff members and **10–84**

Offences) Act 2001, s 14 (Ireland).

186 [2018] IECA 120, para 60.

187 (1975) 61 Cr App R 67. See also *R v Schultz* [1996] 1 Cr App R (S) 451 and *R v Adams* [2000] 2 Cr App R (S) 274.

188 [2020] IECA 48.

customers, including children, present. More than €40,000 was taken though later recovered. Following an undue leniency application by the DPP, the Court of Appeal specified headline sentences varying from nine to 10 and a half years' imprisonment with some reductions in each case to reflect mitigating factors. This case may have involved a post office robbery, but the same considerations would apply to an armed robbery committed in any other setting, including a private residence.

10–85 Largescale robberies are sometimes forestalled as a result of police intelligence and subsequent surveillance. In that event, the participants are likely to be charged with conspiracy (or possibly attempted robbery). Conspiracy is a common law offence punishable with such amount of fine or imprisonment as the court deems appropriate. In practice, the sentence is unlikely to exceed the statutory maximum for the completed offence (which, of course, for robbery is life imprisonment) or, more realistically, the sentence that would be appropriate for the planned offence if completed. Penalties for conspiracy, as a rule, broadly reflect the harm that would have resulted if the conspirators had succeeded in achieving their goal. There will seldom be any ambiguity about their intentions, so their levels of culpability will probably be high, unless perhaps one was participating because of influence or coercion exercised by another. In *People (DPP) v Noonan, Murphy and Saunders*[189] three men pleaded guilty to conspiracy to rob and other associated offences. Their intended targets seem to have been an ATM machine and a cash in transit van. It was claimed that their takings would have been at least €2 million if their plan had succeeded. The Court of Appeal upheld the sentences of 10 years' imprisonment with the last 2two and a half years suspended in each case.

10–86 Under the *Byrne* guidelines, robberies in the middle category attract headline sentences in range of six to 11 years. A sentence in this range will be appropriate where a significant amount of money or other property was stolen or, more commonly, where the victim was subjected to, or threatened with, serious physical violence even if the value of the property stolen was relatively low. An offence may also fall into this category if the offender led the victim to believe that they would be shot or stabbed unless they complied with whatever demand was made of them, even if the offender was not, in fact, carrying any weapon. Recent examples include *People (DPP) v Ormond*[190] in which the appellant had violently robbed the victim of his mobile phone in a public place, and in the course of the struggle led the victim to believe that he would be stabbed by a person accompanying the appellant. The Court of Appeal upheld the sentence of six and a half years' imprisonment with 18 months suspended. A similar sentence was upheld in *People (DPP) v Dalton*[191] for the robbery of mobile phones valued at €11,000 to €12,000. There were

---

[189] [2019] IECA 112.
[190] [2021] IECA 279.
[191] [2023] IECA 220.

three assailants and violence was both used and threatened against the victim. A headline sentence of eight years was identified in this case, and the mitigating factors included an early guilty plea. The appellant in *People (DPP) v O'Dwyer*[192] had robbed a till containing €250 from a shop, having subjected the shop assistant to serious threats, including a threat to shoot her. The trial judge nominated a headline sentence of seven years, but suspended the last three years on account of mitigating factors, notably the appellant's guilty plea. This was upheld on appeal.

A robbery in the lowest category of seriousness may attract a non-custodial penalty, a suspended sentence or a short term of imprisonment. In *DPP v Doolan*,[193] for example, the Court of Appeal substituted 200 hours' community service for an effective sentence of one year's imprisonment imposed by the trial court. In that case, however, the appellant did not participate in the robbery itself but rather seems to have acted as accessory. There were also several mitigating factors including his level of cooperation in the investigation of the offence. It was accepted that a prosecution might well have been impossible without his admissions and cooperation. The robbery in *People (DPP) v Marin*[194] was also placed in the lowest category but there were aggravating factors to justify placing it relatively high within that category. The appellant had robbed an 81-year-old woman of her purse which contained €300. He had used only a minimum level of force to commit the offence and had not inflicted any physical harm on the victim. However, the victim suffered a great deal psychologically as result of the experience. The Court of Appeal upheld the sentence of three years' imprisonment with the last 18 months suspended. **10–87**

Byrne may not have been a formal guideline judgment in the sense identified in *People (DPP) v O'Sullivan*[195] but it is now effectively treated as such. In both *O'Sullivan* itself and later in *People (DPP) v Joyce*[196] the Court of Appeal stressed that *Byrne* provided important guidance on sentencing for robbery. Trial courts should always therefore have regard to the sentence ranges specified in *Byrne*. Some indication of the prison sentences typically imposed for robbery may be obtained from prison statistics. A snapshot of the prison population in late November 2022 showed that there were 93 prisoners serving sentences for robbery, extortion and hijacking. In all probability, most were for robbery. Of these, 11 (12 per cent) were serving sentences of two to three years, 37 (40 per cent) sentences of three to five years and 32 (34 per cent) sentences of five to 10 years. Only three (3 per cent) were serving sentences of 10 years or longer. The remaining 10 (11 per cent) were serving sentences up to two years.[197] All these figures refer to the sentences actually imposed. The headline sentences would have been considerably higher in most cases. **10–88**

---

[192] [2019] IECA 101.
[193] [2014] IECA 22.
[194] [2019] IECA 151.
[195] [2020] IECA 331, discussed further in Chap 13 below.
[196] [2021] IECA 124.
[197] Irish Prison Service, *Annual Report 2022* (2023), 74.

Burglary and Aggravated Burglary

10–89 Burglary consists of entering any building as a trespasser with the intent of committing an arrestable offence therein. It is also committed by a person who, having entered a building as a trespasser, commits or attempts to commit such an offence therein.[198] An arrestable offence is one that carries a maximum sentence of at least five years' imprisonment. Burglary is punishable with a maximum sentence of 14 years' imprisonment, a fine or both. Aggravated burglary is defined as a burglary committed by a person who has with him or her at the time "any firearm or imitation firearm, any weapon of offence or any explosive".[199] It carries a maximum sentence of life imprisonment. Both burglary and aggravated burglary may be dealt with summarily in the District Court in which case the maximum sentence is 12 months' imprisonment, a class A fine or both.[200] Despite the higher maximum sentence which it carries, aggravated burglary will not inevitably be more serious than 'ordinary' burglary. The essence of aggravated burglary is that is committed by a person who is in possession of a firearm or other weapon at the time of the trespass. However, the weapon may not be used or even brandished, whereas in 'ordinary' burglary cases, victims may be seriously assaulted or falsely imprisoned, residences may be ransacked and property of significant financial or sentimental value stolen.

10–90 Irish statute law draws no distinction between residential and non-residential burglary. The same holds true in some other common-law countries, though not in England and Wales where residential burglary carries a maximum sentence of 14 years' imprisonment, as opposed to 10 years for other burglaries.[201] Yet, it is widely recognised, and reflected in judicially developed principles and guidelines, that residential burglary is particularly serious because of its impact on victims. The harm element of residential burglary consists not only in loss of property (if any), but also in the enduring sense of insecurity and fear experienced by persons whose homes have been invaded.[202] In fact, the harm element may be even more diffuse than this. A spate of residential burglaries in a locality can cause great anxiety, fear and distress to inhabitants even if they have not personally been victimised. This holds true especially where burglars have targeted dwellings in remote rural areas. The occupants of such dwellings are often elderly, living alone or both. Fear of home invasion may leave

---

[198] Criminal Justice (Theft and Fraud Offences) Act 2001, s 12.

[199] Criminal Justice (Theft and Fraud Offences) Act 2001, s 13.

[200] Criminal Justice (Theft and Fraud Offences) Act 2001, s 53, as amended by Fines Act 2010, s 10.

[201] Theft Act 1968, s 9 as amended by Criminal Justice Act 1991, s 26(2). See, for example, *R v Chipunza* [2021] EWCA Crim 597; [2021] 2 Cr App R 6; [2021] 4 WLR 81. On sentencing for burglary in England and Wales, see Harris and Walker, note 40 above, at 1465-1478, and Andrew Ashworth and Rory Kelly, *Sentencing and Criminal Justice,* 7th ed (Hart Publishing, 2021), 131-133.

[202] Mike Maguire, "The impact of burglary upon victims" (1980) 20 Brit J Criminology 261; Desmond O'Neill et al, "Effects of burglary on elderly people" (1989) 298 *British Medical Journal* 1618.

such persons in a constant state of anxiety and even cause them to move from their homes to live in a more sheltered or secure environment.[203]

Burglary also amounts to an infringement of the personal constitutional right to the inviolability of the dwelling.[204] The perpetrator may be a private individual rather than an agent of the state, but the state has a responsibility to prevent violations of this right as best it can, and to take effective steps to prosecute and punish the perpetrators. As the Court of Criminal Appeal said in *People (DPP) v Barnes*: **10–91**

> "[The victim's] dwellinghouse has been violated and this is not merely a crime at law but an invasion of his personal rights. Such a thing, especially if repeated, may in itself gravely undermine the wellbeing even of a strong and healthy occupant, and still more that of an older or feeble one. The offence of burglary committed in a dwellinghouse is in every instance an act of aggression, an attack on the personal rights of the citizen as well as a public crime and is a violation of him or her."[205]

As reflected in this statement, residential burglary should be seen as an offence against the person as well as an offence against property. The same might be said of the burglary of other premises that were occupied by persons such as employees or customers when the intrusion occurred. **10–92**

Residential burglary is one of the few offences for which there is currently a formal sentencing guideline. In *People (DPP) v Casey and Casey*,[206] the Court of Appeal said: **10–93**

> "[T]he Court would suggest that mid-range offences would merit pre-mitigation sentences in the range of four to nine years and cases in the highest range nine to fourteen years. The Court recognises that the circumstances surrounding individual offences can vary greatly, and that is so even before one comes to consider the circumstances of the individual offender. While a consistency of approach to sentencing is highly desirable, it is not to be expected that there will be a uniformity in terms of the actual sentences that are imposed. There are just too many variables in terms of the circumstances of individual offences, but even more so in terms of the circumstances of individual offenders, for that to happen. Again, the Court recognises that there is no clear blue water between the ranges. Often the most that can be said is that an offence falls in the upper mid-range / lower higher range In many cases whether an offence is to be labelled as being at the high end of the mid-range or at the low end of the high range for an offence is often a fine call. The judge's legitimate margin of appreciation may well straddle both. In that event, how it is labelled may in fact not impact greatly on the sentence that will ultimately be imposed."

---

203 In *R v Walls* [2021] NICA 19, the Northern Ireland Court of Appeal addressed this aspect of residential burglary at some length.

204 Constitution of Ireland, Art 40.5.

205 [2006] IECCA 165; [2007] 3 IR 130, 147; [2007] 1 ILRM 350, quoted with approval in *People (DPP) v Casey and Casey* [2018] IECA 121; [2018] 2 IR 337, para 31 and in *People (DPP) v Faulkner* [2024] IESC 16, para 6.

206 [2018] IECA 121; [2018] 2 IR 337, para 49,

10–94 *Casey* involved a burglary spree during which the defendants had entered or tried to enter a number of unoccupied residences. This probably explains why the Court of Appeal concentrated on burglary offences falling into the middle and higher ranges. It is to be inferred that those in the lower range should attract sentences of zero to four years. Many non-residential burglaries would fall into this lower category, but so too might some residential burglaries. For instance, a burglar who opportunistically entered a house because the door happened to be open but who ran away once confronted by an occupier would probably merit a sentence in this category. Many burglaries, including possibly some minor residential burglaries, are dealt with summarily in the District Court.

10–95 The Court of Appeal in *Casey* accepted the prosecutor's submission regarding the factors that would place a burglary offence in the mid-range and, quite possibly, in the upper part of that range.[207] These were: (1) a significant degree of planning or premeditation; (2) two or more participants acting together; (3) targeting residential properties, particularly in rural areas; (4) targeting a residential property because the occupant was known to be vulnerable on account of age, disability or some other factor; or (5) taking or damaging property which had a high monetary or sentimental value. The prosecutor had submitted that the following factors would place a burglary in the highest range: (1) ransacking a dwelling; (2) entering during the night a property which was known to be occupied, especially if the occupier was alone; (3) violence used or threatened against any person, whether the occupier or anyone else, in the course of the burglary; or (4) significant injury, whether physical or psychological, or serious trauma caused to the victim of a burglary. To these the Court of Appeal added further aggravating factors: (1) having pervious convictions for similar offences; (2) a confrontation with the occupant of the dwelling, and the more aggressive the confrontation, the greater the aggravation; and (3) evidence that the intruder equipped himself with a weapon while in the dwelling. The last of these was characterised by the court as a serious aggravating factor, particularly if the item was something such as a carving knife that had the obvious potential to be a lethal weapon. The presence of a child or where a child returns home during a burglary is another aggravating factor. This is specifically mentioned in the present English Sentencing Council guideline on domestic burglary[208] and is reflected in at least one Irish case where a heavy sentence was imposed and upheld in these circumstances.[209]

10–96 In practice, the heaviest sentences tend to be imposed where victims of residential burglary (or aggravated burglary) were physically injured by the intruders. The more serious and deliberate the injuries, the more

---

207 [2018] IECA 121; [2018] 2 IR 337, paras 40, 41, 46 and 47.

208 <https://www.sentencingcouncil.org.uk/offences/crown-court/item/domestic-burglary/> accessed 18 November 2024.

209 *People (DPP) v Duggan* [2018] IECA 115 where a 12-year headline sentence, reduced to an effective term of six years' imprisonment, was upheld.

severe the deserved sentence.[210] As the Court of Appeal said in *People (DPP) v Casey and Casey*:

> "A confrontation with an occupant of a dwelling will be an aggravating factor. The more aggressive the confrontation, the greater the aggravation. Evidence that an intruder equipped himself with a weapon while in the dwelling will be a more serious aggravating factor. This is particularly so if the items availed of have the obvious potential to be a lethal weapon, such as a carving knife or a meat cleaver."[211]

A burglary sentence may be increased because of associated conduct. In *People (DPP) v Faulkner*[212] the Supreme Court upheld a sentence of 12 years' imprisonment for a residential burglary in which the appellant had participated with two others. He was the getaway driver and had not entered the residence of the victims, an elderly couple who were out at the time. Unlike his co-defendants who pleaded guilty, he was convicted following trial. (The others had received effective sentences of seven years' imprisonment.) The Gardaí, having been tipped off, were present when the burglary occurred, and when they approached the appellant, he took off at a high speed, driving in a dangerous manner that put other road users at risk.[213] This factor, coupled with the fact that the burglary had been planned and involved the targeting of a vulnerable couple, led the Supreme Court to conclude that the sentence was not excessive. For other residential burglaries, especially where occupants were present at the time (and particularly at night), where the sole occupant was a vulnerable person, where the dwelling was ransacked or where property of significant financial or sentimental value was taken, the headline sentence may be anywhere between three and nine years' imprisonment, depending on the circumstances.[214] **10–97**

In *People (DPP) v Byrne*[215] the Court of Appeal offered the following guideline on sentencing for aggravated burglary which, as noted, carries a maximum sentence of life imprisonment: **10–98**

> "On the basis that a life sentence is likely to be reserved for only the very worst and most egregious offences of this type, the practical reality is that the effective range of custodial penalties caps out at fifteen years, or thereabouts, for all but the most exceptional cases. An effective fifteen-year

---

[210] In *People (DPP) v Kelly and Devine* [2021] IECA 125 headline sentences of 12 years and 9 years were considered appropriate by the Court of Appeal. See also *People (DPP) v Gleeson* [2018] IECA 108; *People (DPP) v Morey and Price* [2018] IECA 367; *People (DPP) v McDonagh* [2021] IECA 197.

[211] [2018] IECA 121; [2018] 2 IR 337, para 47.

[212] [2024] IESC 16.

[213] Concurrent two-year sentences had been imposed for endangerment and dangerous driving.

[214] Examples include *People (DPP) v Harlowe* [2022] IECA 80 (headline sentence of nine years approved); *People (DPP) v Babayev* [2019] IECA 247 (headline sentence of five and a half years approved).

[215] [2018] IECA 120.

range allows for a low range of zero to five years, a mid-range of six to ten years, and a higher range of eleven to fifteen years."[216]

10–99 This may be an informal guideline but it is one to which trial courts should have regard, especially in light of what the Court of Appeal said about the need to observe the robbery guideline given in the same *Byrne* judgment.[217] Headline sentences in excess of 15 years will be appropriate in certain cases. In *People (DPP) v Byrne and others*[218] a gang of seven men invaded the home of a couple and their children in the early hours of the morning. The intruders were carrying various weapons and they inflicted serious injuries on one adult occupant and assaulted the other. Sentences ranging from 12 to 20 years (with three or four years suspended in each case) were imposed by the trial court. The Court of Appeal reduced the 20-year sentences to 18 years (with four years suspended, as in the trial court), and dismissed the appeals by three others.[219]

10–100 On 30 November 2022, there were 311 prisoners serving sentences for burglary and related offences. Of these 126 (40 per cent) were serving sentences ranging from three months to three years, 80 (26 per cent) were serving sentences of three to five years, 92 (30 per cent) sentences of five to 10 years, and 13 (4 per cent) sentences in excess of 10 years.[220] These figures provide no more than a general indication of sentencing patterns and, obviously, only in respect of cases that resulted in imprisonment. Further, they are not disaggregated by reference to the kinds or circumstances of the burglaries involved.

Theft

10–101 A person commits theft by dishonesty appropriating the property of another without the other's consent and while intending to deprive the owner of it.[221] For sentencing purposes, we may include under this heading deception offences and other fraudulent conduct consisting in the wrongful appropriation of property. Theft is an indictable offence but, like all other indictable offences created by the Criminal Justice (Theft and Fraud Offences) Act 2001, it may also be dealt with summarily in the District Court in which case the maximum sentence is 12 months imprisonment, a class A fine (maximum €5,000) or both.[222]

---

216 [2018] IECA 120, para 60.

217 *People (DPP) v Joyce* [2021] IECA 124. See note 196 above and accompanying text.

218 [2017] IECA 136.

219 Other aggravated burglary cases include *People (DPP) v Stokes* [2017] IECA 259; *People (DPP) v O'Loughlin* [2022[IECA 18 (headline sentences of 12 years approved in both); *People (DPP) v Freeman* [2018] IECA 312 (headline sentence of 10 years approved); *People (DPP) v Popovici* [2017] IECA 35 (headline sentence of nine years approved). There was some further reduction in each of these cases.

220 Irish Prison Service, *Annual Report 2022* (2023), 74.

221 Criminal Justice (Theft and Fraud Offences) Act 2001, s 4.

222 Criminal Justice (Theft and Fraud Offences) Act 2001, s 53, as amended by

Following conviction on indictment, the maximum sentence is 10 years' imprisonment, a fine or both. Most detected theft offences are minor in nature and do not call for a penalty exceeding what the District Court may lawfully impose. They therefore come within the constitutional jurisdiction of that court.[223] In 2022, the District Court dealt with about 22,000 theft and other property offences, whereas the number of theft and fraud offences prosecuted on indictment is typically about 350 a year. This figure does not include prosecutions on indictment for robbery and burglary. On 30 November 2022, there were more prisoners (558) in custody for theft than for any other category of offence. Of these, 319 (57 per cent) were serving terms of three years or less, while10 (less than two per cent) were serving 10 years or longer.

Shoplifting accounts for a significant proportion of the theft offences dealt with in the District Court. Most shoplifting offence are minor in nature because of the low value of the items stolen.[224] If this were the sole consideration, a fine, probation order or other non-custodial measure would adequately reflect the gravity of the offence. However, the sentencing of these offences is often complicated by two factors. First, many offenders have numerous previous convictions, sometimes running to hundreds, for similar offences.[225] For sentencing judges, this poses a dilemma to which there is no obvious principled solution. The objections to treating previous convictions as aggravating were discussed earlier in Chap 5, one of these objections being that the offender has already been punished for the earlier offences. In practice, previous convictions for similar offences are treated as aggravating, although any uplift in sentence should be moderate and not result in disproportionately severe punishment for the offence of conviction. Secondly, offenders are typically disadvantaged as a result of addiction, homelessness or both. Short-term imprisonment is by no means the ideal response in those circumstances. All it can hope to achieve is some respite from the offender's conduct within the community and provide temporary accommodation for the offender. A more therapeutic response including measures, if such were available, designed to assist offenders in getting their lives together would be more productive. Data published by the Central Statistics Office show high rates of re-offending among those released from prison for theft-related offences. Of those released in 2017 from sentences for such offences, 71 per cent reoffended within three years. In fact, about 50 per cent had re-offended within a year of release, and those who have served 10–102

Fines Act 2010.

[223] Chap 2 above.

[224] This is not to discount the possibility that high-value items may also be stolen, as has occasionally happened.

[225] See, for example, Andrew Phelan, "Serial thief jailed for shoplifting rum as she clocks up 'record' 857th conviction", *Irish Independent*, 22 February 2023. The defendant had crack cocaine and heroin addictions.

prison sentences for theft are most likely to re-offend in the same offence category.[226]

10–103 Thefts involving large sums of money or valuable property are likely to be prosecuted on indictment, but so too are thefts of smaller amounts where there are aggravating circumstances. From a sentencing perspective, the most difficult question is how much the value of the stolen property should matter. Theft, after all, is quantifiable in a way that assault, for example, is not. Sentence ranges could therefore be constructed according to the value of the property stolen. Formal guidelines, where they exist, often do just that, even if they allow for adjustments to reflect other factors as well.[227] In Ireland, where there is no such guideline, the highest sentences are generally reserved for the theft of large sums of money that resulted in significant hardship or damage to the victims (whether individuals or organisations).[228] Victim impact is always a prominent consideration, and rightly so. The theft of a relatively small amount may cause far more hardship to one victim than the theft of a much larger amount would cause to another. A pensioner who suffers the loss of a few hundred Euro may suffer more than, say, a wealthy corporation deprived of tens of thousands of Euro. Often allied to this is the callousness or indifference with which the offence is committed, a factor that undoubtedly enhances culpability. An offender who took advantage of a vulnerable person can ordinarily expect a custodial sentence, even if the amount stolen was not particularly large. In *People (DPP) v O'Brien*,[229] for example, the Court of Appeal upheld a two-year prison sentence for the theft of €300 from a 74-year-old man who was living in a rural, isolated area. No violence was used or threated; the money was stolen through trickery. The appellant had 61 previous convictions and was already serving a three-year sentence for other theft offences. A two-year sentence for the theft of €300 was undoubtedly very severe, and it should probably have been more lenient, but the Court of Appeal was clearly influenced by the impact of the offence on the victim. More recently, a woman who stole €45,000 from an elderly woman with dementia for whom she was caring was jailed for two and a half years.[230] Again, the sentence might have been lower had it not been for the clear breach of trust and the victim's vulnerability.

---

[226] Information available at www.cso.ie under 'Prison Re-Offending Statistics 2020'.

[227] See, for example, the English Sentencing Council, *Theft Offences: Definitive Guideline* (2015).

[228] *People (DPP) v Hawkins* [2014] IECCA 38, where a seven-year sentence was upheld for the theft by an employee of more than €2.5 million from a member of the band U2.

[229] [2020] IECA 271.

[230] *People (DPP) v Gregg,* Cork Circuit Court, 16 November 2023.

CHAPTER 11

THE RIGHTS AND NEEDS OF VICTIMS

By some accounts, the criminal law originally developed, not in response to the conduct of offenders, but rather in response to the conduct of victims. Absent a coherent body of criminal law and criminal procedure, those who were wronged by others resorted to various forms of private retaliation including blood feuds, duels and lynching. Viewed in this light, the criminal law served a displacement function.[1] It substituted for the vagaries, arbitrariness and, often, the cruelty of private retaliation a more formal and dispassionate system for determining if a legally prohibited wrong had been committed and, if it had been, the punishment to be imposed on the wrongdoer. As David Garland says: **11–01**

> "Criminal justice procedures are intended to turn hot vengeance into cool, impartial justice. They aim to interpose rationality, reflection, circumspection, balance, and collective group interests as a brake upon the unrestrained expression of individual emotions"[2]

A rational, objective and proportionate sentencing system ensures that offenders are punished according to their desert, having regard to the harm they have caused or risked, their degree of culpability and their **11–02**

---

1 John Gardner, "Crime: In proportion and in perspective" in Andrew Ashworth and Martin Wasik (eds), *Fundamentals of Sentencing Theory* (Clarendon Press, 1998), Chap 2, reprinted in John Gardner, *Offences and Defences: Selected Essays in the Philosophy of Criminal Law* (Oxford University Press, 2007), Chap 11. Likewise, in *Munda v Western Australia* [2013] HCA 38; (2013) 249 CLR 600, para 54, the High Court of Australia said that "one of the historical functions of the criminal law has been to discourage victims and their friends and families from resorting to self-help, and the consequent escalation of violent vendettas between members of the community". The gradual state monopolisation of the legitimate use of physical force is regarded as one hallmark of progressive civilisation. See Max Weber, "Politics as a vocation" in *The Vocation Lectures*, translated by Rodney Livingstone and edited by David Owen and Tracy B Strong (Hackett Publishing Co, 2004), and Norbert Elias, *The Civilizing Process*, translated by Edmund Jephcott, revised ed (Blackwell, 2000), first published 1939.

2 Neil MacCormick and David Garland, "Sovereign states and vengeful victims: The problem of the right to punish" in Ashworth and Wasik (note 1 above), Chap 1 at 26. (That chapter consists of a dialogue between MacCormick and Garland.) Garland goes on to quote Francis Bacon: "Revenge is a kind of wild justice, which the more a man's nature runs to, the more ought law to weed it out".

personal circumstances at the time of sentencing. Victims may naturally have their own views as to how those who have injured them should be punished – and those views may tend towards severity or leniency – but a court must always be aware that it is inflicting punishment on behalf of the community and that it must do so in accordance with the applicable rules, principles and standards.[3] Thus, even a plea for leniency by a victim will not necessarily influence a court in deciding on the appropriate sentence. In *R v Konzani*[4] the appellant was sentenced to a total of 10 years' imprisonment on being convicted of three counts of inflicting actual bodily harm. Having been informed that he was HIV positive, he had sexual intercourse with three women without informing them of his HIV status, with the result that each of them contracted the HIV virus. One of the victims had sought a reduction in the sentence imposed for the offence committed against her. However, the Court of Appeal said:

> "We have, of course, reflected on her position. It seems to us, however, that while the sentencing court should always take account of the impact of an offence on its victim, the appropriate sentence should not normally be influenced by the wishes of the victim. Otherwise, there would be wild sentencing inconsistency, and the eventual outcome in each individual case would be influenced by whether the victim was seeking compassion or mercy, vindication or vengeance. It is elementary that this could not form the basis for a sentencing decision, or for that matter for sentencing policy."[5]

11–03 Courts have occasionally mitigated punishment in response to a victim's plea for mercy, though seldom to any great extent. (This is discussed further below.) Victim impact is always a relevant factor in so far as it indicates the harm caused by the offence. As such it falls to be considered when the gravity of an offence is being assessed under the first limb of the proportionality principle as applied in Ireland, and this has long been the case. Ultimately, however, the constitutional obligation to impose a sentence that properly reflects the offender's personal circumstances as well as the gravity of the offence must trump other considerations, including victim preferences.

11–04 One of the more significant developments in common law jurisdictions during the past few decades has been the formal recognition of the rights and interests of crime victims. The same has occurred in many parts of the world, but the change has been particularly noticeable in common law countries because of their traditional attachment to the adversarial

---

3 *People (DPP) v Crowley* [2021] IECA 178, discussed further below; William Blackstone, *Commentaries on the Laws of England*, Bk IV edited by Ruth Paley (Oxford University Press, 2016 (1769)), 5, saying that private wrongs are "an infringement or privation of the civil rights which belong to individuals" whereas crimes are "a breach and violation of the public rights and duties, due to the whole community, considered as a community, in its social aggregate capacity".

4 [2005] EWCA Crim 706; [2005] 2 Cr App R 14.

5 [2005] EWCA Crim 706; [2005] 2 Cr App R 14, para 48.

model of justice.[6] According to this model, the criminal trial is a binary contest between the accused and the state, with the victim, where there is one, relegated (as some would see it) to the role of prosecution witness. This essentially remains the case, but victims now have a more prominent and, at times, influential role at various stages of the criminal process.[7] Reorienting that process to accommodate victims' interests is, of course, problematic, particularly where politicians, often urged on by the media, claim to be 'rebalancing' the criminal justice system in favour of victims when the actual effect, if not the purpose, of such reforms may be to diminish defence rights.[8] Having said this, some procedural reforms, such as the provision of intermediary services for vulnerable victims, can be implemented without compromising the rights of accused persons.[9]

Claims made on behalf of victims may be divided into two broad categories: welfare claims and participation claims. Welfare claims, which are mainly about access to counselling, medical treatment, legal advice, compensation and the like, can be met without upsetting the traditional adversarial balance. Participation claims can be more problematic, depending on their precise nature. As Ian Edwards has persuasively argued, the term 'participation' must be closely interrogated, because it can mean many different things.[10] Inspired in part by Sherry Arnstein's well-known eight-step "ladder of citizen participation" in urban planning decisions,[11] Edwards identifies four possible kinds of victim participation in the criminal process, only one of which is "dispositive" in the sense that it invests victims with some degree of control over outcomes. Where participation is dispositive, the relevant decision-maker must ascertain *and apply* victim preferences. The remaining participation roles are, in Edwards' typology, "non-dispositive" because, while they entail some degree of victim involvement, they do not allow victims to determine outcomes. Such roles include consultation, information provision and expression. Under our constitutional system, the accused person's right **11–05**

---

6 For a survey of current laws and practices, see Jonathan Doak, "Victims' rights in the criminal justice system" in Gerben Bruinsma and David Weisburd (eds), *Encyclopedia of Criminology and Criminal Justice* (Springer, 2014), 5497.

7 Although procedures for involving victims in the criminal process vary across European countries, the victim's formal role in most cases effectively reduces to that of prosecution witness. See Albin Dearing and Holly Huxtable, "Doing justice for victims of violent crime in the European Union" (2021) 45 *International Journal of Comparative and Applied Criminal Justice* 39.

8 Ian Edwards, "An ambiguous participant: The crime victim and criminal justice decision-making" (2004) 44 Brit J Criminology 967; Ezzat Fattah (ed) *Towards a Critical Victimology* (Macmillan, 1992); Kent Roach, *Due Process and Victims' Rights: The New Law and Politics of Criminal Justice* (University of Toronto Press, 1999); Joan Barrett, "Expanding victims' rights in the Charter era and beyond" (2008) 40 *The Supreme Court Law Review* (2d) 627.

9 See *Review of Protections for Vulnerable Witnesses in the Investigation and Prosecution of Sexual Offences* (Department of Justice and Equality, 2020), Chap 8.

10 Edwards, note 8 above.

11 Sherry Arnstein, "A ladder of citizen participation in the USA" (1969) 35(4) *Journal of the American Institute of Planners* 216.

to a fair trial remains paramount, and any claims made on behalf of victims must yield to that right in the event of a conflict. Welfare claims are generally compatible with the Constitution. Indeed, it could be argued that the state, by virtue of its obligation under Art 40. 3 to protect and vindicate personal rights, has a responsibility to attend to the basic welfare needs of crime victims. Participation claims, on the other hand, especially those of the dispositive variety, are almost certain to conflict with the fair trial rights to which defendants are constitutionally entitled. Foremost among these is the right to be tried and, if convicted, sentenced by an independent and impartial tribunal. Victims – and this is no disrespect to them – can scarcely be expected to be impartial if permitted to determine or influence either verdict or sentence.

11–06 Still, there are cogent reasons for according appropriate recognition to victims. Serious offences against the person and against property are usually defined by reference to the harm caused to a victim. An assault, for example, consists of applying force to the body of another person, while theft consists of the dishonest misappropriation of another's property. As Michael Moore has written, victims "are at the centre of the norms whose violation is at the core of the criminal law".[12] This factor alone justifies proper recognition of the victim by law enforcement agencies and courts. The essence of a crime, as distinct from a tort, may be that it is a wrong against the community, and not just against an individual victim, but this should not excuse the marginalisation of victims. After all, the primary objective of core criminal offences is to protect individuals from harm and injury. The state also has a more prudential reason for respecting victim interests. It depends on victims to report serious offences, to cooperate in the investigation of those offences and to testify at trial. Police involvement in such offences is essentially, and almost inevitably, reactive in nature. The police are responding to complaints or reports made to them. (Other kinds of offending, such as road traffic and public order violations, come to light through proactive policing.) Victims may be reluctant to report offences or to cooperate in investigations unless they believe that they will be treated with respect and that their rights and interests will be adequately protected. The effectiveness of the criminal law and its processes therefore depends crucially on the confidence of victims in the criminal justice system and its willingness to treat them fairly.

11–07 The criminal justice system can do little or nothing for a victim unless the alleged perpetrator is convicted or, at least, prosecuted. In the absence of a trial, the victim has no formal opportunity to recount his or her experience, or to describe the impact of the offence. There can be many reasons for this. The perpetrator may escape detection, evade arrest, be able to rely on some kind of immunity from prosecution or die. Where there are no statutory limitation periods on the prosecution of serious crime, diplomatic status is practically the only ground on which immunity may

[12] Michael Moore, "Victims and retribution: A reply to Professor Fletcher" (1999) 3 Buffalo Crim LR 65, 72,

be claimed.[13] That seldom happens but, far more commonly, perpetrators will have died before they can be put in trial. The death of an accused brings criminal proceedings to an end.[14] These 'invisible victims', as they have been called, may be able to find support or help from other sources, but the criminal justice system is largely closed to them.[15] Little can be done about this, but it illustrates the chasm that can exist between crime and harm. Individuals are harmed and often grievously so, not just by other individuals, but also by states, state-sponsored organisations and corporations. Yet, for myriad reasons the criminal law may be powerless or unwilling to respond. Some critical criminologists have developed a new discipline, zemiology (the study of social harm), initially as a competitor to criminology which, whatever else may be said of it, is essentially about crime and that, in turn, is a legal construct.[16] Social harm theorists remind us, as we constantly need reminding, of the limited capacity of the criminal justice system to provide redress for many victims of injustice.

Neither criminal justice nor restorative justice proceedings can assist a victim where the accused, for whatever reason, is unavailable. Both processes require, at the very least, an identifiable accused and, usually, his or her presence. Some victim advocates have therefore developed the concept of parallel justice which aims to separate the pursuit of justice for victims from the criminal process. Susan Herman, a leading proponent of this approach, has identified three basic needs of victims: (1) to be safe; (2) to recover from the impact of the crime; and (3) to regain control of their lives.[17] Such parallel justice is, in fact, provided in a variety of ways, particularly by way of state funded compensation for criminally inflicted violent injuries. The Irish scheme is described at the end of this chapter. Compensation may be available from other sources for persons who have suffered financially as a result of dishonesty or malpractice on the part of professionals, such as solicitors.[18] Non-pecuniary assistance, in the form of counselling, therapy or medical assistance, may be available to victims of sexual and other violent crime. Services of this nature tend **11–08**

[13] The Vienna Convention on Diplomatic Relations 1961 (art 31) confers immunity from criminal prosecution on diplomatic agents and (art 37) on family members forming part of their household. The Convention has the force of law in Ireland through the Diplomatic Relations and Immunities Act 1967.

[14] The death by apparent suicide of Jeffrey Epstein in a New York prison in August 2019 shortly before his trial resulted in the case being struck out but, rather controversially, the judge permitted several of the complainants to testify about the impact of the alleged crimes upon them. See Bruce A Green and Rebecca Roiphe, "Punishment without process: 'Victim impact' proceedings for dead defendants" (2019) 88 Fordham LR Online 28.

[15] Mihailis E Diamantis, "Invisible victims" (2022) 1 Wisconsin LR 1.

[16] Victoria Canning and Steve Tombs, *From Social Harm to Zemiology: A Critical Introduction* (Routledge, 2021).

[17] Susan Herman, *Parallel Justice for Victims of Crime* (National Centre for Victims of Crime, 2010),

[18] On the compensation fund operated by the Law Society of Ireland, see Solicitors (Compensation Fund) Regulations 2018 (SI 548/2018), and <https://www.lawsociety.ie/public/compensation-fund> accessed 27 July 2024.

to be provided by voluntary organisations but these, in turn, are often in receipt of significant government funding.[19] Importantly, however, the availability of these services need not depend on the institution of criminal proceedings against a suspected offender.

11–09 Domestic law on victims' rights has been heavily influenced by international developments, most recently at European Union level. Many instruments adopted by the United Nations, the Council of Europe and other regional bodies have been concerned with protecting certain categories of victims, such as victims of human trafficking, and outlawing certain kinds of victimisation such as torture. At a more general level, the United Nations adopted a Declaration of Basic Principles of Justice for Victims of Crime and Abuse of Power in 1985. The Council of Europe adopted a Convention on the Compensation of Victims of Violent Crimes in 1983, though it has been neither signed nor ratified by Ireland. More significant, however, are two important European Union directives, one dealing with compensation for crime victims and the other dealing more comprehensively with victims' rights. Council Directive 2004/80/EC relating to compensation for crime victims requires member states to have a scheme for compensating victims of violent intentional crimes in a fair and appropriate manner. Ireland has such a scheme, described in the last section of this chapter, which has recently been revised to take account of obligations imposed by the Directive as interpreted by the Court of Justice of the European Union.

11–10 The European Union Directive on the Rights of Victims of Crime,[20] like the Criminal Justice (Victims of Crime) Act 2017 (the '2017 Act') which transposed it into Irish law, was a radical measure conferring a wide range of rights on crime victims, mainly in relation to access to information but also providing for special measures for certain victims and a right to request a review of prosecution decisions. As far as sentencing is concerned, the main provisions are those extending the range of offences in respect of which victim impact evidence may be given (described further below) and a right to be kept informed about prosecution decisions and the trial arrangements. Once the offender is convicted, the victim is entitled to be informed of the date of sentencing and the date of any appeal, whether by the defence or prosecution. If the offender is sentenced to imprisonment, the victim has a right to be informed of the expected release date and of any decisions relating to the transfer or early release of the offender. This is discussed further in Chap 14 below in the context of parole.

11–11 Neither the Directive nor the 2017 Act prevents the adoption of additional legislative or administrative measures to support crime victims. Prosecutors might, for example, adopt a practice of consulting the victim

[19] The Annual Report of the Dublin Rape Crisis Centre 2023 shows that it received government grants of €2.5 million out of a total income of €3.7 million for that year.

[20] Directive 2012/29/EU of the European Parliament and Council.

before deciding to accept a plea to a lesser charge, such as a plea to sexual assault instead of rape. Acceptance of such a plea has obvious implications for sentence, as the penalty ultimately imposed will depend on the offence of which the offender is convicted, whether following a trial or a guilty plea. Yet, a victim may feel a sense of injustice if the offence to which a plea is accepted fails to reflect the harm or injury inflicted by the offender. Ultimately, however, it is the *public* interest, and not victim preferences, that must inform all prosecution decisions. This holds true of the decision to prosecute and decisions as to the charges to be preferred or proceeded with. There can be no objection to a public prosecutor explaining to a victim why a particular course of action is being taken (and there is much to be said for such a practice), but equally there can be no question of a victim being allowed to influence or determine how a prosecution is to proceed. To grant such a role to victims would run counter to the values that public prosecutions are meant to observe and reflect.

1. Victim-Offender Overlap

Criminological research has traditionally tended to treat offending and victimisation as separate phenomena, sometimes to the point of leaving the impression that offenders and victims inhabit two entirely different social worlds. Offenders were 'bad' people (or, at least, the perpetrators of bad acts) who have preyed on 'good' or innocent victims. The reality is often more complex. Recent research has shown that victimisation can lead to offending and, obviously, vice versa.[21] Retaliation within and between criminal gangs and other sub-cultures provides a good example. Much of this occurs in environments where police are mistrusted or seen as the enemy (rightly or wrongly) but where, in any event, those who are victimised are likely to take the law into their own hands by retaliating rather than by reporting a victimising act as a crime.[22] As one American **11–12**

[21] For a review of the literature and research on this topic, see Mark T Berg and Christopher J Schreck, "The meaning of the victim-offender overlap for criminological theory and crime prevention policy" (2022) 5 *Annual Review of Criminology* 277; Mark T Berg and Carrie F Mulford, "Reappraising and redirecting research on victim-offender overlap" (2020) 21 *Trauma, Violence, & Abuse* 16; Anthony Bottoms and Andrew Costello, "The phenomenon of victim-offender overlap: A study of offences against households" in Anthony Bottoms and Julian V Roberts (eds), *Hearing the Victim: Adversarial Justice, Crime Victims and the State* (Routledge, 2011), Chap 5; Janet L Lauritsen and John H Laub, "Understanding the link between victimization and offending: New reflections on an old idea" in Mike Hough and Mike Maxfield (eds), *Surveying Crime in the Twenty-First Century*, Crime Prevention Studies, vol 22 (Willan Publishing, 2007), Chap 4.

[22] Bruce A Jacobs and Richard R Wright, *Street Justice: Retaliation in the Criminal Underworld* (Cambridge University Press, 2006); Mark T Berg, Lee Ann Slocum ad Rolf Loeber, "Illegal behaviour, neighbourhood context, and police reporting by victims of violence" (2013) 50 *Journal of Research in Crime and Delinquency* 75 (finding that assaults and robberies less likely be reported where the victim is involved in crime, especially in high-crime and disadvantages neighbourhoods).

study concluded, those "who disproportionately come into contact with and/or associate with persons who have high rates of offending are likely to be disproportionately victimised".[23] A parliamentary commission established to consider reintroducing parole in the State of Maine has likewise observed:

> "Often, the circumstances that lead a person to commit a violent crime create similar circumstances for the victims of that crime, which can contribute to victims committing a violent crime in the future. This is a contributing factor to why a majority of people who are incarcerated are also survivors of violent crimes themselves. It is crucial that the criminal justice system focus on providing both rehabilitation for offenders and support services for victims."[24]

11–13 In most cases, there is no such overlap; the victim will not have contributed in any way, directly or indirectly, to the offending conduct. Where it does exist, it can lead to a distinction being drawn between worthy and unworthy victims, a concept popularised in another context by Herman and Chomsky.[25] The victim of a retaliatory attack, especially if it is someone with a serious criminal record, may be less readily recognised as a true victim, and may be contrasted with an 'innocent' victim who had no prior involvement, of any significance at least, in criminal activity.[26] Yet, for sentencing purposes this should be irrelevant unless the victim's conduct at the time of the offence was so provocative or threatening as to diminish the offender's culpability to some degree. Offenders may also be victims of events and circumstances that have no direct connection with the crimes they commit. As previously discussed in Chap 9, studies have revealed a strong correlation between adverse childhood experience (including experience of physical and other abuse) and later criminal offending.[27] Incidentally, child soldiers, of whom there are hundreds of thousands in various parts of the world, afford another example of victim-offender overlap. They may well commit atrocities and engage in other conduct amounting to serious human rights violations. To that extent they are offenders but, because of the circumstances in which many of

---

23 MJ Hindelang, MR Gottfredson and J Garofalo, *Victims of Personal Crime: An Empirical Foundation for a Theory of Personal Victimization* (Ballinger, 1978), 122.

24 State of Maine 130th Legislature, *Commission to Examine Re-establishing Parole* (December 2022), 21, <https://legislature.maine.gov/doc/9574> accessed 27 July 2024.

25 Edward S Herman and Noam Chomsky, *Manufacturing Consent: The Political Economy of the Mass Media* (The Bodley Head, 2008), first published 1988.

26 Lynne Henderson, "The wrongs of victim's rights" (1985) 37 Stanford LR 937, 951 referring to the image of the ideal victim as a "blameless, pure stereotype, with whom all can identify". See also Nils Christie, "The ideal victim" in Ezzat A Fattah (ed), *From Crime Policy to Victim Policy: Reorienting the Justice System* (Macmillan, 1986), 17.

27 See, for example, Michael T Baglivio et al, "The prevalence of adverse childhood experiences (ACE) in the lives of juvenile offenders" (2014) 3 *Journal of Juvenile Justice* 1.

them were recruited or conscripted into armed forces, they can often be rightly treated as victims as well.[28]

2. Victim's Interests at Sentencing

Victims may once have had a central role in the criminal process when they were mainly responsible for the initiation and prosecution of criminal charges, but they were progressively marginalised as the process itself became more professionalised.[29] With the establishment of professional police and prosecution services, and the increasing involvement of lawyers in the prosecution and trial processes, victims were deprived of any effective decision-making role.[30] Granted, if there was a contested trial, the victim had (and still has) a crucial role as a witness for the prosecution, but key decisions as to the charges, if any, to be brought and the nature of the evidence to be presented at trial rested with the prosecution. The victim had no role at the sentencing stage and, in the event of a guilty plea, might not even be aware that sentencing was due to take place. There were many instances, even in fairly recent times, of a victim only accidentally discovering that the offender had already been sentenced. This could cause distress, especially where the offender received a non-custodial penalty. The introduction of victim impact evidence, discussed further below, has improved this situation considerably. It means that a victim is made aware of a forthcoming sentencing hearing and has an opportunity to testify about the impact of the offence.[31] **11–14**

The weight to be accorded to victim interests at sentencing was considered in detail by the Court of Appeal in *People (DPP) v Crowley*[32] where the essential question was whether the prison sentences imposed should have been consecutive or concurrent, and whether the totality principle was properly applied. The appellant had pleaded guilty to numerous offences, including assault, theft and criminal damage, committed against six different victims in public places over a period of about three years. Several of the offences were committed while on bail. The trial judge imposed a discrete sentence for each offence, apart from one that was taken into consideration. Some of the sentences were made concurrent but some were consecutive, resulting in a cumulative term of nine years and three months, with the last 15 months suspended. In so doing, the trial judge had stated that "it would do an injustice to any individual injured party to further reduce the sentence which I believe already reflects the totality **11–15**

---

28 Nienke Grossman, "Rehabilitation or revenge: Prosecuting child soldiers for human rights violations" (2007) 38 *Georgetown Journal of International Law* 323.

29 Leon Radzinowicz, *A History of English Criminal Law and its Administration from 1750*, Vol 2, *The Enforcement of the Law* (Stevens and Sons, 1956); John Spencer, "The victim and the prosecutor" in Bottoms and Roberts (eds), note 21 above, Chap 6.

30 Nils Christie, "Conflicts as property" (1977) 17 Brit J Criminology 1.

31 Bottoms and Roberts (eds), note 21 above, is an excellent collection of essays on the role of the victim at sentencing and other stages of the criminal process.

32 [2021] IECA 178.

of the mitigating factors". The judge had recognised the totality principle, but the Court of Appeal found that her approach raised some questions, the first being whether "the duty to impose a just and proportionate sentence on an accused can be subjugated to a perceived obligation to provide justice for an individual victim or victims".[33] The Court answered this question in the negative and reduced the cumulative sentence to eight years and three months, with the last 15 months suspended. In so doing, it said:

> "To put it in very general terms, a court's obligation is to ensure that victims are properly acknowledged as having a legitimate interest in the proceedings, and that they are treated with respect within the process. Moreover, there is a statutory requirement to facilitate them in being heard, if they wish to be heard, concerning the effects of the crime upon them, and to take that evidence into account in assessing the gravity of the offending conduct.
>
> However, in so far as victims have an entitlement to see justice done, that entitlement inures to them not as individuals but rather as members of society. The court's obligation to do justice at sentencing is owed, firstly, to the public at large, including the victims in the case; and secondly, to the accused who has an individual constitutional right to expect and receive a sentence that is proportionate (in the distributive sense) to the gravity of the crime as committed by him in his personal circumstances. The right of an accused to receive such a proportionate sentence was recognised in the case of *State (Healy) v Donoghue* [1976] I.R. 325 as being an aspect of the right of every citizen to a trial in due course of law as guaranteed under Article 38 of the Constitution. However, as the law presently stands, the victim of a crime has no entitlement to expect that a sentence will be crafted to provide individual justice for her.[34]

11–16 The court further said that it could understand the dissatisfaction or frustration expressed by victims who feel that a sentence is unduly lenient. But this, in turn, underscores the importance of trial judges explaining the reasons for their sentence and, where necessary, explaining to a victim that the court's role is to impose a proportionate sentence in each case. Fundamentally, what victims can legitimately expect at sentencing is to see justice done, but they must entertain this expectation primarily as members of society rather than as individuals. The harm they have suffered is, of course, a key determinant of sentence but other important factors, including the circumstances and prospects of the offender (especially if there is a reasonable likelihood of rehabilitation and desistance from further crime) and the broader public interest in maintaining a fair and effective sentencing system, must also be given due consideration.[35]

11–17 Section 5 of the Criminal Justice Act 1993 (the '1993 Act'), while allowing for the reception of victim impact evidence, does not have the effect of

---

[33] [2021] IECA 178, para 62. See also *People (DPP) v Duffy* [2023] IESC 1, para 41.

[34] [2021] IECA 178, paras 63 and 64.

[35] [2021] IECA 178, para 64.

making the victim a party to the criminal proceedings which consists of a binary contest between the state and the accused. The victim remains a witness whose evidence must be weighed and considered like that of any other witness.[36] Of course, the victim is not just any witness. He or she is the person who has suffered the harm, injury or loss inflicted by the offence, and who may have to live with its consequences for a long time to come. The legal system therefore owes the victim a special opportunity to be heard. During the sentencing process, a court makes considerable efforts to get to know the offender, to learn about his or her life experience, previous record and future prospects. A victim is entitled to parity of esteem in this respect. Each victim, like each offender, is a unique individual and it is only by learning about the victim's personal experience that a court can properly assess the impact of the offence. Therefore, to say that the victim remains a witness rather than a party to the case is not to deny that the victim occupies a special position as someone whose evidence is essential, together with any other relevant evidence, for the determination of an appropriate sentence.

Because victim impact evidence can influence sentence, it must always be received and evaluated in a manner that is fair to the offender. At a minimum, the defence should have sufficient time before the sentencing hearing to consider the victim's report or statement and to identify any aspects of it to which objection might be taken. Further, the evidence should be confined strictly to impact that the offence has had on the victim. A victim must not be permitted to allege at the sentencing stage that the offender engaged in criminal conduct beyond that of which he or she has been convicted. Any such allegation appearing in the victim's statement should not be allowed to influence sentence. In *R v Singh*,[37] for example, the victim's personal statement, which was not served until the day before the sentencing hearing, included allegations that the offender had engaged in threatening behaviour although this had not formed part of the prosecution case at trial. The English Court of Appeal held that, in these circumstances. the trial judge erred in treating the alleged threats as an aggravating factor, and it reduced the overall sentence accordingly. Permitting victim impact evidence to influence sentence risks introducing an element of "moral luck" into the sentencing process.[38] As was said in *R v Konzani*[39] (quoted above), a victim may be seeking compassion, mercy, vindication or vengeance. If victim preferences were allowed to prevail, equally guilty offenders might receive markedly different penalties, thereby setting at nought their constitutional entitlement to objectively **11–18**

---

[36] *People (DPP) v C (M)*, unreported, Central Criminal Court, 16 June 1995 (Flood J). See also *R v Gabriel* (1999) 98 OTC 193; 137 CCC (3d) 1, para 83, and *R v Bremner* (2000) 146 CCC (3d) 59 for similar statements in respect of Canadian law.

[37] [2024] EWCA Crim 259; [2024] 2 Cr App R (S) 17.

[38] Andrew Ashworth, "Victim impact statements at sentencing" (1993) Crim LR 498; Thomas O'Malley, "Punishment and moral luck: The role of the victim in sentencing decisions" (1993) 3 *Irish Criminal Law Journal* 40.

[39] [2005] EWCA Crim 706; [2005] 2 Cr App R 14. See note 5 above.

determined proportionate punishment. Thus, it becomes all the more important to confine a victim's evidence at sentencing strictly to the impact of the offence, so that the harm it inflicted can properly be assessed.

3. Victim Impact Evidence in Irish Law

11–19 Sentencing courts are now statutorily obliged to take account of victim impact and to hear evidence from a victim who wishes to testify as to the effect of the offence. This obligation derives from s 5 of the Criminal Justice Act 1993 which, in its original form, applied to sexual and violent offences only. It now applies to any offence that has inflicted harm on a natural person. Subsections (1) to (4) of s 5, in their present form, state:

> "(1) This section applies to an offence where a natural person in respect of whom the offence has been committed, has suffered harm, including physical, mental or emotional harm, or economic loss, which was directly caused by that offence.
>
> (2) (a) When imposing sentence on a person for an offence to which this section applies, a court shall take into account, and may, where necessary, receive evidence or submissions concerning, any effect (whether long-term or otherwise) of the offence on the person in respect of whom the offence was committed.
>
> (b) For the purposes of paragraph (a), 'a person in respect of whom the offence was committed' includes, where, as a result of the offence, that person has died, is ill or is otherwise incapacitated, a family member of that person,
>
> (3) (a) When imposing sentence on a person for an offence to which this section applies, a court shall, upon application by the person in respect of whom such offence was committed, hear the evidence of the person in respect of whom the offence was committed as to the effect of the offence on such person.
>
> (b) For the purpose of paragraph (a), where the person in respect of whom the offence was committed –
>
> (i) is a child under the age of 14 years, the child, or his or her parent or guardian, may give evidence as to the effect of the offence concerned on that child,
>
> (ii) is – (I) a person with a mental disorder (not resulting from the offence concerned), the person or a family member, (II) a person with a mental disorder (not resulting from the offence concerned), who is a child, the person or his or her parent or guardian, may give evidence as to the effect of the offence concerned on that person.
>
> (iii) is a person who is ill or is otherwise incapacitated as a result of the offence, a family member of the person may give evidence as to the effect of the offence concerned on that person and on his or her family members.
>
> (iv) has died as a result of the offence, a family member of the person may give evidence as to the effect of the offence concerned – (I) on the person between the commission of the offence and his or her death (where relevant), and (II) on the family members of the person who has died.
>
> (c) A person who has been convicted of an offence to which this section applies may not give evidence pursuant to paragraph (b) in respect of that offence.

(d) Where more than one family member seeks to avail of paragraph (b), the court may direct the family members to nominate one or more family members for the purpose of that paragraph.

(e) Where the court directs the family members to nominate one or more family members pursuant to paragraph (d) and the family members are unable to reach agreement, the court may, having regard to the degree of relationship between the family members and the person in respect of whom the offence was committed, nominate one or more family members as it considers appropriate.

(4) Where no evidence is given pursuant to subsection (3), the court shall not draw an inference that the offence had little or no effect (whether long-term or otherwise) on the person in respect of whom the offence was committed or, where appropriate, on his or her family members."[40]

Notably absent from this section is any reference to a 'victim'. It refers throughout to "the person in respect of whom the offence was committed". This has the merit of avoiding disputes as to who should be treated as a victim, a matter that has proved troublesome in Canada when multiple statements have been submitted in homicide cases, including some from non-family members.[41] As already noted, s 5 of the 1993 Act originally applied solely to offences of a sexual or violent nature. In 2010, it was extended to include any offence under the Non-Fatal Offences against the Person Act 1997 and to permit impact evidence to be given by family members of homicide victims.[42] In fact, many courts had already been allowing relatives of homicide victims to give such evidence, so the 2010 amendments were effectively formalising an existing practice. As a result of further amendment by the Criminal Justice (Victims of Crime) Act 2017 (s 31), evidence may now be received at sentencing about the impact of any offence with a human victim. The impact may consist of physical, mental or emotional harm or economic loss. Physical harm and economic loss may be relatively easy to assess, as they are matters of which courts have considerable experience. Assessing mental or emotional harm may call for expert assistance, though the English Court of Appeal has held that this is not essential when deciding if a victim has suffered "severe psychological harm" (the issue in the case in question).[43] What is needed, according to the court, is a judicial assessment of the factual impact of the offence, and while expert evidence may be helpful, it is not always necessary. **11–20**

Victim impact evidence may be in the form of a statement from the victim, or a report drawn up by a professional such as a psychologist. Most commonly, however, the evidence will consist of a written statement, oral evidence or both directly from the victim. Any report or statement **11–21**

[40] Criminal Justice Act 1993, s 5 as substituted by Criminal Procedure Act 2010, s 4 and amended by Criminal Justice (Victims of Crime) Act 2017, s 31.

[41] *R v Gabriel* (1999) 98 OTC 193; 137 CCC (3d) 1; Ashley Smith, "Victim impact statements: Redefining 'victim'" (2011) 57 Crim LQ 346.

[42] Criminal Procedure Act 2010, s 4.

[43] *R v Chall* [2019] EWCA Crim 865; [2019] 4 WLR 102; [2019] 2 Cr App R (S) 44.

must comply with the terms of s 5 of the Criminal Justice Act 1993 (as amended) and, in particular, it must deal exclusively with "any effect (whether long-term or otherwise) of the offence on the person in respect of whom the offence was committed" (s 5(2)). Care must be taken to exclude any irrelevant material, especially if it might be unfairly prejudicial to the accused. A victim may not give evidence of the impact of an injury which resulted from an alleged offence of which the offender was acquitted.[44] Section 5 now contains the added safeguard that the trial court may, in the interests of justice, order that certain information relating to victim impact evidence shall not be broadcast or published. This might become necessary where, for example, a person giving impact evidence suggested that the offender was guilty of an offence other than that of which he or she was convicted.[45] Where there are multiple direct victims, each may provide impact evidence. (As noted below, in homicide cases, some limit may be placed on the number of family members permitted to give such evidence.) In sex offence cases, for example, there may be several direct victims. In *R v Trowland and Decker*,[46] where environmental protestors had caused massive public disruption, including delaying half a million vehicles, there were 22 victim personal statements and six business impact statements.

11–22 The Canadian Criminal Code provides for victim impact statements in substantially the same terms as the Irish legislation. It requires that in determining sentence, a court shall consider any statement by a victim "describing the physical or emotional harm, property damage or economic loss suffered by the victim as the result of the commission of the offence and the impact of the offence on the victim".[47] Canadian courts have insisted that victim impact evidence should strictly adhere to this statutory purpose. On no account must victims include in their statements any recommendations as to sentence or any general derogatory comments about the offender.[48] The sole purpose of the evidence is to describe the impact of the offence. The Ontario Superior Court of Justice, for example, has held that a victim impact statement steps over the line when it recommends a penalty, "particularly one incompatible with the dignity and humanity due [to] offenders under our law".[49] (In that case, a victim had expressed regret that the death penalty was no longer available for homicide.) The Criminal Code also provides that in considering a victim impact statement a court shall take account of the portions it considers relevant for the purpose of determining the impact of the offence and disregard any other portion.[50]

---

44 *People (DPP) v S(C)* [2022] IECA 282, para. 45.

45 A problem of this nature arose in *People (DPP) v O'Donoghue* [2006] IECCA 134; [2007] 2 IR 336.

46 [2023] EWCA Crim 919; [2023] 4 All ER 766; [2024] 1 Cr App R(S) 13.

47 s 722(1).

48 *R v Gabriel* (1999) 98 OTC 193; 137 CCC (3d) 1; *R v McDonough* (2006) 209 CCC (3d) 547; *R v Beals* [2023] ONSC 555.

49 *R v Beals* [2023] ONSC 555, para 97.

50 s 722(8).

4. Victim Impact Evidence in Homicide Cases

Where a person has died as a result of the offence, a family member may give evidence about the impact of the offence on the deceased prior to his or her death and also on the family.[51] Although it was not placed on a statutory basis in Ireland until 2010, the practice of receiving impact evidence from close relatives of homicide victims was already well-established as many judges permitted such evidence to be given.[52] Where several family members wish to make impact statements, the court may direct them to nominate one or more of their number to do so. If they fail to agree, the court itself may nominate one or more of them for this purpose. The idea of permitting victim impact evidence in homicide cases probably attracts broad support, but there are some difficulties associated with it. Such evidence cannot affect the sentence for murder which carries a fixed penalty of life imprisonment. It may, of course, be relevant when sentencing for manslaughter or driving offences resulting in death. However, a more principled objection is that evidence of this nature risks treating or appearing to treat some deceased victims as more worthy than others. It might result in "penalties reflecting the comparative worthiness of the deceased relative to other dead victims and/or articulate response of family victims".[53] For this reason, some Australian courts have expressed serious reservations about receiving impact evidence from relatives of homicide victims. **11–23**

In the past at least, New South Wales courts could receive such evidence, but they were prohibited from allowing it to influence sentence. 'Equality in death' provided the main underlying rationale for this exclusionary policy. Allowing information about the particular victim could undermine the objectivity of the sentencing decision-making process. Two leading judicial statements sum up the basis of the policy. In *R v Previtera*[54] Hunt J said: **11–24**

> "It is regarded by all thinking persons as offensive to fundamental conceptions of equality and justice for criminal courts to value one life as greater than another. It would therefore be wholly inappropriate to impose a harsher sentence upon an offender because the value of the life lost is perceived to be greater in one case than another."

Later, in *R v Dang*,[55]Adams J said:

---

[51] Criminal Justice Act 1993, s 5(3) as substituted by Criminal Procedure Act 2010, s 4.

[52] See, for example, *People (DPP) v O'Donoghue* [2006] IECCA 134; [2007] 2 IR 336.

[53] Tracey Booth, "Homicide, family victims and sentencing: Continuing the debate about victim impact statements" (2004) 15 *Current Issues in Criminal Justice* 253.

[54] (1997) 94 A Crim R 76 at 86. For a thoughtful analysis, see Tyrone Kirchengast, "Victim impact statements and the *Previtera* rule: Delimiting the voice and representation of family victims in New South Wales homicide cases" (2005) 24 Univ Tasmania LR 114.

[55] [1999] NSWCCA 42, para 15.

> "The reason why a victim's impact statement cannot be taken into account where a person dies may easily be demonstrated. Assume the deceased was friendless; assume the deceased had no family. It would be monstrous to suggest that that meant for some reason killing her should attract a lesser sentence than would be the case if, as is the situation here, she had a loving family and grieving relatives. Essentially, then, the reason that victim impact statements in cases involving death are not taken into account in imposing sentence is that law holds, as it must, that in death we are all equal and the idea that it is more serious or more culpable to kill someone who has or is surrounded by a loving and grieving family than someone who is alone is offensive to our notions of equality before the law."

11–25 By any standards, this is a powerful argument, and it illustrates the potential injustice of attributing any significant weight to impact evidence tendered by family members or friends of deceased victims. However, it cannot be regarded as a conclusive argument for excluding such evidence altogether. First, and as discussed further below, victim impact evidence can serve more than one purpose. Its primary purpose – indeed its statutory purpose in Ireland – may be to inform the court of the impact of the offence. Yet, it can also have an important expressive function. It allows victims or their families, as the case may be, to express publicly, perhaps for the first and only time, the harm and suffering they have endured as a result of the offence. To that extent, giving the evidence may have a therapeutic benefit, even if it has no influence on sentence.

11–26 Secondly, while the point made by Adams J in *Dang* is well taken, the family circumstances of a deceased victim can shed light on the harm caused by the offence, and it must be borne in mind that harm is one of two ingredients of offence gravity, culpability being the other. If, for example, a homicide victim was the only child of middle-aged parents or a person survived by a dependent spouse and young children, his or her death will have caused significant hardship to those family members, in addition to the obvious harm caused to the deceased.[56] Of course, Adams J was still right to say that a homicide victim without close family members or friends should not be devalued on that account. It would be entirely contrary to principle to impose, for that reason, a more lenient sentence than the offence objectively deserved. But where a court has discretion as to sentence, it can surely take account of particular hardships suffered by others as a result of the homicide, at least where satisfied that the offender, when committing the fatal act, was aware of (or perhaps reckless as to) the victim's family circumstances, a factor that might also be said to increase moral culpability. This argument eventually won out in the United States Supreme Court in the last of three high profile cases on the admissibility

---

[56] See, for example, Paul Gewirtz, "Victims and voyeurs: Two narrative problems at the criminal trial" in Peter Brooks and Paul Gewirtz (eds), *Law's Stories: Narrative and Rhetoric in the Law* (Yale University Press, 1996), 135, 142, defending victim impact evidence in homicide cases in part because it is "a particularisation of a generally foreseeable harm".

of victim impact evidence in capital murder cases. In *Payne v Tennessee*[57] Rehnquist CJ, delivering the opinion of the Court said:

> "We are now the view that a state may properly conclude that, for the jury to assess meaningfully the defendant's moral culpability and blameworthiness, it should have before it at the sentencing phase evidence of the specific harm caused by the defendant."

This statement has rightly been criticised for assuming that resulting harm affects an offender's moral culpability without insisting on any requirement of foresight as to what the particular consequences may be. In *Booth v Maryland*,[58] on the other hand, the majority, while holding that victim impact evidence should not be admitted at capital sentencing hearings, accepted that "a defendant's degree of knowledge of the probable consequences of his actions may increase his moral culpability in a constitutionally significant manner".[59] This approach is more consistent with fundamental requirements of justice than that adopted in *Payne* because of the connection it establishes between foresight of consequences and penal desert. **11–27**

Ultimately, it is a question of striking an appropriate balance between these competing considerations. In the American cases just mentioned, the issue was a matter of life and death because victim impact evidence might well influence a jury to impose the death penalty. Elsewhere, the question will be whether such evidence should affect the severity of a non-capital penalty in those cases where the penalty is discretionary. Clearly, the primary focus must be on the offence itself but factors relating to the offender's culpability when committing the offence remain relevant in assessing gravity. Specific harms suffered by the deceased's family members and the offender's foresight of those harms may therefore be taken into account. As Hill J said in the leading Canadian case of *R v Gabriel*,[60] where a crime results in death, "human experience, logic and common sense surely go some distance to presuming the existence of profound grief, loss and despair". But, as he also said, evidence of the impact of the crime on the victim's survivors "achieves a measure of balance in understanding the consequences of the crime in the context of the victim's personal circumstances, or those of survivors". **11–28**

Fears are also occasionally expressed that sentencers be unduly swayed by family impact statements that are highly articulate, emotional or both. This was certainly a factor in *Booth v Maryland*[61] and to an even greater extent **11–29**

57 501 US 808, 825 (1991). In the two earlier cases, *Booth v Maryland* 482 US 496 (1987) and *South Carolina v Gathers* 490 US 805 (1989), a majority of the Court had held that the admission of victim impact in capital murder cases violated the Eighth Amendment prohibition on cruel and unusual punishment.

58 *Booth v Maryland* 482 US 496 (1987).

59 482 US 496 at 505 (1987), citing *Tison v Arizona* 481 US 137 (1987).

60 (1999) 98 OTC 193; 137 CCC (3d) 1, para 108.

61 482 US 496 (1987).

in *Payne v Tennessee*.[62] However, in these cases, it was a jury rather than a judge who decided if the death penalty should be imposed on a convicted murderer, as is the practice in several retentionist states in the United States. It is therefore understandable that the Supreme Court majority in *Booth* should have concluded that informing the sentencing jury about the personal characteristics of the deceased and the impact of his or her death on the immediate family created "a constitutionally unacceptable risk that the jury may impose the death penalty in an arbitrary and capricious manner".[63] However, in jurisdictions such as Ireland where the selection of sentence is exclusively a judicial task, it is safe to assume that judges will evaluate victim impact evidence dispassionately and objectively, and take account of all other relevant factors when deciding on sentence. There is the additional safeguard of an unrestricted right of appeal against severity of sentence.

11–30 Victim impact evidence in homicide cases may sometimes function to provide a more balanced description of the deceased than emerged at the trial or in the publicity preceding it.[64] Homicide victims will not always have been persons of unblemished character. They may have been involved in crime and may even have precipitated the event that led to their death. There may consequently be a degree of victim-offender overlap as discussed earlier in this chapter. In those circumstances, the picture painted of the deceased during the trial will often be a very negative one. Yet, the deceased, despite having faults and perhaps a record of criminality, was also a human being who may have done much good as well as bad. For example, he may have been conscientious in supporting his family or other dependants. The deceased's family members may naturally be distressed at the one-sided narrative presented at trial. A victim or family impact statement therefore furnishes an opportunity publicly to present a more balanced account of the deceased's life and character.

5. Purpose of Victim Impact Evidence

11–31 Victim impact evidence is commonly said to have informative and/or therapeutic goals. It can be informative in the sense of making the court more fully aware of the harm the offence inflicted on the victim, and therapeutic in terms of furnishing victims with an opportunity to describe what they experienced during the commission of the offence and the impact, short-term and long-term, it has had on them.[65] In Ireland, s 5 of

---

62 501 US 808 (1991)

63 482 US 496, 502-503 (1987).

64 Paul Rock, "'Hearing the victims of crime': The delivery of impact statements as ritual behaviour in four London trials for murder and manslaughter" in Bottoms and Roberts, note 21 above, Chap 8.

65 Marie Manikis, "Victim impact statements at sentencing: Towards a clearer understanding of their aims" (2015) 65 Univ Toronto LJ 85, referring to the instrumental and expressive roles of victim impact evidence.

the Criminal Justice Act 1993, as amended, provides that a court, when sentencing for a relevant offence, must take account of victim impact and receive evidence in that regard. Further, the victim, if he or she wishes to do so, is entitled to testify at the sentencing hearing as to the impact of the offence. The same holds true, or is assumed to be the case, in other jurisdictions. In *Payne v Tennessee*,[66] Rehnquist CJ said: "Victim impact evidence is simply another form or method of informing the sentencing authority about the specific harm caused by the crime in question, evidence of a general type long considered by sentencing authorities".

Others claim that victim impact evidence is primarily or additionally intended to be therapeutic or cathartic. In *United States v Blake*,[67] Weinstein J, while acknowledging the informational value of such evidence, went on to say: **11–32**

> "Victim impact statements may also serve as a catharsis for victims, helping to assuage the bitterness at the fates they have suffered. By participating in the criminal proceeding, victims realise that they are recognised as important by the court. The proceeding is not merely about the criminal, but it also accounts for the person most affected by the crime. Simply giving this person a chance to speak and be heard can have a beneficial effect. Instead of the victim feeling depersonalised and forgotten by the legal processes, she can feel that her situation was properly understood and considered."

Doubts have occasionally been expressed about both the informative and therapeutic value of victim impact statements, and it has said that there is little empirical support for the therapeutic claim.[68] As against this, victim impact evidence undoubtedly has an expressive function.[69] Victims are thereby afforded an opportunity to describe how the offender's conduct affected them, both at the time they were subjected to it and subsequently. In circumstances where the offender and victim are strangers to each other, as is typically true in, say, residential burglary and robbery cases, impact evidence puts a human face on the victim and helps to bring home to the offender how the offence affected that person's life and, in some instances, their family's life as well. Where offender and victim were **11–33**

[66] 501 US 808, 825 (1991).

[67] 89 F Supp 2d 328 (EDNY, 2000). See also Jamie Balson, "Therapeutic jurisprudence: Facilitating healing in crime victims" (2013) 6 Phoenix LR 1017, 1031 ("Historically and at present, the primary function of a victim impact statement has been expressive or therapeutic; to provide crime victims with a voice regardless of the impact it may have on the sentence itself"); Edna Erez, "Who's afraid of the big bad victim? Victim impact statements as victim empowerment and enhancement of justice" [1999] Crim LR 545; Edna Erez, "Victim voice, impact statements and sentencing: Integrating restorative justice and therapeutic jurisprudence principles in adversarial proceedings" (2004) 40 *Criminal Law Bulletin* 483.

[68] Susan A Bandes, "What are victim impact statements for?" (2022) 87 Brooklyn LR 1253.

[69] Julian V Roberts and Edna Erez, "Communication at sentencing: The expressive function of victim impact statements" in Bottoms and Roberts (eds), note 21 above, Chap 9.

well known to each other, as in a case of serial child sexual abuse, the sentencing hearing may well be the victim's first and only opportunity to address the offender directly, and in an environment where, for once, the offender must listen to what the victim has to say. In cases of this nature, the victim will usually have been under the control and domination of the offender while the abuse was being perpetrated, and this may have lasted for many years during which the victim had no voice. Giving such a victim a voice at sentencing is therefore an exercise in justice, apart from any therapeutic benefit it may have. It compensates, however inadequately, for the silence the victim had to endure while being subjected to the abuse. Research suggests that victims feel better when a judge makes a direct refence to their evidence, even if they are not entirely satisfied with the sentence imposed.[70]

11–34 Sentencing is, among other things, a communicative exercise. The court communicates to the offender the wrongfulness of his or her criminal conduct, the harm it inflicted or the risk it posed to others, as the case may be. The offender has an opportunity to respond by, for example, expressing remorse or offering an apology. It is only at sentencing, especially where there has been a guilty plea, that a victim can participate in this communicative process by describing, to the court and the offender, the impact of the offence. That impact is often communicated more effectively by being expressed in the victim's own words rather than being conveyed in the more formal language that courts and lawyers are accustomed to using. The effect of the offence is thereby communicated quite palpably to the offender.[71] Evidence of this nature also has an important educational value for the wider public. Media coverage of victim impact evidence has undoubtedly shaped our collective awareness of the seriousness of certain kinds of offending, and especially sexual offending, and how it adversely affects the lives of victims.

6. Victim's Plea for Leniency

11–35 A victim will occasionally urge a court to treat the offender leniently and, if possible, to impose something other than immediate imprisonment. This typically occurs where there was a close relationship between the offender and the victim. In a case of dangerous driving causing death, for example, the deceased may have been a friend or family member of the offender. Likewise, in a domestic violence case, the offender and victim may have become reconciled, or the victim may wish to spare young children the trauma of having one of their parents imprisoned.[72] In a

---

70 Edna Erez and Linda Rogers, "Victim impact statements and sentencing outcomes and processes: The perspectives of legal professionals" (1999) 39 Brit J Criminology 216.

71 *R v Berner* 2013 BCCA 188, para 14.

72 *R v Mills* [1998] 2 Cr App R (S) 252, sentence for attempted rape of former partner reduced from six to three years' imprisonment when victim told Court of Appeal that she and the offender were now reunited. See also *People (DPP) v*

recent Irish case where the offender was convicted of manslaughter arising from the largely accidental fatal shooting of this sister, his mother (who was also the victim's mother) pleaded with the court not to send him to prison.[73] Pleas of this nature pose a difficult dilemma for the courts. Victim forgiveness has no impact on the gravity of the offence. The harm and degree of culpability would be the same even if there were no such plea. Yet, it might be argued that if there is a general policy to take account of victim impact, evidence of forgiveness on the part of a victim should not be dismissed out of hand. It may, for example, indicate that the offence has caused less psychological harm that would normally be anticipated. Alternatively, it might be treated as a reason for extending mercy. The role of mercy in sentencing provokes intense disagreement among theorists, but in practice it is recognised as a legitimate consideration, though its impact will vary with the circumstances of the case. In any event, a factor that appears to fall under the heading of mercy may also be legally relevant in the sense of coming within a recognised sentencing principle. This was recognised by the Court of Criminal Appeal in *People (DPP) v O'D (R)*[74] where it said:

> "It has never been the practice in this jurisdiction for the victims of an offence to be permitted to express views... as to what the proper sentence might be. In the opinion of the court, s 5 [of the Criminal Justice Act 1993] makes no change in that regard. While a victim or a relative of a victim or a relative of an accused would not be entitled to express an opinion in court as to what was an appropriate sentence, they are entitled always to put forward an *ad misericordiam* plea. As has been pointed out before by this court, the trial court is under an obligation to administer justice rather than mercy but very often the reasons given for the plea of mercy are reasons which are relevant to the assessment of a just sentence."

By way of example, leniency is sometimes sought because the offender's children are suffering as a result of his or her incarceration. As discussed earlier in Chap 5, this is a factor that may properly influence sentence as a matter of principle and not just, if at all, as an exercise in mercy towards the offender.[75] The matter was recently considered by the Supreme Court in *People (DPP) v Duffy*[76] although, as the court acknowledged, it did not directly arise in that case. However, the court essentially endorsed what had been said in *O'D (R)*. O'Malley J, with whom all other members of the Supreme Court agreed, said that a victim's views as to sentence **11–36**

S(T) [2019] IECA 252 which involved rather similar circumstances and where the Court of Appeal suspended part of the ultimate sentence to reflect the victim's plea for leniency and to incentivise the offender's rehabilitation.

73 "Mother of man who fatally shot his sister begs judge not to jail her son", *Irish Times*, 29 November 2022 (*DPP v Boyd*). The man was subsequently sentenced to two years' imprisonment (*Irish Examiner*, 16 December 2022).

74 [2000] 4 IR 361 at 364-365. See also *People (DPP) v McCormack* [2000] 4 IR 356; *Attorney General's Reference No. 38 of 2013 (Hall)* [2013] EWCA Crim 1450; [2014] 1 Cr App R (S) 61, para 86; *R v Nunn* [1996] 2 Cr App R (S) 136; *R v Roche* [1999] 2 Cr App R (S) 105 at 109; [1999] Crim LR 339.

75 See discussion in *People (DPP) v S(T)* [2019] IECA 252.

76 [2023] IESC 1.

cannot sway the sentencing court, but "an *ad misericordiam plea* based on appropriate grounds may be taken into account".[77] As to what appropriate grounds may be, the court seemed to be thinking primarily of offender-related factors of a mitigating nature which the victim was in a unique position to bring to the judge's attention. . The victim might be able to place these matters in a clearer light because of his or her close familiarity with the offender's circumstances.[78] As the Court of Appeal held in *People (DPP) v S(T)*[79] where the matter arose squarely for consideration and which has a valuable discussion of the topic, a court may treat a plea for leniency as one factor in a sentencing decision, but may, and probably should, also have regard to the underlying reasons for the plea.

11–37 In an empirical study of personal mitigation conducted in five English Crown Court centres about 15 years ago, which involved both court observation and interviews with 40 sentencers of varying levels of experience, it was found that sentencers differed considerably on this question. About half of them treated expressions of victim forgiveness in death by dangerous driving cases as a "big impact" factor which, in turn, meant one that would shift a custodial sentence to a non-custodial one or that would halve the sentence length. The others treated it as a factor that would have less impact or none at all.[80]

11–38 As reflected in the passage from *R v Konzani*[81] quoted at the beginning of this chapter, the general policy of the English courts is not to allow a victim's wishes to influence sentence. This certainly holds true in circumstances where a victim urges the imposition of a severe penalty.[82] However, they have been somewhat more flexible when it comes to pleas for leniency. There have been cases, admittedly predating *Konzani*, where the Court of Appeal granted some reduction in sentence to reflect a victim's plea for leniency, mainly in death by dangerous driving cases.[83] In *R v Nunn*[84] there was the additional factor that some members of the victim's family claimed that the sentence imposed on the offender was adding to their grief and anxiety. As noted earlier, the Irish approach more closely resembles those earlier English cases to the extent that, in some circumstances at least, a victim's plea for leniency may have some impact, though a necessarily limited one, on sentence.

---

77 [2023] IESC 1, para 73.

78 This may be inferred from what the court said at [2023] IESC 1, para 42.

79 [2019] IECA 252.

80 Jessica Jacobson and Mike Hough, *Mitigation: The Role of Personal Factors in Sentencing* (Prison Reform Trust, 2007), 16.

81 [2005] EWCA Crim 706; [2005] 2 Cr App R 14.

82 *R v Bird* [2008] ABQB 327, para 60 (Court of Queen's Bench of Alberta) ("Anger, hatred and a desire for revenge are understandable personal feelings, but are not part of the legal process").

83 See, in particular, *R v Roche* [1999] 2 Cr App R (S) 105; [1999] Crim LR 339 where Lord Bingham CJ delivered a significant judgment on the matter, and *R v Matthews* [2002] EWCA Crim 1484; [2003] 1 Cr App R (S) 26.

84 [1996] 2 Cr App R (S) 136.

7. State-Funded Compensation

There are three ways in which crime victims might receive monetary compensation for the harm or injuries they have suffered: (1) civil proceedings against the offender;[85] (2) court-ordered compensation from the offender to the victim as an element of the sentence (or as the entire sentence), following conviction;[86] or (3) state-funded compensation which is not dependent on any civil or criminal proceedings having been initiated against the offender. The first two options are seldom viable simply because the offender will likely be unable to pay any compensation. In some instances, the perpetrator of the crime will never have been identified or apprehended. If identified, he or she may die before any legal proceedings are initiated or concluded. In most others, the offender will not be worth pursuing for civil damages and will seldom have the means to pay any court-ordered compensation, unless of a very small amount, if convicted. **11–39**

The existence of criminal injuries compensation schemes in these islands and in jurisdictions further afield is, in many ways, attributable to the 'power of one'. The idea that the state should compensate crime victims was first championed by Margery Fry (1874-1958), a leading British prison reformer, magistrate (the first woman to be appointed as such) and university administrator.[87] A newspaper article which she published in 1957 arguing for publicly funded victim compensation proved to be enormously influential, and led first to a scheme being established in New Zealand in 1963 and another very soon thereafter in England and Wales.[88] As she noted, the idea was not entirely novel as it had already been mooted by Bentham,[89] but her argument was based on an analogy with social insurance and an appeal to collective responsibility towards victims of violent crime. She argued that "the state which forbids our going armed in self-defence cannot disown all responsibility for its occasional failure to protect". Taxpayer-funded compensation certainly requires justification. **11–40**

---

85 *People (DPP) v Lyons* [2014] IECCA 27, para 63 (although as the Court of Criminal Appeal rightly observed, civil claims are seldom brought in these circumstances).

86 This option is considered in Chap 12 below under "Compensation."

87 Enid Huws Jones, *Margery Fry: The Essential Amateur* (Oxford University Press, 1966); Anne Logan, *The Politics of Penal Reform: Margery Fry and the Howard League* (Routledge, 2018).

88 Margery Fry, "Justice for victims" *The Observer*, 7 July 1957. The article was later republished in (1959) 8 *Journal of Public Law* 191 as part of a round table on compensating victims of criminal violence. It is accompanied by several detailed responses from Glanville Williams and others. On the political response to Fry's article, see Terence Morris "Compensation for victims of crimes of violence" (1961) 24 Modern LR 744. For a more detailed account of the original schemes in New Zealand and England and Wales, see Norman I Siegel, "Compensation for victims of crimes of violence" (1966) 30 Albany LR 325.

89 On historical precedents for Fry's proposal, see Boyd L Wright, "What about the victims? Compensation for the victims of crime" (1971) 48 North Dakota LR 473.

It may not be immediately apparent why the broader community should assume financial responsibility for privately inflicted criminal injuries as opposed, for example, to accidental injuries, even accepting that such an obligation arises only when the perpetrator is either untraceable or unable to pay.[90] One plausible justification is that citizens and, indeed, all residents are entitled to state protection against personal violence. The intentional infliction of such violence represents a failure by the state to provide that protection and it therefore calls for some redress, assuming that this cannot be had from the perpetrator. Additionally, it might be argued that everyone is at risk of such violence and that publicly funded compensation operates as a kind of social insurance that spreads the risk, rather than letting the loss fall entirely on individual victims. It is therefore an exercise in social solidarity which is the main justification indicated in the preamble to the Council of Europe Convention on the Compensation of Victims of Violent Crimes (1983).

11–41 The terms of many criminal injury compensation schemes remind us that victimhood, no less than criminality, is socially constructed. Not everyone who suffers harm or injury is perceived as a victim, particularly if he or she has a criminal record or was involved in criminal or anti-social activity when the injury was inflicted.[91] Compensation schemes, therefore, often reflect broader societal norms and assumptions by distinguishing between deserving and undeserving victims.[92] The present Irish scheme, for example, provides:

> "No compensation will be payable where the Tribunal is satisfied that the conduct of the victim, his character or his way of life make it inappropriate that he should be granted an award and the Tribunal may reduce the amount of an award where, in its opinion, it is appropriate to do so having regard to the conduct, character or way of life of the victim."[93]

11–42 There is a similar provision excluding or reducing compensation where the victim was responsible, through provocation or otherwise, for the offence giving rise to the injuries.[94] Until 2021, awards could not be made where the crime was committed by a member of the same household as

---

[90] For further analysis of this question, see Andrew Ashworth, "Punishment and compensation: Victims, offenders and the State" (1986) 6 *Oxford Journal of Legal Studies* 86.

[91] David Miers, "Compensating deserving victims of violent crime: The Criminal Injuries Compensation Scheme 2012" (2014) 34 *Legal Studies* 242, 258 ("it is a mundane fact that many victims have also been offenders and that in particular instances it may be a matter of chance as to which of two protagonists the criminal justice process subsequently labels as 'the victim'.").

[92] Christie, note 30 above; David Miers, "Victims, criminal justice and state compensation" (2019) 9(2) *Societies* 29, 34.

[93] Scheme of Compensation for Personal Injuries Criminally Inflicted, effective from 20 April 2021, para 13. This was an issue in *Kelly and Doyle v Criminal Injuries Compensation Tribunal* [2020] IECA 342. See also *Cunningham Cummins v Criminal Injuries Compensation Tribunal* [2024] IEHC 143 where compensation was denied to children of the deceased on this ground.

[94] para 12 of the 2021 version of the Scheme.

the victim, but that restriction has now been removed. This 'one roof' rule, as it became known, must have been of dubious constitutionality in any event. It was obviously modelled on an equivalent provision in the original English scheme where it was justified on the basis that if one spouse was awarded compensation for an assault perpetrated by the other, the assailant might end up benefiting from it and, further, that such assaults could be difficult to prove.[95] Obviously, this ignored the plight of children who might be sexually or otherwise physically abused by a member of the same household, a consideration that later led the English Court of Appeal to conclude that the 'one roof' rule, as it applied in those circumstances, was incompatible with art 14 of the ECHR.[96]

Ireland's Criminal Injuries Compensation Scheme was established in 1974 on a non-statutory basis (as it remains) and its purpose was expressly to provide *ex gratia* payments to certain victims of violent crime. In this respect, it mirrored the English scheme introduced a decade earlier. At that time, the British government was at pains to deny that it had any legal responsibility to compensate crime victims.[97] It was doing so essentially as a matter of grace and favour. The Irish position has changed through the influence of EU law. A 2004 Directive on compensation for violent crime victims provides: **11–43**

> "All member states shall ensure that their national rules provide for the existence of a scheme on compensation to victims of violent intentional crimes committed in their respective territories, which guarantees fair and appropriate compensation for victims."[98]

For many years after the adoption of this Directive, there was a widely held view that it applied solely to criminal injuries with a cross-border element, such as where a citizen of one country was the victim of a violent crime in another. However, in 2020 the Grand Chamber of the Court of Justice of the European Union confirmed that the Directive obliged member states to provide a compensation scheme for victims of violent intentional crimes committed within their territory, including for victims who habitually reside in that territory. The scheme should also be available in cases with a cross-border dimension.[99] Ireland responded **11–44**

---

95 *JT v First Tier Tribunal* [2018] EWCA Civ 1735; [2019] 1 WLR 1313 para 10 (quoting from statement by Government spokesman in House of Commons when the compensation scheme was being introduced in 1964).

96 *JT v First Tier Tribunal* [2018] EWCA Civ 1735; [2019] 1 WLR 1313. This, however, was contingent on a prior holding that the entitlement to compensation for criminally inflicted violent injuries, which has been placed on a statutory basis in England, amounted to a property right for the purpose of art 1 of Protocol 1 of the ECHR. The applicant had been raped and sexually assaulted by her stepfather throughout her childhood.

97 Ashworth, note 90 above, at 99.

98 Council Directive 2004/80/EC relating to compensation to crime victims, art 12(2).

99 Case C-129/19 *Italian Presidency of the Council of Ministers v BV* (July 2020), para 55 ("It follows that Article 12(2) of Directive 2004/80 confers the right to obtain

to this ruling by removing the reference "*ex gratia*" compensation in the 2021 revised version of the Scheme. The Court of Appeal has held that the Scheme "must now be seen as the means by which the State gives effect to its obligations under the Directive both as regards cross-border and purely domestic scenarios".[100]

11–45 The Scheme provides for the payment of compensation "in respect of personal injury where the injury is directly attributable to a crime of violence". Difficulties may occasionally arise in interpreting the expression 'crime of violence', but it will almost invariably involve an assault of one kind or another, whether fatal or non-fatal.[101] The Scheme expressly treats arson and poisoning as crimes of violence. It also provides for the payment of compensation to persons who sustained injuries while assisting or attempting to assist in the prevention of crime or in saving a human life, as well as to dependants of a victim who died as a result of a criminally inflicted violent injury. The Scheme is administered by a Tribunal which currently has 14 members, a considerable improvement on the situation some years ago when it was down to one member.[102] A decision on an application may be made by an officer of the Tribunal where the amount claimed does not exceed €3,000 and by one Tribunal member where the amount is between €3,000 and €75,000. Three Tribunal members adjudicate on any claim for €75,000 or more. An applicant dissatisfied with the amount offered may lodge an appeal which will be heard by a differently constituted three-member panel. No application will be entertained where the appropriate compensation is estimated to be less than €500.

11–46 As already noted, an applicant may be denied compensation or granted reduced compensation in certain circumstances, such as where he or she was fully or partly responsible for the injury inflicted. Further, no compensation will be payable to an applicant who has not given the Tribunal all reasonable assistance in relation to medical reports or other matters. Another important limitation is that no compensation is payable for pain or suffering in respect of injuries sustained on or after 1 January 2006. In fact, no compensation has been payable under this heading since

---

fair and appropriate compensation not only on victims of violent intentional crime committed in the territory of a Member State who find themselves in a cross-border situation, but also on victims who reside habitually in the territory of that Member State").

[100] *Kelly and Doyle v Criminal Injuries Compensation Tribunal* [2020] IECA 342, para 81. For a critical analysis of this decision and of the Criminal Injuries Compensation Scheme more generally, see Mark William Murphy, "The right under EU law to compensation for injuries criminally inflicted: The implications of *B.V.* for Irish law" (2021) 23 *Irish Journal of European Law* 219, and Liam O'Driscoll, "Towards a rights-based approach: Victims of violent crime, state-funded compensation and the European Union" (2023) 14 *New Journal of European Criminal Law* 303.

[101] *Earls v Criminal Injuries Compensation Tribunal* [2022] IEHC 679.

[102] *Byrne v Criminal Injuries Compensation Tribunal* [2017] IEHC 28, para 15.

1986. In *AD v Ireland*[103] the applicant, who had suffered serious injuries as a result of rape and other sexual offences, claimed that the unavailability of compensation for pain and suffering violated her constitutional right to bodily integrity. The High Court held that while the applicant undoubtedly had such a right, she did not have constitutional right to compensation, the provision of such compensation being a matter of political policy. The matter was revisited by the Court of Appeal in *Kelly and Doyle v Criminal Injuries Compensation Tribunal*[104] where it was argued that the exclusion of compensation for pain and suffering ran counter to EU Directive 2004/80 as interpreted in *BV* (as outlined above). The Court of Appeal did not reach a firm conclusion on this point, saying that it might well be necessary to make a reference to the Court of Justice of the European Union on the correct interpretation of the Directive in this regard. However, in the circumstances of this case, where the Criminal Injuries Compensation Tribunal had not yet adjudicated on the applicants' claims, such a reference would be premature.[105] However, the High Court has more recently, in another case, made a reference to the Court of Justice where the principal questions are whether the obligation in art 12(2) of Directive 2004/80/EC to provide "fair and appropriate compensation" to victims of violent crime requires that a victim be compensated for non-material loss and, if so, whether non-material loss includes pain and suffering.[106]

The Criminal Injuries Compensation Scheme is intended to be accessible and reasonably informal. The main precondition for a valid application is that the offence giving rise to the injury has been reported to the Gardaí or the Garda Ombudsman, as appropriate, unless it has already been the subject of criminal proceedings. An application should ordinarily be made within three months of the offence, but it must always be made within two years. Applicants are entitled to present their case at a hearing of the Tribunal, and to call, examine and cross-examine witnesses whose reasonable and necessary expenses may be paid by the Tribunal, though it has a discretion in this regard. An applicant may be accompanied by a legal adviser or other person, but the Tribunal does not pay the costs of legal representation. In *Kelly and Doyle v Criminal Injuries Compensation Tribunal*[107] it was argued that the absence of entitlement to legal costs ran counter to various aspects of EU law, including the principle of effectiveness and art 47 of the Charter of Fundamental Rights of the European Union which requires that legal aid be available to those who need it to secure access to justice. However, the Court of Appeal, having analysed the competing arguments at some length, held against the applicants on this ground. This does not necessarily conclude the matter because, irrespective of what may be required by EU law, there are still sound policy arguments for providing some mechanism that would allow **11–47**

---

103 [1994] 1 IR 369.
104 [2020] IECA 342.
105 [2020] IECA 342, para 129.
106 *Blanco v Criminal Injuries Compensation Tribunal* [2024] IEHC 171.
107 [2020] IECA 342.

for the recovery of legal costs by persons who make applications to the Criminal Injuries Compensation Tribunal, as the Law Reform Commission has provisionally recommended.[108] Legal representation and legal aid may not be necessary in every case, or perhaps even in most cases, but some applicants would undoubtedly benefit from representation, especially if there is a possibility that they will be deemed ineligible for compensation under one of the exclusionary rules mentioned earlier.

11–48 Finally, it should be noted that the Criminal Injuries Compensation Scheme still lacks a statutory foundation, but the Tribunal, in the discharge of its functions is obliged to observe the principles of natural and constitutional justice, and the general rules of public law.[109]

[108] Law Reform Commission, *Compensating Victims of Crime*, Consultation Paper (2022), para 6.70.

[109] *State (Creedon) v Criminal Injuries Compensation Tribunal* [1988] IR 51.

Chapter 12

SENTENCING OPTIONS

For much of the 20th century, most Western countries had a fairly narrow range of non-capital sentencing options. Immediate imprisonment, suspended prison sentences, fines, probation and binding over orders were the measures most commonly used for dealing with offenders. Towards the end of the century, community service, compensation, curfew orders, house arrest and supervision orders of various kinds were added to the menu of options in many countries. For present purposes, we need not consider the death penalty which, in Ireland, was entirely abolished by statute in 1990 and constitutionally outlawed in 2001. It has also been abolished in every European country (except Belarus), Canada, Australia, New Zealand and many states of the United States.[1] The same holds true of corporal punishment.[2] This chapter is effectively divided into two sections. The first considers some general issues connected with sentencing options including their effectiveness, relative severity and interchangeability. The second describes the law governing the penalties most commonly imposed for serious offences and the principles applicable to their use. **12–01**

1. Evaluating Sentencing Options

Much of the literature on the effectiveness of sentencing options concentrates on their capacity to prevent or reduce recidivism. Numerous studies have attempted to identify the re-offending rates associated with different kinds of penalty, with particular emphasis on imprisonment **12–02**

---

1 More than 50 countries throughout the world retain the death penalty. It still exists in 27 states of the United States (as well as in the federal and military jurisdictions). For a comprehensive and critical review of the death penalty globally, see Roger Hood and Carolyn Hoyle, *The Death Penalty; A Worldwide Perspective,* 5th ed (Oxford University Press, 2015). The website of the Death Penalty Project is an excellent source of current information, especially for Commonwealth countries: <https://www.deathpenaltyproject.org> accessed 20 July 2024. The Death Penalty Information Centre provides similar information about capital punishment in the United States: <https://deathpenaltyinfo.org> accessed 20 July 2024. See also Amnesty International, *Death Sentences and Executions 2023* (2024).

2 Corporal punishment was formally abolished by the Criminal Law Act 1997 (s 12). It had long fallen into disuse, though it was being imposed well into the 20th century. In *Attorney General v Sherry,* the Court of Criminal Appeal refused leave to appeal against a sentence of seven years' penal servitude and 20 strokes of the 'cat' for armed robbery and wounding (*Irish Times,* 3 December 1926).

and community-based sanctions.[3] Yet, it would be a mistake to assume that re-offending rates, however identified, provide the sole legitimate benchmark of effectiveness. Crime prevention and the encouragement of desistance are undoubtedly important goals of any sentencing system and, indeed, of the broader criminal process of which it is part. This objective has been given statutory expression in some jurisdictions. The sentencing provisions of the Canadian Criminal Code begin by affirming:

> "The fundamental purpose of sentencing is to protect society and to contribute, along with crime prevention initiatives, to respect for the law and the maintenance of a just, peaceful and safe society by imposing just sanctions that have [one or more of the specified objectives]."[4]

12–03 England's Sentencing Code likewise provides that one of the purposes to which a court must have regard when imposing sentence is "the reduction of crime (including its reduction by deterrence)".[5] Ireland may not have any equivalent statutory measure but, here too, crime reduction is undoubtedly one of the aims of sentencing.

12–04 Yet, the effectiveness of any procedure must be assessed by reference to its underlying purpose. A medical intervention might be designed to prevent infection, cure an existing illness or merely give relief from pain, and its efficacy must therefore be judged according to how well it produces the desired outcome. Sentencing, too, has several possible goals, including the punishment of crime, deterring future crime (by the offender and others), rehabilitation and incapacitation.[6] A given penalty might be effective in advancing one or more of these goals, though not necessarily all of them. In many jurisdictions, Ireland included, there is not one officially endorsed dominant sentencing purpose, save to the extent that the principle of proportionality prohibits the imposition of a more severe punishment than the individual offender deserves. But subject to that limitation, courts, if they consider the matter at all, are free to determine the purpose that should guide the choice of penalty in any one case. Effectiveness, then, can be difficult to measure in the absence of any consensus or shared understanding as to the penological purposes that should inform sentencing decisions for different categories of offences and offenders.

12–05 Short prison sentences, the *bête noir* of many penal reformers, must be seen in this light. Even if they fail to prevent re-offending, they may still

---

3 For an excellent analysis of sentence effectiveness viewed from the perspectives of different interested parties in the criminal process, see Jay Gormley, *Reconceptualising the Effectiveness of Sentencing: Four Perspectives* (Sentencing Council, 2024). See also Melissa Hamilton, *The Effectiveness of Sentencing Options: A Review of Key Research Findings* (Sentencing Academy, 2021), and Jay Gormley, Melissa Hamilton and Ian Belton, *The Effectiveness of Sentencing Options on Reoffending* (Sentencing Council, 2022).

4 Criminal Code, s 718.

5 Sentencing Act 2020 (formally known as the Sentencing Code), s 57.

6 Chap 3 above.

be effective in expressing censure or providing deserved punishment for certain offences. As a matter of fact, many offences are punishable with maximum sentences of three, six or twelve months' imprisonment and formal guidelines, where they exist, sometimes recommend custodial sentences as short as a few weeks.[7] This does not, however, dispose of the normative question of whether such sentences should exist or be imposed in the first place. Research suggests that they are much less effective in preventing re-offending than long prison sentences, suspended sentences or community penalties.[8] When interpreting the relevant data, regard must first be had to the research methodology employed. Re-offending statistics are usually based on the number of offenders who committed one or more further offences within a given time frame, typically one to three years after being sentenced or released from prison, as the case may be. The more reliable studies concentrate on proven offences as opposed, for example, to arrests or charges.[9] Statistics compiled by the Central Statistics Office in Ireland show that 53 per cent of those who had spent three to six months in custody re-offended within a year of being released, compared with 31 per cent of those who had served sentences of 12 months or longer.[10] Re-offending rates vary greatly with offence and age. The same statistics show that 78 per cent of those released in 2017 from sentences (of all lengths) for public order or burglary offences were re-convicted within three years, whereas the lowest levels of re-offending were among those who served sentence for sex offences (12 per cent) and homicide and related offences (24 per cent). Eighty-four per cent of those aged less than 21 and 72 per cent of those aged between 21 and 25 who were released from custody in 2017 re-offended within three years of release. The re-offending rates of those placed on probation are lower than for imprisonment. The statistics for 2019 show that approximately one-third of those under 25 who were placed on probation re-offended within a year, whereas the equivalent figure was 14 per cent for those over 45. About one-third of those who received probation for public order or theft offences re-offended within a year. Care must obviously be exercised when drawing conclusions from statistics of this nature. For

7 In Ireland, the Criminal Justice (Public Order) Act 1994, s 6(2), as amended, provides for a maximum penalty of three months' imprisonment, a fine of up to €1,000 or both for threatening or abusive conduct in a public place, while the Non-Fatal Offences against the Person Act 1997, s 2, provides for a maximum penalty of six months' imprisonment, a fine of up to £1,500 or both for assault. The English Sentencing Council's guidelines occasionally recommend sentence ranges expressed in weeks. Under the Definitive Guideline on Theft Offences, for example, the recommended range for the lowest category of general theft is a medium level community order to 36 weeks' imprisonment which obviously leaves open the possibility of a few weeks' imprisonment in certain cases.

8 See Hamilton, note 3 above, and Ministry of Justice, *Transforming Rehabilitation – a summary of evidence on reducing re-offending* (2014). Both have extensive references to existing research literature.

9 Ministry of Justice, note 8 above.

10 The relevant reports are available on the website of the Central Statistics Office: <www.cso.ie> (accessed 15 August 2024) under 'Prison Re-Offending Statistics 2020' and 'Probation Re-Offending Statistics 2019'.

instance, those placed on probation would probably have been regarded as less likely to reoffend than those sentenced to imprisonment. Many other factors must be taken into account when considering the recidivism rates of ex-prisoners, including the nature of their offences, personal circumstances and addiction status.

2. Penal Equivalence and Perceptions of Severity

12–06 Imprisonment is commonly assumed to be the only suitable penalty for serious offences. This assumption is reflected in political and judicial decisions that have resulted in very high prison populations in several countries, notably the United States. Penal reformers therefore argue for expanded use of non-custodial penalties, even for serious offences. They claim that monetary and community-based sanctions can be as effective as imprisonment, whether viewed from a retributive or deterrent perspective. However, this view is not universally shared, least of all by those who emphasise the expressive purpose of punishment. They argue that sentencing is not just about imposing punishment. It also has a distinct and important social meaning; it publicly condemns the offender for having engaged in forbidden conduct. This is undoubtedly true. As Henry Hart wrote, what distinguishes the criminal from the civil sanction is "the judgment of community condemnation which accompanies and justifies its imposition".[11] To adopt his illustrative example, a person involuntarily committed to a psychiatric hospital and a person committed to prison both experience forcible deprivation of liberty and their conditions of detention may not greatly differ. Yet, there is the significant social difference that the psychiatric patient has not incurred the moral condemnation of the community, whereas the prisoner has.

12–07 Scholars and theorists who prioritise the expressive function of criminal punishment over and above, for example, retribution and deterrence, deny that any non-custodial sanction can be truly commensurate with imprisonment when it comes to sentencing serious offences. Dan Kahan argues that alternative sanctions "fail to express condemnation as dramatically and unequivocally as imprisonment" precisely because punishment "is a special social convention that signifies moral condemnation".[12] Imprisonment entails the deprivation of personal liberty which is one of our most fundamental and valued rights, something that cannot be said of a fine, which might be viewed as a price to be paid rather than a punishment for misconduct, or of community-based penalties which, however onerous, are still not as severe or stigmatising as imprisonment.[13]

---

[11] Henry M Hart, "The aims of the criminal law" (1958) 23 *Law and Contemporary Problems* 401, 404.

[12] Dan M Kahan, "What do alternative sanctions mean?" (1996) 63 Univ Chicago LR 591, 592-593. See also Dan M Kahan, "Punishment incommensurability" (1998) 1 Buffalo Crim LR 691.

[13] Robert Cooter, "Prices and sanctions" (1984) 84 Columbia LR 1523, 1524-1525 defines a sanction as "a detriment imposed for doing what is *forbidden*"

Whatever the merits of these arguments, it is safe to assume that, for the foreseeable future, imprisonment will remain the presumptive form of punishment for serious offences. Abolitionism currently has few supporters.[14] However, for many middle-ranking offences, non-custodial penalties can be a viable alternative to imprisonment. The challenge is to devise a means of identifying a reasonable degree of equivalence between a given term of imprisonment and other kinds of punishment.

Criminal penalties can be surprisingly difficult to rank according to severity. Imprisonment might, by common consent, be treated as the most severe punishment, with other measures such as the suspended sentence, community service, fines and probation ranking somewhere below it, though opinions vary as to the comparative severity of those non-custodial options. Yet, a prison term may not inevitably be more severe than any other sanction. Depending on its duration and the conditions in which it is served, it may be less onerous than a community-based measure that imposed severe conditions or restrictions over a long period. Two aspects of modern penal policy combine to underscore the importance of establishing penal equivalence. One is the priority accorded to proportionality among the distributive principles of sentencing. This reflects a desert-based philosophy although proportionality as understood in Ireland also leaves some room for the pursuit of more utilitarian goals. However, the key imperative is that the severity of the penalty should be graded to the seriousness of the crime. The other relevant policy factor is the commitment, at a rhetorical level at least, to treating incarceration as the sanction of last resort, with non-custodial options being preferred whenever possible. Effective implementation of these policies requires some degree of consensus, preferably derived from empirical research, on the 'punitive bite' of different units of punishment. Otherwise, for many offences, it will be difficult to identify a proportionate sentence other than one of imprisonment or detention. **12–08**

Research, limited though it may be, on offenders' assessment of sanction severity has yielded some surprising results.[15] This is particularly true of a survey of more than 1,000 male offenders conducted by Ben Crouch in Texas in the late 1980s.[16] Respondents were presented with 11 pairs of hypothetical criminal sanctions, each pair consisting of a specific probation **12–09**

whereas a price is "a payment of money which is required in order to do what is *permitted*". The idea that a fine is merely a price is, of course, strongly contested. See, for example, Ivó Coca-Vila, "What's really wrong with fining crimes? On the hard treatment of criminal monetary fines" (2022) 16 *Criminal Law and Philosophy* 395.

14 Jeldrik Mühl, *Strafrecht ohne Freiheitsstrafen – absurde Utopie oder logische Konsequenz?* (Verlag Mohr Siebeck, 2015).

15 See Chloé Leclerc and Pierre Tremblay, "Looking at penalty scales: How judicial actors and the general public judge penal severity" (2016) 58 *Canadian Journal of Criminology and Criminal Justice* 354, reviewing research on assessing crime seriousness and sentence severity.

16 Ben M Crouch, "Is incarceration really worse? Analysis of offenders' preferences for prison over probation" (1993) 10 *Justice Quarterly* 67.

term and specific prison term (eg, 10 years' imprisonment versus one year's probation; 10 years' probation versus five years' imprisonment) and they were asked to indicate which sanction they would prefer to face personally. As the summary of results reveals, imprisonment was the strongly preferred option in many instances:

> "[T]wo-thirds of respondents would choose one year in prison over 10 years on probation. Almost half still would opt for prison when the probation term is reduced to five years, and nearly one-third persist in preferring prison even when the alternatives are a seemingly light three years' probation and one year in prison. Even when the prison term rises to three full years against 10 on probation, one-quarter of the sample would choose prison. Thus it is evident that many Texas offenders would choose prison over probation, which society typically defines as less punitive."[17]

12–10 As other surveys of this kind have shown, preferences tend to vary with certain personal characteristics and circumstances. Being older predicted a preference for imprisonment. Married men were more likely to opt for probation whereas unmarried men tended to choose imprisonment. Better educated offenders, who generally had more to lose by going to prison, usually preferred probation. This study, however, had significant limitations. All the respondents were male, and all were beginning to serve prison sentences. Had the sample included offenders of both sexes sentenced to non-custodial measures as well as imprisonment, the results might have been different.

12–11 About the same time as Crouch's study appeared, Joan Petersilia and Elizabeth P Deschenes published the results of their survey of prison inmates in Minnesota, again designed to assess their perceptions of sanction severity.[18] Their sample was much smaller – 48 male offenders – but this time, respondents were asked to compare incarceration with intermediate sanctions as well as probation. Again, imprisonment was not invariably regarded as the most severe sanction. Respondents ranked five years' intensive probation as harsher than one year in prison but not as harsh as five years in prison, the last-mentioned penalty being regarded as more severe than any other. Predictably, a $100 fine was judged less severe than any other sanction. Respondents who were married and had children tended to rank custody as more severe than any other measure, whereas single offenders ranked financial penalties as more severe than did married offenders. Other research has sought to obtain the view of members of the public or criminal justice personnel on the comparative severity of penalties with a view to establishing numerically expressed severity values that could serve to convert one form of penalty to another.[19]

---

17 Crouch, note 16 above at 79.

18 Joan Petersilia and Elizabeth P Deschenes, "Perceptions of punishment: Inmates and staff rank the severity of prison versus intermediate sanctions" (1994) 74 *The Prison Journal* 306. See also the same authors' "What punishes? Inmates rank the severity of prison vs intermediate sanctions" (1994) 58 *Federal Probation* 3, reporting on the same research.

19 See, for example, Maynard L Erickson and Jack P Gibbs, "On the perceived

One problem with surveying offenders' assessment of penal severity is that the results may be heavily influenced by respondents' subjective circumstances or experiences, as seen in some of the studies just mentioned. Efforts must therefore be made to identify more objective indicia of severity, and this is typically achieved by reference to the personal interests that are generally infringed by various kinds of sanctions.[20] As Martin Wasik and Andrew von Hirsch have suggested: **12–12**

> "The more basic the interests infringed, and the greater the extent of their infringement, the more severe the penalty. According to the extent to which the penalty affects a person's survival, physical integrity, psychological well-being, liberty, autonomy, goods, money or reputation, the various penalties could be ranked in order of relative intrusiveness. Regard could be had to the jurisprudential writing on the relative importance of interests, including Feinberg's three-fold grading of welfare, security, and accumulative interests."[21]

The idea, then, is to identify factors that *objectively* render penalties more or less severe. Scholars adopting this approach have looked at research on ranking offence seriousness in order to identify suitable criteria for comparing the severity of penalties. For instance, von Hirsch and Jareborg have made an ambitious attempt to rank offence seriousness by reference to the dimensions of human welfare with which various offences interfered.[22] They adopted the concept of 'living standard' which, as previously theorised by Amartya Sen, included not only material well-being but also non-economic factors such as health, dignity and freedom.[23] They identified four categories of interest that may be adversely affected by crime: (1) physical integrity, (2) material support and amenity; (3) freedom from humiliation, and (4) privacy/autonomy. By analogy, punishments may be evaluated according to the extent to which they remove, diminish or restrict otherwise protected and valued interests such as liberty (in the sense of freedom from physical restraint), freedom from intrusive restrictions while within the community (in the form, for example, of probationary supervision) and the right to private property (which is infringed, to a greater or less extent, by monetary penalties). Mara Schiff developed a highly sophisticated model of penal equivalence based on this kind of analysis, though it would be far from easy to implement in practice.[24] **12–13**

---

severity of legal penalties" (1979) 70 J Crim Law and Criminology 102.

20 Mara F Schiff, "Gauging the intensity of criminal sanctions: Developing the criminal punishment severity scale (CPSS)" (1997) 22(2) *Criminal Justice Review* 175.

21 Martin Wasik and Andrew von Hirsch, "Non-custodial penalties and principles of desert" [1988] Crim LR 555 at 564-565, referring to Joel Feinberg, *Harm to Others* (Oxford University Press, 1984).

22 Andrew von Hirsch and Nils Jareborg, "Gauging criminal harm: A living-standard analysis" (1991) 11 *Oxford Journal of Legal Studies* 1.

23 Amartya Sen, *The Standard of Living* (Cambridge University Press, 1987).

24 Schiff, note 20 above.

12–14 Realistically, it would be difficult to reach a consensus, even with the benefit of empirical research, on exact equivalences between different kinds of penalty. Further, public opinion remains an important factor at sentencing, not in the sense that a court should impose whatever sentence members of the public (however representative or otherwise) seem to want in a particular case, but in the sense that penalties should, in general, reflect the degree of censure that members of the community consider appropriate for the conduct constituting an offence.[25] Nothing less than imprisonment may suffice for a very serious offence, even though a restrictive community-based measure might have the same 'penal bite', whether viewed objectively or from the standpoint of the offender. But this will not always be a decisive consideration. Efforts to identify penal equivalence remain valuable because there will be cases where imprisonment is deserved, but where non-custodial penalty or a combination of such penalties would be equally effective in serving the relevant penal purposes.

12–15 Intensive supervision, especially when accompanied by electronic monitoring, has been characterised as a new form of imprisonment.[26] Offenders subject to such surveillance may not be incarcerated in penal institutions, but their liberty and autonomy are severely restricted. Global positioning systems (GPS) monitoring, where used. permits a person's every movement to be noted and recorded. As Sotomayor J said in *United States v Jones*:

> "GPS monitoring generates a precise, comprehensive record of a person's public movements that reflects a wealth of detail about her familial, political, professional, religious, and sexual associations.... The net result is that GPS monitoring – by making available at a relatively low cost such a substantial quantum of intimate information about any person whom the Government, in its unfettered discretion, chooses to track –may "alter the relationship between citizen and government in a way that is inimical to democratic society."" [27]

12–16 This was said in a case arising from the GPS tracking of a vehicle suspected of being used for drug dealing, but the observation remains valid of GPS monitoring in any context. Intensive supervision involving this kind of surveillance may be imagined as a latter-day panopticon (a prison design proposed by Bentham which would have had inmates under

---

25 Voula Marinos, "Thinking about penal equivalents" (2005) 7 *Punishment and Society* 441.

26 Kate Weisburd, "Punitive surveillance" (2022) 108 Virginia LR 147; Mike Nellis, Kristel Beyens and Dan Kaminski (eds), *Electronically Monitored Punishment: International and Critical Perspectives* (Routledge, 2013); Fergus McNeill, *Pervasive Punishment: Making Sense of Mass Supervision* (Emerald Publishing, 2019).

27 565 U.S.400, 415-416 (2012), quoting from *United States v Cuevas-Perez* 640 F3d 272, 285 (Flaum J, concurring). See also Maya Schenwar and Victoria Law, *Prison by Any Other Name: The Harmful Consequences of Popular Reforms* (The New Press, 2021).

constant surveillance from a central vantage point).[28] One signal feature of a panopticon, according to Michel Foucault, is that the inmate "is seen but he does not see; he is an object of information, never a subject in communication".[29] Intensive supervision is typically a condition of probation or early release from prison and, as such, has traditionally been seen as an incident of punishment rather than as a punishment in itself. More recently, however, courts, especially in the United States, have evinced a willingness to treat intensive supervision and close surveillance as a punishment which, in turn, means that it should be subject to reasonable restrictions in light of the offence for which it is imposed and the offender's circumstances.

3. New Sentencing Options and the Interchangeability Problem

New sentencing options are introduced for a variety of reasons, though reducing reliance on imprisonment is usually the dominant consideration. Because prisons are so expensive to build and operate, governments are always attracted to the idea of less costly alternatives that still have, or are perceived to have, a strong punitive impact. Financial considerations are not always to the fore. Some non-custodial measures may be considered more effective than imprisonment in reducing re-offending and can therefore be justified on crime prevention grounds. During the past half century or so, most countries have expanded their range of sentencing options with the avowed aim, in most instances, of diverting more offenders from custody. In Ireland, for example, community service was introduced expressly for that purpose in 1983. The emphasis has largely been on so-called intermediate sanctions which allow offenders to remain at liberty, though subject to various kinds of conditions, some of which can be quite onerous. During the late 20th century, sanctions of this nature proliferated throughout the United States where imprisonment and probation had traditionally been the only choices available for dealing with mid-level offenders. In addition to community service, the new sanctions included house arrest, boot camps, intensive supervision, electronic monitoring and day reporting centres. However, they soon attracted criticism for lack of effectiveness in some instances and for net widening in others. **12–17**

Critical analyses of the new sanctions may be traced back to responses to the decarceration movement that began in the 1960s and continued for some decades thereafter. This involved the wholesale release of patients from psychiatric hospitals, with initiatives also taken to reduce prison populations.[30] The policy of releasing psychiatric patients was at first **12–18**

[28] Janet Semple, *Bentham's Prison: A Study of the Panopticon Penitentiary* (Clarendon Press, 1993).

[29] Michel Foucault, *Discipline and Punish: The Birth of the Prison*, translated by Alan Sheridan (Penguin Books, 1991), 200.

[30] Bernard E Harcourt, "Reducing mass incarceration: Lessons from the

presented in a benevolent light. It was argued that the development of new medication permitted persons with mental illness to be kept within the community without compromising public safety. The inhumane nature of confinement in total institutions, a term made famous by Erving Goffman in the late 1950s,[31] was also called in aid by proponents of decarceration policies. However, Andrew Scull's *Decarceration*, published in 1977, placed those policies in a radically different light.[32] He located their origin in welfare capitalism and its preoccupation with the cost of welfare provision. As institutional segregation became more expensive, it was replaced with cheaper alternatives such as welfare payments, and many of those released from confinement found themselves living in degrading conditions with no meaningful support.

12–19 The development and deployment of community sanctions (largely intended as alternatives to imprisonment) prompted a rather similar critical response. Some criminologists and social theorists, drawing on Foucault's notion of the dispersal of control, claimed that these measures resulted in more and more people being subjected to various kinds of official control and surveillance, in contrast to earlier times when an offender was either in prison or at liberty.[33] Stanley Cohen, a British sociologist who was to the forefront of this critical movement, contrasted imprisonment which created clear spatial boundaries between incarcerated offenders and the outside world with community corrections where the boundaries were blurred, if not at times obliterated.[34] 'Net widening' became common currency to describe the perceived tendency to use newly-developed community-based and intermediate sanctions, not as an alternative to imprisonment, but as substitutes for less intrusive or controlling measures, such as fines or straightforward probation, that might have been used in past. A similar concern has been expressed about intermittent or weekend imprisonment where it exists. Again, Cohen was a leading exponent of this perspective.[35] Scholars who undertook empirical studies in Canada and elsewhere claimed that prison populations as well the numbers on community programmes were increasing, a conclusion

deinstitutionalization of mental hospitals in the 1960s" (2011) 9 *Ohio State Journal of Criminal Law* 53.

31 Erving Goffman, *Asylums: Essays on the Social Situation of Mental Patients and Oher Inmates* (Doubleday & Co, 1961).

32 Andrew T Scull, *Decarceration: Community Treatment and the Deviant – A Radical View* (Prentice-Hall, 1977); Gerald N Grob, *From Asylum to Community: Mental Health Policy in Modern America* (Princeton University Press, 1991).

33 Foucault, note 29 above.

34 Stanley Cohen, "The punitive city: Notes on the dispersal of social control" (1979) 3 *Contemporary Crises* 339.

35 In addition to his article at note 34 above, see his *Visions of Social Control: Crime, Punishment and Classification* (Polity Press, 1985), p 144 (referring to "the overall intensity of supervision" with offenders "being subject to levels of intervention (including traditional institutionalization) which they might not previously have received (deeper nets)" and new agencies and services "supplementing rather than replacing the original set of control mechanism (different nets)").

that added support to the net widening claim.[36] However, as Maeve McMahon argued in an important critical essay, data of this nature should be interpreted in an even-handed way, rather than constantly emphasising the negatives. She refers, for example, to Canadian findings that about half of those sentenced to community service would probably not have been imprisoned anyway but, as she says, this also suggests that in the other cases community service was most likely used as a substitute for imprisonment.[37]

A more substantial line of criticism, and one of enduring relevance, is that intermediate sanctions may eventually lead to increased levels of imprisonment. As the conditions attaching to probation and other forms of supervision became more numerous and onerous, they were more likely to be breached. The more intense the supervision, the more likely that technical violations will be detected. Imprisonment is the most common sanction for breach of a community order even if it was not considered appropriate for the original offence.[38] Unless carefully designed and fairly implemented, community sanctions will become for many offenders a prelude rather than an alternative to imprisonment.[39] Probation systems in the United States have recently come in for intense criticism precisely for this reason. In some states, probation terms may be as long as the maximum prison sentence permitted for the relevant offence, and this may run to years, decades or even life. The problem is compounded by the nature of some probationary conditions, such as total abstention from alcohol even where alcohol had no role in the underlying offence, and the willingness of supervisors to bring probationers back before court for technical violations, such as missing an appointment. As a result, up to 45 per cent of prison admissions in recent years have been for probation and parole violations, and about a quarter have been for technical violations.[40] **12–20**

---

[36] J Chan and RV Ericson, *Decarceration and the Economy of Penal Reform* (Centre for Criminology, University of Toronto, 1981).

[37] Maeve McMahon, "'Net-widening': Vagaries in the use of a concept" (1990) 30 Brit J Criminol 121, 141.

[38] Michelle S Phelps, "The paradox of probation: Community supervision in the age of mass incarceration" (2013) 35 *Law & Policy* 51, 52; Michael Tonry and Mary Lynch, "Intermediate sanctions" (1996) 20 *Crime and Justice* 99; Katherine Beckett and Naomi Murakawa, "Mapping the shadow carceral state: Toward an institutionally capacious approach to punishment" (2012) 16 *Theoretical Criminology* 221.

[39] Cecelia Klingele, "Rethinking the use of community supervision" (2013) 103 J Crim Law and Criminology 1015, She notes (p 1019) that half of those admitted to US jails and more than one-third of those admitted to prisons arrive there because of having their community supervision revoked. See also Amber Wilson, "Probation and parole revocations: Reviewing over two decades of revocation decisions in the United States" (2023) *Criminal Justice Review* (forthcoming).

[40] CJ Ciaramella and Lauren Krisai "The U.S. probation system has become a quagmire" (March 2023) *Reason*, < https://reason.com/2023/01/26/the-u-s-probation-system-has-become-a-quagmire/> accessed 29 January 2023.

4. Imprisonment

12–21 With the total abolition of capital and corporal punishment, imprisonment is the most severe penalty that may be imposed for a criminal offence. Granted, there is room for argument as to whether, in certain cases, a short term of imprisonment might be less onerous than a heavy fine or a demanding community-based penalty (a topic discussed earlier in this Chapter). Ordinarily, however, imprisonment, since it involves the deprivation of liberty and must often be served in an unpleasant institutional setting, is the penalty offenders most wish to avoid. At one time, penal servitude and imprisonment with hard labour existed as distinct forms of custody, but these were finally abolished in Ireland in 1997, having been abolished in England and Wales 50 years earlier.[41] Imprisonment is now the only form of penal custody available for adults. Any remaining statutory provisions permitting penal servitude are to be interpreted as referring to imprisonment. Viewed more broadly, imprisonment may serve custodial, coercive or punitive functions.[42] It is custodial when used, for example, to detain persons awaiting trial or deportation. It is coercive when used to compel the fulfilment of a legal obligation or court order – in effect, when it is imposed for certain forms of contempt of court. It is punitive when used as a means of punishing convicted offenders.

12–22 Imprisonment is just one form of state-sanctioned custody which also includes detention in young offender institutions and involuntary psychiatric detention. In the not-too-distant past, there were other custodial institutions such as industrial schools where many 'deprived' children were detained, officially for their own good, and so-called Magdalen homes where young women who became pregnant outside marriage were detained, often for long periods. Since the mid-20th century, most Western countries have experienced a marked decline in the number of psychiatric inpatients and a concomitant increase in prison populations.[43] This is often viewed as a manifestation of Penrose's Law, referring to an article published by Lionel Penrose, a psychiatrist, in 1939.[44] On the basis of a cross-sectional study covering several countries, he concluded that there was an inverse correlation between the number of places in psychiatric hospitals and the number of prisoners. More contentious is one of the conclusions drawn from this, commonly known as transinstitutionalisation, meaning that many mentally ill persons who

---

[41] Criminal Law Act 1997, s 11 (Ireland); Criminal Justice Act 1948, s 1. (England and Wales).

[42] Rod Morgan and Alison Liebling, "Imprisonment: An expanding scheme" in Mike Maguire, Rodney Morgan and Robert Reiner (eds), *The Oxford Handbook of Criminology*,4th ed (Oxford University Press, 2007), Chap 32,

[43] For an analysis of this phenomenon in the United States, see Bernard E Harcourt, "From the asylum to the prison: Rethinking the incarceration revolution" (2005) 84 Texas LR 1751.

[44] LS Penrose, "Mental disease and crime: Outline of a comparative study of European statistics" (1939) 18 *British Journal of Medical Psychology* 1.

are no longer admitted to or detained in psychiatric facilities end up in prison.[45]

Detention patterns in Ireland and elsewhere, when viewed across time, bear out Penrose's basic observation about changing patterns of penal and non-penal confinement. In 1951, for example, when the Republic of Ireland had a general population of about three million, there were almost 32,000 in institutional confinement of various kinds. Prisoners accounted for no more than 450 of these, while inmates in psychiatric hospitals accounted for 19,000. There were 6,000 children in industrial and reformatory schools.[46] In fact, in 1958, when the number of psychiatric inpatients peaked at 21,000, the prison population reached an all-time low of 348.[47] Between 1930 and 1968 the average daily prison population never exceeded 700, but from the late 1960s onwards, it increased rapidly, reaching 1,035 in 1972.[48] Overall, during the period 1963 to 2003, the number of psychiatric inpatients decreased by 81.5 percent while the average number of prisoners increased by 494.8 percent.[49] Today, the prison population stands at approximately 5,000 while there are less than 2,500 inpatients in psychiatric facilities.[50] This is not to suggest that there is any established causal connection between the decline in psychiatric detention and the rise in penal detention. Carceral confinement, whether in prisons, psychiatric hospitals or other custodial institutions, entails spatial exclusion imposed for different reasons. In the past, many people were detained in psychiatric hospitals because they were unwanted rather than unwell. Prison populations grew mainly because of higher rates of recorded crime. Increases in serious crime cannot be **12–23**

---

[45] For a discussion of the arguments for and against this hypothesis, see Seth J Prins, "Does transinstitutionalization explain the overrepresentation of people with serious mental illness in the criminal justice system?" (2011) 47 *Community Mental Health Journal* 716.

[46] Eoin O'Sullivan and Ian O'Donnell, "Coercive confinement in the Republic of Ireland: The waning of a culture of control" (2007) 9 *Punishment and Society* 27, 35. See also the same authors' *Coercive Confinement in Post-Independence Ireland: Patients, Prisoners and Penitents* (Manchester University Press, 2012). The Report on Reformatory and Industrial Schools (the Kennedy Report) (Stationery Office, 1970) includes statistics on the population of those schools from 1949 to 1969

[47] For a comprehensive presentation of criminal justice statistics for the first 80 years of the State's history, see Ian O'Donnell, Eoin O'Sullivan and Deirdre Healy, *Crime and Punishment in Ireland 1922–2003: A Statistical Sourcebook* (Institute of Public Administration, 2005).

[48] Oisín Wall, "'Embarrassing the state': The 'ordinary' prisoner rights movement in Ireland, 1972-1976" (2020) 55 *Journal of Contemporary History* 388.

[49] BD Kelly, "Penrose's law in Ireland: An ecological analysis of psychiatric inpatients and prisoners" (February 2007) 100 (2) *Irish Medical Journal* 373.

[50] According to the Irish Prison Service (www.irishprisons.ie) there were more than 5,000 in custody in late July 2024. On the number of psychiatric inpatients, see Antoinette Daly and Sarah Craig, *Irish Psychiatric Units and Hospitals Census 2019 Main Findings* (Health Research Board, 2019). This pattern has been evident since at least 2007 when the number of prisoners exceeded (only slightly at the time) the number of psychiatric inpatients.

linked in any significant way to mental health deinstitutionalisation.[51] What cannot, however, be ignored are the rates of mental illness and intellectual disability among prisoners, and this seems to be a worldwide phenomenon.[52] One Irish study found that for all mental illnesses combined, rates ranged from 16 per cent of male committals to 27 per cent of sentenced men. The equivalent rates for women were 41 per cent and 60 per cent.[53] There were even higher rates of drug and alcohol dependence and harmful use. Reliable estimates of intellectual disability among prisoners are difficult to find, but it seems clear persons with such disability form a significant minority of prisoners.[54]

12–24 Prison experience varies enormously throughout the world. In some countries and regions, imprisonment involves confinement in overcrowded, degrading and highly controlled conditions. Others have decidedly more humane prison regimes. Scandinavian countries are often held up as models in this regard.[55] Their prisons tend to be reasonably small (typically having 100 inmates or fewer) with decent living standards, good quality health and education services and highly qualified prison staff.[56] This 'Scandinavian penal exceptionalism' may sometimes be presented in an idealised way that fails to reflect some of its day-to-day problems,[57] but it still reflects a broader political culture marked by a strong commitment to the welfare state. Ultimately, the

---

51 Pål Hartvig and Ellen Kjelsberg, "Penrose's law revisited: The relationship between mental institution beds, prison population and crime rate" (2009) 63:1 *Nordic Journal of Psychiatry* 51; CJ O'Neill, BD Kelly and HG Kennedy, "A 25-year dynamic ecological analysis of psychiatric hospital admissions and prison committals: Penrose's hypothesis updated" (2021) 38:3 *Irish Journal of Psychological Medicine* 182.

52 Seena Fazel and John Danesh, "Serious mental disorders in 23,000 prisoners: A systematic review of 62 surveys" (2002) 359 (9306) *Lancet* 545.

53 HG Kennedy et al, *Mental Illness in Irish Prisoners: Psychiatric Morbidity in Sentenced, Remanded and Newly Committed Prisoners* (National Forensic Mental Health Service, 2005).

54 Gautam Gulati, Alan Cusack, Shane Kilcommins and Colum P Dunne, "Intellectual disabilities in Irish prisons: Could Article 13 of the UNCRPD hold the key?" (2020) 68 *International Journal of Law and Psychiatry* 101540.

55 Jordan M Hyatt, Synøve N. Andersen, Steven L. Chanenson, Veronica Horowitz and Christopher Uggen, "'We can actually do this': Adapting Scandinavian correctional culture in Pennsylvania" (2021) 58 American Crim LR 1715, 1729-1735.

56 Leading English-language sources on the Scandinavian prison system include John Pratt, "Scandinavian exceptionalism in an era of penal excess: Part I: The nature and roots of Scandinavian exceptionalism" (2008) 48 Brit J Criminology 119; John Pratt, "Scandinavian exceptionalism in an era of penal excess: Part II: Does Scandinavian exceptionalism have a future?" (2008) 48 Brit J Criminology 275; Tapio Lappi-Seppälä, "Penal policies in the Nordic countries 1960-2010" (2012) 13 *Journal of Scandinavian Studies in Criminology and Crime Prevention* 85.

57 See, for example, Thomas Ugelvik and Jane Dullum (eds), *Penal Exceptionalism? Nordic Prison Policy and Practice* (Routledge, 2012), especially the chapter by Peter Scharff Smith, "A critical look at Scandinavian exceptionalism: Welfare state theories, penal populism and prison conditions in Denmark and Scandinavia".

question is whether offenders should be imprisoned *as* punishment or *for* punishment.[58] The answer is surely that custodial punishment consists in the deprivation of liberty, one of our most valued rights, and that it should not entail any additional pains beyond what is necessary to keep prisoners in confinement. Those who argue to the contrary must resort to some notion of lesser eligibility which is associated most notably with Jeremy Bentham who wrote:

> "Saving the regard due to life, health, and bodily ease, the ordinary condition of a convict doomed to a punishment which few or none but the individuals of the poorest class are apt to incur, ought not to be made more eligible than that of the poorest class of subjects in a state of innocence and liberty."[59]

Yet, there are very strong arguments against the idea of lesser eligibility. **12–25**
If the principle that imprisonment should function *as* rather than *for* punishment is taken seriously, it demands that prisoners should retain their rights apart, obviously, from the right to liberty and any curtailments of other rights necessitated by imprisonment. That, indeed, is the view of the courts in this jurisdiction.[60] At a minimum, the human dignity of prisoners must always be assured.[61] In fact, international instruments, including the International Covenant on Civil and Political Rights, are replete with provisions to this effect.[62]

When assessing the severity of custodial sentences, prison experience is **12–26**
no less significant than sentence duration.[63] To be sure, the length of time for which a person is deprived of liberty is an important factor, but it is a

---

[58] The phrase about imprisonment being 'as punishment, not for punishment' is usually attributed to Alexander Paterson. See SK Ruck (ed), *Paterson on Prisons* (F.Muller, 1951).

[59] Jeremy Bentham, "Panopticon; Or, The Inspection House" in John Bowring (ed), *The Works of Jeremy Bentham* (William Tait, 1843), Vol 4. See also Edward W Sieh, "'Less eligibility': The upper limits of penal policy" (1989) 3 *Criminal Justice Policy Review* 159; Ahmed White, "The concept of 'less eligibility' and the social function of prison violence in class society" (2008) 56 Buffalo LR 737 (dealing at length with Georg Rusche's ideas on less eligibility).

[60] *Holland v Governor of Portlaoise Prison* [2004] 2 IR 573; *State (Richardson) v Governor of Mountjoy Prison* [1980] ILRM 82.

[61] *Connolly v Governor of Wheatfield Prison* [2013] IEHC 334; *Kinsella v Governor of Mountjoy Prison* [2011] IEHC 235; [2012] 1 IR 467; [2011] 2 ILRM 509. Dignity as a constitutional value is discussed in Chap 4 above.

[62] International Covenant on Civil and Political Rights, art 10; Kyoto Declaration on Advancing Crime Prevention, Criminal Justice and the Rule of Law: Toward the Achievement of the 2030 Agenda for Sustainable Development (adopted at the Fourteenth United Nations Congress on Crime Prevention and Criminal Justice, March 2021); United Nations System Common Position on Incarceration (April 2021) advocating use of incarceration as a measure of last resort.

[63] Adam Kolber, "The subjective experience of punishment" (2009) 109 Columbia LR 182; Julia L Torti, "Accounting for punishment in proportionality review" (2013) 88 New York Univ LR 1908; Skylar Albertson, "Do prison conditions change how much punishment a sentence carries out? Lessons from federal sentence reduction rulings during the Covid-19 pandemic" (2022) 18 *Northwestern Journal of Law and Social Policy* 1.

mistake to treat it as the only important factor. Measuring severity by time is undoubtedly convenient; as Richard Posner observed, time "has the attractive characteristic of being one-dimensional".[64] Other factors bearing on severity are less easily quantified. David Downes in his now classic comparative study of imprisonment in The Netherlands and England and Wales gave currency to the expression "the depth of imprisonment". [65] He described how differences in custodial regimes rendered imprisonment more or less punitive. The key factors included relations with staff and other prisoners, material conditions including food and accommodation, rights and privileges, contact with the outside world and disciplinary provisions. This insight has since been developed by others, notably Ben Crewe who has analysed prison experience in terms of its depth, weight, tightness and breadth.[66] Prison research can be greatly enriched by a close investigation of this experiential aspect of custody, bearing in mind that the experience can vary not only from one country to another but from one prison institution to another. This research in turn should be of value to courts in determining how punitive a given term of imprisonment is likely to be, depending on where the offender is incarcerated.

12–27 The idea that prisons should be abolished may seem strange given its central role in the penal system. Yet, there have been abolitionist movements since the 1970s. In Europe, it is most closely associated with the Norwegian criminologist, Thomas Mathiesen, whose book, *Politics of Abolition* (1974), stimulated an abolitionist debate.[67] Abolition began to be discussed in the United States about the same time,[68] and it still attracts some scholarly attention.[69] Some forms of imprisonment such as penal servitude, imprisonment with hard labour, and the imprisonment of debtors and children, have been abolished. Today, there is general,

---

64 Richard A Posner, "An economic theory of the criminal law" (1985) 85 Columbia LR 1193, 1212.

65 David Downes, *Contrasts in Tolerance: Post-War Penal Policy in The Netherlands and England and Wales* (Clarendon Press, 1988), Chap 6. See also Gresham Sykes, *The Society of Captives: A Study of a Maximum Security Prison* (Princeton University Press, 1958) where he famously identified the 'pains of imprisonment'; Roy D King and Kathleen McDermott, *The State of Our Prisons* (Clarendon Press, 1995), and Ian O'Donnell, *Prison Life: Pain, Resistance and Purpose* (New York University Press, 2023).

66 Ben Crewe, "Inside the belly of the penal beast: Understanding the experience of imprisonment" (2015) 4 *International Journal for Crime, Justice and Social Democracy* 50.

67 Thomas Mathiesen, *The Politics of Abolition Revisited* (Routledge, 2015) which includes the text of the 1974 work.

68 Joshua Dubler and Vincent Lloyd, "Think prison abolition in America is impossible? It once felt inevitable", *The Guardian,* 19 May 2018. On various abolitionist movements outside the United States, see Máximo Langer, "Penal abolitionism and criminal law minimalism: Here and there, now and then" (2020) 134 Harvard LR Forum 42.

69 Thomas Ward Frampton, "The dangerous few: Taking seriously prison abolition and its sceptics" (2022) 135 Harvard LR 2013; Rachel E Barkow, "Promise or peril? The political path of prison abolition in America" (2023) 58 Wake Forest LR 245.

though perhaps not universal, acceptance of the need to imprison violent offenders (if only for the purpose of temporary incapacitation). The abolitionist debate now focuses largely on the removal of imprisonment as a punishment option for certain kinds of non-violent crime such as theft.[70] But there are also some who argue that well-developed restorative justice practices could remove the need for imprisonment, even for violent offences.[71]

Parsimony in Use of Imprisonment

The Children Act 2001 provides that detention is to be treated as a measure **12–28**
of last resort. Despite the absence of a similar statutory provision in respect of adult offenders, it may be argued that imprisonment too should be the penalty of last resort. Notwithstanding what has been said earlier about the comparative severity of punishments, imprisonment is ordinarily, if not invariably, the most severe penalty available in Ireland and almost all other Western countries. It should therefore be reserved for the most serious cases. This, of course, is a principle that is easy to state but difficult to apply. Criteria for identifying the 'most serious' cases are far from settled or generally agreed. Serious violent crimes undoubtedly fall into this category, as do crimes such as robbery and burglary which violate fundamental rights, such as the right to be secure in one's own dwelling. The same holds true of large-scale drug dealing because of the harm it inflicts on individuals and communities. There is room for disagreement as to whether non-violent acquisitive offences such as theft and fraud should be included among the more serious cases. The other major dilemma relates to previous convictions. Should a prior record of serious offending or persistent minor offending, such as shoplifting, elevate a case to the most serious category, even if the offence of conviction did not do so? At present, the predominant view seems to be that it may although, as discussed in Chap 5 in connection with previous convictions, this practice is difficult to justify in principle.

Legislative intervention has so far been confined to discouraging the **12–29**
use of short prison sentences, though the primary motivation is often to control the prison population rather than benefit offenders. In Ireland, for example, the Criminal Justice (Community Service) (Amendment) Act 2011 requires a court to consider community service as an alternative to a prison sentence of 12 months or less. However, it goes no further than this, which means that very short prison sentences can still be imposed. In England and Wales, the Sentencing Bill 2023, introduced by the Conservative government, proposed to restrict the use of short prison sentences by providing that where a court imposed a sentence

---

70 Christopher Slobogin, "The minimalist alternative to abolitionism: Focusing on the non-dangerous many" (2024) 77 Vanderbilt LR 531; Langer, note 68 above; Andrew Ashworth, *What if Imprisonment were Abolished for Property Offences?* (Howard League for Penal Reform, 2013).

71 Danielle Sered, *Until We Reckon: Violence, Mass Incarceration, and a Road to Repair* (New Press, 2019).

of imprisonment or youth detention of not more than 12 months, it was to suspend that sentence unless it was of the opinion that there were exceptional circumstances relating to the offence or the offender that would justify not suspending the sentence (and there are some other exceptions as well). It is not clear if the present Labour government will proceed with similar legislation, although it has had to take immediate steps to deal with prison overcrowding.

First-Time Offenders and those not Previously Imprisoned

12–30 First-time offenders should be spared imprisonment where at all possible, though it may be inevitable if the offence was particularly serious or violent in nature. One rationale offered for this principle is that individual deterrence and rehabilitation should ordinarily be the key considerations in sentencing first-time offenders.[72] This in turn is based on the prudential policy of persuading and encouraging such offenders, in their own interests and those of the community, to desist from further crime. Even if the offence is sufficiently serious to merit some term of imprisonment, a court should carefully explore all other options to see if any of them might adequately mark the gravity of the offending conduct and, at the same time, provide any help or supervision from which the offender would benefit. Similar considerations apply to offenders being sentenced to immediate imprisonment for the first time, even if they have some previous convictions. The English Court of Appeal once said that the length of a first prison sentence "is more reasonably determined by considerations of individual deterrence; of what sentence is needed to teach this particular offender a lesson which he has not learned from the lighter sentences which he has previously received".[73] However, the policy of making first prison sentences as short as possible, especially for those without previous convictions, may also be justified by reference to desert-based considerations. For many such offenders, it is the experience of being committed to prison that constitutes the most severe element of the punishment, initially at least. The subjective experience of punishment is an important factor in assessing its severity.[74] Therefore, when a court decides that a prison sentence is necessary for an offender of previous good character, it should first determine the appropriate sentence and then ask itself if a shorter term of imprisonment would adequately reflect the circumstances of the case.[75] In *People (DPP) v Bates*,[76] for example, the appellant, a 20-year-old student, was sentenced to 12 months' imprisonment on pleading guilty to careless driving causing serious

---

[72] Canadian courts, in particular, have emphasised this principle: *R v Priest* (1996) 30 OR(3d) 538; 110 CCC(3d) 289 (Ontario CA); *R v Stein* (1974) 15 CCC(2d) 376 (Ontario CA).

[73] *R v Curran* (1973) 57 Cr App R 945 at 947-948. See also *R v Sargeant* (1974) 60 Cr App R 74.

[74] Note 63 above and accompanying text.

[75] *People (DPP) v Durcan* [2017] IECA 3, para 21; *People (DPP) v Maguire* [2015] IECA 350.

[76] [2020] IECA 199.

bodily harm. The Court of Appeal agreed with the trial judge that the offence was at the upper end of the scale of carelessness. However, it considered that inadequate credit had been given for all the mitigating factors, including the fact that the appellant was a person of impeccable good character who had made a positive contribution to society. It therefore reduced the sentence to eight months' imprisonment.

Presumption of Imprisonment

A court is never obliged to impose a custodial penalty unless the offence of conviction carries a mandatory prison sentence and, practically speaking, the only such offence under Irish law is murder. Nonetheless, there are certain offences for which imprisonment is either formally or informally the presumed punishment.[77] In the formal category are those firearms and drug offences that carry presumptive minimum sentences of five or ten years' imprisonment, but a court may impose a sentence below the specified minimum where there are exceptional and specific circumstances to justify doing so. These sentences are therefore presumptive rather than mandatory, and a court may even impose a fully suspended or non-custodial sentence in a truly exceptional case.[78] In the informal category are certain serious offences that are not subject to any presumptive minimum sentences but which, by their nature, call for a custodial sentence of some length unless there are particularly strong or exceptional mitigating factors. As the Court of Appeal said in *People (DPP) v Byrne*: **12–31**

> "[W]e recognise that some offences will be so serious that they effectively carry a presumption against the suspension of a custodial sentence in its entirety. That is certainly true in the case of rape offences, s.15A drugs offences, certain firearms offences and egregious crimes of violence. However, even in such cases existing jurisprudence indicates that a wholly suspended sentence can be imposed in cases where there are special reasons of a substantial nature and particularly exceptional circumstances."[79]

With regard to rape, as the Supreme Court said in *People (DPP) v E(F)*,[80] there is no absolute rule requiring the imposition of a custodial sentence regardless of the nature of the plea, but "a custodial sentence is all but inescapable". Having conducted an extensive analysis of rape sentencing during the previous 20 years, the court could identify only one case in which a fully suspended sentence had been imposed and upheld, and that involved an 86-year-old man who was seriously ill. He had already **12–32**

---

[77] For a more detailed analysis, see Law Reform Commission, *Report on Suspended Sentences* (2020), Chap 6.

[78] On this law as it applies to drug dealing offences, see Chap 10 above.

[79] [2017] IECA 97, para 33.

[80] [2019] IESC 85; [2021] 1 IR 217; [2020] 1 ILRM 517, para 44. In *People (DPP) v Tiernan* [1988] IR 250, 253; [1989] ILRM 149, Finlay CJ said: "it is not easy to imagine the circumstances which would justify departure from a substantial immediate custodial sentence for rape and I can only express the view that they would probably be wholly exceptional".

served a prison sentence for a similar offence committed against a different victim.[81]

12–33 Manslaughter offences, as is well known, can vary enormously in gravity and cases do arise where the circumstances of the offence, the offender or both can justify a suspended or non-custodial sentence. However, imprisonment is all but certain for manslaughters at the more serious end of the spectrum such as where death resulted from an unprovoked act of violence, and particularly if the injuries were inflicted with a weapon brought to the scene. In *People (DPP) v Princs*[82] the Court of Criminal Appeal said:

> "In summary, the offence of manslaughter, particularly voluntary manslaughter where an unlawful act of violence is involved, should normally involve a substantial term of imprisonment because a person has been killed. Only where there are special circumstances and context will a moderate sentence or in wholly exceptional circumstances, a non-custodial sentence, be warranted. Those circumstances are more likely to arise in cases of involuntary manslaughter…."

12–34 The same principle is evident in the analysis of manslaughter sentencing conducted by the Supreme Court in *People (DPP) v Mahon.*[83] The same would apply to causing serious harm contrary to the Non-Fatal Offences against Person Act 1997 (s 4). These are just some examples of offences where, in effect, imprisonment is the presumed penalty, though never mandatory. One might also include human trafficking involving serious exploitation of victims, as in *People (DPP) v Edosa,*[84] and serious fraud offences that caused significant hardship to victims.[85] The English Court of Appeal has held that perverting the course of justice should almost invariably attract an immediate custodial sentence.[86] A preferable approach would be that the punishment for this offence should depend on the nature of the conduct and its consequences, both of which can vary significantly. The offender's personal circumstances must obviously be considered as well.

Rates of Imprisonment: International Comparisons

12–35 The total number of prisoners worldwide is estimated to be 11.5 million, 93 per cent of whom are men and 7 per cent women. However, the number of women prisoners has increased by 60 per cent since 2000, while the number of male prisoners has increased by 22 per cent during the same period.[87] Imprisonment rates are conventionally presented as the number

---

[81] *People (DPP) v K (J),* Central Criminal Court, 22 October 2018.
[82] [2007] IECCA 142.
[83] [2019] IESC 24; [2019] 3 IR 151; [2019] 2 ILRM 81.
[84] [2023] IECA 38.
[85] *People (DPP) v Zaffer* [2016] IECA 321, para 15.
[86] *Attorney General's Reference (R v Graham)* [2020] EWCA Crim 1693; [2021] 2 Cr App R(S) 7; *R v Feve* [2024] EWCA Crim 286; [2024] 1 WLR 3450.
[87] Penal Reform International, *Global Prison Trends 2023,* <www.penalreform.

of incarcerated prisoners per 100,000 of the general population. The *World Prison Brief* which is hosted by the Institute for Crime and Justice Policy Research at Birkbeck, University of London, is a valuable source of information on current imprisonment rates for almost every country in the world.[88] This information, drawn from official sources, reveals significant variations in the use of imprisonment internationally. El Salvador currently tops the list with 1,086 prisoners per 100,000 of the population. The United States is also consistently towards the top of the list, with a current rate of 531.[89] Other high-ranking countries in this respect include the Russian Federation (300), Belarus (345) and Hungary (192). The current figure for Ireland is 93 (as of July 2024) which puts it more or less on a par with Northern Ireland (98) but much lower than Scotland (147) and England and Wales (145). In Western Europe, Scandinavian countries tend to have the lowest imprisonment rates: Finland (52), Norway (55), Denmark (64) and Sweden (80). Further south, we find considerable variations, even in neighbouring countries: Germany (67), Switzerland (77), Italy (105), France (114) and Spain (116).[90]

Imprisonment rates are not, of course, an entirely reliable guide to penal severity. Regard must also be had to conditions of detention. These too can vary considerably, though it is difficult to draw international comparisons because of the essentially qualitative nature of the exercise. What is clear, however, is that prison overcrowding is now rife throughout the world. According to Penal Reform International, the prison systems in 120 countries are operating in excess of 100 per cent capacity, while in 15 countries they are operating at more than 250 per cent capacity. [91] Irish prisons, as already noted, are currently operating at about 112 per cent capacity on average, though the figure for some individual institutions is significantly higher than that. Sentence length and early release provisions are other obvious indicators of severity. **12–36**

Intermittent Imprisonment

Some jurisdictions permit short sentences of imprisonment to be served intermittently, usually at weekends (which is why it is often known as **12–37**

---

org> accessed 18 November 2024.

88 Available at <www.prisonstudies.org> accessed 18 November 2024.

89 Incarceration rates vary considerably within the United States. According to the Prison Policy Initiative (which includes prisons, jails, immigration detention and juvenile detention in its figures), the rate varies from 241 per 100,000 in Massachusetts to 751 in Texas and 1,067 in Louisiana. See Emily Wirda, *States of Incarceration: The Global Context 2024*, <www.prisonpolicy.org/global/2024.html> accessed 18 November 2024.

90 For an in-depth analysis of imprisonment patterns in Western countries, especially during the past 35 years, see Michael Tonry, "Punishments, politics, and prisons in Western countries" in Michael Tonry and Sandra Bucerius (eds), *Prisons and Prisoners* (vol 51 of *Crime and Justice*) (University of Chicago Press, 2022) 7. The remaining essays in this volume represent some of the best of contemporary scholarship on imprisonment and its impact.

91 Penal Reform International, fn 87 above.

weekend imprisonment). The circumstances in which it may be imposed and the manner in which it is served vary from one jurisdiction to another. In Canada, for example, it is available only in respect of sentences of 90 days or less, and offenders remain under probation supervision when not in prison.[92] In some continental European countries, in the past at least, it involved day detention only which meant that offenders did not have be accommodated overnight in prison institutions. In some American states, such as Maryland, intermittent imprisonment is defined as non-consecutive periods of 48 hours or less per week. It is typically served at weekends from 6 pm on Friday to 6 pm on Sunday, or during the offender's non-working hours.

12–38 Ordinarily, imprisonment (as it operates in these islands, for example) entails total isolation. Prisoners are excluded from any form of participation in the life of the wider community.[93] Intermittent custody has the advantage of allowing an offender to serve a custodial sentence while at the same time being able to work, remain self-supporting and maintain family and other social ties. The drawbacks are mainly logistical.[94] Prison accommodation is a scarce resource. As in Ireland at present, prisons are often operating at full capacity or even beyond that, mainly because of the number of long-term prisoners. Finding suitable prison accommodation for weekend or other part-time prisoners would be difficult, especially given the obvious desirability of detaining such prisoners in a facility close to where they live. Admitting and releasing large numbers of part-time prisoners on an ongoing basis would add greatly to the administrative workload of the prison system. Concerns have also been expressed about the possible criminogenic effect of allowing part-time prisoners to mingle with more hardened offenders while in custody. Net widening is yet a further concern. Courts may be more inclined to impose short prison sentences if they can be served intermittently in cases where, in the absence of that possibility, a non-custodial measure might have been chosen instead.

5. The Suspended Sentence

12–39 The essence of a suspended sentence is that it threatens future custodial punishment for a past offence. When imposing such a sentence, a court specifies the term of imprisonment merited by the offender but suspends it for a defined period during which the offender must abide by certain conditions including desistance from further offending. Breach of a condition of suspension during the operational period can lead to the sentence being fully or partly activated. The suspended sentence was

---

92 Canadian Criminal Code, s 732(1). See Québec Ombudsman, *The Consequences of the Increase in Intermittent Sentences in Québec Correctional Facilities* (Québec City, 2018).

93 Hadassa Noorda, "Imprisonment" (2023) 17 *Criminal Law and Philosophy* 691.

94 Nicolette Parisi, "Part-time imprisonment: The legal and practical issues of periodic confinement" (1979-1980) 63 *Judicature* 385.

judicially developed in Ireland more than a century ago,[95] and has been in constant use ever since, but it is now entirely governed by s 99 of the Criminal Justice Act 2006.[96] Any sentence of imprisonment, other than a mandatory sentence, may be suspended in whole or in part provided the offender enters into a recognisance to comply with the conditions of suspension. Irish law is unusual in allowing a determinate prison sentence of any length to be suspended, without any formal limit on the period for which it remains suspended (the operational period). Most other countries confine the suspension power to relatively short prison terms. In England and Wales, for example, a prison sentence, or aggregate sentence where consecutive terms are imposed, may not be suspended unless it is for at least 14 days and not more than two years.[97] Here in Ireland on the other hand, it has been confirmed that owing to the absence of any statutory limit on operational periods, a court may suspend sentence for longer than the custodial element. Thus, a District Court order suspending for five years the last four months of a 10-month sentence has been upheld.[98] However, in that instance the sole condition of suspension was a requirement to keep the peace and be of good behaviour. More onerous conditions might have rendered the sentence disproportionately severe, and a court must always consider all the relevant evidence when determining both the length of sentence to be suspended and the operational period.[99]

Just as there is no formal limit on either the length of a determinate sentence that may be suspended or the operational period, so too are there few formal limits on the range of conditions that may be attached to such a sentence. In every case, it is a statutory condition of suspension that the offender must keep the peace and be of good behaviour throughout the operational period. A court may include such further conditions as it considers appropriate having regard to the nature of the offence, and if it is satisfied that they will reduce the likelihood of re-offending (s 99(3)).[100] Additionally, where a part-suspended sentence is imposed, a court may include conditions requiring the offender (during the suspended portion of the sentence) to cooperate with the Probation Service, be under the supervision of that service or undergo such addiction treatment, course of education or psychological counselling as may be approved by the court (s 99(4)). In fact, there is no obvious reason why some or all of these further conditions may not also be applied to a fully suspended sentence if they are considered likely to reduce the risk of re-offending. However, as discussed further below, courts are not entirely at large **12–40**

95 Nial Osborough, "A Damocles' Sword guaranteed Irish: The suspended sentence in the Republic of Ireland" (1982) 17 *Irish Jurist* 221.

96 *DPP(Purtill) v Murray* [2015] IEHC 782; *Collins v DPP* [2018] IECA 381, para 18.

97 Sentencing Act 2020, s 277, originally enacted in Criminal Justice Act 2003, s 189(1) as substituted by Legal Aid, Licensing and Punishment of Offenders Act 2012, s 68.

98 *Collins v DPP* [2018] IECA 381.

99 *Collins v DPP* [2018] IECA 381, para 27.

100 On the conjunctive nature of this provision, see *People (DPP) v W(D)* [2020] IECA 145, paras 63-64.

in determining conditions of suspension. Any such conditions must be reasonable, relevant and proportionate.

12–41 There are two fundamental principles – they might even be described as golden rules – governing the use of suspended sentences. First, a court must never impose a prison sentence simply because it is being suspended. The court must be satisfied, having regard to all the circumstances of the offence and the offender, and having due regard to the principle of proportionality, that a prison sentence is deserved and appropriate. Only then should it consider the possibility of suspending that sentence in whole or in part.[101] Secondly, a court should never impose a longer than deserved sentence because it is being suspended.[102] Both principles should be strictly observed, and for good reason. A suspended sentence may, after all, be activated in the future. It would be manifestly unjust if an offender ended up serving an undeserved prison sentence or one that was longer than deserved.[103]

Rationale of the Suspended Sentence

12–42 There are some who argue that the suspended sentence is inherently contradictory and ambiguous. On the one hand, a court determines that an offence is sufficiently serious to merit a term of imprisonment while, on the other, it decides that the sentence need not be served if the offender abides by certain conditions for a defined period. Moreover, those conditions sometimes demand no more than desistance from crime, keeping the peace and being of good behaviour. In other words, the offender is merely required, like everyone else, to remain law-abiding. Arguments such as these convinced legislators in some Australian states to abolish the suspended sentence and replace it with various kinds of community penalties.[104] The suspended sentence may, however, be defended by reference to the principle of proportionality, censure-based theories of punishment and the protection of the public which is arguably the ultimate purpose of the penal system.

12–43 The principle of proportionality requires that a sentence must be proportionate to the gravity of the offence and the personal circumstances of the offender. The gravity of an offence may require a headline sentence above the custody threshold, and sometimes significantly above it, but the offender's personal circumstances may bring the case below the threshold. When that happens, an entirely non-custodial penalty should first be considered. Where a court is convinced, having regard to all the circumstances of the case, that a prison sentence is not merited, it

---

[101] *R v O'Keefe* [1969] 2 QB 29, 32; (1969) 53 Cr App R 91; *People (DPP) v Loving* [2006] 3 IR 355, para 33; *People (DPP) v W(D)* [2020] IECA 145, paras 36-38.

[102] *R v Cohen Mah-Wing* (1983) 5 Cr App R (S) 347, 348.

[103] *People (DPP) v Molloy* [2021] IESC 44; [2021] 3 IR 494; [2021] 2 ILRM 278, para 38.

[104] Arie Freiberg, "Suspended sentences in Australia: Uncertain, unstable, unpopular, and unnecessary?" (2019) 82 *Law and Contemporary Problems* 81.

should not put the offender at risk of future imprisonment for the offence in question. To do so would violate the first of the two fundamental principles described earlier. The challenge then is to identify the circumstances in which it is appropriate to impose a suspended sentence as opposed to a non-custodial penalty. The case must first and foremost be one of such gravity that imprisonment is not only deserved but may, in fact, have to be served. Further, the offender's personal circumstances must not only be mitigating but also give reason for hope that he or she will not reoffend or, at least, not in any serious way. A suspended sentence undoubtedly remains a significantly more lenient punishment than actual imprisonment, but it still entails some punishment, especially if it requires observance of onerous conditions. Therefore, the ultimate sentence may be proportionate, especially in light of the offender's personal circumstances.

12–44 As noted in Chap 3, censure-based theories of punishment have been in the ascendant in recent decades. According to these theories, the pronouncement of sentence is intended to express censure or condemnation of the offending conduct, while the punishment imposed – the 'hard treatment' element – reflects the gravity of that conduct. A fine may be sufficiently hard treatment for a minor road traffic offence while nothing less than a substantial term of imprisonment will do for rape or a serious assault. Suspended sentences can be compatible with this theory of punishment to the extent that the stipulation of a sentence of immediate imprisonment (typically by way of a headline sentence) expresses the appropriate level of censure for the offence itself, but there may also be factors present in the case to justify an ultimate sentence that is fully or partly suspended.[105] After all, the deserved level of hard treatment must be determined not only by reference to the offence but also to the offender's circumstances, including prospects of rehabilitation, as they exist at the time of sentence.[106]

12–45 The public interest in crime reduction may also be served by a fully or partly suspended sentence. Where there is credible evidence that an offender is more likely to desist from further crime if made subject to supervision while at conditional liberty rather than imprisoned, suspension of sentence may benefit the community as well as the offender. As the New South Wales Court of Appeal said in *R v Zamagias*:

> "It is perhaps trite to observe that, although the purpose of punishment is the protection of the community, that purpose can be achieved in an appropriate case by a sentence designed to assist in the rehabilitation of the offender

---

[105] *People (DPP) v Schaufler* [2020] IECA 299, para 42.

[106] For further discussion of this argument, see Tom O'Malley, "'That measure of wise clemency': Defending the suspended sentence" (2018) 28 *Irish Criminal Law Journal* 39. But see also Antje du Bois-Pedain, "Constructive sentencing through custody-avoiding sanctions: Theoretical foundations and practical challenges" in Alison Liebling et al (eds), *Crime, Justice, and Social Order: Essays in Honour of A.E. Bottoms* (Oxford University Press, 2022), Chap 10.

at the expense of deterrence, retribution and denunciation. In such a case a suspended sentence may be particularly effective and appropriate."[107]

12–46 Likewise, in *People (DPP) v Cummins*[108] the Court of Appeal, while increasing from two to four years the term of imprisonment for false imprisonment, burglary and other offences, said:

> "We think, however, that having regard to the importance in the public interest not only of deterrence and personal retribution but the achievement of rehabilitation (of which there seems a reasonably substantial prospect at this stage) it is appropriate to suspend part of that sentence. We think that the public interest would be best served by structuring a sentence so that he will be under supervision for a substantial period and would have an incentive to continue on the path of rehabilitation with the prospect of a return to custody if he re-offends or fails to otherwise comply with conditions."

12–47 The utilitarian value of a suspended sentence was recognised by the European Court of Human Rights in *Wilson v United Kingdom*[109]where the victim of a serious assault committed by her husband claimed that the suspended sentence imposed on the offender (a 50-year-old man with no previous convictions) represented a failure by the state to discharge its positive obligation to protect her from personal injury. The court declined to find a violation of the European Convention on Human Rights ('ECHR') in these circumstances, saying:

> "Of course, passing a suspended sentence was a much more lenient response than passing an immediate custodial sentence, but there was merit in the sentencing judge's approach. The virtue of passing an 18-month sentence and then suspending the sentence for three years was that it deterred the applicant's husband from any further violent behaviour towards her for three years, since any further incidents could have resulted in his being made to serve the 18-month sentence. That arguably gave the applicant longer and better protection from her husband than imprisoning him immediately would have done. That approach appears to have worked: there have been no other incidents since the assault on 20 October 2007."[110]

12–48 It must, however, be noted that in other cases, especially where injuries were inflicted by state agents, the court has found a suspended sentence to be an inadequate punishment.[111]

12–49 At a more pragmatic level, suspended sentences help to reduce the prison population, an important consideration at a time of prison overcrowding.

---

107 [2002] NWSCCA 17, para 32. The nature and purposes of the suspended sentence are also discussed in some detail by the High Court of Australia in *R v Dinsdale* [2000] HCA 54; 202 CLR 321.

108 [2018] IECA 413, para 11.

109 (2014) 58 EHRR SE10.

110 (2014) 58 EHRR SE10, para 50.

111 *Okkali v Turkey* (2010) 50 EHRR 43 (see note 116 below and accompanying text).

They also serve a deterrent function; offenders know that they are likely to be committed to prison if they reoffend during the operational period.

The Suspended Sentence as Punishment

Courts in Ireland and elsewhere have insisted that a suspended sentence is a real punishment. This is not a proposition on which there is universal agreement, but it is nonetheless one that may be credibly defended. A suspended sentence is, to be sure, more lenient than the equivalent term of immediate imprisonment and it could even be more lenient than a community-based sanction that included stringent conditions or intensive supervision. That might hold true, for example, if the suspension was conditioned on nothing more than being of good behaviour. Even with such minimal conditions, a suspended sentence remains a punishment because of the so-called Damocles' sword element that leaves the offender in a state of apprehension about having to undergo imprisonment for breaching a condition. Most fully or partly suspended sentences imposed for serious offences include conditions that are inherently punitive, apart altogether from the risk of imprisonment in the event of a breach. **12–50**

The length of the operational period which, as we shall see, must be reasonable and proportionate, and the conditions to be fulfilled are key factors in determining the punitive quality of a suspended sentence. Quite obviously, the more onerous the conditions, the more severe the sentence. In *People (DPP) v Harte*,[112] the Court of Appeal declined to hold that a part-suspended sentence was unduly lenient, largely because of the conditions the defendant was obliged to fulfil, including that he remained drug-free and complied with all directions from the probation officer. Some conditions may require an offender to do no more than the law generally requires, such as desisting from harassing the victim or some other person. Others may require more positive action or impose restrictions on the lifestyle which the offender would otherwise be entitled to pursue. The punitive impact of such requirements was aptly summarised by the Victoria Court of Appeal in *Boulton v The Queen*[113] when dealing with a community correction order that could include conditions very similar to those commonly attached to suspended sentences in Ireland: **12–51**

> "Plainly enough, an order attaching conditions of this kind, whether singly or in combination, is likely to interfere very significantly with the offender's freedom to live as he/she chooses. Compliance with such conditions may require a drastic alteration of daily life. Indeed, by attaching conditions prescribing where the offender must live, and which locations and persons he/she must avoid, the court can effectively require the offender to embark on a new life."

The conditions of suspension and the length of the operational period **12–52**

---

[112] [2015] IECA 121.

[113] [2014] VSCA 342; (2014) 46 VR 308, 322. See Chris Maxwell, "Non-custodial options and the politics of sentencing" (2017) 28 *Criminal Law Forum* 541.

constitute the most punitive element of a suspended sentence. Obviously the enduring threat of imprisonment for failure to abide by the conditions accentuates that punitive dimension. These factors, taken together, represent the 'hard treatment' visited upon an offender whose sentence is suspended.[114]

12–53 It cannot, of course, be gainsaid that a suspended sentence is more lenient than a term of immediate custody (unless, perhaps, it is a very short term). A custodial sentence that is fully or substantially suspended may not adequately reflect the gravity of an offence and, to that extent, amount of an error of principle. This was recognised by the Court of Appeal in *People (DPP) v Rakovac*[115] where a sentence of two-and-a-half years' imprisonment with the last 18 months suspended for a s 15A drug offence was found to be unduly lenient. The court said:

> "[T]he suspended portion of a sentence does represent an amelioration of punishment. But for the suspended portion the offender would suffer a greater level of deprivation of liberty. The punishment for a crime has to be proportionate. We do not consider that the actual level of hard treatment, in the form of deprivation of liberty, required for this offence was proportionate to the gravity of the offending, even taking into account his mitigating circumstances and personal situation."

12–54 The European Court of Human Rights reached a similar conclusion in *Okkali v Turkey*[116] where police officers were given suspended sentences for assaulting a 12-year-old boy while he was in custody. The court found a violation of art 3 of the ECHR (which outlaws torture and inhuman or degrading treatment or punishment), saying that, far from being rigorous, the penalty was not sufficiently dissuasive to deter similar acts in the future and that it afforded inadequate redress for the infringement of art 3. However, as noted earlier, the European Court has found a suspended sentence to be a suitable and appropriate punishment in other circumstance.[117]

The Operational Period

12–55 The absence of a statutory limit on the period for which a determine prison sentence may be suspended – the operational period – is not to be interpreted as leaving courts with untrammelled discretion in the matter. As part of the punishment inherent in a suspended sentence, the operational period should be proportionate in the sense of being rationally related to the purpose for which the sentence is imposed.[118] The conditions attached to a suspended sentence usually restrict a person's life choices to some extent, and the longer they do so, the more punitive the

---

[114] For further discussion, see O'Malley, note 106 above.
[115] [2022] IECA 233, para 43.
[116] (2010) 50 EHRR 43.
[117] *Wilson v United Kingdom* (2014) 58 EHRR SE10.
[118] *People (DPP) v Stronge* [2011] IECCA 79 (length of the operational period is part of the punishment).

sentence, bearing in mind that the threat of actual imprisonment endures throughout that period. In *People (DPP) v Hogan*[119] the appellant had been sentenced to five years' imprisonment with the last 18 months suspended for a period of 10 years. The Court of Appeal varied the sentence to the extent of reducing the operational period to three years. In so doing, it said:

> "We consider that the suspension for a period of 10 years is not proportionate when one considers that portion of the sentence which may fall for consideration as to re-activation should that arise is one of 18 months. Moreover, the length of the operational period of a suspended sentence must be proportionate in the distributive sense and there should be a reasonable prospect of compliance on the part of the offender. In the circumstances, 10 years is too long."[120]

While the suspended sentence was governed by common law, there was a general view, occasionally endorsed by the courts, that the operational period should not exceed the custodial element of the sentence.[121] In other words, a three-year sentence should not be suspended for longer than three years. This was never an inflexible principle, let alone a binding rule. Circumstances might arise where, for example, a relatively short prison sentence should be suspended for a longer period to further some legitimate aim such as incentivising rehabilitation or allowing the offender an opportunity to avail of addiction treatment or other counselling, support or therapeutic service. However, the suspended sentence is now governed entirely by s 99 of the Criminal Justice Act 2006, and this imposes no limit on the operational period.[122] The District Court may never impose a prison sentence exceeding two years (for a combination of offences) but it may suspend a sentence for longer than that. Thus, in *Collins v DPP*[123] the Court of Appeal upheld a sentence of 10 months with the last four months suspended for five years. In that case, the only condition of suspension was that the offender should keep the peace and be of good behaviour. Ordinarily, however, the operational period should bear a reasonable relationship to the term of imprisonment being suspended, bearing in mind the nature of the offence and, in particular, the offender's circumstances. A court should always give serious consideration to the length of time for which it is necessary or appropriate to suspend a prison term. In *People (DPP) v Doherty*,[124] for example, the trial court had suspended three years of a six-year sentence for a period of 10 years. The Court of Appeal increased the sentence to six years with one year suspended for two years. While it did not treat the 10-year operational period as illegal, it regarded it as unnecessary in the circumstances. **12–56**

---

[119] [2022] IECA 236,
[120] [2022] IECA 236, para 39.
[121] *People (DPP) v Hogan*, unreported, Court of Criminal Appeal, 4 March 2002; *People (DPP) v W(D)* [2020] IECA 145.
[122] *Collins v DPP* [2018] IECA 381. See also *DPP v Vajeuskis* [2014] IEHC 265.
[123] [2018] IECA 381.
[124] [2022] IECA 201.

Conditions of Suspension

12–57 As already noted, s 99(3) of the Criminal Justice Act 2006 allows courts considerable latitude in determining the conditions to attach to a suspended sentence. However, they are not entirely at large in this regard. At a minimum, any condition must comply with the principle of legality by specifying clearly and precisely what the offender is required to do or refrain from doing. Conditions of suspension should also be relevant, proportionate and potentially effective. Obviously, a court can never be sure that any measure will succeed in reducing or eliminating recidivism, but it should be satisfied that any condition imposed is likely to assist in that regard. Even more importantly, courts should avoid imposing conditions that an offender has no realistic prospect of fulfilling. As the Court of Appeal has said:

> "What a judge must strive to avoid, however, is unconsciously setting up an accused to fail. Before a suspended sentence is used to reflect mitigation and as an incentive to rehabilitation/reform, a sentencing judge should satisfy himself or herself that there is at least a reasonable prospect that the accused will take the chance provided to him by the proposed suspended sentence, because of the risk that, if a condition of the suspension is breached, the accused could lose all the earned mitigation to which (s)he is entitled."[125]

12–58 One consequence of this principle is that a court must always consider carefully whether to attach a condition requiring abstention from drugs or alcohol if the offender is clearly addicted to any of these substances.[126] There may be little point in including such a condition unless there is a reasonable prospect that the offender can abide by it. Otherwise, there is a strong possibility that the suspension will eventually be revoked. This in turn further underscores the importance of ensuring that a custodial sentence is never longer than deserved simply because it is being suspended in whole or in part.

12–59 As far as relevance is concerned, specific conditions must be selected having regard to the nature of the offence and their capacity to reduce reoffending. Both elements must be considered, bearing in mind that they are expressed conjunctively in s 99(3). They should also be proportionate in the distributive sense of reflecting the gravity of the offence and the offender's circumstances. For the reasons outlined earlier, the conditions of suspension coupled with the operational period may constitute the most punitive element of the sentence. They should not therefore amount to a disproportionately severe punishment. Any condition limiting the exercise of a fundamental right should be no more restrictive than is necessary to achieve a legitimate purpose, whether that be desistance from further

---

[125] *People (DPP) v Broe* [2020] IECA 140, para 77.

[126] Such a requirement is commonly included among the conditions of suspension even where there is evidence of addiction and mental health issues. See, for example, *People (DPP) v Kenna* [2020] IECA 265, but regard must always be had to the caution expressed in *People (DPP) v Broe* [2020] IECA 140, para 77 (quoted above).

crime or the protection of a victim. This general principle was discussed at length by the Court of Appeal in *People (DPP) v W(D)*[127] where the appellant, on being convicted of domestic violence offences, was sentenced to four years' imprisonment with the final year suspended for three years subject to him keeping the peace and being of good behaviour, and with a further condition that he stay away from the victim for 30 years. During that 30-year period he was not to contact the victim directly or indirectly by any means whatsoever and was required to stay away from anywhere the victim lived. There was, of course, a contradiction in the terms of the sentence. On the one hand, the final year was suspended for three years only while, on the other, the restriction on contacting the victim lasted for 30 years. What would have happened if this restriction were breached after, say, 10 years, was unclear. However, there was also the more pressing problem that the appellant and the victim had four children together and it was entirely foreseeable that he would occasionally need to contact her, either personally or through an agent such as a solicitor, in connection with their welfare. The Court of Appeal effectively upheld the sentence but with the important variation that the appellant was not to contact the victim during the three-year suspension period, except through a written communication from a solicitor in connection with the children's welfare, unless invited by the victim to do so. The court held that the imposition of any such condition must conform with what is often known as *Heaney* proportionality, referring to *Heaney v Ireland*[128]where it was held that any legal restriction on a constitutional right must be proportionate in the sense that it: (1) is rationally connected to the objective being pursued and not arbitrary, unfair or based on irrational considerations; (2) impairs the right as little as possible; and (3) is proportionate to the objective in terms of its effect on rights. Applying this test to the impugned condition in *W(D)*, the court concluded:

> "[We consider] that it is disproportionate in the *Heaney* sense insofar as, notwithstanding any legitimate aim that the sentencing judge may have been pursuing, it impacts excessively on the appellant's rights, variously arising either under the Constitution, or the European Convention on Human Rights/ the Charter of Fundamental Rights, including a right of freedom of association with his children, his right as a parent to further develop his relationship with his children, and a right to enjoyment of a family life which involves his children. The condition was arguably so far-reaching in its terms as to amount to an unlawful punishment, not presently available under Irish law."[129]

A sentence should not be suspended, in whole or in part, *solely* to coerce or encourage the payment of compensation. This principle is founded mainly on considerations of equity. An offender should not be permitted, or seen to be permitted, to secure a more lenient punishment than he or she deserves simply because of being able to pay significant compensation to **12–60**

[127] [2020] IECA 145.
[128] [1994] 3 IR 593; [1994] 2 ILRM 420.
[129] [2020] IECA 145, para 93.

a victim. In *People (DPP) v Doherty,*[130] the defendant, who pleaded guilty to a serious assault, was sentenced to six years imprisonment with the last three years suspended on a number of conditions including that he pay €30,000 in compensation to the victim. €25,000 of this was to be paid in annual instalments after the defendant's release from prison. The Court of Appeal found this sentence to be unduly lenient and substituted a six-year sentence with one year suspended for two years but excluding the compensation element from the conditions. However, it then made a compensation order in the sum of €25,000 under the terms of s 6 of the Criminal Justice Act 1993 (described later in this Chapter). In so doing, the court said:

> "We should say that we think that it is inappropriate in any event to impose as a term of suspension of a sentence in whole or in part an obligation to pay sums of money. We reiterate an observation made at the sentencing hearing that in some circumstances the imposition of such a requirement might be optically uncomfortable. The practice is open to the objection, notwithstanding that the objective may be the worthy one of facilitating restitution, that the offender is being afforded the opportunity to buy his way out of all (or as in this case a substantial part) of a custodial term that he would otherwise be required to serve, and which a person in the same position as him, but without means, would have to serve. We think that the more appropriate course where the judge wishes to make provision for compensation is to make a compensation order within the meaning of section 6 of the Criminal Procedure Act 1993, as amended without specific linkage to the period of custody that a person may have to serve. A realistic expression of willingness to co-operate in providing restitution proffered by the accused in evidence, or by his legal representative in presenting a plea in mitigation, can always be taken account of as evidence of true remorse in any discounting for general mitigation."[131]

12–61 As reflected in this decision, a compensation order is by no means incompatible with a suspended sentence. As discussed later in this Chapter, s 6 of the 1993 Act provides that such an order may be made in addition to or instead of any other way of dealing with an offender. In *People (DPP) v Duffy,*[132] the Supreme Court observed that, in a case where a fully or partly suspended sentence was considered appropriate in any event, it did not see any difficulty about making the suspension conditional on the payment of compensation. What a court apparently should not do is suspend a sentence or any portion of it for the sole purpose of facilitating compensation payment. This seems to have been the problem in *Doherty* where a significant portion of the sentence was suspended on condition that the defendant paid what was probably for him a considerable sum of money.

12–62 The conditions attached to a suspended sentence imposed on a foreign national may include a requirement to leave the jurisdiction and stay

---

[130] [2022] IECA 201.

[131] [2022] IECA 201, para 24. This passage was quoted with implied approval by the Supreme Court in *People (DPP) v Duffy* [2023] IESC 1, para 61.

[132] [2023] IESC 1, para 90.

away for a specified period. This may seem tantamount to deportation, but there is a significant difference between the two. The power to deport a foreign national is vested exclusively in the executive, though a court may recommend deportation.[133] Suspending a prison sentence on condition that the offender leave the state does not, strictly speaking, amount to deportation because the offender has a choice, though undoubtedly a difficult one, between leaving the state and serving the relevant sentence in custody. The period of time an offender is required to remain outside the state should be limited rather than open-ended. As the Court of Criminal Appeal said in *People (DPP) v Alexiou*:

> "The court, however, does take the view that imposing an open-ended condition that the accused never return to this country is not, in principle, good practice. If a condition requiring a convicted person to leave the country is imposed the better practice would be to do so for a defined period of time proportionate to the offence. Otherwise, there is a risk that such a condition could have disproportionate punitive effect. Many years later such a person might have good reason to return to the country for a short period of time."[134]

This general principle is reflected in later sentencing decisions and appeal court judgments. In *People (DPP) v Broszczack,*[135] for example, the appellant, on pleading guilty to a s 15A drug offence, was sentenced to seven years' imprisonment with the last three years suspended, one of the conditions being that he leave the country immediately on his release from prison and stay away for seven years. His appeal centred mainly on this condition. He was a 25-year-old Polish national who had been in Ireland for only eight months prior to his arrest. Dismissing the appeal, the Court of Appeal accepted that the conditions attaching to a suspended sentence must always be reasonable and proportionate, but in respect of this case it said: **12–63**

> "The appellant is 25 years of age, and accordingly is not a person who, by virtue of his age, is likely to have particular adjustment difficulties in the event of moving back to his country of origin. He will have none of the exceptional adjustment difficulties that either the very young or the very old can sometimes experience on account of their age when required to cope with disruptive change."[136]

This statement reflects the factors that must be considered when making such an order. A requirement to leave the country and remain outside of it for any appreciable length of time could be even more onerous than imprisonment for a person who had long been resident here and whose family were here, and who would now have to move elsewhere, perhaps to a country with which he or she had no meaningful connection, despite **12–64**

---

[133] Immigration Act 1999, s 3; *People (DPP) v Alexiou* [2003] 3 IR 513.
[134] [2003] 3 IR 513, 527.
[135] [2016] IECA 121.
[136] [2016] IECA 121, para 37. See also *People (DPP) v W(D)* [2020] IECA 145, para 77.

having been born and brought up there. The punitive quality of such a condition will obviously depend on the offender's personal circumstances including the extent to which he or she has integrated into Irish society. But a court must always be careful to ensure that this or any other condition of suspension is not disproportionate to the overall gravity of the offence. Where the condition is simply that the offender leave the jurisdiction for a specified period, it is entirely up to the offender to decide where to go. It is not a matter for the prosecution or the court.[137] Further, a failure to leave despite having freely given an undertaking at sentencing to do so will ordinarily lead to a full activation of the sentence.[138]

12–65 Special considerations apply where the offender is a citizen of the European Union ('EU'). Every person holding the nationality of a member state is a citizen of the EU,[139]and every such citizen has the right to move and reside freely within the territory of the member states, though subject to limitations and conditions laid down in the treaties and other legislation.[140] By virtue of Directive 2004/38/EC, an EU citizen's freedom of movement may be restricted on grounds of public policy, public security and public health. Measures taken on grounds of public policy or public security must comply with the principle of proportionality and be based exclusively on the personal conduct of the individual concerned. Moreover, that conduct "must represent a genuine, present and sufficiently serious threat affecting one of the fundamental interests of society".[141] Previous criminal convictions shall not of themselves constitute sufficient grounds for taking such a measure. An EU citizen who has resided in the host state for 10 years or more may not be expelled except on "imperative grounds of public policy".[142] However, this criterion can be satisfied where, for example, a person was convicted of serious drug dealing offences.[143] Arguably, none of this is directly relevant to a requirement to leave the state as a condition of suspension because this does not, for reasons already outlined, amount to deportation in the true sense of the term. However, the terms of Directive 2004/38/EC and the manner in which they have been interpreted by the Court of Justice of the European Union provide a useful guide to the factors a court should consider when deciding if an EU citizen should be required to leave the state as a condition of a suspended sentence.

Suspension as Mitigation

12–66 It is now common practice to recognise the presence of mitigating factors by partly suspending a prison sentence. Strictly speaking, mitigation

---

[137] *People (DPP) v Abrahams* [2020] IECA 243.
[138] *People (DPP) v Abrahams* [2020] IECA 243.
[139] Treaty on the Functioning of the European Union, art 20(1).
[140] Treaty on the Functioning of the European Union, art 21(1).
[141] Directive 2004/38 /EC, art 27.
[142] Directive 2004/38 EC, art 28(3).
[143] *Land Baden-Württemberg v Panagiotis Tsakouridis* Case C-145/09 (Grand Chamber).

should be rewarded with a reduced rather than a suspended sentence. This is especially true of factors that reduce the gravity of the offence, typically by reducing culpability. In such a case, the offence is less serious than it might otherwise have been, and this should be reflected in the headline sentence. Many other mitigating factors relate to the offender's personal circumstances, including his or her response to the charges. However, these too will usually be more appropriately acknowledged through a reduced sentence. A guilty plea, for example, is widely recognised as a significant mitigating factor, not least because of its value to the legal system and, in some instances, to the victim of the offence.[144] By virtue of its utilitarian value which should be appropriately incentivised, and the fact that it amounts to a voluntary waiver of the constitutionally guaranteed right to trial, it should in principle be rewarded with a straight reduction, and not with a measure that leaves the offender at risk of further imprisonment. In *People (DPP) v M(P)*,[145] the Court of Appeal held that the trial judge erred in not granting a reduction (as opposed to part suspension) for certain mitigating factors. The court then made such a reduction and also suspended a portion of the final sentence to incentivise mitigation.

The Court of Appeal has nonetheless declined to rule out part suspension **12–67** of sentence as a response to mitigating factors.[146] There may be situations where this is appropriate. Certain offender-related factors call for what might be described as conditional mitigation. In other words, some factors such as a guilty plea, previous good character or positive cooperation in the investigation of the offence will already have materialised, or have been established, at the time of sentence and should therefore be rewarded with a straight reduction. However, other factors connected with the offender's present circumstances or future prospects also deserve recognition, but only if the offender responds by desisting from further crime and fulfilling any special conditions. For example, being the sole or primary carer of young children is generally accepted as a personal mitigating factor. But an offender scarcely deserves a reduced sentence on this account unless he or she is committed to adopting a law-abiding and pro-social lifestyle that will benefit the children. Full or part suspension in these circumstances serves the dual purpose of granting mitigation on a recognised ground and affording the offender an opportunity to respond by honouring the conditions of suspension. In a sense, it introduces a communicative element into the sentencing process. The court is offering the offender an opportunity to prove that he or she can successfully adjust to being at liberty, while the offender's response consists in his or her conduct during that period of conditional liberty.[147] Suspension may also be appropriate where the offence is of such a nature that immediate imprisonment would almost invariably

---

[144] Chap 6 above.

[145] [2016] IECA 49, para 28 .

[146] *People (DPP) v Broe* [2020] IECA 140; *People (DPP) v Schaufler* [2020] IECA 299 , para 40; *People (DPP) v Doolin* [2020] IECA 231, para 25.

[147] In *People (DPP) v Lee* [2017] IECA 152, para 37, the Court of Appeal held that

follow, but there are exceptionally strong mitigating factors. Suspension in these circumstances represents a definite concession, even if it leaves the offender at risk of imprisonment throughout the operational period. It therefore operates as a kind of halfway house between a custodial and a community penalty. In *R v Griffin*,[148] for example, the appellant pleaded guilty to conspiracy to supply drugs but, in the words of the English Court of Appeal, there was "exceptionally a very unusual weight of mitigating factors" to be balanced against the seriousness of the offence. The court therefore substituted a suspended sentence for 22 months' immediate imprisonment. (The total value of the drugs found in the appellant's possession was somewhere between £3,000 and £6,000.)

Part Suspension to Incentivise Rehabilitation

12–68 It has now become common practice to suspend part of a prison sentence for the purpose of incentivising rehabilitation.[149] A clear distinction must be maintained between any period of suspension granted for this purpose and part suspension given by way of mitigation. Part suspension to incentivise rehabilitation or desistance from further offending bears a close resemblance to parole. Having served a specified portion of the sentence in custody, the offender is conditionally released, though subject to recall if he or she breaches a release condition. The breach will most often consist in the commission of a further offence. During the transitional period between release from custody and the expiration of the sentence, the offender has an opportunity, possibly with the assistance of the Probation Service, to readjust to life outside prison and become socially integrated. A court should always consider the possibility of part suspension where it has reason to believe that the offender is making progress towards rehabilitation or is demonstrably committed to doing so. As the Court of Appeal said in *People (DPP) v Dent*:

> "While this Court readily accepts that there will always be cases where it is simply unrealistic to expect a judge to suspend all or portion of a sentence, or otherwise incentivise rehabilitation, it is an error in principle to foreclose on such options where there is uncontroverted evidence before the court of a demonstrated track record of progress towards rehabilitation. The possibility of incentivising continued rehabilitation should at least be considered, though having done so a judge may in an appropriate case be justified in rejecting it as a viable option."[150]

12–69 The judicial obligation is therefore to consider part suspension where it seems a viable option, but it need not be granted if there are relevant countervailing factors.

---

there was no error in principle in partly suspending a sentence for the dual purpose of reflecting mitigation and incentivising rehabilitation.

[148] [2023] EWCA Crim 1111; [2024] 1 Cr App R (S) 24.

[149] See, for example, *People (DPP) v Kearney* [2016] IECA 394.

[150] [2015] IECA 169, para 70. See also *People (DPP) v Stokes* [2017] IECA 259, para 27.

12–70 Part suspension may be denied where rehabilitation is either unlikely or unnecessary. There must be a sound evidential basis for concluding that the offender would benefit from the rehabilitative opportunities afforded by the part suspension. Some offenders may not need rehabilitation because, for example, they are not labouring under any particular disadvantage or suffering from addiction. A person who, despite being relatively privileged, deliberately engaged in, say, fraudulent conduct or some kind of financial crime solely with an eye to personal profit might well fall into this category. However, even in these circumstances, there may be reason to believe that the defendant, although not requiring rehabilitation in the conventional sense of the word, is amenable to reform and that he or she will likely desist from further offending if afforded some incentive or opportunity. Part suspension may well be appropriate in such a case.[151] The period of suspension may, however, be reasonably short where the offender is assessed as being at low risk of re-offending.[152] Where part suspension is refused, care should be taken to ensure that the custodial sentence is no longer than strictly necessary in the circumstances.

12–71 At the other end of the spectrum, part suspension may be deemed unsuitable or even pointless because the offender, by virtue of his or her previous record or attitude to the offence of conviction, seems unamenable to rehabilitation or appears unwilling to observe the conditions of suspension. For these reasons, the Court of Appeal has insisted that there must be a sound evidential basis for suspending part of a sentence to incentivise rehabilitation.[153] In *People (DPP) v Doyle*,[154] for example, the Court of Appeal held that the trial judge had properly exercised her discretion in refusing to suspend part of a sentence imposed for criminal damage, demanding money with menaces and other offences. The appellant was a drug addict with numerous previous convictions and, despite having been afforded opportunities to do so, he had made no real progress towards addressing his addiction. The evidential basis to justify part suspension was therefore lacking. On the other hand, previous unsuccessful efforts at rehabilitation should not automatically operate to deny an offender a further opportunity where there is some evidence that he or she is now making genuine efforts to address whatever problem has led to the offending.[155] As research has consistently shown, desistance from crime is usually a process rather than an event. There will be occasional relapses but this does not exclude the possibility that real progress can be made over time.[156]

---

151 *People (DPP) v Kavanagh* [2020] IECA 13, para 15.
152 *People (DPP) v Doherty* [2022] IECA 201, para 21.
153 *People (DPP) v Coughlan* [2019] IECA 173; *People (DPP) v Cummins* [2020] IECA 42, para 21.
154 [2023] IECA 80, para 43.
155 *People (DPP) v Judge* [2017] IECA 148.
156 See note 214 below and accompanying text.

Revocation of Suspended Sentence

12–72 Those provisions of s 99 of the Criminal Justice Act 2006 governing the procedure to be followed when a person was convicted of a further offence during the currency of a suspended sentence proved to be legally problematic, so much so that two of the key subsections were declared unconstitutional in 2016.[157] Remedial legislation enacted in 2017 seems to have addressed these issues satisfactorily.[158] Essentially, as the law now stands, when a person commits a further offence, known as the triggering offence, during the operational period of a suspended sentence, and is convicted of the triggering offence, the court, after imposing sentence for it, must remand the person to the court that imposed the suspended sentence. The latter court shall revoke the suspended sentence unless it would be unjust in all the circumstances to do so. Where it decides to revoke, it may order that all or part of the original sentence be served. Any period of imprisonment required to be served as a result of such revocation shall be consecutive to any determinate sentence of imprisonment imposed for the triggering offence. Where this happens in the District Court, the aggregate of the terms of imprisonment shall not exceed two years. An application to activate a suspended sentence imposed by an appeal court should be brought before the trial court that imposed the original sentence.[159]

12–73 A court may also revoke a suspended sentence if satisfied that the offender has breached a condition of suspension during the operational period. It may do so following an application by a member of An Garda Síochána, a prison governor, a probation officer or the Director of Public Prosecutions.[160] The breach might consist of failure to abide by a special condition such as cooperating with the Probation Service or staying away from a specified person or place, though it could also consist of committing a further offence. Again, the court has a discretion to revoke the order in whole or in part, or not revoke it at all if it appeared that it would be contrary to the interests of justice to do so. Prior to the enactment of the 2006 Act, a suspended sentence had to be activated in its entirety or not at all; that, at least, was the general understanding of Irish common law on the matter. Allowing a sentence to be activated in part, as the law now provides, has the advantage of permitting a court to take account of the nature and circumstances of the breach in deciding how much of the suspended portion should be served. For instance, the commission of a minor offence towards the end of the operational term of a suspended sentence for an unrelated offence would scarcely merit the activation of the entire sentence, especially if this would involve serving a substantial term of imprisonment. An offender who has managed to abide by the conditions of suspension throughout most of the operational period should ordinarily get some credit for having done so, and all the more so

157 *Moore v DPP* [2016] IEHC 244.

158 Criminal Justice (Suspended Sentences of Imprisonment) Act 2017.

159 Criminal Justice Act 2006, s 99(22); *People (DPP) v Dinnegan* [2023] IECA 187.

160 Criminal Justice Act 2006, s 99(13), (13A) and (14). subs 13A inserted by Criminal Justice (Suspended Sentences of Imprisonment) Act 2017, s 2(g).

if he or she was labouring under some disadvantage such as homelessness or addiction.[161] The same would apply where the condition breached was incidental to the overall purpose of the sentence, or where the breach was essentially technical in nature, such as a failure to turn up for an appointment.[162] Ultimately the principle of proportionality should apply to an activation decision as it applies to the original sentencing decision.

6. Community-Based Measures

Any penalty that does not involve immediate imprisonment or detention may be classified as 'non-custodial'. However, this term has fallen into disfavour because many believe it to suggest that custody is the norm and that any other penalty is a deviation, justified or otherwise, from that norm. 'Community-based' punishment has become the preferred terminology. Yet the language of community must also be critically scrutinised. The mid-20th century decarceration movement, especially in the United States but to some extent in Europe as well, was characterised by an optimistic – some would say naïve – expectation that communities would take responsibility for helping those who would otherwise have been detained in prisons or reformatories because of their criminal activities or in asylums because of mental illness. But, as Andrew Scull, a leading historian and critic of decarceration, observed, the reality could be very different: **12–74**

> "Furthermore, it is at least mildly curious to portray modern society as a collection of little organic villages where neighbour will help neighbour and families willingly minister to the needs of their own troublesome members – when surrounded by the reality of the increasingly privatised, rationalised and atomised existence which is characteristic of late capitalism."[163]

It has been said that we did not begin to use the language of community until communities in the traditional sense had largely disappeared.[164] During the era to which Scull was referring, many of those who were spared detention as a result of decarceration policies found themselves abandoned, marginalised or confined to ghettos where their activities, however anti-social, would not trouble the more powerful or influential members of society. Today, we adhere to the language of community in our criminal justice discourse. It has made its way into legislation **12–75**

---

161 By way of contrast, in *People (DPP) v Wall* [2018] IECA 366, the Court of Appeal upheld revocation of a suspended sentence in its entirety for repeated failure to maintain contact with the Probation Service. However, in that case the court had regard to the appellant's prior record in relation to other suspended sentences.

162 *People (DPP) v Abrahams* [2020] IECA 243, para 21.

163 Andrew Scull, "Community Corrections: Panacea, Progress or Pretence?" in David Garland and Peter Young (eds), *The Power to Punish: Contemporary Penality and Social Analysis* (Ashgate Publishing Limited, 1992 (1983)), 148, 152.

164 Nicola Lacey and Lucia Zedner, "Discourses of community in criminal justice" (1995) 22 *Journal of Law and Society* 301.

as exemplified by the Children Act 2001 which has about two dozen sections grouped under the heading 'Community Sanctions'. In England and Wales, the Sentencing Act 2020 (ss 200 to 220) categorises a wide range of measures, including (ironically, one might say) curfews and exclusion orders, as 'community orders'. In Ireland, the Criminal Justice (Community Sanctions) Bill 2014 proposes a new framework for probation, binding over, reparation and similar orders.[165]

12–76 In practical terms, a community order or penalty is one that is fulfilled or served while the offender is at liberty, conditional or otherwise.[166] Offenders remain within 'the community' in the sense of being at large, though in many instances subject to supervision, surveillance or other constraint. It is important, nonetheless, not to paint too bleak a picture. Genuine community engagement with offenders occurs, for example, in restorative justice programmes involving the participation of offender, victim and other interested parties. Voluntary organisations assist with the resettlement of recently released prisoners, and their work is often vital in reducing the risk of re-offending. Businesses, community groups and other organisations often collaborate with probation services in providing work experience or training and educational opportunities for offenders under supervision. But it would still be a mistake to assume that everyone subject to a community order, sanction or penalty is somehow cocooned within a supportive local community that sees itself as having some responsibility for the offender's welfare.

12–77 Compared with imprisonment, community-based sanctions and measures have traditionally received little scholarly attention.[167] This may be partly due to their relative invisibility. Unlike imprisonment, they lack a physical architecture and other signifiers equivalent to officers' uniforms and prison vans. Moreover, imprisonment has a strong presence in popular culture (think of films such as *The Shawshank Redemption, Papillon* and *Birdman of Alcatraz*) and literature.[168] Most people have never been inside a prison, but they still have a vision, accurate or otherwise, of what prison life entails. The same cannot be said of non-custodial sanctions. Mike Nellis once observed that probation "is not very photogenic", meaning

---

165 At the time of writing, all that has been published is a General Scheme of the Bill.

166 The Council of Europe Recommendation No R(92) 16 of the Committee of Ministers defines "community sanctions and measures" as those "which maintain the offender in the community and involve some restriction of his liberty through the imposition of conditions and/or obligations, and which are implemented by bodies designed by law for that purpose. The term designates any sanction imposed by a court or a judge, and any measure taken before or instead of a decision on a sanction as well as ways of enforcing a sentence of imprisonment outside a prison establishment."

167 Gwen Robinson, "The Cinderella complex: Punishment, society and community sanctions" (2016) 18 *Punishment and Society* 95.

168 Examples include *The Autobiography of Malcolm X* (with the assistance of Alex Haley) (Grove Press, 1965); Jimmy Santiago Baca, *A Place to Stand* (Grove Press, 2001) and Brendan Behan's play, *The Quare Fellow* (1954).

that, for want of clear outward manifestations, its purpose and operation remain largely unknown to members of the public.[169] Whatever the reason may be, the level of attention devoted by academic writers and others to imprisonment far outweighs the extent to which it is used as a penalty. The Courts Service Annual Report 2020 shows that of the 195,000 offences (summary and indictable) dealt with in the District Court that year, less than 7,000 resulted in imprisonment compared with more than 35,000 resulting in fines and 8,000 in probation orders.[170] A similar pattern is observable in England and Wales where, in 2019, more than 720,000 adult male offenders were sentenced (by all courts). Of these, 63,357 were sentenced to immediate custody compared to 534,445 who were fined and 86,3919 who were given suspended sentences or community orders.[171]

7. Community Service

Community service orders ('CSOs') were introduced in Ireland in 1983 with the avowed purpose of providing an alternative to imprisonment.[172] When any court, other than the Special Criminal Court, is dealing with an offender aged 16 years or over, and it is of the opinion that the appropriate sentence is one of imprisonment, it may instead make a CSO. (This does not apply where the sentence is fixed by law, as in the case of murder which carries a mandatory life sentence.) A CSO requires the offender to undertake unpaid work for such number of hours, between 40 and 240, as the court specifies. An offender may be subject to more than one CSO at a time, but the aggregate number of hours may never exceed 240. Before making a CSO, a court must be satisfied, having considered the offender's circumstances and a probation report, that the offender is a suitable person to perform work in accordance with the order and that arrangements can be made for the performance of such work. The offender must also consent to the making of the order. The consent requirement seems to have been included, originally at least, to avoid a possible conflict with international human rights provisions outlawing forced labour.[173] Such a conflict is unlikely to materialise, going by the experience of countries that have no consent requirement. A more realistic rationale is that an offender who does not consent to a CSO might be less willing to fulfil the work requirement in which case further court proceedings may be necessary. **12–78**

Where a court is satisfied that the appropriate sentence for an offence would be one of 12 months' imprisonment or less, it *shall* consider community service as an alternative and, provided the relevant criteria **12–79**

---

[169] Mike Nellis, "Representations of British probation officers in film, television drama and novels 1948-2012" (2012) 10 *British Journal of Community Justice* 5.
[170] The most common disposals, accounting for more than 93,500 charges in all, were dismissal, strike out and taking into consideration.
[171] Andrew Ashworth and Rory Kelly, *Sentencing and Criminal Justice*,7th edition (Hart, 2021), 446 (based on official statistics).
[172] Criminal Justice (Community Service) Act 1983.
[173] See, for example, ECHR, art 4.

are fulfilled, it *may* make a CSO. A court may also make such an order where the appropriate sentence exceeds 12 months' imprisonment, though it is not expressly required to consider doing so.[174] Although judges are under a clear statutory obligation to consider community service as an alternative to short prison sentences (12 months or less), they are not expressly obliged to give reasons for not imposing a CSO. The Court of Appeal has held that while judges must take this matter into account, they are not required to state openly that they have done so, although this may be desirable. A failure to make an express statement to this effect will not invalidate a court order. Defence lawyers should always draw this provision to a judge's attention.[175]

12–80 In Ireland, a CSO may be imposed for any offence other than murder or one dealt with in the Special Criminal Court, provided the appropriate sentence would otherwise be one of imprisonment and the offender is at least 16 years of age at the time of sentence.[176] It is not, as in some other countries, an alternative to short sentences only. Naturally enough, it will seldom be an adequate penalty for a very serious offence, but it has occasionally been imposed for relatively serious theft offences[177] and careless driving causing serious bodily harm (although in the latter case the appropriate prison sentence was set at nine months).[178] As against this, there have been cases where it was considered inadequate for serious assault offences, including assaults on Gardai while acting in the course of their duties.[179]

12–81 The CSO, as it operates in Ireland, is both a substitutionary and a stand-alone penalty. It is substitutionary in the sense that it may be imposed only in cases where imprisonment is initially considered to be the appropriate penalty. The justification for this requirement is questionable, not least because it suggests imprisonment as the presumptive sentencing option, even for offences of moderate levels of gravity. Community service should preferably be a sentencing option in its own right, located somewhere between fines and imprisonment on the overall penalty scale. However, once selected, a CSO is a stand-alone penalty in the sense that it may be the sole punishment imposed for an offence rather than being, as in some other jurisdictions, a condition of probation or of a suspended sentence.

12–82 Fine defaulters may also be ordered to perform community service. The Fines (Payment and Recovery) Act 2014 (the '2014 Act') introduced a range

---

174 Criminal Justice (Community Service) Act 1983, s 4 as substituted by Criminal Justice (Community Service) (Amendment) Act 2011, s 3.

175 *O'Brien v Coughlan* [2015] IECA 245, para 12 (upholding this aspect of the High Court judgment [2014] IEHC 425). Leave to take a further appeal to the Supreme Court was refused: *O'Brien v Coughlan* [2016] IESCDET 88.

176 This is confirmed by the Children Act 2001, s 115.

177 *People (DPP) v O'Rourke* [2016] IECA 132.

178 *People (DPP) v McCormack* [2022] IECA 301.

179 *People (DPP) v McAuley* [2017] IECA 325. See also *People (DPP) v Macken* [2018] IECA 75.

of options for dealing with default in payment of fines.[180] It amended the Criminal Justice (Community Service) Act 1983 to provide that where a person fails to pay a fine, and the court is satisfied that it would not be appropriate to make a recovery or attachment order (or where such an order has been made but has not enabled the fine to be collected), it may make a community service order. An unpaid work requirement of 40 to 240 hours may be imposed on a person convicted on indictment for the offence concerned, whereas the number of hours ranges from 30 to 100 in the case of a person convicted summarily of the offence concerned. In deciding on the number of hours, the court shall take account of any part of the fine that has already been paid or recovered. Imprisonment, however, remains the ultimate sanction. A prison committal order may be made where the fine defaulter is deemed not to be a suitable person to perform community service or has not consented to the making of a CSO (in accordance with the Criminal Justice (Community Service) Act 1983, s 4)), or where the defaulter has failed to comply with a CSO already made in response to the fine default. The maximum term of imprisonment to which the defaulter is liable depends on whether the fine was imposed following a summary conviction in which case the maximum period of imprisonment is 30 days or following conviction on indictment in which case the maximum is 12 months.[181]

8. Fines

The fine is the penalty most commonly imposed for minor offences. **12–83**
although it is also available as a penalty for many serious offences.[182] Some summary offences are punishable with a fine only. This holds true, for example, of certain public order offences,[183] the purchase of sexual services[184] and possession of cannabis for personal use (on a first or second conviction).[185] Many other offences are expressly made punishable with a fine, a term of imprisonment or both and, in the case of the more serious offences, the fine is subject to no specified maximum but is instead at the discretion of the court. Thus, assault causing harm is punishable following summary conviction with a maximum sentence of 12 months' imprisonment, a fine of up to £1,500 or both, whereas following conviction

---

180 Pt 3 of the 2014 Act makes the necessary amendments to the Criminal Justice (Community Service) Act 1983 and the Courts (No 2) Act 1986.

181 Where the fine was imposed following summary conviction, the permitted periods of imprisonment vary according to the amount of fine, eg, five days where the fine was not greater than €500 and 30 days where it was greater than €3,000.

182 Jay Gormley, *Fines: A Review of the Sanction, Its Use and Operation, and Research Evidence* (Sentencing Academy, 2022) which has a valuable analysis of fines including the offence categories for which fines are most commonly imposed in England and Wales.

183 Criminal Justice (Public Order) Act 1994, ss 4 and 5.

184 Criminal Law (Sexual Offences) Act 1993, s 7A as inserted by Criminal Law (Sexual Offences) Act 2017, s 25.

185 Misuse of Drugs Act 1977, s 27.

on indictment, it is punishable with a fine (no upper limit specified), a maximum of 10 years' imprisonment or both.[186]

12–84 From a penological perspective, fines have some advantages. They can potentially serve both retributive and deterrent purposes although, admittedly, in practice, they sometimes serve neither. They can be proportioned to the gravity of the offence and the offender's personal circumstances, without causing disruption to the lives of offenders and their families (as happens with imprisonment). In principle, at least, a fine may be imposed for almost any offence although, again in practice, it will rarely be considered adequate as the sole punishment for a very serious offence. In such a case, it is more likely to supplement rather than replace imprisonment. As with other non-custodial measures, a fine may not be publicly accepted as providing adequate censure for a serious offence.[187] Fines, assuming they are collected, provide a net income for the state, unlike other penalties, notably imprisonment, which impose a considerable cost. The effectiveness of fines, judged from the perspective of desert or deterrence, depends largely on the extent to which they can be tailored to reflect an offender's means, an issue considered below in the context of unit fines. One unique feature of the fine as a penalty is that it may be served by somebody else. As Ivó Coca-Vila writes:

> "Since the enforcement of a fine is not based on personal and non-transferable goods – such as life, liberty, physical integrity or honour – but instead on the extremely fungible and transmissible good that is money, the possibility of shifting the cost of the fine to a (consenting or non-consenting) third party who is not responsible for the crime is a constitutive pathological feature of this kind of punishment."[188]

12–85 This may not happen as often as some of the literature suggests, but there is practically nothing to stop a third party, such as a family member or employer, from paying a fine, usually to save the offender from being imprisoned in default. Rendering this practice criminal could prove to be problematic. A law prohibiting one person from paying a fine for another might easily be circumvented by, for example, giving the offender a gift of equivalent value. A company might be prohibited from paying a fine for one of its officers or employees, but it could scarcely be stopped from giving that person a generous end-of-year bonus or paying their golf club fees.

12–86 When imposing a fine, a court must always have regard to the offender's means. This is a long-standing principle which has applied by statute to the District Court since 1914.[189] It is now applicable to all courts by virtue

[186] Non-Fatal Offences against the Person Act 1997, s 3. The maximum fine must now be calculated according to the Fines Act 2010, discussed below. The maximum prison sentence was increased from five to 10 years under the Criminal Justice (Miscellaneous Provisions) Act 2023, s 20.

[187] Kahan, "Punishment incommensurability", note 12 above.

[188] Coca-Vila, note 13 above, at 407.

[189] Criminal Justice Administration Act 1914, s 5.

of the Fines Act 2010 (s 14) which has the express purpose of ensuring that where a court imposes a fine, the effect on the offender or his or dependants "is not significantly abated or made more severe by reason of his or her financial circumstances". A court may direct a convicted person to provide an account of their financial circumstances. Failure to comply with such a direction is an offence punishable with up to five years' imprisonment (or six months following summary conviction). Irrespective of an offender's means, a fine may never exceed the statutory maximum. For rich offenders, even the maximum may not amount to a significant punishment. To address this problem, some countries have adopted unit fine systems whereby a court first determines the appropriate number of "units" of a fine in light of the gravity of the offence. This might be on a scale of one to ten or one to fifty. The offender's disposable income for a defined period (eg, a week or month) is then multiplied by the number of units, and this determines the amount of fine to be imposed. Thus, if A and B were each convicted of an offence considered to merit four units of fine, and A had disposable income of €25 while B had a disposable income of €200, A would pay a fine of €100, while B would pay €800. The essential purpose of this arrangement is to produce equality of impact. It permits a fine to be proportioned to the gravity of the offence while ensuring, as far as practicable, that monetary penalties have a similar impact on people with different financial resources.[190]

Day fine systems of various kinds exist in about half the member states **12–87** of the European Union. They had a famously brief existence in England and Wales in the early 1990s. The Criminal Justice Act 1991 (the '1991 UK Act') (s 18) introduced unit fines in the magistrates' courts. It set out a detailed scheme whereby a maximum number of units, varying from 2 to 50 depending on the level of offence, would be identified for the offence(s) of conviction. The value attaching to each unit depended on the offender's disposable weekly income. This system was well thought through and had been preceded by an experiment with unit fines conducted in four magistrates' courts in the late 1980s.[191] It also seems to have worked quite well after being introduced in all magistrates' courts after the relevant provisions of the 1991 UK Act entered into force in October 1992. Unfortunately, a few cases in which very high fines were imposed for apparently trivial offences (mostly, it seems, because courts had not been furnished with correct information about the offenders' means) led to a media outcry.[192] The government panicked and, in a remarkable *volte-face,*

---

[190] On unit fines generally, see Elena Kantorowicz-Reznichenko and Michael Faure (eds), *Day Fines in Europe: Assessing Income-Based Sanctions in Criminal Justice Systems* (Cambridge University Press, 2021); Sally T Hillsman and Judith A Greene, "The use of fines as an intermediate sanction" in James M Byrne, Arthur J Lurigio and Joan Petersilia (eds), *Smart Sentencing: The Emergence of Intermediate Sanctions* (Sage Publications, 1992), Chap 8; Susan Turner, "Day-fine projects launched in four jurisdictions" (1992) 3(6) *Overcrowded Times* 5.

[191] Martin Wasik and Richard D Taylor, *Blackstone's Guide to the Criminal Justice Act 1991* (Blackstone Press, 1991), 69.

[192] Andrew Ashworth, *Sentencing and Criminal Justice,* 4th ed. (Cambridge University Press, 2005), 306, noting the high-profile case in which a man was

repealed ss 18 and 19 of the 1991 UK Act, as well as significantly amending some of its other provisions, in 1993.[193] Unit fines were therefore given no meaningful opportunity to prove themselves but, had they been retained, they might well have been effective.

12–88 Perhaps there is one lesson to be learned from the English experience, and that relates to the need for some reasonable limit on the fines that may be imposed for minor offences, irrespective of the offenders' means. In principle, there may be nothing wrong with imposing a large fine on a very rich offender, even for a low-level offence. On a more visceral level, however, it is difficult to accept that if two offenders engaged in the exact same conduct (speeding, for example), one could be fined €50 while another could be fined €1,000. There may consequently be an argument for imposing some limit (which would be periodically revised) on the amount of disposable weekly income that could be adopted for the purpose of computing a fine. This, admittedly, would undercut the fundamental policy of matching fines with offenders' means. However, any limit adopted for this purpose could be set sufficiently high to ensure that reasonably heavy fines could still be imposed on rich offenders. Unit fines undoubtedly add to a court's administrative workload because they necessitate an enquiry into the disposable income of each offender on whom a fine is being imposed. Identifying and verifying disposable income could be a time-consuming task, in some instances at least. However, the English experiment, brief though it was, suggests that it is by no means an insuperable task. The same held true of various American experiments with unit fines.[194] In Ireland, the idea of unit fines was twice considered by the Law Reform Commission which recognised that they had some merit but which ultimately decided not to recommend their introduction, partly because of potential difficulties in identifying offenders' means and partly because of the need to avoid any constitutional difficulties that might arise if summary offences were punishable with very high fines as a result of the unit system.[195]

12–89 The Fines Act 2010 (the '2010 Act') introduced a new system for setting and updating maximum fines. Since it entered into force, maximum fines following summary conviction are no longer legislatively expressed in specific amounts (e.g., €1,000) but by reference to one of five classes (A to E). A class A fine means one not exceeding €5,000, class B not exceeding

---

fined £1,200 for dropping a crisp packet on the street, although the reason he was fined £100 per unit is that he had failed to disclose his income to the court.

[193] Criminal Justice Act 1993, s 65. See Andrew Ashworth and Bryan Gibson, "The Criminal Justice Act 1993: (2) Altering the sentencing framework" [1994] Crim LR 101. The abolition of unit fines by the 1993 Act was described as "perhaps the most astonishing *volte face* in the history of the English criminal justice system": Michael Cavadino and James Dignam, *The Penal System: An Introduction*, 2nd ed. (Sage, 1997), 211.

[194] Beth A Colgan, "Graduating economic sanctions according to ability to pay" (2017) 103 Iowa LR 53.

[195] Law Reform Commission, *Report on the Indexation of Fines* (1991) and *Report on the Indexation of Fines: A Review of Developments* (2002).

€4,000, class C not exceeding €2,500, class D not exceeding €1,000 and class E not exceeding €500. The 2010 Act also provides for the conversion of maximum fines specified in older statutes to the new categories. The values attached to each of the five classes may be revised though this has not happened since the 2010 Act entered into force. There is always some concern about increasing the maximum fines attaching to summary offences lest this might take an offence out of the minor offence category and thereby place it beyond the constitutional jurisdiction of the District Court.[196] However, with changes in the value of money, it is improbable that an increase in the value of a class A fine, possibly to as much as €10,000, with commensurate adjustments to the lower categories, would have this effect. Indictable offences, unless dealt with summarily, can carry much higher maximum fines, sometimes running to tens of millions of Euro.[197] Quite commonly, as noted earlier, indictable offences are expressed to be punishable with a fine, without any specified maximum, a term of imprisonment up to a specified maximum or both.[198] In that event, a court has complete discretion as to the fine to be imposed in a specific case, though subject always to the requirements of the proportionality principle.

Fine default is an enduring problem for which it is difficult to find a satisfactory solution. Traditionally, imprisonment was the only sanction for failure to pay a fine, though with growing pressure on prison space, those committed for fine default often spent very little time in custody. The Fines (Payment and Recovery) Act 2014 provides for the option of paying a fine by instalments and introduces some additional enforcement mechanisms including recovery and attachment orders. A court may appoint a receiver to recover the amount due under an unpaid fine, and the receiver may, for this purpose, seize and sell property belonging to the defaulter. Where the defaulter is employed under a contract of employment or in receipt of an occupational pension, the court may order the employer to deduct specified sums from the defaulter's earning and pay those sums towards the satisfaction of the fine in the manner directed by the court. Where it is considered inappropriate to make a recovery or attachment order or where such an order has failed to yield any proceeds, a court may order community service, as described above under 'Community Service'. However, as noted there, imprisonment remains the ultimate sanction where all else fails. **12–90**

9. Probation

Etymologically, 'probation' means 'being put to the test', and this conveys **12–91**

[196] Chap 2 above. See also Law Reform Commission Reports, note 195 above.

[197] Competition offences, for example, can carry fines up to €50 million or 20 per cent of turnover for the previous financial year, whichever is greater (Competition Act 2002, s 8 as amended by Competition (Amendment) Act 2022, s 9).

[198] See, for example, Non-Fatal Offences against the Person Act 1997, ss 3 and 4.

the essence of probation as it developed in the late 19th century as a means of dealing with offenders. Being placed on probation affords an offender an opportunity to prove that he or she can refrain from crime and, in some instances, abide by further conditions for a defined period. Probation orders are primarily intended to assist rather than punish offenders, and they are thus intended to be rehabilitative. What the Saskatchewan Court of Appeal had to say in *R v Taylor* is equally relevant in Ireland:

> "Apart from the wording of the provision, the innate character of a probation order is such that is seeks to influence the future behaviour of the offender. More specifically, it seeks to secure "the good conduct" of the offender and deter him from committing other offences. It does not particularly seek to reflect the seriousness of the offence or the offender's degree of culpability. Nor does it particularly seek to fill the need for denunciation of the offence or the general deterrence of others to commit the same or similar offences. Depending upon the specific conditions of the order there may well be a punitive aspect to a probation order but punishment is not the dominant or an inherent purpose. It is perhaps not even a secondary purpose but is more in the nature of a consequence of an offender's compliance with one or more the specific conditions with which he or she may find it hard to comply."[199]

12–92 As indicated in this passage, probation conditions may be punitive, or be perceived as such by an offender, to the extent that they infringe on liberty or impose some positive obligations. However, the ultimate purpose is to advance offenders' welfare and interests, principally by helping and encouraging them to refrain from further criminal conduct.

12–93 Probation in Ireland remains governed by the Probation of Offenders Act 1907 (the '1907 Act'), one of several progressive measures introduced by the Liberal Party while it was in power at Westminster towards the end of the first decade of the 20th century. Section 1 of the 1907 Act, the key provision for sentencing purposes, differentiates between those who are charged before a court of summary jurisdiction (the District Court) and those convicted on indictment in one of the higher criminal courts. The District Court has the option of dismissing a charge without proceeding to a conviction even if satisfied that the charge is proved. It may also grant a conditional discharge. Where a person is convicted on indictment of an imprisonable offence, the court is limited to granting a conditional discharge.

12–94 Under s 1(1), if the District Court is satisfied that the charge is proved, "but it is of opinion that, having regard to the character, antecedents, age, health, or mental condition of the person charged, or to the trivial nature of the offence, or to the extenuating circumstances under which

[199] (1997) 122 CCC(3d) 376 at 394, quoted with approval by the Canadian Supreme Court in *R v Proulx* [2000] 1 SCR 61, para 32. In *R v Shoker* [2006] 2 SCR 399, 408 the Supreme Court noted that probation had traditionally been viewed as a rehabilitative sentencing tool because "[t]he probationer remains free to live in the community but certain restraints on his freedom are imposed for the purpose of facilitating his rehabilitation and protecting society".

the offence was committed, it is inexpedient to inflict any punishment or any other than a nominal punishment, or that it is expedient to release the offender on probation", it may, "without proceeding to a conviction" (1) dismiss the charge or (2) discharge the person conditionally on his or her entering into a recognizance to be of good behaviour and to appear for conviction and sentence at any time during a period not exceeding three years, if called upon to do so. This is a valuable provision as it permits certain defendants to escape formal conviction even if the court is satisfied that they committed the offence charged. A criminal record, even for a relatively minor offence, may have severe adverse consequences far outweighing any formal punishment imposed. For example, a conviction for possessing even a small quantity of drugs of personal use (contrary to s 3 of the Misuse of Drugs Act 1977) may seriously affect a person's employment prospects or their freedom to travel to certain other countries. Yet, if the drug is cannabis, the most severe penalty that may be imposed on a first or second conviction is a modest fine. The power to spare a defendant a formal conviction is therefore a useful and beneficial jurisdiction for a court to possess. It is all the more important where there is no provision, or only very restrictive provisions, for expunging criminal records.

The District Court may take a wide range of offence- and offender-related factors into account when deciding if it should dismiss the charge outright (commonly described as giving the benefit of the Probation Act) or grant a conditional discharge. The latter option involves probation in the true and literal sense: the defendant is being put to the test for a specified period during which he or she must be of good behaviour or else risk being convicted and sentenced for the original offence.[200] **12–95**

The power to dismiss a charge, even where proved, is obviously one to be exercised judiciously, although it is clearly not confined to first-time offenders. There is nothing in the text of the subsection to prevent its application to repeat offenders, even those who have already received the benefit of the Probation Act. However, the application of s 1(1) has been restricted by several statutory provisions, notably in the area of road traffic law. It may not be applied in respect of most of the offences, including drink driving, created by the Road Traffic Act 2010. The three factors, or sets of factors, a court must consider when deciding if it should apply s 1(1) of the 1907 Act are listed disjunctively. It may have regard to the character, etc of the defendant *or* the trivial nature of the offence *or* the extenuating circumstances in which the offence was committed. A defendant's personal characteristics might therefore justify the dismissal of a charge or the grant of conditional release even where the offence could not realistically be described as trivial.[201] **12–96**

An absolute discharge may not be granted to a person convicted on **12–97**

---

[200] Probation of Offenders Act 1907, s 6(5).

[201] *McClelland v Brady* [1918] 2 IR 63.

indictment. Under s 1(2) of the 1907 Act, a court, having regard to the same factors as are listed in s 1(1), may, as an alternative to imposing imprisonment, discharge the offender conditionally "on his entering into a recognizance, with or without sureties, to be of good behaviour and to appear for sentence when called on at any time during such period, not exceeding three years, as may be specified in the order". A recognisance is effectively a formal undertaking to a court in which a person acknowledges their obligation, under pain of penalty or forfeiture, to fulfil one or more specified conditions. Under s 6(5) of the 1907 Act, where a court is satisfied that a person granted conditional release has failed to observe any of the conditions of the recognisance it may convict and sentence him or her in respect of the original offence. A person granted conditional release under s 1(2) of the 1907 Act will already have been convicted, so the court can proceed directly to sentence. In such a case, the court may impose any sentence authorised by law for the original offence.

12–98 The only conditions that must be specified in a conditional discharge recognisance are that the offender will be of good behaviour and will appear for sentence if called upon to do so during a specified period that may not exceed three years. However, by virtue of s 2 of the 1907 Act, other conditions may be inserted at the court's discretion. First, it may require the offender to be under the supervision of a named person (in effect a probation officer) and an order containing such a condition is characterised in the Act as a probation order. Secondly, the court may insert further conditions "with respect to residence, abstention from intoxicating liquor, and any other matters, as the court may, having regard to the particular circumstances of the case, consider necessary for preventing a repetition of the same offence, or the commission of other offences".[202] A breach of any of these conditions may trigger the enforcement mechanism in s 6 of the 1907 Act. Courts have considerable discretion in selecting conditions for inclusion in a recognisance, provided they have a crime preventive purpose. However, any such condition should be reasonable having regard to the offender's circumstances, a requirement discussed above in connection with suspended sentences. One recurring criticism of probation as it operates in the United States is that it often becomes, in reality, a prelude rather than an alternative to imprisonment because of the frequency with which probationers are incarcerated for technical violations.[203] This is obviously something to guard against.

12–99 Conditions should not interfere with a defendant's human rights any more than strictly necessary, if at all. After all, the purpose of probation is to encourage the person to live an ordinary, productive and law-abiding

[202] Probation of Offenders Act 1907, s 2(2) as substituted by Criminal Justice Administration Act 1914, s 8.

[203] Fiona Doherty, "Obey all laws and be good: Probation and the meaning of recidivism" (2016) 104 Georgetown LJ 291; MS Phelps, HN Dickens and DAT Beadle, "Are supervision violations filling prisons? The role of probation, parole, and new offences in driving mass incarceration" (2023) *Socius* 9.

life, an objective that is difficult to achieve if the person feels unfairly singled out by being subject to restrictions that do not apply to others. American courts have struck down conditions found to be unreasonable or unconnected with the nature of the offence, as when a woman convicted of robbery was given probation on condition that she did not become pregnant while single,[204] or when a young man convicted of drug possession was given probation on condition that he got and maintained a short haircut for the duration of the probation.[205] In the latter case, the condition was deemed incompatible with the defendant's constitutional right to self-expression and unrelated to his rehabilitation,

Section 1(2) applies where a person has been convicted on indictment "of any offence punishable with imprisonment". In the past, questions were raised as to whether the subsection could apply to an offence punishable with penal servitude only, but that is no longer an issue. Virtually all offences triable on indictment will be punishable with imprisonment, but some serious offences might be punishable with a fine only. For instance, s 36 (now repealed) of the Defamation Act 2009 created an indictable offence of blasphemy punishable solely with a fine not exceeding €25,000. Arguably, s 2(2) does not apply to non-imprisonable indictable offences. After all, it further states that a court may grant a conditional discharge "in lieu of imposing a sentence of imprisonment". The dominant legislative purpose was probably to spare an offender imprisonment whenever it was possible to do so, having regard to specified factors (e.g. the offender's age or character). **12–100**

Literally construed, s 1(2) of the 1907 Act permits the grant of a conditional discharge following conviction on indictment for any offence punishable with imprisonment. After all, the trivial nature of the offence is just one of the factors that may be considered for that purpose. Yet as a matter of policy, a conditional discharge could scarcely ever be appropriate for a very serious offence. Clearly, it has no application to an offence, such as murder, which carries an entirely mandatory sentence. Strangely enough, the only express statutory prohibitions on the use of s 1(2) occur in the Air Navigation and Transport Acts 1973-1975 which also are also unique in prohibiting suspended sentences for certain offences. These restrictions seem to have been required by the international conventions to which those statutes were giving effect. Conviction on indictment does not, of course, necessarily imply the commission of a serious offences. Theft, for example, is an indictable offence but, even where an alleged theft is very minor in nature, the accused may opt for jury trial rather than summary disposal.[206] A theft or other acquisitive crime might be committed out of extreme need which could constitute an extenuating circumstance, one of **12–101**

---

[204] *People v Dominguez* 256 Cal App 2d 623; 64 Cal Rptr 290 (1967). Generally speaking, however, there are few legislative restrictions on probation conditions. See Louis Polonsky, "Limitations upon trial court discretion in imposing conditions of probation" (1974) 8 Georgia LR 466.

[205] *Inman v The State* 124 Ga App 190; 181 SE2d 413 (1971).

[206] Criminal Justice (Theft and Fraud Offences) Act 2001, s 53.

the factors listed in both s 1(1) and s 1(2) of the 1907 Act. The same might be said of provocation in an assault case, depending on the particular facts.

12–102 There is very little judicial guidance on the suitability of a conditional discharge for serious offences, though it is unlikely be countenanced for anything other than an offence of a low to medium level for gravity. In *People (DPP) v Jagoe*[207] the Court of Criminal Appeal declined to find unduly lenient a conditional discharge for an assault which, from the limited facts given, seems to have been committed by hitting another person across the face with a bottle. While observing that a conditional discharge would very seldom be appropriate in such a case, the court acknowledged that it was legally permissible since s 1(2) applied to all offences punishable with imprisonment. More recently in *People (DPP) v O'Mahony*[208] the Court of Appeal found an order under s 1(2) to be unduly lenient for an assault committed during a soccer match which left the victim with reasonably serious injuries. A complicating factor in that case, however, was that the trial judge seems to have omitted to make the discharge conditional on good behaviour or to specify a period within which the defendant was to appear for sentence if called upon to do so. In effect, the order amounted to an absolute discharge which is not available under s 1(2). The Court of Appeal held that in view of the nature and gravity of the assault, a discharge under s 1(2) amounted to an error of principle and it substituted an 18-month suspended sentence.

12–103 The 1907 Act (s 3) provided for the appointment of probation officers, but it was only towards the end of the 20th century that a well-resourced professional probation service developed in Ireland. The work of the probation service has greatly expanded in many different directions. In 2019, it dealt with more than 16,500 offenders referred to it by the courts as well as completing 12,500 probation assessment reports and 3,500 community service assessment reports.[209] Probation officers' duties, as specified in the 1907 Act (s 4) include visiting those under their supervision, ensuring that the supervisees observe the conditions of their recognisance, and reporting to the court as appropriate. Importantly, the probation officer has one other duty, namely, "to advise, assist, and befriend" the offender and enable him or her to find suitable employment.[210] The significance of this provision is that it reflects, indeed, mandates, a supportive, caring relationship between the Probation Service and its clients. A recurring criticism of probation reform in other countries, including England and Wales, over the past 30 years is that they have made probation part of the apparatus of punishment and have replaced the traditional ethic of support with a culture of managerialism. The English Criminal Justice Act 1991 rendered all probation orders community sentences and part of the continuum of punishment that ranged from a discharge to imprisonment. Those community sentences

207 [2008] IECCA 128.
208 [2019] IECA 311.
209 Probation Service Annual Report 2019 (2020).
210 Probation of Offenders Act 1907, s 4(d).

then became obliged "to demonstrate their punitive credentials" which, in turn, resulted in probation officers becoming much concerned than previously with enforcing compliance.[211] However, the one-to-one relationship between probation officer and probationer has been a constant throughout much of the history of probation and is rightly seen as critical to successful outcomes.[212] Offenders respond best when their supervising officers show empathy and understanding and become participants in the process rather than enforcers.[213]

In 2014, the Irish government published the heads of a Criminal Justice (Community Sanctions) Bill which it remains committed to enacting. This proposes to repeal the Probation of Offenders Act 1907 and introduce a new range of community-based sanctions, some of which are very similar to existing probationary measures. It provides, among many other things, that a probation officer shall "aim to establish a positive relationship with the person in order to supervise, guide and assist him or her". This is a welcome provision, assuming it is eventually enacted, as it reflects a continuing commitment to a relational vision of probation where the one-to-one relationship between the officer and the offender is accepted as a key element of successful supervision. Further, it is important to be broadminded in measuring 'success' for this purpose. The commission of a further offence during or after the probationary period should not automatically lead to the probation being condemned as a failure. It may have been successful in many respects, such as giving offenders an insight into their offending behaviour or equipping them with coping skills which, in turn, may promote desistance in the longer term. Research shows that desistance is seldom an event in the sense that the offender suddenly decides to stop. Rather it is usually a more gradual process during which the offender 'slows down' and, with appropriate external supports and inner motivation, will eventually desist entirely.[214]As Daniel Glaser once wrote, "those who have lived in both the criminal and conventional **12–104**

---

211 Gwen Robinson and Pamela Ugwudike, "Investing in 'toughness': Probation, enforcement and legitimacy" (2012) 51(3) *Howard Journal of Criminal Justice* 300. See also Mike Nellis, "Probation values for the 1990s" (1995) 34(1) *Howard Journal of Criminal Justice* 19; Mike Nellis, "'Into the field of corrections': The end of English probation in the early 21st century?" (2004) 35 Cambrian LR 115.

212 Ros Burnett and Fergus McNeill, "The place of the officer-offender relationship in assisting offenders to desist from crime" (2005) 52(3) *Probation Journal* 221.

213 Sue Rex, "Desistance from offending: Experiences of probation" (1999) 38(4) *Howard Journal of Criminal Justice* 366.

214 There is now a voluminous body of desistance research. For an evaluation of the main research studies, see Stephen Farrall et al, *Criminal Careers in Transition: The Social Context of Desistance from Crime* (Oxford University Press, 2014). See also Anthony E Bottoms and Joanna Shapland, "Steps towards desistance among male young adult recidivists" in Stephen Farrall et al (eds), *Escape Routes: Contemporary Perspectives on Life after Punishment* (Routledge, 2011), 43; Ros Burnett, "The will and the ways to becoming an ex-offender" (2010) 54 *International Journal of Offender Therapy and Comparative Criminology* 663; H Kemshall et al, "Making desistance real: Implementing a desistance focused approach in a community rehabilitation company (CRC)" (2021) 68 *Probation*

social worlds may walk a zig-zag path between the two".[215] The ambition is obviously to keep them permanently on the conventional path, but that will often require some effort and persistence. An obsession with re-offending when judging the success of probation, as reflected in the British government's 'pay by results' scheme introduced about a decade ago when probation was partly privatised, fails to reflect the core values of probation and the diverse ways in which it can assist offenders.[216]

12–105 Probation officers supervising children are likewise obliged to "visit, assist, advise and befriend the child and, where feasible, the child's parents or guardian or other adult in whose residence the child may be residing".[217] A provision of this nature is even more imperative in the case of child offenders, given that the dominant consideration is to assist and encourage them, not only to desist from further offending, but also to achieve their full potential as they grow into adulthood.

10. Compensation

12–106 Sentencing statutes in other jurisdictions commonly list 'reparation' as a permissible sentencing purpose. This might cover a variety of measures including some kind of restitution or atonement to the community, especially where there is no direct or identifiable victim. Monetary compensation is the most obvious form of reparation when a victim has suffered loss or injury as a result of the offence. In Ireland, the Criminal Justice Act 1993 permits a compensation order to be made by any court for any offence. Section 6(1) provides:

> "Subject to the provisions of this section, on conviction of any person of an offence, the court, instead of or in addition to dealing with him in any other way, may, unless it sees reason to the contrary, make (on application or otherwise) an order (in this Act referred to as a "compensation order") requiring him to pay compensation in respect of any personal injury or loss resulting from that offence (or any other offence that is taken into consideration by the court in determining sentence) to any person (in this Act referred to as the "injured party") who has suffered such injury or loss."

12–107 As thus worded, the subsection applies to all offences, though it can

Journal 347 (stressing the importance of 'identity shift' in the transition of a pro-social identity).

[215] Daniel Glaser, *The Effectiveness of a Prison and Parole System* (Bobbs-Merrill, 1964), 54.

[216] Loraine Gelsthorpe and Madeline-Sophie Abbas, "Supervising offenders in the community: Vision, values and human rights" in Leanne Weber, Elaine Fishwick and Marinella Marmo (eds), *The Routledge International Handbook of Criminology and Human Rights* (Routledge, 2016), Chap 45; Chris Fox and Kevin Albertson, "Payment by results and social impact bonds in the criminal justice sector: New challenges for the concept of evidence-based policy" (2011) 11 *Criminology and Criminal Justice* 395; Lol Burke and Steve Collett, *Delivering Rehabilitation: The Politics, Governance and Control of Probation* (Routledge, 2014).

[217] Children Act 2001, s 259.

scarcely be fully applicable to murder which, since it carries a mandatory life sentence, could not be punished solely with a compensation order. Compensation, where ordered, is payable to the injured party, and that can include a dependant of a deceased victim. It may also be ordered where a person has been given the benefit of s 1(1) of the Probation of Offenders Act 1907, meaning that no conviction is entered even though the charge was proved.[218] The amount may not exceed what the victim would be entitled to recover in a civil action for the injury concerned, and the District Court may not make an compensation order for an amount exceeding its current jurisdiction in tort. Regard must always be had to the offender's means, with account being taken of his or her financial commitments. In this respect, compensation orders differ from awards of damages in tort actions where a defendant's means are irrelevant. A compensation order may be paid by instalments and at such times as the court considers reasonable.

The Children Act 2001 (s 113) likewise provides that where a court is satisfied of the guilt of a child, it may make a compensation order, either instead of or in addition to any other order, and it may direct that the compensation be paid by the child's parent or guardian. However, before doing so, it must be satisfied that "a wilful failure of the parent or guardian to take care of or to control the child contributed to the child's criminal behaviour". When determining the amount of compensation, if any, to be paid, the court must have regard to the means of the parent or guardian. **12–108**

Court ordered compensation of this nature is one mechanism for providing financial redress to crime victims, though it has obvious limitations. First, no such compensation can be awarded unless the perpetrator of the offence has been identified and convicted. Many crimes remain unresolved, and it can never be guaranteed that any identified suspect will be prosecuted or eventually convicted. There is always a certain amount of attrition within the criminal process. The number of persons convicted and sentenced following prosecution typically represents no more than a reasonably small percentage of those who have actually committed offences. This seems to be especially true of sexual offences, domestic violence and other violent offences.[219] Further, many of those who are convicted will lack the means to pay compensation, and the vast majority of those sentenced to imprisonment will never be in a position to do so. Many countries, including Ireland, have therefore established publicly funded compensation schemes for victims of crime, and of violent crime **12–109**

[218] Criminal Justice 1993, s 6(12)(b).

[219] Mandy Burton et al, *Understanding the Progression of Serious Cases through the Criminal Justice System: Evidence drawn from a selection of casefiles* (Ministry of Justice, 2012); D McPhee et al, "Criminal justice responses to domestic violence and abuse in England: An analysis of case attrition and inequalities using police data" (2022) 32 *Policing and Society* 963; Katrin Hohl and Elizabeth A Stanko, "Complaints of rape and the criminal justice system: Fresh evidence on the attrition problem in England and Wales" (2015) 12 *European Journal of Criminology* 324.

in particular. Indeed, the existence of such a scheme is now mandated by EU law.[220] The Irish scheme has already been described in Chap 11 in the context of providing services for victims.

12–110 As a sentencing measure, the compensation order gives rise to two significant issues. First, it may be asked if compensation should ever be imposed as the sole penalty for an offence. Secondly, there is a question about the impact, if any, an offer or payment of compensation should have on the primary penalty imposed for an offence. As to the first of these questions, it is undoubtedly true that a compensation order may be viewed as a punishment by the offender, though this will depend on the amount involved and the offender's means. It may also be welcomed by the victim. Yet, if compensation is the sole order made, as s 6 of the Criminal Justice Act 1993 permits, it results in what is effectively a private transaction between the offender and victim. The payment of compensation from one to the other brings the matter to an end. However, the essence of a crime is that it involves a wrong against society (as well as against the victim where there is one), and the essence of criminal punishment is that it reflects society's condemnation of the offending conduct. As Andrew Ashworth has written:

> "The predominant purpose of criminal liability is to declare public disapproval of the offender's conduct, by means of public trial and conviction, and to punish the offender by imposing a penal sanction (although this may in some cases be no more than a nominal measure)."[221]

12–111 As far as we know, a compensation order is seldom imposed as the sole penalty for an offence. It could, of course, be punitive if the payment called for some sacrifice on the part of the offender, though the debt, so to speak, is being paid to an individual rather than to society.

12–112 The impact that payment of compensation should have on the primary penalty has received a good deal of judicial consideration. Essentially, the law is now well settled. An offer of compensation, even if accepted, will not save an offender from imprisonment where that is the deserved sanction for the offence. Offenders, however affluent, should not be able to buy their way out of imprisonment.[222] Payment of compensation may be treated as a mitigating factor, especially if it imposes a real hardship on the offender.[223] Even then, it can have no more than a limited mitigatory effect. In *People (DPP) v McCabe*[224] the defendant, who pleaded guilty to aggravated sexual assault, offered £15,000 to the victim and this was accepted. He was a farmer who had to sell off his entire herd of cattle

---

[220] Council Directive 2004/80/EC relating to compensation to crime victims.

[221] Andrew Ashworth, "Punishment and compensation: Victims, offenders and the state" (1986) 6 *Oxford Journal of Legal Studies* 86, 89.

[222] *People (DPP) v McCabe* [2005] IECCA 90; *People (DPP) v McLaughlin* [2005] IECCA 91; [2005] 3 IR 198. *People (DPP) v Lyons* [2014] IECCA 27; *People (DPP) v Duffy* [2023] IESC 1.

[223] *People (DPP) v McDonagh* [2020] IECA 323.

[224] [2005] IECCA 90.

to raise this amount. The trial judge imposed an entirely suspended sentence, and this was the subject of an undue leniency application by the DPP. While the Court of Criminal Appeal held that the trial judge erred in treating the offer and acceptance of compensation as a justification for imposing a suspended sentence, it was nonetheless satisfied that there were other mitigating factors that rendered the case sufficiently exceptional to warrant a suspended sentence.

As already noted, s 6(1) of the Criminal Justice Act 1993 permits a court to make a compensation order "instead of or in addition to dealing with [the offender] in any other way". Such orders are seldom made, at least for offences of any appreciable degree of seriousness. It is far more common for an offender to make an offer of compensation that may or may not be accepted by the victim. Section 6 of the 1993 Act which seems to have been inspired, in its essential terms, by s 35 of England's Powers of the Criminal Courts Act 1973,[225] is phrased in open-ended terms. It applies when any court is sentencing an offender for any offence although it cannot, of course, be imposed as the sole penalty for an offence carrying a mandatory sentence. The District Court may not make order compensation for an amount greater than its jurisdiction in tort actions (currently €15,000). Otherwise, the amount "shall not exceed the amount of damages that, in the opinion of the court, the injured party would be entitled to recover in a civil action against the convicted person in respect of the injury or loss concerned". At the same time, the court must have regard to the offender's means and financial commitments. **12–113**

In a serious case, a court would have to undertake quite a complicated exercise to determine the appropriate amount of compensation. If it were a tort action, a court would be furnished with evidence about the nature and impact of the victim's injuries. There might well be conflicting evidence which the court would have to analyse and evaluate before coming to a decision. A sentencing hearing is scarcely an appropriate forum for making such a decision in a serious or complex case, especially with the additional complication that the offender's means and financial commitments must also be ascertained (which may be no easy task) and taken into consideration. Following the introduction of compensation orders in England and Wales in 1973, the Court of Appeal repeatedly reminded criminal courts that civil actions were still available for injuries and damage caused by criminal acts. It accepted that compensation orders could be made in simple, straightforward cases, though they should not involve prolonged instalment payments.[226] In *R v Daly*,[227] for example, two compensation orders had been made against the appellant, one for £37.40 payable at the rate of 50p a week, and another for £1,200, payable at the rate of £3.50 a week. The latter would take about six years to discharge in full, and the appellant earned at most £27 a week. The Court of Appeal **12–114**

[225] Compensation orders in England and Wales are now governed by the Sentencing Act 2020, ss 133 – 146.
[226] PS Atiyah, "Compensation orders and civil liability" [1979] Crim LR 504.
[227] [1974] 1 WLR 133; (1974) 58 Cr App R 333.

reduced the second order to £600 in order to shorten the time over which it would have to be paid. In so doing, it said:

> "It must be remembered by courts making compensation orders that the civil remedy for the damage still exists. The machinery of the compensation order is a quick and simple way of dealing with the claim in simple cases, and in particular it should not be used where the recompense involves a weekly payment over such a long period as the present."[228]

12–115 In Ireland, the Supreme Court has articulated a similar principle largely, it seems, for the same reasons as were outlined in *Daly*, although it did not refer to that case.[229]

[228] [1974] 1 WLR 133, 134; (1974) 58 Cr App R 333, 335.
[229] *People (DPP) v Duffy* [2023] IESC 1, para 97.

CHAPTER 13

STRUCTURING SENTENCING DISCRETION: GUIDANCE AND GUIDELINES

Ireland has traditionally had a highly discretionary sentencing system, as did all other common law countries until quite recently. The main formal constraint on judicial sentencing power was the maximum sentence prescribed by statute for the offence of conviction. Courts of summary jurisdiction were (and remain) subject to more general jurisdictional limits, especially on the use of imprisonment. In Ireland, for example, the District Court may not impose a prison sentence exceeding 12 months for any one offence or two years for a combination of offences. Courts were obliged to have regard to general sentencing principles, such as those described in Chap 5, but these still left considerable scope for exercising discretion. Irish sentencing is now undergoing considerable change in this respect, mainly because of guidelines that have been judicially developed for some commonly prosecuted serious offences. Moreover, the Judicial Council Act 2019 created a Sentencing Guidelines and Information Committee ('SGIC') tasked with the development of formal guidelines for adoption by the Judicial Council. The SGIC has begun its work and is expected to produce various kinds of guidelines in the years ahead.[1] **13–01**

This chapter is divided as follows. Parts 1 and 2 deal with discretion and consistency as those concepts apply to sentencing. Part 3 discusses sentencing guidance and guidelines in general terms. Part 4 provides an overview of American sentencing guideline systems. Part 5 deals in some detail with the evolution and operation of guidelines in England and Wales. Part 6 briefly describes the emerging Scottish guideline system. Part 7 describes the gradual judicial acceptance of sentencing guidelines in Ireland, and it analyses those sections of the Judicial Council Act 2019 providing for the development and adoption of formal guidelines. Finally, **13–02**

---

1 As a consequence of *Delaney v Personal Injuries Board* [2024] IESC 10, in which a majority of the Supreme Court declared unconstitutional s 7(2)(g) of the Judicial Council Act 2019 which required the Council to adopt personal injury guidelines, it seems certain that s 7(2)(h) which is phrased in virtually identical terms and requires the Council to adopt and publish sentencing guidelines is also unconstitutional. As matters stand at the time of writing (July 2024), it appears that the SGIC can continue to work on developing guidelines but they cannot take effect until legislation is passed providing for some other system of adoption.

Part 8 offers some observations on the merits of guidelines and their compatibility with the values that should underpin a sentencing system.

1. Discretion

13–03 It has long been accepted that a political or legal system governed entirely by pre-ordained rules can be neither just nor efficient.[2] More than two millennia ago, Aristotle stressed the impossibility of creating general rules that will produce just outcomes in all the situations to which they apply. As he wrote, "all law is universal, and there are some things about which it is not possible to pronounce rightly in general terms".[3] Because of the legislator's inability to foresee all those situations, some strategy is needed to permit rules to be interpreted creatively or, indeed, ignored entirely if the interests of justice do demand. The strategy Aristotle proposed was *epieikeia*, usually translated for this purpose as 'equity' though it can also mean fairness, decency or clemency. Modern concepts of the rule of law no longer view discretion as antithetical to law. Sir Edward Coke's preference of the 'golden and straight metwand of the law' over the 'crooked cord of discretion' is still occasionally invoked by opponents of discretion, although, in fact, he seems to have been equating discretion with private opinion.[4] Today, however, the predominant view is reflected in Lord Bingham's statement:

> "The rule of law does not require that official or judicial decision-makers should be deprived of all discretion, but it does require that no discretion be unconstrained so as to be potentially arbitrary. No discretion may be legally unfettered."[5]

13–04 In an earlier work, he had defined discretion in terms which capture the essence of sentencing and other legal decision-making:

> "[A]n issue falls within a judge's discretion if, being governed by no rule of law, its resolution depends on the individual judge's assessment (within such boundaries as have been laid down) of what it is fair and just to do in the particular case. He has no discretion in making his findings of fact. He has no discretion in his rulings on the law. But when, having made any necessary finding of fact and any necessary ruling of law, he has to choose

---

[2] Keith Hawkins, "The use of legal discretion: Perspectives from law and social science" In Keith Hawkins (ed.), *The Uses of Discretion* (Clarendon Press, 1992), 11 ("Discretion is a central and inevitable part of the legal order").

[3] Aristotle, *Ethics*, translated by JAK Thomson, revised ed (Penguin Books, 1976), 199. See also Christoph Horn, "Epieikeia: The competence of the perfectly just person in Aristotle" in Burkhard Reis (ed), *The Virtuous Life in Greek Ethics* (Cambridge University Press, 2006), Chap 7. For perceptive analyses of the relationship between discretion and the rule of law, see Lawrence B Solum, "Equity and the rule of law" and Steven J Burton, "Particularism, discretion, and the rule of law" both in Ian Shapiro (ed), *The Rule of Law*, Nomos XXXVI (New York University Press, 1995).

[4] 4 Inst 41; Co Litt 227b.

[5] Tom Bingham, *The Rule of Law* (Allen Lane, 2010), 54.

> between different courses of action, orders, penalties or remedies he then exercises a discretion. It is only when he reaches the stage of asking himself what is the fair and just thing to do or order in the instant case that he embarks on the exercise of a discretion."[6]

The boundaries of permissible discretion in respect of any class of decisions should therefore be clearly defined, and it should be exercised in a rational, transparent, coherent and non-discriminatory manner. Properly used, discretion permits "focused, tailored, case-specific solutions".[7] Ultimately, as Gleeson CJ remarked in *Wong v The Queen*,[8] it must be accepted that all discretionary decision-making will probably result in some degree of inconsistency, but "there are limits beyond which such inconsistency itself constitutes a form of injustice". **13–05**

Discretion should not too readily be equated with choice, as it sometimes is. Choice, after all, can mean freedom to do whatever one wants in a given situation or, more commonly, freedom to select from a range of available options without having to justify choosing one over the others. Of course, discretion always entails making a choice but, when vested in public officials, including judges, it must be exercised in a rational, principled and non-discriminatory manner. As HLA Hart argued, discretion is an intellectual virtue, a near-synonym of practical wisdom, because it is "the power of discerning or distinguishing what in various fields is appropriate to be done".[9] Discernment is key to the proper exercise of discretion which, by this account, is essentially an exercise in judgment. However, Hart was equally clear on the need for discretion within the legal system because of what he called "relative ignorance of fact" and "relative indeterminacy of aim".[10] We cannot predict all the problems and issues that courts and other decision-makers will be required to resolve, and we often have an imperfect understanding of aims. Even scholars who are less than enamoured with discretion accept the practical need for it, provided it is carefully confined, structured and checked.[11] **13–06**

Sentencing is undoubtedly one legal context in which the interests of justice demand a significant element of judicial discretion. It is, after all, **13–07**

---

6 Thomas Bingham, "The discretion of the judge" (1990) Denning LJ 27, later repeated in his address, "Should public law remedies be discretionary" (1991) *Public Law* 64, 67.

7 Daniel Kalderimis, Chris Nixon and Tim Smith, "Certainty and discretion in New Zealand regulation" in Susy Frankel and John Yeabsley (eds), *Framing the Commons: Cross-Cutting Issues in Regulation* (Victoria University Press, 2014), Chap 4.

8 [2001] HCA 64; (2001) 207 CLR 584, para 6.

9 HLA Hart, "Discretion" (2013) 127 Harvard LR 652, 656 (text of paper delivered in 1956). On the context in which the paper was delivered, see Geoffrey C Shaw, "H.L.A. Hart's lost essay: *Discretion* and the legal process school" (2013) 127 Harvard LR 666.

10 Hart, note 9 above, at 661.

11 Kenneth Culp Davis, *Discretionary Justice: A Preliminary Inquiry* (Louisiana State University Press, 1969).

primarily an exercise in judgment rather than calculation.[12] Moreover, what falls to be judged is the offender's moral culpability (broadly construed to include all relevant offence and offender circumstances) which is never amenable to precise quantification. As Lynn Adelman and Jon Deitrich observe:

> "[S]entencing decisions differ from other judicial determinations in that the moral component of the decision is more central. The judge's goal is to arrive at a fair sentence, not to resolve a disputed legal issue. The maxim, "let the punishment fit the crime," refers to moral fitness. This is not to say that sentencing is not also legal. By definition, sentencing is a legal process carried out by legal actors within a legal institutional framework. But when deciding what sentence to impose, a judge seeks to resolve questions of moral culpability and how best to translate such culpability into an appropriate punishment. Because imposing a sentence is in 'substantial part a moral decision, the number of factors that may appropriately affect it is virtually unlimited, as are the weights that may properly be placed on such factors.'"[13]

13–08 Sentencers must also contend with incommensurables. There is scarcely any crime for which a given punishment is intrinsically and universally appropriate. Exceptionally, the death penalty for murder may seem to be truly commensurate, as it involves taking a life for a life. But not necessarily so if the offender had committed several murders or if the perpetrator of one murder can point to personal mitigating factors. The theft of a sum of money might be punished with a fine of the same amount (assuming the offender was able to pay), but even then it has been argued that a commensurate or, a least, an effective sanction should also reflect the probability of being detected.[14] Thus, the fine for stealing €100 where there was a one-in-five chance of being detected should be €500. Consider, however, an unprovoked assault that caused the victim to lose the sight of an eye. Assuming that the infliction of a similar injury on the offender is unavailable as a legal sanction, we must probably resort to imprisonment. Yet the offence itself does not suggest any particular term of imprisonment, whether measured in days, weeks or years, as the 'correct' response. A similar difficulty arises when assessing compensation for personal injuries in tort actions.[15] Judges must therefore select penalties that bear little or no material resemblance to the offending conduct. What is collectively regarded as an appropriate or commensurate punishment for any offence depends on the political culture and prevailing moral sentiment of the time and place. As long ago as the 13th century, Thomas Aquinas argued

---

[12] Tom O'Malley, "Judgment and calculation in the selection of sentence" (2017) 28 *Criminal Law Forum* 361.

[13] Lynn Adelman and Jon Deitrich, "Marvin Frankel's mistakes and the need to rethink federal sentencing" (2008) 13 *Berkeley Journal of Criminal Law* 239, 246. Internal references omitted. See also Antje Du Bois-Pedain, "In defence of substantial sentencing discretion" (2017) 28 *Criminal Law Forum* 391.

[14] Gary S Becker, "Crime and punishment: An economic approach" (1968) 76(2) *Journal of Political Economy* 169.

[15] Philip Sales and Frederick Wilmot-Smith, "Justice for foxes" (2022) 138 LQR 583, 589.

that some principles of natural law translate logically into positive law (eg if there is a principle that one shall not harm any person, it follows as a matter of logical inference that one should not kill or assault another), but that other principles require what he called a determination.[16] In the latter case the civil authorities must determine how exactly they will give effect to the principle. To take Aquinas's own example, there is a fundamental principle that wrongdoers should be punished, but it is up to each jurisdiction to decide on the manner and severity of punishments for various kinds of wrongdoing. That insight remains valid and is reflected in the wide diversity of sentencing practices throughout the world.

Additionally, sentencers must often balance several policy goals, such as desert, deterrence and rehabilitation, which, in the circumstances of a given case, may point in different directions. As Richard Frase has written, "sentencing policy is very complex, requiring compromise and careful balancing of numerous, often competing goals".[17] Unless the goals are clearly prioritised, by statute or otherwise, as they hardly ever are, sentencing outcomes in similar cases will inevitably vary. Different penal purposes can produce different results when applied to the same set of circumstances. Youth or mental disability may be a mitigating factor in a desert-based system but an aggravating factor where deterrence or incapacitation is the dominant purpose. In practice, most jurisdictions operate some kind of hybrid policy (either explicitly or implicitly), and this too has its advantages as long there is guidance on the circumstances in which one purpose should be accorded priority over the others.[18] **13–09**

The major challenge for most sentencing systems is to strike an appropriate balance between discretion and standardisation (which may take the form of rules, principles, presumptive guidelines or some combination of these). Largely unfettered discretion can produce a degree of disparity that will lead to some offenders being treated unjustly. This is not because judges are 'abusing' or 'misusing' their discretion, as is sometimes alleged, but because of the absence of any overarching policies or standards to guide them in exercising it. As Gerard Lynch, a senior American federal judge and academic, has written: **13–10**

> "[I]t may or may not be a good idea to approach the problem of intoxicating and addictive substances by criminal prohibition and severe punishments. But we cannot have a coherent public policy on narcotics if half the sentencing judges are fighting a 'war on drugs' and the other half are pursuing non-punitive treatment options. In a democracy, the legislature or its delegates should decide which policy or combination of policies should be pursued, and judges should follow the policy that is thus adopted. Similarly, the law

[16] Thomas Aquinas, *Summa Theologica,* Question 95, Article 2, translated by the Fathers of the English Dominican Province, 2nd ed (1920), < https://www.nlnrac.org/node/225> accessed 21 June 2024.

[17] Richard S Frase, "Is guided discretion sufficient? Overview of state sentencing guidelines" (2000) 44 St Louis Univ LR 425, 436.

[18] Andrew von Hirsch, "Federal sentencing guidelines: Do they provide principled guidance?" (1989) 27 American Crim LR 367, 370-371.

> cannot claim to be fair and just when the same defendant may serve 15 years in prison or receive a short stay in a treatment programme depending on the policy preferences of the judge before whom he happens to appear."[19]

13–11 Similar observations may be made about the sentencing of any category of offence, and not just drug offences. Some degree of variation in judgment is inevitable, and a price worth paying for permitting judges to craft what they genuinely believe to be the fairest and most effective sentences in specific cases. But unconstrained discretion can lead to indefensible variations in the penalties imposed for similar offences. Discretion must therefore be cabined with reasonable bounds, preferably through guidelines that, at a minimum, require judges to apply the same principles when evaluating offence seriousness and the weight to be attributed to offender characteristics. They should also indicate the nature and severity of punishments appropriate for different offences while, again, leaving reasonable scope for the exercise of judgment in this regard.

13–12 Public preoccupation with judicial sentencing discretion tends to obscure the impact of discretionary decision-making, both before and after sentence, by other actors in the criminal justice system. As already discussed in Chap 1, the judicial selection of sentence is one decision point in a long process that begins with the creation of a criminal offence and, assuming a case runs its full course, ends when the sentence has finally been served.[20] Key decisions by police and prosecutors determine the charges preferred against an accused, and this will influence the ultimate sentence, perhaps to a significant degree, while post-sentence executive decisions may, for example, determine how much of a custodial sentence an offender actually serves. Curtailing or eliminating the discretionary powers of one official or group will not necessarily produce the desired results. In fact, history proves that it seldom does.[21] Judicial sentencing discretion could be eliminated by making every offence punishable with a mandatory penalty. Yet, the inflexibility of such a system could be circumvented by, for example, a prosecutorial policy of charging less serious offences than might otherwise be appropriate (or in some instances declining to prosecute at all), or an executive policy of commuting or remitting penalties that seemed unduly harsh in the circumstances. Reducing discretion at one point in the process can lead to its growth at one or more other points.

---

19 Gerard E Lynch, "Letting guidelines be guidelines (and judges be judges)" (2008) 5(2) *Ohio State Journal of Criminal Law* (Supp), 1, 2.

20 James Q Whitman, "Equality in criminal law: The two divergent Western roads" (2009) 1 *Journal of Legal Analysis* 119.

21 Michael Tonry, "Mandatory penalties" (1992) 16 *Crime and Justice* 243; Michael Tonry, "The mostly unintended consequences of mandatory penalties: Two centuries of consistent findings" (2009) 38 *Crime and Justice* 65; Thomas O'Malley, *Sentencing: Towards a Coherent System* (Round Hall, 2011), Chap 4.

2. Consistency

Public concern about inconsistent sentencing is by no means a modern phenomenon. When most felonies carried a mandatory death penalty, as was true in England during the 18th and early 19th centuries, judges had little discretion in sentencing serious cases. Sentencing disparity, at judicial level at any rate, was not then much of a problem. Instead, it was the executive branch of government that really exercised discretion in terms of deciding whether to uphold or commute the death penalty in individual cases. Capital punishment was progressively abolished during the early 19th century, so that by 1838 only eight capital offences remained. It was replaced over time with transportation, penal servitude, imprisonment and, occasionally, corporal punishment. Judicial sentencing discretion increased accordingly and with it came public dissatisfaction with how it was being exercised. Historical research by Leon Radzinowicz, Roger Hood and David Thomas reveals the extent of the apparent disparity in late 19th century sentencing practice and the criticism it attracted.[22] Leading Victorian lawyers including James Fitzjames Stephen and Edward Fry (both judges) and Montague Crackanthorpe (a well-known barrister) published articles in the monthly review, *The Nineteenth Century,* discussing the purposes of punishment and the merits of structuring judicial discretion.[23] Much of the criticism and commentary sounds familiar today. For instance, we find members of parliament condemning lenient sentences imposed for wife-beating (just as a similar concern might now be voiced about sentencing for domestic violence) and the harsh sentences being imposed for housebreaking and petty thefts.[24] **13–13**

Many efforts were made during this era to confine and structure judicial sentencing discretion, beginning with the work of the Criminal Law Commissioners appointed in 1833 to codify the criminal law and ending, for the time being, with the Alverstone Memorandum drawn up by the Lord Chief Justice and a group of High Court judges in 1901. This was effectively a set of rudimentary sentencing guidelines recommending what it described as "a standard of punishment… which should be assumed to be properly applicable, unless the particular case under consideration **13–14**

[22] Leon Radzinowicz and Roger Hood, "Judicial discretion and sentencing standards: Victorian attempts to solve a perennial problem" (1979) 127 Univ Pennsylvania LR 1288. The authors cover much of the same ground in their book *The Emergence of Penal Policy in Victorian and Edwardian England* (Clarendon Press, 1990); David Thomas, *Constraints on judgment: The search for structured discretion in sentencing 1860-1910* (University of Cambridge Institute of Criminology, 1979).

[23] James Fitzjames Stephen, "Variations in the punishment of crime" (May 1885) 17 *The Nineteenth Century* 755; Edward Fry, "Inequality in punishment" (September 1883) 14 *The Nineteenth Century* 517; Montague Crackanthorpe, "Can sentences be standardised?" (January 1900) 47 *The Nineteenth Century* 103; Robert Anderson, "Our absurd system of punishing crime" (February 1901) 49 *The Nineteenth Century* 268.

[24] Radzinowicz and Hood, "Judicial discretion", note 22 above, at 1308-1309, citing parliamentary debates from 1874 and 1881.

presented some special features of aggravation or of extenuation". It recommended penalties for several commonly prosecuted offences, eg, five years' penal servitude for setting fire to a house or 10 years where life was endangered, three to five years for burglary, five to seven years for the rape of a female over 13 years of age. The memorandum was sent to the Home Office and soon forgotten.[25] Also of interest in retrospect is an article published in 1911 by JS De Vere in which he proposed the establishment of an expert commission which would draw up penalties which it would be reasonable to impose in ordinary cases. The recommendations would carry 'moral weight' only, and would not be binding on the sentencers for whose benefit they were designed.[26] This foreshadowed Marvin Frankel's recommendation to similar effect 60 years later, and described further below.

13–15 Consistency or, more precisely, the apparent lack of it became a major concern of sentencing scholars and reformers in the last quarter of the 20th century. It was the primary motivation for the introduction of formal sentencing guidelines in the United States, England and Wales and elsewhere.[27] A distinction must be drawn between consistency of approach and consistency of outcome. Consistency of approach demands that judges should apply the same principles and criteria when selecting sentence. All offenders should be sentenced according to the same general principles which, in Ireland, are essentially those described in Chap 5.[28] It would scarcely be fair if, for example, judges were free to differ over whether a guilty plea should normally be treated as a mitigating factor. This could result in like cases being treated differently, thereby violating one of the most basic tenets of distributive justice. Judicial consensus on the applicable principles cannot be guaranteed to produce consistency of outcome which some would define as meaning that similar crimes should always attract similar sentences. One leading American study of white-collar crime sentencing, based on extensive interviews with trial judges and an analysis of the sentences they imposed, revealed

[25] The text of the memorandum was published, for the first time apparently, in R.M. Jackson, *Enforcing the Law*, rev. ed. (Penguin Books, 1972), Appendix V. On its subsequent history, see Keith Smith, "Sentencing and review" in William Cornish et al, *The Oxford History of the Laws of England* (Oxford University Press, 2010), Vol XIII, pt 1, chap IV.

[26] RS De Vere, "Discretion in penalties" (1911) 27 LQR 317, 323.

[27] On the prehistory of sentencing guidelines in the United States, see Nancy Gertner, "A short history of American sentencing: Too little law, too much law, or just right" (2010) 100 J Crim L and Criminology 691; Nancy Gertner, "From omnipotence to impotence: American judges and sentencing" (2007) 4 Ohio St J Crim L 523; Douglas A Berman, "Balanced and purposeful departures: Fixing a jurisprudence that undermines the federal sentencing guidelines" (2000) 76 Notre Dame LR 21.

[28] In *Hili v The Queen* [2010] HCA 45; (2010) 242 CLR 520, para para 18, the High Court of Australia said that what is required in the sentencing of federal offences is "consistency in the application of the relevant legal principles, not some numerical or mathematical equivalence". This reflects Irish law as well. See also Sarah Poppleton et al, *A Review of Consistency in Sentencing* (Sentencing Council, 2021), 10.

significant agreement, if not unanimity, about the applicable principles but considerable variation in sentencing outcomes.[29] This should cause little surprise. Judges may, for instance, agree that a sentence should be commensurate with the gravity of the offence and that certain factors should be treated as mitigating or aggravating. Yet, they may well disagree, and probably will, about where exactly a given offence should be located on the overall scale of gravity and about the weight to be attributed to any relevant mitigating or aggravating factors. Further, courts in most countries, including Ireland, have considerable latitude in selecting the fundamental purpose (eg, desert, deterrence or rehabilitation) that should inform their sentencing decisions, even in specific cases.[30] One judge sentencing a young, first-time offender convicted of robbery might, quite legitimately, decide that the case called for a deterrent sentence. Another judge might decide, equally legitimately, that rehabilitation should be the dominant objective. Ideally, therefore, consistency of approach should extend not only to the standard distributive sentencing principles, such as a discount for a guilty plea, but also to the circumstances in which one of the accepted justifications of punishment, as described in Chap 3, should take priority over the others. Consistency in this sense is also closely connected with proportionality which is partly concerned with ensuring that offenders are afforded equal treatment, though this must not be confused with uniformity of outcome. Rather it requires close attention to the circumstances of individual cases.[31] As the United States Supreme Court once said, "consistency produced by ignoring individual differences is a false consistency".[32] However, the criteria for assessing offence gravity and weighing the significance of mitigating and aggravating factors should be applied in a fair and even-handed way.

Consistency of approach is undoubtedly an important sentencing value **13–16**
as it goes some distance towards achieving distributive justice. What it cannot guarantee is moderate sentencing. A system committed to the imposition of harsh punishment, even for minor offences, could be perfectly consistent if the same criteria were uniformly applied when evaluating the comparative gravity of offences and deciding on the weight to be attributed to aggravating and mitigating factors. As Lyndon Harris observes, "consistency is agnostic as to the principle(s) that are sought to be realised and [it] can be present in a regime which pursues any principle(s), whether they might be regarded as flawed, unjust, or even barbaric".[33] Consistency is therefore just one of the values, albeit an

---

[29] Stanton Wheeler, Kenneth Mann and Austin Sarat, *Sitting in Judgment: The Sentencing of White-Collar Criminals* (Yale University Press, 1988), 24-25.

[30] Chap 3 above.

[31] George Letsas, "Proportionality as fittingness: The moral dimension of proportionality" (2018) 71 *Current Legal Problems* 53, 77.

[32] *Eddings v Oklahoma* 455 US 104, 112 (1982). Dante expressed the same idea more bluntly: "He who decides without distinguishing/must be among the most obtuse of men": *Paradiso*, Canto XIII, in Dante, *The Divine Comedy*, translated by Allen Mandelbaum (Everyman's Library Classics Series, 1995).

[33] Lyndon Harris, *Achieving Consistency in Sentencing* (Oxford University Press, 2022), 4.

important one, that should inform a modern sentencing system. Others include moderation, legality, procedural fairness and due regard for the human rights and dignity of those being sentenced.

13–17 Mandatory and mandatory minimum sentences are sometimes, though misguidedly, seen as an effective means of promoting consistency. What they aim to produce is uniformity of outcome; everyone convicted of the relevant offence will receive the same sentence or a sentence that may not fall below the specified minimum. Yet, this kind of uniformity is no less unfair than unwarranted disparity, and may even be more so.[34] Justice is being sacrificed for the sake of formal equality.[35] Mandatory sentences prevent courts from considering all relevant offence- and offender-related factors, and from crafting penalties that fairly reflect the gravity of the specific offence, the offender's culpability and his or her circumstances at the time of sentence.[36] A 'one size fits all' policy of this nature is the very antithesis of just sentencing. As history has shown, once mandatory sentences start to proliferate, and especially if they seem excessively severe in some cases, various strategies designed to neutralise their impact very soon emerge.[37] Prosecutors, juries, judges and those responsible for exercising post-sentence clemency can utilise their powers to spare defendants and offenders from having to undergo harsher punishments than they deserve. Consistency of approach nonetheless remains an important value. And, up to a point, so does consistency of outcome. However, both forms of consistency are best achieved through sentencing guidelines that are sufficiently nuanced to accommodate the variety of circumstances in which particular offences are committed and the relevant personal circumstances of offenders.[38] Mandatory sentences prevent the exercise of that degree of individualised judgment which is indispensable for the attainment of justice.

13–18 All efforts at generating consistency are premised on the assumption that current sentencing practices are vitiated by widespread disparity, though there is seldom any sustained effort to define what disparity is or how its existence can be proved. Disparity may be said to exist when similarly situated offenders convicted of similar offences receive markedly dissimilar sentences. In other words, it occurs when there is no valid reason for a variation in the penalties imposed. It is trite wisdom that no two cases are exactly the same. They may be very similar, but there will almost always be some difference, whether relating to the manner

---

34 J Pina-Sánchez and R Linacre, "Enhancing consistency in sentencing: Exploring the effects of guidelines in England and Wales" (2014) 30 *Journal of Quantitative Criminology* 731, 740 ("uniformity implies a lack of nuance in sentencing decisions, which results in dissimilar cases being treated alike, hence causing deterioration in both proportionality and consistency").

35 Peter Westen, "The empty idea of equality" (1982) 95 Harvard LR 537, 558.

36 Harris, note 33 above, at 179-186.

37 Tonry, note 21 above; O'Malley, note 21 above.

38 Martin Wasik, "Time to repeal the firearms minimum sentence provision" [2017] Crim LR 203 (which has an excellent analysis of this general issue).

in which the offences were committed, the culpability or record of the offenders, or their response to the charges.[39] This holds true even of offenders who participated in the same offence.[40] Establishing disparity is more difficult than it might seem. Newspapers occasionally carry articles describing sentences recently imposed for some offence or other, and claiming to prove, on the basis of this information, that there is widespread inconsistency in sentencing for that offence. They may happen be right in some instances, but disparity cannot reliably be proved without close attention to all the specific circumstances of each case.

Empirical studies often use vignettes, meaning descriptions of (usually fictitious) cases that are circulated to judges who are asked to indicate the sentences they would impose and, ideally, their reasons for doing so. This methodology has the advantage that each respondent judge has the exact same information about each case. The chosen cases should be similar to ones with which the judges frequently deal, and they should include all the information about the offence and offender that would ordinarily be supplied to a judge at a real sentencing hearing. There have been several such research exercises, one of the better known being the Second Circuit Sentencing Study, conducted in the United States in the early 1970s. 50 federal District Court judges of the Second Circuit were furnished with standard pre-sentence reports for 30 defendants and asked to decide on the appropriate sentences. There were significant differences in the suggested sentences, although all the respondents were dealing with the same facts. It was also found that experience on the bench did little, if anything, to reduce disparity.[41] Shortly before that, Roger Hood had conduced similar research with English magistrates on sentencing motoring offences. Again, all participating magistrates were furnished with the same set of papers, and given the same amount of detail about each case as they would typically receive in court. A significant degree of disparity was established. It was mainly attributable to different weights **13–19**

[39] The same applies to an even greater extent when seeking to compare sentencing practices of different countries, because of variations in offence definitions, sentencing traditions and other factors. A rare opportunity to compare like with like arose in relation to the sentencing of piracy which, being a crime of universal jurisdiction, can be prosecuted and tried wherever the suspects are apprehended. A study of the sentencing of 407 Somali pirates sentenced in 15 different countries (apart from Somalia) between 2006 and 2014 showed extensive variations in the sentences imposed in European, African and Asian countries and the United States. The overall average sentence was 14 years but the individual sentences varied from four and a half years in the Netherlands to life imprisonment in the United States. See Eugene Kontorovich, "The problems of pirate punishment" in Michael P Scharf et al (eds), *Prosecuting Maritime Piracy: Domestic Solutions to International Crime* (Cambridge University Press, 2015), 299.

[40] See Chap 5 above under 'Sentencing Co-Offenders'.

[41] Anthony A Partridge and William B Eldridge, *The Second Circuit Sentencing Study: A Report to the Judges of the Second Circuit* (Federal Judicial Centre, 1974).

accorded to aggravating factors and to the sentencing traditions of the benches to which the respondents belonged.[42]

13–20 It is only through carefully designed empirical research of this nature that the existence and causes of disparity can confidently be established. The causes of disparity, where it exists, may vary from one category of offence to another. Judges might, for example, be broadly in agreement on appropriate headline sentences for some offences, but differ over the weight to be attributed to certain offender-related factors. Information of this kind can be critically important when it comes to creating sentencing guidelines. Those responsible for developing guidelines need to be aware of the matters about which judges are most likely to differ and on which detailed guidance may consequently be needed.

3. Guidance and Guidelines

13–21 Sentencing guidelines, whatever form they take, are intended to limit, shape or control the exercise of judicial discretion. They seldom, if ever, consist of inflexible rules in the way, for example, that a statutory maximum sentence places an impermeable upper limit on the punishment that may be imposed for an offence. Guidelines, as the word suggests, are meant to guide rather than dictate. There are very few countries, if any, in which judicial sentencing discretion is either non-existent or entirely unconstrained. Strategies for controlling judicial discretion may be imagined as existing along a continuum with a completely mandatory sentencing system at one extreme and unbounded discretion at the other. The question is where along that spectrum a country happens to lie, accepting that the precise location may change if measures are introduced to curtail or increase discretion further. Guidelines will usually curtail discretion, though not to the same extent as mandatory penalties. Ireland is currently towards the discretionary end of the spectrum while the federal jurisdiction of the United States is closer to the mandatory end. England and Wales now finds itself somewhere between the two.

13–22 At the outset a distinction may be drawn, though solely for explanatory purposes, between guidance and guidelines – not that there is a clear divide between them. Guidance is general in nature and, while undoubtedly intended to inform or structure judicial discretion, it seldom claims to identify or suggest an appropriate penalty in any specific case. It may consist of no more than judicially developed general principles such as those described in Chap 5. The principle of proportionality, the recognised aggravating and mitigating factors, and other distributive principles are all intended to guide judges in selecting appropriate sentences. Statute law may also offer some measure of general guidance. The Criminal Justice Act 1999 (s 29), for instance, provides that when sentencing a person who

[42] Roger Hood, *Sentencing the Motoring Offender: A Study of Magistrates' Views and Practices* (Heinemann, 1972). See review by PR Glazebrook in (1973) 32 Cambridge LJ 330.

has pleaded guilty, a court may, if it considers it appropriate to do so, take into account the stage at which and the circumstances in which the person indicated an intention to plead. This does not oblige a court to take account of these factors in every case, as the words 'if it considers it appropriate to do so' confirm. But it still provides a strong incentive to consider those factors when determining the amount of credit due for a guilty plea.

Appeal court judgments indicating sentence ranges, starting points or benchmarks also provide guidance, though they might equally be classified as guidelines. In fact, they are commonly described as guideline judgments. The English Court of Appeal (Criminal Division) has delivered many such judgments since the mid-1970s, though there has been progressively less need for them since the Sentencing Guidelines Council and, more recently, the Sentencing Council began producing formal guidelines.[43] In *R v Billam,*[44] to take a typical and well-known example, the Court of Appeal indicated four starting points for sentencing rape following a contested trial – five years, eight years, 15 years and life imprisonment, depending on the nature and circumstances of the offence. Here in Ireland, as we shall see, the Supreme Court and Court of Appeal have recently begun to issue similar guidance, though usually in the form of sentence ranges. Sentencing guidance is primarily intended to promote consistency of approach. It seeks to ensure that trial courts will, at the very least, apply the same principles when assessing offence gravity and adjusting headline sentences to reflect aggravating and mitigating factors. Granted, the guidance offered in cases like *Billam* and, more recently, in equivalent Irish cases goes some way towards promoting consistency of outcome. But consistency of approach remains the dominant objective. In Canada, some provincial courts of appeal have developed sentence ranges for certain offences, those ranges being, in effect, "summaries of the minimum and maximum sentences imposed in the past, which serve in any given case as guides for the application of all the relevant principles and objectives".[45] In some provinces, such as Alberta, starting points are used instead. However, the Canadian Supreme Court has stressed that a departure from any such guideline must not, of itself, be treated as an error in principle.[46] **13–23**

Guidelines, as the term is being used here, are usually more formal and detailed, and are typically produced by a commission of some kind rather than a court. They may be divided into two broad categories – numerical and narrative – though these categories are by no means watertight. So-called numerical guidelines are usually accompanied by a significant amount of descriptive text, while narrative guidelines often end up suggesting numbers, in the form of recommended terms **13–24**

---

43 The work of these bodies is described in more detail below.

44 [1986] 1 WLR 349 ; (1986) 82 Cr App R 347; (1986) 8 Cr App R (S) 48.

45 *R v Lacasse* [2015] SCC 64; [2015] 2 SCR 1089, para 57. See also *R v McDonnell* [1997] 1 SCR 948.

46 *R v Friesen* [2020] SCC 9; [2020] 1 SCR 424, para 37.

of imprisonment or levels of fine. The grid-centred guidelines favoured in American jurisdictions may be described as numerical. The federal guidelines grid lists offence levels from 1 to 43 along the vertical axis and criminal history scores from 1 to 6 along the horizontal axis with a recommended sentence, expressed in months' imprisonment, where the two intersect. In fact, the recommended sentence is expressed in terms of a permissible range, e.g., 46 to 57 months imprisonment. The grid itself provides solely for prison terms, starting with 0-6 months and ending with life imprisonment. However, it is also divided into four zones, and offenders whose sentences fall within the first two of these zones may qualify for a non-custodial measure such as probation, while those in the third may qualify for a split sentence, though they must serve at least half their sentence in prison. The Minnesota sentencing guidelines are centred on a rather similar grid, save that there are only 11 offence levels, with the possibility of a sanction other than state imprisonment for offenders whose presumptive sentences fall below a certain number of months' imprisonment. Departure from the guidelines is permissible only where there are exceptional and compelling circumstances. Minnesota has separate grids for sex offences and drug offences. In these and other guideline jurisdictions, both offence and criminal history scores must be calculated according to rules set out in a detailed manual which, in the case of federal guidelines, currently runs to 600 pages.[47] The English guidelines, described below, are more narrative in nature. They specify starting points and sentence ranges but they are primarily concerned with identifying factors that determine the category into which a specific offence should fall, and this in turn will point to an appropriate sentence. Narrative guidelines are generally preferable because they do more to explain the rationale for the recommended sentences. As Martin Wasik aptly puts it, guidelines by numbers provide an "answer" for the sentencing judge but guidelines expressed in words demonstrate the reasoning underpinning the answer.[48]

13–25 One notable feature of many American grid-based guideline systems is that they aim to cover all or most commonly prosecuted offences (or serious offences, at least). This is rendered feasible by their largely numerical nature. Once the guidelines manual or some similar document specifies the weight to be attached to each offence or, more commonly, to variations of particular offences, with additions and subtractions for aggravating and mitigating factors, the offence score can be fairly easily calculated. The offender's criminal history score must then be calculated but, once that is done, the applicable sentence range can readily be identified by referring to the central grid. This so-called big bang approach has the advantage, in theory at least, that all the offences to which the guidelines apply can be considered simultaneously by the framers. Recommended sentences can therefore better reflect the comparative gravity of the various offences,

---

47 United States Sentencing Commission, *Guidelines Manual 2023*, available on Commission's website, <https://www.ussc.gov> accessed 21 June 2024.

48 Martin Wasik, "Sentencing guidelines: Past, present, and future" (2003) 56 *Current Legal Problems* 239 at 257-258.

because in setting guidelines for one offence, the framers are likely to be cognisant of those they are setting for others.

Outside the United States, and particularly in England and Wales, guidelines are developed in a more gradual, piecemeal fashion. The English practice, which is also reflected in similar systems emerging elsewhere, is to establish guidelines on an offence-by-offence basis as well as for more general issues such as guilty plea discounts and the sentencing of multiple offenders. This approach has its own advantages. It may take time (probably a decade or more) to develop a comprehensive set of such guidelines, but the gradualist approach permits detailed consideration to be given to the content of each guideline. Depending on available resources, extensive research and consultation can be conducted before a draft guideline is produced. Further, the guideline-setting body acquires considerable expertise and wisdom over time, and it can learn much from the reaction of the courts to guidelines already adopted. **13–26**

Sentencing guidance, whatever form it takes, becomes all the more necessary when there has been a significant increase in the number of judges and trial lawyers in a given jurisdiction. A broad level of consistency is easier to maintain when criminal justice is administered by a relatively small number of judges and lawyers. In those circumstances, as Gleeson CJ said in *Wong v The Queen*[49] the range of penalties is likely to be well-known, and unwarranted departures from the range can readily be identified. It would, of course, be mistaken to treat that era as a golden age when sentencing was generally consistent, because that was certainly not the case. However, the greater the number of judges and lawyers, the more unrealistic it becomes to rely on the kind of shared wisdom that might have prevailed in former times. In Ireland, the number of trial judges has increased considerably over the last 30 years. In 1995, the maximum number of District Court judges was set at 51, Circuit Court judges at 25 and High Court judges at 20, bringing the total to 96.[50] Today, the total number of judges for all three courts is close to 170.[51] The range of offences with which courts must deal has also expanded greatly during this period. **13–27**

Guideline Creation and Amendment

A sentencing guideline system should be so designed as to ensure that guidelines are created by an independent, expert body; that, once created, they cannot be nullified or altered, except perhaps for strong and compelling reasons, by a political branch of government; and that they are capable of being developed or amended in light of the experience of the courts that are required to implement them. It is now widely accepted that guideline creation is best left to a commission composed of persons who have extensive experience or expertise in sentencing, **13–28**

---

49 [2001] HCA 64; (2001) 207 CLR 584, para 10.
50 Courts and Court Officers Act 1995, ss 9-11.
51 Courts Act 2023, ss 4-6.

though it may also be useful to have one or more members with expertise in decision-making outside the criminal justice system. The commission should be independent in the sense of being insulated from external pressure, political or otherwise. Political decisions, especially in an area like sentencing, are often influenced by transient public controversies, not to mention a more general desire to be seen to be tough on crime. As Marvin Frankel remarked, when arguing for the creation of a sentencing commission in the United States, "legislative action tends to be sporadic and impassioned, responding in haste to momentary crises, lapsing then into the accustomed state of inattention".[52]

13–29 No less important is the procedure for adopting guidelines once they have been drawn up by the commission. There is little point in having guidelines drafted by an expert group if they can be set at naught or substantially amended by a political body that is responsible for their adoption or promulgation. Ideally, guidelines should become effective once they are formally approved by the commission itself. The degree of political control exercised over the content of guidelines varies considerably in the relatively few jurisdictions in which they currently exist. The United States Sentencing Commission, for example, must submit its suggested amendments to the federal guidelines to Congress which has 180 days to alter or reject them (though they have very seldom been rejected). Otherwise, they take effect at the end of the 180 days. The English guidelines take effect once they are adopted by the Sentencing Council itself. No political approval is required. In Ireland, the Judicial Council Act 2019 provides that guidelines drawn up by the Sentencing Guidelines and Information Committee will not take effect until adopted by the Judicial Council which consists exclusively of serving judges, though it now appears that some other method of adoption will have to be devised.[53] In Scotland, guidelines prepared by the Sentencing Council must be approved by the High Court of Justiciary.

13–30 When the United States Sentencing Commission was established in 1984, it was envisaged as being an expert agency, insulated from political influence.[54] Yet, its members were (and continue to be) appointed by the President and confirmed by the Senate, although it must also be bipartisan to the extent that no more than four of its seven members may belong to the same political party and at least three must be federal judges. They have a six-year term of office, and a commissioner may be removed by the President "only for neglect of duty or malfeasance in office or for other good cause shown".[55] Despite all this, a clear majority of those so

---

52 Marvin E Frankel, *Criminal Sentences: Law Without Order* (Hill and Wang, 1973), 119.

53 See note 1 above.

54 Rachel E Barkow, "The evolving role of the United States Sentencing Commission" (2020) 33 *Federal Sentencing Reporter* 3.

55 28 US Code §991(a).

far appointed to the Commission, including judges, have been former prosecutors.[56]

4. The United States

Between 1930 and 1975, all United States jurisdictions had indeterminate sentencing systems based essentially on a philosophy of rehabilitation.[57] Systems differed to some degree from one jurisdiction to another but, in general terms, courts had a wide discretion as to the kind of sentence to be imposed. Further, when imposing imprisonment, a court would often specify a maximum and sometimes a minimum term, rather than a specific term. It might, for example, sentence a person to a prison term of one to 10 years, leaving the relevant parole authority to decide on the release date. The parole authority was therefore in many instances the real sentencer. One other important feature of American sentencing during this era was the absence of merit-based appeals in the federal system and in most states. A sentence could not be appealed unless it was unconstitutional, contrary to statute or the result of a gross abuse of discretion (as was very seldom found).[58] This may seem strange, but it should be recalled that appeals against sentence, as we now know them, were first permitted in Ireland just a century ago, having been introduced in England and Wales in 1907.[59] If similar appeals systems had existed in the United States throughout the 20th century, there might have been less of a perceived need for formal guidelines and any guidelines that were introduced might have allowed more scope for judicial discretion. **13–31**

From the early 1970s onwards, the American sentencing system, and the federal system in particular, came under attack, most notably by Judge Marvin Frankel in *Criminal Sentences: Law without Order*.[60] This short book, running to 124 pages, attracted a good deal of attention when first published in 1973, but in retrospect, it probably ranks as one of the most influential works in the history of criminal law.[61] It ignited a political **13–32**

56 Barkow, note note 54 above, at 4.

57 Kevin R Reitz, "The 'traditional' indeterminate sentencing model" in Joan Petersilia and Kevin R Reitz, *The Oxford Handbook of Sentencing and Corrections* (Oxford University Press, 2012), Chap 11.

58 Edward Kennedy, "Toward a new system of criminal sentencing: Law with order" (1979) 16 Am Crim LR 353, 367. The absence of such a power was emphatically confirmed in *United States v Rosenberg* 195 F2d 583, 604 (2nd Cir, 1952) where the Court of Appeals said: "Unless we are to over-rule sixty years of undeviating federal precedents, we must hold that an appellate court has no power to modify a sentence. 'If there is one rule in the federal criminal practice which is firmly established, it is that the appellate court has no control over a sentence which is within the limits allowed by statute'" (quoting earlier authorities). However, the court did seem to accept there could be some merit in having a system of sentence appeals.

59 Courts of Justice Act 1924 (Ireland); Criminal Appeal Act 1907 (England and Wales).

60 Frankel, note note 52 above.

61 It is so described in Daniel Kahneman, Olivier Sibony and Cass R Sunstein,

movement, in which Senator Edward Kennedy played a leading tole, to reform federal sentencing and this culminated in the passing of the Sentencing Reform Act 1984. This provided for the creation of the United States Sentencing Commission which was charged with the creation of sentencing guidelines. These were adopted in 1987, although a few states – Minnesota, Pennsylvania and Washington – also inspired by Frankel's book, had already adopted guidelines by then.[62] As will be noted later, American-style guidelines have not been adopted elsewhere, but they have been highly influential internationally by demonstrating the possibility of prescribing sentencing outcomes with some degree of specificity.

13–33 Between the late 1970s and early 1990s several states, as well as the federal system, introduced presumptive guidelines.[63] At present, about 20 American jurisdictions have sentencing guidelines. Those guideline systems vary in certain respects. Some are grid-centred, as described earlier, while others require courts to complete worksheets to arrive at appropriate sentences. They also vary in terms of how binding they are meant to be.[64] Presumptive guidelines are intended to be followed, with some scope for departure in exceptional cases, whereas voluntary guidelines are intended for guidance only and have operated with mixed success.[65] The federal guidelines, in particular, have attracted their share of criticism.[66] They became advisory rather than mandatory in 2005 following the United States Supreme Court decision in *United States v*

Noise: A Flaw in Human Judgment (William Collins, 2021), 15. See also Steven L Chanenson and Douglas A Berman, "Frankel at 50: A half-century's perspective on *Criminal Sentences: Law without Order*" (2023) 35 *Federal Sentencing Reporter* 213.

[62] The current guidelines and a great deal of associated information can be found on the Sentencing Commission's website: <https://www.ussc.gov> accessed 21 June 2024. For a detailed account of the creation of the original guidelines, see Stephen Breyer, "The federal sentencing guidelines and the key compromises upon which they rest" (1988) 17 Hofstra LR 1. Breyer, later a Justice of the United States Supreme Court, was a member of the original Sentencing Commission. On the Minnesota guidelines, see Richard S Frase, "Sentencing guidelines in Minnesota, 1978-2003 " (2005) 32 *Crime and Justice* 131.

[63] For a recent account of American guideline systems, see Richard S Frase, "Forty years of American sentencing guidelines: What have we learned?" in Michael Tonry (ed,), *American Sentencing: What Happens and Why?* (University of Chicago Press, 2019), 79. See also Michael Tonry, "Sentencing in America 1975-2025" (2013) 42 *Crime and Justice* 141. The Robina Institute at the University of Minnesota has an excellent website providing detailed information on the current guideline systems in the United States at <https://robinainstitute.umn.edu/sentencing-guidelines-resource-center> accessed 26 June 2024.

[64] Kevin R Reitz, "Modeling discretion in American sentencing systems" (1998) 20 *Law and Policy* 389.

[65] Some advisory guidelines such as those in Massachusetts appear to operate quite successfully in the sense that judges tend to follow them. Others, in the past at least, have been largely ignored.

[66] Kate Stith and José A Cabranes, *Fear of Judging: Sentencing Guidelines in the Federal Courts* (University of Chicago Press, 1998); Daniel J Freed, "Federal sentencing in the wake of guidelines: Unacceptable limits on the discretion of sentencers" (1992) 101 Yale LJ 1681; Nancy Gertner, "From omnipotence

Booker.[67] Federal trial judges must still begin by calculating the appropriate guideline sentence in each case, but they now have more flexibility to depart from it in light of the particular circumstances. In 2022, only 42 per cent of all federal offenders were sentenced within the guideline range.[68] Yet this did not reflect any perceptible trend towards leniency; 93 per cent (of the 64,000 sentenced) were sentenced to imprisonment and the average prison term was 52 months.[69] Presumptive guidelines, in some jurisdictions at least, have been reasonably successful in generating consistency and eliminating discriminatory sentencing practices. Unfortunately, some of them, and especially the federal guidelines, were significantly undermined by the introduction of statutory mandatory minimum sentences for certain offences. Both sentencing commissions and courts are severely constrained by such measures.

5. England and Wales

Until the early 1980s, the sentencing system in England and Wales was very similar to that then operating in Ireland. Maximum sentences were specified by statute and courts had extensive discretion in selecting an appropriate sentence in each case. Such guidance as there was consisted largely of general principles that were mainly of common law origin, although authority for most of them could be found in judgments of the Court of Criminal Appeal, now the Court of Appeal (Criminal Division), that had first been established in 1907.[70] Even in its earliest years, the court had confirmed or established certain fundamental principles including that the maximum sentence should be reserved for the worst case,[71] that a sentence should not be increased merely because the offender had insisted on going to trial rather than plead guilty,[72] and that those who assisted the authorities by providing information should be rewarded with a reduced sentence.[73] Many other general principles were articulated by the court down through the years. Parliament seldom intervened. The Criminal Justice Act 1948, which ran to 83 sections and 10 schedules, effectively **13–34**

---

to impotence: American judges and sentencing" (2007) 4 *Ohio State Journal of Criminal Law* 523.

67 543 US 220 (2005). See also *Gall v United States* 552 US 38 (2007); *Kimbrough v United States* 552 US 85 (2007); *Rita v United States* 551 US 338 (2007).

68 However, this figure rises to 68 per cent when it includes, in addition to the cases sentenced within the guideline range, those sentenced outside the range but the court cited a reason for departure.

69 United States Sentencing Commission, *Annual Report 2023* at <https://www.ussc.gov/about/annual-report-2023> accessed 18 November 2024. . The average sentence length varies greatly with the offence. In 2023, for example, it was 285 months for murder, 82 months for drug trafficking and two months for drug possession. See also Paul J Hofer, "Federal sentencing after *Booker*" in Tonry, *American Sentencing*, note 63 above at 140.

70 Chap 2 above.

71 *R v Harrison* (1909) 2 Cr App R 94, 96.

72 *R v Newman* (1914) 9 Cr App R 134, 136 ("it is not right to give a heavier sentence to a prisoner because he brazens it out").

73 *R v James and Sharman* (1913) 9 Cr App R 142.

codified the formal sentencing law (except maximum penalties) of England and Wales and it survived with few amendments for almost 20 years.[74] All that was to change radically from the early 1990s onwards. Starting with the Criminal Justice Act 1991 which made extensive changes to the law governing sentencing and parole, the Westminster Parliament has produced a raft of highly complex legislation which, in many instances, rendered the judicial sentencing task difficult and prone to error. The English Law Commission did sterling work in producing a draft code embodying all existing statutory sentencing law, apart from maximum sentences.[75] This has since been enacted in the form of the Sentencing Act 2020 which, by its own terms, is known as the 'Sentencing Code'. However, in stark contrast to the 1948 legislation, the Code runs to 420 sections and 29 schedules.

13–35 The recent history of sentencing guidance in England and Wales may be divided into four eras, though they overlap to some extent: (1) the guideline judgment era, (2) the Sentencing Advisory Panel era, (3) the Sentencing Guidelines Council era, and (4) the Sentencing Council era. The first of these may be said to have begun in 1974 when the Court of Appeal decided *R v Willis*[76] which involved an appeal against sentence for sexual offences committed against young boys.[77] The single judge who granted leave suggested that this might be an appropriate case in which to give some general guidance on sentencing offences of this nature. The court, presided over by Lawton LJ, agreed with this suggestion, and dealt at some length with factors that might influence sentence in such cases. More significantly for present purposes, it said:

> "In our judgment, the sentencing bracket for offences [of this kind] which have neither mitigating nor aggravating factors is from three to five years; and the place in the bracket will depend on age, intelligence and education. Few offences, however, have neither aggravating nor mitigating factors. Many have both. When this happens the judge has to weigh what aggravates against what mitigates."[78]

13–36 This short passage was given no special emphasis in the judgment itself and was not even mentioned in the case commentary in the *Criminal*

---

[74] David Thomas, "Sentencing Reform: England and Wales" in CMV Clarkson and R Morgan (eds), *The Politics of Sentencing Reform* (Clarendon Press, 1995), Chap 5.

[75] Law Commission, *The Sentencing Code, Volume 1: Report* (2018). See Julian V Roberts and Umar Azmeh, "Cleansing the Augean stables: A commentary on the Law Commission's Sentencing Code for England and Wales" [2019] Crim LR 694.

[76] [1975] 1 WLR 292; (1974) 60 Cr App R 146. In *R v Guilfoyle* (1973) 57 Cr App R 549, the Court of Appeal had given some very general guidance on sentencing for dangerous driving causing death.

[77] For a summary and analysis of sentencing developments from the early 1970s until about 2000, see Andrew Ashworth, "The decline of English sentencing and other stories" in Michael Tonry and Richard s s Frase (eds), *Sentencing and Sanctions in Western Countries* (Oxford University Press, 2001), Chap 2.

[78] [1975] 1 WLR 292, 295; (1974) 60 Cr App R 146, 148.

Law Review.[79] However, it represented a new frontier in terms of the court's willingness to offer guidance on appropriate sentence ranges. The following year, in *R v Turner*,[80] the court issued another brief guideline of sorts when it held that the normal sentence for taking part in a bank robbery or similar operation where firearms were carried but no serious injury was inflicted should be 15 years' imprisonment. It was not until the early 1980s that the court began to deliver guideline judgments with any degree of frequency. Over the next 30 years, it provided guidance, usually in the form of starting points or sentence ranges, for many offences including drug dealing,[81] rape (as already mentioned),[82] burglary,[83] reckless driving causing death,[84] and theft involving breach of trust.[85] The Sentencing Guidelines Council produced a useful summary of Court of Appeal guideline judgments up to 2005.[86]

The second era began with the establishment of the Sentencing Advisory Panel under the Crime and Disorder Act 1998 (s 81). The Panel was an expert group, eventually with 14 members, appointed by the Lord Chancellor after consultation with the Home Secretary and the Lord Chief Justice. Whenever the Court of Appeal decided to frame or revise a sentencing guideline, it was required to notify the Panel which would research the area in question, carry out such consultations as it deemed appropriate and then furnish advice to the court. Effectively, therefore, the court could no longer develop guidelines without having sought advice from the Panel which was also empowered to propose to the Court of Appeal that guidelines should be formulated for a particular category of offence.[87] Over the next dozen years or so, the Panel produced some **13–37**

---

79 *R v Willis* [1975] Crim LR 177.

80 (1975) 61 Cr App R 67. In *R v Taylor* [1977] 1 WLR 612; (1977) 64 Cr App R 182, the Court of Appeal gave some guidance, but only of a general nature, on sentencing offences of unlawful sexual intercourse with underage females.

81 *R v Aramah* (1983) 76 Cr App R 190; (1982) 4 Cr App R (S) 407; *R v Djahit* [1999] 2 Cr App R (S) 142; *R v Twisse* [2001] 2 Cr App R (S) 9; *R v Aranguren* (1994) 99 Cr App R 347; (1995) 16 Cr App R (S) 211.

82 *R v Billam* [1986] 1 WLR 349; (1986) 82 Cr App R 347; (1986) 8 Cr App R (S) 48. This was superseded by *R v Millberry* [2003] 1 WLR 546; [2003] 1 Cr App R 25; [2003] 2 Cr App R (S) 31.

83 *R v Brewster* [1998] 1 Cr App R 220; [1998] 1 Cr App R (S) 181; *R v McInerney and Keating* [2003] 1 Cr App R 36; [2003] 2 Cr App R (S) 39.

84 *R v Boswell* (1984) 79 Cr App R 277; (1984) 6 Cr App R (S) 257.

85 *R v Clark* [1998] 2 Cr App R 137; [1998] 2 Cr App R (S) 95. .

86 Sentencing Guidelines Council, *Guideline Judgments Case Compendium* (2005) available at: <www.sentencingcouncil.org.uk/wp-content/uploads/web_case_compendium.pdf> accessed 10 August 2024.

87 For further information on the Panel (and the Sentencing Guidelines Council), see Wasik, note 48 above; Martin Wasik, "The status and authority of sentencing guidelines" (2007) 39 Bracton LJ 9; Andrew Ashworth, "The struggle for supremacy in sentencing" in Andrew Ashworth and Julian V Roberts (eds), *Sentencing Guidelines: Exploring the English Model* (Oxford University Press, 2013), Chap 2; Andrew Ashworth, "The sentencing guideline system in England and Wales" (2006) 91:1 *South African Journal of Criminal Justice* 1. Professor Wasik was the first chairperson of the Panel and Professor Ashworth the second.

excellent work which strongly influenced Court of Appeal guidelines on domestic burglary,[88] causing death by dangerous driving,[89] rape and other sexual offences,[90] child pornography,[91] possession of offensive weapons,[92] environmental offences[93] and several others.

13–38 For the first five or six years of its existence, the Sentencing Advisory Panel furnished its advice directly to the Court of Appeal. This changed, however, with the creation of the Sentencing Guidelines Council (SGC) under the Criminal Justice Act 2003 (the '2003 Act') which marks the beginning of the third era of modern English sentencing.[94] The SGC was established in response to the Halliday Report which recommended the establishment of a mechanism for the development of comprehensive sentencing guidance.[95] It consisted of the Lord Chief Justice, seven judicial members and four lay members. It was charged with drawing up sentencing guidelines that could be either general in nature or limited to a particular category of offence or offender, and allocation guidelines for determining if an offence was suitable for summary trial or trial on indictment. Offence-specific guidelines were required to specify criteria for determining offence seriousness, including the weight to be given to any previous convictions of offenders. The SGC was authorised to revise existing guidelines in addition to framing new ones. The Sentencing Advisory Panel remained in existence, but it now reported to the SGC. The Panel could make proposals to the SCG for the framing or revision of guidelines, and the SCG, in turn, whenever it decided to frame or revise a guideline, was obliged to notify the Panel. In either event, the Panel furnished its advice to the SGC rather than, as previously, to the Court of Appeal.

13–39 This arrangement represented an important turning point in English sentencing law. The creation of sentencing guidelines was now assigned to a body other than a court, albeit one with a judicial majority. Further, the 2003 Act (s 172) provided that every court must, when sentencing an offender, 'have regard to' any guidelines relevant to the offender's case, and when exercising any other sentencing function, have regard to relevant guidelines. As we shall see, English courts are now ordinarily required 'to follow' sentencing guidelines. Between 2004 and 2009, the SGC published definitive guidelines for several offences, including

[88] *R v McInerney and Keating* [2003] 1 Cr App R 36; [2003] 2 Cr App R (S) 39, with further clarification in *R v Saw* [2009] 2 Cr App R (S) 54.

[89] *R v Cooksley* [2003] 2 Cr App R 18; [2004] 1 Cr App R (S) 1.

[90] *R v Millberry* [2003] 1 WLR 546; [2003] 1 Cr App R 25; [2003] 2 Cr App R (S) 31; *R v Patterson* [2006] 2 Cr App R (S) 48.

[91] *R v Oliver* [2003] 1 Cr App R 28; [2003] 2 Cr App R (S) 15.

[92] *R v Celaire and Poulton* [2003] 1 Cr App R (S) 116.

[93] *R v Thames Water Utilities Ltd* [2010] EWCA Crim 202; [2010] 2 Cr App R (S) 90.

[94] ss 167 to 173 of the Criminal Justice Act 2003 deal with the establishment and functions of the SGC.

[95] Home Office, *Making Punishments Work: Review of the Sentencing Framework for England and Wales* (2001), known as the Halliday Report. The principal author, John Halliday, had recently retired as a senior civil servant in the Home Office.

causing death by dangerous driving and attempted murder, as well as two on general matters, assessing offence seriousness and reduction in sentence for a guilty plea. It also produced the Magistrates' Court Sentencing Guidelines.

The guidelines system was overhauled yet again by the Coroners and Justice Act 2009 (the '2009 Act') which ushered in our fourth and final era.[96] Both the Sentencing Advisory Panel and the SGC were abolished and replaced with a new Sentencing Council (SC) which still operates. The SC consists of eight judicial members and six lay members. The Lord Chief Justice is President of the SC, though not a member of it. The SC is charged with framing sentencing guidelines which "may be general in nature or limited to a particular offence, particular category of offence or particular category of offender".[97] Guidelines are first published in draft form to allow for consultation and then, after any appropriate amendments have been made, as definitive guidelines. When exercising its functions, the SC must have regard to: **13–40**

(1) the sentences imposed by courts in England and Wales for offences;
(2) the need to promote consistency in sentencing;
(3) the impact of sentencing decisions on victims of crime;
(4) the need to promote public confidence in the criminal justice system;
(5) the cost of different sentences and their effectiveness in preventing re-offending;
(6) the results of any monitoring carried out by the SC (as it required to do under s 128 of the 2009 Act).[98]

Compared with the Criminal Justice Act 2003, the 2009 Act is remarkably detailed in specifying how the SC should go about framing guidelines.[99] An 'offence range', namely the overall range of sentence appropriate for the offence must be specified. Domestic burglary, for example, has an offence range extending from a community order to six years' custody, while aggravated burglary has an offence range of one to 13 years' custody.[100] In addition, whenever practicable, an offence-specific guideline **13–41**

---

[96] ss 118 to 135 and Schedule 15 of the 2009 Act deal with the establishment, composition and functions of the Council. For background and analysis, see Andrew Ashworth, "Coroners and Justice Act 2009: Sentencing Guidelines and the Sentencing Council" [2010] Crim LR 389; Julian V Roberts, "Sentencing guidelines in England and Wales: Recent developments and emerging issues" (2013) 76 *Law and Contemporary Problems* 1.

[97] Coroners and Justice Act 2009, s 120(2).

[98] Coroners and Justice Act 2009, s 120(11).

[99] For more detailed accounts of how the present English guideline system operates, see Julian V Roberts and Anne Rafferty, "Sentencing guidelines in England and Wales: Exploring the new format" [2011] Crim LR 681 (using the guideline on assault occasioning actual bodily harm as an example) and Julian V Roberts, "The evolution of sentencing guidelines in Minnesota and England and Wales" in Tonry (ed), *American Sentencing*, note 63 above, 187 at 205-207 (using the guideline on street robbery as an example).

[100] The Sentencing Council issued a definitive guideline on burglary offences in 2011, but this was superseded by a new guideline in 2022. The new guideline,

should describe different categories of case which illustrate the various degrees of seriousness with which the offence may be committed, having regard to harm, culpability and any other factors particularly relevant to the seriousness of the offence. When this is done, as it usually is, the guideline should go further and specify 'category ranges', namely the range of sentence considered appropriate for each category. Guidelines should indicate either a starting point in the offence range or, where there are categories, a starting point in the range for each category. The guideline on domestic burglary, for example, has three harm-based categories in descending order of gravity, each divided into three sub-categories reflecting different levels of culpability. Thus, in harm category 1, an offence with the highest level of culpability has a staring point of three years' custody and a range of two to six years' custody. For an offence in this harm category with medium culpability, the starting point is two years, and the range is one to four years, while for an offence with the lowest level of culpability, the starting point is 18 months' custody, and the range is six months to three years. This pattern is repeated in the two lower harm categories. For less serious offences in the lower categories, community orders are specified, at least as starting points.

13–42 A guideline also includes a non-exhaustive list of aggravating and mitigating factors to be considered when making any upward or downward adjustment to the sentence that has so far been arrived at. After all, the starting point will usually be about mid-way in the applicable range. Exceptionally, the presence of significant mitigating or aggravating factors might justify moving the offence to a different category from that initially identified. Having taken all these steps, the court will have identified what might be termed a 'presumptive sentence', but there are still more steps to be taken. Any reduction merited by a guilty plea, where there has been one, must then be given as well as any reduction for further factors such as assisting the prosecution. If the offender is being sentenced for two or more offences, the totality principle must be applied in the sense that the court must consider if the aggregate sentence is just and proportionate to the overall offending behaviour. Any compensation or other ancillary order, if relevant, must then be made. Finally, in accordance with s 52 of the Sentencing Act 2020, the court must openly state the reasons for the sentence imposed and explain its effect to the offender.

13–43 As noted earlier, the Criminal Justice Act 2003 (s 172) imposed a duty on courts to *have regard to* sentencing guidelines produced by the SGC. The Coroners and Justice Act 2009 (s 125, now the Sentencing Act 2020, s 59) imposes a stricter obligation by providing that courts must *follow* any relevant SC guidelines unless satisfied that it would be contrary to the interests of justice to do so.[101] The duty to follow the guidelines is further

---

which is more detailed than its predecessor, especially in relation to culpability levels, is available at <https://www.sentencingcouncil.org.uk> accessed 26 August 2023.

[101] This change had been canvassed in the Sentencing Commission Working Group, *Sentencing Guidelines in England and Wales: An Evolutionary Approach*

specified as meaning that, where a relevant offence-specific guideline exists, a court must impose a sentence which is within the offence range (which, as we have seen, is usually quite broad), but where a guideline has case categories (as in the domestic burglary guideline described earlier and most others), a court must decide which category most resembles the case at hand in order to identify both the appropriate starting point and the range. However, where categories exist, there is no separate duty to impose a sentence within the category range. Thus, a court will have fulfilled its statutory duty if, having taken all the steps required by a guideline, it imposes a sentence within the broader offence range rather than a category range. This may seem rather strange, but it was apparently intended to compensate for the imposition of a duty 'to follow' the guidelines which had met with considerable judicial opposition when first proposed.[102] Again, it must be recalled that a court is not obliged to follow a guideline at all if it considers that it would be contrary to the interests of justice to do so.

The SC's functions extend beyond framing new guidelines. When it **13–44**
produces a draft guideline or issues a definitive one, it must publish an accompanying resource assessment indicating the likely impact of the guideline on the resources of the prison, probation and youth justice services. The SC can also revise existing guidelines, as it regularly does.[103] It also has an important monitoring function in terms of investigating the frequency with which and the extent to which courts depart from guidelines, the factors influencing sentences imposed by the courts, and the effect of guidelines on promoting both consistency in sentencing and public confidence in the criminal justice system.

Since 2004, numerous offence-specific definitive guidelines and several **13–45**
others dealing with more general matters such as the assessment of offence seriousness and the discount for a guilty plea have been published by the SGIC and the SC. Many of the offence-specific guidelines cover several distinct offences. The sexual offences definitive guideline, for example, ran to 160 pages and dealt with more than 70 separate offences. It has also been updated a few times since being adopted in 2013. Virtually all commonly prosecuted serious offences are now covered by guidelines produced by the SC since 2010, and almost all guidelines produced by the former SGIC have been replaced.[104] The English guidelines are

---

(2008) (Gage Report). See Julian V Roberts, "Sentencing guidelines and judicial discretion: Evolution of the duty of courts to comply in England and Wales" (2011) 51 Brit J Criminology 997.

[102] Sentencing Act 2020, s 60; Ashworth, note 96 above, at 395.

[103] In 2022/23, the SC published new and revised guidelines for six types of offences, including some sexual offences, domestic violence and terrorism offences.

[104] Sentencing Council, *Annual Report 2022/2023* (2023). The current guidelines for offences dealt with in the Crown Court are available, in alphabetical order of the offences, on the Council's website: <https://www.sentencingcouncil.org.uk/crown-court/> accessed 10 August 2024.

valuable for comparative purposes and can be used with profit in other jurisdictions because, leaving aside the recommended sentences, they provide considered and well-researched lists of factors that are relevant when assessing the gravity of particular offences and identifying offender-related factors that may influence the final sentence. The same holds true of the generic guidelines such as those on discount for a guilty plea and the totality principle, matters of concern in all common law jurisdictions. The principles set out in those guidelines often reflect existing common law, but they do so in a coherent and structured manner. As it happens, the SC's definitive guideline on manslaughter was deployed before the Irish Supreme Court within weeks of it entering into force in England and Wales.[105] Reference was made to it in the prosecution submissions in *People (DPP) v Mahon*[106] on the appropriate categorisation of assault manslaughter for sentencing purposes. The court seems to have been influenced by it to the extent that it adopted a four-fold categorisation of assault manslaughters broadly similar to that in the English guideline. In *People (DPP) v Edosa*[107] a human trafficking case, the Court of Appeal took note of the English guideline on slavery and related offences useful, especially in relation to factors affecting culpability.

13–46 What are not, of course, internationally transferrable are the various starting points and sentencing ranges specified in the English guidelines, and there are various reasons for this. First, maximum sentences, which ultimately inform guidelines, vary from one jurisdiction to another, even for identical or very similar offences. For instance, witness intimidation carries a maximum prison sentence of five years in England and Wales, but 15 years in Ireland. This difference is reflected in the sentence ranges specified in the definitive English guideline for that offence issued in 2023 and in the informal guideline given by the Irish Court of Appeal in *People (DPP) v Lennon*.[108] Secondly, parole and early release provisions may vary. Most prisoners in England and Wales are conditionally released upon serving half their sentences, though many nowadays must serve longer portions of their sentences before being considered for release.[109] In Ireland, on the other hand, a prisoner serving a determinate sentence cannot confidently expect to be released until three-quarters of the sentence has been served, though enhanced remission and temporary release can result in some being released at an earlier point. Finally, and more generally, there is the question of sentencing culture. Countries vary in terms of their use of imprisonment and other forms of penalty and in the punishment typically imposed for various offences.

---

105 Sentencing Council, *Manslaughter: Definitive Guideline* (2018), effective from 1 November 2018.

106 [2019] IESC 24; [2019] 3 IR 151; [2019] 2 ILRM 81.

107 [2023] IECA 38.

108 [2021] IECA 30. The highest category range for this offence in England and Wales is one to four years' custody whereas in Ireland it is 10 to 15 years.

109 As against this, in summer 2024 in response to severe prison overcrowding, the British government was considering releasing some prisoners once they had served 40 per cent of their sentences.

6. Scotland

The Scottish Sentencing Council was established in 2015 under the Criminal Justice and Licensing (Scotland) Act 2010 which gave effect to the recommendations of a specially appointed commission.[110] The Council's statutory objectives are: (1) to promote consistency in sentencing practice; (2) to assist the development of policy in relation to sentencing; and (3) to promote greater awareness and understanding of sentencing policy and practice. The Council, which consists of 12 members including judges, lawyers and lay persons, prepares sentencing guidelines for consideration by the High Court of Justiciary (Scotland's highest criminal court).[111] A guideline does not come into effect unless approved by that court. A sentencing court must have regard to any applicable guideline and state its reasons if it decides not to follow such a guideline. So far four guidelines have been approved: *Principles and Purposes of Sentencing* (2018); *The Sentencing Process* (2021), *Sentencing Young People* (2021) and *Statutory Offences of Causing Death by Driving* (2023). Others, including offence-specific guidelines for rape, domestic abuses and other offences are being developed.[112] The Council has also commissioned research, including a report on public attitudes to sentencing which was submitted in 2019.[113] **13–47**

7. Ireland

In Ireland, judicial attitudes to sentencing guidelines have changed quite profoundly during the past 35 years. Firm resistance has yielded to enthusiastic engagement. In 1988, the Supreme Court declined an invitation to establish sentencing guidelines, for rape on that occasion.[114] It did so for two reasons. First, there was little reliable information available on existing sentencing practice to inform such guidelines (a situation that has not improved very much in the meantime). Secondly, the court felt that, as a matter of policy, it would be inappropriate for it to issue guidelines. Finlay CJ, who delivered the majority judgment, said: **13–48**

> "Furthermore, having regard to the fundamental necessity for judges in sentencing in any form of criminal case to impose a sentence which in their discretion appropriately meets all the particular circumstances of the case (and very few criminal cases are particularly similar) and the particular circumstances of the accused, I would doubt that it is appropriate for an appellate court to appear to be laying down any standardisation or tariff of penalty for cases."[115]

---

110 The Sentencing Commission for Scotland, *The Scope for Improved Consistency in Sentencing* (2006).

111 Criminal Justice and Licensing (Scotland) Act 2010, Sch 1.

112 Scottish Sentencing Council, *Annual Report 2022/23* (2023) is a useful source of information on the Council's work.

113 Carolyn Black et al, *Public Perceptions of Sentencing: National Survey Report* (Scottish Sentencing Council, 2019).

114 *People (DPP) v Tiernan* [1988] IR 250; [1989] ILRM 149.

115 [1988] IR 250 at 254; [1989] ILRM 149 at 154.

13–49 This remained the orthodoxy for the next quarter of a century although, during that period, both the Supreme Court and the former Court of Criminal Appeal produced a substantial body of case law on general sentencing principles with a strong emphasis on proportionality. They did not, however, offer guidance in the form of tariffs, starting points or sentence ranges for particular offences, although indications of appropriate sentence levels for certain offences might be inferred from some of their judgments.

13–50 The next major development occurred in March 2014 when the Court of Criminal Appeal, without any prior warning or attendant fanfare, delivered two guideline judgments, one dealing with possession of firearms in suspicious circumstances and the other with causing serious harm contrary to s4 of the Non-Fatal Offences against the Person Act 1997.[116] In *People (DPP) v Ryan*[117] (the firearms case), the court accepted that it should try to maintain a broad level of sentencing consistency. It was properly a function of an appeal court not only:

> "to attempt to establish the broad legal principles by reference to which any sentencing exercise should be conducted but also to give, where possible, some guidance as to the broad range of sentences which should be imposed, all other things being equal, across the spectrum of severity applicable to an offence under consideration."[118]

13–51 While acknowledging that the Supreme Court in *Tiernan* had doubted the propriety of laying down any "standardisation or tariff of penalty", the Court in *Ryan* said that this should not preclude an appeal court from giving "a broad level of guidance" as to the sentence ranges appropriate for various offences. That is precisely what it did in *Ryan* and in the companion case of *People (DPP) v Fitzgibbon*[119] (the assault case). In *Ryan* counsel had furnished the court with details of cases involving similar offences that had previously been decided by the court itself. There was, however, the complicating factor that the offence in *Ryan* was subject to a presumptive minimum sentence of five years' imprisonment.[120] This clearly had to be factored into any guideline. The court first indicated some of the key relevant factors for assessing the seriousness of an offence of possessing a firearm in suspicious circumstances, such as the nature and quantity of the firearms involved, and any evidence that the possession was connected with a broader pattern of criminality as well as the relevant personal circumstances of the offender. Having considered the earlier precedents and the need to respect the presumptive minimum five-year sentence (unless there were exceptional and specific circumstances to

---

116 For a more detailed analysis of Court of Appeal case law on structured sentencing, see Tom O'Malley, "The path to consistency: A survey of recent sentencing judgments of the Court of Appeal" in Liz Heffernan and David P Prendergast (eds), *Criminal Law and Practice Review* (Clarus Press, 2018),79.

117 [2014] IECCA 11; [2014] 2 ILRM 98.

118 [2014] IECCA 11; [2014] 2 ILRM 98 at 101.

119 [2014] IECCA 12; [2014] 2 ILRM 116.

120 Firearms Act 1964, s 27A, as substituted by Criminal Justice Act 2006, s 59.

justify a downward departure), the court held that an offence at the lower end of the range should ordinarily attract a sentence of five to seven years, an offence in the mid-range a sentence of seven to 10 years and an offence in the top range a sentence of 10 to 14 years (the maximum sentence). However, the court also specified that these were the appropriate ranges before any credit was given for mitigating factors. In effect, therefore, the guidelines were intended to assist in the selection of headline sentences, although the court did not use that term.

Causing serious harm, the offence in *Fitzgibbon*, was not subject to any presumptive or mandatory minimum sentence which meant that the Court of Criminal Appeal had more latitude when it came to indicating sentence ranges. On the other hand, while the firearms offence in *Ryan* carried a maximum sentence of 14 years' imprisonment, causing serious harm carried a discretionary life sentence. In *Fitzgibbon* the court reviewed its earlier decisions, of which there were relatively few, on sentencing for serious assaults and once more adopted a tripartite approach in establishing sentence ranges. An offence in the lower range should ordinarily attract a sentence of two to four years, an offence in the mid-range a sentence of four to seven-and-a-half years and an offence in the top range a sentence of seven-and-a-half years to 12 years. In an exceptionally serious case, a sentence exceeding 12 years, even up to and including life imprisonment, may be appropriate. Again, these were intended to indicate headline sentences before allowance was made for mitigating factors. **13–52**

The Court of Criminal Appeal was effectively abolished in late 2014 (although it continued to sit for some time thereafter to deal with pending cases) when it was replaced by the present Court of Appeal.[121] Although the new court did not deliver a guideline until some years after its creation, it developed a significant body of general sentencing jurisprudence, a practice it has continued. By January 2024, it had issued almost 1,000 sentencing judgments arising from both appeals against severity and undue leniency applications.[122] This has had quite a transformative impact on Irish sentencing law, especially because of the court's strong insistence that it is always best practice for a trial court to nominate a headline sentence before making any allowance for offender-related factors. **13–53**

Court of Appeal and Supreme Court Guidelines

In 2018, the Court of Appeal delivered its first guideline judgment in *People (DPP) v Casey*[123] which dealt with residential burglary. Since then, both that court and the Supreme Court have offered guidance on the sentencing of several offences. The recommended sentence ranges for **13–54**

---

[121] The Court of Appeal was established as a result of the 33rd Amendment to the Constitution adopted in 2013, and the Court of Appeal Act 2014.

[122] These may be accessed through a database maintained by the Judicial Council: <https://judicialcouncil.ie/database-of-court-of-appeal-decisions/> accessed 10 August 2024.

[123] [2018] IECA 121; [2018] 2 IR 337.

most of those offences have already been described in Chap 10. Here, we shall concentrate on four general features of these judicially developed guidelines. First, the guidelines are invariably expressed in terms of recommended sentence ranges as opposed to starting points or tariffs. The Court of Appeal has tended to adopt a tripartite approach with a low, middle and high range for each offence. The Supreme Court has indicated four or five ranges in the two principal guideline judgments it has so far issued, but this was appropriate for the offences in question – manslaughter and rape – which can be committed in a wide range of circumstances.[124] The Supreme Court has also issued a shorter guideline on sentencing for harassment and on the attachment of conditions to suspended sentences.[125] In *People (DPP) v Faulkner*,[126] it summarised the main general principles of sentencing.

Formal and Informal Guidelines

13–55 Secondly, the Court of Appeal has drawn a distinction between formal and informal guidelines. In *People (DPP) v O'Sullivan*[127] it described a formal guideline judgment as:

> "a judgment in which the court says it is providing guidance, in which advance notice was given of the intention to provide guidance, one in which the court attempts to review sentencing for a whole offence or class of offences, and one in which the parties were invited to address the court on aspects of sentencing for the offence or class of offences in question that go beyond issues arising on the facts of the case."

13–56 A strict application of these criteria would mean that there are in fact, very few formal guideline judgments. *People (DPP) v Casey*[128] (on residential burglary) certainly qualifies, as that was one in which general submissions, written and oral, are sought and tendered before the appeal was finally decided. *People (DPP) v Sarsfield*[129] (on s 15A drug offences) is another possible candidate. It does not offer sentencing guidance in the sense of setting out sentence ranges. Rather it dealt with the circumstances in which a court could appropriately impose something less than the presumptive 10-year minimum sentence specified by statute. However, it was a case in which the Court of Appeal sought additional, general submissions and in which it offered some general guidance.

13–57 Additionally, sentence ranges have been indicated by the Court of Appeal

---

[124] *People (DPP) v Mahon* [2019] IESC 24; [2019] 3 IR 151; [2019] 2 ILRM 81 (manslaughter); *People (DPP) v E(F)* [2019] IESC 85; [2021] 1 IR 217; [2020] 1 ILRM 517 (rape).
[125] *People (DPP) v Molloy* [2021] IESC 44; [2021] 3 IR 494; [2021] 2 ILRM 278.
[126] [2024] IESC 16.
[127] [2020] IECA 331, para 30.
[128] [2018] IECA 121; [2018] 2 IR 337.
[129] [2019] IECA 260.

for other offences including robbery,[130] aggravated burglary,[131] cultivating cannabis,[132] defilement[133] and intimidating witnesses.[134] These may be classified as informal in the sense that they did not result from a general review of sentencing practice and principles of the kind mentioned in *O'Sullivan*. Typically, in such cases the court specifies three sentence range with equal divisions from zero to the maximum sentence (or 15 years where the maximum is life imprisonment). Thus, an offence punishable with a maximum of nine years will have ranges of (probably) zero to three years, four to six years and seven to nine years. In effect, most offences are now governed by such informal guidelines in the sense that trial judges, when sentencing for any offence carrying a discretionary prison sentence, will apply a tripartite range even if no guideline has been indicated for the offence in question by the Court of Appeal. This is a perfectly acceptable practice pending the elaboration of more detailed guidance, whether by the appeal courts or the Sentencing Guidelines and Information Committee (discussed below).

The significance of the distinction between formal and informal guidelines **13–58**
has yet to be clearly articulated. However, it is safe to assume that formal guidelines derive their authority primarily from the more extensive analysis of past sentencing practice which is made possible by the additional information furnished to the Court of Appeal once it indicates an intention to issue such a judgment. This analysis may well reveal that previous sentences handed down either by trial courts or the Court of Appeal itself did not fully conform with the predominant sentencing patterns for the offence in question. For this reason, a formal guideline may represent a step change in sentencing for that offence, though that change will be the result of a broader review and a deeper analysis than had hitherto been undertaken of the relevant precedents. This is how the Court of Appeal has interpreted its own guideline judgment in *Casey* on sentencing for burglary.[135] Secondly, it may be surmised that trial courts are obliged to follow formal guidelines unless there is a compelling reason to depart from them. However, it is also clear that the Court of Appeal expects trial courts to have due regard to informal guidelines as well. For instance, the Court of Appeal has stressed on at least two occasions that it regards the informal guideline for robbery in *People (DPP) v Byrne*[136] as important and one that should always be considered.[137] The same might be said of *People (DPP) v Lennon*[138] which may, strictly speaking, be informal but it offers detailed guidance on sentencing for witness intimidation.

---

130 *People (DPP) v Byrne* [2018] IECA 120.
131 *People (DPP) v Byrne* [2018] IECA 120.
132 *People (DPP) v Samuilis* [2018] IECA 316.
133 *People (DPP) v McD* [2021] IECA 31.
134 *People (DPP) v Lennon* [2021] IECA 30.
135 See its remarks in *People (DPP) v Conroy* [2019] IECA 251, para 19.
136 *People (DPP) v Byrne* [2018] IECA 120.
137 *People (DPP) v O'Sullivan* [2020] IECA 331, para 84; *People (DPP) v Joyce* [2021] IECA 124.
138 [2021] IECA 30.

Then, there are cases such as *People (DPP) v Sinnott, Long and Joyce*[139] which, while providing neither a formal nor informal guideline, has a useful analysis of sentencing for money laundering offences. The same might be said of *People (DPP) v Edosa*[140] which is helpful on sentencing more serious instances of human trafficking.

13–59 Incidentally, of the two major guideline judgments delivered by the Supreme Court, only one, *People (DPP) v Mahon*[141] on manslaughter, would qualify as a formal guideline according to the *O'Sullivan* criteria. In that case, the court had sought and received general submissions on the sentencing of assault manslaughter. This was not done in *People (DPP) v E(F)*[142] although in that case the court undertook its own extensive analysis of past sentencing practice for rape (the offence at issue). Further, *E(F)* has been constantly applied by trial courts and appeal courts in the meantime.

Effective Maximum Sentence

13–60 Sentence ranges are easily devised when the offence is punishable with a specified maximum, eg, 12 years' imprisonment. However, several commonly prosecuted offences carry discretionary life sentences. For those offences, the Court of Appeal has generally adopted an effective maximum of 15 years' imprisonment, and it has structured the sentence ranges accordingly. It first did this in *People (DPP) v Byrne*[143] and it has adopted the same approach in later cases.[144] This does not, of course, prevent the imposition of a sentence longer than 15 years, including life imprisonment, in an exceptionally serious case,[145] nor does it prevent a cumulative sentence exceeding 15 years where consecutive sentences are deemed appropriate. In *People (DPP) v Edosa,*[146] which involved human trafficking, the DPP submitted to the Court of Appeal that, in view of the multi-dimensional nature of the harm caused by that offence, an effective maximum of 18 to 20 years might be more appropriate. While the court accepted that there was some merit in that suggestion, it decided to adhere to the 15-year maximum in this case, mainly because it was the first prosecution for human trafficking.

Guideline Revision

13–61 Sentencing guidelines, whatever their provenance, are never set in stone. Even those guidelines formally promulgated by a statutory body such as the United States Sentencing Commission or the English Sentencing

---

139 [2021] IECA 42.
140 [2023] IECA 38.
141 [2019] IESC 24; [2019] 3 IR 151; [2019] 2 ILRM 81.
142 [2019] IESC 85; [2021] 1 IR 217; [2020] 1 ILRM 57.
143 [2018] IECA 120, para para 60.
144 See, for example, *People (DPP) v Samuilis* [2018] IECA 316, para para 45 and *People (DPP) v McD* [2021] IECA 31.
145 *People (DPP) v Edosa* [2023] IECA 38.
146 [2023] IECA 38.

Council are periodically reviewed and revised, in part at least. Judicially developed guidelines are more readily amended as they can be adjusted, if necessary, when a suitable opportunity arises. In *People (DPP) v O'Sullivan*[147] the Court of Appeal adjusted upwards the two higher ranges indicated in *People (DPP) v Fitzgibbon*[148] for the offence of causing serious harm. This element of flexibility may be seen as a strength of judicially developed guidelines, especially in circumstances where, as in *Fitzgibbon*, there were few precedents available when the original guideline was established. However, guideline stability is also important, so revision, whether upwards or downwards, should be undertaken only where it is clear that the existing guideline no longer adequately reflects the gravity of the prevailing manifestations of the offence in question.

Statutory Provision for Sentencing Guidelines

The Judicial Council Act 2019 provides for the establishment of a Sentencing Guidelines and Information Committee ('SGIC') under the aegis of the Judicial Council, the body charged with promoting high standards of conduct among the judiciary and continuing education of judges. The inclusion of the provisions creating the SGIC at a late stage in the passage of the legislation came as a surprise. When the Judicial Council Bill was first introduced in 2017 it provided for the establishment of a Sentencing Information Committee with the function of collating and disseminating information on sentences imposed by the courts.[149] There was little forewarning about the introduction of sentencing guidelines which resulted from amendments tabled during committee stage in the Seanad. The SGIC is one of the committees which the Sentencing Council is required to establish under s 23 of the 2019 Act. It is to consist of eight judges nominated by the Chief Justice (with one of those as chairperson) and five lay members to be appointed by the Government following receipt of recommendations from the Public Appointments Service. Each member of the SGIC is appointed for a four-year term and may not serve more than two full terms. In selecting the lay members, at least two of whom must be women,[150] the Public Appointments Service must try to ensure that they collectively possess knowledge and expertise in certain matters including the prosecution and defence of criminal proceedings, policing, sentencing policy, promoting the welfare of victims, academic study and research in criminal law or criminology, and the rehabilitation of offenders.[151] **13–62**

The functions of the SGIC, as set out in s 23(2) of the 2019 Act, are to: **13–63**

(a) prepare and submit to the Board of the Judicial Council for its review draft sentencing guidelines;

---

147 [2019] IECA 250.
148 [2014] IECCA 12; [2014] 2 ILRM 116.
149 Judicial Council Bill 2017, s 18.
150 Judicial Council Act 2019, s 24(6).
151 Judicial Council Act 2019, s 25(3).

(b) prepare and submit to the Board for its review draft amendments to guidelines adopted by the Council;
(c) monitor the operation of sentencing guidelines;
(d) collate, in such manner as it considers appropriate, information on sentences imposed by the courts; and
(e) disseminate that information from time to time to judges and persons other than judges.

13–64 In the discharge of its information role, the SGIC may collate information on court sentencing decisions, conduct research on sentences imposed by the courts, disseminate decisions of the court relating to sentence, and organise conferences, seminars and meetings relevant to its function. As the 2019 Act is currently phrased, draft guidelines drawn up by the SGIC and any proposal for the amendment of an existing guideline must be submitted to the Board of the Judicial Council (which has 11 judicial members) which must review the draft guideline or amendments and make such modifications as it considers appropriate. Guidelines and amendments are then formally adopted by the Judicial Council which consists, in effect, of all serving judges. The Council must adopt new and amended guidelines submitted to it by the Board as soon as possible but, in any event, not later than 12 months after submission.[152] However, as previously noted, for constitutional reasons some alternative means of adoption will now have to be devised.[153]

13–65 The sentencing guidelines adopted by the Council may relate to sentencing generally or to sentences in respect of a particular offence, a particular category of offence or a particular category of offender.[154] The 2019 Act further provides:

> "A range of sentences may be specified in sentencing guidelines that it is appropriate for a court to consider before imposing sentence on an offender in the proceedings before it."[155]

13–66 This suggests that guidelines may follow the pattern already established in Court of Appeal judgments such as *People (DPP) v Casey*[156] where sentence ranges rather than starting points were indicated. The 2019 Act, unlike the (English) Coroners and Justice Act 2009, makes no reference to offence categories, but it is sufficiently widely drawn to permit the framing of guidelines similar to those produced by the English Sentencing Council under the terms of the Coroners and Justice Act 2009. When framing draft guidelines and amendments, the SGIC shall have regard to:

(a) sentences that are imposed by the courts;
(b) the need to promote consistency in sentences imposed by the courts;

---

[152] Judicial Council Act 2019, s 7(2)(h).
[153] See note 1 above.
[154] Judicial Council Act 2019, s 91(1) which appears to be modelled on England's Coroners and Justice Act 2009, s 120.
[155] s 91(2).
[156] [2018] IECA 121; [2018] 2 IR 337.

(c) the impact of judicial sentencing decisions on victims of the offences concerned;
(d) the need to promote public confidence in the criminal justice system;
(e) the financial costs involved in the execution of different types of sentence and the relative effectiveness of them in the prevention of re-offending;
(f) such factors as the SGIC or the Board considers appropriate relating to the offence concerned and the offender committing the offence for the purpose of specifying a sentence range. [157]

This provision is clearly based on s 120(11) of the (English) Coroners and Justice Act 2009, save that in the 2009 Act, paragraph (f) refers to the results of any monitoring of the guidelines by the Sentencing Council under s 128 of that Act. The reference in paragraph (a) to the sentences imposed by the courts suggests that here, as in England and Wales, sentencing guidelines are intended to be broadly reflective of existing practice. **13–67**

Section 92 of the Judicial Council Act 2019 specifies the extent to which criminal courts are obliged to implement Council guidelines. It states: **13–68**

> "A court shall, in imposing a sentence, have regard to sentencing guidelines relevant to the proceedings before it, unless the court is satisfied that to do so would be contrary to the interests of justice and the reasons it is so satisfied shall be stated by the court in its decision."

This section is an amalgam of s 172 of the (English) Criminal Justice Act 2003 which simply required a court to *have regard to* any guidelines relevant to the offender's case, and s 59 of the Sentencing Act 2020 (re-enacting s 125 of the Coroners and Justice Act 2009) which requires a court to *follow* any guidelines relevant to the offender's case unless the court is satisfied that it would be contrary to the interests of justice to do so.[158] The duty 'to have regard to' is, on the face of it, less constraining than a duty 'to follow' (which, as noted, was included in the Coroners and Justice Act on the recommendation of the Gage Report). However, while s 172 of the Criminal Justice Act 2003 was in force, the Court of Appeal had stressed that it was not open to sentencing courts to disregard what the SGC had to say.[159] They could depart from a guideline in appropriate circumstances **13–69**

---

[157] Judicial Council Act 2019, s 91.

[158] s 92 of the 2019 Act is also very similar in substance to s 6 of the Criminal Justice and Licensing (Scotland) Act 2010.

[159] *R v Oosthuizen* [2006] 1 Cr App R (S) 73. See Ashworth, note 96 above, at 395. The Court of Appeal stressed the same point, even more strongly, in respect of the present duty 'to follow' definitive guidelines in *R v Healey* [2012] EWCA Crim 1005; [2013] 1 Cr App R (S) 33, paras 5 and 6. More recently, in *R v Whirlpool UK Appliances Ltd* [2017] EWCA Crim 2186; [2018] 1 WLR 1811; [2018] 1 Cr App R (S) 44, para 12, the Court of Appeal said, in relation to a guideline for a health and safety offence which included quite detailed tables of fines, that a sentencing court "should not lose sight of the fact that it is engaged in an exercise of judgment appropriately structured by the Guideline but, as has often been observed, not straitjacketed by it." This was later referenced with approval in *R v BUPA Care Homes (BNH) Ltd* [2019] EWCA Crim 1691; [2020] 1 Cr App R(S) 48, para 19.

but not simply because they disagreed with it. A reasoned decision for the departure was required. Section 92 of the Judicial Council Act 2019, especially with its requirement for reasons, is likely to be interpreted in a similar way. For good measure s 93 of the 2019 Act provides that nothing in the Act is to be construed as operating to interfere with (a) the performance by the courts of their functions, or (b) the exercise by a judge of his or her judicial functions. This was presumably intended to forestall, amongst other things, any challenge to the constitutionality of the judicial obligation to have regard to sentencing guidelines. Section 92 of the 2019 Act, as noted, requires a court to have regard to "sentencing guidelines relevant to the offence before it" which raises the question of whether this includes judicially developed guidelines as well as those adopted by the Judicial Council. It seems to cover the latter only because s 2 of the Act (the general definitions section) provides that "sentencing guidelines" shall be construed in accordance with s 91 which is exclusively concerned with guidelines adopted by the Council. However, this should not detract from the obligation of trial courts to follow appeal court guidelines until such time as they are superseded by Council guidelines. The (English) Coroners and Justice Act 2009, in establishing the SC, provides (s 124(8)) that the Court of Appeal may continue in its judgments to provide guidance relating the sentencing of offenders. Guidance, for this purpose, might include matters of a more general nature not covered in any existing guideline.

13–70 Perhaps the most significant feature of the guidelines system introduced by the 2019 Act is that it was not preceded by any consultation or public deliberation about the advantages or drawbacks of introducing formal sentencing guidelines or about the form they should take in this jurisdiction. There was little parliamentary scrutiny of the relevant statutory provisions. The Judicial Council Bill was initiated in the Seanad in November 2017 when it got a second reading. The committee stage in the Seanad was completed in one day in April 2019 and all stages were completed in the Dáil in less than two hours in July 2019.[160] This was in stark contrast to the sequence of events extending over a decade or more that preceded the present guideline system introduced in England and Wales in 2009 and in Scotland in 2015. Granted, the 2019 Act, unlike the equivalent English legislation, does not prescribe the exact form that the guidelines should take; this will be one of the more difficult choices facing the SGIC and the adopting body. There has been some debate elsewhere as to whether bodies charged with creating guidelines should have a lay or judicial majority.[161] The answer in this jurisdiction is now clear: the SGIC has a judicial majority while the Board (which has a revising function) consists entirely of serving judges. The composition of the

[160] All the debates may be accessed at <www.oireachtas.ie/en/bills/2017/70/?tabs=debates>.

[161] Michael Tonry, *Punishment and Politics: Evidence and Emulation in the Making of English Crime Control Policy* (Willan, 2004), 103, arguing that only a minority or bare majority of a sentencing commission should be judges. Judges are in a minority on most American sentencing commissions.

body for adopting them remains to be seen. The regime introduced by the 2019 Act has the potential to produce a fair and coherent sentencing system, especially because of the SGIC's obligation to monitor the application of the guidelines. But, to discharge all its duties effectively, the Committee will need considerable resources, including appropriately qualified support staff to collect and analyse data, and assist in guideline preparation.[162] The English Sentencing Council had an allocation of about £1.8 million in 2022/23 and its staff costs ran to more than £1.4 million.[163] The Scottish Sentencing Council has an annual budget of about £750,000, including £560,000 for staff costs.[164] The Irish SGIC would need a budget at least equivalent to that of the Scottish Council if it is to discharge its functions effectively.

8. Guidance and Guidelines: General Observations

Some major common law jurisdictions including Canada, Australia and New Zealand still have no formal sentencing guidelines resembling those in the United States or England and Wales. They rely mainly on general principles and, in some instances, judicially developed sentence ranges.[165] A sentencing commission charged with drawing up guidelines was planned for New Zealand more than a decade ago but, following a change of government, the idea was abandoned.[166] However, there is a perceptible international trend towards formal guidelines as reflected in recent developments in countries as far apart as Ireland and Ethiopia.[167] The American Model Penal Code: Sentencing, adopted in 2017, which is an admirably comprehensive and thoughtful document, recommends that each jurisdiction should have a sentencing commission charged with the development of guidelines.[168] It envisages guidelines that set forth **13–71**

---

[162] See Jay Gormley, Tom O'Malley, Julian V Roberts, Cassia Spohn and Cyrus Tata, *Assessing Approaches to Sentencing Data Collection and Analysis,* report submitted to SGIC in May 2022 and available on Judicial Council's website: <https://judicialcouncil.ie>.

[163] Sentencing Council, *Annual Report 2022/23* (2023), 67.

[164] Scottish Sentencing Council, note 112 above, at 32.

[165] In *R v M(A)* [2010] NZCA 114; [2010] 2 NZLR 750, for example, the New Zealand Court of Appeal formulated sentencing guidelines in the form of bands or ranges for rape and related offences. Some Canadian appeal courts have also established sentence ranges or starting points for certain offences. See notes 45 and 46 above and accompanying text.

[166] Warren Young and Andrea King, "The origins and evolution of sentencing guidelines: A comparison of England and Wales and New Zealand" in Andrew Ashworth and Julian V Roberts (eds), *Sentencing Guidelines: Exploring the English Model* (Oxford University Press, 2013), Chap 13; Warren Young and Claire Browning, "New Zealand's Sentencing Council" [2008] Crim LR 287; Warren Young and Andrea King, "Sentencing practice and guidance in New Zealand" (2010) 22 *Federal Sentencing Reporter* 254.

[167] Kassahun Molla Yilma and Julian V Roberts, "Out of Africa: Exploring the Ethiopian Sentencing Guidelines" (2019) 30 *Criminal Law Forum* 309.

[168] American Law Institute, *Model Penal Code: Sentencing. Proposed Final Draft* (10 April 2017),

presumptive sentences together with non-exhaustive lists of aggravating and mitigating factors that may justify departure from a presumptive sentence.[169] A 'presumptive sentence' is defined as "the penalty, range of penalties, alternative penalties, or combination of penalties indicated in the guideline as appropriate for an ordinary case coming within a defined class of cases".[170] The Code is obviously addressed to United States jurisdictions only, but its recommendations are worthy of serious consideration in any country that aspires to achieving a healthy balance between consistency and individualisation in its sentencing system.

13–72 The general guidance on which courts have traditionally relied has its advantages, but so also do more formal guideline systems. Ireland is now moving decisively in the direction of formal guidelines. This in turn prompts a number of policy questions, notably: (1) are formal guidelines preferable to judicially developed guidance?; (2) should guidelines aim to replicate existing practice or to change it on some way?; (3) can legal transplants, of sentencing guidelines in this instance, work successfully?; and (4) is it possible to develop an effective institutional synergy between the legislature, the courts and a sentencing commission?

Judicially Developed Guidance Versus Formal Guidelines

13–73 Sentencing guidance included in judgments of senior appeal courts reflect the common law framework in which they are developed. They are informed primarily by the facts of the case or group of cases before the court, rather than by a broader analysis of all the foreseeable offence- and offender-related circumstances that might arise when sentencing the offence in question. This is a defining characteristic of the common law which, as Gerald Postema says, is "the product of reflective practical experience, as opposed to untutored individual intuition or a natural capacity for deductive reasoning exercised in abstraction from concrete details of ordinary life".[171] Custom, as reflected in precedent, is highly valued even though its underlying premises are seldom closely interrogated. The primary objective will always be, as it should, to do justice to the parties before the court. There is, to be sure, some merit in the idea of developing guidelines in the context of real cases, and especially where an appeal court groups several related cases together for purpose of issuing a guideline, or when a formal guideline is being issued. Together they may bring to light relevant sentencing factors that might not occur to somebody charged with developing a guideline in the abstract. But there

---

[169] art 6B.02(1).

[170] art 6B. The Code further provides (art 6B.02(2)) that a presumptive sentence should be proportionate to the gravity of the offence, the harm caused to crime victims and the offender's blameworthiness "based on the commission's collective judgment of appropriate punishments for ordinary cases of the kind governed by each presumptive sentence".

[171] Gerald Postema, "Classical common law jurisprudence (Part II)" (2003) 3 *Oxford University Commonwealth Law Journal* 1 at 10. See also Charles L Barzun, "Justice Souter's common law" (2018) 104 Virginia LR 655, 658-659.

are certain drawbacks as well.[172] Appeal courts usually issue guidelines, on a gradual basis and in an uncoordinated way, for specific offences (eg rape, robbery or burglary) without relating one to the others. This can lead to a lack of cohesion or proportionality between the sentence ranges recommended for different offences. A second obvious drawback is that cases coming before senior appeal courts involve serious offences, and are mostly appeals against severity of sentence, although this situation has changed somewhat since the introduction of prosecution appeals against sentence in England and Wales in 1988 and in Ireland in 1993.[173] Offences that are exclusively or predominantly disposed of in courts of summary jurisdiction are unlikely to receive any attention. Thirdly, the effectiveness of judicially developed guidance depends on the extent to which it becomes known to trial court judges and advocates. This in turn depends on the existence of an effective law reporting system or some other means of disseminating appeal court judgments.

Formal guidelines drawn up by a commission can avoid most of these pitfalls. A commission can undertake a thoroughly comprehensive investigation of the many circumstances in which an offence may be committed and the factors that may legitimately influence sentence. As the English Court of Appeal said in *R v Healey*:[174] **13–74**

> "The Sentencing Council receives a very wide range of information, statistical data, research and opinion, both lay and professional. The collection of information available to it is far wider than the members of this court, individually or collectively, or individual sentencers can hope to have. The Council also engages in a comprehensive consultation programme before it publishes any guideline, frequently with the publication of one, or sometimes a succession, of drafts for discussion. That process frequently involves – and it did in this case – extensive testing of commonly encountered scenarios upon experienced sentencers, namely Crown Court judges and district judges."

A commission is also in a better position to address the coordination problem mentioned earlier by ensuring that guidelines are compatible *inter se*. Problems can admittedly arise where statutory maximum sentences fail to reflect the comparative gravity of the offences to which they apply.[175] Guideline sentence ranges must be chosen by reference to the applicable maximum penalty which, in turn, means that some inconsistency may remain. However, aside from this difficulty, a commission, assuming it has the necessary expertise and research support, has the advantage of being able to frame guidelines that observe ordinal proportionality and **13–75**

---

172 O'Malley, note 21 above, Chap 5, discusses this issue in more detail.

173 Criminal Justice Act 1988, ss 35 and 36 (England and Wales); Criminal Justice Act 1993, s 2 (Ireland).

174 [2012] EWCA Crim 1005; [2013] 1 Cr App R (S) 33, para para 4.

175 Rory Kelly, "Reforming maximum sentences and respecting ordinal proportionality" [2018] Crim LR 450. This problem is discussed further in Chap 1 above.

that are compatible with each other in terms of the sentence ranges and general principles they establish.

13–76 A further advantage of a sentencing commission is that it can keep existing guidelines under review, amend them and, if necessary, replace them with new ones. Unlike an appeal court, it need not wait until a suitable case comes forward in order to consider possible revision. As already noted, English and Irish legislation tasks the SC and the SGIC respectively with amending existing guidelines. Moreover, a commission can monitor the operation of guidelines in a systematic manner by undertaking empirical research on the judicial application of guidelines, and on the extent to which trial courts are departing from them. This too is something which appeal courts are ill-equipped to do, if they can do it at all.

Guidelines and Existing Practice

13–77 In one of the leading works of literary criticism of the 20th century, *The Mirror and the Lamp*, MH Abrams identified two competing concepts of the mind and the imagination. One of these concepts is mimetic to the extent that it reflects the external world, while the other is more productive and creative in the sense that it shines a light on that world and helps us to understand it better.[176] This metaphor of the mirror and the lamp can usefully be adapted to describe one of the more difficult choices facing creators of sentencing guidelines. Should guidelines aim to reflect or replicate existing practice, or should they aim to have a more transformative effect by altering the course of that practice in some way? As noted earlier, the present English guidelines seem intended to mirror existing practice; the governing legislation, after all, requires the SC to have regard to the sentences imposed by the courts. The same holds true of the statutory scheme recently introduced in Ireland. The Minnesota guidelines, on the other hand, were designed to be more transformative.

13–78 One advantage of formulating guidelines that reflect (or largely reflect) existing practice, in so far as it can reliably be ascertained, is that they are more likely to gain acceptance from judges and lawyers. History shows that mandatory penalties, at least when introduced on a widespread basis, are likely to be circumvented if they are perceived to operate unjustly.[177] Guidelines that mandate or recommend penalties that seem excessively harsh are in danger of suffering a similar fate. Indeed, the same might happen if guideline sentences appear too lenient. Most guideline systems leave some scope for departure. The Minnesota guidelines allow for departure where there are substantial and compelling circumstances, the present English law requires judges to follow guidelines unless it would be contrary to the interests of justice to do so, while both Irish and Scottish law

[176] MH Abrams, *The Mirror and the Lamp: Romantic Theory and the Critical Tradition* (Oxford University Press, 1953). Both the phrase "the mirror and the lamp" and the concept it describes were borrowed from WB Yeats's Introduction to *The Oxford Book of Modern Verse* (Oxford University Press, 1936).

[177] Tonry, note 21 above.

requires courts to have regard to guidelines unless it would be contrary to the interests of justice to do so. These various formulations, and especially the Irish and Scottish, could possibly be interpreted by judges, if they were collectively so minded, to allow for departures to an extent that would render the guidelines virtually meaningless. Judges are far more likely to respect and apply guidelines that fairly reflect existing practice and that are sufficiently flexible to accommodate the many different offence- and offender-related circumstances that merit consideration in specific cases.

As against this, guidelines that are rigorously required to mirror existing practice will inevitably end up perpetuating any deficiencies or inconsistencies in that practice. This is a well-known drawback of relying on a sentencing information system as a means of informing or structuring judicial discretion.[178] Sentencing commissions and similar bodies must therefore have some scope to adopt a more normative approach when it appears, for example, that prevailing sentencing practice fails to reflect the principle of ordinal proportionality which demands that more serious offences should ordinarily attract heavier penalties than less serious ones. Or, a commission might conclude that the sentences commonly imposed for some offence simply fail to reflect the gravity of that offence. At least two judgments of the English Court of Appeal in the pre-guideline era, *R v Billam*[179] and *R v Boswell*,[180] were quite explicitly intended to encourage heavier sentences for the offences in question – rape and reckless driving causing death in those instances. Sentencing guidelines designed to have the same effect are unlikely to encounter much resistance unless they demand a significant departure from existing levels. Neither the Judicial Council Act 2019 (s 91) nor the (English) Coroners and Justice Act 2009 (s 120(11)), on which it is modelled, prohibits the adoption of a normative approach. Both the SGIC and the English SC must 'have regard to' the sentences imposed by the courts but, in view of the other matters to which they must have regard, including the need to promote consistency in sentencing and public confidence in the criminal justice system, they are scarcely confined to producing guidelines based entirely on existing practice. Indeed, certain definitive guidelines produced by the English SC were intended to alter existing practice for some offences, including drug offences, and had that effect.[181] **13–79**

Legal Transplants and Legal Translations

The expression 'legal transplants' is invariably associated with a book of that title by Alan Watson in which he claimed that legal rules, and sometimes entire bodies of rules, can successfully be transplanted from **13–80**

---

178 O'Malley, note 21 above, Chap 7.

179 [1986] 1 WLR 349; (1986) 82 Cr App R 347; (1986) 8 Cr App R (S) 48.

180 [1984] 1 WLR 1047; (1984) 79 Cr App R 277; (1984) 6 Cr App R (S) 257.

181 Sentencing Council, *Drug Offences: Definitive Guideline* (2012), See Julian V Roberts, "The evolution of sentencing guidelines in Minnesota and England and Wales" in Tonry (ed), *American Sentencing*, note 63 above, 187 at 198-201.

one country to another.[182] As a Roman lawyer, he tended to concentrate on the reception of Roman law in various European jurisdictions, including Scotland. In later work, he expanded on his thesis, arguing that the causes of 'transplant bias' included the high standing of the donor system and the general prestige of the donor state, a shared legal tradition of donor and borrower, and the accessibility of the borrowed law in written or codified form.[183] Watson's claims have been hotly contested by other comparative lawyers, notably Pierre Legrand, a prominent advocate of difference theory. Responding in one instance to a European Parliament proposal for the establishment of a common European code of private law, Legrand argued that all rules are a reflection of the legal culture in which they are forged.[184] Drawing on the anthropological work of Clifford Geertz and Claude Lévi-Strauss,[185] he rejected the idea of law as an autonomous, self-contained discipline divorced from other social phenomena, and claimed to identify irreducible differences between the common law and civil law traditions. The Watson and Legrand perspectives are not necessarily incompatible. Much of the law in any country is the product of local culture, social conditions and historical contingency, but this does not preclude the possibility that some discrete rules or bodies of rules can successfully be borrowed from elsewhere. A country may become more or less receptive to the influence of foreign law as it undergoes political, economic or social change. Vicki Jackson, a leading scholar of comparative constitutional law, has argued that the response of one jurisdiction to principles and interpretations developed in another may be one of convergence, resistance or engagement.[186] As noted earlier, Irish courts were long resistant to the notion of sentencing guidelines, but now that they have come to accept them, there is an opportunity for constructive engagement with similar developments in other jurisdictions.

13–81 Apart altogether from guidelines, sentencing more generally lends itself to comparative study and analysis, especially if one adopts a functional approach which focuses on concrete issues and problems rather than the formal law.[187] Whatever their structural, systemic and terminological

182 Alan Watson, *Legal Transplants: An Approach to Comparative Law*, 2nd ed (University of Georgia Press, 1974). Jerome Frank had referred to the same concept in "Civil law influences on the common law: Some reflections on 'comparative' and 'contrastive' law" (1956) 104 Univ Pennsylvania LR 887.

183 Alan Watson, "Legal change: Sources of law and legal culture" (1983) 131 Univ Pennsylvania LR 1121 at 1147.

184 Pierre Legrand, "European legal systems are not converging" (1996) 45 *International and Comparative Law Quarterly* 52.

185 Clifford Geertz, *Local Knowledge: Further Essays in Interpretive Anthropology* (Basic Books, 1985); Claude Lévi-Strauss and Didier Eribon, *De prés et de loin* (Odile Jacob, 1988).

186 Vicki Jackson, "Constitutional comparisons: Convergence, resistance, engagement" (2005) 119 Harvard LR109. See also Anne-Marie Slaughter, "Judicial globalization" (2000) 40 *Virginia Journal of International Law* 1103; Sujit Choudhry, "Globalization in search of justification: Toward a theory of comparative constitutional interpretation" (1999) 74 Indiana LJ 819.

187 On the functional approach, see K Zweigert and H Kötz, *An Introduction to*

differences, most countries are grappling with the same fundamental questions: what is the most defensible moral justification for punishment? What range of options should be available to sentencing authorities? How should offence gravity be assessed? Which factors should aggravate or mitigate otherwise deserved punishment? How can a proper or acceptable balance be struck between the individualisation of punishment and the achievement of consistency? As noted in Chap 3, the answer to the first of these questions varies across time and space. But there is a remarkable degree of international consensus (in the common law world at least) on the others. Granted, when it comes to the range of available options, there is a major fault line between those countries that retain and use the death penalty and those that have abolished it. Otherwise, a common law of sentencing can be said to exist in the sense that the same general principles are recognised in most common law countries. An Irish or British lawyer who embarks on the study of Australian, Canadian or New Zealand sentencing will find most of it very familiar, although every national system naturally has some distinctive features as well. The similarity between the general sentencing principles applicable in common law countries is illustrated by the frequency with which their courts cite each other's judgments as persuasive authority. Countless examples of this practice could be given, but two of recent vintage illustrate the point. In *R v Suter*[188] the Canadian Supreme Court referred to an Australian case, *R v Mamarika*,[189] to bolster its conclusion that violent retribution against an offender by members of the public was a relevant collateral consequence for sentencing purposes. In *R v Winders*[190] the New Zealand Court of Appeal drew upon the Canadian Supreme Court judgment in *R v Nasogaluak*[191] when dealing with the question of whether police misconduct during the investigation of the offence could be a mitigating factor at sentencing.

Sentencing guidelines are different in this respect. Unlike general **13–82** sentencing principles that are rooted in the common law (of England in particular), guideline systems are modern developments. Every country will have had its own reasons for introducing guidelines or, indeed, for considering their introduction but ultimately deciding against it. The momentum for structured sentencing may derive from some event, such the publication of Marvin Frankel's *Criminal Sentences* in the United States in 1973,[192] a particularly controversial sentencing decision or intense public dissatisfaction (real or apparent) with existing sentencing practice. The diverse range of circumstances in which guidelines are

Comparative Law, 3rd ed, translated by Tony Weir (Clarendon Press, 1998), in particular Chap 3; Richard Hyland, "Comparative Law" in Dennis Patterson (ed), *A Companion to Philosophy of Law and Legal Theory* (Blackwell Publishers, 1999), Chap 11.

188 [2018] SCC 34; [2018] 2 SCR 496.

189 [1982] FCA 94; (1982) 42 ALR. 94.

190 [2018] NZCA 277; [2019] 2 NZLR 305.

191 [2010] SCC 6; [2010] 1 SCR 206.

192 On this book and its influence, see note 60 above and accompanying text.

introduced and the immediate preoccupations of those who establish the necessary legal framework might suggest that guideline systems are not readily transplantable from one country to another. Experience to date shows that this is only partly true. The grid-centred guidelines favoured in the United States have so far found no imitators elsewhere. They were considered but rejected in Canada, Scotland, and England and Wales.[193] But this is not to say that American guidelines have been without influence. States such as Minnesota, Pennsylvania, Oregon and Washington and the federal system, all of which introduced presumptive guidelines in the 1980s, showed that it was possible to generate more predictable and non-discriminatory sentencing decisions through such guidelines.[194] That experience undoubtedly ignited interest in structured sentencing elsewhere. Consequently, while there may not have been legal transplantation, there was arguably a significant degree of policy transfer.[195]

13–83 The English guideline system looks like being decidedly more transplant friendly, at least in terms of its underlying philosophy and structure, if not in its detail.[196] As already noted, several provisions of the Judicial Council Act 2019 establishing the SGIC and specifying the extent of a court's duty to apply guidelines once formally adopted are directly borrowed from English and Scottish legislation. Certain features of the English system, including its preference for offence-specific guidelines as opposed to a grid-centred system which aims to cover most or all offences, its gradual approach to developing a body of guidelines over time, and its essentially narrative nature probably explain its attraction to other countries, especially in the common law world. Elements of Alan Watson's theory may also be relevant here, including what he had to say about the prestige of the donor state, a shared legal tradition and the accessibility of the borrowed law favouring legal transplantation.[197] These factors go some way towards explaining why the English guideline

---

[193] Canadian Sentencing Commission, *Sentencing Reform: A Canadian Approach* (Supply and Services Canada, 1987); The Sentencing Commission for Scotland, *The Scope to Improve Consistency in Sentencing* (2006); Sentencing Commission Working Group, *Sentencing Guidelines in England and Wales: An Evolutionary Approach* (2008). See also Julian V Roberts, "Structured sentencing: Lessons from England and Wales for common law jurisdictions" (2012) 14 *Punishment and Society* 267 at 269.

[194] Michael Tonry, "Sentencing in America, 1975-2025" (2013) 42 *Crime and Justice* 141, 157.

[195] On policy transfer, see David P Dolowitz and David Marsh, "Learning from abroad: The role of policy transfer in contemporary policy-making" (2000) 13(1) *Governance* 5; Mark Evans, "Policy transfer in critical perspective" (2009) 30 *Policy Studies* 243; Richard Rose, "What is lesson drawing?" (1991) 11 *Journal of Public Policy* 3.

[196] Julian V Roberts, "The evolution of sentencing guidelines in Minnesota and England and Wales" in Tonry (ed), *American Sentencing*, note 63 above at 188, noting that modified versions of the English guidelines exist in South Korea, Uganda, Nigeria, Jamaica and several Gulf states. Ethiopia can also be added to the list: see Yilma and Roberts, note 167 above.

[197] Watson, note 183 above, at 1147.

system might be adopted, in part at least, in Ireland and other countries with a similar legal tradition.

Perhaps a more fruitful way of considering the influence of one country's sentencing guideline system on that of another is to think in terms of legal translation rather than legal transplantation. The concept of legal translation has been effectively employed by Máximo Langer in analysing the spread of plea bargaining throughout different legal systems and traditions.[198] But it may also apply to the international transfer of any aspect of sentencing policy. National variations in the substantive criminal law, the allocation of sentencing powers, early release provisions and, crucially, ideas as to what constitutes severity and leniency mean that the levels of penalty considered appropriate in one country may be totally unacceptable in another. There may also be profound differences of opinion on extent to which judicial discretion should be constrained. However, sentencing structures adopted in one country may still provide a useful conceptual framework for another country, especially one with a broadly similar legal tradition, which is considering introducing some kind of formal sentencing guidance. The proposed penalty levels will, in all probability, differ from those of the host state (to use Watson's term), but the process for arriving at them may be similar. In fact, we already see the English sentencing guidelines 'translating' in this way to other jurisdictions. **13–84**

The way in which formal guidelines were introduced in Ireland raises another question: can transplantation or translation compensate for the absence of prior deliberation? Ireland is unique in having made statutory provision for a guideline system without any preceding analysis of the pros and cons of doing do. There was nothing equivalent to the Halliday, Carter or Gage reports[199] which had informed the evolution of the English system and no experimentation with providing support for appeal court decision-making as occurred with the Sentencing Advisory Panel. It might well be argued that the groundwork already done in England and Wales coupled with the success of the guideline system that emerged from it obviated the need for any similar preparatory work in Ireland. This assumes that Irish guidelines will be similar in form to the English ones, which should not be presumed. For reasons already mentioned they cannot have the same starting point and ranges. As matters now stand, one can only speculate on the extent to which the guidelines eventually **13–85**

---

[198] Máximo Langer, "From legal transplants to legal translations: The globalization of plea bargaining and the Americanization thesis in criminal procedure" (2004) 45 Harvard International LJ 1. See Chap 6, note 12 above and accompanying text .

[199] Home Office, *Making Punishments Work*, Report of a Review of the Sentencing Framework for England and Wales (2001) (Halliday Report); *Securing the Future: Proposals for the efficient and sustainable use of custody in England and Wales* (2007) (Carter Report); Sentencing Commission Working Group, *Sentencing Guidelines in England and Wales: An Evolutionary Approach* (2008) (Gage Report).

developed in Ireland, as opposed to the governing statutory framework, will reflect some element of transplantation.

Institutional Synergy

13–86 The introduction of formal guidelines seldom alters the existing structure and jurisdiction of the criminal courts. It did admittedly bring about one important change in the United States. Merit-based appeals against sentence were unknown in most American jurisdictions during the indeterminate sentencing era, but they became more prevalent once guidelines were introduced.[200] In these islands, the constitutional and legal jurisdiction of trial courts and appeal courts is largely unaffected by the introduction of guidelines, and parliament can, of course, continue to legislate in all areas of criminal law and criminal justice, including sentencing. Guidelines may nonetheless transform the practical function of senior appeal courts in respect of appeals against sentence. Once a comprehensive set of guidelines has been created, covering most commonly prosecuted offences and, perhaps, more general matters such as discounts for guilty pleas, appeal courts will increasingly be concerned with compliance. The question in most appeals will be whether the relevant guideline was properly interpreted and applied, and whether any departure from it was justified. It will probably be many years before this happens in Ireland, because guideline creation takes time, but there is a strong possibility that it will eventually happen. Meanwhile, the Court of Appeal and the Supreme Court will remain entitled to deliver guideline judgments in respect of particular offences and more general sentencing matters not yet covered by guidelines. In an important analysis of the sentencing jurisprudence of the English Court of Appeal for the year 2016, Andrew Ashworth identified six classes of case, categorised according to the function which the court was called upon to discharge in the individual appeals.[201] Those functions were:

(1) application and interpretation of definitive guidelines;
(2) assessing departures from definitive guidelines;
(3) creating or developing offence-specific guidance;
(4) creating or developing guidance on general principles (including sentencing procedure);
(5) interpreting sentencing legislation;
(6) "common law" sentencing.[202]

---

[200] Nancy Gertner, "Supporting advisory guidelines" (2009) 3 *Harvard Law and Policy Review* 261. Massachusetts was one of the states to allow for appeals against sentence.

[201] Andrew Ashworth, "The evolution of English sentencing guidance in 2016" [2017] Crim LR 507. The analysis was based on the 118 judgments reported in the two volumes of the *Criminal Appeal Reports (Sentencing)* for 2016.

[202] By 'common law' sentencing, he was referring to offences for which there was no formal guidance, either in the form of a definitive guideline or a Court of Appeal guideline judgment. Manslaughter was one such example at the time, although it is now the subject of a definitive guideline (Sentencing Council, *Manslaughter: Definitive Guideline* (2018)).

13–87 The highest number of cases fell into the first of these categories. It may well be that by 2030 or possibly sooner, the sentencing case law of the Irish Court of Appeal will be amenable to a similar classification.

13–88 Yet it would be unfortunate if the Court of Appeal (and Supreme Court) were eventually confined to monitoring compliance with guidelines. Appeal court judgments, by virtue of their discursive nature, can engage in moral reasoning in a way that formal guidelines usually cannot. Narrative guidelines (the kind most likely to be introduced here) are preferable to numerical guidelines in this respect, but even narrative guidelines have their limits. Granted, by specifying factors that indicate different levels of harm and culpability, or that tend to aggravate or mitigate, narrative guidelines implicitly convey the reason why some instances of an offence are more or less serious than others. Judgments, on the other hand, can elaborate on these matters in greater detail and more compelling terms. It is widely accepted, for example, that in sentencing for rape, the fact that the offender broke into the victim's dwelling is an aggravating factor, and all the more so if the intrusion occurred during the night. The English Sentencing Council's definitive guideline for rape certainly gives some prominence to this factor. "Forced/uninvited entry into victim's dwelling" is one of the harm elements indicating a category 2 offence with a sentence range of nine to 13 years' custody.[203] Contrast this with the judgment of the Court of Criminal Appeal in *People (DPP) v Keane*[204] which involved a rape committed by such an intruder. The court went to some trouble to stress that the violation of the victim's dwelling was an aggravating factor, and also to explain why this was so. It said:

> "If there is one place in everyday life [in which] a person needs to, and is entitled to, feel safe and secure it must be in his or her own home at night. This must be ten times more true for a mother responsible for three young children asleep in bed. The respondent has been found criminally responsible for invading her family home and raping that young mother in her own bed with her children sleeping nearby…. Thus this was not only a violation of the victim herself, with all the implications referred to at the outset of this judgment, but also the sense of security which citizens feel they have for themselves and their children in the safety of their own home. The fact that the rape took place in these circumstances was to have lasting additional and devastating effects on the victim as well as very negative consequences for her children."[205]

13–89 It further elaborated on this point elsewhere in the judgment. Reasoned, well-crafted judgments have a persuasive power lacking in formal guidelines.

13–90 The existence of guidelines, definitive or otherwise, should not preclude appeal courts from engaging in this kind of moral reasoning.[206] They can

---

203 Sentencing Council, *Sexual Offences: Definitive Guideline* (2014), p 11.

204 [2007] IECCA 119; [2008] 3 IR 177; [2008] 2 ILRM 321.

205 [2007] IECCA 119; [2008] 3 IR 177; [2008] 2 ILRM 321, paras 54 to 57.

206 In *R v Blackshaw* [2012] 1 WLR 1126; [2012] 2 Cr App R (S) 114, for example,

do so, for example, when deciding if a particular offence was located in the right category or if a general principle, such as a discount for a guilty plea, was correctly applied. In fact, it is vitally important that they should do so, because the framing of guidelines should be an ongoing process. Definitive guidelines are not meant to be cast in stone or to remain valid for all time. As stated in the United States Model Penal Code; Sentencing, "sentencing policy should never be viewed as a 'settled' matter, but should be allowed to evolve and must continually be evaluated".[207] English legislation, as noted, charges the Sentencing Council with reviewing and revising existing guidelines as well as monitoring their operation and effect.[208] The experience of the courts, especially as reflected in appellate judgments, is vitally important for this purpose. Two-way communication between the framers of guidelines and those responsible for their application is essential if guidelines are to be truly responsive to the diverse circumstances of the offences and offenders coming before the courts. Further, if they are to retain credibility and support, guidelines must also reflect collective, well-informed opinion as to what might constitute just punishment in specific cases.

13–91 Experience to date in England and Wales shows that guideline-setting bodies and appeal courts can co-operate productively in developing sentencing jurisprudence. This is reflected in several Court of Appeal judgments where the policies underpinning certain guidelines were discussed, analysed and sometimes expanded upon. In *R v Caley*,[209] for example, the court considered the generic guideline on discount for a guilty plea and elaborated on some aspects of it, including the meaning to be ascribed to the 'first reasonable opportunity' for entering a plea. In *Attorney General's Reference No 80 of 2009 (Moore)*,[210] the court discussed the guidelines then existing on assault and domestic violence. It "whole-heartedly" endorsed the latter guideline, and made some useful observations on the seriousness of domestic violence and abuse.

13–92 Rather surprisingly, in *R v Thelwall*[211] the Court of Appeal held that where an offence is subject to a definitive guideline, the citation of previous decisions of the court on the application and interpretation of the guideline is generally of no assistance. The court said that since the sentencing system now proceeds on the basis of guidelines rather than case law, it should be rare for any party to cite case law seeking to

---

the existence of guidelines (to which scant attention was paid on that occasion) did not prevent the Court of Appeal from dwelling at some length on the heightened gravity of offences committed during a riot.

207 American Law Institute, *Model Penal Code: Sentencing. Proposed Final Draft (April 10, 2017)*, comment on §6A.01, p 262. It further states (art 6A(2)(f)) that a sentencing system "must strive continually to evaluate itself, evolve and improve".

208 Coroners and Justice Act 2009, ss 120((9) and 128.

209 [2012] EWCA Crim 2821; [2013] 2 Cr App R (S) 47.

210 [2010] EWCA Crim 470.

211 [2016] EWCA Crim 1755.

express how the guideline should work. This judgment delivered by a court consisting of Lord Chief Justice Thomas, Lord Justice Treacy (then chair of the Sentencing Council) and Mr Justice Leggatt is difficult to comprehend. As Lyndon Harris has pointed out, a prohibition on citing earlier cases interpreting a guideline could produce inconsistency, the very value guidelines are intended to promote.[212] However, more recent judgments suggest that *Thelwall* is not being treated very seriously. In *R v BUPA Care Homes (BNH) Ltd*,[213] the court considered earlier decisions on the interpretation of the relevant guideline (on health and safety offences in that instance).

The need for the kind of institutional synergy being recommended here is recognised in the revised sentencing provisions of the United States Model Penal Code adopted in 2017. What it has to say in this respect merits quoting at some length, if only because the revised provisions and the commentary thereon (running to some 726 pages) are so thoroughly researched and thoughtfully analysed: **13–93**

> "The revised Code does not endorse any and all forms of sentencing guidelines, but only those that allow considerable latitude for judicial discretion and the development of a common law of sentencing through developing case law in the trial and appellate courts. Further, the content of the guidelines, and ongoing projections of their impacts, should be informed by high quality data and research prepared by the commission in an objective, nonpartisan manner. Policy decisions reflected in the guidelines should be made with the input of knowledgeable persons with varied experience from across the criminal justice system and the broader life of the community, and should be taken with awareness of any similar policy initiatives in other jurisdictions. The guidelines should rest explicitly upon the underlying goals of the sentencing and corrections system. They should always be considered a work in progress, to be amended and improved over time as the commission oversees and evaluates the guidelines' performance in light of their purposes. Subsection (2)(a) cross-references Article 6B, which speaks in detail to the vision of sentencing guidelines endorsed by the Institute.
>
> *Collaboration with, not domination of, judicial branch.*
> The revised Code takes pains to avoid the creation of a sentencing commission with authority to eliminate, override, or ignore the discretionary input of sentencing courts and the appellate bench. Ideally, the commission's guidelines will provide a framework, and starting points for analysis, from which the courts may develop a common law of sentencing sensitive to the variations of individual cases. The aspiration stated in this subsection is reinforced elsewhere in the revised Code. See 9 §§ 1.02(2)(b)(i) (one general purpose of sentencing system is "to preserve judicial discretion to individualise sentences within a framework of law")."[214]

So far, we have been considering the relationship between appeal courts and **13–94**

[212] Lyndon Harris, comment on *R v Thelwall* [2017] Crim LR 240 at 242-243.
[213] [2019] EWCA Crim 1691; [2020] 1 Cr App R (S) 48.
[214] American Law Institute, *Model Penal Code: Sentencing. Proposed Final Draft (April 10, 2017)*, comment on §6A.01 (pp 263-264).

guideline-setting bodies. Parliament also has a critical role in cultivating a productive institutional synergy, though sometimes by inaction rather than action. The effectiveness of sentencing guidelines, however carefully crafted, can be greatly diminished by the legislative introduction of mandatory or presumptive minimum sentences to which courts must give priority when sentencing the offences to why they apply. The history of federal sentencing law in the United States during the past 30 years bears ample testimony to this. Other legislative measures may have the same effect. In this regard, there has been at least one positive development in Ireland. The Supreme Court struck down as unconstitutional a law requiring a five-year mandatory minimum prison sentence for a repeat offence of possessing a firearm in suspicious circumstances.[215] The remaining mandatory minimum sentencing provisions have since been repealed.[216] Certain drug and firearms offences remain subject to presumptive minimum sentences of ten years' imprisonment in some cases and five years in others, but a court may impose a sentence below the minimum in certain circumstances.[217] The constitutionality of these provisions does not seem to be in doubt. The Judicial Council Act 2019 (s 29) requires the Minister for Justice and Equality to commence a review of enactments providing for minimum sentences and to consider, among other things, if the continued imposition of such sentences is appropriate in respect of all the offences to which they apply, and the extent to which they are imposed in practice. The review was to have taken place within two years of the section coming into operation (in 2019). It is unclear if 'minimum sentences' was intended to include presumptive minimum sentences such as those applicable to s 15A and s 15B drug offences, or if it referred only to mandatory minimum sentences (which no longer exist). Either way, there is much to be said for reviewing and, indeed, repealing all existing presumptive minimum sentences, at least when there is a constitutionally sound sentencing guidelines system in place. Guidelines could then be developed for drug and firearms offences which would allow for all relevant factors to be taken into consideration, without the complicating presence of presumptive minimums.

13–95 Parliament can also play a more positive role by responding to suggestions and proposals made by a sentencing commission such as the SGIC and to any difficulties that come to light in the judicial application of guidelines. It should also keep maximum sentences under review because, as already noted, they will invariably influence the sentence ranges established by guidelines.[218] Maintaining ordinal proportionality is crucially important for a fair, credible and consistent sentencing system. Maximum sentences

---

215 *Ellis v Minister for Justice and Equality* [2019] IESC 30; [2019] 3 IR 511; [2019] 2 ILRM 420.

216 See Chap 4, notes 42 and 43, above.

217 Thomas O'Malley, *Sentencing Law and Practice*, 3rd ed (Round Hall, 2016), Chaps 16 and 18.

218 In England and Wales, under the Coroners and Justice Act 2009, s 132, the Lord Chancellor may refer to the Sentencing Council any government policy proposal or proposed legislation to assess its impact on prison places, probation

should therefore reflect the comparative gravity of the offences to which they apply. The Judicial Council Act 2019 gives little direction on the form that SGIC guidelines should take. This is not necessarily a bad thing given the absence of any prior research or discussion on the need for sentencing guidelines in Ireland or on the form they should take. The first major task of the SGIC will be decide on the structure of guidelines and the degree of detail they should contain. Further legislation, perhaps along the lines of the (English) Coroners and Justice Act 2009 (Part 4), can later be enacted if this is considered necessary to facilitate the production of more effective guidelines.

---

provision and youth justice services. On receipt of such a referral, the Council must undertake such an assessment and prepare a report on its findings.

CHAPTER 14

SENTENCE IMPLEMENTATION

Non-custodial sentences are usually meant to be served in full. A fine is meant to be fully paid, community service fully performed and probationary conditions fully observed. A custodial sentence, by contrast, is almost never served in full, nor is it intended to be. Most countries have various measures, whether in the form of special or standard remission, credit for good behaviour, parole or temporary release, that result in the vast majority of those sentenced to custody being released, conditionally or otherwise, before their sentences are fully served. This practice has proved to be remarkably resilient.[1] In the United States federal system and some of the states, discretionary parole was abolished when formal sentencing guidelines were introduced. Yet, the laws in those jurisdictions usually allow for some element of remission for good behaviour and for compassionate release.[2] For example, a federal prisoner serving a determinate sentence of more than one year may earn up to 54 days' remission a year for good behaviour.[3] Countries differ, however, in terms of how they allocate powers of sentence modification. The tradition in common law countries has been to confer upon the judiciary the sole power to select and pronounce a sentence, while making the executive branch of government responsible for its implementation. In some continental European countries, decisions on the implementation of sentences, and custodial sentences in particular, are made, in some instances at least, by **14–01**

---

1 Leslie Sebba, "The pardoning power – A world survey" (1977) 68 *Journal of Criminal Law and Criminology* 83 (finding that every country surveyed had some form of executive clemency); Daniel Pascoe and Andrew Novak (eds), *Executive Clemency: Comparative and Empirical Perspectives* (Routledge, 2021). Both works are concerned with clemency rather than parole in the modern sense, but they illustrate the near-universal practice of providing some mechanism for the executive annulment or reduction of judicial punishment,

2 Edward E Rhine, "The present status and future prospects of parole boards and parole supervision" in Joan Petersilia and Kevin R Reitz (eds), *The Oxford Handbook of Sentencing and Corrections* (Oxford University Press, 2012), Chap 26. See also American Law Institute, *Model Penal Code: Sentencing. Proposed Final Draft* (10 April 2017), comment on §305.6 (p 569): "No determinate sentencing system can be absolute, and no purely determinate system has ever existed in American law. All jurisdictions that have abrogated the releasing authority of a parole agency have retained mechanisms such as good-time and earned-time credits, compassionate release provisions, ad hoc emergency contingencies for prison overcrowding, and the clemency power of the executive".

3 18 USC §3624(b).

judicial bodies. Ireland remains firmly within the common law tradition in this regard. The selection of sentence, where there is a selection to be made, is exclusively a judicial task. More specifically, it is the task of the trial judge, subject to any variation later made by an appeal court.[4] But it then becomes the responsibility of the executive to do whatever is necessary to administer the judicially imposed sentence, whether this involves taking the offender into custody, collecting a fine or arranging for the fulfilment of probationary or community service obligations. Moreover, the executive is not obliged to implement the sentence in full or, indeed, at all. Article 13.6 of the Constitution of Ireland provides:

> "The right of pardon and the power to commute or remit punishment imposed by any court exercising criminal jurisdiction are hereby vested in the President, but such power of commutation or remission may also be conferred by law on other authorities."

14–02 The power of commutation and remission was in fact conferred on the Government by the Criminal Justice Act 1951 (s 23) and the Government, in turn, may by order delegate such power to the Minister for Justice.[5] To commute a punishment means to change it to some other form. Remission, as it is used in the Constitution and the legislation made thereunder, refers to 'special remission'" which has the effect of bringing the sentence to an end. Before the abolition of capital punishment, death sentences were often commuted to sentences of life imprisonment. However, very few beneficiaries of such commutation served life, or anything like it, because after some period of time, they were granted remission which effectively brought their sentences to an end.[6] Commutation and remission in this sense are seldom used today because other strategies have been developed for granting early release to serving prisoners.

14–03 Before considering the modification of prison sentences, which is the main concern of this chapter, we should note that the constitutional power of commutation and remission applies to all judicially imposed punishments, whatever their nature. But, aside from imprisonment, it is only in relation to fines that the power has ever become controversial. In 1994, a District Court judge brought judicial review proceedings challenging decisions of the then Minister for Justice to reduce the fines he had imposed in four

---

4 Chap 2 above.

5 Criminal Justice (Miscellaneous Provisions) Act 1997, s 17.

6 Thomas O'Malley, "Sentencing murderers: The case for relocating discretion" (1995) 5 ICLJ 31; Ian O'Donnell, *Justice, Mercy, and Caprice: Clemency and the Death Penalty in Ireland* (Oxford University Press, 2017); David M Doyle and Liam O'Callaghan, *Capital Punishment in Independent Ireland: A Social, Legal and Political History* (Liverpool University Press, 2019). This practice still applies in many countries that retain the death penalty. See Daniel Pascoe, *Last Chance for Life: Clemency in Southeast Asian Death Penalty Cases* (Oxford University Press, 2019). On the terms served by reprieved murderers in Britain until the early 1950s, see *Report of the Royal Commission on Capital Punishment* (1953), paras 644 ff.

cases.[7] The defendants in the four cases were named as notice parties. At that time, the Minister received about 5,000 petitions for remission of fines each year, and more than half of them were granted to some degree. The High Court held that the present constitutional power had to be read and interpreted in light of the prerogative of mercy that had existed at least until the foundation of the State.[8] The operation of the prerogative had never involved a public hearing and there was nothing to suggest that such a hearing was required when sentences were now being remitted or commuted under the Constitution. Nor was the executive obliged to consult the trial judge before exercising the power. However, the High Court went on to hold that the power should be exercised sparingly and that it was only in the rarest of circumstances that the Minister could interfere with a judge's order on the basis that he or she considered it wrong. The most common situation in which the power could legitimately be exercised was when there was a relevant change in the defendant's circumstances since the fine was imposed and outside the normal time for lodging an appeal. The court therefore upheld the constitutionality of s 23 of the Criminal Justice Act 1951 which, as noted, had conferred the power of remission and commutation on the Government. As a matter of fairness to those defendants named as notice parties, the court decided not to quash the Minister's decisions in their cases. However, it granted a declaration to the effect that the Minister had not exercised her powers properly because (1) there was no evidence before her of exceptional circumstances to justify interference with the judicially imposed fines and (2) no purported exceptional circumstances or reasons for the Minister's decisions were recorded.

The state never appealed to the Supreme Court against this judgment. **14–04** There had been a change of government between the time the judicial review proceedings were initiated and the delivery of the judgment and, during that same interval, the District Judge who brought the proceedings had retired. A more restrictive system for assessing petitions for fine reduction was however introduced. It remains regrettable that the Supreme Court was denied an opportunity to rule on the matter. After all, the offender's means as well as the nature and circumstances of the offence must always be considered when setting the amount of a fine. This was a well-established principle even when *Brennan* was decided but it received little attention from the High Court. Granted, a failure on the part of a District Court judge to consider an offender's means is more appropriately addressed by way of an appeal to the Circuit Court rather than a petition to the Minister. More fundamentally, the High Court introduced a restriction on the exercise of the Minister's powers which is not expressly provided for in either the Constitution or the relevant

7 *Brennan v Minister for Justice* [1995] 1 IR 612.

8 On the origins of the common law prerogative of mercy, see Andrew Novak, *Comparative Executive Clemency* (Routledge, 2016), Chap 2. On its modern operation in England and Wales, see ATH Smith, "The prerogative of mercy, the power of pardon and criminal justice" (1983) *Public Law* 398.

legislation. Perhaps this was justified but a Supreme Court decision on the matter would have been welcome.

1. Modification of Prison Sentences

14–05 The term 'parole' is sometimes used broadly to encompass a diverse range of practices for releasing prisoners before they have fully served their sentences. Used in this sense, parole might cover compassionate release by way of executive clemency, time deducted for good behaviour, temporary release and various forms of automatic and discretionary parole authorised by statute or granted by a parole board. In this chapter, 'parole' will be used in that narrower sense to describe statutory arrangements whereby prisoners are either entitled to be released after serving a defined portion of their sentence, or to be considered for early release at some point during the currency of their sentences. The practice of granting parole-type release to prisoners may be traced back to the era of transportation. Those transported to Australia could be granted a 'ticket of leave' after serving a defined portion of their sentences unless they had been of bad behaviour. Those transported for seven years qualified for a ticket of leave (which allowed them freedom within the colony) after four years. Those transported for 14 years or for life qualified after six and eight years, respectively. Later in Ireland, Sir Walter Crofton devised a system whereby prisoners had to pass through three stages before being eligible for tickets of leave. Innovations of this kind inspired the later development of parole in the United States and elsewhere.[9] Modern parole systems bear some similarity to these early experiments to the extent that prisoners are given an opportunity to secure early, conditional release after serving some defined portion of their sentence.

14–06 When penal servitude was introduced as a replacement for transportation, provision was made for some portion of the sentence to be served on licence. At first, the licence period depended on the length of sentence, but in 1891 it was set at one-quarter for male convicts and one-third for female convicts.[10] At that time, penal servitude and imprisonment were distinct forms of custody. It was not until 1898 in England and 1907 in Ireland that a similar arrangement, in the form of standard remission, was applied to

---

[9] Fiona Doherty, "Indeterminate sentencing returns: The invention of supervised release" (2013) 88 New York University LR 958 (which has an excellent account of the systems developed by Maconochie in Australia and Crofton in Ireland). See also Helen Leland Witmer, "The history, theory and results of parole" (1927) 18 *Journal of Criminal Law and Criminology* 24 (which has a detailed account of the development of parole in England); Joan Petersilia, *When Prisoners Come Home: Parole and Prisoner Reentry* (Oxford University Press, 2003), Chap 3; Jacob Schuman, "Supervised release is not parole" (2020) 53 Loyola of Los Angeles LR 587. A more contemporaneous account of Crofton's Irish system is provided by Mary Carpenter, *Reformatory Prison Discipline as developed by the Rt. Hon. Sir Walter Crofton in the Irish Convict Prisons* (Longmans, 1872).

[10] *The Parole System in England and Wales: Report of the Review Committee* (Carlisle Report), Cm 532 (HMSO, 1988), 3-4.

prison sentences. Irish prisoners are still entitled to standard remission of one-quarter and may qualify for enhanced remission of up to one-third. Additionally, in 1960, a temporary release system was introduced by statute which allows the Minister for Justice to grant temporary release (which may become permanent) to a prisoner at any time after being committed to prison. This discretionary release power now operates in conjunction with remission and parole.

Alongside these special provisions there existed the long-established power of executive clemency which allowed the Crown (in effect the Government) to commute or remit punishment for compassionate or other reasons. This, in fact, is the genesis of the Government's power in this country under Art 13.6 of the Constitution to grant special remission, as already described. Clemency may once have been a hallmark of monarchy, but it was readily embraced by republican systems of government including the United States in the late 18th century.[11] **14–07**

The remainder of this chapter will consider these early release mechanisms in more detail. We shall begin with parole which, although a recent innovation in Ireland, provides an opportunity to consider certain fundamental policy questions that are relevant to most forms of early release. Later sections of the chapter will deal with standard remission, temporary release, judicial modification of sentence and general amnesties. Finally, we shall ask if these various early release mechanisms can co-exist in a coherent and efficient manner. **14–08**

2. Parole: Four Policy Questions

Donald West's definition of parole as "a procedure whereby a sentence imposed by a court of justice may be varied by administrative action" remains essentially valid, in these islands at least.[12] The word 'parole' is of French origin where it came to mean 'word of honour'. A prisoner was released on giving his word that he would obey the law while at liberty. Four fundamental policy questions must be addressed before considering the substantive law on parole: (1) How can parole, as a form of early release, be justified?; (2) What should be the criteria for granting parole?; (3) Should early release from prison be automatic, selective or a combination of both?; and (4) To which branch of government should the parole power be allocated? **14–09**

Justifying Parole

The justification for parole or any kind of early release is by no means self-evident. Suppose a state has a desert-based sentencing system in **14–10**

---

[11] Carolyn Strange, "Pardon and parole in prohibition-era New York: Discretionary justice in the administrative state" (2017) 54 Osgoode Hall LJ 909.

[12] DJ West (ed), *The Future of Parole* (Duckworth, 1972). 11.

which custody is used sparingly and prison sentences, where imposed, are both proportionate and moderate. Arguably, all such sentences should be served in full unless, perhaps, a prisoner becomes seriously ill or there are strongly extenuating family circumstances. Any executive reduction of the sentence, save in the exceptional circumstances just mentioned, might result in a penalty that failed to reflect the gravity of the offence, particularly if the sentence was originally chosen by reference to a desert-based rationale.[13] This is one of the standard objections to parole, irrespective of how severe or lenient prison sentences happen to be. Advocates of 'truth in sentencing' argue that judicially imposed sentences should be served in full, rather than be subject to subsequent and, perhaps, arbitrary reduction by other authorities. Otherwise, they argue, offenders will fail to undergo their deserved punishment, penalties will fail to have their intended or presumed deterrent effect, and public confidence in the criminal justice system will be eroded. Arguments of this nature were highly influential in the United States in the 1970s and 1980s when parole was prospectively abolished in the federal system and in several states.[14]

14–11 Yet, there are strong counter-arguments in favour of parole even where most custodial sentences are moderate. All prisoners are eventually released, with the possible exception of a few who, for one reason or another, end up serving whole-life sentences. Most are released simply because they have reached the end of their sentence, with or without the application of remission or good-time credit. In the absence of any kind of parole system, those prisoners will be released automatically without any assessment of whether they are at risk of re-offending, possibly in a violent manner. Paradoxical though it may appear to some, it is for offenders in this category and for society in general that parole is most valuable. The point was well made by Donald West a half a century ago:

> "Since parole is regarded as a privilege, it tends to be given to the better behaved and less serious offenders. On the other hand, in the interests of society and of the offender, it is the more dangerous and desperate cases who stand in greatest need of supervision on release. As the law now stands, unless granted parole, these offenders are released without any supervision whatsoever."[15]

14–12 As Joan Petersilia later argued, abolishing parole means replacing "a rational, controlled system of earned release for selected inmates with automatic release for nearly all inmates".[16] Lord Bingham made a similar observation in *R (West) v Parole Board*:

---

[13] This was the view of the pioneers of modern desert theory, notably Andrew von Hirsch, *Doing Justice: The Choice of Punishments* (Northeastern University Press, 1986 (1976)), and David Fogel, *We Are the Living Proof: The Justice Model of Corrections* (WH Anderson Co, 1975).

[14] Petersilia, note 9 above; Douglas A Berman, "Reflecting on parole's abolition in the federal sentencing system" (2017) 81(2) *Federal Probation* 18.

[15] West, note 12 above, at 23.

[16] Petersilia, note 9 above, at 158. The same point was made a century ago by

> "While… it is true that early release provisions have the practical effect of relieving overcrowding in the prisons, that is not their penal justification. But such justification exists. All, or almost all, determinate sentence prisoners are expected to return to the community on release from prison after serving their sentences. It is in the interests of society that they should, after release, live law-abiding, orderly and useful lives. For a host of practical, psychological and social reasons, the process of transition from custody to freedom is often very difficult for the prisoner. It is accordingly very desirable that the process of transition should be professionally supervised, to maximise the chances of the ex-prisoner's successful reintegration into the community and minimise the chances of his relapse into criminal activity."[17]

The transition from captivity to liberty, which can be particularly difficulty for some prisoners, is better managed through a conditional release system under which selected offenders are subject to supervision and, hopefully, given the necessary support to abide by their release conditions, including desistance from further crime. Desistance research (of which there is now a great deal) has shown that offenders who, on release from prison, find themselves unemployed, without adequate housing and lacking professional or social support may have little confidence in their ability to remain law abiding and, indeed, little incentive in that regard.[18] Additionally, the prospect or possibility of securing early release provides a strong motivation for prisoners to avail themselves of rehabilitative opportunities while in custody and to develop prosocial attitudes that will increase their chances of being granted parole. This, in turn, should help them to remain law-abiding after being released.[19] It cannot be guaranteed to do so, but it should reduce the risk of re-offending which is the best any parole system can hope to achieve. A further advantage of a formal parole system with release decisions made by an expert body is that prisoners who are deemed too dangerous to release can be kept in custody, at least until they have completed their sentences. **14–13**

Parole and other forms of early release are also theoretically justifiable where, for example, incapacitation is the governing policy of judicial sentencing. The entire purpose of the exercise would then be to incarcerate offenders, either indefinitely or for long periods, to prevent them from committing further crimes within the community. Within such a framework, it would make sense to release prisoners once it appeared that they were no longer at risk of re-offending. The purpose for which they **14–14**

Witmer, note 9 above, at 50 who says of prisoners who have never done anything to earn parole need it most: "They, more than the others, require supervision after release, both for their own benefit and for the benefit of society. It is a rank waste if public money to confine them for a certain number of years and then to release them, only to have them drop back into crime again."

17 *R (West) v Parole Board* [2005] UKHL 1, [2005] 1 WLR 350, para 25.

18 See, for example, Stephen Farrall et al, *Criminal Careers in Transition: The Social Context of Desistance from Crime* (Oxford University Press, 2014), 216. See also Chap 12, notes 213 and 214 above.

19 Nancy T Charbonneau and Kathryn E Ferreira, "Sentence administration and parole" in David Cole and Julian Roberts (eds), *Sentencing in Canada: Essays in Law, Policy, and Practice* (Irwin Law, 2020), 200, 201.

were originally imprisoned would, in a sense, have been fulfilled. The same would apply where rehabilitation was the overarching purpose of punishment, as illustrated by the system that operated in the United States for most of the 20th century. Both the federal system and the individual states had indeterminate sentencing systems which in many cases, meant that a court, rather than imposing a specific term of imprisonment, would sentence an offender to a maximum (and sometimes a minimum) term. The relevant parole authority would later decide when the offender was fit to be released, although in the federal system release was generally not permitted until one-third of the sentence had been served.[20] Likewise, if individual deterrence were the governing policy, and it appeared that, for whatever reason, the offender no longer needed to be deterred, early release could be justified. The situation would be more complicated if general deterrence were the governing policy. In that event, no matter how reformed or rehabilitated an individual prisoner might seem to be, the objective of dissuading others from engaging in similar offending might outweigh any arguments for granting early release to the individual in question.

14–15 Early release mechanisms are all the more necessary in countries where harsh prison sentences are routinely imposed. Throughout history, executive clemency has served a useful purpose in mitigating severe penalties which courts were either obliged or inclined to impose.[21] This was true in 18th century England, for example, where more than 200 felonies, most of them property offences, carried the death penalty.[22] A vibrant system of executive clemency was therefore needed to counteract the manifest injustice and inhumanity that a mechanical application of the criminal law would have produced. This was recognised by the leading doctrinal writers and thinkers of the time. Blackstone claimed that one of the great advantages of a monarchy was that there existed a magistrate who could "soften the rigour of the general law".[23] Beccaria devoted a short chapter to pardons in his *Essay on Crimes and Punishments* (1764), but noted at the outset that a fair and humane criminal justice system would have little need for executive clemency:

---

20 Kate Stith and José Cabranes, *Fear of Judging: Sentencing Guidelines in the Federal Courts* (University of Chicago Press, 1998), 18-21.

21 William F Duker, "The President's power to pardon: A constitutional history" (1977) 18 William and Mary LR 475, describing the early English origins of executive clemency.

22 Douglas Hay, "Property, authority, and the criminal law" in Douglas Hay et al (eds), *Albion's Fatal Tree: Crime and Society in Eighteenth-Century England* (Pantheon Books, 1975) is probably the most widely cited work on the operation of the criminal law in this era. However, it has been challenged in some important respects by John H Langbein, "*Albion's* fatal flaws" (Feb 1983) 98 *Past and Present* 96. See also Michael Tonry, "Mandatory penalties" (1992) 16 *Crime and Justice* 243, describing how harsh mandatory penalties were circumvented, historically in England and, more recently, in the United States.

23 William Blackstone, *Commentaries on the Laws of England,* Book IV, edited by Ruth Paley (Oxford University Press, 2016 (1769)), 256.

> "As punishments become milder, clemency and pardon are less necessary. Happy the nation in which they are harmful! Clemency, then, a virtue which has often complemented all the duties which attach to the sovereign's throne, should be redundant in a perfect administration where punishments are mild and the methods of judgment are regular and expeditious. This truth will seem hard to one who lives amid the chaos of a criminal system in which amnesties and pardons are called for in proportion to the absurdity of the laws and the awful severity of the sentences."[24]

Where courts were obliged to impose harsh mandatory penalties, it was essential, if some semblance of humanity was to prevail, that the executive should be able to intervene and exercise what was, in effect, an equitable jurisdiction by substituting a penalty that was more compatible with the demands of justice.[25] The same holds true today, especially in countries such as the United States where crushing prison sentences, often far exceeding the offender's expected life span, are occasionally imposed. In those circumstances, parole can introduce elements of proportionality and moderation that were lacking at the sentencing stage.[26] Growing dissatisfaction with mass incarceration and the sheer injustice of some individual sentences being served in the United States has inspired some recent initiatives such as allowing courts to review long sentences and, at state level, reintroducing parole, at least to some limited extent.[27] **14–16**

Ultimately, then, the strongest arguments in favour of parole are essentially pragmatic and prudential in nature.[28] As already noted, parole involves *conditional* release, a quality that differentiates it from remission which brings the sentence to an end. Parolees remain at liberty only for as long as they abide by their release conditions and these, at a minimum, will include refraining from further criminal activity. A good parole system will try to ensure that, with the assistance of probation or other professionals, released prisoners can gradually readjust to their newfound freedom, use it responsibly and start to rebuild their lives. The prospect of early release provides a strong incentive for prisoners to **14–17**

---

24 Cesare Beccaria, *On Crimes and Punishments,* edited by Richard Bellamy and translated by Richard Davies (Cambridge University Press, 1995), Chap 46.

25 *Bouvier's Law Dictionary* (T & WJ Johnson, 1839).

26 For a discussion of the relationship between parole and proportionality in an American context, see Richard A Bierschbach, "Proportionality and parole" (2012) 160 Univ Pennsylvania LR 1745.

27 Judicial review of long sentences under the First Step Act and similar legislation is described briefly in Chap 3 above. The case of Bobby Bostic, which received much public attention, illustrates this trend. He was convicted on several charges arising from an armed robbery committed in Missouri in 1995 when he was 16 years old. He was sentenced to 241 years' imprisonment with a parole eligibility date for 2091 when he would be 112 years old. All his appeals failed, and the United States Supreme Court refused to take up the case. However, in 2021, Missouri enacted legislation permitting juveniles sentenced to 15 years' imprisonment or more to apply for parole after 15 years. Bostic was released under this provision in November 2022. The trial judge who sentenced him had a change of heart and became his strongest advocate in his quest for parole.

28 Julian Roberts, *Criminal Justice: A Very Short Introduction* (Oxford University Press, 2015), pp 98-101 (summarising the benefits of parole).

participate in rehabilitative programmes during the custodial element of their sentences. Early release, including parole, also helps to relieve prison overcrowding which is a serious problem in many countries. As 'total institutions', to use Goffman's phrase, prisons are difficult to control.[29] Tensions can run high, leading to violence that may culminate in a riot or other major disturbance. The possibility of early release provides prisoners with an incentive to behave well, another important prudential reason for providing such a possibility.

Criteria for Granting Parole

14–18 The criteria for granting parole obviously depend on the purpose(s) it is intended to serve, and they may be quite different from the purpose(s) for which the sentence was originally imposed. The objective of parole might be to promote prisoner rehabilitation, to manage risk by identifying those more or less likely to reoffend if released, to address prison overcrowding or reduce the cost of imprisonment, to provide prisoners with an incentive to behave well while in custody, or some combination of these.[30] In many jurisdictions the primary purpose of parole, when first introduced, was to promote rehabilitation by incentivising prisoners to use their time in custody to prepare for release and to demonstrate during the parole period their willingness and capacity to refrain from further crime and reintegrate into society. However, as mentioned earlier, any form of early release is apt to encounter public opposition as being a kind of 'let off' for offenders, and criticism becomes even more intense whenever a paroled prisoner reoffends. Of late, therefore, legislatures and parole authorities have tended to prioritise risk and to become more risk averse when devising and implementing parole policies. This does not necessarily entail the abandonment of rehabilitative objectives, but it can result in parole authorities being less inclined to take calculated risks, releasing only those who seem to pose a very low risk of reoffending.[31]

14–19 Even if risk of reoffending were the sole or primary determinant of parole release decisions, it could scarcely mean that prisoners should always be released once they no longer seemed to pose any appreciable risk to individuals or the community. Some perpetrators of serious offences, including homicide, might well be assessed at the time of sentencing as presenting no such risk and that, in turn, would call in question the

---

[29] Irving Goffman, *Asylums* (Penguin, 1968) 11 ("A total institution may be defined as a place of residence and work where a large number of like-situated individuals cut off from the wider society for an appreciable period of time together lead an enclosed formally administered round of life").

[30] Arie Freiberg et al, "Parole, politics and penal policy" (2018) 18 Queensland University of Technology LR 191, 203.

[31] On the distinction between 'calculated risks' and 'good risks', see Manuel López-Rey, "Release and provisional release of sentenced prisoners" (1966) 6 Brit J Criminology 236; Stephen Shute, "Does parole work? The empirical evidence from England and Wales" (2004) 2 *Ohio State Journal of Criminal Law* 315.

need for any term of immediate imprisonment. Sentencing decisions are not, however, determined by predictions of future conduct alone. Such predictions may well be factored into the overall sentencing equation, but a court's primary duty is to sentence offenders for what they have done in the past, and not for what they may do in the future. Statutory parole arrangements must likewise reflect the social interest in ensuring that offenders serve at least a portion of the custodial penalties imposed upon them in accordance with established policies and principles of judicial sentencing. This might not apply in exceptional circumstances such as where an offender is suffering from a terminal illness, but that kind of situation is best addressed by way of discretionary executive release. Parole regimes typically provide for some tariff period (even if that expression is not used) which a prisoner must serve before becoming eligible for conditional release. Some Australian jurisdictions permit courts to specify a non-parole period when passing a prison sentence.[32] If a court imposes a six-year sentence with a non-parole period of three years, the offender will serve a minimum of three years.[33] Thereafter, the parole authority will decide how much more of the sentence is to be served in custody.[34] Other arrangements are also possible. In England and Wales, as discussed further below, most prisoners are released on serving half their sentence, but some may not be released except by a decision of the Parole Board. The system recently adopted in Ireland, as we shall see, confines the availability of parole to prisoners serving sentences of eight years or longer but they too will have to serve a defined portion of their sentence before becoming eligible for release. Obviously, becoming *eligible* for release does not guarantee actual release. In effect, therefore, the question is what criteria that should apply when considering the release of *eligible* prisoners – those who qualify for consideration by having served a defined portion of their sentence. Risk of reoffending will normally be the paramount consideration, and this should be assessed as scientifically as possible.

Remorse may become an issue in parole-decision making, just as it may be a relevant factor at sentencing.[35] However, an offender who showed a lack of remorse when sentenced may well have had a change of heart **14–20**

---

32 The principles governing the setting of non-parole periods were discussed in *R v Josefski* [2005] VSCA 265; (2005) 13 VR 85 and *Bertilone v The Queen* [2009] WASCA 149, paras 54-60. Both held that a non-parole period should be the term which the interests of justice require the offender to serve having regard to the circumstances of the offence.

33 Richard Edney and Mirko Bagaric, *Australian Sentencing: Principles and Practice* (Cambridge University Press, 2007), pp 312-321 (describing the arrangements in each Australian jurisdiction); Geraldine Mackenzie and Nigel Stobbs, *Principles of Sentencing* (Federation Press, 2010), pp 197-199; Freiberg et al, note 30 above.

34 In the federal system, the Attorney General, who is responsible for granting parole to federal prisoners, must ordinarily release those sentenced to prison terms ranging from three to 10 years once the non-parole period has been served. See Arie Freiberg, *Fox and Freiberg's Sentencing: State and Federal Law in Victoria*, 3rd ed (Thomson Reuters, 2014), p 883.

35 Chap 5 above.

by the time he or she qualifies for parole. Time spent in custody, coupled perhaps with participation in some kind of therapeutic programme, may have provided an opportunity for sustained reflection on the offence, the harm it caused and the offender's own culpability in committing it. Assessing the genuineness of remorse can, of course, be just as difficult at a parole hearing as at sentencing, but a parole board with a broad range of expertise is probably better equipped to undertake this task than a judge sitting alone. A further difference is that at sentencing remorse is relevant primarily for the purpose of assessing culpability (and, consequently, the appropriate penalty) whereas at a parole hearing it is relevant, if at all, for predicting the risk of recidivism. It is often assumed that genuine remorse reduces that risk. As Judge Posner said in one American case, a remorseful offender "is on the way to developing those internal checks that would keep many people from committing crimes even if the expected costs of the criminal punishment were lower than they are".[36] However, the empirical evidence on the correlation between remorse and reduced recidivism has been described as "equivocal".[37]

14–21 Extreme caution must nonetheless be exercised by any parole authority that allows the presence or absence of expressions of remorse to determine or influence release decisions. The same applies to a prisoner's willingness to admit the offence for which sentence is being served. Most convictions, whether resulting from trials or guilty pleas, are probably safe but that cannot be said of all of them. Miscarriages of justice can and do occasionally occur as illustrated by the case of Andrew Malkinson in England. In 2004, he was convicted of rape and sentenced to life imprisonment. After many years of protesting his innocence and several applications to the Criminal Cases Review Commission, he was exonerated as a result of new and more highly developed DNA analysis. His conviction was eventually quashed by the Court of Appeal.[38] However, by the time of his release, he had spent 17 years in prison. During that time, he was repeatedly denied parole because he refused to admit that he had committed the offence. Ironically, if he had actually committed the offence and admitted it at his first parole hearing, he might have been released many years earlier, not that he should ever have been in prison. Others, including Victor Nealon who also spent 17 years in prison before his conviction was quashed, had similar experiences.[39] Cases of this nature should be foremost in the minds

---

[36] *United States v Beserra* 967 F2d 254, 256 (7th Cir, 1992).

[37] Nicole Bronnimann, "Remorse in parole hearings: An elusive concept with concrete consequences" (2020) 85 Missouri LR 321.

[38] *R v Malkinson* [2023] EWCA Crim 954. See also Andrew Malkinson, "I was wrongly imprisoned for 17 years. Then the state released me into a legal maze", *The Guardian,* 11 May 2024, and Rachel Aroesti, "The wrong man: 17 years behind bars review – dignified, devastating TV" *The Guardian,* 6 June 2024; *Independent Review by Chris Henley KC of the CCRC's Handling of the Andrew Malkinson Case: Report and CCRC Response* (2024).

[39] *R v Nealon* [2014] EWCA Crim 574. He and Sam Hallan were later refused compensation for miscarriage of justice, a refusal upheld by the UK Supreme Court and the European Court of Human Rights: *R (Hallam and Nealon) v Secretary of State for Justice* [2019] UKSC 2; [2020] AC 279; *Nealon and Hallam v*

of parole decision-makers when dealing with applicants who continue to protest their innocence and who cannot, for that reason, be expected to appear remorseful.

Automatic and Selective Parole

14–22 National arrangements for administering parole will be determined largely by the size of the prison population. Treating parole applications on an individual, case-by-case basis is more logistically difficult in a jurisdiction like England and Wales which has a sentenced prisoner population of about 71,000 than in Ireland where the equivalent figure is about 4,000.[40] The task is further eased in smaller jurisdictions if short-term prisoners are ineligible for parole, as is true in Ireland. The early release system introduced in England and Wales in 1991, based on recommendations of the Carlisle Committee, involved a mixture of automatic and selective release.[41] As the English system now operates, a person serving a sentence of less than 12 months is released at the halfway mark, while most of those serving determinate sentences of 12 months or more are conditionally released at the halfway mark.[42] The Parole Board deals mainly with the release of those serving extended determinate sentences,[43] indeterminate sentences (including life sentences), sentences for offenders of particular

---

United Kingdom, App nos 32483/19 and 35049/19 (European Court of Human Rights (Grand Chamber), 11 June 2024).

40 Ministry for Justice, *Offender Management Statistics Quarterly: October to December 2023 and annual 2023* (April 2024), showing that on 31 March 2024 there was a total of 87,869 prisoners in England and Wales, including a sentenced population of 70,999 (of whom 12,344 were recall prisoners). According to daily figures published by the Irish Prison Service, on 1 August 2024, there were 5,048 in custody, including 851 remand prisoners.

41 Criminal Justice Act 1991, giving effect to most of the recommendations of *The Parole System in England and Wales: Report of the Review Committee* (Carlisle Report), Cm 532 (1988). The best account of the development of the English parole system and its (near) current operation is Nicola Padfield, "Giving and getting parole: The changing characteristics of parole in England and Wales" (2019) 11 *European Journal of Probation* 153. For more detailed historical accounts, see Thomas Guiney, *Getting Out: Early Release in England and Wales, 1960-1995* (Oxford University Press, 2018); Stephen Shute, "The development of parole and the role of research in its reform" in Lucia Zedner and Andrew Ashworth (eds), *The Criminological Foundations of Penal Policy: Essays in Honour of Roger Hood* (Oxford University Press, 2003); A Keith Bottomley, "Parole in transition: A comparative study of origins, developments, and prospects for the 1990s" (1990) 12 *Crime and Justice* 319.

42 Recent legislative changes, such as those made by the Terrorist Offenders (Restriction of Early Release) Act 2020 mean that more prisoners must serve two-thirds of their sentence before being eligible for release. See, generally, Richard A Edwards, "Justice for the blackest malefactors? Determinate prison sentences, early release, and the ECHR" (2022) 42 *Legal Studies* 600.

43 These sentences may be imposed on certain violent and sexual offenders under s 226A of the Criminal Justice Act 2003 (inserted by Legal Aid, Sentencing and Punishment of Offenders Act 2012, s 124). Early release of such prisoners is governed by s 246A of the 2003 Act (inserted by s 125 of the 2012 Act).

concern and recalled prisoners.[44] In fact, the term parole now applies solely to those in the categories just mentioned. Yet, the Board, which had 346 members in 2022, still has a heavy workload. In 2022-2023, it made over 29,000 decisions (with 8,000 oral hearings) and 4,000 prisoners were either released or moved to open prisons.[45]

14–23 The system introduced in Ireland under the Parole Act 2019 is entirely selective. Each case will be considered and determined by the Parole Board. The annual number of applications is likely to be significant but not overwhelming, given that life prisoners (of whom there are about 370) will be ineligible for parole until they have served 12 years, and those serving determinate sentences will not be eligible to apply at all unless they are serving sentences of at least eight years.[46] At the end of 2022, there were 272 prisoners serving determinate sentences in excess of 10 years and 769 serving sentences of five to 10 years.[47] Selective parole has much to commend it in principle, as it allows for an individualised assessment of each eligible prisoner's suitability for release. Those refused parole should benefit from feedback on the reasons for the refusal, and this in turn should assist them in identifying any steps they should take to render themselves more suitable for parole in the future. The drawback of the new Irish system, as we shall see, is that it confines parole eligibility to a relatively small proportion of the prison population, though all prisoners will continue to qualify for standard remission of one-quarter of their sentences (with the possibility of one-third in some cases) and will also qualify for discretionary temporary release.

14–24 Discretionary or selective parole means that nobody is guaranteed early release. Prisoners are merely promised the possibility of parole and a fair prospect of being granted it if they fulfil the relevant conditions. This element of hope is nonetheless important, especially for prisoners serving long sentences.[48] Its absence was a decisive factor in *Graham v Florida*[49] where the United States Supreme Court held that the imposition of a life

[44] Jacqueline Beard, *The Parole System of England and Wales*, House of Commons Library Research Briefing No 8656 (2023); Nicola Padfield, *Parole: Reflections and Possibilities. A Discussion Paper* (Howard League for Penal Reform, 2018).

[45] Gavin Dingwall and Megan Millar, *Parole in England and Wales: Recent Reforms and Proposals for the Future* (Sentencing Academy, 2023).

[46] Parole Act 2019, s 24.

[47] Irish Prison Service Annual Report 2022 (2023).

[48] Psychological research has identified a significant correlation between hope and resilience which, in turn, is an important factor in offender rehabilitation. See Krystle Martin and Lana Stermac, "Measuring hope: Is hope related to criminal behaviour in offenders?" (2010) 54 *International Journal of Offender Therapy and Comparative Criminology* 693; Burcu Ozturk et al, "The importance of hope to resilience in criminal justice diversion programs" (2022) 23:2 *Criminology, Criminal Justice, Law and Society* 56, 58 ("A hopeful mindset is a variable that has been consistently linked to resilience.").

[49] 560 US 48 (2010). See Alice Ristroph, "Hope, imprisonment, and the Constitution" (2010) 23 *Federal Sentencing Reporter* 75. For a more detailed and critical analysis of *Graham*, see Bierschbach, note 26 above.

sentence without the possibility of parole (LWOPP) on a juvenile offender for a non-homicide offence amounted to cruel and unusual punishment and was therefore unconstitutional. Significantly, however, the court stressed that what the Constitution required was a realistic opportunity for persons in this category to obtain early release. A state did not have to guarantee eventual release in any given case. The same point was made, even more emphatically, by the Canadian Supreme Court in *R v Bissonnette*[50] where it struck down a statutory provision that permitted consecutive non-parole periods of 25 years to be imposed on a person convicted of two or more first-degree murders. The court held that the inordinately long sentences made possible by this provision could amount to cruel and unusual punishment. Hence, they were incompatible with human dignity which, in turn, required that due regard be had to offender rehabilitation. The court concluded:

> "No crime, no matter how appalling it might be, can justify imposing a punishment that is intrinsically incompatible with human dignity, like a sentence of imprisonment for life without a realistic possibility of parole. Since such a punishment must quite simply be excluded from the arsenal of punishments available to the state, the mere possibility that it may be imposed constitutes an infringement of s 12 of the Charter."[51]

A discretionary parole system, therefore, should provide every qualifying prisoner with a reasonable prospect of early release. The criteria for granting such release should be clearly specified and made known to all prisoners. They should then be conscientiously and dispassionately applied when considering individual applications. **14–25**

Where Should the Parole Power Lie?

Parole decisions might be made by the government (or a government minister), an independent administrative agency or a judicial body. The tradition in common law countries has been to allocate decision-making on parole and other forms of early release to the executive branch of government. Decisions are made directly by the government or by an agency such as a parole board. In some continental European countries, on the other hand, decisions on early release, in some cases at least, are allocated to judges or courts specially appointed for that purpose. France, for example, has a system of sentence implementation courts (*juges de l'application des peines (JAP)*) of which there are about 400. They operate separately from the criminal trial courts where sentences are initially imposed, and they have several functions relating to the administration of sentences, custodial and otherwise.[52] These include granting conditional **14–26**

---

50 [2022] SCC 23.

51 [2022] SCC 23, para 111. s 12 of the Charter of Rights and Freedoms provides: "Everyone has the right not to be subjected to any cruel and unusual treatment or punishment."

52 Martine Herzog-Evans, *Droit de l'Exécution des Peines*, 6th ed (Dalloz, 2022); Martine Herzog-Evsns and Nicola Padfield, *The JAP: Lessons for England and Wales* (Criminal Justice Alliance, 2015).

release and transforming custodial sentences of less than two years into various kinds of community-based measures. In 2006, Belgium established a similar system of implementation courts (*tribunaux de l'application des peines (TAP)*) which deal with applications from prisoners serving more than three years. The point at which prisoners may apply for release depends largely on their previous record, but a non-recidivist prisoner may apply after serving one-third of the sentence.[53]

14–27 Both the administrative and judicial models have their strengths. The principal claim made for the judicial model is that implementation courts evaluate evidence as rigorously as any law court and insist on procedural propriety. The administrative model has the advantage that a parole authority may be so constituted as to include a range of relevant expertise, as is true of the Irish Parole Board.[54] Risk evaluation is key element of parole decision-making. The input of psychologists, psychiatrists and criminologists with expertise in clinical and actuarial risk assessment is therefore vital. A sentence implementation court, like that operating in France, could certainly receive expert evidence from specialists in risk assessment and related matters, but a collective decision-making authority, such as a parole board, permits a more deliberative approach to which others, such as lawyers with expertise in the procedural dimensions of the process, can also contribute. Each application for release or revocation can therefore be considered in a holistic manner. All this, of course, is on the assumption that the administrative parole authority is fully independent and that its decisions are immune from political oversight, amendment or annulment. If, in addition, the authority is required to act judicially in the sense of approaching its task in an unbiased, objective and procedurally fair manner – which, in Ireland essentially means abiding by the principles of constitutional justice – it will be largely equivalent to a court but with the further advantage of a diverse membership encompassing a range of relevant expertise.

3. Parole as Sentencing

14–28 As discussed in Chap 1, sentencing is commonly viewed as a discrete stage of the criminal process – the point at which a judge imposes a penalty on an offender. This is undoubtedly an essential and critically important element of sentencing. The judicial decision determines the nature and severity of the punishment the offender is *liable* to endure. But others may well determine how much of that punishment the offender will *actually* endure. If, as often happens, an executive body is empowered, but not obliged, to release an imprisoned offender at some point before the expiry of the sentence, that body is effectively engaged in sentencing. The criteria it employs in making release decisions may differ from those that shaped

[53] Joséphine Bastard, "Les processus de l'application des peines en Belgique: Temps légal et temps légitime des sorties anticipées de prison" (2018) 98 (1) *Revue de droit pénal et de criminologie* 41.

[54] Described further below under 'The Parole Act 2019'.

the original sentence, but it is still deciding how much of the judicially imposed punishment the offender will undergo. As the Canadian Supreme Court said in *R v Bissonnette*:

> "The length of parole ineligibility is part of an offender's punishment. It is a consequence of conviction and has a significant impact on the offender's interests in liberty and security of the person. What is more, the parole ineligibility period furthers the objectives of denunciation and deterrence that underlie a sentence."[55]

Consequently, parole decisions, no less than judicial sentencing, should be informed by the values of legality, rationality, fairness and consistency of approach. Public protection and risk of re-offending may be more dominant considerations in parole decision-making than at sentencing, but this should not diminish the quality of that decision-making or justify procedural standards falling below those now expected of other public authorities, including courts, when making decisions that affect the rights, liabilities and, above all, the liberty of individuals. **14–29**

Release on parole bears some resemblance to a suspended prison sentence to the extent that both have a punitive dimension. The offender is granted conditional liberty but must live with the threat of parole revocation or activation of sentence, as the case may be, if he or she breaches a release condition during the operational period. Still, the conditional liberty granted to the offender is undoubtedly a mitigation of the punishment that might otherwise have been imposed (in the case of a suspended sentence) or executed (in the case of parole). To that extent, parole release may be seen as part of the overall sentencing process. The connection becomes even stronger when changes in parole regulations adversely affect serving prisoners or when a paroled prisoner is recalled for breach of the release conditions. A new law that restricts eligibility for parole, and that applies retrospectively, may well result in some prisoners spending longer in custody than was envisaged at the time of sentencing. An issue then arises as to the compatibility of such a law with the Constitution and international human rights law. The rules governing parole are generally a matter for the legislature (or the executive if such rule making has been delegated to it), but subject always to any constraints imposed by the Constitution. This was certainly the view of the Canadian Supreme Court in *Canada (Attorney General) v Whaling*[56] which addressed the constitutionality of a statutory provision abolishing early parole even for those already serving prison sentences. The immediate effect was to delay the parole eligibility date for periods ranging from three to 21 months for the three prisoners who challenged the legislation. The Canadian Charter of Rights and Freedoms, strangely enough, has no express provision equivalent to art 7 of the ECHR which prohibits the imposition of a more severe punishment than applied when the offence was committed.[57] It **14–30**

---

[55] [2022] SCC 23, para 58. Internal citations omitted.

[56] [2014] SCC 20; [2014] 1 SCR 392.

[57] It does, however, provide for the *in mitius* principle by providing (s 11(i))

does, however, have a double jeopardy clause which guarantees against being tried *or* punished again for the same offence.[58] The Supreme Court invalidated the impugned statutory provision, holding that by prolonging the period of incarceration of offenders who had already been sentenced, it constituted punishment for the purpose of the double jeopardy clause.[59] The effect of the statutory provision was automatic and it operated without regard to individual circumstances. The court did, however, also hold that retrospective changes to the conditions of a sentence will not ordinarily be regarded as punitive unless, as in this case, they "substantially increase the risk of additional punishment".[60]

14–31 A similar issue arose more recently in both England and Northern Ireland because of the impact of the Counter-Terrorism and Sentencing Act 2021 (the '2021 Act') on persons already serving sentences for terrorist offences. Under the law as it applied when they were sentenced, these offenders were required to serve half their sentences in custody and the remainder while released on licence. The 2021 Act required that they should serve two-thirds of their sentences in custody and, even at that point, a decision on their release would be made by the relevant parole authority. In *R (Khan) v Secretary of State for Justice*[61] the English High Court declined to hold that this violated art 7 of the ECHR, saying that a change to the administration of a penalty, such as a change to early releases provisions, did not amount to the imposition of a heavier penalty than applied when the offence was committed. The Northern Ireland Court of Appeal reached the opposite conclusion in *R v Morgan*[62] in respect of a substantially identical provision in the 2021 Act. Drawing in particular on the judgment of the European Court of Human Rights in *Del Rio Prada v Spain*[63] the court held that the sentences imposed by the trial judge had been redefined and modified by the application of the 2001 Act to a degree that violated art 7 of the ECHR. This seemed more convincing, in normative terms at least, than the decision in *Khan*, as it is beyond doubt that, as a result of the 2021 Act, the applicants in *Morgan* were *in effect* subjected to heavier punishments than applied when they committed the offences or, indeed, when they were sentenced. However, the UK Supreme Court reversed the Northern Ireland Court of Appeal and held that there had been no violation of art 7 of the ECHR.[64] The court began by

that "if the punishment for the offence has been varied between the time of commission and the time of sentencing, [a convicted person has the right] to the benefit of the lesser punishment".

58 Charter of Rights and Freedoms, s 11(h).

59 [2014] SCC 20; [2014] 1 SCR 392, para 83.

60 [2014] SCC 20; [2014] 1 SCR 392, para 63.

61 [2020] EWHC 2084 (Admin); [2020] 1 WLR 3932.

62 [2021] NICA 67. The applicants were sentenced in November 2020 to prison terms ranging from three years to six and a half years, with a provision that they would be released on licence on serving half of those terms. The Counter-Terrorism and Sentencing Act 2021 entered into force on 30 April 2021 and it applied to those already serving prison sentences for terrorist offences.

63 (2014) 58 EHRR 37.

64 *Morgan v Minister of Justice* [2023] UKSC 14; [2024] AC 130.

noting, correctly, that 'penalty' is an autonomous concept, meaning that the way in which a measure or sanction is classified under domestic law is not necessarily conclusive for the purpose of interpreting the ECHR. The European Court is entitled to go behind appearances and decide if the measure or sanction in question is in substance a penalty.[65] However, according to the UK Supreme Court in *Morgan*, this autonomous concept of penalty for the purpose of art 7 is subject to an important qualification, namely, that measures connected with the execution or enforcement of a penalty do not come within its definition. It followed that "retroactive changes to the execution or enforcement of a penalty, whilst a person is serving a sentence, do not fall within the prohibition enshrined in art. 7(1) of the ECHR".[66]

Admittedly, there were earlier British and European authorities to support the UK Supreme Court's conclusion in *Morgan*. In *R (Uttley) v Secretary of State for Home Department*,[67] both the House of Lords and the Strasbourg court held that changes made by the Criminal Justice Act 1991which resulted in the applicant being subject to licence conditions after release from prison did not constitute an additional or more severe penalty for the purpose of art 7. The former European Commission on Human Rights reached the same conclusion in respect of a prisoner who, as a result of legal change, had to spend more time than anticipated in a closed rather than an open prison.[68] More recently, the English Court of Appeal has held that ordinarily judges should not take account of early release provisions, or changes in those provisions, when determining sentence.[69] The problem with all these decisions (apart from that of the Northern Ireland Court of Appeal in *Morgan*) is that while they may be defensible in formal or positivist terms, they fail to grapple with the stark reality that significant changes to parole arrangements can result in a heavier punishment being *served* than could have been predicted or expected when the sentence was imposed.[70] However, the attitude of the courts in the cases just mentioned is that art 7 is primarily, if not exclusively, concerned with prohibiting the judicial imposition of a heavier sentence than applied when the offence was committed, even if later legislative or administrative changes lead a longer or more onerous sentence being served. **14–32**

Article 49 of the Charter of Fundamental Rights of the European Union (CFREU)includes a provision very similar to art 7 of the ECHR. It states: "Nor shall a heavier penalty be imposed than the one that was applicable at the time the criminal offence was committed". Member states must **14–33**

---

65 *Welch v United Kingdom* (1995) 20 EHRR 247.

66 [2023] UKSC 14; [2024] AC 130, para 82.

67 [2004] UKHL 38; [2004] 1 WLR 2278; [2005] 1 Cr App R 15; *Uttley v United Kingdom*, unreported, European Court of Human Rights, 29 November 2005.

68 *Hogben v United Kingdom* (1986) 46 DR 231. See also *Kafkaris v Cyprus* (2009) 49 EHRR 35.

69 *R v Patel* [2021] EWCA Crim 231; [2021] 1 WLR 2997; [2021] 2 Cr App R(S) 47.

70 See comment on *Morgan* by Lyndon Harris at [2023] Crim LR 551, supporting the UK Supreme Court's analysis.

observe the terms of the Charter when implementing EU law. The Court of Justice of the European Union (CJEU) has recognised that art 49 of the CFREU is equivalent to and based upon art 7 of the ECHR. However, in *Minister for Justice v Walsh*[71] a question arose was to whether the CJEU might interpret art 49 differently from the manner in which the Strasbourg court has interpreted art 7 in circumstances identical to those in *Morgan*. The appellant in *Walsh* was resisting surrender to Northern Ireland where he was to be charged with terrorism offences. Like Morgan, he would, if convicted and sentenced, be required to serve a longer prison term than would have been applicable at the time the offence was allegedly committed. The Supreme Court decided to make a reference to the CJEU (under art 267 of the Treaty on the Functioning of the European Union) seeking clarification on the implications of art 49 of the CFREU in these circumstances. The CJEU gave its response in July 2024, having allocated the fictitious name of *Alchaster* to the case.[72] However, the Supreme Court found it necessary to make a second reference asking the CJEU for a direct answer to the question of whether the application of amended rules on early release to a person in the position of Mr Walsh would conflict with art 49.[73] There has been no response to this second reference at the time of writing.

14–34 The factors that a parole authority may or must consider when adjudicating upon applications for release can also render its role akin to that of a sentencing court. Where the governing legislation, or regulations made under it, specify the minimum term a prisoner must serve before being eligible for parole, the key question for the parole authority should be whether the offender, on having served the specified minimum term or longer, can safely be released. However, modern parole legislation is seldom as simple as that, as it often requires that the gravity of the original offence be considered in addition to other matters. This holds true of the Parole Act 2019 which provides (s 27(2)) that in deciding whether to grant parole, the Board *shall* have regard to certain factors including the nature and gravity of the offence for which the sentence is being served and the period of imprisonment already served by the applicant. It must also have regard to any other offence of which the applicant was convicted. By virtue of the obligation to consider the gravity of the offence and the length of sentence already served for it, the Board must essentially engage in a re-sentencing exercise. After all, it is implicitly entitled to refuse parole if it considers that the term of imprisonment already served is an inadequate punishment for the offence. This is a far from ideal arrangement, and its constitutionality may not be beyond doubt. It would be far more satisfactory if the determination of the appropriate penalty were left exclusively to the sentencing court and for the legislature to specify the portion of the prison term that must be served before eligibility for parole arises. The Parole Board could then concentrate solely on the question

---

[71] [2024] IESC 9.
[72] Case C-202/24.
[73] *Minister for Justice v Walsh* [2024] IESC 47.

which it is best equipped to address and that is whether the prisoner can safely be released without creating an undue risk for any individual (such as the victim) or members of the public more generally,

4. The Parole Act 2019

Parole, properly so called, has existed in Ireland since 2001 when a non-statutory Parole Board was appointed by the then Minister for Justice and Equality to review determinate sentences of eight years or longer and life sentences. All cases had to be referred to the Board by the Minister. The general practice was that a sentence of eight years or longer, but less than 14 years, was first reviewed once half of it has been served. Determinate sentences of 14 years or longer and life sentences were reviewed once seven years have been served. By international standards, the Board's case load was rather light. In 2017, 66 prisoners were referred to the Board although in that year it dealt with a total of 346 cases, including second and subsequent applications.[74] Parole was given a statutory foundation for the first time by the Parole Act 2019 (the '2019 Act'). This provides for the establishment of a Parole Board consisting of 12 to 15 members appointed by the Minister for Justice. The chairperson, who must be a serving or retired judge, a practising solicitor or barrister, or a legal academic, is nominated by the Chief Justice. The remaining members must include a practising barrister, a practising solicitor, two psychiatrists, two psychologists, members of the police, probation and prison services and various others. The 2019 Act was brought into operation on 30 July 2021 and the following day was appointed the establishment day for the Board.[75] However, as we shall see, eligibility for parole under the 2019 Act is very narrowly confined to long-term prisoners, as under the previous non-statutory scheme. **14–35**

The 2019 Act has several commendable features, but some drawbacks as well. On the positive side, the Parole Board must include psychiatrists, psychologist and other specialists as well as lawyers. Parole decisions entail predictions about future behaviour and, as such, require an input from persons with expertise in that area. Secondly, the Board is reasonably independent. Members are admittedly appointed by the Minister for Justice (with the chairperson nominated by the Chief Justice). Further, the Minister may remove a member of the Board from office for one of a number of reasons including that "the removal of the member appears to the Minister to be necessary for the effective performance by the Board of its functions".[76] However, release decisions are taken by the Board itself, rather than by the Minister on the Board's recommendation, as was previously the case. Thirdly, the 2019 Act seems to provide for a high level of procedural fairness. Powers conferred on the Board by s 13 of the 2019 Act include a power to direct a written report on a person seeking parole **14–36**

---

74 Parole Board Annual Report 2017.

75 SI No 405 of 2021 and SI No 406 of 2021.

76 Parole Act 2019, s 12(2)(c).

or a parolee facing revocation, to meet with such a person for the purpose of interviewing him or her or to receive oral submissions (through a legal representative or otherwise), to assign a legal representative to such a person and receive written submissions from him or her. Similar rights, including the assignment of a legal representative, may be conferred on a victim who wishes to make representations to the Board. Provision must also be made for granting legal aid to parole applicants, parolees (including those facing revocation) and victims.[77]

14–37 These extensive procedural protections should satisfy the requirements of the ECHR which demands certain standards of fairness, in both release and revocation decisions. In *Waite v United Kingdom*[78] which involved a young offender sentenced to indefinite detention who had his licence revoked without an oral hearing, the European Court of Human Rights said:

> "In matters of such crucial importance as the deprivation of liberty and where questions arise involving, for example, an assessment of the applicant's character or mental state, the court's case law indicates that it may be essential to the fairness of the proceedings that the applicant be present at an oral hearing. In such a case as the present, where characteristics pertaining to the applicant's personality and level of maturity and reliability are important in deciding on his or her dangerousness, art. 5(4) [of the Convention] requires an oral hearing in the context of an adversarial procedure involving legal representation and the possibility of calling and questioning witnesses."[79]

14–38 Likewise, in *R (Osborn) v Parole Board*[80] the United Kingdom Supreme Court, while it stopped short of saying that an oral hearing was required in every case, held that in order "to comply with common law standards of procedural fairness" the Parole Board should hold an oral hearing before determining an application for release or for a transfer to open conditions, whenever fairness to the prisoner requires such a hearing in light of the facts of the case and the importance of what is a stake. The court addressed at length the justifications for such a hearing and cautioned that the Board must be, and appear to be, independent and impartial. It "should not be predisposed to favour an official account of events, or official assessments of risk, over the case advanced by the prisoner".[81]

14–39 However, the 2019 Act also has some significant drawbacks. The least that might be expected of a statute establishing a new parole system is that it would specify exactly the category of prisoners who will become eligible for parole and the portion of sentence they must serve before becoming

---

[77] Parole Act 2019, s 14. Such a scheme has been established. See *Legal Aid Scheme Under the Parole Act 2019* on Parole Board's website: <www.gov.ie/en/organisation/parole-board/> accessed 12 November 2022.

[78] (2003) 36 EHRR 54.

[79] (2003) 36 EHRR 54, para 59.

[80] [2013] UKSC 61; [2014] AC 1115; [2013] 3 WLR 1020.

[81] [2013] UKSC 61; [2014] AC 1115; [2013] 3 WLR 1020, para 2(vii).

so eligible. In other words, it should specify the minimum qualifying sentence, if any, and the minimum qualifying period. Unfortunately, the 2019 Act does neither. Life prisoners are ineligible for parole until they have served at least 12 years, though it is far from clear how that figure was reached or why it is appropriate for all life sentences, whether mandatory or discretionary. However, in the case of prisoners serving determinate sentences, who typically account for about 88 per cent of the sentenced prisoner population, the 2019 Act (s 24(1)(b)) provides that, in addition to lifers, there shall be eligible for parole:

> "a person serving a sentence of imprisonment of a term equivalent to or longer than such term as is prescribed in regulations made by the Minister under subsection (3), who has served at least such portion of the sentence as may be prescribed by the Minister in accordance with that subsection."

Section 24(3) then provides: **14–40**

> "The Minister may, for the purposes of subsection (1)(b), following consultation with the [Parole] Board by regulations prescribe:
> (a) a term of imprisonment of not less than 8 years, and
> (b) the portion of such a term to be served by a person prior to becoming eligible for parole."

What this seems to mean is that those serving prison sentences of less than eight years will be ineligible for parole, though they will continue to qualify for remission and temporary release under the Criminal Justice Act 1960. Moreover, the minimum qualifying period is left to be determined by the Minister following consultation with the Parole Board. One of the factors to which the Minister must have regard when making the regulations is the availability to prisoners of other forms of early release and "the extent to which the objective referred to in paragraph (a) [incentivising prisoners to become rehabilitated] is achieved by such other forms of early release".[82] **14–41**

Overall, then, the 2019 Act represents a half-hearted effort to introduce a modern, effective parole system. Such a system would permit all prisoners, apart from those serving short sentences, to be considered for parole after serving a defined portion of their sentences. In New Zealand, for example, prisoners serving sentences of more than two years, who are classified under the governing legislation as 'long-term prisoners', become eligible for parole after serving one-third of their sentence. Those serving less than two years are automatically released once they have served half their sentence.[83] Likewise in Canada, the Parole Board of Canada deals with parole for offenders serving sentences of two years or more, and with offenders serving sentences less than two years in provinces and territories that do not have their own parole boards. There, persons serving determinate sentences become eligible for parole having served one- **14–42**

---

82 Parole Act 2019, s 24(4)(b).
83 (New Zealand) Parole Act 2002.

third of their sentence or seven years whichever is less. For life sentence prisoners, parole eligibility is set by the court at the time of sentence. For first-degree murder, eligibility is automatically set at 25 years while for second degree murder it is normally set at somewhere between 10 and 25 years.[84] When parole was first introduced in England and Wales in 1967, prisoners serving determinate sentences were eligible for release once they had served one-third of their sentence, subject to serving a minimum term of 12 months, later reduced to six months. However, English parole law has undergone many changes since then.[85]

14–43 Confining parole eligibility to those serving sentences of eight years (and possibly longer given the ministerial discretion to set longer qualifying sentences) deprives most prisoners of the opportunity to be considered for, or to receive, parole. On 30 November 2022, there were 3,409 sentenced prisoners in Irish prisons.[86] Of these 2,001 (59 per cent) were serving sentences of five years or less. Another 769 were serving sentences in the range of five to 10 years, while 272 were serving sentences of 10 years or more, and 367 were serving life sentences. If half of the 769 in the five- to 10-year bracket were serving sentences less than eight years, it would mean that less than a third of the prison population on that date would even qualify to be considered for parole. As of summer 2024, no ministerial order had been made under s 24(3) of the 2019 Act (as quoted above) in respect of determinate sentences and, in fact, the website of the Parole Board states simply that it is an independent statutory body "that considers applications for parole from prisoners serving life sentences once the prisoners concerned have served at least 12 years of their sentence".[87]

The Role of Victims in the Parole Process

14–44 In recent decades, many countries, including Ireland, have adopted measures to integrate victims more fully into criminal process. They have done this mainly by allowing for victim impact evidence at sentencing and more recently, particularly in European Union countries, by guaranteeing victims access to information and support services.[88] As discussed in Chap 11, victim impact evidence at sentencing is defensible on the basis that it informs the court more fully of the harm caused by the offence. It

[84] On the Canadian parole system, see its Parole Board website <www.canada.ca/en/parole-board.html>, accessed 18 November 2024. For description and analysis of the system, see Charbonneau and Ferreira, note 19 above; Anthony N Doob, Cheryl Marie Webster and Allan Manson, "Zombie parole: The withering of conditional release in Canada" (2014) 61 Crim LQ 301; Allan Manson et al, *Sentencing and Penal Policy in Canada: Cases, Materials, and Commentary*, 3rd ed (Emond, 2016), Chap 19.

[85] Notes 41-45 above and the accompanying text.

[86] Irish Prison Service, *Annual Report 2022* (2023), 74

[87] <www.gov.ie/en/organisation/parole-board/> accessed 18 November 2024.

[88] Directive 2012/29/EU of the European Parliament and Council of 25 October 2012 on the rights, support and protections of victims of crime. In Ireland, the Criminal Justice (Victims of Crime) Act 2017 gave effect to this Directive.

can also serve an expressive function in allowing victims to articulate in public, often for the first time, how they were affected by the offending conduct. More recently, however, many countries have begun to allow for victim participation in the parole process and this, in turn, raises important questions as to what role, if any, victims should have in the administration of prison sentences.[89] Parenthetically, it may be added that similar questions can arise in connection prisoner transfer under legislation such as the Transfer of Sentenced Persons Acts 1995 and 1997. This legislation permits foreign nationals serving prison sentences in Ireland to be transferred to their native countries to serve out the balance their sentences. Victims have been known to object to such transfers where it seems that an offender will qualify for release at an earlier point in their native country than they would here.

There can no objection to providing a victim with information about the sentence imposed, where it is being served, the date on which it will expire and any plans to grant the offender early release, by way of parole or otherwise. Victims already have a statutory entitlement to such information under the Criminal Justice (Victims of Crime) Act 2017 (s 8). It is only right that they should be so entitled, especially where the offence was violent in nature and the victim fears for his or her personal safety if the offender is released. Nor can there be any objection to a parole authority informing itself of these victim-related matters. If it grants release, it may use this information to tailor the conditions the offender must observe during the parole period. These might include a requirement not to contact the victim by any means or to stay away from a specified locality. However, just as a victim at sentencing may not recommend or try to influence the penalty to be imposed on the offender, so in parole proceedings, a victim should not be permitted to urge that an offender be denied parole solely on account of the nature or gravity of the offence. Were this to be allowed, it could result in similarly situated prisoners being treated differently simply because some victims might be more forgiving than others – precisely the reason why they are not permitted to make recommendations as to sentence. Parole, like all other criminal justice decision-making processes, must operate fairly. Those being considered for release are entitled to due process, procedural fairness and freedom from any kind of arbitrary discrimination. **14–45**

It is therefore vital that legislation should clearly state the objectives of parole and the criteria for granting it. No less important is the provision of clear information to victims as to what precisely their role is in the parole process and what they can expect from it. Some victims will naturally feel disappointed or distressed if an offender is granted release which they consider to be premature on account of the nature of the offence. This makes it all the more imperative that before victims have any engagement **14–46**

---

89 For a discussion of these questions, see Nicola Padfield and Julian V Roberts, "Victim input at parole: probative or prejudicial?" in Anthony Bottoms and Julian V Roberts (eds), *Hearing the Victim: Adversarial Justice, Crime Victims and the State* (Routledge, 2010), Chap 10; Petersilia, note 9 above, Chap 8.

with the parole process, they should be fully informed as the nature and limitations of their role. The Parole Act 2019 (s 14(1)(f)) requires the Board to make provision for:

> "enabling the relevant victim to make submissions to the Board, whether in person, through his or her legal representative, or in writing – (i) where the Board is considering an application for parole or the revocation of a parole order, or (ii) where the Board considers it appropriate, where the Board is considering the variation of a condition attaching to, or the date of release in, a parole order."

14–47 The 2019 Act (s 14(1)(e)) further requires the Board to provide for the persons who are to be notified of any action it takes, including the 'relevant victim' and the notification must include an explanation of the parole process and details of how the victim may participate in the process.[90] Where the death of a relevant family member was caused by the offence, one or more family members (to be nominated, if necessary, by the Board) may make submissions under s 14.[91] Legal aid may be granted to victims who wish to make a submission to the Board.[92] What is clear, therefore, is that victims may take part in the parole process and be facilitated in doing so. What is unclear is what their role is or, more precisely, the matters in respect of which they may make submissions. The 2019 Act appears to be deliberately vague and open-ended on these questions. In principle, for reasons already outlined, victims should be confined to making submissions connected with any apprehensions they may have about their own safety or the safety of others if the parole applicant is released. It would scarcely be compatible with principle to permit them to argue that the applicant had not endured enough punishment. If victims are not allowed to suggest to a court what the sentence should be, they should hardly be allowed to suggest how much of it should be served in custody. The role accorded to victims in some American parole systems has recently been criticised for causing delays in processing parole applications and in leading to possibly unnecessarily long terms of incarceration.[93]

Revocation of Parole

14–48 Everyone released on parole is subject to recall if found to have violated a condition of release. The violation might involve the commission of an offence, or it might be a so-called technical violation where the parolee fails to abide by a specific condition such as refraining from contacting a victim or associating with members of a criminal gang. Because recall can have an important and, almost invariably, detrimental impact on an

---

[90] 'Relevant victim' means the victim of the offence in respect of which the sentence of imprisonment is being served to which the parole application relates (Parole Act 2019, s 2).

[91] Parole Act 2019, s 3.

[92] Parole Act 2019, s 14(1).

[93] Ráchael A Powers and Jacquelyn Burckley, *Justice for None: How Marsy's Law Undermines the Criminal Legal System* (National Association of Criminal Defence Lawyers, 2024), 27-29.

offender's life, it must be governed by clear rules and implemented in a procedurally fair manner. It is a common complaint in other jurisdictions that parole conditions are overbroad and vague, and that even minor breaches can lead to recall. Certainly, the numbers of recalled prisoners in both England and Wales and the United States are quite striking. Apparently, 14 per cent of sentenced prisoners in England and Wales in late 2020 were recall prisoners.[94] Across the United States, about half of all prison admissions result from revocation of various kinds of conditional release, including probation, parole and supervised release. This has recently led some states to narrow the circumstances in which offenders can be imprisoned or re-imprisoned for minor violations and to limit the custodial term which a person may be required to serve following recall.[95]

Parole revocation exists primarily to protect the public.[96] A conditionally released prisoner who seems disposed to engage in further crime or other harmful behaviour should be liable in re-incarceration if that is considered necessary for preventive purposes. This does not, however, diminish the punitive impact of recall on the offender, as courts have recognised. Hale LJ (when a member of the English Court of Appeal) said that "recall has very serious consequences for the person recalled. Sometimes those consequences will be out of all proportion to the events which have led to the recall".[97] She had previously held that a recalled prisoner seeking re-release should be entitled to the protections afforded to criminal defendants under art 6 of the ECHR[98]. She was in the minority on this point, but other members of the court agreed that recall demanded "a high standard of fair procedure".[99] The United States Supreme Court has been less demanding in this regard. In a trilogy of decisions dating from the 1970s, the court held that a parolee had a limited right to fair procedures when their parole was being revoked, but it still insisted that revocation was not part of a criminal prosecution which meant that "the full panoply of rights due a defendant in such a proceeding does not apply".[100] **14–49**

The procedures for the revocation of parole under the Parole Act 2019 (s 33) have some positive features. First, parole is not to be lightly revoked. The Parole Board must be satisfied that the parolee "poses an undue risk to the safety and security of the public" or that he or she has breached a release condition. Further, it must be satisfied that the revocation is **14–50**

94 *A Parole System Fit for Purpose: A Report by JUSTICE* (Chair: Nicola Padfield) (JUSTICE, 2022) which provides an excellent, critical analysis of the operation of the English parole system.

95 Nancy J King, "Constitutional limits on the imposition and revocation of probation, parole and supervised release after *Haymond*" (2023) 76 Vanderbilt LR 83.

96 *R v Sharkey* [2000] 1 WLR 160, 162-163; [2000] 1 Cr App R 409 (though referring specifically to. s 39 of the Criminal Justice Act 1991).

97 *Rodgers v Governor of HM Prison Brixton* [2003] EWHC 1923 (Admin), para 29.

98 *R (West) v Parole Board* [2002] EWCA Civ 1641; [2003] 1 WLR 705.

99 [2002] EWCA Civ 1641; [2003] 1 WLR 705, 718 (Sedley LJ).

100 *Morrissey v Brewer* 408 US 471, 480 (1972). The other cases are *Gagnon v Scarpelli* 411 US 778 (1973) and *Moody v Daggett* 429 US 78 (1976).

justified "by the gravity of the risk or the breach of the condition, as the case may be". This seems to preclude revocation for so-called technical violations, a practice that has plagued the parole and supervised release systems of other jurisdictions, notably the United States. Revocation on public safety grounds requires evidence of undue risk and, even where, a breach of release conditions is established, it must still be of a level of gravity sufficient to justify revocation. This still leaves a fair degree of discretion to the Board, although, in all probability, terms like 'undue risk' and 'gravity' will eventually be subject to judicial interpretation. Secondly, when considering revocation, the Board must have regard to such matters as it considers appropriate including those specified in s 33(3) which cover any report relating to the parolee, any meeting with the parolee or submissions on his or her behalf any submissions made by a relevant victim. Further, under s 13 where the Board is considering either an application for parole or revocation, it must assign a legal representative to the offender unless he or she proposes to engage one, to meet with that person to receive oral submissions from him or her or from a legal representative and to receive written submissions. The same procedure must be followed in relation to a victim. Also, s 14 which deals with the Board's procedures, requires that provision be made for a number of matters including enabling an offender with a legal representative to attend a meeting of the Board, and present his or her case, either personally or through a legal representative.

14–51 Another potentially valuable provision in s 33 of the 2019 Act is that when the Board is considering a revocation application but is not satisfied that the specified criteria (regarding, for example, the gravity of the breach) have been fulfilled, it may vary a parole condition or release date. This could be used positively to tailor the release conditions in such a way as to minimise the risk of a future breach. Overall, then, the 2019 Act demands a high level of procedural fairness in the conduct of revocation proceedings. The drafters of the legislation were doubtless aware that they had little choice in the matter because of the principles already established by the courts in relation to the revocation of temporary release. As discussed further below under that heading, a person whose release is being revoked is entitled to be heard and given the opportunity to make submissions before the revocation is confirmed.

5. Remission

14–52 Remission brings a prison sentence to an end.[101] Unlike parole which involves conditional release with the possibility of recall and temporary release which, strictly speaking, is for defined periods only and also subject to conditions, remission relieves a prisoner of liability to serve any more

[101] To 'remit' means to forgive further punishment. See *State (Carney) v Governor of Portlaoise Prison* [1957] IR 25 at 27, and Tom O'Malley, "Ireland" in Nicola Padfield, Dirk van Zyl Smit and Frieder Dünkel (eds), *Release from Prison: European Policy and Practice* (Willan Publishing, 2010), Chap 10.

of the sentence to which it applies. When penal servitude was introduced in the mid-19th century, up to one third of a sentence could be served on licence. Remission of ordinary prison sentences was not introduced in England until 1898 and in Ireland until 1907.[102] The relevant statutory provisions, which were identical in both jurisdictions, permitted rules to be made enabling prisoners "by special industry and good conduct" to earn remission of a portion of their sentences and upon a prisoner's discharge "his sentence shall be deemed to have expired". The power to make such rules is now vested in the Minister for Justice and Equality under the Prisons Act 2007 (s 35) which simply states that rules may be made for "the remission of portion of a prisoner's sentence".

Irish law provides for both special and standard remission. Special remission derives ultimately from Art 13.6 of the Constitution, as described at the beginning of this chapter. The Government, in which the power is now vested, may commute or remit any sentence, custodial or otherwise. Therefore, it can quite legally grant remission to a prisoner at any time, even if this amounts to virtual impunity. A few statutory restrictions have been imposed on the exercise of this executive power. It may not be exercised, for example, in the case of a person sentenced for a murder offence within the meaning of s 3 of the Criminal Justice Act 1990 (such as the murder of a member of the Garda Síochána or a prison officer acting in the course of their duty) until the specified minimum term has been served. The same applies where presumptive minimum sentences are imposed for certain drug and firearms offences. As noted earlier, when murder was a capital offence, it was not unusual for a death sentence to be commuted to life imprisonment which would later be remitted after the offender had spent some time in prison. Special remission of this kind is seldom granted nowadays because temporary release under the Criminal Justice Act 1960 will usually serve the same purpose. **14–53**

Standard remission is governed by the Prison Rules 2007 which provide that a prisoner shall be eligible by good conduct to earn remission not exceeding one quarter of the term or, in the case of consecutive sentences, the aggregate term being served.[103] This is effectively an entitlement enjoyed by all prisoners serving determinate sentences, though it may be lost (though typically only partially) through bad behaviour.[104] A prisoner who has engaged in authorised structured activity, such as work, training, education or programmes designed to reduce the risk of re-offending upon release, may apply to the Minister for Justice for enhanced remission, meaning remission exceeding one-quarter but not more than **14–54**

---

[102] Prisons Act 1898 (s 8); Prisons (Ireland) Act 1907 (s 1).

[103] Prison Rules 2007 (SI No 252 of 2007), r 59(1) as substituted by Prison (Amendment) Rules 2014 (SI No 227 of 2014). Standard remission was previously allowed under the Rules for the Government of Prisons 1947 (SI No 320 of 1947), r 38.

[104] *O'Brien v Governor of Limerick Prison* [1997] 2 ILRM 349; *Callan v Ireland* [2013] 2 IR 267; [2013] 2 ILRM 257; *B v Director of Oberstown Children Detention Centre* [2020] IESC 18; [2023] 2 IR 191; [2020] 1 ILRM 469.

one third of the sentence. Formal provision for enhanced remission was first introduced in the 2007 rules but, following amendments made in 2014, the grant of such remission is now very much at the discretion of the Minister who can take a wide range of factors and information from several sources into account.[105] The new regime was introduced in response to a number of High Court challenges from prisoners who had been denied enhanced remission under the original rules.

14–55 Ireland is now the only jurisdiction in these islands to retain standard remission as a distinct form of early release. In England and Wales remission and parole co-existed until the Criminal Justice Act 1991 introduced a new parole system under which, as noted earlier, most prisoners serving determinate sentences were released, conditionally or otherwise, at the half-way mark. Remission was then abolished. Here in Ireland, the Parole Act 2019 retains remission, which is scarcely surprising since only a relatively small proportion of prisoners (those serving long sentences) will qualify for parole under that Act. In contrast to parole, remission has been subject to little detailed scrutiny apart from an investigation by an English committee on prison discipline in the mid-1980s.[106] The report noted that, when originally introduced, remission was intended as a rehabilitative measure and something to be earned by positive good conduct. However, by the 20th century, it had become a right that was subject to forfeiture through bad behaviour, though lost remission could be regained through subsequent good behaviour. The committee was nonetheless convinced that remission, or more precisely the prospect of losing it, was a valuable means of maintaining prison discipline. Some years later, the Carlisle Committee on parole agreed with this general sentiment holding that while the effectiveness of remission in promoting prison discipline was impossible to assess, there had to be some means of increasing the length of time to be served by a prisoner who engaged in misbehaviour of a kind that was insufficiently serious to warrant fresh court proceedings.[107] The Committee however recommended that remission be abolished, saying (para 240) that it was "not persuaded of the case for wiping out part of the total sentence because a prisoner has kept out of trouble while in custody". Instead, all sentenced prisoners should be eligible for parole at some point in their sentence. These recommendations were given effect in the Criminal Justice Act 1991. By then, remission was far more generous in England and Wales than in Ireland. Since 1940 prisoners were entitled to one-third remission and in 1987, as part of an effort to relieve prison overcrowding, it was increased to one-half for prisoners serving 12 months or less.[108]

---

[105] Prison Rules 2007 (SI No 252 of 2007), r 59(2) as substituted by Prison (Amendment) (No 2) Rules 2014 (SI No 385 of 2014).

[106] *Report of the Committee on the Prison Disciplinary System* (Prior Report), Cmnd 9641 (HMSO, 1985).

[107] *The Parole System in England and Wales: Report of the Review Committee* (Carlisle Report), Cmnd 532 (HMSO, 1988), para 43.

[108] Home Office, *Crime, Justice and Protecting the Public*, Cmnd 965 (HMSO, 1990), Chap 6

The merits of standard remission are debatable. As already noted, remission brings a sentence to an end so, for all practical purposes, everyone given a determinate sentence in Ireland can expect to be released on serving, at most, three-quarters of it. Advocates of 'truth in sentencing' would doubtless object to this arrangement, and possibly to other forms of early release, arguing that the sentence imposed should be the sentence served (or, at least, that the two should closely approximate). Further, standard remission is earned simply by keeping out of trouble, as the Carlisle Committee phrased it, rather than by engaging in more positive activities in preparation for release. Eligibility for enhanced remission does, however, depend on prisoners taking positive steps such as participating in treatment or training programmes. As against this, maintaining order and discipline within prisons is a vitally important consideration. Any closed institution with a large population of young males being held against their will, which is a fair description of many prisons, is vulnerable to outbreaks of violence and disorder. It should nonetheless be added that environmental conditions and strained relations between staff and inmates can also be contributing factors.[109] Incentivising good behaviour can be more effective than punishing bad behaviour when it comes to maintaining order within prisons. **14–56**

6. Temporary Release

Temporary release is essentially a form of parole save that, on paper at least, prisoners are released for defined, though often renewable, periods rather than indefinitely. It was first introduced in Ireland by the Criminal Justice Act 1960 (the '1960 Act') which, in its original form, simply allowed the Minister for Justice to make rules providing for the temporary release of prisoners, detainees in St Patrick's Institution (young offenders) and 'criminal lunatics'. Such release was to be subject to conditions. This was replaced in 2003 with a more elaborate set of statutory provision setting out in some detail the purposes for which temporary release may be granted and the factors which the Minister must take into account.[110] Temporary release under the 1960 Act is not to be confused with the executive power to commute or remit punishment under Art 13.6 of the Constitution. It is a distinct statutory procedure.[111] Two fundamental principles may be derived from the case law on temporary release. The first is that release under the 1960 Act is a privilege to be granted by the executive rather than a right vested in a prisoner. As such, once a **14–57**

[109] Anthony E Bottoms, "Interpersonal violence and social order in prisons" (1999) 26 *Crime and Justice* 205. See also Nancy Wolff, Cynthia L Blitz and Ronet Bachman, "Physical violence inside prisons: Rates of victimization" (2007) 34 *Criminal Justice and Behaviour* 588.

[110] Criminal Justice (Temporary Release of Prisoners) Act 2003, s 1. For a more detailed account of temporary release, see Thomas O'Malley, *Sentencing Law and Practice*, 3rd ed (Round Hall, 2016), 628-640, and judgment of Dunne J in *Minister for Justice v Balmer* [2016] IESC 25; [2017] 3 IR 562; [2017] 1 ILRM 1.

[111] *Kinahan v Minister for Justice* [2001] 4 IR 454, 457.

decision (whether to grant or refuse release) is made within the terms of the statute, it is immune from review by the courts.[112] The second is that revocation procedures are subject to closer judicial scrutiny. Where it is sought to revoke the grant of temporary release before the expiry of the sentence, the offender is entitled to a fair hearing before the decision is taken. It was so held by both the High Court and Supreme Court in *State (Murphy) v Kielt*[113] where the applicant, while on temporary release, was arrested and recommitted to St Patrick's Institution where he was charged with having committed two serious offences. Thereafter, he was treated as a sentenced detainee. He successfully challenged the revocation on the basis that it had not been proved that he breached any of his release conditions and that he had not been afforded an opportunity to be heard before his release was revoked. In the High Court, Barron J held that a hearing is required whenever a person's rights (which include the right to liberty) are threatened. He said:

> "In my view, the essentials of a valid hearing in the present case required at the least: (1) evidence from which it would have been fair to hold in favour of the allegation; (2) notification to [the applicant] of the nature of such evidence sufficient to enable him to prepare a defence; (3) time for [the applicant] to prepare a defence; (4) an opportunity to make that defence. Such a hearing should have been held and should have been seen to have been held. Such hearing did not have to be of a very formal nature, provided that the minimum requirements to which I have referred were met."[114]

14–58 The Supreme Court agreed and held that the fact that the applicant had been charged with an offence did not rebut his presumption of innocence in respect of that charge which should not have been automatically treated as a breach of release conditions.[115]

14–59 Temporary release will remain the primary early release mechanism for most prisoners before they qualify for standard or enhanced remission, even with the entry into force of the Parole Act 2019. As already noted, that Act applies solely to prisoners serving life sentences or determinate sentences of at least eight years. For the majority of prisoners, those serving less than eight years , temporary release remains their only hope. How the various forms of early release may be reconciled is considered further below.

---

112 *Dowling v Minister for Justice* [2003] 2 IR 535, 541; *Lynch and Whelan v Minister for Justice* [2010] IESC 34; [2012] 1 IR 1 at 25; *Minister for Justice v Balmer* [2016] IESC 25; [2017] 3 IR 562' [2017] 1 ILRM 1, para 95 (Dunne J); *People (DPP) v Tiernan* [1988] IR 250, 256; [1989] ILRM 149; *Murray v Ireland* [1991] 1 ILRM 465. 472; *Doherty v Governor of Portlaoise Prison* [2002] 2 IR 252, 263.

113 [1984] IR 458; [1982] ILRM 475 (High Court)

114 [1984] IR 458, 465-466; [1982] ILRM 475, 479-480 (High Court)

115 [1984] IR 458, 468; [1985] ILRM 141 (Supreme Court). See also *Dowling v Minister for Justice* [2003] 2 IR 535.

7. Judicial Modification of Sentence

Ordinarily, a court has no role in the implementation of a sentence which it imposes, but some jurisdictions allow for exceptions to this principle. We are not concerned here with breach proceedings which are common enough. In Ireland, for example, a person who fails to fulfil the terms of a community service order may be brought back before court which may revoke the order and deal with the offender in any way in which he or she could have been dealt with for the offence of conviction.[116] Likewise, a suspended sentence may be later activated in whole or in part where the offender has been in breach of a condition of suspension. Sentence modification, in the sense in which the term is used here, refers to a practice whereby the original sentencing court may later review the sentence and possibly reduce or mitigate it in some way. Many American states traditionally permitted modification in this sense, and some still do. Judges in the State of Maryland, for example, had a very broad discretionary power to modify a sentence at any time while it was being served, provided a motion to modify had been served within 90 days of the sentence being imposed. Once that time limit was observed, the court could decide when to consider it, and that was often many years later.[117] Nowadays, a court must exercise its revisory power within five years. **14–60**

Judicial modification of sentence has not been unknown in Ireland, though here we usually refer to reviewable sentences. As discussed earlier in Chap 9 on the sentencing of children, it was for some years a common practice in this country for a judge, when imposing a determinate prison sentence, to order that the offender be brought back before court after serving a specified portion of that sentence. The expectation, if not the guarantee, was that if the offender had behaved well in prison and did not appear to pose an unacceptable risk of re-offending, the balance of the sentence would be suspended. However, in *People (DPP) v Finn,*[118]the Supreme Court, while stressing that its observations were obiter, cast serious doubts on the constitutionality of this practice which it ultimately described as undesirable, and said that it should be discontinued. Courts no longer impose such sentences on adult offenders, although when sentencing for a s 15A or s 15B drug offence, a court may list the sentence for review after one-half of it has expired, though only if it is satisfied that addiction was a substantial factor leading to the offence.[119] Nowadays, it has become common practice for courts to partly suspend prison sentences at the outset which means that the offender is guaranteed release on having served the custodial portion, and possibly earlier. Reviewable sentences of detention are often imposed on child offenders and, as noted in Chap 9, this practice is currently assumed to be constitutional. **14–61**

---

[116] Criminal Justice (Community Service) Act 1983, s 8.

[117] Steven Grossman and Stephen Shapiro, "Judicial modification of sentences in Maryland" (2003) 33 Univ. Baltimore LR 1.

[118] [2001] 2 IR 25; [2001] 2 ILRM 211.

[119] Misuse of Drugs Act 1977, s 27(3J) as substituted by Criminal Justice Act 2007, s 33, and amended by Criminal Justice (Amendment) Act 2021, s 6.

8. General Amnesty or Collective Pardon

14–62 A general amnesty or collective pardon involves the simultaneous release of a large number of prisoners, often granted to mark some special occasion or to relieve prison overcrowding.[120] It rarely occurs nowadays, in these islands at least. At one time, in predominantly Catholic countries, there was a tradition of granting an amnesty to some prisoners at the beginning of each Holy Year. (Since about 1300, a Holy Year is declared every quarter of a century, though the idea of a prisoner amnesty on such occasions dates back to Mosaic law). In 1950, for example, Spain granted an amnesty to 13,000 prisoners to mark that Holy Year while in Ireland a more modest 113 prisoners were released to mark the occasion.[121] However, the impact, in Ireland at least, was not very dramatic as it merely involved releasing those with less than a month to serve and granting 50 per cent remission to others, subject to a total remission of three months. The Government stated that it was taking this step as an indication of its complete harmony with the spirit of the Holy Year.[122] This act of clemency backfired quite spectacularly in the case of one released prisoner, Thomas Ryan, who, a few days after his release, went to a church and stole the collection box. For this he was sentenced to four months in prison, a penalty he gladly accepted. He said that he had had a good time in prison, especially over Christmas, but he had been left starving after his release.[123]

14–63 Large-scale release of prisoners is most likely to occur nowadays as a solution to overcrowding. The most notable recent example occurred in Italy in 2006 when almost 22,000 inmates (about one-third of the total prison population) were released at the beginning of August of that year. The sole purpose was to relieve overcrowding as the prison system was then operating at 130 per cent capacity. Those serving sentences for certain offences including terrorism, kidnapping, organised crime and serious sex offences were excluded from the scheme, but all others had their sentences reduced by three years. This meant that anyone serving less than three years was immediately released. There was no post-release supervision but, as a disincentive to repeat offending, any released prisoner who was reconvicted within five years and who received a prison term of two years or more would have to serve the unexpired portion of their amnestied sentence in addition to the new one.[124] General amnesties of this nature

[120] *Burdick v United States* 236 U.S.79, 95 (1915) ("Amnesty is usually general, addressed to classes or even communities, a legislative act, or under legislation, constitutional or statutory, the act of the supreme magistrate.").

[121] "Spain gives Holy Year amnesty to 13,000", *Irish Press,* 31 March 1950. Irish amnesty reported in *Irish Independent,* 20 December 1949.

[122] *Evening Herald,* 20 December 1949.

[123] "Jailed again as he wished", *Irish Times,* 21 January 1950.

[124] Paolo Buonanno and Steven Raphael, "Incarceration and incapacitation: Evidence from the 2006 Italian Collective Pardon" (2013) 103(6) *American Economic Review* 2437; Francesco Drago, Roberto Galbiati and Pietro Vertova, "The deterrent effects of prison: Evidence from a natural experiment" (2009) 117(2) *Journal of Political Economy* 257; Alessandro Corda, "Sentencing and penal policies in Italy, 1985-2015: The tale of a troubled country" in Michael Tonry

seldom have any significant long-term impact unless accompanied by deeper policy and structural reforms designed to limit the future use of imprisonment. This is borne out by the Italian experience. There, the prison population may have declined drastically overnight with the general release in August 2006, but it quicky rose again, reaching almost 68,000 in 2010. In 2020, it stood 53,000.

9. Reconciling Early Release Provisions

Ireland now has several early release mechanisms: special remission, standard remission, early release and parole. We may discount special remission for present purposes, but we should add part-suspension of sentence because this, too, is a form of conditional release. Prior to the introduction of parole, the system was fairly straightforward. Every prisoner serving a determinate sentence was entitled to one-quarter remission, with the possibility of enhanced remission of up to one-third, at the Minister's discretion. A prisoner might be granted temporary release, in theory at any point during the sentence, but typically towards the end which would, of course, be reached once the prisoner qualified for remission. In effect, therefore, everyone serving a determinate sentence, unless he or she had persistently engaged in bad behaviour, could look forward to release on remission after serving three-quarters of the sentence at most, with the further prospect of being granted temporary release before that. Where a part-suspended sentence was imposed, remission was applied to the custodial portion, though temporary release was also possible. All these provisions still apply. Standard remission does not apply to life sentences for obvious reasons. There is no identifiable term to be reduced, but life sentence prisoners have long qualified for temporary release, which often became permanent, and they now qualify for parole. **14–64**

The introduction of formal parole under the Parole Act 2019, while welcome in many respects, complicates matters as far as long determinate sentences are concerned. Let us assume that Minister for Justice will eventually make an order under s 24 of the 2019 Act specifying eight years as the minimum sentence to which parole can apply (though the specified term may be longer) and further specifying the portion of such a sentence that must be served before eligibility for parole arises. This portion can scarcely be more than one-half, as prisoners will remain entitled to remission on serving three quarters of their sentences. It may even be one third, as in other jurisdictions such as Canada. No obvious problem would arise in reconciling parole and remission in these circumstances. Eligibility for parole would arise well before the sentence expired with remission. A prisoner serving eight years (96 months) will ordinarily **14–65**

(ed), *Sentencing Policies and Practices in Western Countries* (Vol 45 of *Crime and Justice*) (University of Chicago Press, 2016), 107, 145-147; Alessandro Barbarino and Giovanni Mastrobuoni "The incapacitation effect of incarceration: Evidence from several Italian collective pardons" (2014) 6(1) *American Economic Journal* 1 (dealing with eight collective pardons issued between 1962 and 1993).

be entitled to remission on serving 72 months or, if granted enhanced remission, on serving something between 64 and 72 months. A prisoner would be due consideration for parole on having served 32 months (if the specified portion were one-third) or 48 months (if it were one-half). Either way, there would be a meaningful gap between the parole eligibility date and the expiry of the sentence with the grant of remission.

14–66 Temporary release and part-suspension of sentence may be more difficult to reconcile with parole for long-sentence prisoners, once that is introduced. The Parole Act 2019 provides (s 6) that it is without prejudice to the Minister's power to grant temporary release under the Criminal Justice Act 1960, the power to commute or remit punishment under the Criminal Justice Act 1951 and the entitlement of prisoners to earn remission. It further provides (s 2(3)) that, for the purpose of calculating the length of a prison sentence or the portion of such a sentence, there shall be included any time spent on temporary release pursuant to the 1960 Act, excluding any time during the currency of a sentence is suspended. This implies that a prisoner who is eligible for parole may still be granted temporary release. While the law on the matter may be clear, it gives rise to the more difficult policy question of whether temporary release, except perhaps for a short period and for a specific purpose or reason, should be granted to a parole-eligible prisoner before being considered for parole or, indeed, after being refused parole. After all, the main advantage of formal parole is that it enables decision on early release to be made by an independent body with an appropriate range of expertise which is in a position to consider all relevant information about prisoner who is seeking release. Temporary release decisions, by contrast, while no doubt made as carefully as possible, are made by the executive in a far less structured manner than parole decisions. The advantages of formal parole could therefore be substantially diminished by the wholesale grant of temporary release to parole-eligible prisoners.

14–67 Questions will also arise about the part suspension of sentences for offenders who will become eligible for parole. As it now operates, the part-suspended sentence bears some similarity to parole because it entitles an offender to be conditionally released after serving a defined portion of the sentence, although subject to recall to serve out some or all of the remainder of the sentence if found to be in breach of a condition of suspension. The difference, of course, is that the decision on part suspension is made when sentence is being imposed in contrast to parole where the release decision is made by an expert body during the currency of the sentence. Further, an offender given a part-suspended sentence is entitled to be released once the custodial portion, less remission, has been served, irrespective of whether the prison authorities consider him or her to be suitable for release at that point. Ultimately, however, both the part-suspended sentence and parole give offenders an opportunity to show that they can desist from further crime during the period of conditional release and to re-establish themselves within the community. As a matter of policy, it seems preferable that courts should not partially suspend parole-eligible sentences. The primary objective of the part-suspended sentence is to incentivise rehabilitation but that is also the primary or, at least, a salient purpose of parole. As already suggested, a specialised parole board is probably better placed to evaluate an offender's amenability to rehabilitation at some point during the currency of the sentence than is a court at the time sentence is being imposed. In desisting from imposing part-suspended sentences on parole eligible offenders, courts can be assured that those offenders will be duly *considered* for parole at a certain point during their sentence as guaranteed under the 2019 Act. What is not, however, guaranteed is that they will be released at that point or, indeed, at any time until they have served their sentences in full. One problem with the 2019 Act, which may require an amendment, is that it does not specify how the length of a part-suspended sentence is to be computed for parole purposes. Is a 10-year sentence with the last three years suspended to be treated as a 10-year sentence in which case the offender will (probably) be eligible for parole or as a seven-year sentence in which case he or she will certainly not be so eligible? This matter will require attention before s 24(3) is brought fully into effect.

10. Supervised Release Without Parole

Whatever its official purpose, parole permits offenders to be supervised in the community between the time of their release and the expiry of their sentence or their recall to prison (if that should happen). The benefits of this post-release supervision, provided it is conducted effectively and fairly, have already been noted. Essentially, it helps offenders to readjust to freedom, rebuild their lives and, hopefully, desist from further crime. A similar result may be achieved, or at least pursued, by ordering an offender to remain under supervision after serving the full sentence (less any applicable remission). This has become an increasingly common strategy for ensuring that offenders are supervised following release. It bears a close resemblance to parole in terms of its purpose but there is the significant difference that parole shortens the custodial term of a prison sentence whereas supervised released adds to the overall sentence. A breach of supervised release conditions may be an offence in itself, as it is in Ireland under sex offender legislation, or it may result in recall to prison for some or all of the supervised release period. This distinction has been well recognised in the United States where, following the abolition of parole in the federal jurisdiction under the Sentencing Reform Act 1984, courts were empowered to attach a term of supervised release to a prison sentence and, by all accounts, they routinely do. Since the implementation of this legislation in 1987, about one million people have been sentenced to supervised release by the federal courts. Some, in fact, are sentenced to lifetime supervised release. Otherwise, the average term, during the period 2005-2009, was 41 months.[125] It is now 47 months.[126] There was very **14–68**

125 Doherty, note 9 above; Schuman, note 9 above.

126 United States Sentencing Commission, *Annual Report 2023*, showing that 82.5 per cent of those sentenced in federal courts were ordered to serve a period

little Supreme Court jurisprudence on this practice until *United States v Haymond,*[127] decided in 2019. By a bare majority, the court invalidated a statutory provision which required the imposition of a minimum five-year sentence on a sex offender who committed a further sex offence while on supervised release after having served the original sentence. Gorsuch J, who delivered the plurality opinion, rejected the Government's argument that the procedures following breach of supervised release conditions were essentially the same as those formerly applicable to parole revocation. He said that while parole violations "generally exposed a defendant only to the *remaining* prison term authorized for his crime of conviction," supervised release violations may expose an offender "to an additional... prison term well *beyond* that authorized by the jury's verdict".[128] In *Apprendi v New Jersey*[129] the court had held that "any fact that increases the penalty for a crime beyond the prescribed statutory maximum must be submitted to a jury, and proved beyond a reasonable doubt." In *Haymond,* the district court, as was the prevailing practice, concluded on the preponderance of evidence (the civil standard), that the defendant had committed the new offence while on supervised release. Gorsuch J therefore concluded that the statutory provision permitting this procedure violated the *Apprendi* principle. Breyer J concurred with the plurality, though on the basis that the revocation procedure under the impugned statutory provision operated "less like an ordinary revocation and more like punishment for a new offence". It therefore violated the constitutional right to jury trial.[130]

14–69 In Ireland, a court, when imposing a prison sentence on a sex offender, must consider imposing a term of post-release supervision during which the offender's conduct will be supervised by a responsible person.[131] The aggregate of the term of imprisonment and the supervision period shall not exceed the maximum for the relevant offence – though it must be borne in mind that the maximum sentence for many serious sex offences is life imprisonment. The statute further provides that the term of imprisonment imposed shall not be less than would have been imposed in the absence of any post-release supervision order.[132] This was presumably intended to prevent courts from treating the supervision period as part of the deserved punishment for the offence. One might question the compatibility of this provision with the principle of proportionality which, it must be recalled, is constitutionally mandated in Ireland, unless the offence carries a mandatory penalty. Post-release supervision, however it may be formally classified or described by statute, is part of the sentence imposed for the

---

of supervised release. This rose to 88.7 per cent when immigration cases were excluded.

[127] 139 S Ct 2369 (2019).

[128] 139 S Ct 2369, 2382 (2019).

[129] 530 US 466 (2000).

[130] 139 S Ct 2369, 2385-2386 (2019).

[131] Sex Offenders Act 2001, Pt 5. Some, mainly minor, amendments have been made to this Part by the Sex Offenders (Amendment) Act 2023.

[132] Sex Offenders Act 2001, s 29(3).

offence. Even if its objective is to protect the public or promote offender rehabilitation, it still imposes a burden on the offender who must abide by the relevant conditions and face a further criminal penalty if found to be in breach of them.

A mandatory condition of supervised release under the Sex Offenders Act 2001 is that the offender must remain under the supervision of a probation officer and comply with any conditions specified in the court order.[133] A court has considerable discretion in determining the more specific conditions provided they are appropriate in light of the stated purposes of supervision which are to protect the public from further offending, including sexual offending, and to rehabilitate the offender.[134] As in the case of parole release and suspended sentences, conditions should be carefully chosen so as not to set the offender up to fail. For instance, any condition restricting an offender's access to computers, use of social media or similar technology must take account of present-day realities. It is now virtually impossible to lead anything resembling a normal life with access to computer-based technology.[135] This was recognised by the United States Supreme Court in *Packingham v North Carolina*[136] where it invalidated a state law that made it a felony for a registered sex offender "to access a commercial social networking Web site where the sex offender knows that the site permits minor children to become members, or to create or maintain personal Web pages". According to the court, a restriction of this breadth violated the First Amendment free speech guarantee. It barred access "to what for many are the principal sources for knowing current events, checking ads for employment, speaking and listening in the modern public square, and otherwise exploring the vast realms of human thought and knowledge". However, the court also said that there was no constitutional impediment to enacting more specific laws, even if speech was the medium of the prohibited conduct. **14–70**

Breach of a supervised release condition under the Sex Offenders Act 2001 (s 33) constitutes a summary offence carrying a maximum penalty of £1,500, 12 months' imprisonment or both. Proceedings for such an offence may be brought and prosecuted by a probation officer.[137] This arrangement obviates the difficulties associated with the revocation process at issue in *United States v Haymond*[138](described above). In Ireland, a breach is a distinct offence which, if prosecuted, must be tried by a court applying the criminal standard of proof. Further, the court has a discretion as to sentence which may not, in any case, exceed 12 months' imprisonment. **14–71**

---

[133] Sex Offenders Act 2001, s 29(1).

[134] Sex Offenders Act 2001, ss 28 and 30.

[135] Eric J Chan, Dale E McNiel, Renee L Binder, "Sex offenders in the digital age" (2016) 44(3) *Journal of the American Academy of Psychiatry and the Law* 368.

[136] 582 US 98 (2017). See note in (2017) 131 Harvard LR 233.

[137] Sex Offenders Act 2001, s 33(4), inserted by Criminal Law (Human Trafficking) Act 2008, s 13.

[138] 139 S Ct 2369 (2019).

INDEX